U.S. Capitalist Development
★ Since 1776 ★

U.S. Capitalist Development
★ Since 1776 ★
Of, By, and For Which People?★

DOUGLAS DOWD

M.E. Sharpe

Armonk, New York • London, England

Library of Congress Cataloging-in-Publication Data

Dowd, Douglas Fitzgerald, 1919-
U.S. Capitalist development since 1776: of, by,
and for which people? / Douglas F. Dowd.
p. cm.
Includes bibliographical references and indexes.
ISBN 1-56324-166-8.—ISBN 1-56324-167-6 (p)
1. United States—Economic conditions. 2. Capitalism—
United States—History. 3. Income distribution—United States—History.
4. Wealth—United States—History.
I. Title.
II. Title: US capitalist development since 1776.
HC103.D753 1993
338.973′009—dc20
93-16219
CIP

Printed in the United States of America

The paper used in this publication meets the minimum
requirements of American National Standard for Information
Sciences—Permanence of Paper for Printed Library Materials,
ANSI Z39.48–1984.

BM (c) 10   9   8   7   6   5   4   3   2   1
BM (p) 10   9   8   7   6   5   4   3   2

For Anna

*Who are you indeed who would talk
or sing to America?
Have you studied out the land,
its idioms and men?*

—Walt Whitman, *Leaves of Grass*

Contents

Figures and Tables

Figures

Tables

Preface

When, on July 4, 1776, the United States of America came into existence by dissolving "all political connections between them[selves] and the State of Great Britain," they did so with a momentous and stirring declaration that still today is one part of those many factors pushing people toward democracy over the world: "We hold these truths to be self-evident, that all men are created equal, that they are endowed by their Creator with certain unalienable Rights, that among these are Life, Liberty and the pursuit of Happiness." In the early 1970s there was a great hustle and bustle in the land, as thousands of people and hundreds of institutions began to make preparations to celebrate the 200th birthday of that great event. I was among them. Originally, I wrote a book entitled *The Twisted Dream*, its intent being to show what had gone wrong with "The American Dream," and why; to analyze the yawning gap between the magnificent ideals and the disturbing realities of our nation.

To do so, it was necessary to show that the dream itself had been defective. After all, among the dozens of signers of the Declaration were many slaveholders; and if some of those, like Jefferson, had their reservations about designating human beings as property, most did not. And although the Civil War of less than a century later was not fought only over the dissolution of slavery, it may be asserted that it would not have been fought at all if that issue had not been at its hot center. That is, the attachment to slaveholding could not be undone without war—the bloodiest war in all of history, up to that time.

These matters were clearly on President Lincoln's mind on November 19, 1863, when, standing on the bloodiest battleground of that bloodiest war, he could find only one justification for it: "That this government of the people, by the people, and for the people, shall not perish from the earth." But the Civil War meant more than the end of chattel slavery in the United States. Among the several conflicts between the North and the South (and the West) that led inexorably to war were those arising from the frustrated needs of the rising industrial and financial capitalists of the North, needs frustrated by the decisive powers of the South in the government—in its legislative, judicial, and executive branches. When the North won the war, it also garnered virtually exclusive powers to control the destiny of the nation, for decades to come. What this came to mean was the emergence of the most powerful industrial capitalist nation in the world, a nation whose politics, society, and culture, as well as its economy, would be dominated by and for an always smaller fraction of its people.

That this has been so *The Twisted Dream* sought to pin down and explain. It was first published in 1974. A revision seemed necessary only three years later, in response especially to the worst recession since the 1930s, combined with prolonged and rising inflation. The years since 1977 have produced changes both in degree and kind, going well beyond surprise—to amazement, shock, and bewilderment. They seem to have produced almost, but not quite, another world. And they led me to produce another book, both very much like and very different from *The Twisted Dream*; and with a different title.

Standing high on the list of stunning developments are of course the reforms sought by Gorbachev in the late 1980s, and the consequent social earthquakes in what was the Soviet Union and in what once was its Bloc, a process whose main characteristics seem without a historical reference point. Also at the top of the list of immense changes, and much closer to this book's concerns, has been the accelerating drift toward hard conservatism in the economic, political, and social life of the United States. What during the Carter era could be thought of as a set of unconnected policy shifts—some deregulation, some increases in military expenditures, some pressure downward on social expenditures—soon emerged as a major redirection of the U.S. social process, its symbol Ronald Reagan and its consequences forbidding, with, as yet, no end in sight.

That these two sets of dramatic changes have some common origins and will continue to interact with each other over the indefinite future perhaps goes without saying; but the process of interaction has been and will be intricate, as will be discussed in later pages. Among the most important links we shall examine is of course the meaning of the end of the Cold War. Its economic and related political demands contributed greatly to the demise of the Soviet economic system. But what was a burden to their economy was seen as a boon to our own system, at home and abroad—although, belatedly, the recognition is now spreading that we too have in numerous and complex ways been weakened by our addiction to the Cold War's economic and political ways and means.

I believe the earlier editions retain much of whatever validity they originally had, but this edition has had to be altered a very great deal—not just in the "addition" of recent developments or the "subtraction" of now irrelevant discussions (or mistaken judgments), but also in something equally important. When a work of history is written with the present and the future in mind, as this one has been, the ever-changing present also means that the past will and should be viewed differently in at least some degree. Different questions must be asked, emphasizing this more and that less or not at all. Thus, by way of example, because the past decade or so has seen an accelerating celebration of "the free market," along with innumerable policies presumably justified by its virtues both in the United States and elsewhere, it becomes important to take a closer look at both the ideology and the realities of the free market in our past: what was standing off in the political wings earlier now occupies center stage, and historical analysis is needed to help us "get our heads screwed on straight."

What has not changed, however, are my original reasons for writing the book, except, perhaps, for a sense of greater urgency in response to the strong conservative, even reactionary drift of the United States. It therefore seems appropriate to repeat the largest part of the original Preface to *The Twisted Dream*, with a few minor changes. It is that which now follows.

The United States is in the midst of a developing social crisis, at once economic, political, and moral, simultaneously domestic and international. This book seeks to identify and explain the nature of and the reasons for this crisis.

The complexity of society and the rapidity of social change in the United States are kaleidoscopic in their appearance and bewildering in their effects. Underlying both the complexity and the change is a coherent pattern that establishes the limits and the possibilities of social change, a set of fundamental institutions that may and must be understood as a *system*. The United States is an advanced industrial *capitalist* system, and the leading nation of the world capitalist system.

The very notion of a social system implies that all facets of social existence—economic life, politics, social behavior and attitudes, education and culture—continually interact with each other through the system of which they are a part. Rapid change and intermittent conflict are inherent to the functioning of the modern capitalist system. When substantial conflicts persist or become irreconcilable, the system is losing its ability to absorb or resist efforts to share its benefits in new ways. It then moves toward crisis.

The crisis that began in the 1970s and that continues in the 1990s is one of U.S. and therefore of world capitalism. It results from the renewal and strengthening of dynamically related conflicts within and between the United States and the other powerful capitalist nations, and between all of them and the rest of the world. This is by no means the first crisis of capitalist society and very probably not its last, just yet.

Capitalism was born in what is now seen as the European crisis of 1560–1660. Two centuries or so later, the capitalist world was once more rocked by abortive revolutions and, in the United States and France, by civil war. The ensuing decades were marked by explosive industrialization and imperialist expansion. The major powers enjoyed relative social stability, for a while. The twentieth century's first pervasive crisis was a direct outcome of that earlier industrialization and imperialism. The resulting stresses and conflicts produced World War I, the first major anticapitalist revolution, and then a breakdown of the world capitalist system. The central elements of that breakdown, all in dynamic interaction, were numerous fascist states, the world's most serious depression ever, and World War II, the most destructive of all wars.

The two world wars and the social upheavals connecting them in the interwar period pounded the major powers to their knees, exposing both their external and their internal weaknesses—for all but the United States: our domestic and global economic and military strengths grew as others' declined. From 1940 on, the rising power of the United States was inextricably interwoven with war and cold war, enormous and continuing military expenditures, and the expansion of our overseas influence and power. But for our society, as for so many others in the past, the diet that gave us our strength was also the source of our growing troubles.

As the 1970s proceeded, the hot center from which the troubles of the United States seemed to have emerged was our prolonged involvement and attenuated defeat in Indochina. The appearance is based on more than illusion, but confuses effects with causes. Indochina was a vortex pulling the United States in deeper year after year, from 1946 and the Truman presidency, until 1975, after the abrupt end of the Nixon presidency. That the United States for so long could find no way either to give up on the area or to overcome the Indochinese peoples was not a result of particular personalities—there were, after all, so many very different personalities involved in those thirty years—or of this or that mistake or accident. The United States, as the leader of the world capitalist system and the colonial/neocolonial possessions so vital to that system, explicably and inexorably played out its role, in Indochina and elsewhere. The burdens were heavy; but so were the gains. All empires meet their limits; ours were first met in Indochina, and since that terrible war we have sought and found other means (always brief, when also bloody) to pursue our ends.

But other problems easily if not obviously as troublesome for the rule of the United States also began to appear in the 1970s, those among and between the members of the Rich Man's Club of capitalist nations: Japan and the leading members of the European Economic Community (EEC).

What had made for the gains of empire, already by the mid-1960s, had begun to make for serious strains—in the form of increasing international competition, domestic unrest and economic imbalance, and looming national and international instability. All of these were both resolved and intensified (sometimes because of the nature of the resolution) as the 1970s gave way to the successes and excesses of the Reagan era.

What some saw as the beginning of the "American century" in 1945 rested upon a combination of economic and military strength; the 1990s began with what appears to be an equally unchallengeable military position, but an economy increasingly fragile, dependent upon external financial support, and bereft of the Cold War which played a critical economic and political role at home and abroad in our decades of being Number One. Well before World War I, the philosopher William James, apprehensive of what lay ahead, said "We must find the moral equivalent of war" to give unity and direction to our society. Now we must find the moral equivalent of cold war. What should be seen as a set of beckoning opportunities for the creation of a safer and saner, a more decent and just society, is by no means seen that way. Not yet.

These are heady assertions, neither to be accepted nor rejected without systematic inquiry and analysis. Most of us in the United States have had little or no exposure to such analysis; even worse, the "best-educated" in social analysis typically have been trained much as the feet of Chinese women used to be: bound from childhood, resulting in a crippled elegance.

If we are in the midst of social crisis, and if it is a crisis of capitalist society, the manner in which such a society moves through time, and why, must be comprehended. We must learn to think in analytical terms that are historical and that bridge the gulfs now separating the social sciences from each other, and all of them from history. And if the system that requires this study and this understanding is a capitalist system, then we must learn the imperatives and the modes of capitalist development.

Conventional, or mainstream, social science is utterly weak in the face of this challenge. Its characteristically narrow, segmented, and static (that is, nonhistorical) analyses are doubtless useful and necessary for some range of purposes; for today's needs and possibilities we need something more and something different, more (in the poet Stephen Spender's image) than "lectures on navigation while the ship is going down."

The public has every right to expect that those who have studied and taught in the areas of economics, political science, sociology, and history would be well-equipped to understand the system within which and because of which the present crisis stirs; every right to assume that courses at all levels of formal education and an accompanying literature would clarify the nature of our system and how it has come to this pass. Such expectations are almost always thwarted, as so many students and teachers have discovered. One can go through high school, college, and graduate school in the social sciences and history without either the obligation or the opportunity to engage in serious discussion let alone systematic analysis of the nature and development of U.S. capitalism, the facts of its existence, or its place in the larger world capitalist system.

In economics, the subject matter is the functioning of an effectually hypothetical "market economy," with the institutions and the life processes of capitalist economy and society ignored, assumed away as not requiring more than casual comment or, more usually, given a quick and approving glance and taken as permanent and beyond question: The best of all possible worlds.

Economists must study theory and usually study facts, but the selection of *which* facts to study—concerning, say, product or labor markets, matters of employment, foreign trade and investment, and the like—and *how* to study them is determined by the questions arising out of the theory. That theory is carried out on such a high- and wrong-headed level of abstraction that the matters most crucial for contemporary understanding are blurred and flattened, much as the great heights of modern air travel make it virtually impossible to distinguish between a plateau and a valley, one city or even one nation from another, a person from a goat. Chapter 1 seeks to show how and why this lamentable state of affairs came to be in economics (and by extension in the other areas of social inquiry). I have sought to make this failure understandable both to those who have and those who have not studied economics, a study that should be compelling and informative but which is typically boring and obfuscating.

The problems of abstraction in studying economics apply to the other social sciences as well: while students of economics fail to study the connections of "economic" with vital and interdependent "noneconomic" relationships and processes of their capitalist society, political scientists and sociologists normally abstract from the economic setting of capitalist society; historians, meanwhile, generally pursuing what British historian J.H. Hexter has called "tunnel history," burrow through one branch or another of a history (political, diplomatic, military, etc.), walled off from each other and in abstraction from the socioeconomic system that gives the historical process its particular dynamics. There are, of course, exceptions—some books, some teachers—but only rarely do they play a significant role in the curriculum of even the most diligent students of our society.

There are always some working in educational institutions who seek to bring their schools, their students, themselves back to life. Of course that remains true in our time and place at all levels of education, as teachers and scholars seek to remedy the grave defects of social study. The task they and we face is formidable. This book is an attempt to make it somewhat less so.

If this seems arrogant on my part, it may be softened somewhat by adding that what I have written is cast as nothing more than a general perspective, a synthesis of the main paths along which critical inquiry has moved (without which I could have done very little) and might and should continue to move. Numerous suggestions for further reading are scattered throughout the text as footnotes and at the ends of chapters to aid those who wish to continue the effort on their own.[1] I have sought to write a book that can be read by any person of any age or prior education (or previous condition of servitude), assuming only a serious concern with society. I have not sought to "give both sides to every question," to be neutral; but I have given due consideration to fact and logic, and have sought to be objective.

The theme that ties the book together is the perception of the United States as a *capitalist* society, and capitalism as a social system that requires, offers, and through oligarchic rule imposes two principal conditions on society: expansion and exploitation. It is a work of synthesis, combining what I believe to be valuable from Marx, Veblen, and Keynes with more recent and lesser-known works in economics, history, and other social studies. The book sees the achievements, the problems, and the tragedies of U.S. history as stemming from the needs and the ability of U.S. capitalism to expand and to exploit in ever changing ways.

This is a critical analysis based, of course, on my own system of values and perceptions, which I wish to make explicit at the outset. Although I have lived what I consider to be a privileged existence, since my own education began I have come to be horrified by the unnecessary cruelties and deprivations in our own and others' societies. Very early I came to the conclusion that although human beings as such need not live badly or at each others' throats, they must continue to do so for as long as they live, directly or indirectly, under capitalist institutions.

Capitalism's claims to fame have rested on its presumed ability to enhance production and freedom. But the production it undoubtedly enhances has been achieved at the cost of terrible distortions to the human spirit and to nature, and its products are as unevenly and unjustly distributed as its freedoms. When the choice has arisen between maintaining capitalist power or reducing human freedoms—and the choice has arisen many times—freedom has been forced to give way to power. It is doing so today, as these words are written. All know that oppression did not begin with capitalist societies, nor is it by any means confined to them now; but the entire world—including that portion that has called itself communist—has increasingly moved within a system of capitalist power and standards for the past few centuries. The most powerful set the tune to which others dance.

The people of the United States have both the need and the opportunity to throw off the incubus of capitalist relationships. For reasons that I trust will become apparent in this book, the time is long past when any reasonable calculation of advantages from capitalism can be seen as exceeding its costs to ourselves, to others, and to nature. If the United States emerges from the ongoing crisis without a significant alteration of its capitalist institutions in directions that have human and environmental, rather than capital's, needs as guiding standards, it will do so by becoming more centralized, more militarized, more oppressive, and more heartless, at home and abroad. We have already gone much too far, for much too long, in those directions. The human spirit, like our air and water, has been dangerously poisoned; we dare not allow its vitality to be weakened further, as surely will be so if current social processes continue uninterrupted.

Facing the crisis entwining slavery and civil war, Abraham Lincoln said to his people, "We must disenthrall ourselves." And so must we. We can and must begin to find ways to free ourselves from the deadly weight of acquisitiveness, mutual distrust, and combativeness, and begin to see our lives, our fellow human beings, and our environment as requiring and enabling cooperation and peace, equality, and genuine economic and social democracy, not just the political democracy that we rightly prize.

No particular group, let alone an individual, can specify what must be done, and how, and when, and where, and by whom to move toward a society combining decency with sanity with safety with justice with well-being for all. If and when a movement in such directions were to begin to take hold, its further steps would have to be thought through and accomplished by those taking the steps, in the times, places, and circumstances where they act. In the concluding chapter I shall put forth a substantial but still desperately brief discussion of what some in the United States have been trying to do, and my own judgment as to what else might be sought for and done. In anticipation, I can say here that it is my judgment that a society that would move toward economic, political, and social democracy would be moving away from capitalist institutions and aims and toward those of a democratic socialist society. Whatever else might be necessary for such an effort, social understanding and political participation based on that understanding head the list of priorities.

Except for my acknowledgment of assistance from many friends and colleagues, there ended the original Preface. At the time of its writing (1973), I had considered, but set aside as unnecessary, an explicit discussion concerning my many references to and quotations from the works of Marx, and also, for different reasons, from those of Thorstein Veblen. Today I believe it necessary to do so.

The collapse and drastic reconstruction of what have been called communist regimes has been almost universally taken to justify or even to equal a complete repudiation of Marxian analysis. There are several points to be made in this connection. Marx spent his entire adult life seeking to understand the capitalist process, what he called "the economic laws of motion of capitalist society." (It was Marx who gave capitalism its name, as he did also to the industrial revolution.) Marx's writings were analytical, not programmatic. He was responsible for a few epigrams concerning what might characterize a postcapitalist society—for example, when he made his famous distinction between socialism, where the guiding principle would be "from each according to ability, to each according to *work*," and communism, where the principle would be "from each according to ability, to each according to *need.*"

But Marx was also explicit to the effect that his work was historical, theoretical, and philosophical, not the "provision of kitchen recipes for the future," much less the founding of an ideology. Certainly, many proponents and members of socialist/communist societies have commonly referred to the latter as "Marxist." A study of Marx's works makes it clear that he would not have seen them as such. (As it may be doubted that Christ would have seen the Crusades, the Inquisition, or the many political parties with the designation "Christian" as reasonable representatives of his beliefs.[2] As might similarly be said of Freud, and, more to the gist of this book, Adam Smith.)

Marx's ideas are used often by me because for understanding the capitalist process they are the most incisive. And this is a book about the capitalist process. It has been wisely remarked, much less in the United States than in Europe, that whether one is an opponent or a supporter of capitalism, one needs to understand it—and that to understand capitalism, although it requires much more than reading Marx, requires at least that: it is a necessary, though by no means a sufficient condition.

That Marx studied the capitalist process for decades is well–known; less understood is that his first relevant publication (in 1844) had to do with the effects of capitalism on the human spirit, on our increasing "alienation." What Marx had to offer was only a part of what we must know, but it is a vital part. And Marx's supporting view of human nature, of our needs and possibilities, is analytically compelling, as I hope to show in Chapter 1. (One of the reading suggestions at the end of that chapter is the fine book of the late William Appleman Williams, *The Great Evasion*, where he assesses just how foolish and costly it has been that Marx has so assiduously *not* been studied in the United States.)

And then there is Thorstein Veblen, of whom most who read these pages have probably never heard. A quick look at the index of authors quoted will show more listings for Marx and for Veblen by far than any others, and that they are about equal in number of citations. Veblen

(1857–1929) was born on a farm in the United States, the son of Norwegian immigrants. He took a Ph.D. in philosophy at Yale, and then another in economics at Cornell, and proceeded to become, in my judgment, the most profound student of U.S. capitalism. He learned from Marx's works, but he was also his penetrating critic.

Veblen is not unknown in the United States, indeed there is in some sense a "school" of his intellectual descendants ("institutionalists"); but he is studied only rarely. He was a relentless critic of the principal controlling institutions of the modern world: capitalism, the State, organized religion, patriotism and militarism, and what he saw as the corrupted university. His eleven books and innumerable articles were mostly concerned with the social processes and relations and ideology (taken together, the "institutions") of capitalism, and with the ideas, the ideology, and the economic and social theories that grew alongside and in some degree facilitated the development of the capitalist world. His emphasis was on the United States.

So, I have depended greatly on Marx and Veblen for helping me to make my points. As will be seen, they both differed and agreed on vital matters. Veblen, unlike Marx (and inacurately), saw himself as apolitical, and his writings did not easily lend themselves to the development of a political movement in his name. Thus Veblen did not become an object of political opposition, as Marx did. But because Veblen's analyses were so deeply critical of the status quo, how it evolved and where it was going, his works never entered the mainstream of the social sciences. Now he is scarcely mentioned and seldom read; he is being allowed to disappear. Veblen deserves a better fate, and we today need his understanding.

Finally, a comment meant to lower levels of impatience, frustration, puzzlement, and even anger, that might plausibly arise due to certain problems having to do with the structure of the book and the meaning of its most important terms. Earlier, I asserted that "capitalism as a system requires...expansion and exploitation." Those three terms, like many other "big words" in social analysis, cannot, indeed should not, be defined easily or briefly. They are simultaneously abstract, and historical, and "loaded": that is what makes them "big words." To clarify the meaning of *capitalism*, I have devoted a good part of the first and all of the second chapter, and much of what is discussed in the remaining chapters is also a part of its "definition."

As a requirement for the capitalist process, *expansion* is accepted by almost everybody—Adam Smith, Karl Marx, and Milton Friedman, for example. But most who accept it do so without exploring the whys and wherefores. That will be done systematically in Chapter 2 at some length, and discursively throughout Chapter 4.

Exploitation is another matter. Just as vital as expansion, it is seen neither as a fact nor as a requirement for capitalism by almost anybody. "Expansion" has a nice sound to it, just as nice as the sound of "exploitation" is nasty. To my knowledge, exploitation as such has never been advocated by *anyone*, but policies leading to its increase and spread have been and are advocated by many—Adam Smith as well as today's mainstream economists, for example. Consequently, although I can rest easy in not putting forth my "definition" of expansion until Chapter 2, I shall have to give at least an introductory explanation of exploitation when the term is first used, early in Chapter 1. I shall use a long footnote for that purpose, and frequently for other purposes as well.

I hope these remarks, plus frequent glances at the indexes of subjects and of authors will be helpful in making the book a minimally trying experience. Indeed my larger hope is that this will be seen as a book that can, where desired, substitute for a classroom, used as a starting (or continuing) point for many years of reading and thought. Thus all the reading suggestions.

If this book reaches any of its goals, it is in no small measure due to the substantial help I have been given by many friends with whom I have been associated professionally and politically for a few or for many years. Many have been thanked in earlier versions of this book, but I should like once more to express my gratitude to Bruce Dancis and to Daniel and Patricia Ellsberg for their critical comments in the past, as also to my old friend and colleague Chandler Morse, now passed on, who worked so hard on more than one draft. Of all those I have known, he represented most what is best about the United States and the academic world. I should also like to express my debt to the works of Paul M. Sweezy, James O'Connor, and James Cypher, without which I doubt very much I could have found a workable analytical framework for what follows. And, as good friends they have been supportive over the years.

For this latest edition I was helped early on by the critical comments of my colleague at Johns Hopkins in Bologna, Professor John Harper; and in various ways Professor Paul Leigh of San José State University was most helpful. Nor can I close without thanking my stars for the editorial assistance of Barbara Thayer and Linda Frede-Tripicco.

Notes

1. An asterisk (*) following the title of the works cited indicates that the book is available in paperback.

2. Soon after these words were written, a regular contributor to the *Wall Street Journal* made something of the same point concerning the fate of both Marxism and Christianity.

Acknowledgments

The following publishers have granted permission to quote or reproduce graphic materials from their books: W.W. Norton, Frank Levy, *Dollars and Dreams: The Changing American Income Distribution* (1988); Brookings Institution, David J. Ravenscraft and F.M. Scherer, *Mergers, Sell-Offs and Economic Efficiency* (1987); M.E. Sharpe, Inc., for Richard DuBoff, *Accumulation and Power*, and Lawrence Mishel and David M. Frankel, *The State of Working America*; Grove Press, Inc., Francis Moore Lappé and Joseph Collins, *World Hunger: Twelve Myths* (1986); Chatto & Windus, Michael Ignatieff, *The Needs of Strangers* (1984); and Prentice-Hall, Edwards, et. al., *The Capitalist System* (1986).

– 1 –

Economics and Economies, Past and Present

O this is not spring but in me
there is a murmuring of new things.
This is the time of a dark winter in the heart
but in me are green traitors....[1]

"The American Dream" has always been complex, never single-minded. Both in its nature and in the struggles fought over its realization, the dream has encompassed a broad range of economic, political, and social aspirations. Still, what stands out most in U.S. history, what has most persistently and effectively absorbed the energies of its people, is without question the individual and national aim of economic advancement —accompanied each step along the way by its vital companion, geographic expansion. Sitting at the center of our personal and national self-esteem has been the pride of material achievement; the frame of reference for national policy has had its limits and its directions set mostly by what is compatible with economic criteria; as a people, what has most frequently moved us to political excitement have been economic hopes and fears—until, perhaps, yesterday.[2]

The United States has long been the business society *par excellence*, with few questions asked, except in periods of perceived hard times: for farmers and urban workers in the last decades of the nineteenth century, workers and some urban intellectuals before World War I, and perhaps a majority in the depression-wracked 1930s.

1

Then, in the 1960s, the grounds for opposition and protest changed, as many, especially, but not only, the young, argued that our business society at its best (as it was, in the 1960s) is none too good: it is cold and dehumanizing, unjust, abrasive, and bellicose. The widespread dissent affected the society in important ways, some positive, some negative. But the inability of the dissidents or their arguments to achieve lasting influence or power was due less to their own political naiveté than to the stubborn great strength of capitalist ideology, militarism, and racism in the United States.[3]

All that, taken together with the emerging U.S. and world economic crisis of the 1970s, soon called "stagflation," paved the way for a swing back to a 1920s-like enthusiasm for the political economy of "rugged individualism"—with Ronald Reagan alternately playing the roles of Harding, Coolidge, and Hoover (while perhaps imagining himself as Teddy Roosevelt).

Even as the 1960s, their struggles and their personnel, faded into memory, however, it soon became politically impossible to ignore looming natural and social disasters, many already accomplished, others well on their way: the poisoning of the air, the soil, the rivers, streams, lakes, even the oceans; the steady destruction of the atmosphere; the seemingly insoluble problems of waste disposal (nuclear and chemical, and Himalayas of garbage) in a society which, as will be argued later, cannot have its version of "prosperity" without always more waste; and, joined to the spoliation of nature, a comparable process of social deterioration: poverty that becomes crueler as it also spreads and deepens, shuddering systems of transportation and education, and the most scandalously inadequate *and* costly health care system of the industrial world.

But perhaps all this is not too high a price to pay for a strong economy? Perhaps no, probably yes; but now it is commonly acknowledged that the U.S. economy is considerably weak in its production sector, and always more so in confrontation with the Japanese and German economies. Connected with that, the decade of the 1980s produced what has seemed to be the greediest and most unconstrained generation of capitalists ever who, as the economy was "financialized," assaulted, rendered fragile, and even destroyed significant elements of its industrial and financial capacities. All this and more moves a growing number of hitherto indifferent citizens to a state of perplexity and worry that allows them too to wonder if a business society at its best is good enough, and sane or safe enough, perhaps also because its best now becomes a memory.[4]

Be that as it may, those now concerned to rid the United States of the ugly and threatening dynamics that transform dream into nightmare must also question a long-standing assumption about the capitalist social process. Our ingrained belief has been that personal and national *economic* improvement would prevent, eliminate, or facilitate the resolution of *noneconomic* problems. Now, by contrast, it seems increasingly likely that our very means of achieving economic success—in industry, agriculture, and the services—have worsened, even created, that lengthening list of social and environmental "problems" plaguing our society.

Thus, in later chapters it will be argued that racism (and other forms of oppression), neither initiated in nor confined to capitalism or to the United States, has been "good for business" (not only by keeping wages lower than they otherwise might be, but also by deflecting the politics of the white population away from issues vital to them); that the spread of coercion and militarization in our domestic and foreign policies and the dependence upon military production, whatever their important harmful effects on the economy, nature, and society, have, through their vast expenditures, been decisive in avoiding serious economic depressions and, not less important, instrumental in creating and shaping the vital world economy since World War II; that the plight of virtually all our cities, burdened by intractable fiscal, environmental, educational, and health crises, though complex in its origins, has been much worsened by that businesslike callousness that can never find sufficient reasons for the well-off to pay the (tax) costs of a decent society.[5]

And all this is closely connected at the local and national levels to corruption in private and public life, by no means confined to the United States, that far outdistances anything that happened in the scandalized Twenties, Fifties, or Sixties. To which it may and must be added that going hand in glove with the quantitative economic achievements of the U.S. economy in recent decades has been the ever-tighter grip of centralized and concentrated power, economic and political, business and governmental, which, taken together with the always advancing secrecy, manipulation, and dishonesty that such a pattern requires and enables, presides over all: another very large, very frightening skeleton in the closet of this proudly democratic, free market society. It must be a sorry time to be young.[6]

Hidden within that melancholic dirge are of course some cheerier notes, not the least of them that many seek to set aright what so badly goes askew. But nothing will be set aright without understanding why it is wrong. The question *why*, when asked of social processes, is always *historical*; whatever else is also necessary, understanding of a social present requires understanding of how it came to be.

"The American Dream" that now seems so twisted became so over time, but it was inherent in key elements of the dream itself. For present purposes, the dream's beginning may be related to two events of the year 1776, putting together dramatic ideas with dramatic social changes. The first was Adam Smith's *Wealth of Nations*; the second was the *Declaration of Independence*. They had considerably more in common, in origin, intent, and consequences than is usually supposed. In the intervening centuries the laudable spirit that motivated both events has been vitiated by the emerging domination of the troublesome "key elements" referred to above: a fervent, expansionist, and unquestioned (if also understandable) nationalism, and often blind dependence upon "the invisible hand" of market competition and economic individualism to render unnecessary any broader or deeper guiding social ethic.[7]

What has ensued since 1776, what became economics and what the United States has become, have moved in directions neither expected nor intended by their originators. Adam Smith and Thomas Jefferson (who wrote the *Declaration*) were not in agreement, the former seeking industrialization and the latter an "agrarian democracy," but we may be certain that both would have been deeply affronted by what has been created in their name.

To understand the how and the why of that history requires understanding the dynamics of capitalist development (at least), which in turn requires understanding how very much a capitalist *economy* requires of its associated *social* and *political* framework (and all the more so as time goes on).

The defining characteristics of a capitalist economy are that the means of production—mines, mills, factories, land, and so on—are privately-owned, and operated for the profit of the owners. *All* decisions —what and whether to produce, when, how much, where, who and how many to hire (or fire); whether to expand or contract productive capacity and change technology; advertising, marketing, and financial decisions; all these and other decisions are made by a relatively few individuals for their individual or corporate benefit, and the "bottom line."

The "free market economy," today's term for capitalism, is thus one in which those privileged, clever, or ruthless enough to have acquired productive assets are entitled to use them as they see fit, to their own

anticipated advantage. The ideology that developed along with the capitalist process presumes that the benefits of such a system will be shed on
all, from the owners down to the entire population: they will "trickle
down."

Capitalism has existed for only a brief fraction of history, no more
than two centuries anywhere, and much less than that everywhere else.
The seeds were planted in medieval Europe, especially in the trading
cities of Italy, and given much nourishment by the overseas expansion of
the sixteenth and seventeenth centuries. By then, the first recognizably
capitalist economy, that of the Dutch, appeared. But it was not until the
late eighteenth century, in Britain, that capitalism may be said to have
become an unstoppable development.

Special circumstances, in a process of violent change, were required
to bring capitalism into existence; its continuation has depended upon a
precariously balanced set of social institutions and economic processes:
power *must* be held by the relatively few who own productive property,
or by others who move in harmony with the needs of capitalism, in order
to allow the *exploitation*[8] intrinsic to capitalist development; and the
economy must continually *expand*, both in its production and in its
geographic sway. The interaction of these imperatives over time weaves
together the economic, political, and social relationships that give
capitalism its life, its strength, its dynamics, its virtues, and its defects.

Adam Smith and those called "the founding fathers" (men like
Jefferson, Madison, Hamilton, Franklin, etc.) were sophisticated thinkers,
discerning of the complex web of relationships and processes required
and enhanced by capitalist development. But, much as they disagreed
among themselves, they viewed these matters through the rose-colored
lenses of the upper crust of society. Their optimism and their social
values led them to emphasize the real gains possible from capitalist
development while minimizing or ignoring its social and human costs—or
to assume that the material successes of capitalism would render such
costs negligible.[9]

There have always been some who have thought otherwise; now
there are many more. These are the critics who sense, who believe, and
who understand that the social costs of capitalism are far too high and
that much of its material achievement is not achievement at all: that too
many are exploited and oppressed (and befuddled) in too many ways for
too little and for the benefit of too few, that capitalist economic expansion is heedless, too costly to human beings and to the rest of nature.

The historical and analytical support for these assertions constitutes the heart of this book. Suppose for the moment that the assertions are valid. It would seem that to understand their whys and wherefores it would be necessary to understand what is now called *economics*. That is not so, but it is necessary to develop an analytical perspective on the U.S. *economy*. It is both fortunate and unfortunate that mastery of economics is neither sufficient for gaining the needed perspective, nor necessary in order to do so.

Quite apart from an ideological basis (and bias) that accepts the status quo, mainstream economics is neither broad enough in its reach nor deep enough in its penetration to suit today's analytical needs. This is not to overlook the existence of valuable elements within it which, happily, could and should be incorporated into a more appropriate framework. But thinking and working *solely* within the framework of conventional ("neoclassical") economics does more to obstruct than to provide the possibilities of understanding the U. S. economy; it does not so much lubricate as act like sand in the gears of thought.[10]

Much the same can be said of the analytical state of affairs in the other social sciences and in history. What is needed badly are not further refinements of existing conventional economics and of the other social sciences, but the development of a dynamic social science that starts with our world, our needs, our possibilities. Central in that development must be a dynamic new *political economy*, one that allows us analytically to integrate contemporary with historical developments, and economic with political and social life.

This book is an attempt to take a step along that long and difficult path, a step that, were it to succeed, would contribute to a perspective helpful in the development of more specific and more theoretical inquiries. Now some definition of terms is necessary, in order both to clarify and to demystify "economics."

Classical and Neoclassical Economics

When the term *economics* is used here or, generally, by contemporary economists, the reference is to conventional ("mainstream") *economic theory*. Today's economics is an outgrowth and modification of classical political economy; as such, it is called neoclassical economics (not, it will be noted, neoclassical political economy). The usage of these classifications is by no means standardized. Marx, for example, saw classical political economy ending in the early nineteenth century, and Keynes viewed *all* economists up to himself as classicists. Here classical political economy will be seen as having its first great thinker in Adam Smith, and its last in John Stuart Mill (1806–1873). Neoclassical economics will be viewed as having begun to take hold in the 1870s, with its ultimately most influential thinkers being Alfred Marshall (1842–1924) and John Maynard Keynes (1883–1946). Karl Marx (1818–1883) and Thorstein Veblen (1857–1929), unlike the classical and neoclassical economists, were profound critics of capitalism and of the economists of their own time; their ideas and their social values provide much of the guiding framework for this book's analysis.

All these thinkers were unusually sensitive to the nature, the needs, and the possibilities of their times; all were theorists; all were critics, reformers, or revolutionaries. Most decisive of all, and it was this that made them great, was that the values, analyses, and purposes they expressed coincided with significant social interests in their day, and were thus reflected in practice. They not only studied society; in some measure they changed it. And all were concerned with capitalism—lovingly, worriedly, or angrily.

Adam Smith (a Scot) was the first to be so concerned in a fully systematic manner, and the first theoretician of capitalism as a *system*. He laid the groundwork of what became the methodology of classical political economy, altered in form but not in ideology by neoclassical economics, thoroughly criticized, transformed, and transcended by both Marx and Veblen.

All theory, social or physical, works from and within a *methodological* framework, which guides the theorist in what is examined, what ignored, what emphasized, what relegated to secondary consideration, what taken as "given" and what come to be the main "variables" to be studied and analyzed. For social theorists, methodology is developed in accord with basic social values, with their conceptions of human nature and of society, with their initial conception of which problems most require analysis and resolution.

Classical political economists had much the same set of social values as their successors, the neoclassicists. But the needs of early capitalism in Great Britain were very different from those of Britain after, say, 1870. The classicals were concerned with establishing the conditions—economic, political, and social—within which capitalism and industrialism could emerge from the remaining and important confines of the precapitalist tradition; the neoclassicists were working with an already well-established industrial capitalist society, with different needs and possibilities.

As will be seen, Smith and David Ricardo (1772–1823) theorized in order that political constraints holding back economic development could be understood as doing just that; John Stuart Mill, writing some decades later, synthesized classical thought while at the same time seeking to puzzle through the harsh consequences of the developments that this thought had facilitated. Classical political economists all constructed analyses that encompassed developments over time, and all related economic to political and social relationships; it was this that made their economics *political economy*.

It is the absence of these characteristics that is a defining factor in identifying neoclassical economics up to the present (and notwithstanding the important contribution of Keynes). The lofty abstractions and rigorous assumptions of neoclassical economics gave it what strength it has possessed; its present grave inadequacies are also owing to that analytical narrowness. Neoclassical economics retains some uses for contemporary purposes, but those uses do not include adding to the possibility of comprehending the dynamics or the costs of modern capitalism—which must be understood by both the supporters *and* the critics of capitalism. Let us now proceed to examine what Adam Smith and the colonial revolutionaries had in common.

Mercantilism, Capitalism, and Political Economy

Both Smith and the revolutionaries were fighting against British mercantilism, Smith to get it off the back of constrained British capitalism, the colonists to get it off their own backs. Smith correctly saw that mercantilistic restrictions were holding back the dynamic potential of the British economy; the colonists correctly perceived that the same system as applied to the colonies not only held back and distorted, but also skimmed the cream from their own economic development—as remains true for presently dependent "neocolonial" societies. Smith had to undertake a full analysis of how capitalism works; much to their surprise, the colonists had to set off a national revolution.

It was Smith who introduced the concept of "mercantilism," or what he called the *mercantile system*.[11] Its importance in his argument and his day requires examination of the term; the fact that much of what capitalist economies practice nowadays may be seen as "neomercantilist" increases the importance of doing so. First, it will be fitting to examine the times in which mercantilism came into being, and seek to extract the essence of those times in order to understand not only the term but its continuation in practice today.

The "mercantilist period" is generally seen as extending from the sixteenth through the eighteenth century. The societies involved directly were the new nation-states of Western Europe. Although each of these societies practiced mercantilism in different ways and over different stretches of time during the three centuries, all were faced with the same general set of conditions, and all held two aims in common: wealth and power. As the new nation-states struggled for power, territory, and gain all over the globe, they created an epoch of constant warfare. In the seventeenth century, when the mercantilist system was at its peak, there were at most four years *not* marked by international war.

The mercantilist period opened with the expansion of Europe into the Americas, Africa, and Asia. Maritime trade and navies were essential and dangerous, costly and profitable. Piracy and warfare were inseparable from trade, whose running mates were plunder and slavery. National economic strength was linked to national military strength. Not to win was to lose; national autonomy required national aggressiveness. It was the birth of the modern world, whose defects are thus congenital. If we owe much to those earlier centuries, in our cultural, political, and technological advance, they also kept us on the always tortuous paths of militarism, imperialism, and racism, with variations supplied by modern nationalism and capitalism. Then as now, all these were tightly intertwined.

Trade and control over resources in the overseas areas were highly interdependent: spices (which signified hundreds of different commodities, from condiments to medicines), sugar, tea and coffee, gold and silver, and slaves obsessed the economic, political, and military figures of that era. Private fortunes and national strength waxed and waned as rivalry and wars for domination of the sea lanes and the lands they connected saw first the Portuguese and the Spanish, then the Dutch and, by the eighteenth century, the French and the British struggle for leadership. The seventeenth century was dominated by the Dutch; the nineteenth by the British. The Dutch had wrested control from the Spanish; the British from the Dutch and French. The decisive element in both cases was the ability to devise an appropriate blend of private and public institutions to enhance the profit and power needed for national strength.

The Dutch depended upon their ability to make the most of water resources. Fishing led to shipbuilding and shipping, thence to a complex pattern of overseas trade, premodern industry, and finance. So bereft of landed resources they had to build sea-walls (dikes) and windmills to be able to farm adequately, the Dutch nevertheless by the close of the seventeenth century had the strongest economy and the most dynamic empire of the time. The British, steadily copying Dutch technology (in shipbuilding, for example) and business techniques, took advantage of their much larger population, their agricultural and mineral resources and location (fronting on both Europe and the Atlantic), and their centralized political system to put together the first modern industrial society. The energetic development of capitalist institutions and impulses was both cause and consequence of the successes of the Dutch and the British; the undoing of the Spanish and the French is largely explained by their global political ambitions and their complicated failures to break the crust of medieval and dynastic social and political molds.

Adam Smith sought a *laissez-faire* State for Great Britain, that is, a State that would serve as a "night watchman" over economic life rather than as a fussing and intrusive parent. He saw the latter role as characterizing the mercantilist State.[12] More specifically, there was virtually no area of economic life untouched by State controls, subsidies, or regulations. Overseas trade was entirely carried by the numerous Crown-chartered trading monopolies, the most famous of which was the East India Company. Industries deemed critical by the State were similarly vested with monopolies of production. The supply of labor, the conditions under which labor worked, and its possibilities of geographic movement were subject to intricate regulations. The manner in which the land was farmed was unregulated, but the conditions of land tenure (affecting control and sale of land) were subject to nonmarket constraints. Finance was dominated by taxation and, at the end of the seventeenth century, the Bank of England was chartered so as to gain a virtual monopoly over banking. The French cry of *laissez-faire, laissez-passer!* symbolized Smith's position: freedom of enterprise and movement.

Smith was a good historian. He knew that the mercantilist network of private-public privilege and power had served a vital role. He also knew that the military and economic risks of the early modern period required the protection and subsidization of the State; that the State's security required a strong economy and access to the resources of overseas colonies to have the strength to preserve itself. But he saw that what had been useful and necessary in one historical setting had become harmful, precisely because the success of mercantilist policies had made them unnecessary.[13]

What was harmful about mercantilism? In ways that very much suggest contemporary processes, the intimate cooperation between the State and its private economic favorites had ultimately created a locus of power that inexorably mixed corruption with economic stultification. Access to the favors of the Crown was the key determinant of private economic activity. Although the activities thus encouraged strengthened some of the muscles of Britain's economy, others remained undernourished. Trade, industry, and finance by Smith's time required freedom more than parental protection; the laws and customs surrounding labor and the land held back their "rational" utilization. For Smith, not the State but the "law of supply and demand," the free market, was the best determinant of what should be produced, who should produce it, how it should be produced, and how the production should be distributed. This meant the elimination of *all* Crown-granted monopolies, *all* restrictions on trade, and the transformation of land and labor into commodities.[14] The only State activities deemed worthwhile by Smith were those that private business could not—or should not—undertake: defense, justice, and "certain public works" (by which Smith meant roads, and perhaps education).

World trade had expanded enormously in Smith's lifetime, and increasingly so as the eighteenth century drew to an end. The sea lanes were for Britain and its powerful navy becoming safe enough to allow a sharp distinction betwen mercantile and naval voyages, something quite impossible in the seventeenth century. Trading opportunities multiplied, but trade monopolies continued in the ruts of the past. The industrial revolution was growling beneath the surface while Smith wrote; but the aging industrial monopolies granted by the Crown impeded the possibilities. Surplus labor was bottled up in parishes where work was unavailable; the new industries would need that labor in the growing towns and cities. And so on. *Laissez-faire*!

Smith was unquestionably correct in arguing that the mercantilist policies of the State were holding back private economic initiative. In seeking to bring about an unhampered capitalist economy he was also, consciously or no, helping to create a society in which the possession and use of private property in the means of production would determine almost the entirety of both the qualitative and the quantitative aspects of social existence. Smith believed that by replacing State power with *market competition* as the dominant force in the economy, power itself would be dispersed. But he failed to see how very strong and effective the impulses would become to replace "*state* mercantilism" (Smith's target) with "*private* mercantilism." In Britain and the United States—the closest approximations to the Smithian ideal of laissez-faire capitalism in the industrializing nineteenth century or since—private economic power in the form of the giant corporation grew even more rapidly than the economy; in the process it was able to use the relatively weak State to protect, aid, and abet it in the carving out of private economic baronies. But what transpired in the nineteenth century appears quaint when compared with the power and behavior of the supercorporations that now characterize the economies of all the leading industrial nations.

Competition, Power, and Property

Smith relied upon market competition, what he called the "invisible hand," to transform individual self-seeking into social well-being. Smith was a wise, observant, and humane person, and in no way innocent concerning the proclivities of businessmen, "an order of men," he said, "whose interest is never exactly the same with that of the public, who have generally an interest to deceive and even to oppress the public, and who accordingly have, upon many occasions, both deceived and oppressed it."[15]

Smith's analytical enemy was the State, the Crown, what we would call the government. That was appropriate enough in his era. Monopoly in his day was not privately achieved, but publicly granted. The truly private enterpriser did not and could not gain pervasive market power, which the small-scale technology of the time did not then allow. (The first factory, tiny by modern standards, did not begin to produce until 1815.) Thus it was reasonable for Smith, distrustful though he was of businessmen, to believe that distortions of economic life *and* of public life both had their origins at the power center of society—in the State. He knew that businesses would do what they could to avoid market competition in what they sold for the very reasons that competition is deemed socially valuable: it pushes down their prices and their profits. He also knew that those same businesses would value competition among those from whom they bought, for obverse reasons. What he failed to take into account was how very effective businesses would be in combining their *economic* with their *political* activities to lessen competition in their selling markets (among other aims). The combination was made all the more effective in the late nineteenth century as the development of modern industrial technology rendered small-scale production and therefore competitive market structures less tenable, while access to political power by the larger business firms became both easier and more necessary. Smith's shortcomings in these respects are more comprehensible than those of modern economists. It was one thing for him not to be able to foresee the future; it is quite another for modern economists not to take seriously facts of past and present.

One important source of Smith's optimism concerning the consequences of laissez-faire capitalism was a certain myopia regarding the relationship between property and power, and the decisive connection between that relationship and capitalist development. Smith was not blind on this matter, far from it:

> Whenever there is great property, there is great inequality. For one very rich man, there must be at least five hundred poor, and the affluence of the few supposes the indigence of the many. The affluence of the rich excites the indignation of the poor, who are often both driven by want and prompted by envy to invade his possessions. It is only under the shelter of the civil magistrate that the owner of that valuable property, which is acquired by the labor of many years, or perhaps of many successive generations, can sleep a single night in security.... The acquisition of valuable and extensive property, therefore, necessarily requires the establishment of civil government.[16]

But Smith was myopic if, as was true, the aim of his analysis was to benefit the society as a whole rather than the few most privileged within it. The last sentence of the foregoing quotation, at least in substance, could have been written by Karl Marx, who saw "the executive of the modern state [as] but a committee for managing the common affairs of the ruling class." But Smith did not perceive the private owners of productive property as a "ruling class." There is a great analytical, to say nothing of political, difference between Smith's belief that property must be protected from the propertyless, and Marx's belief that the existence of a small class of property owners and a large population of the propertyless sets the entire tone and direction of social development.

Smith believed that property had to be protected by the State; he also believed that society could and would be protected from property by the forces of market competition. That was not to be.[17]

The guiding theme around which the analysis of this book revolves, and that will be emphasized and elaborated upon again and again, is that capitalism thrives not only by economic and geographic *expansion*, which Smith advocated and facilitated, but as well by labor *exploitation*. Nobody *advocates* exploitation, but Smith, by arguing for the systematic elimination of sociopolitical constraints on business activity provided, doubtless unintentionally, a basic rationale for it. The exploitation of labor was intense and universal long before Smith wrote, and he recognized it clearly in his own day; and the means he proposed for increasing "the wealth of the nation" had as their ultimate end the improvement of the lot of the common people.[18] But the evolution of the Smithian social framework meant that his own social hopes would be brutally swept aside, and that human exploitation would be intensified in ways and to a degree unimagined by Smith.

Writing a century and a half after Smith, and thus with the benefit of hindsight, R.H. Tawney (1881–1966) attacked laissez-faire economics by contrasting it with medieval social thought, in these scathing words:

> ...to found a science of society upon the assumption that the appetite for economic gain is a constant and measurable force, to be accepted, like other natural forces, as an inevitable and self-evident *datum* would have appeared to the medieval thinker as hardly less irrational or less immoral than to make the premise of social philosophy the unrestrained operation of such necessary human attributes as pugnacity or the sexual instinct.[19]

Classical Political Economy and Industrial Revolution

The impact of Smith's *magnum opus* was triggered more by his times than by the ideas themselves, as is generally true of influential thought. At a critical moment, Smith had put together preexisting ideas into a new and compelling whole. His basic argument was not universally accepted, either ideologically or economically; the tendencies energized by the industrial revolution accomplished in fact what his persuasiveness alone could not do.

Smith was the broadest in vision and highest in optimism of the classicists. In his *Essay on Population* (1798) and his *Principles of Political Economy* (1820) the Reverend Thomas Malthus (1766–1834) substituted apprehension for optimism. Malthus developed two sets of arguments in these books, one more economic and the other largely social and political; but they were interdependent. Whether or not attributed to him, all his ideas have once more gained a relatively wide audience, and it will be worthwhile to examine them.[20]

Malthus was a pessimist. Economics came to be called "the dismal science" in part because of the gloominess of his anticipations. His gloom centered on two probabilities, both of them imperfectly but vividly argued: (1) the prospect of population growth outrunning resources, and (2) the likelihood of what we call stagnation or chronic depression, which he called "gluts of production." As a parson whose emotional attachments were to the rural virtues and his family's substantial rural properties, Malthus did not share the enthusiasms of Smith regarding industrial capitalist development. This led him to peer more critically at such prospects, albeit literally as a reactionary. Taken seriously in his own time, Malthus came to be scorned by economists over the ensuing, largely buoyant nineteenth century. In this tumultuous and bloody century, with its rapid population growth and its terrible depression of the 1930s (not to mention wars, and other upheavals) he is once again taken seriously.

As subsequent discussion will argue, if Malthus was right at all, it was for the wrong reasons. Despite a constant barrage of arguments to the contrary, (1) there is a sufficient supply of food (and other natural resources) for the world's people now (and can be into the indefinite future), and (2) while intermittent "gluts" cannot be avoided in a capitalist economy, they need not endure or be seriously harmful in their consequences. (The case for these assertions will be made in Chapters 6 and 4, respectively.) When there are problems such as Malthus anticipated, they are created by our social institutions; and by changing those institutions they can be resolved, or at least mitigated.[21]

What has made Malthus *seem* to have been right for the right reasons have been certain consequences of the normal functioning of industrial capitalism. His argument about population expansion has a compelling quality to it, as is true of many highly abstract notions. The limits of development are set, Malthus said, by the "fact" that population increases geometrically (1, 2, 4, 8, 16, 32...) but that subsistence (that is, production, especially of food) increases only arithmetically (1, 2, 3, 4,

5, 6...). He was subsequently derided because technological development intervened to allow production, including food, to *increase* more dynamically than he foresaw, at the same time that industrial development led to a *decrease* in the rate at which population grows.

So, by the end of the nineteenth century, economists believed that optimism, not pessimism, was solidly grounded in fact. However, neither they nor today's mainstream economists understood what imperialist expansion did, and still does, to upset the apparently benign relationships then apparent. When international capitalism rushed into imperialism in the closing decades of the past century, a considerably more powerful process in its impact than the expansions of the sixteenth, seventeenth, and eighteenth centuries, one consequence was *increased* population growth rates in the imperialized areas (because of improved public health) while simultaneously there was engendered in those same areas a process of retrogressive development, or underdevelopment.[22]

In short, the technological and socioeconomic developments that reduced population rates of growth in the industrialized countries exacerbated those pressures in the imperialized areas (of Africa, Latin America, and Asia)—and we do no more here than note the depletion of resources and environmental problems created by the same processes of economic and geographic expansion. Industrialization proceeding under capitalist auspices has, of course, been materially beneficial to perhaps a quarter of the world's population, but very much at the expense of the rest; ultimately, it now appears, it may be very much at the expense of all.

But in this, as in so many cases where comfort confronts misery, the relatively few who are comfortable attribute their well-being to their virtues and the ill-being of the many to the latters' personal defects, most frequently their laziness (although in the entire world, those who work hardest have the lowest incomes—as we shall see was noted by John Stuart Mill). Chapters 5 and 7 will pursue these arguments more fully.

In his other major argument, concerning "gluts," Malthus partially anticipated both Marx and Keynes, and their theories of capital accumulation and the causes of depression. Put simply, production takes place for profit in a capitalist economy; profit depends upon sales in buoyant—that is, sellers'—markets; the level of "effective demand" (a concept used also by both Marx and Keynes) is a measure of total sales, a level determined by the combination of sales to businesses (for equipment, etc.) and consumers; the former depend upon the actual and expected state of business, the latter upon the purchasing power of consumers. Since the state of business is partially and importantly dependent upon consumers' purchasing power of which the mass of consumers do not have enough, the economy will periodically or even persistently be faced with gluts—that is, with inadequate levels of effective demand. Malthus therefore argued the need for what he called "unproductive consumption," anticipating Keynes in his conviction that private (capitalist) prosperity would come to depend critically upon public spending.[23]

David Ricardo was the most illustrious successor to Smith, in his effective contributions both to political change and to political economy. Ricardo developed two "principles" of lasting importance in economic thought and practice. The "principle of diminishing returns" argued that increases in the use of one factor of production (say, labor) in combination with another, fixed factor (say, land), would initially bring increasing efficiency but subsequently increasing *inefficiency*. He used that argument to support increased imports of cheaper foreign grains, and thus carried forward Smith's aim of freeing the British economy from politically imposed handicaps; in this case the protective tariffs on imported grains (called "corn" in Britain). The Corn Laws made the price of bread unnecessarily high in Britain; the price of bread was the major determinant of wages; and wages were the strategic factor in manufacturers' costs. Therefore, the Corn Laws provided an unearned income (Ricardo, as was common then, called such incomes "rents," that is, returns to power, not production)[24] to the better-off landowners and reduced the profits (by increasing wage costs) to manufacturers. (Ricardo, like Smith and Marx, saw wages as being determined by the costs of subsistence, mostly food—mostly bread.) Thus, industrial development was held back by protective tariffs on grain, and they in turn were due to the political power of the large landowners. Ricardo argued the necessity of abolishing the Corn Laws in 1817. They were abolished in 1846, and Britain went to full "free trade."

International free trade, free trade by and for all nations, was the focus of his second principle, the "principle of comparative advantage." Put simply, all nations would be best off if each nation specialized in the production of that in which it was *relatively* most efficient. Such a pattern of production would maximize worldwide economic efficiency; but it would also freeze the world structure of production, so that the relatively most efficient in industrial production (by good fortune, Britain) would continue to industrialize, while the most relatively efficient hewers of wood and drawers of water would go on doing just that. That the former would have high incomes, military strength and a host of other advantages, and the latter would not, was not emphasized by Ricardo (nor by his followers in mainstream economics today); but it was quite clear to Alexander Hamilton, whose various "Reports" argued clearly and effectively that the new United States of America, rather than follow the Ricardian precept, should protect its "infant industries" if it was ever to be able to advance economically beyond its colonial status.[25]

Ricardo's analytical focus was considerably narrower, and his level of discussion considerably more abstract than Smith's. Having made a fortune in the London stock exchange Ricardo knew the real world well, and when in his arguments he abstracted from reality, it was a reality with which he was familiar. The reasoning in his *Principles* was largely *deductive*, based on logic; Smith was not by any means illogical, but his reasoning was largely *inductive*, derived from history and observation. In the past century and more, economics has been shaped by Ricardo's mode of reasoning (absent his sense of reality), and carried to extremes of abstraction requiring and allowing a rigidly limited reference to the real world. The arguments could be (and many theorists proudly proclaim this) used equally well—and uselessly—regarding "war games," sports, or other activities whose aim is, in effect, to win. In sum, the theorists who dominate the study and practice of economics and who take Ricardian method as the basis of their logical methods, unlike Ricardo himself, normally neglect the observable facts of our own, very different world, in favor of seeking always more elegant and abstract theorems.[26]

The decade of the 1840s saw the full triumph of free trade for Great Britain, both at home and in its foreign economic relationships; it also brought forth the last major work of classical political economy, and its great synthesis: *The Principles of Political Economy* (1848), by John Stuart Mill. In the very moment of its triumph, efforts to "interfere with the free market," to reintroduce protection for labor, were underway, sponsored by the "Tories" (mostly agrarian in their power) and religious groups. These were the so-called Factory Laws, which sought to limit the working hours and working dangers of women and children—almost unimaginably harsh for the modern mentality, even for those familiar with conditions in the poorest countries: children five to ten years old, working in coal mines and textile mills, dawn to dusk (more than twelve hours in midyear), with absolutely no safety provisions, with thirty minutes for rest and food in the entire working day; and they and the women always in constant fear of beatings and sexual mistreatment.[27]

These horrors came to be known to Mill through the activities of reform groups, which in turn led to governmental inquiries. While Mill was learning, so was Karl Marx, whose *Communist Manifesto* (written with Friedrich Engels) was also published in 1848—the year in which, the Manifesto begins, "a specter is haunting Europe...." Marxian ideas will be brought into focus shortly; now the continuity and change in the development of conventional economics is resumed.

John Stuart Mill, writing seventy years or so after Smith, could reflect on the economy and the economics that Smith had helped to create. By then, both were very different from what Smith had proposed; Mill lived at a time when the human suffering—the "satanic mills"—as well as the economic achievements of capitalism were evident. Furthermore, the problems facing the society were not those of a struggling new capitalism but those beginning to reveal "the failures of success." Or so it seemed to Mill. He did not foresee the renewed explosion of economic growth that lay ahead: industrialization spreading over Europe, North America, and Japan, a new wave of technological advance, a "second industrial revolution," giving vitality to capitalism through the cheapness of its metals, its fuels, its transportation and communications, its foodstuffs and raw materials; and, a necessary condition for all that, the completion and deepening of the imperialist conquest of the entire world by the major powers.

In 1848, Mill believed that the period of major vitality and expansion was drawing to a close. He pondered the probability and the implications of a "stationary state" (that is, a nonexpanding economy), which he, like some today, saw as desirable. He believed that the long hours of work were unnecessary, and the conditions of work in mine and mill inhumane; he saw the need for at least mild forms of social intervention. The increase of production had occupied the thoughts of Smith and Ricardo; for Mill the main problem was that of the extreme inequality of income distribution. He was an urbane and humane believer in capitalism, believing still in 1848 that political liberty and human decency were compatible with capitalist institutions. He was not rigid in his attachment to capitalism, however, as revealed by this passage from his *Principles*:

If, therefore, the choice were to be made between Communism with all its chances, and the present state of society with all its sufferings and injustices; if the institution of private property necessarily carried with it as a consequence, that the produce of labour should be apportioned as we now see it, almost in an inverse ratio to the labour—the largest portions to those who have never worked at all, the next largest to those whose work is almost nominal, and so in a descending scale, the remuneration dwindling as the work grows harder and more disagreeable, until the most fatiguing and exhausting bodily labour cannot count with certainty on being able to earn even the necessaries of life; if this, or Communism were the alternative, all the difficulties, great or small, of Communism would be but as dust in the balance.[28]

It is widely believed that by the time he died in 1873, Mill had become a socialist (and that he became so through his long association with and love for Harriet Taylor, herself a socialist). The mild ("gradualist") nature of British socialism in the late nineteenth century and up to the present, it is worth noting, has depended considerably more upon Mill than Marx, both in its analysis and its politics; whereas, in sharp contrast, continental developments were generally Marxist or anarchist.

Industrial Capitalism and Neoclassical Economics

Classical political economy may be viewed as an attack upon and critique of the dying remnants of the feudal and mercantilist epochs. It was an economics of *development*. Development is a process extending over substantial time, taking on its pace, direction, and forms because of the connections *within* the economy and *between* the economy and the larger society.

Neoclassical economics came into being when industrial capitalism was seen as fully established, in the 1860s and 1870s, most especially in Great Britain. In the hands of some, that economics served as an apologia for "free market" capitalism, as a sustained argument showing why Marx was wrong, and why even moderate social intervention in economic life (such as that advocated by Mill, for example) would harm the society. The harsh arguments of Malthus, seeing a large part of the population as immoral, useless, and growing too rapidly, were fundamental then, and still are.

Of great significance also, however, was the function of this economics in meeting the more narrowly economic needs of the business world. Those needs, by then, were not for the abolition of political constraints on businesses, already accomplished in Britain in the decades preceding the 1870s. Neoclassical economics took the political setting for granted (as "given"), as not to be changed, and *political economy* became *economics*. Economics soon became the "science" of economizing. It became, in the words of one of its most influential spokesmen, "the science which studies human behavior as a relationship between ends and scarce means which have alternative uses."[29]

The rationale underlying this theoretical focus was that relative to the rapidly growing demand for resources, as not only Britain but other nations underwent industrialization and demographic growth and restructuring (a smaller percentage of their growing populations producing food, for example), the supply of those resources, seen as finite, was already or would soon become dangerously scarce: therefore, economize, maximize efficiency. In fact the last quarter of the century saw the supplies of almost all resources expand at least as rapidly as demand, as the technologies of discovery, transportation, and production all improved swiftly—and as prices fell spectacularly (steel by 90 percent, for example) from the 1870s on. But this was (and is) an economics of *logic* in which the facts of the real world might be annoying but are not allowed to interfere with the reasoning.

A "science" of economizing and maximizing is quantitative in its procedures and content (although the "quantities" are posited rather than real, and are just as easily—and usually—represented by symbols rather than numbers). *Qualitative* relationships are left unexamined. Not being concerned with development, but with making the most of a good thing, neoclassical economics could, and still does, ignore historical (that is, real) time; its analysis is static, not dynamic. Social and political institutions, technological change, technology itself, the structures and functions of wealth and power—all this and much more could quite *logically* be taken as given. Those who developed neoclassical economics decided· upon these "givens" deliberately and in keeping with those analytical problems they chose to emphasize (as all theorists of all disciplines must and do). Their contemporary, and usually much less (methodologically) self-conscious, descendants often seem not to know what is even on the list of what is being ignored; as one wag has put it, some students *and* their professors may now believe that "society," rather than being the subject matter of the social sciences, is but a synonym for "parameters."

In sum, neoclassical economics works within a framework that places both the social process and social relationships outside its ken, except insofar as posited abstractly for purposes of the argument. This is so for the works of all neoclassical economists, including the two greatest, Alfred Marshall and John Maynard Keynes, and despite the quite different questions they confronted.

Economic theory today divides itself into two major sectors, *microeconomics* and *macroeconomics*.[30] The fundamentals of the former are found in Marshall's *Principles of Economics* (1890) and of the latter in Keynes's *General Theory of Employment, Interest, and Money* (1936). Marshall was the great synthesizer of neoclassical economics; Keynes, finding it necessary in the midst of the disastrous depression of the 1930s to alter a key assumption of that economics (having to do with savings and interest rates), may very well have opened a floodgate in his attempt to plug a hole in the dam.

The classicists, to repeat, were concerned with bringing about change, and the changes were both controversial and substantial. The difference between their focus and that of the neoclassicists is aptly suggested by the epigram on Marshall's title page: *Natura non facit saltum*—nature does not make leaps. It was not the intent of neoclassical economics to provide useful arguments for even gradual let alone "leaping" social or economic changes; maximum efficiency and maximum profits were their bywords—an explicable response to the felt needs and perceived interests of business toward the end of the nineteenth century, especially for Britain, the dominant industrial capitalist power.

Marshall saw nature and society as ruled by the "principle of continuity." Change was at the *edges* of life, slow, incremental, "marginal"—all this, by the way, when the world was changing more rapidly and abruptly in every way than ever before in history, and mostly for reasons of economic development.[31] However, in a world where natural resources, skilled labor, and capital were all *thought* to be stubbornly scarce, the economic problem came to be that of making the most of what was available, of economizing, of maximizing efficiency. By an almost magical process, a theoretical sleight of hand, the processes of maximizing efficiency also came to be those of maximizing the profits and minimizing the losses of business. In turn this meant no interference in the labor market (that is, trade unions or worker protections, etc.), among other dictates of this economics, a creamy topping for an already rich cake from the point of view of business.

Mainstream economists, then as now, would deny sleights of hand, the favoring of business, and almost all the rest of the foregoing. Increased efficiency and market rationality are quite simply the means to the best economic end, best for all people, all societies. Economics thus focused on the ("micro") unit where such efficiency would be achieved. That was the individual firm (assumed to be small and quite powerless in the face of the market), using materials, equipment, and labor in the most efficient combinations. The economy would get the most for least when all firms produced where their costs and outputs and sales were optimally in balance ("equilibrium"), with workers minimizing the "disutility" of labor, and consumers maximizing "utility," a state of mind subjective, unknowable, and unmeasurable. (So much for science.) With all participants portrayed as maximizing and minimizing individuals, there are no classes, and thus no class problems or other forms of social conflict, and no basis for social interference in the economy.

The "laws of supply and demand" are of course much more complicated than this, and some of that will be treated later. More important at this point is the conception of human nature and of society that the classical economists handed down to the neoclassicists, and the latters' modifications of that conception. A digression on this important question is essential, after which we shall proceed to a brief discussion of Keynes.

Human Nature and Conduct

All competent social theorists begin (literally or figuratively) with a working conception of human nature and how that presumed nature contributes and responds to social relationships and processes. When we unconsciously absorb these ideas, through our formal and informal education, we are also induced to accept or reject social principles and proposals without a knowing basis for doing so. The meaning and the validity of any social theory rests upon its treatment of the raw materials of that theory: the nature of our species and of the process of social change. The most profound analytical differences between those who have uncritically accepted capitalism and those who have not are to be found in this area of analysis; the other differences follow.

Smith was a philosopher held in high esteem (largely because of his first book, *The Theory of Moral Sentiments*) before he turned his talents to economic affairs. He believed in an inherent "natural order" superior to anything human beings might seek to create, and that the wisest form of social organization is that which allows people to act as nearly as possible in harmony with the dictates of that "natural order." Those dictates, if not interfered with by human and especially governmental meddling—such as that of mercantilism—would lead to an "obvious and simple system of human liberty."[32]

According to Smith, human beings are actuated by six motives: self-love, sympathy, the desire to be free, a sense of propriety, a habit of labor, and "the propensity to truck, barter, and exchange." Let us be ourselves, said Smith, and the beneficence of Providence will provide that social order which, though not perfect, is the best to be had. The best we can do for ourselves is to let the natural order realize itself: anything else is harmful. This in turn implies allowing the self-interest that characterizes us to assert itself without interference.

In practical and political terms, this meant ridding society of the State's meddling and allowing a laissez-faire capitalist society to emerge, and "it's each for himself and God for all." The subsequent development of capitalism led to an added phrase: "as the elephant said, while he danced among the chickens."

Smith's conception of human nature was narrow, by comparison with Marx, Veblen, and John Dewey, for example; but it was narrowed still more by the neoclassical economists. For Smith's six human propensities or attributes, neoclassical economics substituted *homo economicus*, thus compressing human nature into a mold of rational economic maximization, entirely lacking what Smith called "sympathy"—that is, any feeling or concern whatsoever for anyone other than ourselves.[33] Neoclassical economics, still today, works with the long-discredited conception of "man as hedonist," a rational and calculating person who seeks to maximize pleasure (by consumption) and minimize pain (by not working). Thorstein Veblen, an early and relentless critic of that economics (and of U.S. capitalism), ridiculed these notions of human nature in this observation:

The hedonistic conception of man is that of a lightning calculator of pleasure and pains, who oscillates like a homogeneous globule of desire of happiness under the impulse of stimuli that shift him about the area, but leave him intact. He has neither antecedent nor consequent. He is an isolated, definitive human datum, in stable equilibrium except for the buffets of the impinging forces that displace him in one direction or another.

Self-imposed in elemental space, he spins symmetrically about his own spiritual axis until the parallelogram of forces bears down upon him whereupon he follows the line of the resultant. When the force of the impact is spent, he comes to rest, a self-contained globule of desire as before.[34]

Marx and Veblen viewed the classical and the neoclassical conceptions of human nature and society as culture-bound and ahistorical, much though they may have disagreed about other matters. Both saw our species as a *part* of nature, rather than as one set apart from or against nature; more to the present point, they saw human beings as *transforming* nature and (most clearly in Marx) as thereby transforming themselves, as part of nature. And they perceived human nature as being distorted —Marx used the term alienated (see below)—by the social conditions of capitalism. As for society, given this conception of the relationship between human beings and nature, it followed that no form of social organization is "natural": all societies are created by human beings, all in a process of continuous change, all are historically dynamic, all give rise to processes and relationships which are self-displacing. The difference between Marx and Veblen on this score was not on the question of permanence or change, but on the question of how the process of change works out, and the directions in which it moves. Marx was profoundly optimistic, Veblen just as gloomy.

In addition to these differences between the classical-neoclassical economists and Marx and Veblen, there is a striking difference regarding work. For Marx, the main motive forces of history revolved around the production and reproduction of life. For him, an animal's life—and people are animals—is its *activity*, what it does; first and foremost what humans do is to produce and reproduce the stuff of life (or the species would not have survived). Work is not only natural, but fulfilling. Under capitalist conditions, however, people do not *work* for themselves, they *labor* for others—for those who own and control the means of production, the means of life, who decide what will be produced and why—for profit—it will be produced, and by whom the workers, because they are propertyless and thus powerless, are exploited. Under such conditions, Marx said, the worker is *alienated*:

First, the work is external to the worker, ...it is not part of his nature; ...consequently, he does not fulfill himself in his work but denies himself, has a feeling of misery rather than well-being, does not develop freely his mental and physical energies but is physically exhausted and mentally debased. The worker, therefore, feels himself at home only during his leisure time, whereas at work he feels homeless. His work is not voluntary but imposed, *forced labour*. It is not the satisfaction of a need, but only a *means* for satisfying other needs. Its alien character is clearly shown by the fact that as soon as there is no physical or other compulsion it is avoided like the plague.[35]

Because the basic productive life under capitalism is necessarily alienating, Marx saw workers as therefore further alienated from nature, from themselves, from other human beings, and from their essential and distinctive nature as human beings (which he called species-being). For the conventional economists' mechanical view of humans, Marx substituted a dynamic view, where human beings, nature, and society move in a process of continuous, mutually transforming interaction. Fundamentally, Veblen agreed.

Veblen's views were put forth in *The Instinct of Workmanship* (1914). Before examining those ideas, it is necessary to show how he uses the term *instinct*, for many criticisms leveled at Veblen have sought to dismiss him as being unscientific for merely using the word. After stating that "instinct" is a concept of "too lax and shifty a definition to meet the demands of exact biological science," Veblen goes on to state:

"Instinct," as contradistinguished from tropismatic action, involves consciousness and adaptation to an end aimed...at the conscious pursuit of an objective end which the instinct in question makes worthwhile.... The ends of life, then, the purposes to be achieved, are assigned by man's instinctive proclivities; but the ways and means of accomplishing those things which the instinctive proclivities so make worth while are a matter of intelligence.... Men take thought, but the human spirit... decides what they shall take thought of, and how and to what effect.[36]

Veblen's "instinct of workmanship" overlaps with Marx's notion of work as the life activity of human beings, in the sense that workmanship and what Veblen calls the "parental bent" refer to the production and the reproduction of life. The sense of workmanship has for Veblen a "sub-instinct," that of "idle curiosity." It is this latter that accounts for the growth of technology, science, and culture, and that makes human beings transformers of themselves, society, and nature. What Veblen calls "the regime of private property" (and Marx called capitalism), he argued, leads people to shirk labor and to become reduced as human beings. And he finds another "instinct," that of "sportsmanship." This is his ironic way of referring to the combative, warlike, and ultimately self-destructive processes that have littered so much of history.

If Veblen is gloomier than Marx, at least part of the reason is that he sees workmanship and sportsmanship as running a terrible race, between life- and death-giving activities, and he saw little reason to believe that a society controlled by "force and fraud" would allow the race to be won by life. We shall have occasion to return to these questions later. Now we turn our attention back to the nature, evolution, and inadequacies of neoclassical economics.

Transformation and Failure of the Market Economy

The narrow and mechanical view of human nature and of the basic outlines of nineteenth-century Britain as the representation of an essentially unchanging "natural order" verge on the ludicrous today. Even as the analytical framework of neoclassical economics was being constructed, the processes of social change were consigning it to irrelevance. The market economics of Marshall assumed a competitive and small-scale (quaintly so) economic structure. Its "representative firm" was the center of Marshall's "model." Were such a firm to exist today, it would only be as a display at Disneyland. Without that "representative firm" that economics makes no sense at all.

In the very years in which Marshall put together his grand synthesis of neoclassicism, monopolies were moving to center stage; today all the industrial powers are characterized and dominated by monopolistic (technically, "oligopolistic") structures of ownership and control, by super-corporations unimaginable in their complexity and sweep to a Marshall, ignored not only in the theory but also in the policy recommendations of the economics profession. (As we shall see in Chapter 3, the exuberant free market economists who surrounded Reagan, and still surround Bush, have encouraged and applauded the policies that have made what as recently as the 1970s were already supercorporations take off to even more staggering dimensions.)

Marshall's theoretical model also assumed and advocated an unobtrusive State. All industrial States are today necessarily and continuously interventionist, and largely at the behest of big business—those with economic power. Behind all the free market arguments the unspoken question is not *shall* the State intervene, but *how*, and, equally important, for whose benefit and at whose cost. It was noted above that the "economics of scarcity" (also called "the economics of choice") was developed in the late nineteenth century, when the world's resources were becoming more plentiful than ever; and that is spectacularly even more so in this century. Our problems are not those of inadequate resources and productive capacities for the world's population; they are problems of distribution, of economic direction, and of the quality and safety of both products and productive processes. Not nature, but the ways in which economies are organized, by, for whom, and for what, are the causes of the terrible scarcities that afflict a good three-quarters of the world's peoples.[37]

At the close of the nineteenth century, Marshall's era, there was one unchallengeable power: Great Britain. The war that exploded in 1914 was a symptom of, among other great changes, the inability of Britain any longer to rule the world at all, to say nothing of unchallengeably. Since then, the world has been in a constant state of tumult, in its economics, its politics, its structures, its ways and means. An "economics of choice" might well be useful as a *part* of our economic/political thinking and behavior; allowed to be the major, let alone the *only*, way in which we guide our social existence, such an economics in today's world has become something more than a bad joke; it is positively dangerous: spray deodorants and automobiles respond to market incentives; the riddled ozone layer and the warming atmosphere do not.

One might be excused for thinking that the extraordinary turbulence of the period that began as the nineteenth century ended, a period now almost a century old, and which has encompassed two major and many "lesser" wars, many revolutions and counterrevolutions, and among other upheavals, the worldwide depression of the 1930s—would have led mainstream economists to reevaluate their theories. The depression did seem to begin that process of rethinking; however, as we shall see, the changes brought about were *theoretically* peripheral, though of great practical importance; and they were temporary. The reevaluations that have taken place in the economics "establishment" in the recent past, and that now dominate both theory and policy, have been all too "successful" attempts to transport both micro and macro neoclassical economic theory and policy back to their late nineteenth century state.

Depression, Keynes, and War

The central importance of economic and geographic expansion for the maintenance of capitalism is so great that we shall devote much of Chapters 4 and 7 to explaining why that is so, and under what conditions the need has and has not been met. Here our attention will be confined to the alteration of economics and of capitalism induced by the *failure* of expansion between the two world wars.

Great Britain was economically stagnant throughout the entire 1920s, suffering from a languishing business community and an average of 10 percent unemployment throughout the decade.[38] The entire capitalist world collapsed after 1929, and the collapse was most devastating in the two most highly industrialized nations, the United States and Germany. The enormity of that depression is suggested by the fact that industrial production in both the United States and Germany fell by 50 percent. Since World War II, in contrast, it has never dropped more than a few percentage points, and then for very brief periods—in large part, as will be shown in later chapters, because of governmental intervention.

The economists were caught off guard by the depression. The facts were plain and large, but the theory could not handle such (or any) facts. Neoclassical macro theory (essentially monetary theory), until it went through a revision after 1936, taught that when unemployment occurred it was "voluntary"; that is, it happened because workers were demanding excessive wages.

When unemployment in the United States rose to (a very conservatively estimated) 25 percent of the labor force in 1933, and long bread and soup lines became a daily sight throughout the nation (there was no unemployment compensation, no social security, nor any other interferences with the free market for labor), it became somewhat difficult to believe that it was unrealism concerning wages that placed all those unemployed on all those lines. There were no jobs to be had at any wage for them. The problem lay elsewhere, and it was this that brought Keynes to his (for then) radical conclusions.

The theoretical sticking-point for neoclassical theory was "Say's Law." Jean-Baptiste Say (1767–1832), who tried to spread Smith's free market ideas in still mercantilist France (with no success), also sought to show the theoretical impossibility of a depression. He argued that "supply creates its own demand."[39] That is, everything that is produced will always be sold at normal prices, either to consumers or businesses, because (1) the value of production creates consumer purchasing power to the same value, and (2) that portion of income not spent on consumer goods but saved is offset by business purchases of investment goods. The key notion underlying Say's argument was that consumers would reduce their expenditures and save only because the rate of interest paid for savings would induce them to do so; and that the rate of interest is determined by the demand of investors for funds (with which they would purchase the difference between consumer goods bought and total production). In short, consumption and investment are reciprocally motivated; if consumption declined it was because investment rose to exactly the same degree. QED: supply creates its own demand. Given that neat argument, it followed, among other things, that there could be no involuntary unemployment. The jobless are evidently lazy, witless, useless, seeking excessive wages, or all of the above. Justice is done.

Keynes's *General Theory of Employment, Interest, and Money* jiggled one assumption in that theory and came out with opposite conclusions. He showed that consumption and investment are not reciprocally motivated; that savings are related more to changes in money income than to the rate of interest.[40] Thus, not only could depression and high (involuntary) unemployment occur, but in the normal and "rational" functioning of industrial capitalism they were downright likely; and, Keynes argued, without governmental intervention to supplement private (consumer and business) demand, the economy could get stuck in a trough of depression with no tendency to escape.

Up to the time of the *General Theory*, neoclassical economics had served to show why governmental intervention was both unnecessary and undesirable. Keynes, though himself a basically conventional (and highly esteemed) neoclassical monetary economist, was led by the events to believe that intervention was necessary in order to save capitalism itself. Capitalism had matured; it had to take care.

Like all the great economists who had preceded him, Keynes was not so much a creator of new ideas as one who integrated others' ideas when the times compelled attention. Swedish economists had for several years been developing the basic ideas presented in the *General Theory*, and Keynes was assisted by a group of young and brilliant economists such as R.F. Kahn, Joan Robinson, and Michael Kalecki.[41]

Depression or no, resistance among economists to the new ideas was strong and lasting (and lasts still), as Keynes had anticipated. "The difficulty," Keynes wrote in the Preface to the *General Theory*, "lies, not in the new ideas, but in escaping from the old ones, which ramify, for those brought up as most of us have been, into every corner of our minds."[42] If anything, the opposition to Keynesian ideas in terms of their practical implications was even greater among "men of affairs" than economists. They did not relish being told that thrift was not necessarily a virtue, or that not only government spending but deficit spending (that is, an excess of government expenditures over taxes) and perhaps even socialized consumption and investment had become at least intermittently necessary. For these U.S. businessmen and politicians, the blocks to understanding and acceptance were all the higher, given the British citizenship and aristocratic mien of Keynes—who did not suffer fools gladly—theorists being suspect enough in any case.

In the late 1930s, President Franklin Roosevelt and Congress responded, both too little and too late, to the prescriptions of "the new economics." Widespread acceptance came only after the practical experience of World War II and the Cold War taught economists, politicians, and businessmen that, like it or not, the ideas worked to maintain employment and increase profits. The first economics textbook to incorporate Keynesian ideas was Paul Samuelson's *Economics* (1947), initially banned in several states as being "communistic." The first administration after World War II to absorb and apply the ideas systematically was that of John F. Kennedy; by 1970, even the arch-conservative President Richard Nixon proclaimed "I am a Keynesian."

Keynes died in 1946. It is doubtful that he would have been pleased with that narrowing and alteration of his ideas that allowed their acceptance even in the farther reaches of conservatism. Such an evolution requires explanation of what Keynesian theory accomplished and what it left undone; and, how it thereby came to be something Keynes, himself, explicitly opposed: "military Keynesianism." Only the bare bones of the theory as he and his co-workers developed it have survived. Not only policy makers but also most economists are unaware of (and/or against) the body of arguments and policies surrounding those bones. He caused some mainstream economists to reexamine a few of their premises; but the main structure of their economics remained intact and has gone on to house always finer webs of counter-factual "analysis."

If we look further into what Keynes wrote (not only in the *General Theory* but also in numerous essays), we see that he came to the conclusion that the long-term prospect for industrial capitalism was a continuing tendency for the economy to function at high levels of unemployment and unused productive capacity—what has come to be called stagnation. This is due to the inability of a mature industrial capitalist economy profitably to absorb the output of ever-increasing productive capacity. However, in a private, that is, "pre-Keynesian" economy, the engine that makes both consumer incomes and business profits rise so as to be able to *absorb* increased productive capacity is precisely that same process of *increasing* productive capacity (called net real investment).

Fundamentally, then, the problem has the following dimensions as Keynes saw it: (1) increases in productive capacity are enduring (lasting, say, ten to twenty years or more), while increases in consumer incomes and the purchases thus financed that are made possible by increased investment are relatively short-lived (lasting, say, one to two years); (2) this is so because out of every round of increased income, there is a round of savings (the rate tending to rise), that is, a withdrawal of consumer purchasing power; (3) this in turn is a consequence of the highly unequal distribution of income innate to a capitalist economy, leaving most of the population with far too little purchasing power, while a small fraction has incomes that are in excess of their spending habits. The latter therefore save, as their incomes rise (the data show that all the net saving is done by the best-off 10 percent of the population; the savings of the rest are offset by their borrowing).[43] (4) And all this means that what Keynes called "the deflationary gap," if it is not to have negative effects, must be offset by increases in real net investment. But that is where we began, and that is also where the troubles begin—troubles that, according to Keynes, require an ongoing, in effect permanent commitment for the government to fill that savings gap by its own spending whenever necessary. If that spending is on social consumption and social investment (for example, on subsidized public housing, education, health facilities, and the like), such policies amount to a redistribution downward of real income, ultimately financed by someone's taxes. Whose? Those who would prefer to do the net savings. Quite apart from any other problem with this reform program, there is this key fact: Those who do the net savings are also those with the most economic and political power, not at all inclined (or so powerless) as to be treated that-a-way.

Keynes, a critic of capitalism, but one who could not countenance any other social system, believed (evidently with reluctance) that only a much reformed capitalism could survive. That made him what came to be called a "Left Keynesian." As will be discussed in Chapters 4 and 8, such social policies became quite common from the 1960s on throughout Western Europe, and also in the United States, where the reform program, which included the "war on poverty" and related measures, was made acceptable in critical part by having substantially heavier government expenditures on the military and superhighways—yielding, in the 1960s and 1970s the United States "warfare/welfare state."[44]

By the mid-1970s there was a growing and already serious economic crisis, affecting all the major industrial countries. The socio-economic-political consequences of that crisis translated slowly but surely into the conservative ideas and policies of the late 1970s and since, as will be discussed in Chapters 4 and 8. Now, a few summary words on some shortcomings of Keynesian theory and policies, which may shed light on some reasons for those subsequent changes.

Keynesian economics constituted a significant improvement over what preceded it, but at least three matters have rendered it inadequate for the present. First, as suggested above, its acceptance was never more than partial, and (in the United States, by comparison with Sweden, for example) never put in practice in the manner Keynes proposed. Keynes knew there was a strong need for *structural* changes in the economy—in production, consumption, income distribution—but those called "Keynesians" today (except for the promising new "post-Keynesians") continue to analyze and prescribe in terms of marginal adjustments and aggregative policies, rendering what Keynes saw as qualitative problems into quantitative puzzles. Their effect is to maintain the very structures and practices that have generated the problem. Second, Keynes developed a theory for an economy whose dynamics were held to their national dimensions; the internationalization of the United States and all other economies requires a substantial theoretical alteration, not just an "adjustment," to come to grips with a tightly integrated and advanced industrial world economy. Third, the theory Keynes developed was meant to apply to a fundamentally private economy, with government activities brought in to resolve troublesome developments. The government is not in his model, nor should it have been for his purposes, but now it is very much in the economy. As will be seen in Chapter 4, the State's large role both resolves and creates problems.

The economy is still privately dominated (not least because of the enormous political power that those with economic power have), but the structure of the economy is heavily and permanently infused with government as spender, taxer, employer. Even, or we may say especially, Ronald Reagan, whether as governor of California or president of the United States, expanded the role of the government in all these respects, although he and his cohorts transformed the *uses* of the government substantially to favor the already well-off at the expense of those not at all so.

In different words, Keynesian theory pounded cracks in the wall of neoclassical laissez-faire philosophy and capitalist practice; in doing so, it necessitated a different theory, one that would provide understanding of a global monopoly capitalist system (where the State and the world economy play vital roles); whilst Keynes's theory was geared to a national economy with laissez-faire institutions.

Not least among the missing elements is a theory of power, in Keynes as in the rest of neoclassical economics. The principal tendencies of contemporary economics are to mathematize and refine the micro and macro economics of the past, leaving one caught between tears and laughter, as our times demand analyses at once broader and deeper than any now existing.

Toward a New Political Economy

The foregoing very long examination of the evolution of economic analysis has usually been harshly critical; we may now soften that somewhat by noting two not insubstantial areas offering promise. First, as pointed out earlier, conventional economics, though dominated by its theory, has long been connected to many fields of "applied economics," touching on virtually every aspect of economic life—agriculture, public finance, labor, international trade, etc. These fields have collected and organized vast bodies of published data—without which a work such as this would be impossible. The large defect of these data is that the criteria for their collection have derived either from a theory that provides poor direction, or from a hodge podge of conflicting analyses. We gain understanding not merely by looking at or for facts, but by looking for and at them with appropriate questions. The main virtue of the published data is that when they are put to the service of promising analyses they represent a large body of work that has been done, and which, with care, can help us to compose more useful analyses.

Second, there are existing and potential promising analyses close to hand. Some of that has been put forth in preceding pages, both as a critique of the mainstream and as valuable in itself; and for many years now there have been spreading attempts to put together the work of those in the past, such as Marx, Keynes, and Veblen, with the available collections of data, while developing new analyses and organizing contemporary data. It is seldom true that human beings must start from scratch in resolving their problems; nor is it true for us now. What follows, then, are some brief comments on what needs to be and is being done to meet our needs for better understanding of the capitalist process.

Those now seeking to change the various aspects of social analysis are responding to a society that is changing rapidly and under great stress, and that places large numbers of people under immense suffering and apprehension. The major characteristics of that society in the United States and elsewhere interact in such a way as to threaten much of what has not already been damaged or destroyed. Some reading those words might wonder what causes this lament: Has there ever been a time when so many have had so much? True enough, but neither has there been a time when so many more, more than ever in history, have had so dangerously little; nor when the fates of the privileged and the desperate have been so closely interwoven. Nor has there ever been a time when the avoidance of social disaster must be accompanied by taking large steps, soon, for saving the natural environment, a crisis caused directly by the powerful economic processes of just this century. To meet these challenges, we need a biochemistry of the social process, but we are still in the hands of alchemists.

The strong criticisms of conventional economics running through this chapter are not meant to suggest that economics—and even less, theory as such—is useless. Neoclassical economics (or "marginalism") is a theory of minor adjustments within a given social and economic framework. It cannot, though it often does, make any pretense of providing understanding of socioeconomic structures and processes, or of when and why it might be necessary to seek structural changes in production, consumption, trade, income distribution, investment, or, say, the structure of power. Minor adjustments to enhance efficiency are always called for, in any economy; marginalism of the micro or the macro variety will be useful for that question, and only it, so long as that is so.

Now, however, *structural* changes are badly needed, and society has the right to expect something more than marginalist theory from its economists. But what is meant by "society"? The economics profession sees itself as serving society as a whole, a presumption not shared by those who started the profession, the classical political economists. Ricardo, on the opening page of his *Principles*, presented the principal focus of political economy as the distribution of income; and his theory was explicitly designed to enhance the category of profits at the expense of land rents—with wages seen merely as a necessary cost, to be held to the subsistence minimum. Ricardo placed the interests of one propertied class against another's in his theory, as it was in reality.

Contemporary economic theory sees no classes, no interests, only the maximizing of efficiency to the presumed benefit of all, and economists see themselves not merely as neutral, but as analyzing a society in which not neutrality, but rationality is the sole issue. And they have provided a theoretical foundation for a capitalism whose structures and functions are for the overwhelming benefit of a small minority. Although all should seek to be *objective*, that is, pay due accord to fact and logic, nobody can be or should seek to be socially *neutral*—if the term means not caring about social outcomes.

Confusion on this matter is one reason why so many conventional economists are taken aback by the politically forthcoming, self-styled "radical," "institutionalist" (usually signifying followers of Veblen), and, among others, "post Keynesian" economists, whom they criticize for being "political." But those who wish to keep things the same, whether they are conscious of that or not, are every bit as much as political as those who wish to change those same things. Everyone cares; spare us, especially in the social "sciences," from those who are indifferent.[45]

Caring is not enough, of course. We need an appropriate framework of analysis (and a politics to pursue its implications). Whatever else it needs to be, this framework must be informed by history. What is changing cannot be understood except as a part of a process that leads to change. To study historically is to study in terms of *connections*; it is to take far fewer matters as *given*. Conventional economics shies away from such modes of inquiry; political economy in the past did not. The political economy we need cannot.

A place to begin anew, whatever else it depends upon, should include the insights of Marx and Veblen. Even their combined works are necessarily inadequate for the needs of our time, but they provide a strong foundation upon which to build a modern political economy.

The range of Marx's inquiries was as broad as society itself, although he bore down systematically and thoroughly only on economic analysis in *Capital*. Almost all conventional social scientists, and not least the economists, have rejected the possibility of Marx having said anything of much use to those living in capitalist society—and most have done so with the confidence that comes from never having bothered to read Marx. Veblen is a name that is virtually unknown in professional circles, except perhaps as that quaint man who coined the term "conspicuous consumption" about a century ago.

The indifference and scorn meted out to these two analytical giants is made comprehensible by their own arguments, which explain the manner in which critical theories are deflected by an intellectual status quo, as well as by other elements of the social power structure. As Marx put it, "the ruling ideas of any era are the ideas of its ruling class." The works of both Marx and Veblen help us to understand why basic impulses toward change in economics and in the society seem almost always "to die a-borning." It is a matter of the staying power of a status quo, quite apart from the enormous difficulties facing those who would change ideas, let alone society. Those out of power have little to work with and much to oppose; those in power have much to work with and little to oppose—until, perhaps, society finds itself in a crisis, and the balance between its virtues and its defects begins to tilt unfavorably.

It appears that the United States entered the first stages of an enduring crisis in the 1970s, characterized economically (and oversimply) as "stagflation." The processes of crisis do not reveal their causes or produce their consequences suddenly; left unresolved, or "resolved" with policies meant to preserve the old order, however, crisis spreads and deepens. Meanwhile, the social consciousness of all, of the powerful and the weak, is stimulated and enhanced; rubbed raw. And those in power find it always more necessary (and more complicated) to tighten their hold on the reins of the social process, to concentrate power even more, and to use it always more harmfully.[46]

Since the 1930s, economics has been in a process of transformation as it has sought to cope with a whole new range of pressing questions and developments: depression, endemic inflation, business monopolies and trade unionism, modern public finance, economic growth and development, poverty, ecology, and complicated international changes. Attempts to inform all this by theory have accompanied these tumultuous changes; but in the mainstream, the hard core of the theory used has been neoclassical theory—a theory that assumes away change and takes as "given" the very matters requiring analysis.

If we think of theory as a compass to guide us, then we may note that a defective compass is worse than none at all: errors become systematic and cumulative. This should not be taken as an argument for substituting hunches and intuition for analysis: the need is to develop better, indeed a radically different, theory. What its outlines might be must be integrally related to the social concerns and aims of its makers; what can be said in this book in those respects will appear mostly in the closing chapter.

Whatever else might characterize that theory, it must come to terms with history. In a time of rapid and troubling change, the minimum basis for understanding is that we know how we got where we are, and why; in a time when change cuts through all quarters of social existence, we must know how the various aspects of social existence connect and interact. The specialization of social inquiry that has given us "economics," "sociology," and "political science," and the innumerable fields within each of those, has led to analytical compartments hermetically sealed off from each other—and from the very reality they presume to explain. The social analysis our times require must take society for what it is, an organic and dynamic whole. Were such an analysis to develop, many specialized efforts of conventional social science could take on a new and positive meaning.

In the years since the 1960s attempts have been made to move in these directions in all the social sciences. In economics the most noteworthy and early development was the emergence of The Union for Radical Political Economics (URPE), in 1968. It survives as a serious, respected, and dynamic organization. In addition to its theoretical journal, *The Review of Radical Political Economics*, noted earlier, URPE has a monthly magazine that explains well and clearly the principal issues of the day, *Dollars and Sense*. We shall make reference to useful articles in both publications in the chapters that follow.

Neither the tasks set by URPE for itself, nor those set by their counterparts in other areas, will be easily or quickly fulfilled, any more than a decent and safe society can be easily or quickly created. Among the many matters compelling immediate attention is the need to comprehend the whys and wherefores of capitalism as a social system, in its nature and contemporary workings, especially in the United States, to which we now turn.

Reading Suggestions

In this and succeeding chapters we shall list books to facilitate the concerned reader's ability to push beyond the general perspective offered here. Many more references could be listed; the criterion guiding these selections is a combinatiuon of accessibility, readability, breadth, and depth. An asterisk (*) following the book's title means it is available in paperback editions.

The kind of understanding we all need combines facts with analysis; the kinds of facts and analyses we need are, some of them, to be found off the beaten track. For "facts," which are always chosen and organized from an analytical/value standpoint, we have already noted *Dollars and Sense*, published by the Economic Affairs Bureau, One Summer Street, Somerville, Mass. 02143. Another handy and comprehensive source of facts is the book put together by the Center for Popular Economics, Amherst, Mass., with which *Dollars and Sense* shares many contributors: *A Field Guide to the United States Economy** (New York: Pantheon Books, 1987), coordinated and written by Nancy Folbre. It is probably the most readable and comprehensive (and least expensive) of such works, with more than two hundred pages of charts, graphs, and illustrations covering all aspects of the economic process. For those who are intimidated by statistics and wish not to be, Lucy Horwotz and Lon Ferleger's *Statistics for Social Change** (Boston: South End Press, 1980) will be a great boon. Now we turn to books of analysis and history.

Robert L. Heilbroner, *The Worldly Philosophers** (New York: Simon and Schuster, 1953) is a brisk introduction to the lives and works of the major figures in the development of economic thought. If it is occasionally a bit breezy, that is perhaps an unavoidable accompaniment of the author's unusually readable style. Eric Roll, *A History of Economic Thought** (Englewood Cliffs, N.J.: Prentice-Hall, 1946) is not brisk, but it does penetrate more deeply than Heilbroner, and is very useful in relating the classicists and neoclassicists to each other and in placing Marx with respect to them. Leo Rogin, *The Meaning and Validity of Economic Theory: A Historical Approach* (New York: Harper's, 1956) is the most incisive analysis of how and why economic theory developed, up through Keynes. Unfortunately, the author died before he completed the book, and parts of the text reflect this. It remains a superb analysis. (As do the several methodological essays in Veblen's *Place of Science in Modern Civilization*, noted earlier.)

The shortcomings of conventional analysis may be studied from various standpoints. Joan Robinson, *Economic Philosophy** (Chicago: Aldine, 1962) is a cheerful but slashing critique of conventional theory by one who has made contributions both to it and to Marxian analysis. An excellent, mostly but not entirely Marxian collection of essays is E.K. Hunt and Jesse G. Schwartz, eds., *A Critique of Economic Theory** (Harmondsworth, England: Penguin Books, 1972). Benjamin Ward, in his *What's Wrong with Economics?* (New York: Basic Books, 1972) laments the methodological inconsistencies and inadequacies of conventional theory, and is all the more devastating because of his seeming detachment. Sidney Schoeffler, *The Failures of Economics: A Diagnostic Study* (Cambridge, Mass.: Harvard University Press, 1955) is a technical critique of economic theory from a coolly logical standpoint, an attempt to reform from within that the profession has studiously ignored since its publication many years ago. A very interesting book concerned with the development of theory in the *natural* sciences, Thomas Kuhn, *The Structure of Scientific Revolutions* (Chicago: University of Chicago Press, 1962), which seeks to show how and why the hard core of scientific theory, its "paradigms," undergoes change and displacement, has stimulated much controversy on the degree to which his analysis applies to *social* thought.

A new and excellent collection, "Schools of Thought in Economics," put out by Edward Elgar Publishing, Chattenham, England includes of interest for our focus *Post-Keynesian Economics*, edited by Malcolm C. Sawyer (1989), *Institutional Economics*, 3 volumes, edited by Warren J. Samuels (1992), *Radical Political Economy*, edited by Samuel Bowles and Richard Edwards (1990), and *Marxian Economics*, edited by J.E. King (1990). See also Howard J. Sherman, *Foundations of Radical Political Economy* (Armonk, N.Y.: M.E. Sharpe, 1987).

Brian Burkitt, *Radical Political Economy: An Introduction to the Alternative Economics** (New York: New York University Press, 1984), examines dissenting thought going back to the early nineteenth century and up to the present, all critical either of conventional thought and/or of capitalism in its own day (ranging from Owen through Marx, "Fabianism" and "syndicalism," to contemporary radical analysis). The book is excellently organized, and the discussions clear. James Weaver, ed., *Modern Political Economy: Radical and Orthodox Views on Crucial Issues** (Boston: Allyn & Bacon, 1973) provides a good collection of contrasting views. Two excellent introductory texts well and usefully off the beaten track are E. K. Hunt and Howard Sherman, *Economics** (New York: Harper & Row, 1985) and Tom Riddell, et al. *Economics: A Tool for Social Understanding** (Reading, Mass.: Addison Wesley, 1987). The latter book is unique in being not only seriously useful, but also very funny along the way. Many of the criticisms of economics made in this chapter have their sociological counterpart in C. Wright Mills, *The Sociological Imagination** (New York: Oxford University Press, 1967).

The best introduction to Marxian economic theory is Paul M. Sweezy, *The Theory of Capitalist Development** (New York: Monthly Review Press, 1968; originally published in 1942). Dudley Dillard, *The Economics of John Maynard Keynes** (Englewood Cliffs, N.J.: Prentice-Hall, 1948) does for Keynes what Sweezy did for Marx, for those who wish to "do" Keynesian theory. In a less ambitious way, I have sought to do something of the same for Veblen, in my *Thorstein Veblen** (New York: Washington Square Press, 1964). A work demonstrating that realistic and important economic thought has not always required radicalism in viewpoint is J. M. Clark, *Studies in the Economics of Overhead Costs* (Chicago: University of Chicago Press, 1923). Clark sought to integrate "micro" and "macro" processes into a dynamic whole connected with the facts of modern industrial life in the United States. Clark's father, J. B. Clark, was perhaps the most eminent of the turn-of-the-century United States neoclassical economists. Interestingly, Veblen had studied with the father, and many of his arguments were directed against J. B.; but the son, J. M., studied with Veblen, and was much influenced by his down-to-earth approach.

An original interpretation of U.S. history is provided by William Appleman Williams, in his *Contours of American History** (Chicago: Quadrangle, 1965); and, also worth reading is his *The Great Evasion** (New York: Quadrangle, 1964), noted earlier, wherein Williams challenges the usual assumption that Marxism is irrelevant to our "unique" development. Others of Williams's books will be cited in later chapters.

Finally, the matter of "alienation" has been discussed in this chapter, and there will be reason to bring it up again later. Much has been written about that complicated and worrisome question. A readable introduction to most of its dimensions is Eric and Mary Josephson, eds., *Man Alone: Alienation in Modern Society** (New York: Dell, 1962), and, on a more particular level, Studs Terkel's *Working** (New York: Pantheon, 1962), whose subtitle is "People Talk About What They Do All Day and How They Feel About What They Do." It is an illuminating and unsettling glimpse of how alienating most jobs are, compiled from interviews. For a down-to-earth long look at the nature and meaning of racism in the United States, see Terkel's latest book, *Race: How Blacks and Whites Think and Feel About the American Obsession** (New York: The New Press, 1992). Terkel is a Chicago-based journalist and TV/radio commentator.

Pushing deeply into Marx's views in this respect are three books, the first by Istvan Meszaros, *Marx's Theory of Alienation** (New York: Harper Torchbooks, 1970), the second by Bertell Ollman, *Alienation: Marx's Conception of Man in Capitalist Society** (Cambridge, England: Cambridge University Press, 1976). Shlomo Avineri, *The Social and Political Thought of Karl Marx** (Cambridge, England: Cambridge University Press, 1971), treats the question of alienation with great clarity, and also goes more broadly into Marx's philosophical position. None of these could be classified as light reading, but they are well worth the effort.

Notes

1. Kay Boyle, "O This Is Not Spring." From *Collected Poems*, copyright 1938, Kay Boyle.

2. One cannot ignore the "excitement" that our numerous small and large wars have generated (and have been generated by). Military and nonmilitary violence have been omnipresent in our history; so much so that they are taken for granted, barely acknowledged, like a very large skeleton in our historical closet. Economic achievement, in contrast, is proudly up front.

3. The term "racism" did not even enter the political vocabulary of the nation until the 1960s. The relatively small numbers of whites who consciously opposed the elements of racism saw themselves as seeking to reduce or end "discrimination," or "prejudice," or, among other euphemisms, "mistreatment." It was in the context of the civil rights

(and, subsequently, the "black power") movement that "racism" became the term identifying the oppression of black and other people "of color." And it was then also that the analytical term "institutionalized racism" was first applied. That racism—rather than, say, class or income—has increasingly become the dominating political issue in the United States (whether openly or covertly) is argued at great length and strongly in "Race," by Thomas Byrne Edsall with Mary D. Edsall, in *The Atlantic Monthly*, May 1991, Vol. 267, No. 5. The same theme is pursued at greater length, and with a wealth of supporting data in Andrew Hacker, *Two Nations: Black and White* (New York: Macmillan, 1992).

4. See Bennett Harrison and Barry Bluestone, *The Great U-Turn: Corporate Restructuring and the Polarizing of America,** (New York: Basic Books, 1990) for the main developments, which will be examined in detail in Chapters 3 and 4. "Financialization" and its connected developments will also be discussed in Chapters 3 and 4, and again in Chapter 8 where the political background that encouraged it will be examined.   Table 2 in Chapter 3 presents data that show the relative decline of corporate profits compared to interest, and related matters pointing to the alteration of our economic structure away from industry and toward finance, as its heart.   Meanwhile, here it is worth noting a book that, its publication predating the recently emerging and well-known scandals of the financial system (e.g., the collapse of the thrifts, the Bank of Credit and Commerce International [BCCI], CIA and drug connections, etc.), carefully documents many of the developments that led to them. See R.T. Naylor, *Hot Money and the Politics of Debt* (New York: The Linden Press/Simon and Schuster, 1987).

5. The late Joseph Pechman, one of the two or three most widely respected tax authorities in the United States, had much the same thought, when he said: "It may be that, at some distant future date, the rich will have enough income to satisfy not only their own needs, but also to help relieve the tax burdens of those who are less fortunate. In the meantime, the tax system will continue to disgrace the most affluent nation in the world." *Tax Reform* (Washington: Brookings Institution, 1989), p. 27. Of course, the rich, who have become considerably richer in the past decades, and spectacularly so in the 1980s, become not more but less inclined "to help relieve" as indicated by their intense campaign to have capital gains taxes reduced (with the fervent support of President Bush). For those who seek to be rich, not just comfortable, there can never be "enough income."

6. It was pleasant to believe, in the 1970s, that Watergate, whose crimes and lies caused the resignation of President Nixon (preceded by the financial corruption causing the resignation of Vice President Spiro Agnew), was a turning-point in these respects. There was the Freedom of Information Act, and new electoral laws, and an atmosphere which, among other developments, seemed to promise, if not a squeaky clean government, at least one that was not plumbing new depths. And then, the ever-deepening well of corruption of the continuing "Reagan era," in which we may find an Attorney General who must resign, Irangate, the military fig leaf that barely conceals the outrageous connections between the White House, the CIA, the drug trade, criminal banks (BCCI, once more), and Noriega, the S&L disaster that ties petty with large crooks and all of them with the House and the Senate, the son of the President, and, on Wall Street, Michael Milken and Ivan Boesky and Drexel Burnham and Salomon Brothers, and...to turn away from own shame, financial scandals on high in Japan, and Britain, and Germany, and Italy and.... Doubtless, greed, corruption, and itch for power have always been with us as a leading social disease, but in this generation the disease seems to threaten plague.

7. It is worth noting that the Bill of Rights, that most praiseworthy aspect of U.S. political democracy, came as an afterthought; that it was fiercely struggled over, and only with difficulty achieved, as the first ten *amendments* to the Constitution. It is worth noting, too, the surveys showing that well over half of our people have little or no knowledge of the Bill of Rights and that (e.g., from a Gallup poll of the 1950s) when people are told of its contents—and especially the insistence on freedom of speech and assembly—a majority are opposed. And perhaps even more notable, it was not until more than three-quarters of a century after 1776 that slavery, and the "free market" for the sale of human beings was, only with great resistance, legally abolished. Those are among the disturbing elements of our reality; but also worth noting is that the Bill of Rights *was* made part of our Constitution, and that slavery *was* abolished.

8. When we use the word "exploitation" as regards natural resources it has a neutral sound. But when used in reference to labor, as here, it suggests an unjust use of power: not an attractive relationship to consider as *essential* to the well-being of one's economy. It is unsurprising, therefore, that nowhere in neoclassical economic theory is the notion of exploitation seen as even a possibility of capitalist reality. Wages, interest, profits, and rent are all "returns to the factors of production,"

received in proportion to contributions to production. Wages are a return to labor, the other three to property ownership. Nowhere is the question asked as to why most have no property and a few have all of it: a historical question. It is worth noting here that classical political economists theorized within the framework of the so-called "labor theory of value"—which assumed that labor alone creates value; that is, the other forms of income are not a reward to production, but to the power of ownership (as will be seen below, when Ricardo is discussed). And, all agreed, wages were equal to subsistence, that is, no more than necessary to keep the worker and his family alive. Marx agreed, and went on to argue, with a logic difficult to refute, that the relationships thus posited were those of exploitation. But one need not accept the labor theory of value and its numerous now (but not then) unrealistic assumptions to see that exploitation remains pervasive and essential. Often in the following pages exploitation will be discussed and explained, and especially in Chapter 2. There the historical process in Britain mostly responsible for creating an exploitable working class, the "enclosure movement," will be examined. But what happened then and there is only one variation of a complicated theme, at the center of which is *power*: for one group to exploit another group implies a relationship of power versus powerlessness, whether we refer to exploited medieval serfs otherwise powerless to survive the military anarchy of their era, the Africans enslaved because they didn't have the power to hold off their captors, or the "free workers" in a capitalist society—still today—who, owning no productive assets, have no power to survive without working for others, on the others' terms. Naturally, those with power will set terms favorable to themselves, and they will be the terms of exploitation (of which, much more later).

9. Jefferson, as noted earlier, was not an advocate of industrialization; indeed he was opposed to that and to the urbanization it would bring with it. His dream was that of a nation of small farmers and artisans. It is something more than an irony that, seeing abundant land as one of the underlying needs for such a society, he presided over the first major geographic expansion of the United States, the Louisiana Purchase of 1803 which, over subsequent decades was significant in the development of large-scale plantation agriculture and, later, industrial capitalism.

10. The numerous criticisms of neoclassical ("mainstream," "conventional") economics made throughout the book have reference to the guiding *theory* of the profession. Much that is valuable is done in the so-

called "applied fields" of economics: in public finance, industrial organization, labor and industrial relations, international trade, etc. When that work is guided solely by the guiding theory, it is in my judgment close to useless, as I shall argue later. When it is valuable, as often it is, it is not because of but despite the theory. It seems reasonable to assert that we need a different theory; and to wonder why, other than for ideological/political reasons, this theory so helpless to explain our economy for us persists and strengthens its hold, always.

11. Adam Smith, *An Inquiry into the Nature and Causes of The Wealth of Nations.* McCulloch edition (London, 1869), Book IV.

12. "State" is capitalized here, to distinguish it from the usage in the United States that almost always refers to the separate "states." This narrow question and the much more complicated set of matters concerning the State are discussed in Chapter 8.

13. A misleadingly calm but comprehensive survey of the mercantilist period at its height throughout Europe is given by G.N. Clark, *The Seventeenth Century** (London: Oxford University Press, 1950). A series of analyses emphasizing the change and conflict of the period is Trevor Aston, ed., *Crisis in Europe, 1560–1660** (London: Routledge, 1965). An excellent study of England for the period stretching from 1530 to 1780 is Christopher Hill, *Reformation to Industrial Revolution* (New York: Pantheon, 1968).

14. A commodity is something produced for the market, for sale, in the hope of profit, rather than, say, for use. The processes by which land and labor became commodities in England in the eighteenth and nineteenth centuries are studied exhaustively by Karl Polanyi, *The Great Transformation** (New York: Holt, Rinehart, and Winston, 1944). Unless the laborer is a slave, it is not her or his person that is the commodity; in a free market economy, it is the workers' labor power (as Marx termed it) that becomes the commodity, and thus their incomes and working conditions free of all but market constraints. When, as is customary, there are more workers seeking work than there are jobs available—those Marx termed "the reserve army of the unemployed"—the bias of the market is thus on the side of the buyer of labor, not the sellers. That "bias" in the market for labor is in part the result of the political power of the employing class; nor does their power over the labor market end there, of course. As will be seen later, workers in the United States did not gain the meaningful right to organize and to strike until the mid-1930s. During

the years since then and through the 1960s, workers were able to increase their wages and improve their working conditions (most importantly, hours and safety) directly, and through their enhanced political power they were able to win pensions, health care, and paid vacations. All the foregoing benefits have been sharply reduced since the 1970s as the economy has weakened and the politics of conservatism have strengthened.

15. Smith, *Wealth of Nations*, p. 215. This view of Smith's, in these years of boyish free market celebrations, has been found embarrassing. George Gilder, seen by many as the social philosopher of contemporary free market campaigns, goes rather far in the opposite direction from Smith, when he views businessmen as conscious philanthropists, whose aim is the wellbeing of the underlying population; and he explicitly compares business with the "potlatch" of the tribes of the Northwest United States, where each chief vies with others in generous giving. See his *Wealth and Poverty*, (New York: Basic Books, 1981).

16. Ibid., p. 561.

17. Problems surrounding Smith's position in this and related areas will be explored again in Chapter 2. The data on property and income in the United States will be presented and analyzed in Chapter 5.

18. A readable presentation of Smith's main argument, and one that also centers in upon Smith's humanitarian and communitarian purposes, is Eli Ginzberg, *The House of Adam Smith* (New York: Octagon Books, 1964). A masterful treatment of the basic ideas of Smith and of his times is Samuel Hollander, *The Economics of Adam Smith* (Toronto: University of Toronto Press, 1973).

19. In *Religion and the Rise of Capitalism** (New York: Mentor, 1950), p. 35. Published first in 1926.

20. Everyone who makes a social argument has, consciously or not, "an axe to grind" (present company included). Malthus lived at a time when the rapid social changes taking place in Britain, to be discussed in the following pages and in Chapter 2, had resulted in, among other things, a great number of unemployed in the countryside. The laws and customs of the time meant that the landowners were responsible for supporting the poor in their parish. Malthus, a parson from a landowning family, was much occupied with the problem from that standpoint, which sheds light on his attitudes and his analyses. The Malthusian arguments that have not only lasted but have been used as a basis for public policy

most recently are those manifesting what can only be seen as his hatred for the poor. John Hess, in his excellent essay, "Malthus Then and Now," *The Nation*, April 18, 1987, shows the similarities between the views of certain of today's social scientists and politicians (not least the much-loved Reagan) and those of Malthus, with side-by-side quotations, among which is this, from Malthus's *Essay On Population*: "Instead of recommending cleanliness to the poor, we should encourage contrary habits. In our towns we should make the streets narrower, crowd more people into the houses, and court the return of the plague. In the country, we should build our villages near stagnant pools.... But above all, we should reprobate specific remedies for ravaging diseases."

21. The post–World War II years have seen such a mitigation of the problem of "gluts," in that those years have seen only minor recessions and no severe depression. The policies employed are subject to diverse criticisms, as will be discussed in Chapters 4 and 8.

22. As will be discussed in Chapter 7, the areas colonized in the sixteenth through the eighteenth, imperialized in the nineteenth and early twentieth, and neocolonialized in the late twentieth centuries, by those processes have had their economies, governments, and cultures displaced and/or destroyed in always more ways and at always increasing rates. Their resources have been taken for foreign gain and use; of at least equal importance, they have been robbed of their traditional ways of life—which though not modern in type or level—were not only *theirs* but usually more supportive of what for them was a decent life than that which replaced them. The invading power—whether Spain, Holland, France, Great Britain, Germany, Italy, the United States, or Japan—takes into those societies much of what is wrong in its own society, and little of its virtues; and destroys or plunders what is valuable in the weaker country. The result is "retrogressive" development which, to make matters worse, is a process perhaps impossible to reverse.

23. Productive consumption for Malthus (and others of the classicists, and also Marx) was that which maintained the population whose work maintained the economy. "Unproductive consumption" we might today call luxury spending, or in contemporary economics jargon, "discretionary" spending. Malthus had in mind that (especially) the landed classes must, in effect, live it up—which the gentry and the aristocrats quite generally did (see, for example, Fielding's *Tom Jones*). Marx distinguished between the consumer spending of the capitalist class (the largest part of which would fall under Malthus' "unproductive consump-

tion") and the spending of the working class, entirely devoted to subsistence—that is, what allowed them to continue working and reproducing themselves. Keynes, viewing the matter from another angle, believed that private spending had to be supplemented by public spending, to make up for inadequate effective demand, and that the best outlets for such (deficit financed) spending were in what he called "social consumption" (e.g., public housing) and "social investment" (e.g., bridges).

24. This power derived from the ownership and control of what was then the most vital productive asset: agricultural land. This was also one of the key bases for political power—in this case the political power that landowners had in Parliament giving them the opportunity to pass, for example, tariff laws setting profitably high domestic prices for "corn." Marx transformed this notion quite appropriately to see the ownership of the productive assets of industry as giving the owners power to keep workers' wages low along with harsh working conditions, as well as power in the larger society.

25. Interestingly, Hamilton was basically a "mercantilist" in his beliefs, and Jefferson at least partially "Smithian," in opposing strong central government (but not so, in opposing industrialization). Hamilton's arguments won the day for several decades after our independence; so much so that the theoretical architect of subsequent German mercantilism, Friedrich List, came to study U.S. practices in the early nineteenth century. Also interesting in this connection is that in the meetings creating the General Agreement on Tariffs and Trade in 1947 (aimed at constructing a free world economy without protective tariffs) the "underdeveloped" countries argued that they should have the right to protect their "infant industries," and used Hamilton's arguments against the United States to make their point.

26. I cannot resist recounting a revealing, not to say unsettling, incident in my introductory economics course. It is my custom to begin the course by relating the interdependent developments of capitalism and economic thought. In discussing Ricardo I had noted that he depended much on logic and little on facts (and made it clear that his great work was in 1817). In a subsequent exam, a student informed me that Ricardo's problem was that "he didn't have a fax."

27. For an authoritative treatment of these conditions, as well as for the development of British industrial capitalism in the entire period, see E.J. Hobsbawm, *Industry and Empire* (New York: Pantheon, 1968). And read Dickens's *Hard Times*.

28. *The Principles of Political Economy* (New York: Peoples Edition, 1872), p. 128. When Mill wrote, "communism" and "socialism" were interchangeable terms.

29. Lionel Robbins, *The Nature and Significance of Economic Science* (London: Macmillan, 1932), p. 16.

30. Technically speaking, the subdivision is into more than two parts. There is welfare theory, capital theory, wage theory, general equilibrium theory, trade theory, monetary theory; or, in some versions, distribution theory, the theory of markets, and the like. For present purposes, the twofold division suffices. For a penetrating critique of neoclassical welfare economics, whose final meaning is the welfare of the property-owning class (naturally), see Herbert Gintis, "Neoclassical Welfare Economics and Individual Development," *Occasional Paper, No. 3* of the Union for Radical Political Economics (July, 1970). (Hereafter URPE.)

31. Writing at a time when Darwin's *Origin of the Species* (1867) was most influential, this could be construed as a Darwinian view—the latter having underscored the enormous slowness of the processes of evolution. Interestingly, Marx (whose *Capital* also came out in 1867) admired Darwin, but saw the *qualitative* change of the Darwinian process as fitting in with his own views. Marshall himself would have been unhappy with the mathematization of those who followed him. The only math found in his *Principles* is relegated to appendices. And Marshall was a knowing student of economic realities. See his *Industry and Trade* (London: Macmillan, 1919).

32. Just where the tendencies to "meddle" come from in human and social behavior, other than from the nature of our species, is a question (among many others of the same sort) neither Smith nor his followers confront. Thus, in the free market view it is "meddling" in human affairs to require safety provisions in a dangerous factory, but that same factory is not "meddling" in human affairs when it discharges poisonous chemical wastes in the soil or streams nearby, the customary practice in the absence of governmental "meddling."

33. It may be believed that those who see our species as being so utterly selfish developed their ideas by looking into the mirror. For a different view, see the fine essay by Amartya Sen (an economist and philosopher), "Individual Freedom as a Social Commitment," *New York Review of Books*, June 14, 1990. Among other relevant observations is this: "In many economic and social theories today, human beings are

seen as strict maximizers of a narrowly defined self-interest, and given that relentless compulsion, pessimism about social rearrangements to reduce inequality will indeed be justified. But not only is that 'model' of human beings depressing and dreary, there is very little evidence that it is a good representation of reality.... Indeed among the things that seem to move people, whether in Prague or Paris or Warsaw or Beijing or Little Rock or Johannesburg, are concern for others and regard for ideas" (p. 54). For a substantial and convincing treatment of this and closely related questions, see Alfie Kohn, *The Brighter Side of Human Nature: Altruism and Empathy in Everyday Life* (New York: Basic Books, 1990).

34. In *The Place of Science in Modern Civilization* (New York: B.W. Huebsch, 1919; Russell and Russell, 1961), pp. 73–74. This book contains the bulk of Veblen's methodological essays, including a critical but friendly analysis of Marxian political economy. A reading of the quoted passage puts one in mind of the manner in which a space capsule is manipulated—quite remarkable considering when it was written.

35. *Karl Marx: Early Writings,** translated and edited by T.B. Bottomore (New York: McGraw-Hill, 1963), pp. 124–25. This book contains the so-called "Economic and Philosophic Manuscripts of 1844," where Marx's theory of alienation, which lies at the base of much of his later thinking, was first expressed. These manuscripts were unpublished until 1932. Veblen died in 1929. Although he could not have known of these ideas directly, his own views are strikingly similar.

36. *The Instinct of Workmanship** (New York: Macmillan, 1914), pp. 2–6. A sunflower acts "tropismatically."

37. Forty years ago, using very much the same criteria for the judgment of "three-quarters" just noted, I published (in the *Antioch Review*) an analytical essay concerning the underdeveloped areas entitled "Two-Thirds of the World." So bad has gone to worse. All the development projects and strategies have accompanied a further descent into misery for most of the people in the world. A tragic and still generally misunderstood early instance of this kind of problem was the famine that struck Ireland in the years 1846–47 (the very years in which the free market philosophy became fully practiced in Britain—whose colony Ireland was, and in the North, still is). During the famine, "caused" by the insect of potato blight, and as Ireland was exporting large quantities of food to England (dairy products, meat, vegetables, etc.), the colonial administration quite self-consciously and systematically enforced the new social rules of free marketry. Of a population of not more than

eight and a half million, at least a million starved to death—"the greatest human catastrophe of the nineteenth century anywhere in the world...relative to the size of the population," as E.J. Hobsbawm, says (op. cit., p. 73). Making changes for time and place, the famines of our days and years which regularly decimate the populations of the Third World are not much different: now too, those countries are exporting food, from food supplies controlled by foreign companies. We shall examine this and related questions in Chapters 6 and 7.

38. Britain's export-dependent economy, though generally prosperous in the twenty years preceding World War I, was *relatively* falling behind the always stronger German and U.S. economies. That weakness, combined with the widespread economic nationalism after the war, meant Britain was unable to generate sufficient exports to keep its factories and its workers occupied. Aggravating the problem was the preponderance of the financial sector in Britain's policy determination, and its insistence on behaving as though the world was back in the 1870s. See Alfred E. Kahn, *Great Britain in the World Economy* (New York: New York University Press, 1946).

39. The presently dominant "monetarists" and "supply-side economists" represent a further over-simplification of what were originally over-simplified notions. Of which, more later.

40. Confirming Keynes's analysis once more was the experience of the 1980s. Guided by the monetarists (the analytical pre-Keynesians given a Second Coming by the conservative political revival of recent years) and their sidekicks the supplysiders (often but not always the same people), the changed tax laws of the Reagan years substantially lowered taxes on the top 20 percent of income receivers (and especially on the top 1 percent) with the rationale that it would increase savings, lower interest rates, and spur real investment, with consequent renovation of the U.S. economy, more jobs, and so on. What happened was that savings declined to their lowest rates in memory, interest rates rose as private and public debt increased, real investment declined and speculative financial investment soared, and the U.S. economy continued on its path toward ever greater weakness and fragility. That the whole thing was a cruel hoax is revealed, jot and tittle, by Reagan's first budget chief, who presided over the meetings that worked these dirty deeds. See David Stockman, *The Triumph of Politics* (New York: Harper & Row, 1987). Stockman also shows that these policies had the deliberate aim of creating deficits—this from Reagan, who had campaigned for years as a would-be

budget balancer—that could serve as a rationale for cutting social expenditures. And it all worked, just as they hoped; but not just as the gullible public was told (concerning which, more in Chapters 4 and 8).

41. Joan Robinson, herself a noted neoclassical economist at the time, subsequently sought to reintegrate Marxian theory with what is valuable in conventional theory. Kalecki (of Poland) was even then a brilliant Marxist. He anticipated and broadened the basic ideas of Keynes, and did much to enrich theory before his death in 1970. See *The Last Phase in the Transformation of Capitalism** (New York: Monthly Review Press, 1972), a collection of his essays.

42. *The General Theory*, p. viii.

43. "Net saving" is total saving less borrowing. Almost everyone borrows—for a mortgage, an auto, a vacation, whatever—and a very high percentage saves—in a thrift account, an insurance policy, etc. But one has to have a fairly high income to be able to spend and borrow *and* save net. Ten percent have such incomes. The data may be found regularly recorded in U.S. Department of Commerce (monthly) *Survey of Current Business*.

44. For useful discussions of U.S. and European practices since World War II, see Andrew Shonfield, *Modern Capitalism** and his *The Use of Public Power* (Oxford: Oxford University Press, 1965 and 1982, respectively).

45. The professional journal of the radical economists has been noted earlier, *The Review of Radical Political Economy*. The institutionalists, essentially followers of Veblen, have more than one outlet, but most important is *The Journal of Economic Issues*. *The Journal of Post Keynesian Economics* is self-descriptive (although it should be noted that not all of its articles depart from the mainstream). Critiques of conventional theory in all the social sciences, as well as an identification of some "key problems" and alternative analyses are set forth well in Robin Blackburn, ed., *Ideology in Social Science** (New York: Vintage, 1973).

46. The economist who has done the most insightful work on this process, beginning in the 1970s, who before others saw what was happening, is James O'Connor, first in *The Fiscal Crisis of the State* (New York: St. Martin's Press, 1973), and then, analyzing the social and political spread of the continuing economic deterioration, *Accumulation Crisis* (New York: Basil Blackwell, 1984). More recently, and more abstractly, he has written *The Meaning of Crisis* (New York: Basil Blackwell, 1987), which, although it treats more recent developments,

might well be read before its predecessors. As might be guessed, he is a radical, not a mainstream economist.

– 2 –

Capitalism

Unhappy, eagle wings and beak, chicken brain
Weep (it is frequent in human affairs) weep for the terrible
magnificence of the means
The ridiculous incompetence of the reasons, the bloody and shabby
Pathos of the result.[1]

Capitalism is a world economic system with a global division of labor. Its emergence and development over the past few centuries has been the dominant force in world history. Capitalist nations have certain basic characteristics in common; each capitalist nation also has defining characteristics that set it apart from and often in conflict with the others. For certain analytical purposes, the defining national adjective—U.S., Japanese, British, German—is critical; for other purposes the noun "capitalism" is decisive. For our purposes it is essential to grasp the meaning of both. As Maurice Dobb put it:

> Capitalism is not a system that is cut to a certain pattern and remains the same for all time. Product of a complex process of historical development, capitalism is itself continually subject to historical development. It changes from one decade to the next, it is different in many respects in one country from what it is in another country, according to the specific features of that country and according to the peculiarities of that country's history... But that does not mean that it is not valuable to pick out and to study certain *general features* of capitalism—to isolate and analyze certain relationships that are typical of capitalism in all its varied forms and manifestations. In fact it is essential to do this as a *preliminary* to a more detailed study, if we are to see the wood for the trees—if we are to grasp the general lie of the land as well as be acquainted with each separate bit of it.[2]

The principal focus of this book is on the nature and development of capitalism in the United States. The latter part of this chapter will examine capitalism's beginnings and some of its features that are specifically those of this nation; the rest of the book will analyze its development to the present. But first we must discuss in general the origins, the meaning, and the imperatives of capitalism.

The first social arrangements we may call capitalist emerged in Western Europe, and began to take hold in the seventeenth century; it became an irreversible socioeconomic system first in Great Britain in the years when classical political economy was taking shape. Capitalism spread from Britain to what became the "major powers" by the end of the nineteenth century. Those nations *became* major and powerful because they could and did move toward industrial capitalism. The "minor powers" (in Europe and the rest of the world) were under the formal or informal rule of the industrial capitalist states, all functioning within the framework of a British-dominated world economy—until its violent decomposition early in this century.

Its birth was a unique historical development: the many capitalist societies that have come into existence outside of *Western* Europe since then (such as the United States and Japan) have not done so spontaneously, but as an extension or complicated consequence of European capitalism. That such a system emerged at all, and when and where it did, resulted from the specific, distinctive features of *Western* European feudalism; in turn, those features were owed to the combination of German tribalism with the legacy of classical (Greco-Roman) antiquity.[3]

Thus, when capitalism as such emerged, it was in a specific historical context; the same is true, even more specifically, of capitalism in different countries. The ways in which, say, British capitalism evolved are due to the particular temporal, spatial, historical, and cultural characteristics of Great Britain. But all these were in turn strengthened, weakened, shaped, and distorted over time by the driving general forces of a developing world-economic system, a global division of labor under capitalist auspices—developing, it is important to note, in a *political* context of competing nation-states. As Wallerstein puts it,

> [Three] things were essential to the establishment of such a capitalist world-economy: an expansion of the geographic size of the world in question [by comparison with medieval Europe], the development of variegated methods of labor control for

different products and different zones of the world-economy, and the creation of relatively strong state machineries in what would become the core-states of this capitalist world-economy.[4]

As a given society moves through time it never totally loses the traces of the cultural characteristics that set it apart from others: the ways we think and feel, what we take to be valuable, possible, beautiful, terrible, and so on, continue to mark a people, whether under the impact of feudalism, capitalism, or socialism. However, the special power of capitalism as a system of production has been due to its ability—indeed its need—to subordinate all social relationships to its dynamism. Marx and Engels put it vividly in *The Communist Manifesto*:

> The bourgeoisie [i.e., capitalists] cannot exist without constantly revolutionizing the instruments of production, and thereby the relations of production, and with them the whole relations of society. Conservation of the old modes of production in unaltered form was, on the contrary, the first condition of existence for all earlier industrial classes. Constant revolution-izing of production, uninterrupted disturbance of all social conditions, ever-lasting uncertainty and agitation distinguish the bourgeois epoch from all earlier ones. All fixed, fast-frozen relations, with their train of ancient and venerable prejudices and opinions, are swept away, all new-formed ones become antiquated before they can ossify. All that is solid melts into air, all that is holy is profaned, and man is at last compelled to face with sober senses his real conditions of life and his relations with his kind.[5]

What is it about capitalism that gives it such power? What needs does such a social system have, what imperatives must it satisfy, that drive it so forcefully through time and space and tradition?

The answers to these questions cannot be supplied fully here, but a serious attempt to make headway on them can at least begin. That attempt will revolve around examining the three prime needs of capi-talism: for expansion, for exploitation, and for rule by what amounts to an oligarchy.[6] More questions are raised: What makes expansion necessary? What makes it happen? What gives the process its push, its direction, its rate, its quality, its consequences? To answer those questions requires careful inspection of the socioeconomic relations within a given capitalist society and of those between it and other societies. Whatever else such relationships entail—and they entail very much indeed—their unwavering requirement is labor exploitation. And, feeding and being fed by the interaction of expansion and exploitation is a dynamic system of economic, political, and social power that buttresses, depends upon, and guides the process of socioeconomic development.

The Heart of the Matter: Expansion and Exploitation

Throughout its history, capitalist profitability has required, and capitalist rule has provided, ever-changing means and areas of exploitation. The central relationship making this possible is that which has to do with ownership and control of productive property: a small group that owns and controls, and the great majority of the population that does not, and whose propertylessness requires them to work for wages simply to survive: in Marx, the capitalist class and the working class. These may be seen as the bones and muscles of capitalist *social relations*—the necessary but not the sufficient condition for capitalist development.

Given these social relations, the strength of each capitalist enterprise and of national and global capitalist economies varies in accordance with the volume, scope, and rate of capital accumulation, what we term here "economic expansion." In turn, the economic expansion relates closely to the processes of extensive and intensive *geographic expansion*. Expansion may be seen as the essence of the capitalist *process*, as its heartbeat. The full meaning, the widespread recognition, and the political consequences of capitalist social relations have been effectively obscured or blocked in the leading industrial capitalist nations mainly by their recurring ability to meet this need for expansion—the primary explanation for the containment of class conflict in those societies, and most of all in the United States, historically the most expansive.[7]

Because expansion and exploitation are fundamental to the strength and the survival of capitalism, an inquiry into their causes and consequences necessarily carries deeply into the nature and the dynamics of that system. Here we shall make only a brief and abstract foray into that territory; subsequent chapters will get down to the specifics of the United States[8]

To repeat, *expansion* is a process; *exploitation* is a set of relationships. Neither functions adequately without the other; it is their interaction that is decisive: the process moving within the relationships, changing them and being changed by them, sustained by and helping to sustain them. The means and ends of business require and lead to expansion: these means and ends in a society in which most of the people are economically powerless, and/or socially and politically oppressed (because of their race or sex, most importantly) produce and sustain exploitation.

The direct aim of the capitalist business is to make a profit; when it fails to do so, it goes under. Except for brief and exceptional circumstances, profit cannot be made unless businesses function within a process of economic expansion, as manifested in the growth of markets—that is, expansion of the markets in which commodities are *sold*. This is so whether or not a business is able successfully to exploit its labor force, the prime condition surrounding the *production* of commodities: the most exploitive industries (e.g., those employing migratory agricultural workers) are not usually the most profitable. Conversely, even in expanding markets, profits cannot be made unless production is carried on in an exploitive context. This was especially so in the relatively competitive conditions of the nineteenth century, when profits depended squarely upon direct labor exploitation, given expanding market conditions.

In Chapter 4, when contemporary expansion processes are analyzed, it will be seen that the combination of monopolistic structures, modern advertising and consumer debt accumulation, overseas economic processes, and the taxing and spending activities of the modern capitalist State have made for sources of profitability going well beyond simple labor exploitation (which, in any case, when the focus is global, is always more present).[9]

The dependence on expansion and exploitation has not decreased as capitalism has moved from relatively competitive to monopolistic structures; what has changed are the nature and the determinants of the expansion process and the burden and the forms of exploitation and oppression. Let us look more closely at the importance of expansion.

Bigger Is Better; More Is Not Enough: The Political Economy of Expansion

The need for continuous expansion rises out of the motivations of business and the key institutions of capitalism: private ownership and control of the means of production in the hands of the very few and their use to make profit, depending upon and perpetuating a starkly unequal distribution of income, wealth, and power. More specifically:

1. Production is for profit, not use; it is production for sale, for the market. Although profits may be made *possible* by labor exploitation in the production process, they can be *realized* only in the market. The full realization of profits thus depends upon market buoyancy, on the relative *scarcity* of commodities compared with the demand for them, which gives sellers relative power over buyers. In turn, the most generally beneficial and socially acceptable basis for market scarcity (as compared with natural disasters or monopolistic restrictions of supply) is the overall expansion of the economy, brought about by and further contributing to expansion in productive capacity.

2. Capitalism rests upon individualistic ownership, control, and direction of production, upon capitalist competition within and between industries and national economies, also in the era of monopoly capitalism. But there is a major difference between competitive and monopoly capitalism: competition in the earlier era (which we may say had ended before World War I began) led to *falling* prices and perhaps to expanding markets, whereas in our time competition (or, better, rivalry) leads to "nonprice" tactics (advertising and sales promotion, trivial product changes, packaging gimmicks, etc.) and *higher* prices, thus increasing the *need* for expanding markets.[10] If the disproportionalities and gluts that unavoidably arise from unplanned production are to be kept within bounds, and the sharp edges of domestic and international competition are to be blunted, expanding markets are essential.

3. Technological innovation (in both products and productive techniques), a normal and accelerating process under conditions of industrial capitalism, requires market expansion if the increased productivity and production that make technological change profitable are to occur. In addition, the largest part of such innovation takes place in and most affects the capital goods industries (machinery, heavy chemicals, metallurgy, electronics, and the like), the heart of an industrial economy. These industries depend upon expansion in the rest of the economy (as well as in their own sectors) if they are not to suffer losses through excess productive capacity.

4. Capitalist exploitation and capital accumulation depend upon and perpetuate a highly unequal distribution of income and wealth. As will be discussed in detail in Chapter 5, the large majority of the population

lives at levels of socially defined subsistence (nowadays including TV, cars, etc.), while a small minority (perhaps 10 percent) is able to consume freely *and* save at relatively high levels. If capitalist savings are to be positive in their economic effects, they must be matched by continuous expansion of real investment, by increases in construction and productive capacity. That only takes place in the expectation of profit, which is to say in the context of actual and expected market scarcities—in turn dependent upon expansion.

5. Capitalism has always depended upon debt financing to some important degree for its production and investment activities. Such dependence has increased both in degree and in kind over time—spectacularly so after World War II, and wildly so in the years after 1980—and extends throughout all spending activities: of consumers for all kinds of purchases, of governments at all levels and everywhere, of businesses not only for working capital and real investment, but for mergers (especially for "leveraged buyouts"). Debt financing, as it has increased at accelerating rates has, because of both its means and its ends, become a major problem in and of itself, as it also exacerbates the problems of other areas, both financial and nonfinancial." To make matters scarier, business debt financing, especially since the 1980s, has turned increasingly to the issuance of "junk bonds" (with their high interest rates) and short-term (under one year) borrowing, which require even more rapid expansion of sales to provide the corporate incomes to pay off *their* debt; just as increasing personal and governmental (tax) incomes (from economic expansion) are required to provide jobs, support markets, *and* to refinance and further expand *all* debt. The legend of the sorcerer's apprentice comes to mind.

6. From its beginnings, capitalist economic expansion has depended upon intermittent and deepening waves of *geographic* expansion. Increasing access to exploitable cheap labor, natural resources, and broader markets has lifted the volumes of trade, investment, and production for the core (center or imperialist) national economies. This has allowed the maintenance or increase of profits and, in raising the level of socially defined subsistence, has helped to reduce social conflict in the core countries, but at the expense of external populations. There have doubtless been sociopsychological consequences of this imperialism also, taking the form, for example, of attitudes of superiority and vicarious power which, in association with the cultivation of patriotism and bellicosity in the nation-states of capitalism have also contributed to

their political stability. Anything that might do so is good news for capitalism, given the potentially explosive nature of its highly unequal distributions of income, wealth, and power.[12]

The interaction of *all* these "needs"—rather than the importance of any one of them—defines capitalism's dependence upon continuous expansion. The recurring inability of global capitalism to fulfill all of them in adequate combination throughout its history up through World War II provides the major explanation for its tendency toward intermittent economic crisis and toward internal and international conflict. Subsequent experience, in contrast, has been quite successful in satisfying these needs in North America, Western Europe, and Japan.

In those decades there has been sustained economic expansion (in the context of a "new" world economy) and a notable reduction of conflict within and between the core capitalist nations. Economic expansion reduces social conflicts over the distribution of income, and the reduction of social conflicts helps the system to expand even more. Thus, that the United States was able to have relatively healthy rates of expansion throughout almost all of its history is an important part of the explanation for the relatively low levels of class conflict in the United States, by comparison with Europe.[13]

Returning now to the compulsive quality of expansion under capitalism, let us examine further the historical meaning of business competition and rivalry, and the impulses of and relationships between capitalists. We must take a closer look at the class structure of society, the relationships between the powerful and the powerless, which underlies the profitability accompanying expansion. Engels caught an important part of this very well, when he wrote:

Competition is the most complete expression of the battle of all against all which rules in modern civil society. This battle, a battle for life, for existence...is fought not between the different classes of society only, but also between the individual members of these classes. Each is in the way of the other, and each seeks to crowd out all who are in his way, and to put himself in their place. The workers are in constant competition among themselves as the members of the bourgeoisie among themselves.[14]

It is fairly easy to see how and why workers would compete among themselves for jobs; nor is it difficult to imagine business competition.

But why does the competition require and lead to expansion? Capitalism emerged full-blown only when the traditions and restrictions of earlier times had been swept away. It was also a time of rapid geographic expansion and the ever-swifter growth of technology and science. The expanding production sought by Smith took place in a context of increasing productivity, brought about by technological improvement. Once set loose, the rate of technological change became increasingly rapid and pervasive in its impact.

A competitive capitalist economy is one in which the only protection a given firm has is its own strength. That strength finally depends upon its profitability. In the modern world this means that each firm must adopt the latest in technology, for both defensive and offensive purposes. With all or most firms in a given industry doing so, both production and productivity increase. The market must expand to absorb the increased production. In the normal course of such processes, some firms succeed and others fall by the wayside. The surviving firms continue to expand, in themselves and by gobbling up others. The result is large-scale production, large-scale ownership, and large-scale control: a tendency toward monopoly.[15] Along with economic expansion, both facilitating it and required by it, is geographic expansion—of foreign markets, of access to increasingly needed foodstuffs and industrial raw materials, and of profitable foreign investments. Again, *The Communist Manifesto*:

> The need of a constantly expanding market for its products chases the bourgeoisie over the whole surface of the globe. It must nestle everywhere, settle everywhere, establish connections everywhere.

But there is more involved. The aim of profit under capitalist conditions, as earlier in the mercantilist period, sets up a corollary aim: *power*. Control over productive property is the *sine qua non* of profits; property and profits *are* private power, and private power has access to State power; such access allows protection and enhancement of an already privileged position. Smith knew that State power was essential to protect the unequal division of property in society, with the propertied on one side and the propertyless workers on the other. Power inheres in property ownership, and power begets power both at home and abroad, as powerlessness begets powerlessness.

The emergence of laissez-faire capitalism depended upon the

abolition of State mercantilism. What Smith had correctly viewed as obstacles to the full increase of productive powers in the mercantilist era was also a system of protections and privileges. Labor was obliged to work, but it also had the *right* to work and in principle the *right* not to starve: as a partial continuation of the medieval world, it was a time of rights and obligations. Capital, to the degree that it had the favor of the State, was likewise insulated from the market. Laissez-faire capitalism placed individuals' and enterprises' fates in the hands of impersonal market forces, forces which changed swiftly and at times violently. In the absence of the protections and privileges of labor and capital of the mercantilist era, such had to be obtained (if at all) through private efforts. It was a contest the powerless could not win.

Ownership of the means of production was (and remains) the prime source of advantage. The means of enhancing that advantage for both offensive and defensive purposes was to move toward monopoly—the control over supply. For those whose incomes come from their work rather than from property, means of controlling *their* supply were even more indispensable. This is what trade unions, professional associations, licensing, and the like, achieve. Both for capital and for labor, the seeking and the achievement of such ends require access to or the protection of State power. Although neither labor nor capital can produce without the other, in a *capitalist* society capital retains the clear advantage over those who must work or starve, an advantage measured not simply by laws that until well into this century made effective trade unions illegal, but by the predominance of an ideology that, in sanctifying property, also places the propertyless outside the pale of rights and privileges.[16]

Businessmen and all others agree that production is for profit, and that expansion is good and necessary. But neither they nor conventional social scientists grant that exploitation is an actual, let alone a necessary, accompaniment of profits and business success. Mainstream analysis leads few to think in terms such as these; it fails even to raise questions that might lead us to check a concept such as exploitation against social reality. Yet how is one otherwise to comprehend a situation in which incomes are distributed "almost in an inverse ratio to the labour," as John Stuart Mill said, unless one recognizes that some are being exploited by others and that that relationship can persist, as Smith said, "only under the shelter of the civil magistrate"?

Such assertions and such questions require explanation, all the more essential because the existence of systematic and persistent exploitation is rejected, ignored, or treated in an aloof manner in conventional social analysis. The requisite explanation is necessarily historical: how did a small number of people gain the power to exploit the majority of the population?

Exploitation and Capitalism

Workers as such do not own or control productive assets. To produce they must work with materials and equipment owned by capitalists; to survive, they must produce. As Marx put it, "…the labourer purchases the right to work for his own livelihood only by paying for it in surplus-labour…"[17] By "surplus-labour" Marx meant unpaid labor—that is, exploited labor. Exploitation as a concept leads directly to power as a reality.

The power of the employer derives from his position in the scale of income and wealth, his control over the means of production, and his related political and social power and prestige.[18] All these are inextricably knotted together. Conventional economics begins and ends with the capitalist producing for profit; it ignores the fact that what makes the process possible is the control over property exercised by the capitalist and the power preceding and accompanying the achievement of that control. Having ignored the relationship, conventional analysis is therefore under no obligation to explain its existence.

How did these capitalist property and labor relationships come to be? Has it always been thus? Why and how does it persist? We need not posit some golden idyll of a dim past to answer that as capitalism came into being it did so on the wreckage of medieval property relationships. In the medieval world, private property as we understand the term did not exist. Neither land nor labor were commodities; neither could be bought or sold. The fundamental form of wealth was land, which was "held" (thus "land tenure" where tenure is from the Latin word "to hold"), never "owned." All that had to change, not just for land, but for everything; and land tenure was the bedrock institution. Let us examine what Marx called "the classic case," that of England.[19]

The rights to the land, for lord or serf, were the rights of "usufruct": that is, the rights to the produce of the land. The holding of this land was consequent upon a feudal "contract," in which those granted land (always those in the upper, free, nonserf strata) were obliged to provide "aid and counsel" to their lord (who was also obliged to *his* lord). Aid and counsel took the form of military, political, and religious service. The serf and his family were required to work the lands and to provide other forms of necessary labor for their lord. The serfs were attached to the land hereditarily, generation after generation on the same estate.[20] The various strata of lords—knights at the lowest level, emperors at the highest—found their status within each generation. They were "free" to form their contracts. Free meant "honorable." They were the gentlemen (and the ladies) of the medieval world. The serfs worked three to four days a week (generally) for their lord, farming his land, repairing the paths and bridges on his estate (measured in the thousands of acres for substantial lords, and in what we call "counties" for those among the very most substantial, the counts). The rest of the week, the serfs worked for themselves.

The work the serfs did for their lord was surplus labor, not necessary for their own subsistence; it was the degree of their exploitation. It was, in its day, their taxes (their lord being both their "employer" and their "government"), paid in labor power. Custom and force in varying measure held the serfs to their tasks (in the east of Germany until about the twelfth century, almost as slaves: "Slavs") and the land on which they performed them. That simplicity gave way as the medieval world gave way to the modern, altering economic, political, and social structures and processes.

The medieval structures began to break down around the twelfth and thirteenth centuries in an irregular pattern, depending very much upon specific location and circumstances. In that era of weak and very slow transportation and communications, social uniformity was as rare as it is relatively common in our own time.[21]

The more or less constant warfare of early medieval Europe, an outcome of the breakup of the Roman Empire, had moderated by then, because of the success of feudalism in bringing about relative peace—while also undermining the reasons for its own continuance as a social system. Peace allowed improvements in agricultural production and trade, and population grew. The labor payments of serfs began to be "commuted" into money payments called "quitrents," an early version of what we call rent. In England, serfs became "copyholders"—still not owners, but free in themselves and also free to use and sell the entire produce of their lands. Farming practices remained unchanged; the holding of land was not yet a commodity. The copyholders were the "sturdy yeomanry" of renaissance literature. Their conditions were transformed and displaced as full commercialization began to take hold—as the towns and cities grew, new and powerful nation-states were born, technology improved, and overseas expansion from Europe became the hallmark of the sixteenth, seventeenth, and eighteenth centuries.

Alongside that set of changes, becoming disturbing in the sixteenth, substantial in the seventeenth, and a landslide in the eighteenth century, was the so-called "enclosure movement" in England, which enclosed with a hedge or fence a whole estate (of, say, ten thousand acres) with its many "open fields" into one "enclosed" or unified farm, displacing many copyholders by one owner. That process, impelled by the gains to be made by a larger-scale and increasingly commercial agriculture producing wool and grains, entailed the transformation of a once populous and free peasantry, farming its own lands (and with their own tools or "capital" doing light industrial work, mostly in textile production, in the so-called "domestic" or "putting-out" system), into a propertyless and "free" working class.[22] It should be noted that this mass of people could not find jobs in factories until the latter came into existence, after 1815: in consequence, there was at least a whole generation, from the 1770s on, that was helplessly unemployed, demoralized, and treated cruelly by the emerging Malthusian ideology that taught contempt and hatred of the poor. Thus was born the working class of England.

By 1820 or so, almost all the agricultural land of England had been enclosed, to become the property of two to three thousand families by the close of the century. When the process of enclosure was done legally, as was not infrequent, the legalities were accomplished through the "Justices of the Peace" and through Parliament. Until the reforms of the 1830s both institutions were dominated by landowners. Again, justice was done.

By the time Adam Smith wrote his *Wealth of Nations* the medieval and Elizabethan institutional structures were in a shambles. The power of the Roman Catholic Church was broken in the sixteenth century in England, to give way to the "divine right of kings," which, by the close of the seventeenth century had begun to give way to the "divine right of capital." Land was well on its way to becoming a commodity, and by the opening years of the nineteenth century so was labor, no less and no more than any other article of commerce, free from obligations and free of protection.

68 – U.S. CAPITALIST DEVELOPMENT SINCE 1776

All this seems natural to us now, but it was a process fought against every step along the way by those—among them workers and others ethically or politically motivated— to whom the new ways were painful, unnatural, and immoral. Only today is the view growing in the United States, but with painful slowness, that sheer commercial considerations should not be dominant either for land (meaning "nature") or labor (meaning human beings). Engels observed the connection between the two in 1843: "To make the earth an object of huckstering—the earth which is our one and all, the first condition of our existence—was the last step toward making oneself an object of huckstering. It was and is to this very day an immorality surpassed only by the immorality of self-alienation."[23]

The enclosure movement in England, and its role in creating a wage-earning, propertyless and powerless, and therefore easily exploitable class of workers, was not unique to England in all of its respects, but it was when taken as a whole. The exploitation of labor has had more diverse roots and has taken on forms other than wage labor in global and national capitalist developments. We need only mention the critical role imported black slaves played in the agricultural production of the New World—and not least in the United States and its capitalist development—to see that exploitation is an outcome of powerlessness, and that powerlessness is the outcome of many sociohistorical combinations and permutations. Powerlessness in one's work, as in other aspects of our lives, is also demoralizing: alienating. The problem is not work, which can and should be natural and fulfilling to human beings; nor is it property, which is necessary for the work to be done. The problem is the conditions within which work takes place, and who controls the property. "Wages," Marx said, "are like the oil which is applied to a wheel to keep it running."[24] Like the commodities they produce, workers in industrial capitalism become things.

Faith, Hope, and Competition

Something else, perhaps most momentous of all, happened as the medieval gave way to the modern world. One of England's most searching political philosophers put it this way:

The movement from feudalism to capitalism is a movement from a world in which individual well-being is regarded as the outcome of action socially controlled to one in which social well-being is regarded as the outcome of action individually controlled.[25]

That was the change given its fullest rationale by Adam Smith: the fate of society, and of the individuals in it, was entrusted to the outcome of a no-holds-barred economic contest. The only rules were those protecting property; all else was in the laps of the gods. No doubt, in the setting of the eighteenth and nineteenth centuries, such an economy would grow and change at rates that were, by previous standards, extraordinarily high, as dramatically portrayed in *The Communist Manifesto*:

> The bourgeoisie, during its rule of scarce one hundred years, has created more massive and more colossal productive forces than all preceding generations together. Subjection of nature's forces to man, machinery, application of chemistry to industry and agriculture, steam-navigation, railways, electric telegraphs, clearing of whole continents for cultivation, canalization of rivers, whole populations conjured out of the ground—what earlier century had even a presentiment that such productive forces slumbered in the lap of social labor?

As the industrial revolution gained strength, the State loosened its hold on the economy, and laissez-faire capitalism emerged, the structure of power in Britain underwent continuous change. The improving technology meant a dynamic economy, and it also meant always more muscular business firms, and the growth of a new and powerful private-State pattern of power—a pattern all the more insidious because those who had to be controlled were more difficult to identify. And those who had to be controlled were in fact in control.

When Smith argued for a "free market" system, he did not do so trusting in the character or intentions of capitalists. As he noted in a famous observation, "...people of the same trade seldom meet together, even for merriment and diversion, but the conversation ends in a conspiracy against the public, or in some contrivance to raise prices."[26] His fears on that score were neutralized by his key assumption that a highly decentralized market structure, and its "invisible hand" of competition, would frustrate the conniving businessmen. But it was the very success of his economic system in increasing productivity and production with what became a large-scale technology that rendered that hope vain.

Smith tripped over another matter of greater weight: the distribution of income and wealth, and the ways in which those structures affect both the process of expansion and the possibilities of exploitation. For this shortcoming, Smith had less excuse than for his failure to anticipate fully the future of technology. The distribution of income and wealth when Smith wrote was of course already highly unequal, and rapidly becoming more so. They were the years of high turmoil associated with the enclosure movement, a process impoverishing the multitudes while placing more wealth in very few hands. It was a contemporary of Smith's, after all, whose epic poem "The Deserted Village" has done so much to tell us—if romantically and sentimentally—what was lost when efficient agriculture was gained:

> Ill fares the land, to hastening ills a prey,
> Where wealth accumulates and men decay:
> Princes and lords may flourish, or may fade;
> A breath can make them, as a breath has made;
> But a bold peasantry, their country's pride,
> When once destroyed, can never be supplied.[27]

England had ceased to need a "bold peasantry" while Goldsmith wrote; to further its economic growth it needed instead a docile and powerless labor force that would work under wretched and dangerous conditions in mine, mill, and factory. England got much of what it needed through the enclosure movement; other capitalist nations found both similar and different means to create or to import a powerless labor force. The conditions of Irish workers brought into England (Ireland was the first, and its North is now the last, English colony) were even worse than for the English, and the great British historian Macaulay found the conditions of the German workers worse still, leading to his characterization of them as "degenerate dwarfs." That he was not entirely off the mark (setting aside his ugly language) is suggested by this observation concerning Germany: "In 1828 General von Horn warned the Prussian Government that these [Prussian] districts could not supply their quota of army recruits since the health of young factory workers was being undermined."[28]

What Smith failed to foresee regarding technology and private power is less egregious as a defect for a moral philosopher than his failure to grasp what would become of a society freed from virtually all social constraints but those of the market. He was, of course, right in believing that the abolition of constraints would allow the capitalist economy to grow apace; indeed, the prime reason for the *economic* powers of capitalism is that (by comparison with other social systems) it *is* socially unconstrained, that in releasing individual energy and removing external (and internal) inhibitions, there is nothing to prevent the economy from becoming a juggernaut. It must be noted that this system works best when it brings out the worst in its people: greed, aggressivity, distrust, selfishness, ruthlessness, an ever-narrowing "individualism," and ultimately an amoral, heartless, even mindless society.[29]

Economic growth taken alone is neither desirable nor undesirable. It must be judged in terms of its larger meanings to human beings and to nature, in what it elicits and what it deflects or suppresses in human beings; in what it does to the nature of human relationships; how it serves human needs; how it encourages human possibilities. In establishing competition as the ruling principle of social existence, a capitalist society makes combative relationships necessary for all, makes such relationships "normal": not just between workers and employers, or workers and workers; not just between nations; but also between the various ethnic and "racial" groups, between men and women—a kind of continuous war, all the more threatening because it is seen as "natural" rather than only our "dark side," extruded and exacerbated by social institutions that do little to bring out the best in us.

If there are quantitative rewards in such a society for those who are victorious, there are qualitative losses for all. This has been so even after the reintroduction of some social constraints, as represented in the reforms of the 1930s and subsequently, for basic attitudes and processes of competition and combativeness not only are deeply embedded, but remain "practical." Human inclinations other than naked self-interest narrowly defined are pushed into the realm of the impractical, the "idealistic," those who manifest them scorned as "do-gooders." As Tawney observed in 1920,

> It is obvious, indeed, that no change of system or machinery can avert those causes of social *malaise* which consist in the egotism, greed, or quarrelsomeness of human nature. What it

can do is to create an environment in which those are not the qualities which are encouraged. It cannot secure that men live up to their principles. What it can do is establish their social order upon principles to which, if they please, they can live up and not live down.[30]

To which may be contrasted, as Tawney points out, "the compound of economic optimism and moral bankruptcy which led a nineteenth-century economist to say: 'Greed is held in check by greed, and the desire for gain sets limits to itself.'"[31]

What classical political economy (John Stuart Mill as a partial exception) ignored in the capitalist process was the starting-point for Marx. He saw competitive capitalism as an inhumane and dehumanizing social system, dependent upon greed for its energy and exploitation for its fuel. He took for granted that it would increase production and productivity immensely over time; given its dynamics, he also saw that monopoly would replace competition. Even after a century or more of evidence confirming Marx's judgment,[32] conventional analysis and current free market ideology remain unabashed by the central, dominating role of giant business complexes, and their obsessive concern for the bottom line, come hell or high water. What Marx took for granted is seen analytically as aberrant, dismissed as unimportant, or not seen at all.

The transition from competitive to monopoly capitalism was facilitated by but not solely *due* to technological change. It was the increasing scale and complexity of production *combined with* the major impulses of those who controlled the means of production that led to monopoly (and today's structural consequence of "oligopoly"). The concentration and centralization of capital that is characteristic of all industrial capitalist societies today (the United States neither most nor least so) arises out of, not despite, competitive capitalism. It is one of the chief ways the system moves through time.

Those who survive this struggle do so by absorbing or by destroying the lesser firms, a process called "creative destruction" by Joseph Schumpeter. Capitalism is a predatory form of economic organization. For Smith's optimism to have been well-founded, limits would have had to have been set on the size of the bigger fish. Set by whom, the bigger fish? In the absence of any explicit institutions other than market competition designed to control aggrandizement—and free market capitalism excludes any such, in principle—the bigger fish become always more unreachable and untouchable, always more immune to any constraints on their behavior or further enlargement. It is they who are best able to respond effectively to changing technology, and are best able to survive intermittent blasts of recession and depression. Nor is their destruction always creative. The history of the United States, most capitalistic by far of all capitalist nations, reveals these processes most clearly.[33]

Capitalist Paradise: The U.S.A.

A generalization readily agreed upon by both foes and supporters of our system is that capitalism and industrialism have been more firmly and thoroughly established in the United States than elsewhere.[34] How and why this came to be is explained by all those matters that contribute to industrial capitalist development, so much more abundantly present here than in other societies, and by the manner in which they have interacted in our history. Let us note first the most obvious of these contributing factors—our geographic, natural advantages—and place them in the United States social context.

Anything and everything that might facilitate the emergence of capitalist institutions and the progress of industry was available in our colonial period. All that was lacking was control over our own destiny; and that was achieved in the War for Independence. Most obvious and striking of our advantages has been our physical setting.

No nation has matched the quantitative or qualitative abundance of the natural resources of this country, whether the reference is to climate, terrain, soils, coasts, bays, rivers, lakes, forests, and minerals, or to the convenient locations of each of these with respect to each other.[35] Nor can the vast oceans that have given us almost total security from military assault be ignored as a developmental advantage. All these are obvious. But there other and less obvious advantages, institutional and historical, which were of perhaps overriding importance in our evolution as a capitalist society.

The times and social conditions under which colonial North America and the United States came into being were most auspicious. As such, we had no medieval past, and thus no tradition of social controls of our own to deny or destroy. On this continent, all that had to be destroyed were the Native American and Mexican communities standing in the way of our "manifest destiny." The settlement and development of North

America, as a colony of the British, represented the leading social edge of British development, rather than the British past. In the seventeenth century, and even more in the eighteenth, that meant a Britain moving rapidly toward capitalist institutions.

Attempts to implant traditional agricultural forms (such as manorialism in upstate New York) or stringent social codes (such as theocratic institutions in Massachusetts) were made; the strong winds of commercialism and the extraordinary opportunities of the time and place combined to blow away such social structures. There were very few people on this continent in comparison with the rich resources of the land. Labor was short in supply; workers were wanted in shipping, trade, fishing, petty industry, and agriculture. This was an especially severe problem for those who wished to exploit the rich soils of the southern colonies. Serfdom was impossible; slavery, with its absence of freedom, was not.

Commercial slavery began well before the significant settlement of the colonies. The African slave trade was well-established by the sixteenth century; slaves were widely used in Latin America and in the Caribbean, especially for sugar cultivation. As the southern colonies began to grow tobacco for the market, and even more so when rice, indigo, and especially cotton plantations grew in number and importance, North America became the principal user of African slaves. The most conservative estimates of the number of Africans enslaved and carried to the Americas range from fifteen to twenty millions; and it is estimated that from 50 to 85 percent of these died in the deadly "middle passage."[36]

The nonslave labor force of the colonies was made up of immigrants, many coming as indentured servants, which meant working three to seven years to pay for their passage. Arriving mostly as adults, immigrants were a boon to the young economy: their childhood, their unproductive years, had been "paid for" in their home countries. This remained an advantageous characteristic of the expanding United States labor force up to World War I, and then again after World War II, as millions, from Asia and Central America, continue to provide abundant cheap labor, and help to keep wages down and profits up.

In addition, another feature concerning the labor force should be noted: those who came voluntarily to this country, whether propelled or drawn by religious, political, or economic considerations, were clearly desirous of or suited to the nontraditional shape of the growing society.

Their characteristics contributed to that growth; as the characteristics of the very recent immigrants, eager to "make it" in the capitalist paradise, also contribute to social conservatism.

From its first days, and setting aside those enslaved or conquered, the United States was a land of enterprisers—small or large farmers, artisans or petty manufacturers, domestic and foreign traders, low or high financiers, innkeepers, and so on. It was a capitalist society from birth; or, if not quite then, as soon as it could crawl. By the mid-eighteenth century, the colonies had the ability to walk but were increasingly held back by British capital and British power. What mercantilism had been to British capitalism at home, both in its positive and its negative aspects, British regulations were to colonists (as Smith had noted).

Few indeed were the colonists who foresaw either the need or the possibility of war against Britain, until the mid-1770s. Once war broke out, the ability of the colonists to fight successfully was enhanced not only by the ocean between but also by the diverse interests and rivalries distracting the British from a sole preoccupation with the North American colonies: for example, the Caribbean sugar colonies were seen as more important economically (and strategically) at that time. And, of course, Britain had to contend with its European rivals, especially the French, who aided the colonial struggle directly and indirectly.

Of great importance to the young economy both before and after the war were the expansive trends beginning to take hold in the world, with the coming of the nineteenth century. The old structures of power were cracking up in Europe, and new waves of economic and geographic expansion were transforming the world. In that setting, the United States found new and growing sources of trade, of technological innovation, of capital, and of immigrants. Added to our already substantial advantages in resources, attitudes, and labor supply, this dynamic new world context propelled United States economic development along its path toward industrialism with an unmatchable set of advantages; and the relative ease of our economic development did much to obscure and to suppress the social conflicts associated with capitalist development.

Next we should characterize the role of the State in our history. In rebelling against the British, the colonists were also rebelling against the role of centralized State power. Consequently, even though the war brought them to a pitch of patriotism and nationalism that would still be considered intense by world standards, an affection for a central government did not result.[37] This did not mean, however, a distaste for governmental assistance when necessary and useful. Thus, our first decades as a nation saw a minimal role of the *federal* government and a vital role for the separate *state* governments. The federal government was very Smithian, as it presided over a unified foreign trade policy, a uniform currency, and a national policy for absorbing, buying, and conquering the lands to the west. The state governments were considerably more mercantilistic; they played a decisive role in developing transportation (roads, canals, and railways), banking, and, among other matters, business and labor laws.

The upshot, for the first half-century of our existence as a nation, was far from laissez-faire capitalism. Here we may note very briefly (and more fully in Chapter 8) four different periods regarding the role of the State in United States economic life. The first has just been noted, as the United States period of limited, Hamiltonian mercantilism. The second period, replacing mercantilism after Jackson's presidency, amounted to the beginnings of United States-style laissez-faire capitalism.[38] It came to its roaring climax in the decades after the Civil War, called by Mark Twain the Gilded Age, and by Vernon Parrington the Great Barbecue.

The third phase, a response to both the instabilities and the beckoning possibilities of maturing industrial capitalism, began to develop as this century opened, and it found coherence during Wilson's presidency. It involved increased concentration of State power in Washington, both consequence and ongoing cause of the increasing concentration and centralization of economic power in the corporate world of industry and finance—all hastened by the onset of World War I. It was accompanied by the first waves of overseas imperialism, begun when the United States went to war in Cuba and the Philippines.[39]

Historian Gabriel Kolko has called this the beginnings of "political capitalism" in the United States. Although the 1920s saw a decade-long detour from that evolving "neomercantilism," the depression of the 1930s (and FDR's "New Deal") and World War II combined to renew the broadening and deepening of the role of the State in almost all aspects of United States economic life, well beyond the policies of the Wilson years, as will be seen in Chapters 4 and 8. The fourth phase began in the late 1970s and in the 1980s and became a tidal wave of efforts seeking to remove the regulatory role of the State from the economy and its protective role from the society. What the overall consequences of this conservative shift have been to date, and whether, like the seeming reversal of the 1920s, this is merely a prelude to a further strengthening of the State, or something much different, are matters to be examined later.

Mirror, Mirror, on the Wall...

The people of the United States tend to view our national history as having made astounding economic achievements with a minimum of the coercive and violent practices associated with other nations' histories, and as having taken place within a political and social context at once humanitarian, egalitarian, and democratic—with, to be sure, here and there a wart, but who's perfect? Such a view requires blindness (and depends upon and supports numbness) to certain basic features of our development. The blindness is systematic and pervasive (and very much connected with our scornful disinterest in history: "History is bunk," said Henry Ford, at the peak of his career).

Largely overlooked, neglected, or brushed off almost as a youthful indiscretion by our people is the enormous fact of slavery for over two centuries of our history, and its role as a central determinant of our economic development until at least the mid-nineteenth century. Also neglected, and in a connected way, are the other forms of labor exploitation that hastened and shaped our economic achievements. Nor, until quite recently, has more than minimal attention been paid to the relationships between our rapid economic growth and the spoliation of nature that cheapened the direct costs (and increased the profits) of that growth.

What Veblen called the "trained incapacity" to comprehend our history of human and resource exploitation has made it terribly difficult for us to comprehend or control the consequences of our past. Not least among these is that major historical blind-spot in our social perspective that prevents us from seeing or understanding our history of almost continuous geographic expansion.

Economic expansion was noted earlier as being essential to capitalist health; now we shall focus upon the key role played in that process by our geographic expansion. Capitalism began and continues that way; the settling of the North American colonies was, of course, an instance of geographic expansion for the British. The United States has been and remains critically conscious of the incessant attempts of *other* nations to enlarge their geographic influence and control; we have spoken harshly of British, or French, or German, or Japanese imperialism. Only rarely, however, do our histories speak of United States imperialism; instead, we read of "westward expansion," or "manifest destiny." We do not view our process of geographic expansion on this continent as imperialism (although it was probably the most successful of all such processes, anywhere, anytime), but as simply a filling of the space up to "our" natural boundaries. We do not see our history as one of exterminating or penning in the Native American population, or of holding back and pushing away the other contenders (French, British, Spanish, Mexican, Russian) for geographic control, but rather as merely securing "our" lands, lands that were in some unexamined sense "ours" to begin with, or "ours" when we could get around to settling and exploiting them.

Given such views of the expansion on this continent, it was natural and easy as this century began to see our extra-continental expansion—into the Caribbean and the Pacific first, and directly and indirectly over the face of the entire globe later—as having much the same qualities. If the rest of the world was not "ours" in the same sense as actual settlement, it was—is—ours to protect, to assist, to shape, to lead, to make or to keep "free." As subsequently became the case with Korea and Indochina (and with similar as well as diverse reasoning, Panama and Iraq), they were "ours" to destroy if necessary, in order to save them—or something.

A line from Jamestown to the present marks our entire history. Its importance must be measured first in terms of what it has meant to those we have killed, caged, or shoved aside. But only at our peril can we overlook the importance to our past and our future that the studied innocence (or arrogant justification) of that line had meant in shaping United States policy and United States consciousness, and how it connects with our treatment of human beings (including ourselves, of course) and nature here at home.[40]

Later chapters will elaborate upon all the foregoing generalizations concerning United States capitalist development. Here a few summary points may be of use. The United States had the easiest, swiftest, and most successful process of economic achievement of any society in history, whether we measure by the level or composition of production, by productivity, or by per capita real income. Most capitalist of all nations, the United States has had less open and sustained class conflict than all other capitalist nations. As a people we have seen more hope for ourselves *within* the system than our counterparts elsewhere; when we have moved to struggle—whether as workers seeking unions, or as those racially or sexually oppressed—we have almost always adopted both the means and the ends of those who rule and profit in the system.

Perhaps the best way of explaining the economic and the social strength and stability of United States capitalism is to see that it has possessed *within its own boundaries* and capacities so much of all that is essential for capitalist development, which other nations have possessed in much lesser part, or not at all. Even better, where the United States was lacking a key element, an abundant domestic labor supply, we not only were able to import labor—slave, indentured, and free—but the diversity of its composition—in color, religion, ethnic origin, etc.—contributed to the continuation and strengthening of racism: in the past and still today a vital means of diverting attention from economic and social inequalities.[41] No other capitalist nation has had such diversities in its domestic labor supply, nor has any other (with the possible exception of the Union of South Africa) been able to use racism at home in ways that combined economic with political advantage: just think of the almost innumerable deprecatory names we have for the various colors, national, and religious origins that make up our population. Taken together with our ease of geographic expansion, this "racial" resource helps to explain the most successful and prolonged process of economic expansion among capitalist nations.

A Summing Up

Having come to be as a nation created in the name of minimal State power, the United States now functions as a highly centralized State at home. As the first society to fight a successful war for national independence, the United States now sits in the midst of a complex web of neocolonial relationships constructed in this century in the name of what William Appleman Williams aptly terms "anticolonial imperialism."

Nor should we fail to note that the land whose Declaration of Independence speaks in inspiring ways of human dignity and freedom has as its most fundamental and unresolved question an intensive form of racism practiced from our first years, and no less so after our independence. We continue despite repeated warnings from many quarters that if racism has not already been our undoing, it will one day be so. Much the same may be said about our destruction of the environment, the deadly qualities of our air, and the poisoning of our water supplies.

In short, in creating the world's most powerful economy, the United

States has also produced a society teeming with troubles. The troubles are connected in such a way that we must speak not of "social issues" but of an enduring and worsening social crisis. Racism and imperialism and poverty were not invented by capitalism or the people of this country. But the development of United States capitalism has nourished those monsters. Their effects are to create fear, tension, hatred, and violence, and these cannot be viewed as separable from the nature of the socioeconomy that has allowed or encouraged them to flourish.

United States capitalism is the acme and the epitome of capitalism. As such it departs further and further from inherited noncommercial values; in the process, institutions and attitudes supportive of noncommercial values—the family, human solidarity, trust, among them—are vitiated, weaken, and disappear. At the same time, many people become increasingly aware of the essential inhumanity and amorality of a society so much dominated by profit making and wealth-garnering, and the subjection of the human spirit and human activities to machine-like conditions. The tension between these two developments, between the natural course of capitalist development and the increasing resistance of the human spirit, lies at the root of our ongoing social crisis.

Human beings are everything that the species has been, thought, felt, done. We are our poems, our soaring bridges, our concentration camps, our gardens, our love, our brutality, we are Bach, Reagan, Charlie Chaplin, Picasso, Doonesbury, Hitler. We are the most constructive and the most destructive of all species, we imagine and dream, hope and fear as no other. In short, we are full of marvelous and dreadful possibilities. Our history proves it.

Having said all that, we may also assert something difficult to remember in these greedy and bloody times: human beings are inherently moral, possessed of feelings of sympathy, empathy, solidarity with our kind, and the *need* to lead creative and loving lives. These attributes continue to emerge and manifest themselves, now as in the past, alongside the continuation of our baser capabilities. One need not be a Shakespeare or a Goethe, one need merely look around, to see people as something more than creatures of material self-interest. All the major religions, psychiatry, and the landmarks of our literature, art, and music remind us of what we have been and what we can be, as do the numerous struggles fought by so many people for their own and others' dignity throughout history. These are not sentimental or "idealistic" observations; were we not such a species, we would not have survived.

The crisis in which we now move shows itself first as a crisis of economic and political life; its root, however, is moral. A historical turning point is suggested by the metaphor of crisis, the resolution of which will take us closer to the realization or to the destruction of our species' needs and possibilities. The resolution is unlikely to be favorable within a social framework that encourages a warped individualism and a crass materialism. That there are alternative possibilities, none easy to achieve, goes without saying. In the concluding chapter some of these will be examined.

Reading Suggestions

For two books that seek to explain the ways and means of capitalism, in overlapping but contrasting analyses, see Samuel Bowles and Richard Edwards, *Understanding Capitalism* (New York: Harper & Row, 1985), and Robert L. Heilbroner, *The Nature and Logic of Capitalism* (New York: Norton, 1985). R.H. Tawney has already been noted for some of his books. He is deservedly among the most influential and respected historians of the rise of capitalism (and in *The Acquisitive Society*, cited earlier, for his critique of it). He has also provided a subtle and profound analysis of the manner in which, as capitalism began to emerge, religious thought changed its meaning, though not always its words, from the sixteenth to the eighteenth centuries—a process that has also occurred with our nonreligious terms more recently. See his 175-page introduction to Thomas Wilson, *A Discourse Upon Usury* (London: Bell, 1925), itself the work of a sixteenth-century divine. E.P. Thompson, *The Making of the English Working Class** (New York: Vintage, 1966) has written that history "from the bottom up," and in doing so has inspired the work of a new generation of historians. A closely reasoned historical analysis of capitalism by a leading Marxist is Maurice Dobb, *Studies in the Development of Capitalism** (London: Routledge, 1946). The difficulties and violence associated with economic development in the capitalist era have been studied carefully by Barrington Moore, Jr., *Social Origins of Dictatorship and Democracy** (Boston: Beacon Press, 1966). Chapters on the English Civil War of the seventeenth century, the French Revolution, and our own Civil War are especially insightful. J.L. and Barbara Hammond wrote many books on the consequences of evolving industrial capitalism in Britain, all of them combining penetrating analysis with great detail, all of them heartbreaking in what they show happened to the ordinary people of Britain in the decades of the Industrial Revolution, not least among them *The Bleak Age** (London: Pelican Books, 1947).

Two comprehensive views of the origins and nature of capitalist development, both affected by and considerably different from Marx, are Thorstein Veblen, *The Theory of the Leisure Class** (New York: Macmillan, 1899) and Joseph Schumpeter, *Capitalism, Socialism, and Democracy** (New York: Harper & Row, 1942). Schumpeter was a leading conservative economist and critic of Marxism. C. Wright Mills, was also a critic, but a radical one, in his *The Marxists** (New York: Dell, 1962).

The succeeding chapters will be much concerned with various aspects of the economic history of the United States. Frequent reference will be had to one or another of the books in a very useful series published in the 1950s and 1960s by Holt, Rinehart and Winston (New York), entitled *The Economic History of the United States*. The separate volumes are generally valuable in themselves and each has a most useful bibliography. It seems appropriate to list all these books together here for handy reference: Curtis P. Nettels, *The Emergence of a National Economy, 1775–1815*; Paul W. Gates, *The Farmer's Age: Agriculture, 1815–1860*; George R. Taylor, *The Transportation Revolution, 1815–1860*; Fred Shannon, *The Farmer's Last Frontier: Agriculture, 1869–1897*; Edward C. Kirkland, *Industry Comes of Age, 1860–1897*; Harold U. Faulkner, *The Decline of Laissez-Faire: 1897–1917*; George Soule, *Prosperity Decade: From War to Depression, 1917–1929*; Broadus Mitchell, *Depression Decade: From New Era Through New Deal, 1929–1941*; Donald L. Kemmerer, *The U.S. Economy, 1940–1960*.

Richard B. Du Boff, *Accumulation & Power: An Economic History of the United States** (Armonk, N.Y.: M. E. Sharpe, Inc., 1989), provides an incisive analysis of United States history focusing on what he conceives to be "the central organizing process of capitalism in the United States—private investment carried out to assure profitable growth for the corporate sector of the economy" (p. xi).

Howard Zinn has written a valuable and unique history of the United States whose "focus is not on the achievements of the heroes of traditional history, but on all those people who were the victims of those achievements, who suffered silently or fought back magnificently": *A People's History of the United States** (New York: Harper & Row, 1980), which stretches from colonial times into the 1970s, with a revision published in 1984 that begins with the opening of this century and goes into the 1980s: *The Twentieth Century: A People's History of the United States.** (The quoted statement above is from p. ix of the latter book.) Finally, an incisive analysis of United States history from the late nineteenth century to the 1970s is Gabriel Kolko, *Main Currents in Modern American History** (New York: Pantheon, 1984).

Notes

1. Robinson Jeffers, *Eagle Valor, Chicken Brain.* Reprinted by permission of Jeffers Literary Properties.
2. Maurice Dobb, *Economics of Private Enterprise** (Sydney: Current Book Distributors, 1944), p. 3.
3. This important argument cannot be pursued further here; it is, however, especially vital for understanding the political "side" of capitalism (which we examine in Chapter 8), so frequently neglected by both supporters and critics of the system. For a comprehensive and powerful statement of this position, see the two volumes by Perry Anderson, *Passages from Antiquity to Feudalism* and *Lineages of the Absolute State* (London: NLB, 1974), especially pp. 397–431 of *Lineages.*
4. Immanuel Wallerstein, *The Modern World System: Capitalist Agriculture and the Origins of the European World-Economy in the Sixteenth Century* (New York: Academic Press, 1974), p. 38. By the "sixteenth century," he means 1450–1640. "Variegated labor" refers to three distinct forms of labor control: wage labor, sharecropper/tenancy, and serf/slave labor, which work in core, semi-peripheral, and peripheral economies, respectively. The "core" economy stands as technologically/economically advanced in relation to the others.
5. *The Communist Manifesto* may be found in innumerable editions and contexts—as a pamphlet, part of a book, etc. It is contained, along with many thoughtfully selected quotations from Marx, Engels, and Lenin, and useful introductory remarks by the editors, in Howard Selsam, David Goldman, and Harry Martel, eds., *Dynamics of Social Change** (New York: International Publishers, 1970).
6. None of these is unique to capitalism, of course, singly or in combination. What is unique are the particular functions served, their hows and whys, and the ways in which these processes and relationships

combine and interact in the capitalist process. It is not the similarities between social systems (or, for that matter, between different animals) that give them their special character, but their differences.

7. Those who call for the cessation or slowing of economic growth on grounds of ecological damage, must—but seldom do—contend with the fact that they are thereby calling for a new, or very much modified, socioeconomic system, not just the ecological defanging of the present one. This vital question, and related matters (including the need for a very complex alteration of growth rates and patterns, in terms of products, techniques, and geographic areas) will be pursued in Chapter 6.

8. Probably the most helpful book of readings to accompany this book, or for gaining a grasp of the nature and functioning of the capitalist system, whether regarding the matters under discussion in this chapter or more generally, is Richard C. Edwards, Michael Reich, and Thomas E. Weisskopf, eds., *The Capitalist System** (Englewood Cliffs, N.J.: Prentice-Hall, 1986). For this chapter, see their Chapters 2 and 3.

9. In turn, this allows us to think of exploitation as being "done to" not only workers in the process of production (the generic meaning of the term), but also to consumers and citizens, keeping in mind that in the industrializing nations of the nineteenth century the average person had a very narrow access to what today are called consumer goods and less formal political power (non-property-owners could not vote in Britain until 1867, nor any women in either the United States or Britain until this century).

10. Consumers' abilities to put up with these processes without complaint seem to be endless. A few years ago it became customary, in the context of always rising automobile prices, for the spare tire in a new car to be considerably smaller than the other four, capable of being used for only 3,000 miles, and then only with the warning (well-hidden in the trunk) that one should drive with great care, etc. And then there is the now common "downsizing" (a euphemism that Orwell, in his *1984*, failed to anticipate in particular, but did in general), whether in candy bars, or soap detergents, or whatever, where as one gets less, one pays more. The detergent example is particularly interesting: The big box has now been replaced with one far smaller, at a higher price per wash, its predecessor having been largely devoted to giving the appearance of muchness. The change was caused by the rivalry among producers for shelf space in the increasingly powerful supermarket chains (Safeway, etc.), who wish to be able to display and sell more products with the same space.

11. Most costly to date has been the savings and loan bailout, to be discussed in Chapter 4. The debt problem was already seen as threatening in the mid-1970s when, compared to now, it was relatively minor. See two useful articles: "The Debt Economy," *Business Week*, October 12, 1974 and, on a deeper level, Hyman P. Minsky, "Financial Resources in a Fragile Financial Environment," *Challenge*, July/August, 1975. Professor Minsky is both authoritative and was already then alarmed; we shall have reference to his work again later in the book.

12. Chapters 7 and 8 are much concerned with these matters, and will seek to support the foregoing generalization. From time to time, after wars, there has seemed to be reason to hope that gullibility of this sort might lessen substantially—after World War I, after World War II, after the Korean War, after the Vietnam War, for example. But Grenada, Panama, and the Gulf wars show just how hardy this poisonous weed can be, and that its cultivation is, up to now, to be taken for granted.

13. The expansion itself has to be explained, and that will be attempted in Chapter 4, where the discussion will locate the explanation within the institutions of what is called "monopoly capitalism" and the Cold War, where both will be viewed as global in scope and functioning. Such matters will also be brought forth in Chapters 3, 7, and 8. And, as will be seen in Chapters 4 and 7, like all processes of capitalist development, major and minor, these also transformed themselves, yielding from the 1970s to the present, a complex and enduring set of crises.

14. Frederick Engels, *The Condition of the Working-Class in England in 1844** (London: Allen & Unwin, 1950), p. 75. Published originally in 1845.

15. See "Large-scale Production," by Myron W. Watkins, in *The Encyclopaedia of the Social Sciences*. This fifteen-volume work, available in almost all libraries, is an invaluable source of information and analysis concerning institutions, social processes, notable thinkers, etc., despite (perhaps also because of) its being published in the 1930s. A later version (entitled *The International Encyclopaedia of the Social Sciences*) does not contain this essay (or others that may be noted).

16. In all industrial capitalist societies, labor has gained various forms of protection—maximum hours, minimum wages, safety conditions, various types of privately and publicly financed insurance, etc.—but only after considerable political struggle in their industries and in the larger society. And it must be noted that unless the efforts that have brought such achievements into being are continued, the sociopolitical pressure of

capital tends to diminish the gains and push labor back from comfort and safety. That such is so has been all too clearly demonstrated in the past decade and more, not only in Britain and the United States, but in virtually every advanced society in Western Europe. This will be examined in more detail in Chapter 8.

17. Karl Marx, *Capital** (New York: International Publishers, 1967), vol. I, p. 515. Originally published 1867.

18. In modern capitalism, the "employer" may be the small owner of a shop, or a large corporation. In the latter case, generally it is management, rather than owners, who exercise the power of property. Although there has been a large (if diminishing) stir concerning the differences between decisions made by owners as compared with managers, a matter to be looked at in Chapter 3, it may be said that for what is being discussed here, it makes no sensible difference. The "stir," for those interested, was begun by A.A. Berle and Gardiner Means, in *The Modern Corporation and Private Property* (New York: Macmillan, 1932).

19. Of R.H. Tawney's many profound studies, two of those concerned with the early rumblings of what was to become a social earthquake were *Religion and the Rise of Capitalism**, noted earlier, and *The Agrarian Problem in 16th Century England** (New York: Burt Franklin, 1959, first published in 1912.) For Tawney, the religious institutions that were transformed in the processes of the Reformation and the transformation of agrarian institutions represented by the "enclosures" wc shall note momentarily represented the breakup of the two most fundamental (and closely related) sets of institutions in European history; and when that could and did happen, everything else could and would give way. For better or for worse, they were the dams holding tradition in place.

20. The serf and his family presumably received protection from their lord; except that, depending upon region and time, many who became serfs had been free and had their freedom wrested away from them militarily by those who subsequently were their "protectors." And, as regions came to be militarily stabilized over the centuries, the serf continued to give service, but for needs no longer existing. As the readings in note 21 will show, there was no one pattern at any time, or over time in any one place.

21. The diversity of the pattern in various parts of Europe, and the forces at work, are analyzed at their best in *The Cambridge Economic*

History of Europe, Vol. I: The Agrarian Life of the Middle Ages (Cambridge, England: Cambridge University Press, 1942) edited by J.H. Clapham and Eileen Power. See also, in *The Encyclopaedia of the Social Sciences*, "Feudalism," by Marc Bloch, which provides a succinct and illuminating analysis of European feudalism and its decline. His own *Feudal Society** (Chicago: University of Chicago Press, Phoenix Books, 1964), in two volumes, is the classic study, rich in wisdom and detail. Bloch was a member of the French Resistance; he was executed by the Nazis in a field, early in World War II.

22. In the course of developing his "labor theory of value," in volume I of *Capital*, Part I, Marx makes the important historical point that the small landholders, who produced both agricultural and industrial products, were producing commodities (C) to exchange for money (M) in order to buy other commodities (which he writes C-M-C)—production for their own use, mediated by selling and buying. Marx saw this as the early stage of capitalist development, what he called "primitive accumulation." As the small holders were displaced, the process changed to one of buying commodities in order to sell them as a means of buying more commodities (M-C-M'), all with the end of profit, of capital accumulation. M' represents an increase over M, due to the extraction of "surplus value" from C, where C is the commodity labor power.

23. From his *Outlines of a Critique of Political Economy,** quoted in Meszaros, op. cit., pp. 314–315. For the social upheaval consequent upon all these changes, see the definitive work on the period in all its respects, Paul Mantoux, *The Industrial Revolution in the Eighteenth Century** (London: Cape, 1928), especially chapter 3. First published 1906. William Lazonick, "Karl Marx and Enclosures in England," RRPE, vol. 6, no. 2 (Summer 1974) is a superb discussion both of that history and of the historiography of enclosures.

24. Bottomore, *Karl Marx: Early Writings*, cited earlier, p. 138. Stephen A. Marglin, "What Do Bosses Do? The Origins and Functions of Hierarchy in Capitalist Production," RRPE, vol. 6, no. 2 (Summer 1974), is an important analysis showing how the organization of work under capitalist conditions itself contributes to exploitation, whatever else it might mean. His emphasis is the long period into the nineteenth century. Harry Braverman, *Labor and Monopoly Capital** (New York: Monthly Review Press, 1974) shows this and much more for this century, with its "scientific management" of labor. His apt subtitle is *The Degradation of Work in the Twentieth Century*. That perhaps a third of

the working population in contemporary industrial capitalist societies consumes goods and services whose composition and level would have been unimaginable even fifty years ago allows many to believe that the observations concerning alienation and related matters in the text are no longer valid; there is at least as much reason to believe that today's consumeristic drives are a manifestation of a deepening alienation and demoralization (of which, more subsequently).

25. Harold J. Laski, *The Rise of European Liberalism* (London: Allen & Unwin, 1936), p. 28.

26. *Wealth of Nations*, p. 130.

27. Oliver Goldsmith (1728–1774) was Irish, but the setting of his poem was England. This is but a fragment of a very long poem. The sixteenth century enclosures had earlier prompted Sir Thomas More to observe that "shepe are eating men," as lands were converted from arable (food producing) into pasturage for the expanding wool trade. In the past hundred years or more, as will be discussed in Chapters 6 and 7, much higher numbers of "bold peasantry" or their counterparts have been "destroyed" under the impact of imperialism and neocolonialism, and now find themselves in degrading work or unemployed, crowded into hostile cities, or wandering their old lands, ill and hungry.

28. W.O. Henderson, *The Industrial Revolution in Europe, 1815–1914** (Chicago: Quadrangle, 1968), p. 23. This book is a useful source for developments in Europe, to balance our emphasis on Britain and the United States. Also see Thorstein Veblen, *Imperial Germany and the Industrial Revolution** (New York: Viking, 1946) for a searching and witty comparison and analysis of British and German development. First published 1915, wherein, it is interesting to note, Veblen anticipated what would become German fascism by the 1930s.

29. There have been many, especially in this century, who have argued that when the system works "well" in these ways it is also moving toward self-destruction. I am one of those. And it is undeniably true that the most pervasively and deeply dynamic years in capitalist history, the years of the 1950s and 1960s, were precisely those when the market was constrained, when economic growth and stability were most impressive, and when living conditions rose markedly for a large percentage of the inhabitants of the leading capitalist nations. They were the years of "Left Keynesianism" and "social democracy." As I shall try to explain in Chapter 4, the larger framework within which these developments occurred—"military Keynesianism," neocolonialism, the Cold War, and

their ways and means—produced a socioeconomic crisis whose first casualties were the very achievements noted above, and the growth of a conservative capitalist politics that shows no signs of abating. It was as that crisis was beginning to show itself that the perceived need arose to write the original version of this book.

30. R.H. Tawney, *The Acquisitive Society** (New York: Harcourt Brace Jovanovich, 1920), p. 180.

31. Ibid., p. 27. A quotation Mr. Ivan Boesky might have used to dignify his commencement address lauding greed to the students at the University of California, Berkeley in 1986, only shortly before he was apprehended and sent to prison—literally and figuratively carried away by his own greed. Mr. Boesky was held in the Llompoc, California "facility," from which he was freed after a relatively brief confinement. His crimes, amounting to billions of dollars of frauds and swindles, for which investors and taxpayers will pay for many years, and his punishment (he is reputed to be still very rich), may be compared with the time spent in maximum security "facilities" by those who steal, let us say, some thousands of dollars.

32. And Veblen's, at the very beginning of this century, in his first book strictly concerned with the U.S. economy: *The Theory of Business Enterprise* (New York: Charles Scribner, 1904). The "judgment" spoken of refers to the points cited in the sentences immediately preceding, not to all of Marx's expectations.

33. The passage of the Sherman Anti-Trust Act in 1890, and its subsequent amendments, far from contradicting the foregoing paragraph, strongly confirms it, as discussion in Chapter 3 will show. Suffice it to say here that the law was used in its first twenty years or so almost exclusively to prevent workers from achieving a "monopoly." Its major impact on business organization has been to push firms into oligopolistic rather than purely monopolistic forms—not only as more profitable in the long run, but as forms preserving the fiction of competition, making it all the easier to fend off controls. There have been many kinds of regulation put in force, going back to the first of its kind, the Interstate Commerce Act of 1886, and up through the occupational health and safety, and environmental protection acts, and other such legislation from the 1960s and 1970s. From the beginning to the present there have been at least two major problems with such legislation, as is well-known: First, those who are to be regulated—whether railroads, banks, utilities, advertisers, radio and TV stations, or whatnot—use their substantial economic and

political power, directly and indirectly (campaign contributions, lobbying, political advertising, etc.), to influence and or control the regulating agencies; second, whether or not laws (speeding, or pollution, or work safety, or any other) will be effective or not depends upon the potential law-breaker's knowledge of the probability of enforcement. Occupational health and safety laws remain intact, but the Reagan years saw the staff for their enforcement dwindle to an impossibly low level. And that is more the rule than the exception.

34. Japan and Germany (and other nations) are of course heavily industrialized; but their organizing institutions have not been even remotely those of market capitalism, neither at the "beginning" or now. Profits have been sought, and eagerly; and workers have been much exploited; and expansion has been necessary and sought after; of course. But from the beginning the State has been at the center of the industrialization process, and the guiding ideology has always reflected that. And there have been many other departures from "market capitalism," in those and other capitalist nations, which was realized to a substantial degree only in Britain, the United States, and, stretching the point a bit, in Switzerland.

35. One reason for this is, of course, the "continental" size of the United States. The only other continental powers were the ex-U.S.S.R. and China. China is rich in resources, but much of the reason *is* its great size, with, in any case, lesser levels and kinds than those of the United States. The abundant natural resources of the ex-U.S.S.R. are less than "meets the eye," both because their weather is daunting, especially in the winter, and because, as one resource specialist has put it, not only are they distant from each other, but "their rivers run the wrong way." In the United States, coal could be shipped to iron to make steel cheaply, on lakes and downstream rivers, and were not all that far apart. They are far apart in the ex-U.S.S.R., and the coal has to go upstream. (Coal goes to ore, not vice versa.)

36. W. Schulte Nordholt, *The People That Walk in Darkness** (New York: Ballantine, 1970) is an excellent and comprehensive treatment of the slave trade from its beginnings; and it has a comprehensive bibliography for further study. Included are two classics deserving special notice here: Eric Williams, *Capitalism and Slavery* (Chapel Hill, N.C.: University of North Carolina Press, 1944), and Eugene Genovese, *The Political Economy of Slavery** (New York: Vintage Books, 1967).

37. As noted earlier, Hamilton believed some governmental interven-

tion in the economy to be desirable and necessary—with respect to tariffs, transportation, and banking—but he argued for nothing resembling mercantilism in its full form. Madison, as often noted, wrote in the *Federalist Papers* (#10) of the need for a government strong enough to keep "factionalism"—what we might call power and class struggles—at their distance from the main social process. He probably could have persuaded Smith on that point, as it was not meant to impinge on the market.

38. The most famous of Jackson's acts had to do with what came to be seen as "the destruction" of the Second Bank of the United States—the then counterpart of the Federal Reserve System created in 1913. Between the 1830s and 1913, the United States, alone among industrial capitalist nations, lacked any meaningful central bank. This is discussed in more detail in Chapter 8, along with reading references.

39. The presidential administrations involved in the new directions were those of Theodore Roosevelt and Woodrow Wilson. Roosevelt combined a belligerent overseas imperialism with "trust busting," a concern for natural resources, and—after reading Upton Sinclair's *The Jungle*, concerned with the horrors of the meat-packing industry—food and drug regulation. Wilson's first administration saw the Federal Reserve System created, along with the Federal Trade Commission, tariff reform (downwards), and the federal income tax. We shall examine these and other developments again in later chapters.

40. Historians did not even begin to pull this history together until very recently. See Richard W. Van Alstyne, *The Rising American Empire** (New York: Oxford University Press, 1960) and William Appleman Williams, *The Contours of American History*, noted earlier, for two books that trace our expansion to its earliest beginnings. Studies influenced by these initial breakthroughs are relied upon in Chapter 7, where our geographic expansion is a central topic.

41. Wallerstein, *The Modern World System*, cited earlier, discusses this point systematically, pp. 85–86. The term "racism" is used loosely when applied to religious and ethnic animosities, if one sees it as a term regarding color. But the whole matter is sunk in confusion when one understands that science does not accept the notion of "race" at all. In agreement with that, when I use the term here it is in its conventional sense, in order to communicate.

– 3 –

Business as a System of Power

They pass through the great iron gates—
Men with eyes gravely discerning,
Skilled to appraise the tonnage of cranes
Or split an inch into thousandths—
Men tempered by fire as the ore is
and planned to resistance
Like steel that has cooled in the trough;
Silent of purpose, inflexible, set to fulfillment—
To conquer, withstand, overthrow....
Men mannered to large undertakings,
Knowing force as a brother
And power as something to play with,
Seeing blood as a slip of the iron,
To be wiped from the tools
Lest they rust.[1]

"The business of America," President Calvin Coolidge once remarked, "is business." More pointed, while also reflecting the further advance of *big* business, was the famous statement some decades later of Charles Wilson (of General Motors, and Secretary of Defense for President Eisenhower): "What's good for General Motors is good for America." These pithy assertions, and others of their genre—"The public? The public be damned!" (Cornelius Vanderbilt)—have been much maligned by those with a loftier vision for the United States. But as matters now stand—that is, in the absence of fundamental institutional change—it is unquestionably true that when business is bad, the people are worse off; when GM and the other giant corporations are in trouble, so is not only the whole economy, but all the society.

93

In short, the United States is a business society, for better or for worse, in sickness or in health, 'till death do us part. It is, indeed, *the* business society, even in comparison with all other capitalist societies. Unlike the others, we pretty much began that way, and become always more so as time passes. If in our day deep questions have arisen concerning the performance of our society, is it not because business calculations, rather than natural and human needs and possibilities so much dominate the entirety of our lives? As Edward S. Herman puts it, after underscoring very much the same long list of severe problems noted in our preceding pages,

> The motives and power of the large corporation—and the system of large corporations—will have obvious and large bearing on the capacity of societies to address these problems in the coming decades. In such a context, corporate diligence in the pursuit of profits has no simple relationship to wel- fare...[for] most of the problems just enumerated are the built- in and cumulating negatives of the same drive for profitable growth that produced the huge productivity advances of the past. Some of these problems are the undesired secondary effects of the means corporations employ to pursue profitable ends. Others flow from the corporations' power to limit the problems that may be addressed and society's power to deal with them.[2]

That ours is so fully a businesslike society and the most fully developed of capitalist societies allows two major inferences about the historical development of the United States. First, *all* social activi- ties—the production of all goods and all services from carrots to computers and from mechanics to ministers—have flourished or languished dependent upon the degree to which they have satisfied the finally financial criterion of *marketability*. Indeed, most of our people seem unaware that other, qualitative, criteria exist to be taken seriously. From the necessary evaluation of a business firm in terms of its income statement and balance sheet, U.S. society has moved insensibly to evaluating virtually all activities in similarly quantitative and pecuniary terms: What does it cost? How much does he make? Will it sell? Is it profitable? So it is with our ways of speech, with paintings and movie stars, with professors and journalists, with religious personages. The society has left or created no comfortable resting-place for means of evaluation other than "the bottom line."

Second, if business criteria have made their way into all walks of life, the prime reason is that capitalist development has been so successful in its own terms in the United States. No other country has had so long and so impressive a history of expansion, production, and productivity, with, over time, our levels of per capita real incomes.[3] Capitalism stresses material achievement as its promise. U.S. capitalism fulfilled that promise. If, in the process, large sections of the population have been shunted aside, exploited and oppressed, left outside the charmed circle of material well-being drawn by "the American dream," then that is by no means unique to the United States where, in fact or in illusion, a clear majority has seen itself as blessed to reside in the most blessed of all nations.[4]

To say that U.S. capitalist development has been successful for so long is to point to two other major aspects of our development: the persistent and remarkable profitability, and the easy and comprehensive access to power, prestige, and authority by U.S. businessmen, and those who live by their criteria (that is, doctors, lawyers, engineers, politicians, etc.). These two processes have sustained and reinforced each other and they bear closer examination, which of necessity will continue to focus largely on the questions of *expansion* and *exploitation*, the alpha and omega of capitalist development.

Onward and Upward with King Cotton

We have noted that expansion has two directions: upward, the growth of the economy in its productive capacity, and outward, the expansion of the land surface under the control or influence of the national economy.

The temporal and social advantages for U.S. capitalism noted at the close of Chapter 2 were facilitated mostly by our *geographic* realities and possibilities. The meaning of the North American colonies to the British was slight by comparison with what could be made of the continent stretching westward from the lands the British had settled on the Eastern Seaboard. Given the limited military and maritime technology of the time, the new United States had virtually a free hand in moving into the wide open and very rich spaces to the west of the original thirteen colonies, and much more was made of the eastern land space because of that expansion into the West.

Consider briefly what access to the West stimulated and allowed and, less obviously, what it *required* (most especially, canals and railroads). For the South, the western lands were both a lifesaver and a boon—a lifesaver because the South's techniques of cultivating tobacco and cotton quickly depleted the soil; a boon because the new and even richer lands (richest of all, the Mississippi valley) fitted most profitably into rapidly expanding markets in the Old World (most importantly, cotton for England's burgeoning textile mills). The South's movement westward into Alabama, Mississippi, and Louisiana meant, of course, the wholesale destruction of Native Americans and of their remarkable and healthy societies, as well as a vast increase in the numbers of black slaves imported and bred for plantation cultivation.[5]

But the South's geographic and economic expansion was an essential part of the developing *world*-economy and, of course, profitable—to the plantation owners, to the northern merchants and shippers and financiers tied into plantation agriculture. Still more, the U.S. economy depended very much upon the dynamism, the foreign exchange, and the internal trade generated by King Cotton in the first half of the nineteenth century.

The importance of the South's economy in the United States was reflected in its power in the national government. By any measure, of population, land, or capital, the South's power was disproportionately high, whether the reference is to the legislative, judicial, or executive branch of the federal government. That power, not the moral issue of slavery, was the central issue leading to the Civil War; when the South lost, it was because the economic power of northern industry, agriculture, and finance had surpassed it.

If we may judge the intentions of warriors by what they do after victory, the organization and functioning of the U.S. government during and after the Civil War tells us that northern intentions were to adapt federal power to the needs of industrial, not planter, capitalism; and the former slaves were abandoned to the not-so-tender mercies of their former masters—as ruthlessly exploited and oppressed sharecroppers. Freed from chattel slavery, most frequently they became debt slaves, free (as they were no longer valuable assets) to starve.[6]

The North's economic strength rested on the commercial, industrial, and financial activities that had their small beginnings in colonial New England, New York, Pennsylvania, and New Jersey. The beginnings were small because of the less bountiful agricultural possibilities in the North as compared with the South. However, forced to diversify and to improvise, by the 1830s the small beginnings had become a torrent of economic life, with still greater dynamism lying squarely ahead.

Much of the North's early development had depended on the South, for the merchants of the North were heavily involved in the slave trade and in the associated rum and general mercantile trade, in a series of "triangular" patterns linking North America with the Caribbean, Africa, and Europe. Veblen had a characteristically insightful and sardonic view of those northern activities, emanating from the center of Puritanism in the United States:

> The slave trade was never a "nice" occupation or an altogether unexceptionable investment—"balanced on the edge of the permissible." But even though it may have been distasteful to one and another of its New England men of affairs, and though there always was a suspicion of moral obliquity attached to the slave-trade, yet it had the fortune to be drawn into the service of the greater good. In conjunction with its running-mate, the rum-trade, it laid the foundations of some very reputable fortunes at the focus of commercial enterprise that presently became the center of American culture, and so gave rise to some of the country's Best People. At least so they say. Perhaps also it was, in some part, in this early pursuit of gain in this moral penumbra that American business enterprise learned how not to let its right hand know what its left hand is doing; and there is always something to be done that is best done with the left hand.[7]

The North's process of economic development soon became the most dynamic industrialization process in the world up to that time; it was weaning itself from its heavy southern diet even in the years it was gaining the most from it. Of the several factors that loom large in northern economic development, one whole complex related to westward expansion. It was as vital as it was timely.[8]

The Dream Unfolds: Westward the Course of Empire

It is impossible to speculate beyond a certain point on what the United States would have been like had its geographic scope been confined to that of the original colonies: certainly a less imposing Rambo; more likely, not Rambo at all. For the states north of the Mason-Dixon line, the trans-Appalachian West was not merely a beckoning frontier; it was a seemingly endless expanse of land teeming with excellent soils, waterways, minerals (including gold and silver, and oil), and forests—and an array of wildlife almost beyond imagination.[9]

To exploit those lands, the United States had to import rising millions of people, dig canals, and build the largest rail network in the world—30,000 miles by 1860, 53,000 by 1870, twice that by 1882, and over 210,000 miles by 1904—import capital, and employ a technology that could master the great spaces and complex needs of such a land. But these needs had another side to them: they offered boundless possibilities to a society dominated and led by people with their eyes on the main chance: financial gain.

The millions of immigrants contributed not just labor power, but imagination and enterprise.[10] The transportation network required new private and public financial institutions, and it constituted an enormous demand for a whole range of products—most importantly, metals and machinery and coal, the heart of nineteenth-century industrial development. A new technology was required to dig canals, to tame the plains and mountains with rails and powerful locomotives, and to exploit the surface and subsurface resources of this vast country. All this, taken together with a persisting labor shortage, meant that the United States became the first of all industrial nations to develop a comprehensive machine technology for all aspects of production—agricultural, mineral, manufacturing, and transportation.

The resulting high labor productivity, combined with the widespread ownership of land (relative to Europe) yielded a level and a distribution of income that provided the first *domestic* mass market for modern production. By the end of the nineteenth century, the structure of U.S. production in both consumer and capital goods was broader and deeper than anywhere else in the world; and the process had just begun.

With unprecedented swiftness, the United States filled in its continental boundaries, and in doing so created an economy that dazzled the world. But the unprecedented swiftness was matched by unprecedented rapacity—a heedless exploitation of natural resources, and a pattern of human exploitation whose viciousness was obscured, on the one hand, by the widespread expectation that *everyone* would someday rise in the socioeconomic structure and, on the other, by the equally widespread indifference to the conditions of those who had no such prospects.[11]

From all this, a process of economic expansion whose buoyancy and profitability, despite intermittent business panics and crises, transformed the northeast quadrant of the United States into a businessman's El Dorado. Meanwhile, cities grew like mushrooms over the face of the nation—New York, Philadelphia, Boston, and Baltimore, of course; but also Chicago, Cleveland, Cincinnati, St. Louis, New Orleans, Omaha, and San Francisco. The growth of the cities, like the growth of the economy, was a response to business needs and possibilities; as for anything more complicated, that could wait—or be forgotten (as will be discussed in Chapter 6).

Survival and success in the expansion process required passing the test of the market, the test of a fully commercializing society. Those who survived grew in strength, and they garnered the society's power, prestige, and authority. *Power* means the ability to decide (even what will be decided about), to influence, to control; *prestige* refers to the deference received by those highly placed in society; *authority* resides in those who have the weight of law, of custom, and of society's deepest values vested in them. To have one is normally to have had or to be on the way to having the others.

In the United States, already by the close of the nineteenth century the strength of the business impulse had swept aside all noncommercial contenders for power, prestige, or authority—except those political and social figures who knew where the power lay. In practice, this meant a multitude of things; most especially it meant that what business needed, business got. When complications arose, it was almost always when one business group was in contention with another business group—small versus big business, national versus international firms, farmers versus railroads, for instance. Having said this, we now turn to the evolution of U.S. business as "a system of power."[12]

The Road to Hell Is Paved

Adam Smith's hopes for a benign capitalist order rested squarely on his prescription for a vigorously competitive economy. In such an economy, all firms would be small; the percentage of a given industry's output produced by one firm (or by a few firms) would be insignificant as a percentage of the whole industry output. Without control over supply, each business would have to function in response to the free market; *with* control over supply, the powerful firm (alone or in combination with a small group of others, as in oligopoly) could control the market. Smith's policies were designed to eliminate the control provided by State-granted privileges and monopolies. He did not examine the future dyamics of the kind of private economy he sought. Marx and Veblen did, and many others have followed in their paths—without, however, altering the core of economic theory, or the sacrosanct policies of free market capitalism that depend on that theory for their dignifying support.

The *general* development of capitalism was first analyzed and explained by Marx, who sought to understand "the economic laws of motion of capitalist society." The factual basis for his analysis was Great Britain in the mid-nineteenth century, the leading (virtually the only) industrial capitalist society of the time. As a contributing journalist to the *New York Tribune* in the 1850s and 1860s Marx had occasion to observe and comment upon U.S. developments; he never did more than that.[13]

It was left to Veblen to undertake the first systematic critique of U.S. capitalism. Born in the United States (1857) almost a half-century after Marx's birth, Veblen was well-situated to study the more advanced and specifically U.S. experience, as he did in two books noted earlier, *The Theory of Business Enterprise* (1904) and *Absentee Ownership* (1923).[14] Veblen did not have to imagine or speculate on the course of capitalist development since the time of Marx or Smith. He lived and wrote when the full sweep of U.S. business and industrial practices was in evidence. His starting-point was to distinguish between "business" and "industry":

> The industrial arts are a matter of tangible performance directed to work that is designed to be of material use to man.... [The] arts of business are arts of bargaining, effrontery, salesmanship, make-believe, and are directed to the gain of the business man at the cost of the community, at large and in detail. Neither tangible performance nor the common good is a business proposition. Any material use which his traffic may serve is quite beside the business man's purpose, except indirectly, in so far as it may serve to influence his clientele to his advantage.[15]

In brief, business is about making money; industry about making goods.

Veblen was by no means unique in noting the aggressiveness and the "effrontery" of businessmen. But he combined that widespread view with a larger critical analysis that doomed him to the role of a lonely prophet. In his *Theory of Business Enterprise* he foresaw the two leading developments of U.S. capitalism as centering on the drive for monopoly and the steady buildup of the forces of economic depression; in *Absentee Ownership* he was able to look around him and see his expectations confirmed. Another major probability he anticipated was an "increased unproductive consumption of goods," by which he meant the need to manipulate and persuade the population to buy unnecessary and trivial commodities, and the growth of arms production, accompanied by what he called "a strenuous national policy."

Precisely because the kind of competitive economy Smith desired would entail effective price competition, Veblen argued, businessmen would energetically move to eliminate the competitive structure that allowed and required it. Their view of price competition was effectively suggested when they described it as "cutthroat: regulation by the knife." Businesses, monopolistic or otherwise, continue to "compete." But the forms taken by modern business rivalry are not such as to reduce costs, prices, and profits to some optimal level, as predicated in the competitive model; quite the contrary. Price competition has been replaced by two major forms of business rivalry: (1) "nonprice competition," which takes the form of price-*increasing* advertising, packaging, and other forms of sales promotion; and (2) efforts to gain special privileges at all levels of government—to stabilize prices, to gain governmental contracts, to influence taxing and spending, labor and foreign policies, and the like.[16] To recall an earlier observation, the *State* mercantilism that Smith fought against has been revived and joined by a *private* mercantilism. We can do no better than quote Veblen again:

This decay of the old-fashioned competitive system has consisted in a substitution of competitive selling in the place of that competitive production of goods that is always presumed to be the chief and most serviceable feature of the competitive system. That is to say it has been a substitution of salesmanship in the place of workmanship; as would be due to happen so soon as business came to take precedence of industry, salesmanship being a matter of business, not of industry; and business being a matter of salesmanship, not of workmanship.... Competition as it runs under the rule of this decayed competitive system is chiefly the competition between the business concerns that control production, on the one side, and the consuming public on the other side; the chief expedients in this businesslike competition being salesmanship and sabotage. Salesmanship in this connection means little else than prevarication, and sabotage means a business-like curtailment of output.[17]

The hoped-for effects of a competitive economy need not depend upon the existence of textbook forms of "perfect" or "pure" competition, with hundreds or thousands of tiny firms in each and every economic activity. But such effects do depend upon the existence of pervasive and effective competition which, as the data below will show, has little to do with the realities of the U.S. (or any other) industrial economy. A competitive economy is one in which firms have no choice but to respond to the market; the "representative firm" is simply without the power to set the terms upon which the market must respond to it. In such an economy there could be monopolies, but they would be under constant scrutiny and regulation, or temporary. In the former case, which economists call "natural" monopolies, the monopoly is justified by the technology of industry, as is typically so for utilities—where it would be economically foolish to have duplicative facilities, as in large-scale gas or water works. The aim of the regulating is to combine the advantages of large-scale production with the pricing results of a competitively structured industry, with prices set so as to attract the optimal amount of capital into the industry, but without the profits of monopoly. In numerous instances of regulated utilities, it is the rule, not the exception that those who sit on the regulatory commissions' boards are predominantly from or in sympathy with those being "regulated." Temporary monopolies are presumed to disappear as soon as the new technology or unusual market circumstances giving rise to them are countered by long-run competitive forces.
What would *not* be, in an effectively competitive economy, is what exists in all the major capitalist countries today: patterns of concentrated power in all of modern manufacturing and mining, and increasingly in trade, large-scale construction, finance, and other hitherto competitive sectors—all this against the background of a State apparatus that, far from restraining private economic power, responds to it, represents it, and paves the way for it. Almost everyone is by now familiar with part of the pattern as in recent years the so-called "military-industrial complex" has become a continuing focus of critical discussion. The relationships exemplified in that substantial area of the economy (all the more substantial when the network that it supports is taken into account) are not new; they are merely the latest (and because of their "product,"

among the most exposed) development in the "family ties" between business and government in the United States and elsewhere. The military-industrial complex is of course most importantly a product of wars (with strong seeds for it planted as early as the Civil War); but like so much in today's economy, that particular "complex" helped to create and was helped in its own creation by those same processes of which the super-State and the supercorporation have been the result. This and other vital roles played by the State are the focus of Chapter 8.

Returning now to the question of business competition in the U.S. economy, and assuming that the textbook model is neither necessary nor possible—nor, perhaps, even desirable[18]—did anything even approximating an effectively competitive market economy ever exist in the United States? Until the past decade or so, the conventional term for such an economy has been "the free enterprise system," at whose center sit the fact and the rights of private property, which "permits the security, independence, and civic virtue of its holder." But, as Lustig points out,

> ever since private property assumed the functions of capital—at a point that can be fixed fairly accurately as at the beginning of the eighteenth century—market property has become...a vehicle of aggrandizement—restless, unsettling, and corrosive of the real possibilities of civic virtue. The habit of calling the American economy "free enterprise" obscures this by implicitly confining attention to relations of *exchange*. But it is more accurate to recognize the economy as capitalist..., because *capitalism* identifies a system of *production* [and] relations of exchange.... are shaped and limited by those of production.... Capital was never a simple auxiliary of the market; the market, rather, was a historical auxiliary of capital.[19]

Still, for at least the first half of the nineteenth century, but certainly not by its last years, the U.S. economy may have been effectively competitive. What processes displaced relatively small firms by giants, market competition by collusion, rivalry, and monopoly? And how and why?

The Invisible Fist

The capitalist system posits the business firm as its dynamic center, of course. The "entrepreneur" is expected to respond to stimuli and to overcome obstacles so as to produce what society needs and wants. But to do this, he must possess one form of power: ownership of productive assets. To the degree that he succeeds, he is likely to gain more economic power, and other forms of power as well.

In practice, the dice are loaded in favor of those who own and control society's productive assets; and they are a tiny percentage of the population (see Chapter 5). By design and by default, those who are *not* property owners are weak in influence and power. It is necessary to note that for the competitive system to work well economically and socially in Smith's terms, those who are powerful must be *frustrated* in what they seek—that is, profits and power. The social rationale for a competitive capitalist economy is thus very curious indeed: market competition will prevent those who have power in the society from realizing their aims. In reality, of course, capitalists are not such passive creatures nor could they survive if they were. Thus in practice the benign principles are abandoned, except for their half-lives in textbooks and political rhetoric.

The point may also be made this way: Social and economic policies are decided upon and implemented by those with power. The laissez-faire society is one in which all sources of public policymaking over the economy are in principle eliminated. What is left is private economic power alone, in the hands of those who own and control the means of production. Not, certainly in the hands of the propertyless wage-earner; nor, by design, in the hands of Church or State.

So in a society devoid of social controls other than the market, the capitalist will do what he can to mitigate the one threat to his strength and profitability: he will seek to eliminate his competitors, by absorbing them or defeating them. But if a capitalist economy is made socially "safe" only by competition, what then remains of the social rationale for capitalism in the modern world? Where economists, essayists, and political functionaries are not sublimely indifferent to this vacuum in our "social philosophy," their carelessly held optimism about the social process rests on what Edward S. Herman calls the "modern liberal illusion" that somehow it is all working out o.k., or if it isn't, it will; after all, there are responsible people (neither beholden nor known to the underlying population) who are looking out for the larger good and the long run. "My own view," says Herman, "is sharply different. 'As if by an invisible hand,'" the collectivity of autonomous yet interdependent business units, sharing the same broad outlook and profitable growth objectives, pushes society and governments in directions of its own choosing and preference, allowing the government to ratify *faits accomplis* and to pick up some of the debris.[20]

Until the years just after the Civil War, the U.S. economy may be said to have been effectively competitive, if ever. During that early period, businessmen's desires were no less profit-oriented than after the 1870s; what was different was technology and the extraordinary onrush of events associated with westward expansion (given an added boost by the industrial demands and financial boons of the Civil War). In the last quarter of the century, the westward movement began to stabilize, while large-scale technology spread throughout the production process, constituting a "second industrial revolution."

In the period before the Civil War (roughly speaking), there were, of course, large as well as small firms. The largest firms tended to be found in transportation, communications, finance, and trade. The occasional large *manufacturing* firm (in textile machinery, for example) had no substantial influence on the economy as a whole, which was changing its structure and growing rapidly. Once more, however, the impact of large-scale technology after the war deserves emphasis.

Times change, but the seller's impulse toward monopolization is a constant in economic history: Thales, the ancient Greek philosopher, is known for his attempts to corner the market in olive oil; in the 1970s the Hunt brothers of Texas almost cornered the market in silver; and in 1991, Salomon Brothers, among the most respected of Wall Street firms, confesses to having sought to corner the market in U.S. Treasury bonds several times. That impulse becomes necessary and, when successful, much more profitable when it joins with the economics of large-scale industry. Efficiency associated with modern industry is owed to the scale of production. This in turn entails not only widespread specialization in production, but also much in the way of expensive and long-lasting plant and equipment (and high "fixed costs" payable irrespective of the level of output and sales). The normal ups and downs of capitalist economic expansion and the intermittent glutting of markets combine with these large-scale plants to yield to destructive competition—price competition which means selling below cost in bad times to minimize the losses associated with high fixed costs. When that happens, or in order to keep it from happening, the number of firms in a given industry shrinks, leaving the giants to endure and to prosper—until the next bout of troubles. Eliminating competitors diminishes the prospects of price competition, while it also *increases* the possibilities of enhancing profits in both good and bad times by controlling—that is, holding back —supply, which is impossible in a competitively structured market.[21]

Thus the key characteristic of modern business behavior becomes that of dominant firms ("oligopolies") restricting supply, while engaging in a variety of rivalrous "nonprice" tactics and strategies, from advertising to political lobbying. Business is enabled thereby to dictate and sell at its chosen price, while the processes both of supply and demand are distorted. No less important is that the large firms in the same process gain broad power over the social as well the economic process—in a society that systematically and in principle foregoes locating that social power in *non*economic institutions, subject to democratic control.[22]

From Mergers to Monopoly: The Giants Feed

Until about 1860, the corporate form of business was largely confined to transportation and finance. With few exceptions, the emergence of corporations in manufacturing awaited the new, large-scale technology that emerged and spread after the Civil War.

From the early 1870s until the late 1890s the entire industrial capitalist world underwent what was seen as "the great depression." In that quarter-century of falling prices, there were really two serious depressions, 1873–1878 and 1893–1897, but neither approximated the depression of the 1930s in duration, severity, or hardship—nor its accompanying political convulsions.

The most prominent feature of the downturns of the 1870s and 1890s was downward pressure on profits, rather than massive unemployment. That pressure was due to the steady and dramatic lowering of prices through the period, in turn the result of great increases in productive efficiency, combined with the inability to cut off domestic or foreign competition in the context of relatively free world trade and relatively competitive market structures.

Consequently, that same period saw the first widespread attempts to control price competition through one form or another of business reorganization. "Gentlemen's agreements" not to cut prices, profit pools, and trusts (maintaining the separate identities of the companies) were all tried; none worked well, and the form that finally took hold was the merger, taking place within what came to be called the *combination movement*.

By the late 1890s, mergers, wherein many firms are combined under one identity and ownership, became the rule; the years between 1897 and 1905 witnessed their first spectacular explosion. As Du Boff points out,

> Around the turn of the century all those forces making for big business coalesced in a tidal wave of mergers and consolidations. Nothing like it had been seen before, nor anything like it since, although...at least three later merger movements have taken place in manufacturing and mining. A total of 2,653 large firms disappeared through merger from 1898 through 1902. [Those] numbers may seem small by today's standards, but for the economy of 1900 they were staggering; in terms of real GNP that economy was fifteen times smaller than the economy of the late 1980s.[23]

During the whole first period, 1897–1905, over 5,300 industrial firms came under the ownership and control of 318 corporations, the most advanced and powerful firms in the economy, indeed, at that time, in the world—led by the first billion-dollar merger, in 1901, the United States Steel Company, a combination of twelve large corporations, themselves having combined from over seven hundred companies in earlier years.

Subsequently, the merger movements between the two world wars, of the 1960s, and that which took hold in the 1970s and took off in the 1980s (and has yet to stop) rose to even greater absolute heights, in terms of numbers of companies and value of the acquisitions (Figure 3.1); but relatively the 1898–1902 episode remains the greatest, not only quantitatively but for what it signified, and what it solidified.[24] There has not been, and cannot be, a turning-back to the presumably idyllic days of a free market economy—except in that professional and political rhetoric that appears to assume that only government can make a market unfree.

The first waves of mergers were an outcome of expanding technology and businesses' aims of avoiding competition and of making profits. Until World War II, technology usually led to centralization of productive facilities in a particular location (steel in Pittsburgh, autos in Detroit, etc.). In recent decades technological development makes it possible and

Figure 3.1
*Constant-Dollar Volume of Manufactuing
and Mineral Firm Acquisitions, 1895–1985[a]*

Value of Acquired Firms
(billions of 1972 dollars)

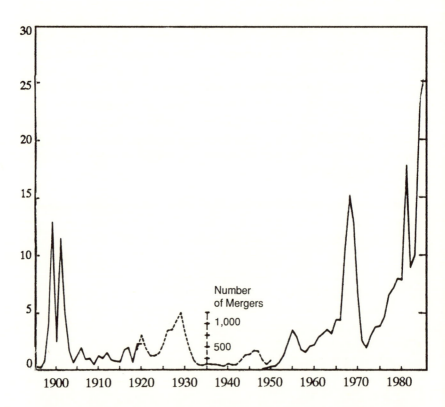

a. Data on the value of manufacturing and mineral company acquisitions are not available for the years 1921–47. The broken line reflects the number of acquisitions in those years.

Source: David J. Ravenscraft and F.M. Sherer, *Mergers, Sell-Offs and Economic Efficiency* (Washington, D.C.: Brookings Institution, 1987), p. 21.

profitable to decentralize productive facilities geographically. At the same time, precisely because the technological realities suggest decentralization, business "realities" underscore the necessity of insuring the continuity of centralized control: thus adding one more stimulus to mergers.

But there seems to be no end to such stimuli. The most recent and ongoing wave of mergers ("takeovers") mixes in two additional motives: (1) the general slackness in the economy which has been common since the 1970s has been both a partial cause and consequence of, among other matters, excess productive capacity, reducing the incentive for real investment in new productive facilities, connected to which has been (2) the "financialization" of the economy. Table 3.1 organizes some data for the years between 1929 and 1990 that show how the relationship between corporate profits and net interest has changed, and how the share of manufacturing has declined.[25] The latter process combined with the tax laws to make it very profitable for "leveraged buyouts" (normally financed with "junk bonds") to become the cutting edge of contemporary business dynamics. We have departed supersonically from the playing fields of Adam Smith.

Table 3.1
Changes in Distribution of Income between Corporate Profits and Interest, and Manufacturing Profits, 1929–1989
(billions of current dollars)

Year	Total Corporate Profits	Manufacturing Profits	Percent of Manufacturing Total	Net Interest	Corporate Profits as % of Net Interest
1929	10.5	5.2	50	4.7	204
1939	6.5	3.3	50	3.6	153
1949	31.1	16.2	52	2.6	1,076
1959	52.3	26.4	50	10.2	504
1969	81.4	36.7	45	34.6	253
1979	214.1	87.5	40	158.3	126
1989	286.1	96.1	31	445.1	70

Source: *Economic Report of the President, 1991* (Washington, D.C.: U.S. Government Printing Office), pp. 311, 388–89.

In raising these points about business organization and functioning (the realm of "microeconomics") we necessarily verge into the territory of the accumulation ("macroeconomic") process. Further movement into that area will be undertaken in the following chapter, when we shall try to understand the disasters now arising throughout the entire financial world: savings and loan *and* commercial banking institutions, the insurance industry *and* pension funds, etc., in the United States, and numerous financial scandals elsewhere (in Japan, Germany, and Italy, plus the Bank of Credit & Commerce International [BCCI]), all of which relate to each other and to crime, drugs, and Statecraft, among other matters, in ways that are simultaneously disgraceful, dangerous, and very profitable.

Initially, mergers took place in each industry as it began to employ modern, large-scale technology. Sometimes the process was more like warfare than business in the late nineteenth century.[26] Mergers spread from transportation to manufacturing, to utilities and finance, to mining and construction and trade; by now they are the dynamic mode in all significant business, including entertainment, hotels, various services, and even agriculture, long (if inaccurately) considered the final preserve of effective competition.

In addition to the unsettling qualities of post–World War II mergers already noted, there is an additional point to be noted; namely, in recent decades, over and above the usual gobbling up of little fish by much bigger ones, the process now includes the mergers of supercorporations. *Fortune*, the "magazine of big business," underlined the process in its issue of April 1973;

> ...from 1964 through 1966, there were 293 mergers in which the acquired companies had assets of more than $10 million; in the final three years of the decade there were 530. The average size of the transactions, $38 million in the first period, rose to $64 million during the second. In the peak year of 1968 the nation's top 200 industrial firms acquired a total of ninety-four large companies, with aggregate assets of more than $8 billion.

A glance at Table 3.2 will show that what was happening in the late 1960s was chicken feed compared with what became common in the late 1970s, itself much outdone by the spectacular mergers of the late 1980s. As the table shows, of the twenty-five giant mergers from 1979 to 1987,

Table 3.2
The Twenty-five Largest Nonbank Mergers by Current Dollar Value 1979–1987

Buyer	Seller	Dollar Value (billions)	Year
Standard Oil of California	Gulf Oil	13.4	1984
Texaco	Getty Oil	10.1	1984
DuPont	Conoco	8.0	1981
British Petroleum	Standard Oil of Ohio	7.6	1987
U.S. Steel (now USX)	Marathon Oil	6.6	1981
General Electric	RCA	6.4	1986
Mobil	Superior Oil	5.7	1984
Philip Morris	General Foods	5.6	1985
General Motors	Hughes Aircraft	5.0	1985
R. J. Reynolds	Nabisco	4.9	1985
Allied Corp.	Signal Companies	4.5	1985
Burroughs	Sperry	4.4	1986
Société Nationale Elf Aquitaine	Texasgulf Inc.	4.3	1981
Connecticut General	Insurance Company of North America	4.2	1981
Occidental Petroleum	Cities Service	4.1	1982
USX	Texas Oil & Gas	4.1	1985
Shell Oil	Belridge Oil	3.7	1979
Baxter Travenol	American Hospital Supply	3.7	1985
Campeau	Allied Stores	3.5	1986
Capital Cities Communications	American Broadcasting Company	3.5	1985
Unilever	Chesebrough-Ponds	3.1	1987
Occidental Petroleum	Midcon Corp.	3.0	1985
Nestlé	Carnation	2.9	1984
Hoechst	Celanese	2.7	1987
Monsanto	G.D. Searle	2.7	1985

Source: Du Boff, *Accumulation and Power*, p. 135

the *smallest* had a value of $2.7 billion, the largest $13.4 billion—as compared with $8 billion for the acquisition of ninety-four large companies in 1968. United States Steel was noted earlier as the first billion-dollar corporation. Its name is now USX, the significance of which is that steel is no longer its dominant product: note on the table, USX bought two giant oil companies (for $10.7 billion) while, not so incidentally, it was closing steel plants, laying off workers, and gutting the life out of "steel towns."[27]

Throughout all of this merger activity there have been several subprocesses. At first, mergers were in one industry, where all the merging firms produced much the same product and were in direct competition with each other. These continue, of course, and are called *horizontal* mergers, in which competitors in a given industry come under the ownership and control of one company (one steel company buying out another). Along-side those mergers, another form, *vertical* mergers, began to appear, gaining much strength in the 1920s. There a company buys out its suppliers and/or its customers (for example, Ford gaining its own steel facilities; U.S. Steel buying up coal mines and a bridge building company).

Horizontal mergers lead to concentrated market power in a given industry, and to *oligopoly*: a few dominant sellers in an industry. Vertical mergers strengthen the hand of already powerful firms, while also creating higher barriers to entry for would-be new firms. In the late 1920s and early 1930s another merger form became noticeable, and after the 1960s the dominant form (and typical of the current takeover move-ment): the *conglomerate* merger, where the firms acquired are only distantly related, if at all, to the industry of the acquiring firm (Grey-hound Bus buys a pizza maker and a deodorant soap company). In the vast merger movement of recent decades, all these forms—horizontal, vertical, and conglomerate—have been operating, with the conglomerate (and most especially the "multinational" version, of which more in a moment) taking the prizes for the drama that became vivid first in the 1960s, with the "new conglomerates."

The birth and expansion of these hydra-headed giants was dominated by eight companies: ITT, Gulf & Western, Ling-Temco-Vought (LTV), Tenneco, White Consolidated, Teledyne, Occidental Petroleum, and Litton Industries. "Each of these companies made acquisitions during the 1960s totaling more than a half-billion dollars, for six the asset value was over a billion dollars."[28] Of the various important aspects of this movement, one worth noting here is that it sped up the process of bringing traditionally "small business" industries—for instance, food processing, nonelectrical machinery, and textiles—under the control of giant corporations.

The early merger movements, both horizontal and vertical, led to the *concentration* of economic power within the affected industries. When we add the conglomerate mergers to that earlier movement, and especially their most recent manifestations (including growing connections with the financial world), we must also add *centralization* to the concentration of economic power. Furthermore, combined with the concentration and centralization of *private* economic power is the associated concentration and centralization of *public* power. The concentration and centralization of State power shows itself in the enormously enhanced powers of the federal government today as compared with, say, 1900: it is revealed even more pointedly in the extraordinary powers increasingly arrogated by the presidency—and, conversely, the declining powers of Congress, the separate states, and the cities.[29]

The government at all levels represents the interests of many groups in the United States, of course—doctors, organized labor, the aged, the poor—but it represents most and best the interests of the most powerful business corporations. Lustig makes a searing indictment of the result:

Modern American society thus captures the worst of both modern and medieval worlds. Corporatist to its core, it creates mechanistic rather than organic social relations. It forces agglomeration, but without community. It mandates corporatism, but without diversity. It imposes close interdependence, without trust. And it justifies hierarchy without enforcing accountability.[30]

Let us now examine some data representative of the position of the supercorporations in the U.S. economy (and society).

Facts Are Stubborn Things

There is no mystery as to the size or the identity of the giant corporations, those of the United States or elsewhere. *Fortune* annually publishes its "Fortune 500," a compilation of the assets, sales, employees, profits, and other data concerning the largest industrial companies in the United States (and other compilations, including the largest 500 companies in the world); these data (like similar information put together in

Forbes Magazine) are derived from a multitude of governmental and private sources, all open to the public eye. Many economists are fully aware of these data, and all could be; but the profession does not alter conventional economic theory to fit the data: to do so would require abandoning the entire structure of the theory and the policies and politics it dignifies.

First we look at data concerning the top industrial (manufacturing and mining) corporations of the United States. There are about fourteen million enterprises in the United States, about one million of which are industrial. And roughly 200,000 of the industrial firms are incorporated. Those corporations do about 90 percent of the business of all industrial enterprises. Keep in mind that GNP (gross national product, the measure of the economy's total output of goods and services) was about $5.5 trillion in 1990, the year for which the data apply (all derived from *Fortune*, April 22, 1991):

1. The *sales* of the Top 500 industrials were $2.3 trillion; their *assets* $2.4 trillion; their *employees* numbered 12.4 million; and their *net income* (profits after taxes) came to $93.3 billion. Amounting to less than .25 percent of all industrial corporations (and a tiny fraction of all industrial enterprises), these 500 firms made approximately three-quarters of all industrial sales, employed well over half of all industrial workers, and took in about three-quarters of industrial profits.

2. The Top 100 of this powerful group had 71 percent of the 500's sales, 75 percent of their assets, and the same percentage of their profits. And the Top 50 had 57 percent of the Top 500's sales, 63 percent of their assets, and 52 percent of their profits; and of the Top 100's, the Top 50 had 81, 83, and 73 percent of sales, assets, and profits, respectively.

3. And then there are the supergiants, the Top 10: General Motors, EXXON, Ford, IBM, Mobil, GE, Philip Morris, Du Pont, and Chevron. They alone had almost 30 percent of the Top 500's sales, 36 percent of their assets, and 28 percent of the 500's profits (and correspondingly higher percentages of the Top 100 and the Top 50). GM, the largest company in the world, made sales of $126 billion in 1990, a bad year for them (they ran losses of $2 billion). It is interesting to note the relative constancy of this powerful group: all but two of the firms in 1975, for example, are still in the Top 10. The two missing are Gulf Oil (bought by USX) and Chrysler, which fights for sheer survival in the struggling U.S. auto industry, their places taken by Du Pont, the chemical giant, and Philip Morris, one of the major takeover artists of the 1980s. The four oil companies in the Top 10, the main beneficiaries of the Gulf war, had

combined aftertax profits in 1990 of $12.9 billion, about 14 percent of the profits of the Top 500. EXXON alone had profits of just $5 billion. (With such profits, they could afford to pay for weekly house cleaning for all Alaskans, not just the damage done by the *EXXON Valdez*.)

4. In short, the concentration of economic power in the entire economy, dominated by the giant industrial (and financial, and transportation, and utility, and other) corporations, is reproduced in an even tighter pattern among the Top 500 corporations; and as is true for the economy and society as a whole, the meaning of that pattern of concentrated power neither begins nor ends with numbers and percentages.

5. Some facts of a different sort. The Top 500 do more and more business, slowly or rapidly, over time, but they do not hire more and more workers. They employed 14.6 million in 1970, 13.1 million in 1987 but only 12.4 million in 1990. Between 1978 and 1989, before the recession that began in 1990 and its dwindling jobs occurred, total manufacturing employment had fallen by 4 percent; but employment by the Top 500 fell by 21 percent. The enormous flexibility of these supercorporations means they can increase their sales, assets, and profits while reducing jobs in the United States. For them, almost all of them multinational corporations, it is a simple matter to locate production facilities elsewhere in the world ("outsource"), where labor is cheaper, and where there are other benefits, among them lower taxes and U.S. tax breaks.[31] Flexibility is in itself a form of power, as the lack of it (for workers, not least) is a form of weakness.[32]

The foregoing data have been largely concerned with the domestic U.S. economy and the corporations that, taken together, constitute the hard core of power in the United States. But for many years now it has become analytically misleading to posit a boundary between the domestic and global functioning of our economy. As touched upon earlier, by far the most important development of business power since the 1960s (the years in which today's highly integrated world economy became a reality) has been the *multinational* (or transnational, or supranational) corporation. And, of course, the same tendencies that created concentration and centralization of business power in national economies (along with decentralization of production) have been repeated internationally—if with important variations (as will be discussed in Chapter 7). The main features of multinational corporations are an integral part of the functioning of the U.S. global system; here we will examine only the general shape of the development.

With Good Intentions

The multinational corporation (MNC) has its origins and its headquarters in one nation, but it buys, sells, invests, and produces in many nations. The MNC is now common to all the leading and lesser capitalist nations. However, as the late Stephen Hymer pointed out,

> The multinational corporation is in the first instance an American phenomenon. Its precursor is the U.S. *national corporation* created at the end of the 19th century when American capitalism developed a multi-city continent-wide marketing and manufacturing strategy.... Though many U.S. corporations began to move to foreign countries almost as soon as they completed their continent-wide integration, the term multinational came to prominence only after 1960.... National firms think in terms of the national market; *multinational* firms see the whole world as their oyster and plan manufacturing and marketing on a global scale.... The shift in business horizons is closely connected to the aeronautical and electronic revolutions which made global planning possible.[33]

Fortune has also published a "Top 500" listing for the largest industrial corporations in the *world* (July 29, 1991), virtually identical in organization with that for the United States—sales, assets, profits, etc. It is the "Rich Man's Club" of the world. As in the United States, so in the world, at least in 1990: GM is the world's largest nonfinancial company. And the United States still has the largest number of giant MNCs of any nation, 164 of the 500, Japan second with 111 (its largest also an auto company, Toyota). Then the numbers trail off to 43 for Britain, 30 apiece for France and Germany, and many fewer for all others (surprisingly, 11 for South Korea which having lived under a quasi-fascist dictatorship and within the supporting embrace of the United States for the decades of its modernization is not much of an advertisement for the free market; nor are the most forceful of all economies these years, Germany and Japan).

In general, the MNCs of the world are among the very largest corporations in their own countries. Also, as might be expected, the emergence of this phenomenon for U.S. corporations coincided with (both as cause and consequence) our taking up a dominating status in the world economy after World War I, but more particularly, self-consciously, and by design, after World War II. The growth of the MNC has been most spectacular since the 1960s, years in which the U.S. economy has become thoroughly internationalized, and the world's economies (and, to a lesser but noticeable extent, its culture) "Americanized." The dynamic center of any future power struggle in the world economy will surely find the MNCs (financial and nonfinancial) taking leading roles, both openly and behind the scenes.

The increasing tendency of U.S. corporations to locate their facilities (productive and otherwise) all over the world has continuing and vital consequences for the functioning of the United States as well as other economies—as do others' tendencies to locate their facilities in the United States. As will be seen in Chapter 7, the combination of the modern technologies of transportation, communications, and production, taken together with the creation of a "new world economy" of reduced trade barriers between nations, has made this process of multinational geographic flexibility an inexorable process, resisted only at great cost by any one corporation. That the U.S. economy has been "hollowed out" considerably more than any other is due to a set of past and present processes that cannot be effectively explained by good or bad leadership, character, or any such traits. In Chapters 4, 7 and 8 (concerned respectively with accumulation, world economy, and the State) the facts and the analysis concerning this complicated recent history will be attempted.

Meanwhile, let us return to the corporate world in the United States. The emergence of the MNC in the United States, like the emergence of the national corporation, was facilitated by the State, much accustomed to responding to business needs and possibilities first, and asking and being asked questions about what it all might mean to society later —usually too late. The internationalization of the U.S. economy and the "Americanization" of the world economy could not have been accomplished without great changes in our global military posture, by comparison with *any* earlier period; nor could that have happened without a change in the ways our people have come to view the various dimensions of militarism.

Thus, there is an additional and vital matter to be stressed in viewing the evolution of U.S. business as a system of power: its relationship with the State and within that the relationships between business, elected officials, and the military. Here only the bare outlines of this matter will be suggested, with fuller discussion postponed to later chapters.

Among the justifications for capitalism as a system was one which, running contrary to the obvious facts, is still frequently (one might say, always more frequently) put forward. It claims that a "free enterprise" system minimizes the role of the State, while encouraging everybody to pursue their rational material interests. One presumed advantage of such a system is productive efficiency; another is maximum material well-being; still another, a government swayed only by rational (that is, material) considerations, scrutinized by a rational citizenry.

In this century, however, the United States has found itself faced with a set of realities where neither need nor possibility could be met satisfactorily, even safely, by a "free market" economy. This had begun to be realized before World War I by the then largest corporations (coinciding with the so-called "Progressive Movement"), as they set about to develop what Kolko calls "political capitalism."[34] And the war itself gave substantial impetus to that "politicization" of the U.S. economy.

But it was the economy-breaking depression of the 1930s, and its growing left- and right-wing political movements, a frightening period indeed for the supporters of capitalism, that revealed the stark alternatives facing the capitalist world: find, and where possible control, extramarket institutions to make this system work without deadly crisis, or go into the dustbin of history.

World War II almost was that dustbin. The United States came out of war stronger than it or any other nation in history had ever been, absolutely and relatively (all other nations battered to their knees by the interwar period and by the war itself). Unchallengeable, the United States was both able and inclined, using both carrots and sticks, to take a broad variety of steps that allowed capitalism to be revived, changed, and strengthened. It was not a free market economy that brought cooperation and economic expansion to the major powers of the capitalist world; it was a powerful state working with powerful corporations, and doing so within the framework of an absolutely indispensable Cold War (as will be argued in Chapters 4, 7, and 8).

The costs and benefits (as economists like to say) of the post-World War II system were both substantial. The benefits have been much publicized and understood; the costs less so, neither for the rest of the world nor for ourselves. Among the generally unrecognized costs are those related to the Cold War, the spine of the postwar system. I refer to the inexorable militarization of the U.S. economy and of U.S. society—its culture and its politics. Our economic "miracles" came not from a fairy princess, but through a Faustian bargain: better Cold War than cold breadlines.

Sitting at the very center of these developments were not military but corporation and political personnel and pressures. Out of it came a "military-industrial complex" which, already seen as a threat to our social health by President Eisenhower as he left office, has over time become a spreading cancer. What these gloomy words refer to, and the support for them, will emerge later.[35]

Suffice it here to say that virtually all our people saw these developments, combining economic, political, military, and ideological needs, possibilities, and appeals, neither as malign, imagined, or unreal; they learned to see the Cold War as a set of responsibilities thrust upon our economic and moral strength—thrust upon us by hostile, crafty, enigmatic, and essentially irrational foreigners. (President Johnson once remarked during the Vietnam war, "those foreigners weren't reared like us.")

That many, let alone all of the developments of the past half-century were thrust upon us is subject to dispute. Be that as it may, those processes have had the at least temporary effect, salubrious from the viewpoint of U.S. capitalism, of allowing a large majority of our people to believe in the reality of traditional conceptions of "American virtues," a consequence anticipated by Veblen in 1904, in the closing words of *The Theory of Business Enterprise*:

> The largest and most promising factor of cultural discipline—most promising as a corrective of iconoclastic vagaries—over which business principles rule is national politics.... Business interests urge an aggressive national policy and businessmen direct it. Such a policy is warlike as well as patriotic. The direct cultural value of a warlike business policy is unequivocal. It makes for a conservative animus on the part of the populace... [and] directs the popular interest to other, nobler, institutionally less hazardous matters than the unequal distribution of wealth or of creature comforts.... There can, indeed, be no serious question but that a consistent return to the ancient virtues of allegiance, piety, servility, graded dignity, class prerogative, and prescriptive authority would greatly conduce to popular content and to the facile

management of affairs. Such is the promise held out
by a strenuous national policy.[36]

Brave New World

In this chapter we have stressed the emergence of the today's giant
corporation and the associated solidification of the business power that
occupies the center of a triad of concentrated economic, political, and
social power. Before going on to the next chapter, it seems appropriate
to pause briefly to examine the modern evolution of some of the
connections between economic, political, and social power, while setting
aside a fuller discussion until later in the book.

The analytical core of this book is its insistence on the need for
capital to be able to exploit, to expand, and to rule. In all industrial
capitalist societies, the existence of concentrated economic power is the
basis for the ability of business to achieve and to maintain its oligarchic
rule and, along with that, to exercise the main purposes of that rule: to
meet its needs for a relatively powerless labor force and an ever-
expanding economy.

But the powerful processes of industrialization that brought the giant
corporation into being just as inexorably carried the spread of threats to
business supremacy: popular education, democratic political institutions,
trade unions, socialist, and, in the colonial world, revolutionary independence movements—each tending to strengthen all the others, and constituting a set of imposing challenges to what had been the easy rule of
capital. We may say that the outbreak of World War I both sped up and
made chaotic the subsequent development of these actual and potential
disturbances to oligarchic rule. The war years also saw the birth of what
are now established technologies and techniques for mass persuasion.

All major wars are outcomes of complex processes combining
economic with political and social developments, and the war that broke
out in 1914 was no exception. To oversimplify, the central core of the
many processes leading to war was the intense nationalism characteristic
of the preceding century and the national economic needs arising out of
the industrialization process, needs that could not then be met simultaneously by all those involved. The possibilities of economic imperialism
were running out, and the institutions of competitive capitalism, dying on
the vine, were totally unsuited to making the kinds of economic, political,
or social adjustments that would make continuing expansion and

international and social peace possible—the sort of changes that were made much later, in the 1950s and 1960s, in the world of U.S. dominated global monopoly capitalism.

The war devastated all of Europe in obvious and, more dangerously, in hidden ways. But for the United States World War I was a great boon (as, even more so, World War II became). The ways in which that was so have been already been noted in part, and will be noted further in the next chapter. But there is one particular set of changes especially relevant to our focus here on the political and social challenges to business supremacy: I refer specifically to the invention of the radio and the development of propaganda techniques.[37]

World War I was by no means the first to utilize or require propaganda. To mention no other, our "splendid little war" in Cuba and in the Philippines is seen as having been significantly prompted and vitally supported by the "yellow journalism" of the turn of the century, specifically that of William Randolph Hearst.[38] But World War I constituted a particular problem for the Wilson Administration, in that Wilson had campaigned for re-election in 1916 on what today we would call a "peace platform." To make matters more complicated, there was considerable antagonism to *both* Germany and Great Britain in the United States. Wilson had somehow to increase the animosity against Germany and dissolve that against Great Britain. What have later become the techniques of modern advertising, of "public relations," were well-suited to that purpose. As Edward L. Bernays, Wilson's propaganda advisor, put it, after the war "business realized that the great public could now be harnessed to their cause as it had been harnessed during the war to the national cause, and the same methods would do the job."[39]

The existence of democratic political institutions makes it essential that ways be found to capture the "hearts and minds" of the population. Radio, developed and used for tactical military purposes as the war began, was used neither for propaganda nor for advertising until after the war. It did not become a consumer good until the 1920s, and not until the end of that decade had it become widely owned in the United States, let alone elsewhere. By the 1930s it had become a powerful technique both for business and political purposes, in all the industrial countries.[40]

Films had of course been common before World War I, and were even more so in the 1920s. But it was not until the advent of the "talkies" as the 1920s ended that films joined ranks with radio, newspapers, and magazines to constitute a major tool for influencing consumer tastes and behavior and political behavior and thought. With television, after World War II, the array of propaganda weapons was complete; and TV was the equivalent of nuclear weaponry in that armory.

What mass production required in terms of mass consumption was part of the same process that established the state of permanent tension between democratic institutions and political persuasion. The main power in a capitalist society is in the hands of those with economic strength, and it is to both their business and long-run political advantage and need to be the dominating influence in the world of information and entertainment. They are; and they began to become so as the techniques and the technology of mass persuasion were born, early in this century. By our time, like the goods-producing sector of the economy, the media sector had come to be dominated by giants, the newest, most ominous part of business as a system of power:

> Modern technology and American economics have quietly created a new kind of central authority over information—the national and multinational corporation. By the 1980s, the majority of all major American media—newspapers, magazines, radio, television, books, and movies—were controlled by fifty giant corporations. These corporations were interlocked in common financial interest with other massive industries and with a few dominant international banks.[41]

The upshot of these developments, combining business needs and outlook with business power and modern media techniques/technology, has been a society that moves to the tunes and rhythms set by business aims, ways, and means. Consequently, in the preceding chapter it was argued that "the special power of capitalism as a production system has been its ability—indeed, its need—to subordinate all social relationships to its dynamism." To seek to bend the modern institutions of education and political democracy to the needs of business has been the major test of contemporary capitalism; and to gain the ability to do so has been its major success. Not only the techniques of persuasion were at work in that success; what was also necessary, and what also required the society's main processes to be shaped in conformity to the needs of capital, was to find ways to assure an effectively continuous process of economic expansion. The elements of that problem and the institutions created for its attempted resolution occupy the following chapter.

Reading Suggestions

One good way to begin further reading in this area is Thurman Arnold, *The Folklore of Capitalism* (Garden City, N.Y.: Blue Ribbon Books, 1941), a thorough and skeptical study of the leading ideas and institutions of U.S. capitalism. Arnold had reason for his skepticism: At one time head of the Antitrust Division of the Justice Department (appointed by FDR), he was "booted upstairs" and out for taking those ideas and institutions too seriously, especially the ones lauding the free market. A.A. Berle (along with Gardiner Means) was noted earlier as having set forth a disturbing thesis (the divorce of ownership from control) in *The Modern Corporation and Private Property.*

Later, Berle took another potentially explosive issue, indicated by its title: *Power Without Property* (New York: Harcourt Brace Jovanovich, 1959), and, characteristically, let it slide out of sight. John Kenneth Galbraith is a witting and witty troublemaker, and though by no means a radical, his troublesomeness, and perhaps even more his graceful writing style, have placed him beyond the pale for most of the economics profession—despite that in the following seven books of his, he, like Berle, uses a fine mind to underscore problematic areas in the socioeconomy, but moves from those troubles, somehow, always to a comforting set of conclusions (and then in his next book, undermines those conclusions and repeats the process). See his *American Capitalism** (1956), *The Affluent Society** (1958), and *The New Industrial State** (1967) (Boston: Houghton Mifflin).

Much has been said about the State and big business, in the various dimensions of that relationship. Some books to help follow up: Walter Adams and Horace M. Gray, *Monopoly in America: The Government as Promoter* (New York: Macmillan, 1955), and, more recently and somewhat broader in scope, Walter Adams and James W. Brock, *The Bigness Complex: Industry, Labor, and Government in the American Economy* (New York: Pantheon, 1986).

Early regulative processes, containing important hints of what the future would hold, are examined by Gabriel Kolko, *Railroads and Regulation 1877–1916* (Princeton, N.J.: Princeton University Press, 1965) and, more broadly by far, *The Triumph of Conservatism* (New York: Free Press, 1963).

A valuable and classic study of the area is Clair Wilcox and William G. Shepherd, *Public Policies Toward Business* (Homewood, Ill.:

Richard D. Irwin, 1975). Studies of governmental regulation are, of course, numerous and quite diverse in orientation. A mix providing different perspectives includes Alfred E. Kahn (who as President Carter's man deregulated the airlines with initially "pleasing" competitive results but subsequently leading to tighter concentration than ever), *The Economics of Regulation*, 2 vols. (New York: Wiley, 1971); Roger Noll, *Reforming Regulation* (Washington, D.C.: Brookings Institution, 1971); and Alan Stone, *Economic Regulation and the Public Interest* (Ithaca, N.Y.: Cornell University Press, 1977). It is very difficult to have laws developed and passed that will regulate business in the broad social interest, in the consumers' interest, etc. And if that hurdle can be conquered, it remains *very* difficult to have them *enforced.* Two books that analyze these realities are Mark Green, *The Other Government: The Unseen Power of Washington Lawyers* (New York: Grossman, 1975) and Lawrence P. Feldman, *Consumer Protection: Problems and Prospects* (St. Paul, Minn.: West Publishing, 1976).

There have been numerous references in footnotes to studies of mergers and the functioning of concentrated industries, etc.; F.M. Scherer, *Industrial Market Structure and Economic Performance* (Skokie, Ill.: Rand McNally, 1980) and David J. Ravenscraft and F.M. Scherer, *Mergers, Sell-Offs, and Economic Efficiency* (Washington, D.C.: Brookings Institution, 1987), the basis for our Figure 3.1, are both excellent for data and analysis, especially concerning the recent past. For a concise analysis indicated in its title, see William G. Shepherd, *Market Power and Economic Welfare* (New York: Random House, 1970). For lighter, but still informative reading, see Morton Mintz and Jerry S. Cohen, *America, Inc.** (New York: Dell, 1971).

Both the United States and the rest of the world had a long love affair with the U.S. automobile industry. Two books are good reading in this connection, one concerned with the man who was its giant-sized hero, the other for the sad story of the decline of that industry: Keith Sward, *The Legend of Henry Ford** (Ford, who once proclaimed, "machinery is the new Messiah!") (New York: Holt, Rinehart and Winston, 1948), and Emma Rothschild, *Paradise Lost: The Decline of the Automobile-Industrial Age* (New York: Vintage, 1973), concerned with more than the automobile, and most presciently.

For a serious and probing analysis of the conformism that is the hallmark of the "brave new world," see Russell Jacoby, *Social Amnesia* (Boston: Beacon Press, 1975). A large part of our conformism in recent decades has revolved around the Cold War. That will be discussed at some length later in the book, but an excellent and neglected study of it worth looking at is Lawrence Wittner, *Cold War America* (New York: Harper & Row, 1978).

Finally, a book that speaks to the closing themes of this chapter, the ways in which the modern corporation seeks to become dominant not only over its markets, but its society: John McDermott, *Corporate Society: Class, Property, and Contemporary Capitalism** (Boulder: Westview Press, 1991).

Notes

1. Lola Ridge, "The Legion of Iron," From *The Ghetto and Other Poems*, published by B.W. Heubsch. Reprinted by permission of David Lawson.

2. From his *Corporate Control, Corporate Power** (Cambridge, England: Cambridge University Press, 1981), p. 250.   There will be many references to this comprehensive and profound study of the nature (statistical, behavioral, analytical) of the modern corporation in the United States, in my judgment the most authoritative and informative—and alarming—work of its kind.   Herman, Professor of Finance at the Wharton School, University of Pennsylvania, often displays the stance and the wit of Veblen, but not the latter's frequent ambiguities.

3. This kind of generalization is not muted by the great economic successes of Japan and Germany since the 1960s—a brief period by comparison with the U.S. experience; and, as we shall see in Chapter 7, significantly aided and abetted by the role played by both countries in the U.S. cold war strategy.

4. One important though subtle aspect of our past, contributing greatly to our political stability as a nation, has been that, as a nation of immigrants, even when a first generation family worked hard and yet lived badly, it could have the usually realistic hope that the children would be economically and socially better off. As will be shown in Chapter 5, that hope became considerably less realistic as the 1970s opened.

5. And there is something to be learned about ourselves as a people when it is understood that not infrequently those deeply involved in ruthless slaughter became our most popular heroes in their own time (and subsequently); for example, Andrew Jackson. (See Zinn, op. cit., for this

and related matters.) A comprehensive historical treatment of racially oppressed groups in our history is the two-volume work by Paul Jacobs, Eve Pell, and Saul Landau, eds., *To Serve the Devil** (New York: Vintage, 1971). Volume 1, *Natives and Slaves*, traces the early history of the treatment of Native Americans, African slaves, and Chicanos. Volume 2, *Colonials and Sojourners*, examines the lesser-known histories of Hawaiians, Chinese, Japanese and Puerto Ricans in the U.S. context. In addition to a brief narrative history, the authors have collected valuable documents wherein the affected peoples speak for themselves; and there is an excellent bibliography for further study. A fine anthology concerning Afro-Americans is Eric Foner, ed., *America's Black Past** (New York: Harper & Row, 1970).

 6. C. Vann Woodward, *Reunion and Reaction** (New York: Doubleday; Anchor, 1956) provides a definitive interpretation of the sordid "Compromise of 1877 and the End of Reconstruction." In that infamous "deal" the North agreed to look the other way as regards the treatment of the freed slaves, in exchange for unlimited access to the South's investment possibilities (in natural resources, railroads, mining, etc.). The consequences of that deal, neither the first nor the last of its kind in our history in or out of this country, include the conservative-racist coalition still central to our "social stability."

 7. Thorstein Veblen, *Absentee Ownership and Business Enterprise** (New York: Huebsch, 1923; Viking, 1954), p. 171.

 8. Pre-Civil War history is rich in details that are skimmed over or ignored here. See the works of Nettels, Gates, and Taylor suggested at the close of Chapter 2. For the post–Civil War period, Shannon and Kirkland provide support for most of our generalizations, as does Du Boff, cited earlier, in his Chapters 2, 3, and 4, for the entire nineteenth century. Also see Harold Vatter, *The Drive to Industrial Maturity** (Westport, Conn.: Greenwood Press, 1975) for a useful and original analysis of the period 1860–1914.

 9. We shall have much to say about waste in Chapter 6. Perhaps it was in the expansion to the West that our people absorbed their strongest lessons on how to waste. The soils were used with abandon (giving rise to the Dust Bowl of the 1930s, among other tragedies, natural and social), and abandoned for presumably better soils beyond the horizon: as Veblen remarks, the farmers pushing west were as much land speculators as farmers. But how we treated the buffalo is perhaps more telling: It is usually assumed that around 1800 there were anywhere from

fifty to sixty-five million buffalo in North America. The Native American tribes used the buffalo for clothing, shelter, and food; the intruders did likewise, at first, but as civilization spread into the West, it became a common sport to take a train ride across the plains, seated on benches facing outward, to shoot buffalo randomly, leaving them to rot. By 1900 there were estimated to be 1,500 buffalo in the continental United States. Now there are some thousands, raised for buffalo meat; and near Yellowstone Park one can pay $200 to shoot a (passive) buffalo and have one's photo taken with the carcass.

10. A useful factual and analytical study of the entire immigration process up into the early twentieth century is Oscar Handlin, *The Uprooted* (Boston: Atlantic Monthly Press, 1951). The important surge of immigration that began in the 1840s was much facilitated by the revival of indentured labor during the Civil War, and became a headlong rush from 1861 on. Between 1861 and 1920, over twenty-eight million people came to the United States as immigrants. Movement to the West was principally by the "native-born," but their rush to take up western lands was reinforced and made possible by the filling up of eastern cities by the newcomers. Toward the close of the century immigration was induced largely to work the mines and the mills spreading over the whole country, and the immigrants were then coming from Eastern and Southeastern Europe (and for building the western railroads, from China), rather than the United Kingdom and Western Europe—with profound social and political results.

11. The conditions and the history of workers in their major aspects will be dealt with in Chapter 5. Meanwhile, those interested will find it illuminating to read any one of several novels that explore the lives of ordinary people in the past. See, for example, Upton Sinclair, *The Jungle* (slaughterhouse workers, turn of the century Chicago), O.E. Rolvaag, *Giants in the Earth* (Dakota farm life, nineteenth century), T.S. Stribling, *The Store* (southern tenants, post–Civil War), A. Cahan, *The Rise of David Levinsky* (Jewish immigrants, late nineteenth century), Pietro di Donato, *Christ in Concrete* (Italian immigrant building workers, early twentieth century), James Farrell, *Studs Lonigan* (slum conditions, Chicago, early twentieth century), and Agnes Smedley, *Daughter of Earth* (autobiographical novel, late nineteenth–early twentieth century). Such a list could be very long, of course, and also continually rewarding. The same may be said for some films, such as "The Emigrants" (Swedish), which portrays the harsh conditions pushing people toward the United

States, or "The Grapes of Wrath" (from the Steinbeck book), placed in the Dust Bowl of the 1930s, which shows how hard life could be for those long here.

12. This perspective is put forth most explicitly by Robert A. Brady in *Business as a System of Power* (New York: Columbia University Press, 1943) an analysis of the patterns of power and the socioeconomic directions of the major capitalist powers—Great Britain, France, the United States, Japan, Italy, and Germany—in the decades leading up to World War II. The book is, of course, dated in detail; it is not "dated" in its major conclusions as to the sociopolitical thrust of the capitalist system. Brady, very much an independent thinker, was greatly influenced by Marx and Veblen; and he affected the development of this book's viewpoint, for I studied with him at the University of California (Berkeley). An illuminating study of the modern evolution of capitalist "social philosophy" in the United States also influenced by Brady is that of R. Jeffrey Lustig, *Corporate Liberalism: The Origins of Modern American Political Theory, 1890–1920* (Berkeley: University of California Press, 1982). The effects of business power on the process of economic growth will be taken up in my Chapter 4; its relationship to the distribution of income and wealth, and the organization of labor, in Chapter 5; business power in the cities, in agriculture, and as affecting the environment in Chapter 6; business power in the world, occupies Chapter 7; and Chapter 8, "The State," will seek to bring all this together.

13. And much of what he did say was without benefit of adequate observation, understandably, as he was in Great Britain. He was especially off the mark in his view of the Civil War as an expression of class struggle. For astute criticisms of Marx by a Marxist, and noted student of the South's history, see Eugene Genovese, *In Red and Black** (New York: Vintage, 1972), especially Chapter 15.

14. Brady's book, just noted, continued in the path of Veblen (combined with Marx and his own strengths). After World War II, Paul Baran and Paul Sweezy, focusing entirely on the United States, sought to do for contemporary industrial capitalism what Marx had done for its first appearance. The capitalism Marx had studied in Britain was economically, ideologically, and politically that of competitive capitalism; that of the United States had become economically and politically that of (as they titled their book) *Monopoly Capital* (New York: Monthly Review Press, 1966), which has not deterred it from remaining ideologically Smithian/-Malthusian. The business structures and market processes of monopoly

capitalism are discussed in this chapter; the larger system will be analyzed in terms of its larger institutions in Chapter 4.

15. *Absentee Ownership*, p. 107.

16. See Joe S. Bain, *Industrial Organization* (New York: Wiley, 1968), for lucid discussions of both market structure and behavior.

17. *Absentee Ownership*, p. 78. This was written in 1923; Veblen makes it clear elsewhere that the process of "decay" began many decades earlier. For details, see Faulkner, cited above, *Decline of Laissez-Faire*, and Arthur Robert Burns, *The Decline of Competition* (New York: McGraw-Hill, 1936).

18. Up to this point we have been questioning the existence of meaningful competition. There is a larger question to be raised: supposing that such a "Smithian" economy did exist, would its long-run social and environmental consequences be beneficial to human beings and nature? This is really another question, and one that will be taken up seriously in our final chapter. Granted that the free market has a vital, even essential role to play in *any* healthy economy (and society), what are its boundaries, what matters require decisions and judgments that are not and cannot be based on purely quantitative (let alone also purely short-run) relationships? Thus, and only as a few examples: is it wise to pit human beings against each other for jobs so as to keep wages as low as possible? to have farmers produce in terms of market criteria even though in the process the soil is overused, "mined"? Should the ill, the disabled, the old find comfort only if they can "pay"? Should access to a decent education be determined by the incomes of students (or their parents)? to recreation? Smith would have to answer "yes" to all these and many other questions of their sort. And his followers today (not least the theoretical gray eminence of the free market philosophy in the United States, Professor Milton Friedman) do say just that: And let the devil take the hindmost. And behind that question is a larger one: Cannot we be trusted to develop social arrangements good for us, and nature? Smith said "no," his distrust of human judgment so great that he believed the "impersonal laws of supply and demand" were the best we could do. So say his followers still, perhaps again looking only at their mirrors.

19. R. Jeffrey Lustig, "Freedom, Corporations, and the New Whiggery," in Fred E. Baumann, ed., *Democratic Capitalism? Essays in Search of a Concept* (Charlottesville, Va.: University Press of Virginia, 1986), pp. 141–143. (My emphasis.)

20. *Corporate Control, Corporate Power*, p. 297. To which may be

added Lustig's observation: "[C]apitalism turns not on greed but on the need to concentrate ever-larger units of wealth under private control. This need eventually forces the transformation of more and more goods and social relations into either capital.... or commodities, from the sale of which capital can be gained. It is not surprising that postwar America has seen the penetration of corporate capitalist organization beyond the marketplace into neighborhoods, health care, sports, and even the distribution of knowledge. Private property emerges from all of this as an artifact and crystallization of power. This has rarely been a topic for polite conversation on these shores. The market was supposed to have dispensed with the need for thinking about all that; it was supposed to have diffused power in a multitude of mutual agreements.... But because the continued survival of capitalist properties requires growth and growth requires the expropriation of holdings from small owners, because that property also requires centralized control over the people within its domain, and because its owners possess the ability to forcefully reshape patterns of social life by their decisions, property emerges as an obvious vehicle of power" (ibid., p. 142).

21. In production, one of the few competitively *structured* areas is that of agriculture. Precisely because that structure exists, with its omnipresent danger of "overproduction," the pricing and output policies of agriculture are almost entirely done within a *governmental* control framework, something which began in the late 1920s, and which persists to the present, always at the behest of the farmers (of which, more in Chapter 6).

22. In the economic sphere, the most vital activity employed to avoid price competition while seeking to increase market share is, of course, advertising. If we are bothered by it at all, mostly it is because it can be annoying, interrupt our TV watching, etc. (although often it is more entertaining than the program it sponsors). But that advertising, whatever its intentions, has had other and more serious consequences and has occupied considerable thought and writing. Among the most compelling books are Stuart Ewen, *Advertising and the Social Roots of the Consumer Culture* (New York: McGraw-Hill, 1976), Jerry Mander, *Four Arguments for the Elimination of Television* (New York: Morrow, 1978), and Herbert Schiller, *The Mind Managers* (Boston: Beacon Press, 1971). Advertising expenditures in the United States are by far the highest in the world. In 1988, for example, they were $118 billion dollars, about 20 percent higher than those for all the nations of the European Economic

Community and Japan combined, even though their populations are almost double our own, taken together.

23. *Accumulation and Power*, p. 57.

24. Though that earlier process was *relatively* the most important, it is still worth noting a few of the numbers of the dizzying 1980s: "Between 1983 and 1986 alone, some 12,200 companies and corporate divisions, worth almost a half-trillion dollars, changed hands. The merger-acquisition-takeover business amounted to nearly a fifth of the 1986 market value of all trade stocks." Bennett Harrison and Barry Bluestone, *The Great U-Turn: Corporate Restructuring and the Polarizing of America** (New York: Basic Books, 1990), p. 59. And the race was by no means over by 1986.

25. Some manifestations of "financialization" of the U.S. economy: between 1960 and 1985, GNP rose about four times, total outstanding debt about eight times, and the financial sector as a percentage of goods production rose from 29 percent to 40 percent. As pointed out earlier, a high percentage of financial activity is in speculation. After 1977, industrial production rose only 25 percent, while futures speculation increased by 370 percent. See "The Logic of Stagnation," *Monthly Review*, October 1986. In the late 1920s the economy was possessed by a similar frenzy of speculation, though of lesser magnitude, not only absolutely but relatively. See Soule, op. cit., Chapters XIII and XIV, and John Kenneth Galbraith, *The Great Crash* (Boston: Houghton Mifflin, 1976), throughout.

26. Tactics ranging from outright gun battles (in the fight to control the Erie Railroad, for example) to the most relentless financial "terrorism" (in Rockefeller's successful steps toward an oil monopoly) are related in detail in Matthew Josephson, *The Robber Barons* (New York: Harcourt Brace Jovanovich, 1934), for the period 1861–1901. The basic history and central problems of combination and competition are treated thoroughly in the classic by George W. Stocking and Myron W. Watkins, *Monopoly and Free Enterprise* (New York: Twentieth Century Func, 1951). Alfred Chandler, Jr. has written several substantial books dealing carefully (and tranquilly) with the rise and behavior of big business in the United States, perhaps the most representative of which is his *The Visible Hand: The Managerial Revolution in American Business* (Cambridge, Mass.: Harvard-Belknap Press, 1977).

27. In 1991, for reasons best known to itself, USX, remaining one corporation, divided its accounting systems into two, one just for oil, the

other for everything else: steel, real estate, etc.

28. John M. Blair, *Economic Concentration: Structure, Behavior and Public Policy* (New York: Harcourt Brace Jovanovich, 1972), p. 285. This is probably the most comprehensive study of the whole process, up to 1970, and still essential, both for its factual and its analytical strengths. The author spent his life working on the problems of big business in the Federal Trade Commission (FTC). His data on conglomerates are drawn from Federal Trade Commission, *Economic Report on Corporate Mergers* (Washington, D.C.: 1969), the best overall study of the conglomerate movement.

29. This development will be analyzed more fully in Chapter 8. In recent years, beginning in the Johnson administration and accelerating under Nixon, the Supreme Court has become subject to always more obvious and crass political considerations (which is not so much to point to a pure past as to an always more corrupted present), which has the effect sought, namely, to place more of the power of the judiciary in the White House. A careful and outraged analysis of the process in its early days is Louis M. Kohlmeier, Jr., *God Save This Honorable Court* (New York: Scribner's, 1972), whose conclusion it is that "President Nixon's place in history is secure: Nixon politicized the Supreme Court more dramatically than any President in history" (p. 281). Since those days, the Court has become so thoroughly politicized that it is now taken for granted, much like the dirty air.

30. *Corporate Liberalism*, p. 247. In the presidential campaign of 1912, Woodrow Wilson, presenting himself as a potential caretaker of the public welfare against the depredations of big business, said: "Suppose you go to Washington and try to get at your government. You will always find that while you are politely listened to, the men really consulted are the big men who have the biggest stakes—the big bankers, the big manufacturers, the big masters of commerce.... Every time it has come to a critical question, these gentlemen have been yielded to, and their demands treated as the demands that should be followed as a matter of course. The government of the United States is a foster child of the special interests." Quoted by Robert Sherrill, in "S&Ls, Big Banks and Other Triumphs of Capitalism," *The Nation*, November 19, 1990, a major and valuable essay, to be referred to often in our examination of the S&L disaster in Chapter 4. The "special interests" used to be seen as those "big men" and their companies; one of the triumphs of the mind managers in the past decade is that now it is those who have little or no

access to political power who are classed as those "special interests" and any legislation that might protect them seen as a form of vile corruption. Like the lobbyists, the mind managers earn their high incomes.

31. Among the best-known of innumerable legislated favors for MNCs is that which allows oil companies such as EXXON to count the "royalties" it pays to (for example) the rulers of Saudi Arabia as deductions from their U.S. tax liabilities. More than once this has meant that EXXON and other such companies end up the tax year paying *no* taxes and with a net income from the government. A moment's reflection will show that this goes beyond deducting costs from gross income. Who says there's no such thing as a free lunch? More generally, the MNCs normally shift and juggle their accounts from one nation to another, depending upon tax systems, to minimize their total taxes.

32. Regarding this and related matters, more will be said momentarily, as the multinational corporation is discussed; and considerably more than that in Chapter 7, where the discussion will be continued and expanded to include an examination of "restructuring," and what *Business Week*, in a famous feature essay of March 3, 1986 by the same name, called "The Hollow Corporation."

33. And today, it must be added, not just possible but essential for profits and for survival. The quotation is from an unpublished manuscript of Stephen Hymer, "The United States Multinational Corporation and Japanese Competition in the Pacific," which he gave me permission to use in this book's first edition, just before his accidental death at an early age, in 1974. All who knew Hymer and his work saw him as uniquely brilliant. Fortunately, some of his work has been published. See his "The Multinational Corporation and the Law of Uneven Development," in Jagdish Bagwati, ed., *Economics and World Order* (New York: Macmillan, 1972), a portion of which is reproduced in Edwards, et al., *The Capitalist System*, op. cit., pp. 62–66, and "The Multinational Corporation and the International Division of Labor," in *The Multinational Corporation: A Radical Critique* (Cambridge, England: Cambridge University Press, 1979), Stephen Hymer, et al., eds.

34. See his *Main Currents*, esp. pp. 15–23. As is customary in such developments, it is likely that the main consequences of their efforts were neither comprehended nor intended.

35. A reasonably full discussion of the militarization of the U.S. economy and society will be divided between Chapters 4 and 8. Two references are worth pointing to here: C. Wright Mills, in his *Power*

*Elite** (New York: Oxford University Press, 1956) was probably the first to note and to analyze the central position of the military in the power structure of the United States—while noting that the military's position in that structure was defined by civilians; and Seymour Melman, in one of his many books in the area, detailed the processes and structures that in some sense *are* the military-industrial complex: *Pentagon Capitalism** (New York: McGraw-Hill, 1970).

36. Op. cit., pp. 391–93.

37. Some would define propaganda as just another, not very nice, word for education. When that is not cynical, it is wrong. Education seeks to illuminate, to stimulate thought and reflection. Propaganda aims at something like the opposite: it seeks to sell, to control, to deceive. Whether for commercial or political aims, propaganda has the aim of causing the listener, reader, or watcher to do something for the specific benefit of the "sponsor." As such, there are no generic differences between a beer ad, a political candidate's "commercial," or the hoopla supporting a war. The person who more than any single other who was in at the modern origins of both propaganda and advertising in the United States was Edward L. Bernays, Woodrow Wilson's advisor in what was initially an unpopular war, and the creator of numerous advertising techniques in the 1920s and 1930s. See his memoirs: Edward L. Bernays, *Public Relations* (Norman: University of Oklahoma Press, 1952). (It is doubtless irrelevant, but nonetheless interesting that Bernays is Sigmund Freud's nephew. Bernays, now 100, lives still.) For an interesting, amusing, and revealing look at a later perfection of the craft, see Joe McGinniss, *The Selling of the President, 1968** (New York: Trident Press, 1969). The author, a conservative journalist, was invited to accompany the Nixon campaign, an experience he found sobering. The book's cover shows a cigarette package with Nixon's head emerging, along with the rest of the product.

38. Journalism played a role; but for the economic and political background of that and broader developments, see the conclusive study of William Appleman Williams, *The Roots of the Modern American Empire** (New York: Random House, 1969).

39. Bernays, op. cit., p. 87.

40. See H. D. Lasswell, *Propaganda Technique in World War I* (Cambridge, Mass.: MIT Press, 1971; first published 1927), and Walter Lippman, *Public Opinion* (London: Allen & Unwin, 1932).

41. Ben H. Bagdikian, *The Media Monopoly* (Boston: Beacon Press,

1983), p. xv. Later, the author (a professor of journalism at the University of California, Berkeley), points out that 21 of the Top 50 media companies are among the Top 500 Industrials, more than double the number twenty years ago (pp. 20–21.) For an excellent analysis of aims and means in these respects, see Herbert I. Schiller, *The Mind Managers.* (Further discussion of these and related matters are presented in Chapters 7 and 8, and other references are noted.)

− 4 −

Growth and Development, Prosperity and Depression

As I sd to my
friend, because I am
always talking,—John I

sd, which was not his
name, the darkness sur-
rounds us, what

can we do, against
it, or else, shall we &
why not, buy a goddamn big car,

drive, he sd, for
christ's sake, look
out where yr going.[1]

A capitalist economy cannot stand still. It must *grow* or shrink; it must continually change its patterns of production, consumption, and trade—that is, *develop*—or cease to grow; irrespective of growth and development, it will continually *fluctuate*. At any time and over time, the capitalist economy is marked by unevenness, uncertainty, and instability.

Why is all this so? What are the characteristics of, and differences between, fluctuations, growth, and development? How do they relate, separately and in combination, to the defining traits of capitalism—its need to expand and to exploit? Earlier we touched on some of the relevant explanations; here we shall explore them at greater length.

However much they may disagree on other matters, all economists who have studied capitalism—from Smith through Marx, Marshall, and

137

Keynes—agree on the necessity of expansion. Disagreement centers upon what is *required* for expansion, what is associated with the process, the likelihood or not of expansion over time, and the consequences of expansion, whether at adequate or inadequate rates. How these matters are treated distinguishes classical from neoclassical economics, and both of those from dissenting or radical economics.

The classical political economists, and especially Smith and Ricardo, developed analyses whose aim was to enhance the possibilities of economic growth and development. John Stuart Mill's examination of the probabilities and problems of a "stationary" economy brought the period of classical economic thought to a close. In the 1870s, as Mill's life came to an end, neoclassical economics had come to the fore. Until the astounding depression of the 1930s, that economics gave little sustained or even serious attention to the processes of growth and development. Neoclassical monetary theory, capital theory, and trade theory may be said to have been *related* to such questions, but distantly. Their theories took growth and development (and almost everything else) for granted; so why systematically examine the life processes, the realities, of economic growth? And, as we stated earlier, development—any kind of significant structural change—was neither sought nor discussed in neoclassical economics. Given the kinds of problems businessmen saw themselves as facing in the late nineteenth century—centering mostly on real or imagined market scarcities of capital, labor, and resources—and given the essential harmony between the viewpoints of businessmen and economists, this was an understandable neglect. All that was rudely upset by the depression of the 1930s and by the adjustments of neoclassical theory put forth by Keynes and his associates.

Alongside the aloof attitude of neoclassical economists, and developing in the same years (in the half-century or so after 1870), there *was* a body of analysis that sought to approach questions of growth, fluctuations, and development directly (if not always in those terms). The analyses came to be called "business cycle" or "fluctuations" theory, and until about 1970 or so, an economics major could (and at many universities one had to) take undergraduate and graduate courses in such studies—which almost universally concerned themselves with, among other things, the facts of what today we might call "aggregative" or "macroeconomic" processes. Although that "field" of economics has virtually disappeared by now, it at least left a substantial and continually valuable body of data that can be used by economists who wish to keep their feet somewhere near the ground.

The significance of that work did not become meaningful until after the depression of the 1930s was well underway; nor did business cycle studies divert the smooth flow of the calm mainstream of neoclassical theory. In the United States, Veblen was unquestionably the most influential thinker in this area, although his influence was not always acknowledged by those he directly or indirectly instructed: J.M. Clark and Wesley Clair Mitchell, directly (as his students), and Joseph A. Schumpeter, indirectly. Economists in general went on their cheerful way, unruffled by serious concern with the prospects of untoward booms or slumps, while serious business cycle analysts managed to overlook the gloomy expectations of Veblen's analysis—which in turn was indebted to European, including Marxian, contributions.[2]

In the decade or two preceding the onset of the 1930s depression, the seriousness of the problems of expansion and contraction was only barely recognized, in short, as revealed by the credibility given to "theories" that explained aggregative movements in terms of sunspots, or (among others as laughable but not as amusing) by an inverse statistical correlation with the length of women's skirts in Australia. It took a disaster to prompt either the economics profession or its principal audience (the business world) to pay heed to the relationship between such disaster and the normal functioning of a capitalist economy.

Joseph A. Schumpeter, a very conservative but not a very conventional economist, was one who—like Veblen, J.M. Clark, and Mitchell —stood as an exception to those who saw business downturns as temporary aberrations. Although, like Keynes, he accepted much of neoclassical theory, Schumpeter could not do so for the vital questions of growth and development. "Analyzing business cycles," he said,

> means neither more nor less than analyzing the economic process of the capitalist era.... Cycles are not, like tonsils, separable things that might be treated by themselves, but are, like the beat of its heart, at the essence of the organism that displays them.[3]

Schumpeter (like Keynes), was an ardent though not starry-eyed supporter of capitalist society; his studies of capitalist development, pursued very much as a doctor studies the organic processes of human beings, told him that the best one could hope for was to prolong its inevitable disappearance. He developed this position most fully in his *Capitalism, Socialism, and Democracy.* The healthy dynamic of capitalism for Schumpeter was what he called "creative gales of destruction"—gales powered by technological innovation, leading to the elimination of *old* patterns of competition and monopoly by *new* patterns of both. In this view, but in few others, he was close to Veblen and Marx, despite his quite different value system. They saw the life and death of capitalism more as undertakers than as doctors.

Writing in the heyday of both neoclassical economics and rampant U.S. industrialization, Veblen combined a dour analysis of capitalist growth and development with a dim view of the associated economics:

> There are certain saving clauses in common use.... Among them are these: "Given the state of the industrial arts"; "Other things remaining the same"; "In the long run"; "In the absence of disturbing causes." Now,...the state of the industrial arts has at no time continued unchanged during the modern era; consequently other things have never remained the same; and in the long run the outcome has always been shaped by the disturbing causes.... The arguments [of the neoclassical economists] have been as good as the premises on which they proceed.[4]

For Veblen, the process of capitalist growth and development hurried through time under the domination of three major trends: a steady increase in monopolization, a continuing increase in technological strength, and a chronic tendency toward depression. Monopoly results from the native impulse of the businessman to eliminate competitors— "buy cheap and sell dear." Technological advance "...has in recent times been going forward at a constantly accelerated rate, and it is still in progress, with no promise of abatement or conclusion."[5] But why should depression be the outcome of monopolization and technological improvement? That takes us to Veblen's distinction between business and industry.

Business is a matter of making money; what business will produce, in what quantities, and when, is determined by actual and prospective market conditions. The advance of technology means ever-increasing production and productivity; the combination of consumer and investment expenditures with the ability of monopolistic business to hold back production—Veblen called it "businesslike sabotage"—places steady downward pressure on the economy, relieved only intermittently by stimuli coming from outside the "normal" functioning of the economy.

Thus, Veblen asserted,

Since the [1870s]..., the course of affairs in business has apparently taken a permanent change as regards crises and depression. During this recent period, and with increasing persistency, chronic depression has been the rule rather than the exception in business. Seasons of easy times, "ordinary prosperity," during this period are pretty uniformly traceable to specific causes extraneous to the process of industrial business proper; [e.g., in] the one now drawing to a close, it was the Spanish-American War, coupled with the expenditures for stores, munitions, and services incident to placing the country on a war footing, that lifted the depression and brought prosperity to the business community.[6]

The remedy Veblen saw for this tendency toward chronic depression (already in 1904), put forward sardonically as always, was for the "vested interests" to *create* these stimuli, for them to develop means of "unproductive consumption," through a "strenuous national policy," and a "popular concern for the national integrity." Those who find this view out of keeping with what appears to be a different set of realities since 1904 may be reminded that the U.S. economy was saved from contraction by World War I (and the expenditures in the United States by the warring powers from 1914 on, as well as our own before and after 1917) and an ensuing "prosperity," that it sank into deep depression in the 1930s from which it recovered only after our entrance into World War II, and that our economic buoyancy since has been accompanied by both Cold War and hot war involving, as we shall see, expenditure by the United States on military goods and services here and over the globe amounting to five *trillion* dollars since 1946.[7] These and other characteristics of the U.S. developmental process will be traced more fully later in this chapter. But first, let us look briefly at Marx's treatment of certain of the essential traits of the expansion process. There are explicit and implicit differences between his and Veblen's analyses, as well as common ground.

Marx spoke not of economic growth or development, but of the process of "capital accumulation." This was for Marx the rope on which capitalism climbed through time, aided by intermittent knots of expansion and threatened by periodic frayed stretches, which he called crises (and which are now called recessions or depressions). Marx believed also that this was the rope with which capitalism would ultimately hang itself —with the generous help of the working class, itself a product of capital accumulation.

More exactly, for Marx both the expanding and the contracting phases of capitalist development are negative as well as positive in their meaning. Expansion means expanded production and profits, *but* the point comes when it also means overproduction and upward pressure on wages; contraction means depressed production and losses, *but* it also replenishes the vital "reserve army of the unemployed," reduces competition through the destruction of weaker firms, and usually lays the basis for renewed expansion and the continuing tendency toward monopoly.

Marx saw the process of capital accumulation, or expansion, as energized by what each individual capitalist *wishes* to do and what he and all other capitalists *must* do: seeking to make profits in competition with others in the context of an ever-changing technology, the surviving capitalists and the economy are driven to "accumulate," or expand. The capitalist, Marx said,

> shares with the miser the passion for wealth as wealth. But that which in the miser is a mere idiosyncrasy, is, in the capitalist, the effect of the social mechanism, of which he is but one of the wheels. Moreover, the development of capitalist production makes it constantly necessary to keep increasing the amount of capital laid out in a given industrial undertaking, and competition makes the immanent laws of capitalist production to be felt by each individual capitalist, as external coercive laws. It compels him to keep constantly extending his capital, in order to preserve it, but extend it he cannot, except by means of progressive accumulation.

Therefore,

> Accumulate, accumulate! That is Moses and the prophets! Accumulation for accumulation's sake, production for production's sake....[8]

A full treatment of Marxian and Veblenian analysis along these lines would show that Marx had a more coherent and more powerful economic theory than Veblen. On the other hand, the looseness of Veblen's analysis, and the later period in which he wrote, allowed him to bring in the behavior and the meaning of modern monopolistic business organization and of the State, as well as that of imperialism, in ways that Marx (who died in 1883) could not.[9] What seems clearly essential now is to combine the strengths of Marx, Veblen, and Keynes with contemporary data and analyses, an effort already begun by Baran and Sweezy, in their *Monopoly Capital* (and followed by many others, as we shall see). Next, let us explore what is meant by fluctuations, growth, and development, in general, and in the experience of the United States.

Fluctuations and Instability

In proceeding first to explain the pervasiveness and persistence of business fluctuations in a capitalist economy, it should be emphasized that fluctuations and instability are not *defects* in such an economy. The price of such instability may well be high for particular firms, industries, and workers at any time, but for a capitalist *economy's* health over time such fluctuations are essential. In what is no more than a suggestive analogy, we may think of the role of business fluctuations in a capitalist economy as comparable to the processes of inhaling and exhaling, of hunger and surfeit, of ingestion and digestion, in our bodies—and add that artificial attempts to control or enhance those processes often have undesirable side-effects as, we shall see, has been the case with attempts to "iron out" fluctuations. And, extending the analogy a bit more, we may point out that it is not our normal processes as such that are harmful, but the quality of the air, the quantity and composition of the diet, that make for health or sickness in our bodies.

So: business fluctuations are inherent in a capitalist economy. To rid the economy of them would require ridding it as well of its basic institutional characteristics: private ownership of the means of production, and the right and the will to use those productive assets to make profits at the independent decision of the business firm. A capitalist *economy* is in its nature unplanned, however much each *enterprise* may plan. The economy is, of course, complex in its many parts. It becomes always more so as industrialization broadens and deepens specialization in all aspects of the economy—in agriculture, trade, industry, finance, and the broadening variety of services. Time must pass between the initial decision to invest and produce; that is, decisions made on the basis of one set of market signals are realized well or badly in markets that exist later. And all this is made substantially more complex by virtue of the mediating role of money and finance, to say nothing of the impact of foreign trade, investment, and speculation.[10]

As noted in Chapter 3, competition, taken in its own terms, is intrinsic to the economic and the social health of a capitalist society; so is instability. However, just as businessmen have acted when they could to mitigate or eliminate competition, they have also done what little they could to mitigate the harmful effects of instability on their own firms. But competition is "only" an industrywide phenomenon; instability is economywide, nationally and internationally. Consequently, no matter how effective steps may be to eliminate market competition when taken by an individual company, the substantial amelioration of instability has depended upon economic intervention by the State. Such intervention became neither significant nor persistent until the onset of the depression of the 1930s. This marked a major change in the role of the State *and* in the structure of the economy (by virtue of the spending, taxing, and employment role of the State: There were more government employees in 1992, than in all of manufacturing). What these changes reflected was the necessity for a *developmental* change if adequate growth rates as well as the mitigation of instability were to be achieved.

If capitalism is *inherently* unstable, and if the United States was capitalist from its earliest beginnings, then our economic history should have been characterized by continuous ups and downs, as indeed it was. Table 4.1 recounts this performance for the United States since 1800.

Growth and Development, Nineteenth Century

With such a dramatic pattern of economic seesawing throughout our history, why were no persistent and deliberate counteracting steps made part of the State's functions until the past generation or so? It is not far-fetched to make an analogy with a young man who gets periodic hangovers, or an occasional broken leg from skiing. Why does he not take more care, place himself under the advice of a doctor?

The nineteenth century was the U.S. economy's careless youth, a period of rapid expansion every which way, as our geographic boundaries and structure of production were both filled in and expanded. It was a

Table 4.1
Prosperity and Depression, Expansion and Contraction
1800–1992

1800-1807	Prosperity	1883-1885	Mild Recession
1808-1809	Depression	1886-1890	Vigorous Prosperity
1810-1814	Gradual Recovery and Boom (1814)	1891	Minor Recession
1815	Panic	1892	Recovery
1816-1818	Depression	1893	Stock Market Collapse
1819	Panic	1894-1897	Mostly Depressed Years
1820-1821	Mild Depression	1898-1907	Prosperity
1822-1824	Prosperity	1907	Panic
1825-1826	Recession	1908	Depression
1827-1836	Growing Prosperity	1909-1914	Semistagnation
1837	Panic	1914-1918	War Prosperity
1837-1843	Generally Depressed Conditions	1919	Mild Postwar Recession
1844-1848	Mild Prosperity	1919-1920	Prosperity and Inflation
1849-1856	Vigorous Prosperity	1921-1922	Sharp Recession
1857	Panic	1922-1923	Prosperity
1858	Depression	1924	Recession
1859-1860	Revival and Prosperity	1925-1926	Recovery
1861-1862	Generally Depressed Conditions	1928-1929	Boom
1862-1865	War Prosperity	1930-1940	Deep Depression; Short "Boom," 1937
1866-1867	Depression	1940-1945	War Prosperity
1868-1872	Prosperity	1946	Recession
1874-1878	General Depression	1947-1948	Recovery
1879	Recovery	1948-1949	Recession
1880-1882	Prosperity	1949-1953	Recovery

Table 4.1 (cont.)			
1953-1954	Recession	1973-1975	Sharp Recession
1954-1957	Recovery	1975-1980	Recovery with Severe Inflation
1957-1958	Recession	1980	Recession
1958-1960	Recovery	1980-1981	Recovery
1960-1961	Recession	1981-1982	Severe Recession
1961-1969	Sustained Expansion	1983-1990	Expansion
1969-1970	Slowdown and Inflation	1990-1992	Recession
1970-1973	Weak Recovery and Inflation		

Source: Joseph A. Schumpeter, Business Cycles, cited earlier, Vol. I, Chapter VII, Vol. II, Chapter XIV; Robert A. Gordon, Economic Instability and Growth, cited earlier, Chapter 5; Richard Du Boff, Accumulation and Power, cited earlier, Chapter 6.

period of extraordinary buoyancy, both because of domestic possibilities and the manner in which they were supported by the economic developments over the rest of the globe. Each of the century's numerous crises and panics was followed by successively higher peaks of economic activity. Optimism was understandably the rule; for those at the top levels of business, and for many others as well, it was justified. There was neither the inclination nor the need for a "doctor's care."

In the early twentieth century, the U.S., European, and Japanese economies (that is, all those that had been undergoing industrialization) were approaching or had reached "maturity"; and business contractions, market instability, and insecurity all became more dangerous, on both economic and political grounds. The consciousness of this grew in the United States, especially among the most powerful corporate leaders (but not, usually, among small businesses). In turn, this consciousness led to a transformed view of the proper role of the State, one different from laissez-faire. What was sought, as Kolko puts it, was some greater degree of predictability, security, and stability, all very much jeopardized by the precariousness of an industrial capitalist society; what was gained was not much more than a mild principle of social control:

…many businessmen increasingly saw politics as the arena in which to find solutions for wasteful competition, inconsistent state regulations, the easy entrance for new firms into their industry, and potential crisis. What was politically impossible for the moment because of divisions within the industry might prove relevant in another year—and often did. Meanwhile, the numerous federal acts and agencies created during the "Progressive Era" left an important, if incomplete, basis for later reforms. In addition to the railroad regulatory system there was now a Federal Trade Commission and a Federal Reserve Board, food and drug legislation, a meat inspection that the biggest firms had much desired, and diverse other laws.[11]

The postponement of any more vital economic functions for the State at that time may be explained by the outbreak of World War I, its deflecting impact in terms of expansion in the war years, and the ensuing years of expansion until 1929. A closer examination of these developments is now in order.[12]

In Chapter 3 we dwelt upon the dynamic interaction between economic and westward geographic expansion in the nineteenth century. Viewed from the perspective of this chapter, we may observe that process as almost chaotic; we may also understand how its individual and social costs were both softened (for many) and obscured (for almost all) by the generally rapid quantitative expansion and the developmental changes accompanying it. In addition, prior to the stage of advanced industrialism of this century, troubles in one part of the economy were felt less immediately *and* less seriously in the rest of the economy than in the twentieth century.

The advance of productive efficiency is related to an ever more extensive specialization of function, or division of labor, in turn implying increasing economic and social interdependence. Greater productivity is thus paid for with greater precariousness. Our chronological listing of expansions and contractions shows many depressions and "panics." The very term "panic" suggests the spread of trouble over the economy; in some cases in the nineteenth century it spread like a prairie fire.[13] What was noteworthy about such instances, however, was that their origins were almost always in the loose and speculation-dominated *financial* system of the nation, which in turn was usually responding to land and railroad speculation.

But underneath that turbulent surface was a deepening and spreading industrial system, providing ongoing buoyancy to the economy and optimism to its businessmen. There was no felt need for an activist State to set limits to bad times; experience suggested that the bad times would not last long or become dangerously threatening. Depression, when it occurred in the nineteenth century, does not signify either deep or lasting (recorded or known) unemployment, until the massive depression of the 1930s.[14]

As was pointed out in Chapter 3, the generally depressed years between 1873 and 1897 were years of steadily falling prices, due to the combination of rapid technological advance and the tying together of world markets, resulting in foreign competition plus intense domestic competition. Both in Europe and the United States, a major response to the conditions of those years was a growth of monopolies, trusts, imperialism, cartels, and tariff protection. The substantial storms of that period came to seem minor compared with the typhoons that swept the world in the first half of this century; indeed, the last half of the nineteenth century came to be seen as a "Golden Age."

World War I and the New Era

There are at least two important matters requiring explanation for the period from 1914 to 1929: first, the sustained quality of its expansion, by comparison with earlier periods; second, the manner in which that long expansion connects with the unprecedented collapse after 1929. The prosperity of the fifteen years preceding 1929 was quite unusual in our history; drastically more so was the depression, in its severity, its duration, and its pervasiveness. Something new was going on; it probably began before World War I, in the period we have called "semistagnation."

In seeking analytically to integrate the prosperity preceding 1929 with the depression following it, we place ourselves in the arena of growth and development analysis, not short-term business cycle theory or the abstract income and employment theory of Keynes. We are thus taken to an exceptionally complicated area of analysis; here we can only point to the major elements of what such an analysis must put together.

First we should note that in the years preceding World War I, the United States had reached the limits of economic complexity then allowed by technology, real income, and business conditions—although the limits reached in the United States were significantly beyond those attained elsewhere, whether the reference is to productivity, the balance between consumer and capital goods production, the total of all production, or the scale of individual plant production. Second, although the years after 1909 are conventionally seen as a period of recovery from the panic and depression of 1907–1908, if there was a recovery it was quite uneven and feeble. The uncertainty and rocky quality of the U.S. economy had its counterpart in what was, if anything, a worse situation in Europe, where what was by then an emerging North Atlantic economy had begun, by 1914, to slip toward major economic troubles. Because each segment of the capitalist world interacted with all the rest, these developing weaknesses in the two strongpoints of the world system were ominous portents of the disaster that exploded in 1929, but which had been showing its signs throughout the 1920s.[15]

Much of the talk about the causes of economic difficulty in the United States in the decade before 1914 pointed to the inadequacies of the financial system. Because those inadequacies were quite real, and their consequences vivid, they took attention away from deeper problems (as is true today):

An inefficient and inelastic credit system, however, was by no means the only cause for the unstable condition of American economic life between 1907 and 1914. High finance had overloaded railroads and other corporations with fantastic capital structures; industrial "trusts," as in the case of United States Steel after the panic of 1907, were reluctant to adjust prices to decreasing demand. Wages were barely keeping up with the increased cost of living, whereas unemployment in manufacturing and transportation amounted to 12 percent or over in 1908, 1914, and 1915.... [Despite] a vigorous speculative advance...in the early months of 1914 on both the London and New York stock exchanges..., the world saw no revival in trade and industry. In the United States the recession of 1913 sank into a depression in 1914 with an increase in gold exports, a decline in foreign trade, a weakening of commodity prices, and an increase in unemployment.[16]

What Faulkner portrays here as a condition of substantial instability, Baran and Sweezy see as the onset of *stagnation*. Stagnation is another term for chronic depression where, in the absence of "external stimuli" such as war, the economy tends to limp along with unutilized productive capacity, depressed business, and high unemployment (like Britain in the 1920s).

Pointing to the increasing severity of the contraction phases of the business cycle from 1908 until the war, and to a sharp increase in unemployment over the same years (averaging 6.6 percent, from 1908 until 1915), Baran and Sweezy conclude that the years after 1907 displayed:

> the kind of "creeping stagnation" with which we have become familiar.... If there is any other interpretation of these facts, we are certainly ready to consider it on its merits. But until we know what it is, we shall feel justified in concluding that if the First World War had not come along, the decade 1910–1920 would have gone down in United States history as an extraordinarily depressed one.[17]

The outbreak of the European war in August 1914 entirely altered the economic prospects of the U.S. economy. Instead of having to struggle with what might well have been a serious depression, both national and international, the United States found itself faced with rapidly growing demands from abroad for its production and its capital. Internally, this meant that a likely downturn was replaced by a strong upswing in business and jobs, and an even further expansion of our industrial system. It also gave an added boost to the concentration and centralization of power, and explicit business-State coordination and planning, when the United States entered the war in 1917. A full panoply of new war agencies brought representatives of agriculture, industry, and labor into the government, where they were schooled in new ways to gain and to use power.[18]

Out of war needs, the U.S. economy was able to generate rising instead of falling incomes for a whole range of "ordinary people," along with sustained and high profits for the business world (including farmers). This, taken together with the technological developments facilitated by the war, laid the basis for the "New Era" of the U.S. economy in the 1920s. Added to the advanced development of durable *capital* goods was the introduction on a mass basis of a broad range of durable *consumer* goods (such as automobiles and home appliances) and a vast boom in residential, commercial, and public construction (of buildings and especially of roads). Similar developments on such a scale did not take hold in other industrial economies, if at all, until much later—and on a mass basis, radios excepted, not until after 1950.[19]

Another important outcome of the war is the manner in which it speeded up and facilitated the emergence of the United States as the strongest power in the world economy—a position more than symbolized by the change from our *owing* other countries (especially to Britain) more than $3 billion before the war and being *owed* (again, especially by Britain) over $6 billion after the war. (World War II, in this and many other respects, had quite a bit more of the same consequences, as will be discussed later.)

The domestic meaning of our new world role after the war was not vital to the prosperity of the 1920s, both because the postwar upsurge in economic nationalism (protective tariffs, etc.) placed stringent limits on U.S. possibilities abroad, and because domestic prosperity reduced our need to look far afield for substantial export possibilities—except for our cotton, tobacco, and grain farmers, who were placed in serious trouble by the combination of their wartime expansion and the collapse of export markets in the 1920s.

Nevertheless, seen in a long-term perspective, World War I and its aftermath were critical in placing the United States in the forefront of world economic powers; after 1940, the United States was able to take conscious advantage of what had come within reach when the European powers entered upon the suicidal path of World War I.

With all the enormous stimuli provided during and by World War I, it is not difficult to understand the subsequent "prosperity decade." But what brought it to an end? And, more to the point (for capitalist expansions always come to an end), why was the depression of the 1930s so terribly deep? and so very long? and why, even more, was World War II—like the depression itself, the deepest, most widespread, and most damaging of all wars—required to lift us out of that depression?

One way to begin (but only to begin) to answer such questions is to dwell for a moment on the word "prosperity." Like so many pleasing terms used to describe our history, it has to be viewed with an eye to who uses it and what they mean by it. Up until very recently, almost all of those informing us about our society—as historians, economists, sociologists, journalists, politicians, et al.—have been in or from the upper ranks of society, among the comfortable beneficiaries of the society's achievements. As Veblen said, speaking of professors of social science, "their intellectual horizon is bounded by the same limits of commonplace insight and preconceptions as are the prevailing opinions of the conservative middle class."[20]

Thus, to say that the U.S. economy was prosperous in the 1920s, as these words are commonly used, is quite compatible with the existence of widespread and growing misery in the same time and place. In 1989, in the *Economic Report of the President* (to Congress) President Ronald Reagan said: "And by reducing taxes and regulatory bureaucracy, we have unleashed the creative genius of ordinary Americans and ushered in an unparalleled period of peacetime prosperity" (p. 3).

As Chapter 5 will demonstrate, the taxes on "ordinary Americans"—four-fifths of the population—rose significantly in the 1980s, as their incomes stagnated or fell; while, in the same years and for the same reasons, the taxes of those at the top declined as their incomes rose—and as the U.S. economy came to resemble more that of Britain in the 1920s than the United States in its heyday. Doubtless Reagan believed what he said, as doubtless he did for utterances even less credible; what is more curious is the continuing popular support from virtually all quarters of society he received (and receives?), including from those damaged by these and others of his policies.

In the 1920s, as today, "prosperity" was compatible with serious economic problems in a broad range of industries. But "the system" was doing just fine; it was expanding in its production and power, it was yielding all sorts of new and attractive products for a significant percentage of its population, and it was setting new records for returns to owners of productive assets and of securities and real estate. The period was one in which perhaps a third of the population of the United States was realizing the dream of material abundance, and when many of the components of that abundance, including the shining new array of consumer durable goods, hadn't even existed only a few years before.

The railroads had already begun their long decline; they, coal mining, cotton textiles, and staple agriculture (grains and cotton, especially), where most of the farm population worked, were all in serious trouble, all shrinking. Naturally, those who depended on those industries for their jobs were in even more serious trouble.

Unemployment statistics before the 1930s are notoriously unreliable as, for different reasons, they are still today.[21] Estimates for the years 1920–1929 range from an average of 5 percent to something over 13 percent unemployed. Even if we accept the conservative lower figure, we are faced with a jobless rate that suggests something other than "prosperity" for those directly involved and the even larger number—their families, for example—indirectly involved. To which it must be added that five percent or more unemployed in the 1920s (and the percentage was more likely double that) had a harsher meaning than today, for at least two reasons: (1) average income levels are significantly more comfortable today; and (2) in those years there was nothing in the way of a "social net" to break the fall into joblessness. But, it is relevant to note that one way in which the Reagan years mimicked the Harding/Coolidge/Hoover era is that the unemployment insurance benefits created in the 1930s now cover many fewer than twenty and thirty years ago, and the time of coverage is substantially shorter.

Nor is it unimportant to make another set of comparisons—remembering that the 1920s and the years since the late 1970s have as many differences as similarities. The 1920s are seen as *the* prosperous decade, and the 1980s as *the* great expansion. But in both periods the very substantial income gains and tax reductions for the top tenth of the population were simultaneous with a sinking into hard times and desperation for a much larger number in the bottom two-thirds of the population. It was estimated that in 1929 a family income of $2,000 (in 1929 prices and incomes) was necessary to supply just basic necessities. But 40 percent of families had incomes below $1,500 a year, and 71 percent were under $2,500.[22] In the next chapter, where the focus is the distribution of income and wealth, we shall examine the changes in the post–World War II years, and note more similarities between the 1920s and the 1980s. In both periods, and not only in them, it is almost as though we are observing two different economies, two different worlds. And in an important sense, as will now be discussed, we are.

The Dual Economy

From its first years, the U.S. economy has contained industries that were lively, while growing alongside them others were stagnating and depressed; it would have been remarkable had that not been so, given the rapidity of technological and economic change in the modern world. And, of course, like the rest of the world, we have always had groups of people making high, medium, and low incomes—or, until after the Civil War, making no money income, if they were slaves. However, until the years just before World War I, such differences did not constitute a firm basis for *duality* in the economy and society.

As the term duality is used here it is meant to suggest more than simply some differences between groups and sectors in the economy, and the people attached to them. It signifies the evolution of two systematically diverging paths of change—one dynamic, yielding profits and power, the other marked by difficulties, stagnation, and weakness. Such a "bifurcation" began to appear in the decade or so before 1920, as the U.S. economy developed into the industrial and organizational patterns which, as we approach the present, seem to settle like concrete, and tend toward a permanent hardening.[23]

Students of recent U.S. economic development will object to the idea of any "settling in" process for the U.S. economy. After all, this century has seen an extraordinary amount of change in products, techniques, and patterns of distribution and finance, along with a great increase in real per capita income. All that is, of course, indisputable. The important aspect of that dynamism, however, is that it has been carried by what O'Connor calls the monopolistic sector and the State sector; meanwhile, the competitive sector has drifted into something like a backwash—increasingly dependent upon the monopolistic sector and the State for viability or even livelihood, and increasingly resentful of both.

The prosperity of the 1920s was attributable to the dynamism of the monopolistic sector: high rates of technological innovation in production, and a whole new spread of expensive durable consumer goods, combined with an associated and enormous expansion in (especially) the petroleum and construction industries.[24]

If one were to locate the hot center of this dynamism in the 1920s, it would be in the expansion of the automobile industry. The latter meant the connected growth also of industries directly (metals, machinery, paints, leather, rubber, and glass) and indirectly (petroleum, highway, residential housing and service station construction, etc.) involved in the production and the use of the automobile. In its heyday, the automobile industry could claim that one out of six jobs in the United States was tied into its existence, even if they also would deny that theirs is the instance par excellence of a monopolistic and overweening industry, with GM as the virtual symbol of U.S. economic power.[25]

In the 1920s, great pride was taken concerning our "new era." Very few who wrote about it, and least of all economists, paid much attention to its seamy side. But there were some. Veblen, already in 1923, had come down hard on monopolistic dominance and the likelihood of severe depression, and writers such as Sinclair Lewis (in his *Main Street* and

Babbitt, for example) and F. Scott Fitzgerald (in *The Great Gatsby* and *Tender is the Night*) had seen the emptiness of middle-class existence accompanying economic "successes." But the "seamy side" refers to more than moral decay. It was economically where most of the people lived, depending for their jobs on the competitive sector and its "sick industries."[26] "An economic system based on private investment decisions thus tends to produce a *dual economy* both in the structure of industries and in the structure of the labor force," said Professor Bluestone in his statement to the Joint Economic Committee in 1972. This pattern was well underway already in the 1920s; and its development sits at the center of a full explanation for the severity of the depression of the 1930s.[27]

In the midst of the prosperity of the 1920s, trouble had begun to develop even in the dynamic sector. The impulses of the corporate leaders of that sector, and their power to realize their impulses, disguised the trouble and postponed the collapse. It is likely that the collapse was therefore somewhat more severe than it otherwise might have been. The troubles appeared in the two leading industries of the time: automobiles and housing construction.

First, we look at the automobile industry.[28] There are three kinds of car buyers (other than for business fleets): new owners, those replacing an old with a new car, and used-car buyers. By 1924 new car buyers were no longer the focus of the auto industry's attention; given the distribution of income and the small percentage of the population able to pay for a new car, their numbers had inexorably begun to decline. What was needed was stepped-up replacement, and a large, cheaper used-car market to support it. In turn, this led to what has since become the hallmark of consumer goods production and distribution: deliberate product obsolescence, extensive advertising, and consumer finance. GM took the lead in all three; advertising, yearly model changes, trade-ins, and living in constant debt were thereby elevated to what many take to be "the American way of life." These developments also postponed the day when the industry would find itself with chronic excess capacity, as in the 1930s. However, as Soule points out:

> ...installment buying could not obviate the eventual retardation of expansion. There was certain to come a time when all families who would utilize installment loans were loaded up with all the debt they could carry. In the long run the only

possible means of keeping these new industries expanding would have been to augment the cash purchasing power of the consumers through sufficient increases in wages and salaries or through sufficient reduction in retail prices.[29]

There is a vital set of differences between the twenty years or so encompassing the prosperity of the 1920s and its ensuing depression, on the one hand, and the almost half-century since World War II. Although there have been ten recessions in the latter period, they were relatively minor until the mid-1970s and early 1980s, with none showing signs of becoming a major depression. What differentiates the two periods is the substantially changed role of the State. The change is well-symbolized by the following data on government expenditures, which do not, however, inform us on the full meaning of expanded State power (whose details will be discussed in Chapter 8).

Thus: In 1929, the combined expenditures of federal, state, and local governments, as a share of gross national product (GNP),[30] were about 10 percent, in 1975 had tripled to just over 30 percent, and for 1990 had risen still more to 37 percent. Also of great—in some sense, even greater—significance is that in 1929 total government expenditures were about sixty percent of total *private investment* expenditures, whereas in 1975 the situation was reversed, with private investment only forty percent of government expenditures; and in 1990 the percentage had declined to about thirty-six percent. Looked at analytically, the reversal is even more striking: aggregative analysis teaches that the economy's health depends upon three types of domestic expenditure—private investment, consumer, and government, and that consumer expenditures are derived from the incomes generated by the other two. In 1929, private investment expenditures were almost twice those of the government; today government expenditures are almost three times as great as gross private domestic investment.[31]

We have here one mark of just how much the structure of the economy has changed since the 1920s. If the structure, and therefore also the functioning, of the economy has changed so much, the economic theory that presumes to tell us how the economy works must change accordingly; but it has not. Keynesian theory considers private investment as *the* key variable. As was noted in the first chapter, neither the role of government nor of our relationships with the world economy have been incorporated into the theory in any satisfactory manner—nor can that happen, without a theory of the State, plus at least some integration with a dynamic theory of global economic processes. Wherever such a theoretical advance might carry us—and as yet it has too little strength to carry us more than a few steps—it would surely be in the direction of a "new political economy."

Before resuming our analysis of the movement from prosperity into depression, a further comment on the concept of the dual economy is in order. As we have seen, in the 1920s duality had already become pronounced. The monopolistic sector and those benefiting from it moved dynamically through the 1920s; the competitive sector lagged behind, afflicting those dependent upon it. What was relatively insignificant then, as the foregoing discussion shows, was the third sector, the State sector. Governmental expenditures were not only small as a percentage of GNP, they were also dominated by state and local (mostly for education and roads) rather than federal spending: in 1929, of the total of $10.3 billion, $7.8 billion was state and local.

The significance of this is that states and localities must move *with* the direction taken by the economy; the desired role of the State is to move in the opposite direction—to stimulate a weak economy, and restrain an inflating one. States and localities do not have the fiscal/economic power (or, by their constitutions, the right) to operate in the desired way, and in the 1920s no pressures were being placed on the federal government to do so—indeed, not until the mid-1930s, six years after the onset of depression, were even the smallest of appropriate steps undertaken (of which, more below).

Collapse and Depression

As seen by contemporaries, the 1920s was a period not just of boom, but of an expansion that would never cease. Then as now, after a run of prosperous years, memory and thought were replaced by boyish optimism. Irving Fisher, the leading U.S. economist of the time, proclaimed only a few months before the depression began that the economy had solved the problem of the business cycle, and that it was settled on a high plateau of endless prosperity. The well-off believed him; within a year, many of them, especially those involved in the feverish speculation of the late 1920s, were desperate enough to commit suicide from the shock of their losses.[32]

Individual losses for speculators were indeed great, but of more importance was what happened to the economy. The collapse was so substantial as to be virtually incomprehensible to those born after World War II. Between 1929 and 1933, GNP fell from $104 billion to $56 billion; per capita disposable income fell from $678 to $360; the income of farm proprietors fell from $5.7 billion to (in 1932) $1.7 billion; and unemployment rose from 1.5 million to 12.8 million—25 percent of the labor force.[33]

The quantitative disasters suggested by those numbers are impressive enough, and they were staggering to those enduring them; but, quantitatively there was more to the collapse than that and more still when its qualitative impact is taken into account. The depression left no sector of the economy standing upright in the United States or elsewhere. The entire capitalist world underwent a terrible collapse, worst of all in Germany and the United States among the leading countries, and even worse for the already much poorer dependent economies of the Third World. Each nation had its own particular crisis, with differing political and social consequences, but all shared in what was a global catastrophe —which led squarely to the considerably more deadly catastrophe of World War II. The United States was already the largest of the national economies, and, as W. Arthur Lewis said,

> It is clear that the center of the depression was the United States of America, in the sense that most of what happened elsewhere has to be explained in terms of the American contraction, while that contraction is hardly explicable in any but internal terms. The slump was also worse in the United States than anywhere else (with the possible exception of Germany, whose severe contraction was a direct result of American events).[34]

A recession or a depression is a process of economic contraction which, whatever else it means, implies a serious underutilization of the society's productive resources. Unemployment is the most tragic measure of such underutilization, but as such it does not capture the attention of business leaders unless it leads to social turbulence. What is of greater importance to those in business is the implication of shrinking markets for the profitable use of their productive assets. Just how far markets contracted in the 1930s is well-signified by figures for capacity utilization. Industrial producers usually find it desirable, depending upon their technology, to utilize capacity at rates lying between 85 and 95 percent. Already by 1928, the figures had begun to drop below 85 percent; but witness what happened in the 1930s:[35]

1930:	66 percent	1935:	68 percent
1931:	53 percent	1936:	80 percent
1932:	42 percent	1937:	83 percent
1933:	52 percent	1938:	60 percent
1934:	58 percent	1939:	72 percent

When business is bad in a capitalist society, everyone is in economic trouble. Therefore, we may find a close correlation between the foregoing capacity utilization figures and the following (understated) unemployment rates for the corresponding years:[36]

1930:	8.7 percent	1936:	16.9 percent
1931:	15.9 percent	1937:	14.3 percent
1932:	23.6 percent	1938:	19.0 percent
1933:	24.9 percent	1939:	17.2 percent
1934:	21.7 percent	1940:	14.6 percent
1935:	20.1 percent	1941:	9.9 percent

The decline in utilized capacity and the rise in unemployment after 1929 and the persistence of bad news in both respects until the United States entered the war in 1941, was matched by the performance of the economy as reflected in Table 4.2 which, showing the various components of GNP over time, also indicates that the long slump after 1929 had not ended even by 1939, when real GNP (measured in constant dollars) was almost exactly that of 1929.

Table 4.2
Selected Categories of Gross National Product or Expenditure
(in billions of 1982 dollars, for selected years)

Year	Total GNP	Personal Consumption Expenditure	Gross Private Investment	Net Exports	Government Purchases		
					Total	Fed.	S&L*
1929	710	471	139	4.7	94	18	76
1939	717	481	86	6.1	144	54	90
1943	1,243	540	50	–23.0	709	638	71
1944	1,381	557	56	–23.8	791	723	68
1949	1,109	695	169	18.8	226	120	106
1959	1,629	979	270	–18.2	398	222	176
1969	2,423	1,457	410	–34.9	591	296	296
1979	3,192	2,004	575	3.6	609	236	373
1989	4,118	2,657	690	–54.1	798	335	463

*"S&L" signifies state and local purchases. A minus sign for net exports signifies an excess of imports over exports of goods and services, that is, net imports.

Source: Economic Report of the President, pp. 286-89, 381.

In examining Table 4.2, note first the comparative magnitudes of the components—personal consumption, investment, net exports, and government purchases of goods and services; and note especially how their relationships have changed over the past seventy years or so. The one stable relationship in that period is between GNP and consumption, which fluctuates around two-thirds of GNP over time. The most volatile components have been gross private domestic investment and net exports; and that which has risen most as a percentage of GNP since 1929 is government *purchases* which, along with government *transfers* (taken together equaling government *expenditures*) equals about one-third of GNP.[37]

As might be expected, consumption expenditures dropped seriously after 1929 (to $379 billion in 1933). Population increased from about 122 to about 132 million between 1929 and 1939; the fact that total consumption expenditures were about the same in both years of course means that per capita consumption was lower in 1939 than it had been ten years previously—and it was even lower in the intervening years. Gross private domestic investment almost vanished by 1933 ($23 billion in 1982 dollars, $3 billion in 1929 dollars), and *net* investment did vanish (where "net" refers to increasing productive capacity, while "gross" includes support and maintenance of existing capacity).

During that worst year, 1933, utilization rates in industry were at about the halfway mark, and expectations for the future were extremely gloomy, at best.[38] Private investment did not begin to approach its 1929 proportion of gross national product until after the war, during which time, in response to rapidly growing domestic, military, and foreign markets, it rose steadily.

The government columns of Table 4.2 are especially notable, given the general understanding—or misunderstanding—most have about the *spending* impact of the New Deal in the 1930s. Until 1940, federal purchases remained consistently lower than state and local purchases, which themselves remained stable through the decade. Between 1940 and 1941, when President Roosevelt was said to have completed the transition from being "Dr. New Deal" to "Dr. Win-the-War," federal purchases more than doubled, after which they rose to the point where in 1944 total government purchases amounted to about *half* of GNP, with no decrease of consumption in those same years.

A further discussion of the New Deal is now appropriate, for it amounted to a major social change that continued to be built upon up through the 1960s—and which has been "put in reverse" since the late 1970s.

The New Deal and World War II

The period of the New Deal was intensely controversial and, not for the first or the last time in our history, one in which both supporters and opponents of the new policies took positions they would later alter or abandon. To understand the period it is necessary to make at least two distinctions: first, between the subperiods of the New Deal, and second, between the two main activities that gave it its name: deficit spending and institutional reforms.

First, we should distinguish the three phases of the New Deal, or, more properly, of the Roosevelt Administration, for after 1938 there were no further "New Deal" policies. FDR was first elected president in 1932, and died in 1945, at the beginning of his fourth term. (The two-term limit was enacted after the war, and in important part as an anti-FDR move.) The policies of the first New Deal extend from 1933 into 1935; those of the second, or "real" New Deal lasted into 1938. From 1938 on, FDR is generally seen as having become preoccupied with the onrushing world war.

Consistent with his electoral campaign, when he first took office Roosevelt stood for little in the way of institutional change: he was a conservative, not a liberal.[39] But he was, of course, the new president, faced with our most severe depression, already in its fourth and worst year. Essentially and initially, FDR pursued the policies laid down by his predecessor, Herbert Hoover; but the unforgettable spirit of Roosevelt gave them a hopeful sound.

FDR was at one with the Democratic Party of the time, also conservative: in the campaign of 1932, "National Democratic party leaders criticized Hoover not because he had done too little but because he had done too much. [Their] main criticism…was that [Hoover] was a profligate spender. In seeking to defeat progressive measures, Republicans in Congress could count on the votes of a majority of Democrats on almost every roll call."[40]

In his Inaugural Address in 1933, FDR said "We have nothing to fear but fear itself." Unquestionably a good tonic for the fallen spirits of the workers, farmers, businessmen, and speculators of the United States, it was, of course, not enough for a body as weak as the U.S. economy. In that respect, the first few months of the "New Deal" (given its name in that same address) were not materially encouraging: the federal government spent less in FDR's first five months than had been spent by Hoover in the same period of the preceding year.

Like Hoover, Roosevelt faced massive unemployment, and an almost total collapse of agricultural, industrial, and financial markets:[41]

Item: The Dow-Jones dollar average per share of sixty-five stocks (different from its present index method) fell from $125 to $36 between 1929 and 1933.

Item: The average number of bank suspensions in 1928 and 1929 was 566; in 1930, 1931, and 1932 the average number 1,700. (But even 566 should have caused some dampening of the euphoria so common in 1928–1929.)

Item: Merchandise exports fell from $5.2 billion in 1929 to $1.7 billion in 1933.

Item: The value of building construction of all sorts was $4 billion in 1925, $3 billion in 1929, and $500 million in 1933.

Item: Farm prices (at wholesale) fell by more than half, 1929–33.

As noted earlier, at least one-quarter of the labor force was unemployed in 1933.   In this early period of FDR's presidency he emphasized "relief and recovery"; the second New Deal, beginning in 1935, undertook the more controversial "reform."   The distinction is somewhat too sharp, as will be seen; the point remains that the "liberal" reforms of the New Deal await 1935, for reasons now to be discussed.

The major steps taken by Roosevelt in 1933 were taken in the name of emergency and in a context in which no opposition to the new president was feasible.   Roosevelt had what was (for the first time in our history) called "the honeymoon of the first hundred days."   He closed *all* the banks for four days, by proclamation; he embargoed the export of gold; with Congress he created the Agricultural Adjustment Administration (AAA—one of the many "alphabet soup agencies"), which followed the path laid down by Hoover in 1928 in supporting farm prices at the high-level 1910–14 average, and went beyond Hoover in also limiting farm production.   FDR legislated several "emergency relief" acts that provided simple money relief and work relief, and that also continued and expanded Hoover's Reconstruction Finance Corporation (used to bail out financial and utility companies), a forerunner of the sort of financial assistance given to Lockheed in 1971, and Chrysler and Continental of Illinois in subsequent years—leading straight up to the present Resolution Trust Corporation for the savings and loan bailout.[42]

To attempt to bring some order out of the shambles in the securities markets—due in no small part to the assorted malpractices and downright crookedness characterizing the stock and bond markets then as now—the Securities Act of 1933 and the Securities and Exchange Act of 1934 were passed, providing for supervision and regulation of stock and bond markets.   The powers of the Federal Reserve System were expanded, and deposit insurance was enacted to prevent a recurrence of the disastrous "bank runs" of 1933,   when panicky depositors understandably but hopelessly lined up to retrieve money that wasn't there for all (nor is it ever, in good times or bad, in a fractional reserve banking system such as exists in all modern economies). The Home Owners Loan Corporation was created to refinance home mortgages—that, and much more.

These were exciting changes at the time, not because they were radical or even liberal, but because they were governmental, a dramatic switch from the Harding/Coolidge/Hoover years. In nature they were all conservative in two senses: meant to keep the system from falling apart, and designed to benefit its property-owners. Most indicative of the conservative-mindedness of these first years was the National Recovery Administration (NRA), established by the National Industrial Recovery Act (NIRA) of 1933—although "right-wing" is a more accurate term than conservative to describe the NRA if right-wing is meant to suggest a design to disrupt and reverse the process of social change (even that modest one of the years 1900–1930) and to place even more power in the hands of the already powerful.[43]

The NRA, originated and pressed for by the leaders of the largest corporations, was meant deliberately to replace the "free market," the ideological heart of capitalism, the approved and impersonal arbiter of supply and demand, with hundreds of "code authorities." These usually consisted of the leading representatives of the business trade associations in each industry, associations in which policies were normally and naturally established by the most powerful firms. In the guise of establishing codes of "fair competition," the code authorities could set prices, below which no member company (and all had to belong) could sell. That is, the NRA made price competition *illegal* and agreements to restrict production (and other agreements) common. In effect and in fact, the NRA suspended the antitrust laws, which, seldom more than a nuisance, had at least been that.[44]

The NRA was declared unconstitutional in May 1935, on grounds of illegal interference in interstate commerce by a Supreme Court FDR angrily called "nine old men," as he promptly set about to force several justices out to be replaced by men more suited to his politics—a process for which he was roundly and rightly criticized, but which has become the norm. The minimum-price setting goals of the NRA were thereafter taken care of by the spread of "fair trade laws," which endured until they were stricken down by the courts in the 1950s and 1960s—a period of expanding markets. The NIRA also, in its Section 7A, gave labor the right to organize and to bargain collectively, but provided no means of enforcement to make those "rights" meaningful.[45] That would be provided by the Wagner (National Labor Relations) Act of 1935. Some slight economic recovery had taken place by 1935, but there were still 20 percent officially unemployed, and business conditions were still far from buoyant. Social unrest was spreading over the country in all regions, evoking memories of the Populist movement of the 1890s, only more so. After a long period of decline, socialist ideas took on a new life and received increasing attention; and for the first time explicitly fascist groups began to organize successfully. Neither those on the Right or the Left had any national electoral significance in the United States (as they did in other nations at the time), but their growing appeal on local and state levels and in workers' circles began to move to the front of the political stage.

The Communist Party of the United States probably had its greatest influence in this period, mostly through its successful organizational activities in trade unions, its efforts to organize against racism, and because its politics generally supported the second New Deal. The Socialist Party, which had been significantly strong in the years just before and during World War I but which had declined after the early 1920s, revived in the mid-1930s, also constituting a supporting bloc for the New Deal, perhaps making it somewhat more reformist. Father Coughlin's National Union for Social Justice was the leading (by no means the only) fascist-type group, most effective in and around Detroit, serving up a poisonous stew combining racial, religious, and class hatred with economic appeals. Both the demagogically appealing and vicious sides of Populism ran through these movements of Right and Left, as they did in Huey Long's "Share the Wealth" movement in Louisiana, and Upton Sinclair's "End Poverty in California" movement. The turbulence grew and spread as the depression persisted.[46]

Roosevelt was repeatedly and pointedly made aware of all this politically threatening (at least to him) dissatisfaction. The Second New Deal was his response; his overwhelming reelection in 1936 was his reward for moving with the political winds of the time. The years 1933–35 were not entirely illiberal, nor were those of 1935–38 entirely liberal. But the change in emphasis was as obvious at the time as it is in retrospect.

For the aged and infirm, especially, the Social Security Act of 1935 was a beginning, if a weak one. Unlike the social policies of other nations, in the United States, benefits are tied to contributions, rather than coming from a progressive income tax. Thus, in this as in other respects, the rich can continue *not* to pay for the alleviation of the misery of the poor, irrespective of age, infirmity, or whatever; but a crack in the wall of social unconcern had been made. By far the most controversial aspect of the New Deal was the Wagner Act, which not only reaffirmed the right of workers to organize and bargain collectively "with representatives of their own choosing," but spelled out a list of unfair practices by employers and set up a National Labor Relations Board to adjudicate disputes.

This "Magna Carta" of labor was a watershed in U.S. history—for whose application labor has had to fight continuously until World War II, and then again in much of the period after the war—most especially the past decade or so. The major cause of labor disputes and strikes between 1935 and 1941 was union security, presumably *guaranteed* by the Wagner Act, and despite the fact that the Supreme Court upheld its constitutionality in 1938. As with the depression itself, it took a large and long war to bring even a temporary end to the perennial conflict between labor and business. The war's greatly enhanced production in itself created a shortage of labor, quite apart from the 16 million men and women who went into the armed forces, and was historically the most significant force for lowering racial and sexual job barriers. Its cost-plus contracts (then as now) assured large profits for business, and lowered business opposition to a free hand for labor to organize in war plants. And the State got maximum production for the war. The resulting honeymoon for capital and labor didn't last beyond the war.[47]

Secular Stagnation?

So, after a dozen years, the Great Depression finally came to an end, requiring the most massive war in history and its attendant demands upon capital and labor to turn the trick. Why had the depression been so stubborn? The only promising attempt to come to grips with that question during the depression years originated with Professor Alvin Hansen of Harvard, the "translator" of Keynes's *General Theory* into the U.S. setting. Keynes's focus was abstract and short-run, not historical; Hansen applied and broadened the static theory to the historical conditions of the United States, and in doing so he developed what was called a theory of "secular stagnation."

Hansen argued that three main factors contributed to the long-run economic expansion of the United States throughout the nineteenth and early twentieth centuries: (1) rapid and sustained population growth, (2) geographic expansion over the continent, and (3) intermittent waves of technological change (especially the railroad in the nineteenth and the automobile in the twentieth century). These processes in combination had resulted in an interacting and long-term expansion of both investment and consumer expenditures. Thus the normal cyclical contractions of capitalist accumulation were swiftly ended and followed by ever-higher levels of output, employment, and income. However, Hansen argued, both population growth and geographic expansion had diminished by the 1920s, and the burden of continuing expansion thus fell heavily on technological change which, though continuing, could not be expected to rise to the challenge alone.[48]

Nor did the economics profession rise to Hansen's analytical challenge. Narrow though his argument was for what it purported to explain, it was both too broad and too unsettling, and it was casually dismissed. The normal tendency of conventional economists to ignore the bearers of bad news was aided and abetted in this instance by the onset of World War II. In the long expansion that took hold during and after the war, Hansen's stagnation thesis became nothing more than a quaint memory, if that. Those few among the mainstream older economists who had once grappled with the argument saw the sustained expansion as a clear refutation of Hansen's dour analysis. On both logical and subsequent factual grounds, they can be shown to have been mistaken.

Hansen had not maintained that stagnation could not be overcome; rather he had proposed that to *offset* the inability of the "private" economy to create satisfactory levels of production and jobs, the State would have to fill the gap. Since World War II the State has, of course, done just that—in ways that go beyond (and ethically, beneath) anything proposed by Hansen or Keynes. As has been suggested earlier, and will be pursued further below, massive military expenditures, facilitation of U.S. overseas expansion, underwriting of "social consumption and investment" (as in welfare and highway expenditures) and extraordinary debt accumulation, as well as an active monetary and fiscal policy, were all employed by the State to transform stagnation into expansion. The ensuing growth did more than rescue mature capitalism, however; we shall see that its ways and means, the ways and means of global monopoly capitalism, also bred further structural imbalances—and a new and different process: stagflation, a combination of a chronically weak with a chronically inflating economy. The 1980s Reaganomic cure for this problem may well turn out to be worse than the disease, as the old saw puts it. Now we have a slow economy, slow inflation, and a paralyzed government; the 1991–9? recession is the first and only recession of the past half-century in which the State has used none of the fiscal tools available to combat recession which also helps to explain why it lasted longer than any recession of the years since World War II. If anything, what the State has done has aggravated the problem, as will be discussed further below.

Mainstream economists, having successfully ignored Hansen's theoretical challenge, and having failed to integrate the role of the global monopoly capitalist State into their analysis of economic behavior, now put one in mind of doctors who, having administered enormous doses of drugs to suppress the symptoms of disease, go on to diagnose and prescribe for the patient as though he is unaffected by either disease or drugs. Thus, in a widely used text of the 1970s by a Harvard economist, we read:

> As it turned out, the postwar economy of the United States was far more buoyant than the stagnationists had anticipated, and it is reasonable to say that these theorists had been unduly influenced by the Great Depression of the 1930s.[49]

Below we continue with our examination of the changes wrought during and after World War II that allowed such illusions to be sustained, and the processes associated with them up to the present. Because the State was so thoroughly involved in almost all those changes, much of the discussion will be reserved until Chapter 8.

Warfare, Welfare, and Economic Growth

The Roosevelt years were dubbed "New Deal," so it was probably inevitable that succeeding administrations would give or be given their own nicknames: Truman's "Fair Deal" was followed by what Adlai Stevenson called Eisenhower's "Big Deal." Kennedy initiated his "New Frontier," which in the wars and invasions in Indochina and Cuba was found to have more of a geographic than institutional meaning—though there were both in Johnson's "Great Society." Nixon's years came to be called the "Crooked Deal," an epithet that might well have been reserved with even more justice for the Reagan years, although some prefer the

"Raw Deal." Whatever might be said of the labels, the repetition of the term *deal* is not without its own meaning. Since the 1930s, what Kolko calls "political capitalism" has indeed meant a continuous series of deals between various power blocs within the United States and between them and foreign power groups.

The basic techniques of this modern political economy, more than vaguely reminiscent of the mercantilistic era, were rediscovered in the Wilson administration, especially during World War I. The booming optimism of the 1920s caused relaxation among the powerful; but the frightening depression implanted once more the processes of powerbrokering. Despite the antigovernmental rhetoric of both major parties in the past dozen years or so, the big deals not only continue, but multiply. It is a game played at the top by and for those at the top; the rest must wait for something to trickle down: or organize their own latent political power.

Neither the institutional reforms nor the deficit spending of the New Deal had substantial effect before World War II. But the institutional and functional precedents had been established, along with the habits and experience of control and intervention. When accompanied by the largesse of a war economy, the stage was set for the emergence of a new political economy in the postwar years: in the war years, business, labor, and agriculture had all learned just how useful and bountiful an intrusive and generous State could be.[50] The largest impact of the New Deal was not in its own time, but in the 1950s and 1960s. For purposes of this chapter, that impact can be best understood in terms of its effects on the process of economic expansion. (Domestic policies that affected relationships between classes and other social groups at home, and foreign policies that promoted economic expansion will be examined in Chapters 5 and 7.)

The aggregative or macroeconomic behavior of the economy after World War II is nothing less than striking, when compared with any previous period. Since 1946 GNP has never fallen at all in current dollars and fallen substantially less than 1 percent in constant dollars, even in the two deepest recessions (mid-1970s and early 1980s). Even more significant is the record of disposable personal income (the income of persons after federal income taxes and transfers): after 1946, it never fell once, by any measure. This means that aggregate purchasing power has never fallen, though its per capita and distributional patterns have changed, both for better and worse in that period of several decades.

The key to the process of sustained growth is to be found in the record of governmental purchases, and in that category, the most vital component has been purchases geared to the military: perhaps the biggest deal of all was that which made military and social expenditures mutually, even enthusiastically, acceptable by the giant corporations at the top and those nowhere near the top whose purchasing power was sustained by the Cold War. Shortly we will argue that when that arrangement began to crack at its seams, producing stagflation and lowered profits, a rightward turn of the political economy was constructed—placing a good four-fifths of the population at the fringes of or well beyond the charmed circle of comfortable consumption.

Almost half a century has passed since the end of World War II. In that long process, we may distinguish two main periods. The first, in which the economy worked well for at least the top two-thirds of the population, stretched from the close of the war until about 1974; the second, which takes us to the present, has been one of developing and spreading crises, on the one hand, and a steady deterioration of the economic condition of at least the bottom two-thirds of the population (as will be detailed in Chapter 5). We look first at the buoyant period.

Between 1946 and 1975 federal purchases of goods and services totaled almost $2 *trillion*. Of that, 75 percent, or $1.5 *trillion* was for "defense" expenditures; over 10 percent of the remainder was for highway construction. This says nothing about state and local purchases, which rose steadily from about $10 billion in 1946 to $208 billion in 1975.[51] When all this is put together with exports of goods and services, which rose one-and-one-half times in the same years (a process also aided substantially by State policies), it becomes easy to understand why the U.S. economy suffered no major relapse from buoyancy in the two decades following 1945. Naturally, going along with this was a steady increase in private investment and in consumer expenditures with the explosion of suburban housing and commercial developments, and the rapid spread of automobile and consumer durable goods ownership.[52]

The policies that underlay this expansion were initiated at the top levels of business, government, agriculture, and labor; and they were almost universally supported throughout the nation. Consciously or unconsciously, since the depression the people of the United States have allowed and encouraged the creation of a political economy that, whatever else it has meant, was designed never to allow a repetition of severe depression: it is the political economy of global monopoly capitalism. Some of the features of this system have been pointed to earlier, and still others will be examined in later chapters; here it seems appropriate to summarize the main developments within that system that have shaped the accumulation process since World War II.

None of these developments now to be noted was unique to the post–World War II era, but all have been more extensive and potent, their existence more consciously enhanced and coordinated than earlier; nor could any one of these have persisted or had its effects except in mutually supporting combination with all the others. Outstanding among these developments were the following:

1. a vast increase in both the absolute and the relative power of supercorporations—within and between industries, sectors, and nations;

2. an equally striking increase in both the quantitative and the qualitative role of the State at all functional and geographic levels;

3. the strengthening and spread of "consumerism" in the United States and its replication in all the leading and, in yearning, most of the lesser capitalist and noncapitalist economies;

4. the recreation and strengthening of a global capitalist empire, under the leadership and control of the United States;

5. the concomitant growth of a "military-industrial complex";

6. an extraordinary accumulation of debt by persons, businesses, and governments;[53] and

7. required and facilitated by all these changes, the extension and refinement of mass communications techniques for commercial and political exhortation and manipulation: the lubricant of global monopoly capitalism.

Taking hold in the early 1950s and running strongly by the early 1960s, sustained economic expansion became the rule and the continuing expectation in the capitalist world among businesses, consumers, and governments. A major consequence was a state of growing economic euphoria, with an accompanying relaxation of customary prudence —whether the reference is to producers or consumers, borrowers or lenders, companies or governments. Interestingly, *none* of the seven major institutional stimuli just listed could find support in the traditional social philosophy of capitalism—neither monopoly nor its giant State, neither imperialism nor militarism, certainly not consumerism, with its emphasis upon spending and leisure, rather than thrift and work: "Neither a borrower nor a lender be; a penny saved is a penny earned; waste nothing," admonished Benjamin Franklin—words that seemed like wisdom itself as this century began, but that amount to economic treason as it ends.

The strength and the pervasiveness of the economic expansion into the 1970s deflected attention from and altered attitudes about such ways and means, as it also obscured the negative possibilities that might flow from what had become a carefree economic process. In the late 1960s, U.S. economists, echoing their predecessors of the late 1920s, came to believe that "the business cycle has been tamed,"[54] just as a new and monstrous variation of it was being born: stagflation.

Stagflation

In 1973, of the twenty-four nations that comprise the Organization for Economic Cooperation and Development (OECD), accounting for over 90 percent of world capitalist production, over half had double-digit inflation rates; in 1974, only two (West Germany and Switzerland) did not. In the dependent nations of the Third World, annual inflation rates were running anywhere from 35 percent to ten times that. And in the same years, a worldwide recession took hold, bringing rising unemployment and shrinking world trade and production.

As the 1960s drew to a close, inflation in the United States was running at only about 2 percent annually, and unemployment was under 4 percent; between 1979 and 1980, inflation was 10 percent, and unemployment passed the 7 percent level, not descending below that for another seven years (and having risen to almost 10 percent, 1982 and 1983). Since the mid-1970s, unemployment rates in Europe have tended to range just below or just above ten percent—whether the focus is on France or Italy, Britain or Germany.

In short, the free and easy days were a thing of the past. As the foregoing developments began to appear in 1973 and 1974, they were seen as aberrations, an outcome of the dramatic oil price increases imposed by the Organization of Petroleum Exporting Countries (OPEC). Oil, which is required in almost all of contemporary industrial, and increasingly, agricultural production, is the most vital product in world trade. Its price rose by more than five times between December 1973 and a year later; and in the late 1970s rose again: a barrel of oil whose price was about $2 in 1972 cost as much as $35 in 1979. There can be no doubt that the OPEC actions caused economic trouble. But it was trouble that made a bad situation worse: world economic conditions, including those of the United States, had begun to deteriorate *before* the oil crises. (Note above the double-digit rates of inflation for 1973: OPEC changed prices only in the last month of that year.) Something had begun to go wrong earlier; indeed, OPEC's actions were in important part prompted by their need to obtain rising oil prices to meet the inflating prices of the commodities they imported.

What was the nature of the serpent that had entered the paradise of endless economic expansion with price stability? The answer, as always for such matters, is that what had made the system work so well had also produced the conditions for its undoing. Another set of changes was called for, changes in policy, attitudes, ways and means. In the mid-1970s it was by no means clear what the direction and nature of changes in the United States or other OECD nations would be; by the early 1980s the process had become obvious, led by Margaret Thatcher in Britain, and by Ronald Reagan in the United States. In its essence it was a set of policies whose aim was to reassert the dominance of capital in the socioeconomic process by moving to the Right. It involved much, not least of which was a substantial transformation of what has been termed global monopoly capitalism.

For purposes of clarifying this major social turn, it will be useful to focus on "consumerism," one of the central characteristics of the expanding system after World War II. It was emphasized earlier that each of the key characteristics of monopoly capitalism functioned effectively only in dynamic combination with all the others. Consumerism embraces both the exhortation of the mass public to buy, and buy, and buy—"shop 'til you drop"—and its continuing *ability* to do so. That ability depended upon an average level of disposable personal income—purchasing power—that evolved in the 1950s and 1960s whose origin was a strong trade union movement and a liberal social expenditure policy.

The key to the creation and maintenance of consumer purchasing power was, of course, continuous economic expansion; within that process, and also supporting it, was a de facto agreement, the "labor-capital accord," that evolved both in the United States and Europe, requiring the active cooperation of the State, that assured benefits to all parties, and that took the heat out of class conflict: (1) capitalists enjoyed the right to do what they would, when and where and how they chose, with support or at least acquiescence from the trade union movement (in the United States) and the Left (in Europe), up to and including rapid technological change and overseas adventures, while (2) "labor" could expect real incomes to rise in keeping with, or sometimes in excess of, increased productivity, could expect a low ceiling on unemployment and a floor beneath the lowest incomes, along with health, pension, and welfare benefits, and could expect union security and a selective access to political power. As class conflict was suppressed or abandoned, socialist aspirations were dimmed or extinguished. The economic and political bargaining of organized labor and most of the Left, at least tacitly and often explicitly, accepted capitalism as permanent.

In doing all this capital had allowed its costs and its taxes to rise (without interfering with rising profits, for the economy was expanding rapidly), and labor, while its income was rising, had allowed its bargaining and political teeth to be pulled—leaving it weakened and helpless in the face of the sharply conservative political assault that began as the 1970s ended.[55]

But why the conservative assault? At the heart of an explanation, if the main thesis of this book has validity, must sit the conditions surrounding exploitation, expansion, and oligarchic rule. All three had been changed in important ways in the postwar decades; but those changes were themselves subject to change as the "new" system evolved. In the heyday of monopoly capitalism, the process of economic expansion—the most vigorous and widespread in history—had made it possible for exploitation to be lessened in the industrialized countries (while being increased in the neocolonial world), and for political rule to be shared to some degree. When the rate of expansion began to slacken, everything had to change. We must examine elements of the deteriorating process more carefully.

The social relations that were necessary and beneficial for the revival of capitalism after World War II had by the 1970s begun to be the source more of problems than solutions. Stagflation, a difficult problem in itself, was in an important sense a manifestation of a much deeper malaise. In the language of sociology, what had been *functional* for capitalism—the set of arrangements termed monopoly capitalism—had come to be increasingly *dysfunctional*. That is, the global postwar system had in the 1970s begun to decay, where the metaphor is meant to suggest a process that is protracted and confused (and confusing), rather than swift and obvious. The ways and means that had enabled capitalism to regain health and strength began to eat away at its vitality. The developments of that process were numerous and can be noted here only in their most prominent manifestations:

1. The era of the supercorporation and the superState is perforce an era of vast and unavoidable private and public bureaucracy. The costs, wastes, and inefficiencies associated with their existence, functioning, and continuing growth come to compete with the positive effects of the incomes generated in and by them—as, with the passage of time and altered circumstances, the essential functions of bureaucracy serve less for creating new bases of strength and more for seeking to hold on to what has been gained earlier. Or, even costlier, such bureaucracies become virtually functionless, almost pure dead weight. This has been an especially prominent feature in the United States, where, for example, "management" personnel are a substantial multiple of those in, say, Japan.

2. The normal practices within and between businesses, and especially big businesses, and between businesses and politicians and governments—classified as "corruption"—have, with the exfoliation of giant corporate and State entities and of their functions, deepened and spread to new and always more spectacular levels, producing financial and political quagmires for businesses and governments. Some of these instances will occupy our attention in later pages.

3. The creation by North American, European, and Japanese capital of productive capacities for durable consumer and capital goods was, of course, a major stimulus in the long expansion. By the 1970s these facilities had already become seriously duplicative, producing intense competition for critical raw materials and for markets, with consequent whipsaw effects—the competition for raw materials yielding upward pressures on costs, the competition for markets causing downward pressures on sales and profits. The growth of excess productive capacities from the 1970s on—in autos, appliances, metals, chemicals, electronics, etc.—has slowed but not stopped, for even in weak markets, given the normally anarchic organization of world production and investment, capacity has increased.[56] This excess capacity, which always appears within and between capitalist nations, is the central development leading to the deteriorations we have noted, and others—including those connected with financial fragility—still to be discussed.

4. The stupefying increases in the levels of debt and the spread of casual financial practices from the 1960s on—involving individuals, businesses, and governments, nationally and globally—were essential to finance and to sustain the unprecedented expansion. Already in the 1970s alarums were being raised about precarious debt/revenue ratios for all concerned, ratios whose threat to financial stability can only be lessened

through heightened economic expansion. That in turn, however, requires further, indeed accelerated indebtedness—as the 1980s have all too vividly and painfully shown. It cannot be said that there is an identifiable amount or ratio of debt beyond which certain disaster awaits. But it can be said that at the same time that the heedless expansion of debt in a weak economy threatens a financial crack, it also makes any movement toward recession more difficult to reverse. In addition, both problems, financial collapse and recession, are likely to be greater the longer their postponement.[57]

5. The replacement of traditional imperialism by neocolonialism (see Chapter 7) was vital in providing Third World economic stimuli and support for the expansion of the major powers. The military expenditures required, stimulated, and facilitated by that effort, and by the concomitant and associated Cold War with the Soviet Union and China, also did much to sustain economic expansion. However, the great increases in military expenditures since the 1950s—most costly, and most wasteful of all State expenditures—taken together with the several wars they have accompanied, have provided a hard basis for inflation, and not only because they are, economically speaking, almost pure waste. Military expenditures clearly contributed to economic expansion, and placed a floor beneath tendencies toward recession. But their technological tendency over time to provide "more bang for a buck" also came to mean "fewer jobs for the buck." *If* government expenditures were made on school construction or public housing, instead of on missiles, for example, it is calculated by government agencies and others that 30 to 100 percent more jobs would be created per dollar of that expenditure—and space expenditures create fewer than one-third the jobs of straight military expenditures.[58]

6. The swift alteration of rural/urban and occupational patterns, and, within the cities, of the pre–World War II urban political economies, was an integral and profitable ingredient of the postwar accumulation process. Investment and incomes boomed with the expansion of industrial and residential suburbs, shopping malls, and all that attended such developments; more recently attention has had to focus upon the loss of city jobs and tax bases, together with the need for rising expenditures which, as that need rose, faltered and declined—thereby increasing the need still more, for purposes both of decency and social stability. As will be seen in Chapter 6, virtually all major cities face a seemingly intractable set of economic, political, and social problems, intensified greatly by the rising needs and justifiable demands of a variety of urban groups   which,

whether granted or, as is now almost always the case, refused, add to the cities' fiscal problems. Much of the fiscal crisis of the cities is attributable to the decades of high federal expenditures on the military, combined with increasing income deficiencies for the urban population, as economic expansion slackened.

7. Last but by no means least has been the increasingly perverse impact of consumerism. Unquestionably a major effect and cause of the long expansion and of the political stability associated with it, consumerism necessarily depends upon the combination of rising incomes and upon the mass media and its universal audience for purposes of persuasion. The entire population, not just those of middle and high incomes, has been taught to accept, to want, and in an important sense to need, a level and composition of consumer goods that is quite simply beyond the present or potential income capacities of at least half of the population, as data in the next chapter will show.[59]

Consumerism, which means, creates, and depends upon rising expectations throughout the population, has thus raised the popular definition of what is economically necessary to keep the social peace. At the same time, related processes both at home and abroad have lowered the economy's ability to satisfy that definition for one-third to one-half of the population. This is a unique development in capitalist history. It comes now not because of some new inequality in the distribution of income and wealth—although it is now more unequal than at any time since 1947. Severe inequality is a constant in the history of capitalism, essential if capitalism is to exist and accumulation to occur. What is novel today is the social definition of an adequate level and composition of consumption which, as a *necessary* accompaniment of the postwar boom years, has produced in the same process a new and higher level of socially necessary *waste*: in today's advertising, sales promotion, deliberate product obsolescence, and trivial product change, in its retricted use of productive capacities in industry and agriculture, in its vast bureaucracies, in its large-scale use of personnel, technology, and resources dedicated in always higher percentages to profitable but socially uscless and dangerous speculation, and among other areas and most draining of all, in its military expenditures—normally about $300 billion annually for the United States, about $1 trillion in the world[60]—not only pure waste, but large-scale waste and spoliation of presumably scarce raw materials and costly technology (while not forgetting what it means in terms of wasted and distorted human effort, injury, and destruction).

Benjamin Franklin's axiom, "waste not, want not," has been translated, for the needs and in the language of those who preside over contemporary capitalism into "waste, and want not."

Magoo Country

Much of what is now attributed to the Reagan presidency—increased military and decreased social spending, deregulation, etc.—in fact had its beginnings in the relatively benign Carter presidency. Both administrations were responding to the inability of the liberal corporatism of the 1960s any longer to provide for economic growth, "satisfactory" profits, politically acceptable levels of unemployment, or foreign economic challenges. Those challenges from abroad had become substantial and were growing as the 1970s proceeded and they took on worrisome dimensions in the 1980s; we shall note their nature only in passing here, and give them prolonged attention in Chapter 7.

Both administrations were responding to the unprecedented and persisting combination of stagnation and inflation, rising business costs and declining profits, and the associated and increasing difficulties of competing with foreign firms both at home and abroad. At the same time, progress toward environmental protection, occupational safety for workers, medical care for the old and the poor, and consumer protection —all achievements of the immediately preceding years—were met by business demands for deregulation and taxpayer "revolts" from both high and middle income levels.[61]

Although Carter and Reagan both pushed in the same direction, they did so in different degrees and in a different spirit. There was no meanness, indeed a certain reluctance in the conservative directions undertaken by Carter; Reagan relished the cuts in social expenditures, enthused over the vast increases in military expenditures, gushed as he signed deregulation legislation: "All in all," Reagan said, as he signed the Garn-St. Germain bill opening wide the gates for the corruption of the thrift industry, "I think we've hit the jackpot."[62]

The relatively mild changes in governmental policies of the late 1970s, when compared with the drama of the early 1980s, may be explained by the fact that when Carter took office in 1977 it was still possible to see the crisis of the 1970s as aberrational; by 1981, the new president (or, more accurately, those advising and pressuring him) could be sure that the economic path had become dangerously rocky. And then, of course, there were the vast differences in the person of and the personnel surrounding the two presidents—Carter an intelligent and well-informed conservative, deeply religious and sensitive to moral issues, surrounding himself with people at least competent in domestic and foreign affairs.

And Reagan? None of the above: crafty, perhaps, but intelligent doesn't sound right; wildly uninformed; not conservative, but irresponsibly reckless; his religious attitudes evidently political rather than personal; and his ethics those of the small-town poolhall. As for the people surrounding him, suffice it to say that his Attorney General (the guardian of our laws) was ushered out of his office under a cloud of corruption. And as *he* left the White House,

> Happy and loved in his traveling little cone of light, he left behind a country more cynical about politics than at any time in recent memory, a scandalous S & L mess we shall be paying for into the next century, a national debt that cripples our ability to help others or ourselves. But Mr. Magoo never has to see the devastation he leaves in his wake.[63]

In Chapter 3 we briefly examined how the structure of business organization became more concentrated and perilous in the 1980s; in what follows the intent is to discuss the various dimensions of the accumulation process from 1980 to the present. The last section of this chapter will explore the nature and problems of the vital and fragile financial sector—hanging over the cliff of disasters even beyond those of the S&L debacle, brought to us through that "jackpot" achieved in 1982, only one of many such triumphs of recklessness and greed.

In Carter's last year in office, 1980, unemployment was running at about 7 percent, and the annual inflation rate was 10 percent—with, for one month, a rise to 18 percent. The recession of 1980 did not last out the year. When Reagan took office in 1981, it is now generally recognized that through a highly restrictive monetary policy a recession was deliberately caused—with the advice and counsel principally of Paul Volcker, Carter's appointed head of the Federal Reserve.[64] Unemployment rose to just under 10 percent in 1982 and 1983, as both labor's strength and the inflation rate fell, the latter to 6 and then 3 percent in the same years. It was then that Reagan broke the air controllers' strike, in a manner reminiscent of the 1920s.

From 1983 until the summer of 1990 the economy expanded: the longest expansion in U.S. economic history, the Reagan supporters have announced—neither for the first nor the last time, inaccurately: that honor belonged to the expansion that began under Kennedy, strengthened under Johnson, and ended in Nixon's first year. And there was a major difference between those two very long expansions: the earlier one increased the production, the productivity, and the economic well-being of a clear majority of the population, with an aggregated deficit of only $64 billion for the eight years of the Kennedy and Johnson administrations, but of $1,820 billion (that is, almost $2 trillion) for the two administrations of Reagan. In his eight years the U.S. economy wasted most of that spending on the military. When Reagan took office, the United States was the world's largest creditor; when he left it, we were the largest international debtor in world history—to say nothing of our national debt. All this while (and partially because) a wrecking crew was at work in both the industrial and the financial sectors.[65]

Reagan came into office promising to balance the budget (as he had promised when campaigning for governor of California), and left having been the largest and most profligate spender in the nation's (or California's) history—while still damning the big spenders and calling for a balanced budget. Mr. Magoo.

There is more to be said about the Reagan years, and some of it will be in our discussion of the State in Chapter 8. Here it seems useful to point to a terrible irony of the 1980s, one that continues in the 1990s. The swing toward a hard conservatism in the past fifteen years or so has had a social (anti-abortion, etc.) as well as an economic dimension. Sitting at the center of its economic position has been a wholesale condemnation of governmental intervention in the economy—and most publicly and effectively, against government taxing and spending. As we have seen, spending rose in the Reagan years as never before in our history: his regime accumulated more debt than in all of preceding U.S. history, rising from one to over three trillion dollars. And tax collections did not go down, but up. (Again, repeating California history.)

What should be, but evidently is not clear to the anti-government enthusiasts who supported the Reagan (and now Bush) policies, is that it is not government or taxing and spending as such that is the problem. Rather it is *who controls* the government, the *incidence* of taxation (who pays, and in what proportions), and the direction or *composition* of government (who benefits).[66] Reagan, who came into the political spotlight as an "anti-Keynesian," surrounding himself with monetarist (essentially laissez-faire) economists, has been the biggest "Keynesian" of all time; the economic expansion of his administrations was the most deficit-engineered ever. But his was "military Keynesianism."[67] It provided jobs and profits, but did so as what economists call the infrastructure, the basis of the economy, was allowed to deteriorate, perhaps beyond the danger point.[68] And, of course, as the economic conditions of the bottom half of our population fell to a level that may be described as scandalous, even obscene—not just because this is a very rich country, but because its government has spent so much on weapons of destruction while letting its people languish or suffer. As for taxes, to be sure income taxes were reduced, but the total taxes of those in the bottom 80 percent of the population rose (largely because social security taxes went up), while those at the top declined (of which more in the next chapter).

So, both taxes and spending have risen in this new era, and continue to do so. But the composition of spending benefits those already well-off, and the incidence of taxation does the same—"as wealth accumulates and men decay." But the Reagan story doesn't end there; we must also look at how the spirit and the practices of those years facilitated the "greed and glitz" that became the hallmark of the 1980s.

House of Cards

The story now to be told is both sordid and frightening; maximum brevity is merciful, and will be attempted. It is well to begin with the reminder that the spirit meant to provide energy to the vital capitalist expansion process, though of course selfish in its origin, is not supposed to become its perversion, greed. Capitalists are supposed to be rational in their attempts to "accumulate, accumulate!" And although those powerful in business have always been able to design many of the laws within which they function, they are also supposed to function within those laws, once established. The 1920s showed that capitalists do not always live by the rules of their own game; the 1980s showed something more: when the rules are changed or bent to suit relatively excessive behavior, some significant number of people—from business and government, from the world of crime, and just plain greedy individuals—will violate even those loose rules, run wild, and place the entire system in jeopardy. It has been said that civilization is a thin veneer; the sleazy ethics and deregulative solvents of the Reagan administration, combined with the vulnerable economic conditions of the time, steadily dissolved that veneer.

The trail that leads to the financial jungle of the 1980s has its beginning in the excess capacity that began to emerge in the late 1960s and that became pervasive in the 1970s. Lots of investible funds rolling around loose from the heady years of expansion, but why put them into the expansion or improvement of more productive capacity? Why not put them into takeovers (and borrow lots as well to finish the job), both profitable and helpful and useful against excess capacity? Or, for those in the top 1 to 5 percent, well, there is a certain limit to more consumption; three Ferraris, five vacation homes, ten fur coats?[69]

The 1970s became a time in which banks searched for borrowers and rich individuals searched for places to put their surplus cash. The banks found, often created, many borrowers in the Third World, those same borrowers who, in 1982, began the continuing process of default on their hundreds of billions of dollars of loans. Bankers, once the most prudent of people, taught homeowners to borrow on their still unpaid-for homes, for trips, boats, etc., as richer individuals sought maximum returns from money-market funds, CDs, options, and the like. And giant corporations, especially the multinationals, found it both possible and necessary to become speculators in foreign exchange. The list of those who began to live as though in a gambling casino, instead of a capitalist economy, lengthened as the 1960s became the 1970s, and came to dominate the main tendencies of U.S. capitalism. Reagan's metaphor of "jackpot," doubtless unconsciously used, was right on the button.

The savings and loan disaster is the best-known of the many financial bombs either ticking away or already exploded. Given that it is likely to cost the taxpayer at least $500 billion—some say, not at all carelessly, over $1 trillion, before all the bills (that is, our taxes for them) are paid—and given that the S&L explosion (or one of them) has already happened, that is understandable. But other major elements of the financial system—commercial banks, insurance companies, pension funds, and investment companies—are already in deep and growing trouble, and largely for the same kinds of reasons—some combination of greed, mismanagement, and a government that has looked the other way or, not at all rarely, encouraged malpractice.

By now there have been many books written on these developments, and those interested are threatened with drowning in them. Because of the general issue's importance, it is important to gain a general understanding of it before plunging in. For that purpose I commend the reader's attention to the efficient and powerful Sherrill essay noted in Chapter 3,[70] where, in addition to providing a thorough survey of the S&L road to hell, he shows that, as is true of so much else that has been discussed already in this book, what happens in one area of the economy is virtually always dynamically connected with others.

The failure of about one-third (so far) of S&Ls has very much to do with those (including President Bush's son) who were allowed to own and direct them in the 1980s, always greedy, usually sharpies, often criminals. But the economic environment in which they were operating made their frauds and mismanagement both compelling and possible. These "thrifts" (now a very quaint word) and their crimes and misdemeanors overlapped with the frequent crimes and misdemeanors associated with junk bonds, the connected LBO (leveraged buyout) mania and the tax laws encouraging them,[71] and, of course, with the felonies of high-powered financiers such as Michael Milken and Ivan Boesky. Fraudulent and reckless behavior, allowed and encouraged by the government, became easy and immensely profitable in the entire financial sector.

Sherrill points to the "pirates of a fraudulent system of communism forced to scuttle their own ship, and...the pirates of a fraudulent system of capitalism beginning to do the same...,[a] system just as bogus and defeated in its own way, offering neither the risks of true capitalism nor the safeguards of true democracy"—a condemnation justified by the realities. Deeply involved and participating in the corruption and failure of the S&Ls were various levels of government—the presidency, the bank regulators, the Congress, the CIA and FBI, for example—and a generous representation from the highest levels of business and finance. The truths of how our financial sector has become so rickety, and so riddled with criminality, are quite simply shocking, even.to one who has long been a critic of the system. It is a system that has gone on a drunken spree, but those who will have the long hangover, the ordinary citizen and taxpayer, were never invited to the party. It helps not at all to know that what has taken place in the United States, in many respects, also does so elsewhere. One can barely pick up a newspaper in the 1990s without reading of deep financial scandals in Japan, Italy, Britain, Germany, France, and other countries, or fraudulence such as that of the BCCI that ties together all these and many other countries, their banks, and their governmental agencies.[72]

The fragility of the financial system of the United States is made all the more ominous when we note some connected facts: the U.S. economy has become increasingly "financialized" in its structure and functioning; the United States is integrally and inextricably tied into a world economy, all of whose participants are just as interdependent; and the U.S. financial system, fragile enough in itself, is all the more so because financial fragility marks the entire world—especially and most ominously, Japan, the supposed Gibraltar of contemporary capitalism. We shall examine this in greater detail in Chapter 7.

And Now, the Bad News

In October 1987 the world thought the financial crack had arrived. When the smoke cleared and almost everything was still standing, optimism took hold once more, showing itself in financial and real activity: 1987 was not 1929. Many thought "not just yet"; most thought "we've got it licked." And there was some truth in both positions. What was done in 1987 to contain the financial collapse would not have been seen as necessary until too late in 1929, and then it *could not* have been done. The crash of 1929 had shown what is possible, and more important, the reforms of the 1930s (so much hated by the very people at the top protected by them), not least those giving more powers to the Federal Reserve System, enabled the liquidity of the financial system to be maintained.[73]

As Reagan left office, the view had begun to grow once more that perhaps, just perhaps, the expansion would be endless—despite the hell of foreign competition and the high water of debt, among other "disturbing causes." Recession began to take hold in midsummer of 1990. It was at first disbelieved—and, by the Bush administration, denied; then it was explained as a consequence of the Gulf war; and when that war ended, each month was said to be its last; and so it has gone and goes as 1992 draws to an end. Herbert Hoover came to be mocked for his repeated announcement that "prosperity is just around the corner." For us now living, it is recovery that is repeatedly "just around the corner." President Bush, in a lapse, in fact used those very words in the spring of 1991. Perhaps it is? We cannot know, of course; but we can try to identify the principal elements of the recession and the environment in which it occurs, and then make a guess. One reason for thinking this will be a prolonged recession (at the least) is a striking one: this is the first and only recession since the 1930s when the State has done nothing—or worse—to pull the economy out of it. "Or worse" points to the fact that not only has *no* spending or tax reduction taken place by the federal government for such purposes, but that the states and localities are in a process of spending reduction and tax increase, with, at the same time, many thousands being laid off. The only step urged and achieved by Bush has been reduction in interest rates. There have been some modest reductions.

The latter have been aimed at increasing business and consumer borrowing and, therefore, spending. Business, as Keynes taught long ago, invests because it expects to make profits from expanded capacity. They are not doing so now. Consumers spend because they need things, can afford them, and/or can borrow for them. Consumers have for the past decade or so been seen as "the engine of economic expansion," a position with little analytical support—except when the expansion is already going on. They need more and better-paying jobs and are getting neither as they "hunker down." And the Fed's lowered interest rates have not touched the rate on plastic—always near 19 percent—and are not expected to.

If there is to be renewed expansion, the engine has to be either that of the State or business investment. The State is paralyzed by its ideology and by its unwillingness and fear of adding to the Mt. Everest of debt. Perhaps the stimuli will come from the world economy, buying more of our exports, adding to our jobs, giving consumers more income and ability to borrow? But Britain, and subsequently all the other English speaking countries, preceded us into recession and stay there with us, including Canada, our biggest customer. Japan, thought to be invulnerable to recession in 1991, in fact had a negative GNP for the last quarter of that year, as it struggled with massive drops in real estate prices and a fall of over three-fifths of the value of its stock prices—a process that continued through 1992—with consequences for the rest of the world, and especially the United States that are cause for great concern. France, Italy, the Low Countries and Scandinavia, plus Spain, Portugal, and Greece are all in slack or worse times. Germany nervously involved in rearranging itself economically as well as politically to accommodate the former GDR, had negative GNP growth for the last three quarters of 1991. (See Chapter 7.)

And then there is the problem of financial fragility, which shows no signs of going away. Indeed, as warned earlier, the financial problem is itself worsened by recession,[74] and threatens to add collapse to recession, as it also makes it more difficult to turn a recession around. To make matters worse, the normal stimuli from the White House that accompany an election campaign did not occur in 1992. So, the economy could recover, though from what source(s) it is hard to see; or it could collapse, as we shall see later, from international financial weakness combined with global recession. One early warning signal is that Japan, counted upon as a source of capital in the past ten years or more, in 1991 began to have a net *inflow* of capital.

Lord of the Flies

The deterioration and the developments of the past two decades or so have been rooted in the "new capitalism" of the post–World War II era, and the financial recklessness we have noted may be seen as the predictable latest stage of that system. We argued earlier in this chapter that the major institutional developments within which all this has functioned could not have found support in the traditional social philosophy of nineteenth century, competitive capitalism. That social philosophy had to be displaced, and it was, but by what? Whatever the defects and associated cruelties of what may be called the ideology of capitalism, it was at least the work of political, social, and economic thinkers and theorists. By what social philosophy, devised by which Madison Avenue and Wall Street philosophers, do the rulers and the ruled of contemporary U.S. capitalist society live? It is simple, and can be summed up simply in three words: "More!—Why not?" It is the social philosophy of greedy children, of a decadent society.

That society came into being in part by accident, in part by design, guided neither least nor most by the effort to forestall forever the evil of another 1930s depression. But its achievements now appear as increasingly problematic, and are associated with an accumulation of socioeconomic problems with the dimensions of a social crisis. That not many see it at all this way is due in part to the alteration over time of our social standards: in seeking to master the art of quantitative gain, we have not only engendered qualitative deterioration, we seem also to have lost the ability to distinguish between "good" and "bad," so long as there is "More." One indication of that is the process by which, in the midst of the highest accumulation of commodities in history, our attitudes toward those who live on or over the bare edge of survival become increasingly hostile. We come to blame, to fear, finally to hate the victim.

There are, of course, other and better ways to approach such matters; among them is an understanding of the facts of the distribution of income, wealth, and power, the subject of Chapter 5. There it will be useful from time to time, in noting the immense differences between those at the top and those at the bottom of those distributions, to recall that after 1973, as the levels and the distribution of real income worsened significantly for the bottom four-fifths of our population, the changes were accompanied by a process of high-handedness and cold-heartedness from a State that was at the same time distributing not just meat and potatoes, but also champagne and caviar to those at the top.

Reading Suggestions

The more or less technical matters discussed above can be better understood and appreciated if also approached through "lighter" works, both fictional and nonfictional. Such works help us to taste both the bitter and the sweet flavors of the interwar period. Here is a very short listing of such books.

A substantial percentage of people today are still responding to the trauma of the years between the two world wars, due either to their own or their parents' experience. They were years of middle-class euphoria in the 1920s and of despair in the 1930s; surprisingly to many, they were bitter years for the militarists, for antimilitarism was dominant (a residue from World War I). F. L. Allen, *Only Yesterday** (New York: Harper, 1931) is a classic and enjoyable history of the 1920s. Studs Terkel, whose book *Working* was noted earlier, also put together a remarkable and most readable book that records the voices of people of all types and ages who lived through the depression, and it is a fine, often moving, sometimes funny, way to capture the feel of the period: *Hard Times** (New York: Pocket Books, 1970).

Among the works of fiction, all easily available, especially informative is the trilogy of John Dos Passos *USA: (The 42nd Parallel, 1919, The Big Money)*. For the 1920s anything of Sinclair Lewis and of F. Scott Fitzgerald. William Faulkner's many novels beautifully illuminate life in the Mississippi Delta in the decades before World War II, as, for Los Angeles, does *Oil!* by Upton Sinclair. John Steinbeck's *Grapes of Wrath*, of course, but also his *In Dubious Battle*, a penetrating story based on a farm workers' struggle in the Salinas Valley of California. There are many books by and about African-Americans, of course. Two

I have found most valuable are Ralph Ellison, *Invisible Man*, and Richard Wright, *Native Son*. Because the past few decades are less likely to need recalling for most readers, I mention only Clancy Sigal, *Going Away*, which deals with the years 1930–60, and then with a big and wild jump into the 1980s, Tom Wolfe's *Bonfire of the Vanities*, which explores the greed, the glitz, and the social deterioration of the very recent past. Finally, for fiction, see the short stories collected in Harvey Swados, ed., *The American Writer and the Great Depression** (Indianapolis: Bobbs-Merrill, 1966).

Back to dryer stuff. For those who wish to look into the business cycle analyses of an earlier time, see Robert A. Gordon and Lawrence Klein, eds., *Readings in Business Cycles* (Homewood, Ill.: Irwin, 1965) and Wesley C. Mitchell, *Business Cycles and Their Causes** (Berkeley: Univ. of California Press, 1963; written in 1941). To understand the Keynesian theory that is so relevant to the past half-century, Dillard's book, cited earlier, is an apt summary. Useful controversies coming from right, middle, and left have been brought together in Robert Lekachman, ed., *Keynes and the Classics** (Boston: D.C. Heath, 1964), and his *National Income and the Public Welfare** (New York: Random House, 1972) is a clear and succinct statement of income and employment analysis. For a valuable and broad survey of theoretical positions, see Howard J. Sherman and G.R. Evans, *Macroeconomics. Keynesian, Monetarist, and Marxist Views* (New York: Harper & Row, 1984). See also Robert D. Cherry, et al., *The Imperiled Economy, Book I: Macroeconomics from a Left Perspective** (New York: Union for Radical Political Economics, 1987). *Challenge: The Magazine of Economic Affairs*, is continually informative; its July/August 1991 (Vol. 34, No.4) issue is especially so. Two essays pertinent to the current recession are Wallace C. Peterson, "The Silent Depression," and David A. Levy, "A Contained Depression."

The depression of the 1930s is treated exhaustively in terms of both its economics and politics in Broadus Mitchell's *Depression Decade*, which we have cited earlier. Charles P. Kindleberger's *The World Depression 1929–1939** (Berkeley: Univ. of California Press, 1973) is a careful and readable analysis of the global disaster. For a mainstream view of the global stagflation of our time, see Michael Bruno and J.D. Sachs, *Economics of Worldwide Stagflation* (Cambridge, Mass.: Harvard Univ. Press, 1987). Articles of Hyman Minsky have been noted earlier. They and others have been put together in his *Can "It" Happen Again?*

Essays on Instability and Finance (Armonk, N.Y.: M.E. Sharpe, 1982) and *Stabilizing an Unstable Economy* (New Haven: Yale University Press, 1986).

Turning to the post–World War II era, Harold G. Vatter's *The U.S. Economy in the 1950s* (New York: Norton, 1963) is a useful introduction, and the book by Donald L. Kemmerer, *The U.S. Economy 1940–1960*, is also helpful. A strong framework putting together the politics with the economics of the postwar world is found in Chapters 7 through 11 of Kolko's *Main Currents...*, noted earlier. James O'Connor's *Fiscal Crisis of the State*, noted earlier, was an early warning signal for both the economic and the political developments of the late 1970s and following years, and his *Accumulation Crisis* a penetrating analysis of the manner in which the individualism of capitalist ideology has become deformed and contradictory in contemporary capitalism. Howard Sherman's *Stagflation** (New York: Harper & Row, 1977) was the first (and still useful) book to explain the emergence of that phenomenon.

James Cypher has been mentioned more than once, as an authoritative voice on military expenditures. His substantial and penetrating essay, "Monetarism, Militarism, and Markets: Reagan's Response to the Structural Crisis," *MERIP Reports* 14, no. 9, Nov.–Dec. 1984, brings together the main dimensions of that administration's policies. Over the past fifteen years or so, the editors of the *Monthly Review*, Harry Magdoff and Paul M. Sweezy, have written and subsequently combined into books numerous essays that shed light on the developments of the 1970s and 1980s: *The End of Prosperity** (1977), *The Dynamics of U.S. Capitalism** (1979, *The Deepening Crisis of U.S. Capitalism** (1980), *Stagnation and the Financial Explosion** (1987), and *The Irreversible Crisis** (1988), all published by Monthly Review Press, New York.

In Chapter 8 we shall have reason to note many books dealing with the State policies of the Reagan years, but here a few are relevant to mention, as they deal with the wastefulness and counterproductiveness of those policies. See Edward N. Wolff, *Growth, Accumulation, and Unproductive Activity* (New York: Cambridge University Press, 1987), Edward Nell, *Prosperity and Public Spending* (Boston: Unwin Hyman, 1988), and, more narrowly, Seymour Melman, *Profits without Production* (New York: Knopf, 1983)

For two collections of essays in U.S. history, treating of developments throughout the century, but especially useful on the 1930s and since, see R. Radosh and Murray Rothbard, eds., *A New History of Leviathan** (New York: Dutton, 1972), and Barton J. Bernstein, ed., *Towards a New Past: Dissenting Essays in American History** (New York: Vintage, 1972).

Notes

1. Robert Creeley, "I Know A Man," from *For Love*, reprinted by permission of Charles Scribner's Sons. Copyright © 1962 by Robert Creeley.
2. A comprehensive and very useful study of this area of economics, in its historical development and its contributions up to about 1960, is Robert Aaron Gordon, *Business Fluctuations,** 2nd ed. (New York: Harper & Row, 1961). Gordon provides a thorough (and rare) integration of Keynesian analysis with historical and then current data; chapters 12 and 13 examine "the variety of business-cycle theories." Gordon's more recent *Economic Instability and Growth: The American Record** (New York: Harper & Row, 1974) examines the data from 1919 to 1970, and is the historical excerpt from and extension of the earlier book.
3. Joseph A. Schumpeter, *Business Cycles: A Theoretical, Historical, and Statistical Analysis of the Capitalist Process, two vols.* (New York: McGraw-Hill, 1939), vol. I, p. v. This massive (and invaluable) work ranges throughout the capitalist world in terms of its title. Schumpeter was given the mantle of greatness by his contemporaries, but his approach and his ideas were given short shrift by them. (Gordon, just cited, is an exception.) Schumpeter was an Austrian, and Austria's finance minister in 1919. From 1932 until his death in 1950, he taught at Harvard, having left Austria in 1925.

Along with Britain, Austria was the principal source of neoclassical economic theory; there it tended strongly to emphasize the ideological, especially the antisocialist aims always present in that body of thought. Like Keynes, Schumpeter was a "man of the world," and an essayist whose mind roamed far beyond the usually narrow confines of the discipline. See the recent and admirable collection of his essays, *Joseph A. Schumpeter: The Economics and Sociology of Capitalism*, edited by Richard Swedberg (Princeton, N.J.: Princeton University Press, 1991). See also Schumpeter's *Capitalism, Socialism, and Democracy*, cited earlier. It is pleasant to note that Schumpeter thought his best student at Harvard was Paul M. Sweezy, subsequently the leading Marxian thinker in the United States; and Sweezy has returned the compliment regarding Schumpeter as his professor. Perhaps there is hope for our species, after all.

4. Thorstein Veblen, *The Vested Interests and the Common Man** (New York: Huebsch, 1919; Viking, 1946), pp. 85–86.

5. *Absentee Ownership*, p. 251.

6. *Theory of Business Enterprise*, p. 250.

7. The five trillion dollars just noted sounds like a lot, as indeed it is; but it is unquestionably a substantial understatement of the facts. There are two matters requiring comment on this area of government expenditures. First, they are called "defense" rather than "military" (or "war") expenditures, just as what was called the Department of War since the inception of the United States came to be called the Department of Defense, in 1947. What are added up as defense expenditures excludes several large expenditures on past, present, and future wars. For example, looking at federal expenditures for 1992, interest on the public debt was $292 billion. A very conservative estimate of how much of that interest was for debt accumulated for military purposes past and present would be $150 billion. And there are payments for veterans and their facilities, $29 billion; and foreign military aid, about $9 billion; and the military part of the NASA budget, another $9 billion (again, an understatement, for that is only about two-thirds); and another $2 billion plus for the Department of Energy, almost all of whose expenditures have to do with nuclear weapons technology. Taking all these and other conservatively estimated expenditures as reasonably qualifying as military expenditures raises the stated $299.3 billion (one hears of how much trouble is taken to keep the figure *just* under $300 billion) by a good 50 percent. (The data are from the U.S. Treasury press release, August 24, 1992, and *Economic Report of the President, 1991*.) Second, we are told that our "defense" expenditures are less than 10 percent of GNP and only 26 percent of the federal budget. *That* understatement is due to a marvelous trick pulled off by LBJ during the Vietnam war when not only did he lie to his own budget director about its costs, 1966–67 (understating by $10 billion), but he had social security contributions and expenditures, which are paid for and disbursed entirely *outside* the federal budget, placed for accounting purposes *in* the budget—where they remain. Thus, if total government expenditures are $1 trillion, and military expenditures are $300 billion, the latter are 30 percent, and that is including, let us say, $300 billion of social security "expenditures" in the $1 trillion. Take out

the latter $300 billion, and it was never there before LBJ and shouldn't be there now, and, the $300 billion of military expenditures become more than 40 percent. And if one adds to the $300 billion of official military expenditures the others noted above, the federal budget has more than half going to the military. Now you see it, now you don't. As we'll see later, to add to the abracadabra, the social security trust fund, whose rising yearly surplus now exceeds $50 billion, is borrowed from by the government, is classified as "off budget" (now you see it, now you don't), and to that extent the offical annual deficit is understated. In other words, the announced roughly $290 billion deficit for the fiscal year ending September 1991 was in fact closer to $350 billion. The predicted deficit for fiscal 1992, $350 billion, would be over $400 billion with these adjustments.

8. It could make one feel sorry for the capitalist. The first passage is from *Capital*, vol. I, p. 592, and the second from p. 595.

9. "Above all, Veblen was, and remains alone in assigning a decisive role in the development of capitalism to the reciprocating interaction of business principles and national politics. Others have described the economic impact of war, the psychological effects of militarism, the cultural incidence of nationalism; and none can deny that these forces have become increasingly important, if not actually dominant, in the world of the twentieth century. Yet only Veblen has built all these elements into a reasoned and coherent theory." Paul M. Sweezy, "Veblen on American Capitalism," in Douglas F. Dowd, ed., *Thorstein Veblen: A Critical Reappraisal* (Ithaca: Cornell University Press, 1958), p. 195.

10. Gordon, *Business Fluctuations*, Chapters 1 and 8, provides an excellent explanation of instability and its causes. The role of financial speculation on a global scale has expanded enormously in the past two decades or so, as the world economy has become ever more integrated and more vital, and as electronic communications and calculations have surpassed imagination. It is now generally understood that, conservatively estimated, at least $150 billion worth of global financial transactions take place every *day*, and that about 90 percent of that is for speculative purposes, only 10 percent for trade and investment. See Susan Strange, *Casino Capitalism* (Oxford: Basil Blackwell, 1986) for a useful introduction and analysis.

11. Gabriel Kolko, *Main Currents in American History*, cited earlier, p. 13.

12. Intensive examination of the growing and changing role of the State is postponed until Chapter 8. Those wishing to explore these matters now, however, may do so in Faulkner, *Decline of Laissez-Faire*, and in two major revisions of U.S. history centering upon these developments: Gabriel Kolko, *The Triumph of Conservatism: A Reinterpretation of American History, 1900-1916** (New York: Quadrangle, 1867), and James Weinstein, *The Corporate Ideal in the Liberal State: 1900-1918** (Boston: Beacon Press, 1968). Weinstein discusses, among other matters, the substantial opposition of small business to State intervention—a pattern that continues.

13. For a thorough and entertaining historical examination and analysis of such matters, see C.P. Kindleberger, *Manias, Panics, and Crashes* (New York: Basic Books, 1978).

14. Serious industrial unemployment was first noted for the years 1895–97, when industrialism may be said finally to have taken hold. But after two or three years, that unemployment was replaced by more and often better jobs, as the economy muscled out and sped up. By contrast, the depression and unemployment that began in 1929 continued past the outbreak of World War II. In 1939, unemployment was over 17 percent, and still at 10 percent in 1941.

15. Dudley Dillard, *Economic Development of the North Atlantic Community* (Englewood Cliffs, N.J.: Prentice-Hall, 1967), is a useful introduction to the development of European–U.S. economic processes and relationships. As for the troubles of the 1920s in Europe, it is significant that Britain, still seeing itself as the world's economic giant, suffered from sustained high unemployment and general business weakness throughout the entire decade. That the arrogance of power fades belatedly, if at all, is evidenced by the fact that one of Britain's respected economic historians in what was then a widely used textbook, in 1926 portrayed the United States as largely an agricultural society, in comparison with Britain. Given Japan's current importance, readers may wonder about its role in the 1920s. Japan, like the United States, benefited greatly from World War I (though for different reasons), and its industrial economy was essentially constructed by the 1920s. But it had very limited access to the world economy before 1914 and the breakdown of world trade after the war worsened matters. Moreover, Japan lacked both a domestic consumer market and sufficient resources for its industries. By the mid-1920s its economy was already showing signs of difficulty and stagnation. The problems were resolved by the

militarization of Japanese foreign policy, its economy, and its politics: it became fascist. See Brady, Business as a System of Power, op. cit., Chapter III.

16. Faulkner, *The Decline of Laissez-Faire*, pp. 31–32. This book is rich in information concerning all aspects of U.S. economic and political developments in the twenty years before 1917. What is striking, however, is that the author's devastating recital of facts—devastating to a relaxed view of U.S. capitalism—is accompanied by an essentially complacent analysis. Kolko, in *The Triumph of Conservatism*, working with the same facts, takes them to quite different conclusions. Where Faulkner sees the upshot of what he has reported to be a revival of "the reform movement" (p. 382), Kolko concludes his book with a chapter entitled "The Lost Democracy."

17. The authors go on to make clear that they are not saying the depression of the 1930s would have taken place after 1910, for "by 1915, the automobile era was already well under way, and the great shake-up in living patterns and consumption habits which it brought with it would probably have created a boom...." *Monopoly Capital*, p. 234. Their analysis concerning 1907–1915 begins on p. 228. Their demurrer about "by 1915," may be more positive than justified. As argued in the text that follows immediately, the "new era" of the 1920s owed very much indeed to direct and indirect economic consequences of the war. In the late 1930s, Harvard economist Alvin Hansen developed his theory of stagnation, which will be discussed later in this chapter.

18. See George Soule, *Prosperity Decade*, Chapters I–III for the detailed story.

19. The "mass basis" referred to is defined economically; that is, in terms not of the "masses" having access to the relevant products, but of a sufficient number of buyers to justify mass production. A fair estimate is that not more than a third of the people of the United States were able, in the 1920s, to buy throughout the range of consumer durables. (As the United States had a population over 120 million, the largest of the industrial countries, by far, this constituted a mass market.) There were refrigerators and gas and electric stoves in those years, for example, but for a good two-thirds of the population, the icebox and the wood-burning or coal stove had to serve; and for that large majority, an automobile was at best something to dream about. See George Soule, ibid., especially Chapter XIII.

20. In *The Higher Learning in America: A Memorandum on the*

*Conduct of Universities by Businessmen** (New York: B. W. Huebsch, 1918; Sagamore Press, 1957), pp. 135–136. This quotation is from the Sagamore edition. Originally written in 1908, it was not published for a decade. Veblen identified the basic elements of what he saw as university corruption, some of which were among the matters rebelled against in the student movements of the 1960s. Veblen was not as surprised as many are still that in a business society the universities (and much else) would live under business criteria. His own career in the universities was erratic and limited.

21. It was not until the 1930s that systematic attempts to gather and analyze aggregative data (concerning jobs, investment, savings, etc.) were institutionalized—a consequence of the depression taken together with the recognition that information was necessary to analyze the problem. Today's inadequacies are political in origin, as are the inadequacies of many public data. Only those are counted as unemployed who are known to be seeking work; and those who are working only part-time but wish full-time jobs are counted as fully employed. Those who have been unemployed longest, the "hard-core" jobless, and who finally give up looking, are not counted. It is widely accepted by economists that the "real" rate is a good 50 percent higher than the "official" rate of unemployment. Those in power frequently redefine categories when the new definition is favorable to their political cause. That should cause no puzzlement; but the meek acquiescence in this continuing (bipartisan) shell game by those in the media and the academy is close to disgraceful.

22. Du Boff, *Accumulation and Power*, p. 87. The estimates were those of the Brookings Institution.

23. Economic duality as a concept helps to solve some puzzles of the U.S. economy, but complicates understanding of those regarding, say, the economies of the Third World. (See Chapter 7.) In the forefront of developing these ideas in the United States have been James O'Connor, *Fiscal Crisis of the State** and Barry Bluestone and Bennett Harrison, in their *The Deindustrialization of America** (New York: Basic Books, 1982), and *The Great U-Turn*, cited earlier. Bluestone first (to my knowledge) put forth the notion at the *Hearings* of the Joint Economic Committee on the *Economic Report of the President*, in 1972. O'Connor's argument moves along some similar paths, but with a different terminology.

24. Economists can rightly object that the construction industries —building materials and supplies, contractors, and the building trades

workers—are competitive in structure, with thousands upon thousands of separate firms. However, they might also know that the *organization* of construction in any given locality has been monopolistic, through trade associations, building codes, and cooperating trade unions. More recently, giant corporations such as Bechtel have begun to lessen some of the competitive *structural* characteristics of the industry. And of course a substantial percentage of construction—highways, most obviously, but not solely—is State-financed and organized.

25. See, for example, Federal Trade Commission, *Report on the Automobile Industry** (Washington, D.C.: U.S. Government Printing Office, 1939), Keith Sward's *Legend of Henry Ford*, noted earlier, and the case studies of the automobile (and other) industries in Walter Adams, ed., *The Structure of American Industry* (New York: Macmillan, 1961), or Leonard W. Weiss, *Case Studies in American Industry** (New York: Wiley, 1967). The incredible socioeconomic power and impact of both autos and petroleum are underscored by Barry Weisberg, *Beyond Repair: The Ecology of Capitalism* (Boston: Beacon Press, 1971), Chapter 5. Such matters will be examined in our Chapter 6, when environmental questions are analyzed.

26. Some of the data are revealing: Productivity rose between 1920 and 1929 such that a given volume of manufactured goods could be produced in 1929 with only 70 percent of the man years of labor required in 1920; employment in manufacturing rose only slightly in the period despite great increases in production, because of that increased productive efficiency. Meanwhile, employment in mining fell by 200,000. Overall employment rose by 16 percent, while the labor force (those working and seeking work) rose by 21 percent. As manufacturing, mining, and agriculture hired fewer people, jobs opened up in distribution, finance, and services—but not enough jobs, as indicated by the gap between them and the labor force. For data of this sort, and much else besides, consult U.S. Bureau of the Census, *Historical Statistics of the United States, Colonial Times to 1970* (Washington, D.C.: U.S. Government Printing Office, 1975). The annual *Economic Report of the President** is useful and convenient for a broad range of data, but its scope is narrower both in subject matter and time. Also, it must be noted that although the statistical appendices (well over one hundred pages) are conventionally reliable, the other (usually) three hundred or so pages are shaped more by the president's concern for the next election, both in subject and treatment, than by the desire to illuminate the state of the economy.

27. Because of the importance of the United States in the world economy, and vice versa, a complete explanation of the severity of the depression must give serious importance to the weaknesses of the world economy in the 1920s, and its utter collapse as the 1930s began. But much of that explanation fits well within a "dual economy" framework for the world economy—with the industrial nations dynamic, and the raw-materials supplying (Third World) nations always exploited and usually depressed. That will become part of the discussion of Chapter 7. For the 1920s, and an explanation of the 1930s depression that depends squarely on the weakening position of the Third World countries, see W. Arthur Lewis, *Economic Survey, 1919–1939** (London: Allen & Unwin, 1949), especially Chapter 12. This small book provides a useful summary of developments in the major industrial nations in the interwar period.

28. Paul M. Sweezy, "Cars and Cities," *Monthly Review* (April 1973), provides a succinct historical analysis of the automobile industry in its broader meanings, as well as its impact on the environment, which will be taken up in our Chapter 6.

29. *Prosperity Decade*, p. 288. But, despite great increases in productivity, "administered pricing," that is pricing controlled by giant firms working in collusion with each other, saw to it that prices did not decline in the 1920s. As for wages, Soule shows they rose 8 percent in manufacturing and railroads, stayed the same for farm laborers, and declined 14 percent for miners. Meanwhile (1923–1929), corporate profits rose 62 percent, while national income rose by 21 percent; and tax policies were changed to lower most the taxes paid as a percentage of income for those with the highest incomes and least for those toward the bottom: a 31 percent reduction for those with incomes above $1 million and a 1 percent reduction for those with incomes of $5,000 annually. In the 1980s we discovered that consumer debt could be extended much beyond what Soule thought possible (as of 1991 it amounted to 85 percent of disposable income, as compared with 30 percent in 1929), and that tax policies favoring the rich could be even more imaginative—and popular with almost everyone, rich and poor, if accompanied by racist and militaristic politics. In Soule's period, the arts of mind-management for economic and political purposes were neither so necessary nor as well-developed as recently.

30. GNP, as briefly noted in Chapter 3, is defined as the dollar value of the total annual output of *final* goods and services (where "final" means that a good is counted only once—for instance, cotton cloth going

into shirts is not counted until the shirt is sold at retail, except for what might be inventoried at the end of the year in intermediate stages). GNP only counts marketed goods and services; it takes no account of many valuable activities that are not marketed, such as housework and community service, but the cost of oil spill cleanups is counted, as are smog devices, nuclear weapons, and the like. Recently, total production has come to be measured as GDP (gross domestic product) = GNP less net receipts of factor income from the rest of the world. A GNP of $5 trillion would mean a GDP of perhaps $15 billion less.

31. The figures are all taken from *Economic Report of the President, 1991*.

32. Prof. Fisher's remark, and other such attitudes, are recounted in Charles H. Hessian and Hyman Sardy, *Ascent to Affluence: A History of American Economic Development* (Boston: Allyn & Bacon, 1969), p. 628.

33. More realistic estimates place the percentage at closer to one-third of the labor force. The data are taken from *Historical Statistics of the United States and Economic Report of the President*.

34. Lewis, *Economic Survey*, p. 52. Lewis notes that U.S. national income, a narrower figure than GNP, "contracted by 38 percent, and the unemployment figure increased to fifteen millions." The official U.S. figure, noted earlier, was 12.8 million. In 1929, U.S. industrial production was 46 percent of the total industrial production of the twenty-four most important producers in the world (Lewis, p. 57).

35. The data to follow are those of Donald Streever, *Capacity Utilization and Business Investment*, University of Illinois *Bulletin*, vol. 57, no. 55 (March 1960), p. 65, quoted in Baran and Sweezy, *Monopoly Capital*, cited earlier, p. 242. As Du Boff, op. cit., p. 121, shows, there has been a steady and ominous drop in the rates from the late 1960s, when they averaged near 88 percent, to the late 1980s, when 80 percent was the average.

36. *Economic Report of the President, 1991*, p. 323. In anticipation of our examination of the postwar period, we note here some unemployment data for the war and postwar years: unemployment sank to its historic low in 1943, 1.2 percent (when the State was buying about half of GNP), and stayed under 4 percent until the recession of 1958, when it rose to 6.8 percent, fluctuating between that level and 5 percent until 1964. The years of lowest unemployment in the 1950s were those of the Korean War, and in the 1960s those of the most intense military buildup for the Indochina War, 1965–1970. Then, until 1975, when the rate rose

to 8.5 percent, it averaged about 5.3 percent, and about 6.5 percent for the rest of the 1970s. Between 1980–1985 the rate was never below 7 percent, and for two years was over 9.5 percent. For the rest of the 1980s the rate moved down to its lowest level since 1970, 5.5 percent. Since the beginning of the recession in 1990, the rate has been over 7 percent.

37. "Transfers" are defined as payments received in the accounting period (usually the year), but not for contributions to production in that (or perhaps any) period.   There are business transfers and government transfers (at all levels of government), and they include pensions, welfare payments, social security, veterans' benefits, etc. In 1990, federal transfer payments were $488 billion, as compared with federal government purchases of $416 billion. It should be noted that the figures are in "1982 dollars," a procedure aimed at achieving comparable magnitudes by "deflating" for price changes over time. An example of the difference the procedure makes is that in "current dollars" GNP for 1929 was $103 billion, while in "constant (1982) dollars" it was $710 billion.

38. The low rates of gross private domestic investment in the war years (see Table 4.2) may be explained by looking at the high rates of federal purchases. The government built and paid for new war plants and the expansion of existing facilities—in steel, airplanes, tanks, machine guns, textiles, etc.—all of them easily convertible (and converted) to civilian products, which were sold off at bargain basement prices (in some cases $1) to private corporations after the war. The conversion of military to useful facilities that occurred after World War II could of course be repeated "after the Cold War." There was no need for political pressure to do so after World War II; because there is considerable resistance to conversion from business and the State now, there is considerable need for a politics from below to bring it about (of which, more in the last chapter).

39. As the term "liberal" came to be used in the United States in this century, it was meant to suggest interventionist governmental policies, reformist in nature, designed to curb the excesses of capitalism, to keep it from self-destruction by dangerous depressions or inflations, and to blunt its harsh edges for the underlying population. This is almost the complete opposite of what it has meant to be a liberal in Britain or on the Continent. There the term has stood for "free market" or laissez-faire capitalist policies. Thus the sharp criticisms against "liberals" in the United States in the past fifteen years or so have been made by what

would be called "liberals" in, say, England or Italy.

40. William E. Leuchtenberg, *Franklin D. Roosevelt and the New Deal** (New York: Harper & Row, 1963), p. 3. The Democratic Party at that time was dominated by its southern members. The "Solid South" was the term used to designate the South, meaning it was solidly Democratic, solidly *white*, for blacks could not vote in the South until the struggles of the 1950s and 1960s. In turn, the electoral invulnerability of southern Democrats meant the South's senators and representatives held positions of seniority on virtually all congressional committees, enabling them to hold sway over governmental policies in a measure at least as great as before the Civil War. The liberal southerner Lyndon Johnson, who "ran" the Senate for many years before he became president in 1963, was a follower of FDR and the New Deal, and more than a symbol of how much the South had changed between 1932 and the post–World War II years. More recently, of course, racism is again an effective weapon for holding back and reversing liberal social change—the difference now being that racist politics are used nationally, not only in the South.

41. See Broadus Mitchell, *Depression Decade*, cited earlier, p. 40. This is an unexciting but indispensable history of the economy of the period; and it has a full bibliography for further work. Taken together with Leuchtenberg's political history and bibliography, it will enable the diligent reader to get a good grip on the depression years, especially if some of the general and fictional works noted in the Reading Suggestions at the end of this chapter are studied. The data that follow immediately in the text are from Mitchell, pp. 438, 128, 444, 447, and 448, respectively.

42. As the list of first New Deal acts continues, it will be noted that the meat and potatoes furnished to businesses was accompanied by crumbs for the jobless. That only changed in 1935, as will be seen, when political unrest rose to levels making it clear that FDR would not be reelected without beginning to serve the needs of the whole nation—at least to some noticeable degree.

43. For many it is probably useful to pause here to show what "right" and "left" mean in political discourse. The terms began to be used in the years of the French Revolution, when the sitting of parliamentary members went in an arc from left (liberal) to right (conservative). As the years have passed, Left has come to signify a politics in the socialist direction, and Right a politics in the fascist direction. And what is fascism? It came into being in the midst of social crisis, first in Italy

in 1921–22 (under Mussolini), and subsequently in many countries, most notably Japan in the late 1920s and Germany in the early 1930s. To oversimplify, it may be said that the Left wishes to replace capitalism with socialism, and the Right to preserve capitalism, even if (for some because) that means eliminating all democratic institutions (including, not least, trade unions), and even if (again, for some because), as has always been so, that means militarizing the society (and ultimately, as has happened in all fascist societies, allowing the militarists—which all fascists are—to gain power at the expense even of the capitalists). For some small percentage of business leaders, this has been an ugly choice. Consequently, many in fascist countries have found themselves, almost always belatedly, opposing the monster they helped to create. It may be noted that fascism began in the crises that accompanied and followed World War I: it is always a politics whose success depends upon social breakdown and desperation, usually accompanied by fear and hate. For the German case, see Robert A. Brady, *The Spirit and Structure of German Fascism* (New York: The Viking Press, 1937). Brady's was the first book in English to explain and to attack this development. On his title page he uses Shakespeare's King Lear to warn, all too appropriately: "If that the heavens do not their visible spirits/ Send quickly down to tame these vile offences/ It will come,/ Humanity must perforce prey on itself,/ Like monsters of the deep." Sixty million were killed in Europe alone in World War II.

44. See Brady, *Business as a System of Power*, cited earlier, pp. 12–13, 144, 218, 244–45, 295, and Chapter VI.

45. As will be seen in Chapter 5, there had, of course, been unions before the NIRA, and they were legal. But two major problems, among many others, meant that for all but some skilled craft unions with local monopolies (plumbers, for instance), the right to have a union was more apparent than real: first, the major weapon of the union is its ability to place pressure on employers through the strike—but the laws of the land saw that as an illegal incursion on the rights of property, and would generally enjoin strikes (meaning that continuation would lead to imprisonment); second, those attempting to organize a union were easily fired (or, worse beaten up, even killed), with no recourse. Section 7A did not resolve either of these problems, but it opened the door to such a resolution.

46. For a discussion of the crisis and the politics of the period, see Kolko, *Main Currents*, Chapters 4 and 5, and Irving Bernstein, *The*

Turbulent Years: A History of the American Worker, 1933–1941 (Boston: Houghton Mifflin, 1970). For an excellent history of the rise and fall of socialist strength in the United States, see James Weinstein, *The Decline of Socialism, 1912–1925* (New York: Monthly Review Press, 1967).

47. The Taft-Hartley Act of 1947, literally written by the National Association of Manufacturers, was designed to limit and reduce the strength of unions. Although vetoed by President Truman, it was made into law by a Congress which, in overriding the presidential veto, revealed how very strong the voice of business was (to say nothing of is) in Congress, and how temporary the peace between capital and labor. As later discussions will show, since the 1960s organized labor has undergone a substantial decline in its numerical and its political strength, with painful consequences for both organized and unorganized workers.

48. Hansen wrote many articles and books in development of the stagnation thesis. The most appropriate single book for present purposes is his *Full Recovery or Stagnation?* (New York: Norton, 1938). For a more "radical" stagnation theory that systematically relates monopoly structures to the accumulation process, see Josef Steindl, *Maturity and Stagnation in American Capitalism* (New York: Monthly Review Press, 1976; first published in 1952). Baran and Sweezy's *Monopoly Capital* relies greatly on Steindl's analysis. A review of stagnation theory, and a useful criticism of its strengths and weaknesses, is H.R. Smith, "The Status of Stagnation Theory," *Southern Economic Journal*, 15 (October 1948 and January 1949).

49. Richard T. Gill, *Economics* (Pacific Palisades, Calif.: Goodyear, 1975), p. 139. As it turned out, while the ink was drying on those words the U.S. economy was wallowing in stagnation, bridged by the serious recessions of the mid-1970s and early 1980s, and accompanied by serious inflation—both bulldozed away by the most massive deficit spending in not just our, but the world's history. Nobody's right all the time.

50. A suggestion of how minimal the New Deal years were in terms of federal spending is given by the fact that in no year of the 1930s, despite massive unemployment, did the federal deficit rise to $5 billion; and in only one (election) year, 1936, did it exceed $4 billion—perhaps $30 billion in today's dollars. The deficit anticipated by the Bush administration for this (1992) fiscal year is more than ten times that amount.

51. It is important to note that in those years, a critical part of state and local purchases was financed through federal grants-in-aid, and that

the transfer payments (welfare and the like) of states and localities were more than covered by the federal grants: for example, in 1973 total purchases were $160 billion, federal grants were $40 billion, and state and local transfers were $30 billion. (*Economic Report of the President, 1991*, p. 382.) One reason for the fiscal disasters of states and localities in recent years, which spread rapidly, is that federal grants-in-aid have been sharply reduced: for 1989, purchases were $626 billion, federal grants $118 billion, and state and local transfers $146 billion. (All current, not constant dollars.) Note that in 1973 federal grants were just 25 percent of state and local purchases and greater than their transfer payments, but that in 1989 the percentage had fallen to about 19 percent and that transfers exceeded federal grants. This transformation was done in the name of giving more power to the states and localities; what they were given was a set of incurable problems, while the federal government was left free to increase its military expenditures always more. This was only one of the blades in the Malthusian ripsaw that was sharpened for expanded use in the 1980s.

52. As the 1960s came to an end, a little more than two-thirds of the population owned their own homes, just about double the figure for a generation earlier. As the 1980s ended, home ownership was in steady decline, edging down toward 60 percent, and doing so at an accelerating rate. The reasons for this included the inability to make mortgage payments, high interest rates, falling real income, and high prices for homes—the last due to a decline in low-cost housing as supportive federal housing policy virtually disappeared.

53. In its article of February 2, 1987, entitled "Deep in Hock," the *Wall Street Journal* had several charts showing that between 1960 and 1987, the ratio of debt to GNP rose over 20 percent, corporate debt as a percentage of net worth rose from under 90 to over 115 percent, nonbusiness bankruptcies rose from under 200,000 to over 500,000, household debt rose from under 25 to over 30 percent, and that interest costs as a percentage of federal spending rose from slightly over 9 percent to just under 14 percent. Subsequently, all these percentages have, of course, risen further. For example, by the fall of 1991 there were already 700,000 declared personal bankruptcies, with the year not yet completed, and household debt plus mortgage debt amounted to 85 percent of disposable income. If one looks only at corporate debt, the picture darkens further. In its March 15 issue, the *WSJ* showed that nonfinancial corporations' debt, significantly outstripping their growth of

revenues, had risen from $586 billion in 1976 to almost $2 trillion in 1987; that in a mere three years, from 1984 to 1987, their ratio of interest payments to earnings had risen from 40 to 49 percent; that corporate debt as a percentage of GNP had risen from under 32 percent in 1976 to over 40 percent in 1987; and that corporate liquidity ratios (the percentage of cash and receivables to debt due within a year) had fallen from 90 to 83 percent between 1980 and 1987.

54. The optimism of those years was less foolish than in the 1920s, however, given the data of the time. Between 1947 and 1972, "...real GNP grew at a rate of 3.7 percent per year, real disposable income per person at 2.3 percent per year. Civilian unemployment averaged 4.7 percent of the labor force, the lowest quarter-century average...since 1890.... Corporate profitability...rose substantially over most of the period, peaking in the mid-1960s (Du Boff, pp. 111–12).

55. Much of the foregoing is a paraphrase of arguments made in my *The Waste of Nations: Dysfunction in the World Economy* (Boulder: Westview Press, 1989), p. 28. For an excellent summary of the waxing and waning of the "capital-labor accord," see "The Rise and Demise of the Postwar Corporate System," in Edwards, et al., *The Capitalist System*, cited earlier, pp. 379–90. Also see Michael Kidron, *Western Capitalism Since the War** (London: Penguin, 1970), and the two books of Shonfield, cited earlier.

56. This has been true of many industries in the past decade or so, most illustratively in autos: The world automobile industry can produce about fifty million cars annually at what it calls efficient rates of production, but for many years now a forty-million year has been seen as a good one. In those same years, *new* plants have opened up not only in Korea and Brazil, for instance, but also in the United States.

57. For worries expressed in the 1970s, see "The Debt Economy," *Business Week*, October 12, 1974, and Hyman P. Minsky, "Financial Resources in a Fragile Financial Environment," in *Challenge*, July/ August, 1975. Discussion and references concerning the current situation will be put forth later in this chapter.

58. James Cypher has written much and well on the various dimensions of military expenditures. For present purposes, see his "The Basic Economics of Rearming America," *Monthly Review*, November 1981, and "Military Spending, Technical Change, and Economic Growth," *Journal of Economic Issues*, March 1987. As for the trade-off between military expenditures and other types, Cypher convincingly

makes the case that military expenditures are in no sense an alternative to more useful spending; as we now see with the Cold War over, the Bush administration argues for more military expenditures while arguing that any other kinds are impossible.

59. Compare the data just quoted from Du Boff (see note 54) concerning 1947–1972 with the following: "From 1973 through 1987 real disposable income per head grew at 1.4 percent annually, well below the 2.3 percent rate of the boom years. The highest previous civilian unemployment had been 6.8 percent, during 1958, but that rate would now be almost a luxury, as unemployment averaged 7.2 percent from 1973 through 1987. Clearly the hard times that many Americans began to feel were no illusion" (op. cit., p. 113). And after that was written, the long recession began to take hold.

60. See R.L. Sivard, *World Military and Social Expenditures* (Washington, D.C.: World Priorities, 1983 and subsequently), and Saadet Deger, *Military Expenditures in Third World Countries* (London: Routledge & Kegan Paul, 1986).

61. It was noteworthy in the 1970s and 1980s, and remains so in the 1990s, that taxpayers complain about social expenditures that meet serious human (including their own) needs—health, welfare, education, environment, etc.— while only rarely if ever noting that military expenditures get the lion's share of the government pie, are the most wasteful and corrupt (the $700 toilet seat, etc.), and the most useless to them and others—except for the corporations and the Pentagon. There is no better measure of just how successful the propaganda of the past half-century or so has been.

62. Stephen Pizzo, et al., *Inside Job: The Looting of America's Savings & Loans*, cited earlier, p. 12.

63. Garry Wills, "Mr. Magoo Remembers," a review of Reagan's *An American Life*. For those too young to remember, Mr. Magoo was a movie cartoon character, almost totally blind, a vivacious and likeable old man, always cackling and laughing to himself, bouncing through life like a loose cannon, always leaving others in trouble. The essay is in *The New York Review of Books*, December 20, 1990—in which, more than incidentally, Wills (who has done a thorough biography of both Nixon and Reagan), sees Reagan as a consummate liar, or fool, or both.

64. Volcker's professional experience was as an international banker, and ridding the economy of inflation was his principal aim, come hell or high water. This was Reagan's first year in office, with no impending

election campaign soon to be fought, and in addition to sharing the anti-inflation bias of Volcker (rather than the anti-unemployment bias of most people), it was his and most of his advisors' view that a stiff recession would be good discipline for, among others, trade unions. For an illuminating discussion of this matter, see William Greider, *Secrets of the Temple* (New York: Simon and Schuster, 1987), and the memoirs of Reagan's first budget director, David Stockman, *The Triumph of Politics*, cited earlier. It has long been the view of a significant segment of the big business world (and especially its financial sector) that a recession is like a spanking for a child: it may hurt, but it's good for (someone else's) character. When the 1954 recession began, I recall a full-page ad paid for by Bankers' Trust of New York (in the *New York Times*) headlined: "What's Wrong with a Little Recession?"

65. Probably the best discussion and analysis of the process is given by Harrison and Bluestone, *The Great U-Turn*, and *The Deindustrialization of America*, op. cit. These two economists were in the forefront of those showing that the many jobs created in the Reagan years were low-wage, temporary, and low-security. Emma Rothschild, in two brilliant and devastating essays in *The New York Review of Books*, shows that and considerably more. See "Reagan and the Real America," and "The Reagan Economic Legacy," June 30 and July 21, 1988, respectively.

66. A lucid and brief explanation of these relationships and structures, how they work out in economic terms, and thus what the conventional political options are is Francis M. Bator, *The Question of Government Spending: Public Needs and Private Wants* (New York: Harper & Row, 1960). Though written some time ago, the principles it elucidates remain valid—perhaps always more so.

67. Keynes deplored and mocked military spending—"building dreadnoughts and sinking them in the Atlantic"—and explicitly recommended "social expenditures." The most astute analyst of military expenditures in the United States has been James Cypher. Two of his works were noted earlier; one that is focused on our present point is "Capitalist Planning and Military Expenditures," *RRPE* 6 (Fall 1974).

68. The infrastructure refers to what makes it possible for the economy and society to function smoothly and efficiently, and it is in large part publicly-funded: rail and mass transit systems, streets and highways, bridges, ports and airports, waste disposal and water treatment facilities, and even its national forests, parks, and recreation areas. The listing is taken from Du Boff, op. cit., p. 121, who goes on to show how

public spending for such facilities has almost vanished: e.g., dropping from $63 billion in 1964 to $12 billion in 1984. See Chapter 6, below.

69. Five percent of 250 million people is 12.5 million people. Between 1980 and 1990, the incomes of the top 1 percent (2.5 million people), rose 73.7 percent, from $316,000 to $549,000 a year, 42 percent of which was from capital. The data are from Lawrence Mishel and David Frankel, *The State of Working America, 1990–91* (Armonk, N.Y.: M.E. Sharpe, 1991), p. 34, upon whom we shall depend for much more in Chapter 5.

70. Robert Sherrill, "The Looting Decade: S&Ls, Big Banks and Other Triumphs of Capitalism," *The Nation*, November 19, 1990. The occasion for the article is a review of some of the books on the subject. One, that by Stephen Pizzo, et al., has already been cited. Two of the several others are especially worth noting here: Martin Mayer, *The Greatest-Ever Bank Robbery: The Collapse of the Savings and Loan Industry* (New York: Scribner's, 1990), and Brooks Jackson, *Honest Graft: Big Money and the American Political Process* (New York: Knopf, 1990).

71. A largely technical but still readable analysis of this development is John B. Shoven and Joel Waldfogel, *Debt, Taxes and Corporate Restructuring* (Washington, D.C.: Brookings Institution, 1990).

72. The reader is reminded of Naylor's *Hot Money*, where the emphasis is on important and shady international processes and relationships.

73. It was soon forgotten that despite the Fed's swift and effective action, a major explosion was only narrowly averted. Almost by chance, an unheralded figure in the Chicago commodities market was able to maneuver so as to prevent the collapse from spreading there—and thus further. Today's instant communications patterns were helpful there; also lacked in 1929.

74. Companies, whether small or large, depend on cash flow from sales to keep them solvent when they have high debt loads. Data provided earlier showed that such loads are at their historically highest levels. And consumers need jobs and/or transfer payments to stay level. Personal and business bankruptcies (quite apart from banks) had broken all records in 1991.

– 5 –

Income, Wealth, and Power

Who can make a poem of the depths of weariness
bringing meaning to those never in the depths?
Those who order what they please
when they choose to have it—
can they understand the many down under
who come home to their wives and children at night
and night after night as yet too brave and unbroken
to say, "I ache all over"?
How can a poem deal with production cost
and leave out definite misery paying
a permanent price in shattered health and early old age?
When will the efficiency experts and the poets
get together on a program?
Will that be a cold day? Will that be a special hour?
Will somebody be coocoo then?
And if so, who? [1]

Capitalism is a system whose vitality is given to it by everyone trying to make as much money as possible, come what may. It is a contest in which for all but a few, the dice are loaded for or against winning. The few are exceptional individuals who, despite all odds against them, climb high on the ladder; or those other few who, despite everything favoring them, manage to fall toward the bottom. The odds are determined by a complex of factors: when and where one is born; the income, wealth, and power—the class—of one's parents; one's color; one's sex; often, one's ethnic or religious identity; and, neither the least nor the most important—although we are taught to believe it is the principal or only determinant—one's abilities and energy. It is an abundance of these latter (plus, all too often, ruthlessness) that allows some few to beat the odds and move to the top; as their lack allows some few among the "well born" to sink toward the bottom.

From its beginnings to the present, capitalist development has taken place within interrelated structures of income, wealth, and power, all characterized by great inequality. Although its past and present are marked by constant changes in technology, in products, in markets, in institutions and in attitudes, capitalism's unequal structures of income, wealth, and power have changed little, or only temporarily, or not at all, or toward more inequality—depending upon time and place.

Inequality is intrinsic to capitalism, essential to its birth, nourishing and nourished by its existence. It is another way of viewing the existence of exploitation. Without inequality, neither capitalism's capital nor its working class would exist, nor could the expected profits that generate real investment: there could not be economic expansion; there would not be capitalism. The inequalities of capitalist society, and their perpetuation, are the name of the game, what it's all about—*its* bottom line.

Variations in the patterns have of course occurred. Given the complexity and the rapidity of capitalist development and its constant changes in technology, products, and markets, in its economic, demographic, and geographic structures, and in its institutions and attitudes, variations have been and remain unavoidable. Especially after the crises and convulsions of the first half of this century, there were alterations *lessening* inequality in the structures of income, wealth, and power, and, as will be discussed, the alterations were substantial. Given the eruptions and violence of the first several decades of this century, it is understandable that those still in power in the capitalist world found it both necessary and desirable to make concessions to what was a relatively well-organized working class. However, since the profits crisis of the 1970s there has been an increasing tendency to lessen or to eliminate what was earlier achieved.[2] We now examine the main paths to our day.

Them That Has, Gits

In the nineteenth century and earlier, a simple divison between property-owners and the propertyless wage-earner was both cause and consequence of the unequal distribution of income and wealth. In our time, a more complex cause and effect relationship exists: (1) there is usually an important difference between the earning power of the assets of *big* business and those of small business; (2) substantial income and wealth distinctions must be drawn between those who "own" *professional* skills (lawyers, doctors, engineers, etc.) and those who do not, for those skills and the professional associations that limit entrance and enhance fees provide almost all their holders with incomes in the top ten (or five or one) percent;[3] (3) in the nonprofessional ranks of labor, there are substantial differences in the incomes of those whose earnings are protected and sustained by strong trade unions, weak trade unions, and the unorganized workers. Within the foregoing *class* divisions, further distinctions must be made because of racial and sexual barriers.[4]

Those who possess income-earning *wealth*—stocks and bonds, real estate, etc.—use it to increase their *incomes*, and then again their wealth, and then again their incomes in a manner considerably more rapid than that available to those whose incomes depend upon work alone. Apart from anything else, this alone explains how "the rich get richer." And it should go without saying that wealth is a principal means to become, or to be able to influence those powerful in the political world, and, among other matters, to see to it that interference with the maintenance or further accumulation of wealth is kept to a minimum.

When we look at historical variations within the basic patterns of *income* distribution in the United States, what stands out is the long-run direction in which they have moved, the small number of lasting changes toward lesser inequality, and the extent of overall *sociopolitical* effort that was required to accomplish them.

The period of least inequality in the United States was in the decades preceding 1850—leaving out of account the enslaved African-Americans and the Native Americans, who were more than 15 percent of the population in 1850. After 1850 there ensued a century-long period of *increased* inequality, with only slight interruptions. Then, after 1947, there was a movement toward lesser inequality until about 1973. Since then income inequality has once again increased, presently reaching the levels of 1947. And whatever the changes in income distribution, the patterns of wealth and power have become more concentrated. We may now look more closely at that history, and at connected questions.[5]

The historically lowest levels of inequality for whites in the period before 1850, although they cannot be pinned down with reliable data, are suggested not only by impressionistic and anecdotal information, but by the economic structure and processes of the period: widespread and growing access to land, a shortage of nonslave, nonindentured labor, and light rather than heavy industrial production.[6] The years after 1850 constituted a major turning-point in U.S. capitalist development, when both heavy and light industrialization spread and deepened. From then on, income and wealth came to be held in a steadily more unequal pattern, as the size of farms grew and the smaller farmers disappeared (one basis for the Populist Movement late in the century), industrial production became large-scale and business units became bigger, and the power of business in the increasingly active State became always more influential. The economic transformation was accompanied by a geographical shift in power, leading to and flowing from the convulsion of the Civil War.

It is vital to note here that as the *distribution* of income in the post–Civil War period became more unequal, the *levels* of per capita income were rising. An important by-product of rising real incomes then, and generally in U.S. history, has been that despite frequent harsh exploitation, there has been relatively little class conflict. To which it may be added that relative social peace is helpful to the process of capital accumulation—and, the opposite of a vicious circle, rapid capital accumulation makes social peace more likely.

As we now examine the data from the 1920s to the present, lightly in the earlier years and more intensively for recent decades, all the data to be noted will have been derived from the decennial federal census, and from aggregated income tax forms. There is good reason to doubt the detailed accuracy of both those sources of information, quite apart from sampling errors, but the general outlines provided by the data over time remain worth studying. There is one major reservation, however, and that concerns the systematic understatement of high incomes and the understatement of the real *wealth* of the very wealthy. This understatement, which was casual before World War II, became institutionalized with the substantial general increases in taxation of the later New Deal and World War II; and it may be said that each new tax law is accompanied by dozens or hundreds of amendments that provide for exemptions, legal avoidance, or whatever.[7] As Kolko puts it,

After 1941...the complexity of the [income] statistics increased with the advent of tax laws which placed an immense premium on the rich underreporting and deferring their income or devising covert ways of receiving it.[8]

The statistical data for various periods now to be presented are both dry and skeletal. To suggest what the data represent in terms of daily life, we preface them with a few representative facts:

• Automobile possession increased by 14 million in the 1920s, and only 3 million in the decade of the depression. When World War II began, after more than a generation of automobilization, there was less than one car for every three adults. Today there is slightly more than one car for every adult.
• When World War II began, the proportion of population living in owner-occupied homes was 44 percent. The percentage rose to 67 percent in the 1970s, and has declined since.
• And living in those homes was often more than one family: one family in fourteen lived in a household headed by another family or person, usually a relative; about one-quarter of the over-65 population lived in households headed by their children.
• The average house, still in the mid-1940s, was impoverished by current standards: one-third had no running water; two-fifths had no flush toilets; three-fifths had no central heat; four-fifths were heated by coal or wood; one-half did not have an electrical refrigerator (as compared with an ice box); one-seventh did not have a radio; almost nobody had air conditioning; and TV was not yet a mass product.
• Meat and fowl consumption were about one-half and one-third, respectively, of today's levels. "On the whole, the 1947 diet is what we would call stark."[9]

As we proceed to offer some tables of income distribution, it is well to keep in mind that at times the data refer to the *dollar level* of incomes, or they also may refer to percentage *shares* in national personal income, and they may be before or after taxes. One must make note of just what it is that is in focus. We begin with a distribution showing how many lived at what level of income in three time periods: Among the many matters these data reveal, they tell us how badly off most of the people were at the end of the "prosperity decade." When President Johnson declared his "war on poverty," he asked his advisors (in 1964) for a number that would establish the "poverty line," at or below which a family would be deemed to be living. The figure was set at $3,000. The figures in Table 5.1 are in 1962 dollars. It may be seen that in 1929 over half of the population was living at or below that amount; and even after the buoyant economic years of the war, 30 percent still were. (By 1969 the percentage had dropped to just over 12 percent, and by 1972 to just over 11 percent. It has risen ever since, to over 14 percent in 1991.)[10]

Table 5.1
*Distribution of Families and Incomes by Income (in $1962)
for 1929, 1947, and 1962*[11]
(in percent)

Income Level	1929	1947	1962
Under $3,000	51%	30%	21%
Between $3,000 and $6,000	34	40	31
Between $8,000 and $10,000	3	7	11
$10,000 and over	5	9	19

For those same years, we may now examine the distributions in percentage (not dollar) terms.

Inequality is plain enough when we note in Table 5.2 that the highest fifth in 1929 received more than half of all income, and the lowest fifth in 1947 and 1962 received in the neighborhood of one-tenth of the income of that in the highest fifth. Even starker is the relationship between the Top *5 percent* and the rest: in 1929 they received more than

Table 5.2
*Family Personal Income Received by Each Fifth
and Top 5 Percent of Families and Unattached Individuals
for 1929, 1947, and 1962*[12]

Year	Lowest fifth	Second fifth	Third fifth	Fourth fifth	Highest fifth	Top 5 percent
1929	12.5%		13.8%	19.3%	54.4%	30.0%
1947	5.0	11.0	16.0	22.0	46.0	20.9
1962	4.6	10.9	16.3	22.7	45.5	19.6

the bottom *60 percent*, and from 44 percent to 55 percent of the highest fifth. When the data are divided into tenths, we also find that the top tenth regularly receives about two-thirds of the highest fifth's share. Thus, for family income, as for ownership and control in industry, the structure that comes to mind is that of a pyramid with a wide bottom and a needlelike top, most of the people on the bottom, most of the income at the top. When we examine the data on wealth distribution, we shall see that it is even more unequally held than income. Shortly we shall turn to the changes in the distributions of income and wealth in the 1970s and 1980s. As a bridge between the years noted above and those to follow, Table 5.3 shows "changes in living standards" between 1949 and 1984.

Table 5.3
Change in Living Standards in the 1950s, 1960s, and 1973–84
(1984 dollars)

	1949	1959	Growth per Decade	1969	Growth per Decade	1973	1984	Growth over 11 Years
Median Family Income	13,540	19,300	+42.5%	26,700	+38.3%	28,200	26,433	-6.2%
Tax Burden at Median Family Income (%)	12.2	13.1		20.9		20.9	22.4	
Income Share of Lowest Quintile of Families (%)	4.5	4.9		5.6		5.5	4.7	
Percent of All Persons in Poverty	(est.) 32.0	22.4		12.1		11.1	14.4	
Government Expenditures								
Per Person	1,509	2,409	+50.7	3,774	+56.6	4,124	4,792	+16.2
National Defense	377	849		968		728	910	
Payments to Individual	334	469		798		1,138	1,721	

Source: Frank Levy, Dollars and Dreams, pp. 47, 56, 66.

There are several striking changes revealed by those figures. Note that between 1949 and 1969, twenty years, the real income of the median family doubled; that it rose slightly in the next four years, but that it had *declined* between 1973 and 1984.[13] Also note that over the entire period, and even more so when we take the figures through the whole 1980s, the tax burden of the median family has increased—as we shall see that it has decreased for those at the top. The author of the foregoing data, in summarizing them, says that "...twenty-six years of income growth [1947–1973] followed by twelve years of income stagnation [1973–1985] is the major economic story of the postwar period."[14] The latest available data for his study were for 1985. As we shall see momentarily, by 1989 incomes had risen slightly, but so had inequality. There is much else to be noticed just looking at those few figures; we will leave them noting the inverse relationship between the drop in income share of the lowest quintile, and the rise in the rate of poverty—inverse, but not coincidental.

Many times in the preceding chapters, the 1970s have been portrayed as in "crisis," and the 1980s as those in which "Reaganomics" took a heavy toll on the bulk of the population's material well-being. We now turn to a variety of statistical supports for those generalizations. We look first at those on the top, for what they could make happen for themselves is a part of the explanation of what was made to happen for 80 percent of the rest of the population.

Table 5.4
Average Income of the Top 5 Percent Compared with the Bottom 80 Percent for 1947–1989
(1989 dollars)

Year	Average Family Income for Families in the:		Ratio of Average Income of Top 5 percent to Average Income of Bottom 80%
	Top 5 percent	Bottom 80 percent	
1947	60,701	12,357	4.9
1967	89,274	21,915	4.1
1973	109,131	25,919	4.2
1979	118,249	27,317	4.3
1989	148,591	28,743	5.2
Change, 1979–89			
Level ($)	+ 30,343	+1,426	21.3
Percent	+ 25.7	+ 5.2	4.9

As the authors who put together Table 5.4 go on to emphasize,

In 1947 the richest 5 percent of the population had $4.90 of income for every $1 received by the bottom 80 percent. By 1967 inequality had lessened—so that the ratio improved to $4.10 to $1. Since 1979 this ratio has increased, so much that inequality in 1989 exceeded the level in 1947.[15]

Let us now examine data for the very top income receivers, those in the Top 5 percent.

Table 5.5 Before-tax Income Shares (in percent)[16]			
Year	Top 1% of tax units	Top 2% of tax units	Top 5% of tax units
1952	8.7	12.1	18.7
1963	8.8	12.3	19.4
1967	8.8	12.3	19.6
1972	8.0	11.4	18.7
1977	7.8	11.3	18.9
1981	8.1	11.5	19.0
1986	14.7	18.2	26.6

Pechman's conclusions from his own data are worth quoting at length:

First, between 1952 and 1981 the very rich in the United States did not enjoy larger increased incomes, as defined in the tax code, than the average income recipient. Since 1981, their share of total income has been rising sharply, indicating that their incomes have been rising much faster than the average. Part of this increase reflects a large increase in capital gains, but salaries at the top have also been rising faster than the average.[17]

Pechman goes on to underscore the obvious: "Clearly, this improvement in the income shares of the top 15 percent could come only at the expense of the lower 85 percent...," and adds something significant, either unknown or not understood by those whom it principally affects; namely, that after 1979 and even more after 1984, unemployment compensation and social security benefits became taxable. Thus, "the lower classes have not been able to hold their own in the private economy; even the large increases in government transfer payments did not prevent an erosion of their income shares" (ibid). Made worse by the fact that in the recession that began in 1990, unemployment compensation payments had been lowered and their time span reduced.

Just how kind the 1980s were to those already very rich, or quickly becoming so, the millionaires, is shown by these comparisons between the 1960s and 1970s, on the one hand, and the 1980s, on the other:

	Number of tax returns declaring income over $1 million:	Rate Per One Million Returns (adjusted for Inflation)
1968	1,122	51
1978	2,092	41
1985	17,312	186
1987	34,994	338
1988	65,303	595[18]

Looking at the same kind of development from a different angle, we may note that "Since 1982, according to *Forbes*, the amassed fortunes of the wealthiest 400 individuals in the United States has increased 300 percent—from an individual average of $230 million to $682 million. By 1989 these fortunate individuals had a combined net worth of $272.5 *billion*."[19] Figure 5.1 shows the considerably improved situation of the Top

Figure 5.1
The Worsening Distribution of Income

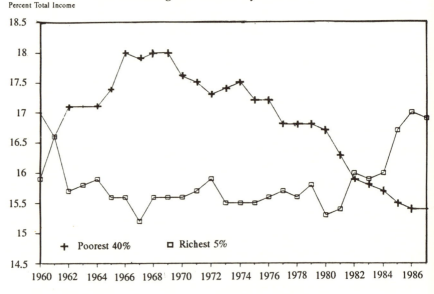

Source: Dollars & Sense, December 1988, p. 23. Their data are derived from U.S. Department of Census, *Money Income of Households, Person, and Families in the United States*, Series P–60.

5 percent at the same time that it shows the plummeting deterioration of the bottom 40 percent, from the 1970s into the 1980s.

Now, in Table 5.6, we change our focus from the very rich to the distribution of income for the whole population over the span from 1947 to 1989, using census data (excluding capital gains and undistributed profits and, as well, transfer payments).

Table 5.6
Shares of Family Income Going to Various Fifths and to Top 5 Percent

	Lowest Fifth	Second Fifth	Third Fifth	Fourth Fifth	Top Fifth	Total	Breakdown of Top Fifth	
							Top 5%	Next 15%
1947	5.0	11.9	17.0	23.1	43.0	100	17.5	25.5
1967	5.5	12.4	17.9	23.9	40.4	100	15.2	25.2
1973	5.5	11.9	17.5	24.0	41.1	100	15.5	25.6
1979	5.2	11.6	17.5	24.1	41.7	100	15.8	25.9
1989	4.6	10.6	16.5	23.7	44.6	100	17.9	26.7
Point Change								
1979–89	–0.6	–1.0	–0.1	–0.4	+2.9	0	+2.1	+0.8

Source: Mishel and Frankel, *The State of Working America*, p. 20.

What stands out in Table 5.6 is the decline in income of the bottom four-fifths of the population—that is, 200 million people—when compared with the rise of the top, and especially the Top 5 percent, which claimed over two-thirds of the gains for the highest fifth. Even more striking is what happens when all capital gains are included, as in Table 5.7 (from Mishel & Frankel, op. cit., p. 24; 1990 figures are estimated).

When one examines either the dollar or the percentage figures, they are not merely striking, but shocking—especially as regards the Top 1 percent.

For those already rich in 1977—with average incomes of $281,383—to almost double their incomes between then and 1990, while the incomes of the bottom 50 million people fell by almost 10 percent, and when such a fall meant terrible increases in poverty and homelessness, is one of the more dramatic meanings of the policies carved out in the Reagan years.

What but unlimited greed can account for the efforts of those already so rich to become so much richer? As the authors conclude, "The average income *gain* of the richest one percent of families in the 1980s is nearly double the average income level of the next best-off [also very rich] 4

Table 5.7
Income Growth among Top Fifth and by Fifth, 1977–90
(1990 dollars)

Income Group	Average Family Income in: 1977	1980	1990	Percent Change 1977-90	1980-90
All	36,247	36,138	41,369	14.1	14.5
Top Fifth	78,965	81,589	105,209	33.2	28.9
Top 1%	281,383	315,648	548,970	95.1	73.9
Next 4%	97,739	100,534	125,800	28.7	25.1
Next 5%	69,335	69,439	82,154	18.5	18.3
Next 10%	54,407	55,505	63,663	17.0	14.7
Bottom Four Fifths:					
Fourth	42,148	41,957	44,908	6.5	7.0
Middle	31,311	30,268	30,964	–1.1	2.3
Second	20,205	19,237	19,348	–4.2	0.6
Lowest	8,531	8,082	7,725	–9.5	–4.4

percent of the population and is more than 5 times the average family income in 1990" (ibid.). The substantial declines in income for those at the bottom, it should be remembered, take into account their receipt of transfer payments. This recent redistribution of income *upwards*, increasing already great inequality, was the inexorable outcome of the combination of the slowed economy of the 1970s, on the one hand, with the high military spending and Malthusian conservatism of the 1980s.

The foregoing point brings into focus a generalization relating changes in the *level* of the national income with changes in its *distribution*. When the national income rises, along with economic expansion, the biggest absolute gainers are those with the highest shares: 10 percent of a bigger pie is much larger than 1 percent of that same larger pie. In addition to the simple arithmetic of the change, it is also true that those at the top, with their ability to expand their incomes through investment, have their fortunes enhanced even more through the economy's successes: the rich grow richer because they are in a strategic position to take advantage of the increased opportunities of expansion.

It is also true, of course, that the incomes of *all* will rise as the economy moves into expansion and thus toward fuller employment; but the *share* of those in the lower "fifths"—those whose incomes depend upon work, rather than property—will decline. As expansion continues, and brings full employment (say 4 percent or less unemployed),[20] down the *share* of the lower income groups will tend to rise, accompanied by falling profit rates, due both to rising wages as labor becomes scarce, and to softening markets for commodities. When contraction begins and recession continues, there are, of course, fewer jobs and falling incomes for those still employed; and though the process also means falling *incomes* for those at the top, their *share* once again rises—and, of course, they are less likely to suffer from privation, as those in the bottom 80 percent do. To all of which it may be added that a striking departure from this set of generalizations has taken place in the years since the 1970s, as those in the bottom four-fifths have *not* had an increase in their relative share during the periods of expansion, and have seen their real incomes decline, since 1973.

This development is a consequence of many factors, the two most important of which are "the deindustrialization of America,"[21] and the fiscal policies that were put into play since the late 1970s.

Also important to note is that over time the *absolute* gap between those at the top and those at the bottom tends to widen, even though relative shares may remain constant or change slightly toward less inequality. For example, Table 5.7 shows that the (constant) dollar difference between the top and bottom fifths widened from $70,000 in 1977 to $97,000 in 1990, and that the gap between the top 1 percent and the top 20 percent widened from $202,000 to $444,000. An examination of *any* other time periods would show the same tendency.

The poor may or may not see their money incomes or their income shares rise; in general they do well to hold on to their relative share. But even when that is accomplished, poverty increases when the *absolute* gap widens. Poverty is a *social* condition. A family in the United States receiving many times the money income of a family in India, for example, can be poorer than the Indian family. *Absolute* poverty exists when starvation and accompanying illness and early death enter the picture, when poverty is physical as well as social. But poverty is always first and foremost social. Marx put it well:

Rapid growth of productive capital calls forth just as rapid a growth of wealth, of luxury, of social needs and social pleasures. Therefore, although the pleasures of the labourer have increased [through higher wages], the social gratification which they afford has fallen in comparison with the increased pleasures of the capitalist, which are inaccessible to the worker, in comparison with the stage of development of the society in general. Our wants and pleasures have their origin in society; we therefore measure them in relation to society; we do not measure them in relation to the objects which serve for their gratification. Since they are of a social nature, they are of a relative nature.[22]

This view helps to clarify why it is often in periods of economic expansion (such as the 1960s) that social protest tends to rise among those at the bottom of the heap.

As we shall see in Chapter 7, what is true of the distribution of income and wealth and the widening gap between rich and poor *within* a capitalist country is also true of the widening gap *between* rich and poor nations in the world economy. Both the absolute and the relative differences between the industrialized and nonindustrialized societies have widened substantially in the post–World War II decades of sustained economic expansion—and turbulence has increased in that same period, though not for that reason alone. Our focus up to now has been income; now we turn to the distribution of wealth.

The Accumulation of Wealth

The old saw that "the rich get richer..." has more to it than spite and envy. The rich own and control almost all of society's income-earning assets, and, as noted earlier, that wealth yields incomes that in turn are invested in more wealth—and all of that also means great power.

Wealth measures the sale value of possessions and property. Almost everyone owns something of value, but the society's income-producing assets, the most vital of which is its corporate stock, is owned by a very small percentage of the population. The considerably more unequal distribution of wealth than income, shown in Table 5.8, is directly connected to political power. These connections mean that the wealthy are strategically positioned to neutralize the apparent redistributive income and wealth effects of governmental income, estate, and inheritance taxes.[23]

Those data are for 1983. The authors of the table add information emphasizing the upward redistributions of the 1980s:

In the 1980s, the financial assets owned primarily by the wealthy grew considerably, while tangible assets, which are spread out more

Table 5.8
Percent Distribution of Wealth and Income, 1983
Shares of Total

Family Income Group	Net Financial Assets (%)	Net Worth (%)	Income (%)
Upper 2 percent	54	28	14
Next 8 percent	32	29	19
Bottom 90 percent	14	43	67[24]

evenly, increased only slightly. This caused the distribution of wealth to become yet more unequal...[the] average net worth of the richest 0.5 percent of families rose 6.7 percent between 1979 and 1989, while the average net worth of families in the bottom 90 percent actually fell by 8.8 percent. This means that the gap in overall financial security between the rich, on the one hand, and the middle class and the poor, on the other, has widened even further. In addition, there has been a striking increase in the wealth gap between older and younger families.[25]

If wealth is essentially the preserve of a few at the top, household debt is considerably more democratic. Earlier, (note 24) we pointed out in the data for wealth that in the bottom 90 percent there were 20 percent with negative net worth and 54 percent with negative financial assets; and in an earlier chapter we saw that *all* the net saving is done by the top 10 percent of income receivers. This is merely a roundabout way of saying what we all know: most people can't get along without borrowing, and then borrowing more, and then finding themselves at the edge of trouble, or over it. As Mishel and Frankel point out (op. cit, p. 161),

Two measures of the total debt burdens of households, debts as a percent of assets and as a percent of personal income, have each grown markedly in the 1980s after a long period of relative stability. Household debt leapt from 66.8 percent of personal income in 1979 to 80.2 percent in 1989, and from 14.9 percent of household assets in 1979 to 17.1 percent in 1989...the lowest fifth of families had an average yearly debt payment of 24 percent of income in 1970...[and] 34 percent in 1983, while burdens among upper income families actually fell off slightly.

So there we have a large part of the story—the top 2 percent with over half of the financial assets of the nation, and over half of that owned by the top 1 percent, while the bottom 90 percent share only 17 percent of the national income-producing wealth. But the top 2 percent have "only" 14 percent of the nation's personal income. Why has not all that wealth been translated entirely into income? First, because wealth produces income, one reason that the law of the rich is "never live off capital." Second, the higher incomes that would be involved, if allowed to go even higher through converting wealth to income (which would also lower the "prices" of the assets), would be taxed away, at least in part. Third, wealth in the form of stock ownership means increased wealth in reserve, through undistributed (and personally untaxed) corporate profits. Fourth, wealth means power. And last, in the case of those at the top, on what would they spend those higher incomes? "Accumulate! Accumulate!" is what they have quite sensibly and characteristically done.[26]

Whether or not there is great inequality in the distribution of income and wealth is not debatable; and as such, it is not debated. But what, if anything, to do about it, whether it is desirable or possible to move toward less inequality—such questions are very much debated. Setting aside radical voices, however, the arguments that range around this matter see property rights and privileges as sacrosanct, and do not question the basic institutions that have created and that require great inequality. Thus *Business Week*, in three major and useful essays in the 1970s on the distributions of income and wealth, all consistent with the data noted above, concludes its essays in a state of bemusement: "Neither side can come up with hard answers as to how [income distribution] can—or should—work." And, "some inequality may serve as an incentive for growth in a profit-oriented economy." "Some" inequality is not what their own data show. The worst-kept family secret about the relationship between capitalist development and *great* inequality in the distribution of income and wealth is that they are Siamese twins.[27]

Nobody, and least of all the rich, needs to be told that wealth is the key to high incomes. Nor could anyone reasonably doubt that being male and white is irrelevant to one's income. What is less rarely discussed or understood are the systematic and longstanding *class* relationships allowing the gains from property, and that perpetuate the low incomes of *all* workers—irrespective of gender, color, ethnic or religious background, whatever. Discussion of such matters is normally in the nature of asides, disclaimers, or, at best, with the unexamined assumption that some goodwill, some social intelligence, and some time are likely (if anything could) to rid U.S. society of such patterns.

A critical analysis of capitalist development shows otherwise. The causes of existing patterns of income and wealth are far from accidental and, so far as basic patterns are concerned, unchangeable. Capitalism *requires* expansion; expansion *requires* savings and investment; the required savings depends upon incomes exceeding consumption needs and desires, and the required investment depends upon past and expected profits; persisting profitability in the economy is the telltale sign of both expansion and exploitation; it *requires* people who *must* work for what they can get even when that does not meet consumption needs and means they work part of the time "for nothing," that is, for the benefit of the employer and of capitalist expansion. If the alternative to being exploited for those with little or no income-earning property is harsh, it is harsher still for the man of color, still more for women as compared with men, and worst of all for women of color—a discussion of which will conclude this chapter.

The Accumulation of Misery

From time to time in the foregoing pages, it has been argued that the definitions of important social realities—such as unemployment, poverty, etc.—have not descended on us from the heavens, nor been found graven on a stone tablet somewhere; rather they are made and changed by those with the power to do so. For our purposes here, that means the State. Thus the definitions of who is unemployed, or poor, are transmitted to us through a government agency and its documents, which in turn is responding to congressional or presidential directives. There is more to it than that, however.

The data on income and wealth used by academics and others are collected and organized for governmental and public use by the Bureau of the Census and the Internal Revenue Service, with some important related data on wages, etc., collected by the Bureau of Labor Statistics (and GNP data by the Department of Commerce, etc.). The data finally made available depend upon the organizing categories of the collectors, the questions asked, and the procedures (the nature and breadth of the research sample, for example) of collection. But this in turn depends upon what the various levels of power in the State want to know—and what they want the public to know. That varies over time, as will be noted in a moment. What varies is what data are sought, and what funds are allotted to search out the information.

Thus, after this longish prologue, it may be said that the kinds and quantities of information available for analysis have changed greatly in this century, and in abrupt waves in the past fifteen years or so. It was noted in Chapter 4 that systematic data on unemployment were not collected until the 1930s. Reasonably substantial data concerning levels of well-being and poverty had to await the 1960s. And in our own day all such efforts have been transformed and some have been abandoned, for a variety of reasons—almost all of them political.

In the 1977 edition of this book, the present section began as follows: "Every year the Bureau of Labor Statistics (BLS) calculates the annual money income that a family of four (husband, wife, eight-year-old daughter, and thirteen-year-old son) needs to enjoy a 'moderate but adequate standard of living' in the 'average American city.' ...The BLS also calculates budgets for a 'lower' or 'austere' level of living, within a 'minimum budget,' and one for a 'higher' level which 'allows for some luxuries.' The moderate budget may reasonably be viewed as 'the American standard of living,' if in a pinched version. It allows, for instance, for one suit every three to four years for the father, and three street dresses for the mother every two years; it assumes a new TV every ten years, a new refrigerator every seventeen years, a toaster every thirty-three years. The adults are entitled to nine movies a year, with none for the children (who presumably watch the ageing TV set). It includes no allowance for savings to meet periods of unemployment, illness, or higher education for the children. A *used* car may be purchased every four years (the 'higher' budget allows a *new* one every four years). And out of the budgeted amount, social security, income, and other taxes must be paid. The lower or 'austere' budget pares everything down to food, clothing, and shelter, leaving virtually nothing for other items."

The BLS no longer calculates those budgets, and not mostly because it costs money to do so. The information one could derive from their data had become politically embarrassing, to say the least. Following the paragraph quoted above, government data were used to show that in 1975 "the average factory workers in durable goods production—those with the strongest unions—earned only a little over the urban 'lower' level and were almost one-third shy of meeting the 'moderate' budget, unless, of course, more than one person in the family worked." And then it was pointed out that in 1975 the median family income, $12,840, as against a 'moderate' budget of $15,500, produced a deficit of $2,660. It was in just those years that it became necessary for "more than one person in the family" to get a job, as, after 1973, family real income began the decline from which it has yet to recover: and it was also in just those years that the BLS ceased to collect and publish such data. If and when the government of the United States moves back and away from the imposed austerities of recent years, perhaps the BLS will once more resume its organization and presentation of such budget data—if the BLS has not been cut from the budget.

Even in the absence of current data for such budgets, and even with intermittent definitional changes of poverty, we are able to put together a reasonably informative picture; and the import of even this limited information suggests why a fuller statement would not be casually funded by the State at this time.

Before proceeding to the grim facts of poverty in the United States, it is important to understand that usually, as above, we are discussing *quantitative* data and standards. Even when the numbers are embellished by the *kinds* of expenditures they allow, for clothing, appliances, and the like, it does not adequately suggest what the money income levels of the majority of people in the United States, least of all the poor, mean in terms of the *quality* of life. To have too little money for sufficient purchases and possessions in a society that defines the good life by such standards is bad enough in itself, and considerably worse when there is too little income to maintain decent and safe levels of health and comfort. The bureaucrats who define standards such as "lower" can hardly imagine what life is like for an urban family of four that pays excessive rents to a slumlord for a cramped apartment which, and among other terrible defects, has faulty plumbing and heating at best, peeling and perhaps poisonous paint, and numerous rats. Most people cannot identify with those whose health is chronically poor because of rotten housing and poor diets and who must suffer the indignities of the inadequate health care meted out to the poor—and many millions who are not called "poor." In short, in this as in so many other instances of social measurement, quantitative standards, useful and necessary though they are, often disguise as much as they reveal; and in doing so, they mislead as much as they instruct. Let us now turn to the enduring disgrace in the United States of so much poverty amidst so much plenty—and, as will be shown in the next chapter, alongside so much sheer waste.

The degree to which so many of our people have walled themselves off from this ugly side of our reality was well-captured by the late Michael Harrington when in 1962 he wrote of "the invisible poor."[28] In that year, as the United States was still congratulating itself on having to face the problems of "the affluent society" (the title of Galbraith's 1958 book), there were by conservative estimate (see Wilcox's quote below) nine million *families* plus five million unrelated individuals living at annual incomes below the official poverty line—that is, about one-fifth of the nation. Even though poverty cannot be understood in purely quantitative terms, it would be a step in the right direction to use accurate and meaningful quantitative definitions—such as that noted earlier, where those with less than half the median family income would be considered poverty-stricken. However, given that the State's definitions have become *the* definitions, it is important to show in even more detail just how inadequate, one could say ludicrous or even obscene, those definitions are.

It was in 1964 that the government, responding not only to Harrington's book, but even more to the civil rights turmoil of the time, first defined a "poverty line" so as to estimate the number of poor then in the United States. This was done by the Council of Economic Advisors, at President Johnson's order. It is worth quoting a respected textbook on just how the CEA arrived at its figure:

The Council's estimate was based upon a study by the Social Security Administration of the income needed to support a nonfarm family of four. The SSA had established two standards for such a family, both based on estimates of dietary costs prepared by the Department of Agriculture: [1] a "low-cost" budget, permitting the minimum diet consistent with the food preferences of the lowest third of the population and adequate to avoid basic nutritional deficiencies.... The resulting budget stood at $3,995. This called for a far higher level of expenditure than welfare agencies were allowing for families receiving public assistance. *To meet the administrative need of these bodies*, the SSA prepared... [2] an "economy budget" based on a *deficiency diet designed for temporary or emergency use*... set[ting] the total budget at $3,165. On the basis of this figure, the CEA adopted $3,000 as its family poverty line..., [and] $1,500 as the line for a single individual. It thus found...some 35,000,000 people, a fifth of the nation, to be in poverty in 1962.[29]

The Council of Economic Advisors was the key agency advising the president for the definition of poverty in 1964. It is entirely a presidential servant, its directorate appointed by him without need for congressional approval. As such, it is a thing of politics. The Bureau of Labor Statistics is not entirely independent of the White House, but it is basically a civil service operation. Its estimates for 1975, discussed above, calculated $9,800 as necessary for a "minimum budget for food, clothing and housing, with little left over." Using the CEA poverty line, the figure for 1975 (taking into account rising prices since 1964) was $5,500, only 56 percent of the BLS figure.

There is another disturbing aspect of the poverty definition—which determines benefits under many programs—and that is that although the pattern and the costs of consumer expenditures have changed substantially since 1964, there have been only minor changes in the definition. The only major adjustment is that which raises the dollar line in keeping with changes in the Consumer Price Index. Although that index is altered from time to time, its alterations are in terms of the "average consumer"—which those in poverty are far from being. Probably the most important statistical difference between the poor and others is that the poor must spend a higher percentage of their income for housing; and, more's the worse, housing prices have risen disproportionately in recent decades: In 1952–53, the *average* household spent 34 percent of its budget on housing, and in 1982-84 that had risen to 42 percent; but in 1985 it was estimated that half of *low*-income renters spent at least 65 percent of their incomes on housing. Patricia Ruggles, the author of a recent study on this question estimates that "today's line would have to be 50 percent higher than it is now just to match the standard of living provided by the 1967 poverty line. [Were that procedure used], nearly one in four Americans would be considered poor, almost double the official rate."[30]

Despite the many ways in which poverty has been understated since Johnson's "war" against it began in 1964 there has been a continuing attempt to redefine the line downward, or, if possible, to define it out of existence. Among the most straightforward of these efforts was that of President Nixon's head of the Office of Management and Budget (Roy Ash, previously CEO of Litton Industries, one of the larger conglomerates). He was reported by the *New York Times* on April 4, 1973 as "quietly examining the possibility of doing away with federal use of the word 'poverty' and of changing income figures used to define the poor, 'because current usage exaggerates the [rising] number of poor.'"

So the extent of poverty in the United States is understated both quantitatively and qualitatively. Before looking at the relevant data, we should ask about its whys and wherefores, its historical and qualitative dimensions. To begin with, the persistence of poverty, and its tendency to spread and deepen, can be seen as a set of vicious circles. To be born poor—certainly not the baby's fault?—is to live in inadequate housing in overcrowded, often dangerous neighborhoods, with bad schools and little or no recreational facilities; it is to be mired down in an atmosphere of cynicism and hopelessness, of illness and crime, of price-gouging in neighborhood stores, of job discrimination, and, neither least important nor last, of political nonrepresentation. The psychological/emotional impact of living so can only be imagined or read about by those who have not experienced it directly; but it takes little imagination to perceive that those who are born poor are likely to stay poor and to have children who, through no fault of their own, will stay poor—with here and there the exception that proves the rule. But even, perhaps particularly, in a rich society like the United States, there is more to it than vicious circles for the tens of millions of people for whom poverty is a natural state, for whom poverty has become institutionalized.

Thus, we may ask a frequently useful question in economic and social affairs: do any benefit from the persistence of poverty? And who pays? The popular and political answer suggests that nobody except the welfare recipient, the blameworthy poor person, benefits, and that the upper layers of society pay. The realities show otherwise. Two essays analyzing poverty will be noted here, one from the liberal the other from a radical standpoint.

The liberal argument lists and discusses thirteen "functions" of poverty: (1) It ensures that society's "dirty work" will be done. (2) The very low wages of the poor subsidize a variety of economic activities that benefit the affluent (for example, domestic servants), and the poor pay a disproportionate share of all taxes (see Chapter 8). (3) Poverty creates jobs for middle-income people who "serve" the poor, such as social workers, and prison guards. (4) The poor buy goods that others wouldn't, which is profitable to those who produce and sell them. The foregoing are *economic* uses of the poor; the remaining nine "uses" are social and political. They include the self-defined elevation in moral and social standing that middle-class attitudes toward the poor allow to middle- and upper-income groups; the absorption by the poor of the costs of socioeconomic change, being powerless to do otherwise—such as being pushed out of their housing for freeways, urban renewal, and the like; their availability as cannon fodder for wars; their utility as a basis for arguing against liberal social change.[31]

Howard Wachtel, a radical economist, does not dispute the foregoing points, but he points out that all that is said about the *uses* of poverty is consistent with the common attitude that places the *causes* of poverty in the individual shortcomings of the poor themselves, rather than in a social process over which they have no control. Those who blame the poor for being poor see them as depraved, shiftless, stupid, and so on. But the facts are that most of the poor (1) work full-time but at wages that leave them and their families underneath the official poverty line; or they work half-time because they cannot get full-time jobs; (2) are handicapped and unable to work; or (3) are retired with low or no pensions, having worked at a disadvantage all their lives.[32]

But surely the poor can lift themselves up and away from the vicious circles of poverty by the education that in turn allows better jobs? Except that the best schools are in the most affluent districts of every city, and the worst are for the poor—worst in terms of facilities, environment, administrative attitudes and, perhaps the most subtle but not the least vital, the almost universal "tracking system." The latter, from the earliest years of schooling, classifies children according to tests and performance that seldom take account of cultural background, with the consequence that poor children are placed in curricula in primary and secondary schools that virtually assure they will be trained only for lower income jobs, if that.[33]

Education can and should be a process in which the young not only realize their creative and practical possibilities in terms of their life's work, but also where human beings learn to appreciate and to understand nature, society, culture, and themselves. Instead, and especially for the poor, schools have taken on the quality of disciplinary barracks or, for the well-off, recreational centers—boring, disillusioning, and embittering students, teachers, parents, and taxpayers.

Given the concentration of economic and political power in our society it may be assumed that if the powerful—including George Bush, the self-styled "education president"—had the will to change the educational situation, they could find the ways. When an effort *is* mounted, as in the recent "America 2000" education initiative, its goal is to make the U.S.A.

competitive in the world economy—to train, not to educate. Meanwhile, deterioration continues, creating an ever-widening poisoned and stagnant pool of young lives with neither zest nor hope.

Without further comment on the inadequacies of governmental definitions and data, let us now—finally!—present some facts regarding poverty in the United States. Even with the understatements and blurred edges provided by officialdom, the picture is one of bleakness for tens of millions of our people. Instead of the usual series of tables, I have chosen to reproduce some of the more striking conclusions found in the impressive study from which I have already quoted many times, that of Mishel and Frankel, *The State of Working America.* Their tables supporting these statements will be found on the pages cited at the end of each conclusion:

• The poverty rate rose from 11.1 percent in 1973 to 12.8 percent in 1989, increasing the number of officially poor from 26.0 to 31.5 million. Decreased governmental aid and lower wages are largely to blame for the increase (pp. 166–67). (On September 26, 1991, the Census Bureau announced that the poverty rate for 1990 had risen to 13.5 percent; that is, there were 33.6 million people in poverty in the United States, as officially measured: two of every fifteen. *International Herald Tribune*, Sept. 27, 1991.) In September, 1992 the Census Bureau announced that 35.7 million people, 14 percent of the U.S. population, were poor in 1991.

• Not only are there more poor; the poor are also poorer. The average income deficit (the dollar gap between actual incomes and the poverty line) per family member rose 8.9 percent between 1973–79 and another 11.9 percent between 1979–89. And the percentage of the poor who have incomes below half of the poverty line, which was 32.9 percent in 1979 had risen to 38 percent in 1989 (pp. 168-69).

• Minorities are two or three times as likely to be poor. In 1989, 10.0 percent of whites, 30.7 percent of blacks, and 26.2 percent of Hispanics were poor (p. 171).

• Within each race/ethnic group, children (under 18) are the age group most likely to be poor: 54.3 percent of all black children and 41.3 percent of Hispanic children live in poverty (ibid.). Child poverty increased from 14.2 percent in 1973 to 16.2 percent in 1979 and then to 19.6 percent in 1988.

• Women are more likely than men to be poor: in 1989, 14.4 percent of women and 11.2 percent of men were poor (ibid.).
• Poverty among whites rose from 9 percent to 10 percent between 1979 and 1989, while falling slightly for blacks and Hispanics (pp. 171–72).
• Poverty rates for the elderly (over 65) dropped from 29.7 percent in 1967 to 12.0 percent in 1988, due to transfer payments. Without such transfers, the rate would have been 52.0 percent in 1988. But many of the elderly are now just above the poverty line and therefore vulnerable to cuts in benefits (pp. 172–73).
• The increase in poverty in the 1980s was due partly to declining governmental aid to the poor. For example, government taxes and benefits removed 39.7 percent of persons in female-headed families with children from poverty in 1979, but only 22.8 percent in 1988 (p. 177).
• Only 25 percent of poor persons aged over 15 were employable yet did not work at all during 1988 (p. 181).
• In 1989, 22.4 percent of poor working adults worked full-time, year round, while 34.1 percent worked at least 50 weeks and remained poor (p. 183).
• Whites have consistently made up the majority of poor female-headed families, and between 1979–89, 59.1 percent of the increase of poor female-headed families was for whites (p. 185).
• Although the impression is widespread that those who are poor are minorities, or female-headed families, we have seen above that female-headed families are white in the majority, and it is also true there are more married-couple families in poverty than female-headed families: 40.2 percent as against 37.8 percent. And of those married-couple families, 64.3 percent are poor because of low hourly earnings, because they were made up of full-time, full year workers (p. 187).

There is much more that could be cited that goes in the same direction; that is, opposite to the direction portrayed by the dominant politicians in the United States, and duly reported in the media. That this systematic flow of misinformation has been and continues to be used as one of several levers to redistribute the national income *upward*, at the demonstrable expense of a good four-fifths of the people of this country, is less to be explained by the stupidity of the latter than by its longstanding susceptibility to ideological and racist reasoning which, in this television era, has been developed to always more persuasive levels. But there is more to it than that.

The reference is to a unique and central characteristic of the United States, whose workers have created a *trade union* but not a *labor* movement, a vital distinction to be discussed below later in the chapter.

Oligarchic Democracy

How patterns of such inequality and misery are maintained, in what is not only the richest but, by its own standards, the most democratic country in the world, cannot be explained without examining the role of *power*—the power to idealize, defend, and enhance the prerogatives of private property and production for profit. The holders of such power in capitalist society have been seen by its critics as "the ruling class" (Marx), "the vested interests" (Veblen), and, among other designations, "the power elite" (C. Wright Mills). The terminological differences connect with analytical contrasts between these three theorists. But whatever their differences, they agree on one fundamental point: the commanding holders of social power are few in number, and at their center sit those who own and control what is most valued in capitalist society: its productive wealth.

We the people of the United States are a strange lot when it comes to questions of power, and even more, of its blood brother, class. Consider the following generalizations, all of them quite common and accepted: Workers hate their bosses. You can't beat City Hall (or their state and federal equivalents). Government at all levels is a nest of corruption. The media are in the service of powerful business interests. Schools and churches and social occasions differ greatly in keeping with the levels of wealth and income of those participating.

Despite all these and many other such views, *class analysis* of the United States is absent, or rejected and scorned, not only by conventional social scientists, but quite generally by the very people who hold the attitudes noted above.

The contrast between popular attitudes and popular understanding and politics is by no means so common in the industrial capitalist countries of Europe—all of which have an organized Left, centered on one degree or another of anti-capitalist policies. The absence of *class* politics is "as American as apple pie." In recent years, as the political economy of the world has been "Americanized," the European Left tends more toward accommodation with than elimination of capitalism, but the generalization still holds.

Why is the overwhelming majority of the population in the United States so oblivious of what has seemed so obvious elsewhere? Some of the reasons were summarized in Chapter 2, where the natural, social, and temporal blessings surrounding U.S. development and *making* it different were noted—including its predominantly immigrant population. Here we must enlarge the explanation. Among all capitalist societies, the United States alone had no precapitalist history. For other societies, that was a history of clear-cut *class* relationships, with power graded in terms of class. And when, for example, medieval institutions gave way to capitalist institutions, class structures, though changed in character, remained clearly evident.

The United States was born in a *nationalist* war. Understandably, at the time that struggle could be seen as a social revolution, but there is a sharp distinction to be made between the two. Nationalism unites people of different classes in a common cause against the controlling *outsider*; a social revolution seeks to overthrow the preexisting *internal* structure of power. Many of the conflicts in the Third World in recent decades have been both anti-imperialist and anticapitalist, which helps to explain their great difficulties and as well as their potency and ongoing obstacles.

Seen in this way, the American Revolution does not appear as a social revolution. Its internal structural effects were peripheral and far from permanent. Setting aside the differences between a monarchy and a republic—and as the 19th century began, Britain was monarchical only in form—the new United States were not *sociopolitically* all that different from Great Britain; but they did gain control over their own destiny then, as much as any society has (and more, given our resources and location). Madison, Hamilton, Washington, and almost all the other giants in our Pantheon of "revolution" were in no sense social revolutionaries, or even liberals, except for Jefferson, with his dream of a small-holders' democracy. (Tom Paine would qualify as a radical, but his is not a household name in the United States.) They were quite at home with an oligarchic structure of power based on private property.

Notwithstanding, the people of the United States both in the past and in the present have seen themselves living in a society characterized by widely diffused power and a fluid social structure—where movement from one level to another (with the different "levels" defined by income and wealth, not class)[34] is a matter of pluck and luck and effort. And of course a great measure of fluidity has existed and still does, in comparison with other societies. What has been important about that fluidity for present purposes, however, has not been its existence, but that along with social mobility has gone a *continuation* of the relative power of classes —indeed, as has been argued earlier, an increasing concentration of power at the top.

The continuity of class structure is not as puzzling as it might seem at first glance. The upward mobility has, of course, been that of *individuals*. Those who have risen occupationally and financially have been absorbed and co-opted by the stratum into which they have moved—and happily so. This came as no surprise to Veblen, who saw the "underlying population" (which Marx called the working class or proletariat) wanting to "emulate," to be like, rather than to overthrow or supplant those above them. The formal and informal educational process—"socialization"—has been the prime agent in this process of co-optation. Once a "lower-class" person makes her or his way on to the upper reaches of the social ladder—whether in a corporation, in the university, in the military, the professions, or the government—the absorption process is intensified. Or, ostracized, one falls or is pushed down the ladder. Social fluidity for individuals is one matter; class structure and the concentration of social power are another. They can and do exist side by side, most especially in the United States.

One consequence has been analytical confusion in the social sciences, another and connected result has been a virtually unchallenged role for the class that has gained and held power by virtue of its wealth and its control of the upward mobility ladder.

But has there not been class *struggle* in the United States, between capital and labor? Certainly, as we shall soon see, but it has taken particular forms that require careful analysis if their meaning is to be understood; and such struggle has attenuated almost to the vanishing point by now. Kolko, relying upon Veblen, has pointed to a key characteristic of the process in the United States:

American society could also be understood as a class structure without *decisive* class conflict, a society that had conflict limited to smaller issues that were not crucial to the existing order, and on which the price of satisfying opposition was relatively modest from the viewpoint of the continuation of the social system. In brief, a static class structure serving class ends might be frozen into American society even if the interests and values were those of a ruling class.[35]

The power of the ruling class in the United States has come principally from its ownership and control of the nation's productive wealth, which is a matter of class. But that power has also been enhanced and strengthened by the depth and persistence of fearful, hateful, and scornful racial, ethnic, religious, and sexual attitudes and the activities accompanying them. Whatever else in the United States may have held back the consciousness and organizational strength of the working class, these divisions have surely been vital sources of weakness. Nor, of course, have such matters been confined to the United States, nor to differences in skin color. Discussing Ireland as a British colony, and the conditions of Irish workers in England (in a letter written in 1870), Marx said:

And most important of all! Every industrial and commercial center in England now possesses a working class *divided* into two *hostile* camps, English proletarians and Irish proletarians. The ordinary English worker hates the Irish worker as a competitor who lowers his standard of life..., feels himself a member of the *ruling* nation, and so turns himself into a tool of the aristocrats and capitalists of his country *against Ireland*, thus strengthening their domination *over* himself. He cherishes religious, social and national prejudices against the Irish worker. His attitude toward him is much the same as that of the "poor whites" to the "niggers" in the former slave states of the U.S.A. The Irishman pays him back with interest in his own money.... This antagonism is artificially kept alive and intensified by the press, the pulpit, the comic papers [1870!], in short, by all the means at the disposal of the ruling classes. This *antagonism is the secret of the impotence of the English working class*, despite its organization. It is the secret by which the capitalist class maintains its power. And that class is fully aware of it.[36]

Before examining further how such *non*class relationships have functioned, we shall briefly explore the development of trade unionism in the United States—the main avenue taken by U.S. workers to offset their weaknesses in the face of business power.

Nothing to Lose, But...

The trade unions of the United States, by comparison with similar groups in other capitalist countries, are politically conservative. Neither in principle nor in practice are they class conscious; they do not seek basic institutional changes, they have not formed themselves into a *labor* movement, as in other capitalist societies. A trade union movement seeks to work *within* the system to improve the material lives of its members; a labor movement also seeks those ends, at the same time that it works to change the *system*, its power structures and its direction, not only its patterns of rewards.

For trade unionism to succeed at all, some institutional changes have been necessary, of course; but they have if anything strengthened the system. U.S. unionism has generally been characterized as "business unionism," or, sometimes, "pork-chops unionism." There have been exceptions to these generalizations in very early or very bad times, but they have died out or been crushed.[37]

Right after the Civil War, groups such as the Knights of Labor formed which had as an important part of their aims a reconstitution of society, along lines which were then considered radical, though they would not seem so today. Even the very conservative American Federation of Labor (AFL) in the 1890s faced a moment when whether or not it would become socialist was debated—and rejected. Before World War I, about one-third of AFL members were also members of the Socialist Party. In the depression of the 1930s, the newly formed Congress of Industrial Organizations (CIO) worked closely with New Dealers seeking broad social reform. And the most radical labor organization of all in the United States, the Industrial Workers of the World (IWW, called the "Wobblies"), was uncompromisingly anticapitalist, its members tending toward socialism or anarchism. The IWW was ruthlessly crushed by the events surrounding World War I, which it opposed, by the "Red Scare" in the 1920s, and by the force of deeply hostile public opinion—not least of all that expressed by the AFL—which more than once resulted in lynchings. Today, a few of the left-leaning unions that emerged out of the 1930s depression have managed to hang on to life and members, but only when they have been able to succeed at *business* unionism.

In addition to what has been said earlier, how may the general conservatism of U.S. trade unions be explained? It begins with the origins and the hopes of workers in this country, and with the socioeconomic context within which they worked. From its beginnings, and until the 1920s, ours was a land of labor shortage—when the labor supply is set against the amount of land open to cultivation and the rapid rate of economic growth. But there is one important proviso: the "labor shortage" was not as intense as it appears in retrospect if the several millions of unemployed and severely underemployed blacks and whites in the U.S. South are taken into account. From 1865 until the 1930s, migration from the underdeveloped South to the labor-hungry North was a mere trickle. Whites chose not to leave for an "enemy country" and blacks were generally restrained—by force of circumstance or by sheer force—from doing so. World War I and World War II, the agricultural depression of the 1930s, and the mechanization and chemicalization of southern agriculture in the decades beginning with World War II slowly and then suddenly unlocked the substantially unused labor supply of the South—substituting, in recent years, substantial urban for rural unemployment and underemployment.[38]

Given the foregoing institutional or artificially created labor shortage, the labor supply was persistently inadequate, despite a rapid rate of population growth. That rapid increase was due in part to the high birth rate among residents, but the vital addition was due to heavy immigration, partly a result of the positive lure of the United States, partly due to the negative push of population pressures and political, social, and economic discontent in the countries of origin. Acting as a link between the labor shortage and the influx of labor were U.S. agents in Europe (and, later, in Asia), working for shipping companies, potential employers, or land companies. They hawked the virtues of life in the United States much as soap and beer are advertised today. The population rose from 31.5 million in 1860, to 63 million in 1890, and to 106.4 million in 1920, about 29 million of which was accounted for by immigrants.[39]

In the period between the Civil War and 1920, the proportion of male immigrants to the total immigration never fell below half, more often than not was above 60 percent, and in many years was above 70 percent. The men were overwhelmingly between 15 and 50 years old, ready and eager to become members of the labor force, no questions asked. Our total population more than tripled in this period. Still, in 1920 a congressional committee was told "there is a labor shortage in practically every industrial activity. It amounts to not less than that of 5 million men." From then on, excepting the peak years of World War II, labor moved into surplus.

But in those long and important formative years, the United States was one of the countries where people were more likely to be needed than needy, poor though many were throughout. Wages and working conditions were terrible, even brutal, but except for the most highly skilled "urban trades" (carpenters, plumbers, etc.), effective unions did not form. Why not?

One part of the explanation is the heavy percentage of foreign-born in the labor force. For immigrants, the United States seemed a land of unparalleled opportunity and social mobility. Bad though conditions were, they were better than the even harsher conditions of the home country, which usually meant the conditions of the peasantry. Here there was hope, at least, hope for themselves and especially for their children; hopes more often than not realized in the second generation. Why fight the bitter fight for unions if, perhaps, next year, or ten years from now, you might no longer *be* a worker?

Add to this the uncertainties and the hardships and the dangers of becoming involved in a union organizing drive and it may be understood why unions had difficulty in attracting converts. Employers' opposition to unions was unremitting and relentless, and they were greatly assisted by their allies in the courts and in the press—to say nothing of the pervasive view that *individual* hard work was the sure way to economic well-being. But the multiplicity of languages, religions, and national and cultural backgrounds of the labor force also rendered communication and solidarity among workers most difficult. Employers did what they could to drive these wedges in deeper: "divide and rule" is as useful a stratagem for employers as it was for the British Empire.[40]

Employers' determination to resist union organization took many forms: discrimination against union men on the job and in hiring, the use of labor spies within plants and unions, physical force or its threat, so-called "yellow-dog" contracts (where the job depended upon signing away the right to join a union), and moving plants to nonunion areas in response to union activity. The press cooperated along the way in alerting the general public to anarchism, communism, and other schemes to destroy all that is good. Local police, state militias, and federal troops could be relied upon to maintain "law and order," when and if the occasion arose, and private police (like the "Pinkertons") could do the job when it became especially nasty—which it often did. And then there were the laws of the land and their interpretation by a friendly judiciary.

The law did not forbid unions as such. But it did make the rights of labor quite explicitly secondary to those of property. In 1842 it was decided that a trade union was *not* a conspiracy (in *Commonwealth v. Hunt*); workers had a right to organize. But local, state, and federal courts up until 1930 interpreted that decision as meaning the right was effective only when it did not interfere with employers' rights—and strikes were seen as such interferences. Unions without the right to strike are like armies without weapons. Antitrust legislation was used more frequently against unions ("combinations in restraint of trade") than against business until 1914, when the Clayton Act exempted unions from such laws; but in 1921 that too was reversed (*Duplex Printing v. Deering*).

By 1915, about 8 percent of the labor force was in unions (2.5 million workers). World War I and its accompanying upswing in production and the need for cooperation between business, labor, and government allowed the figure to double. Although the labor force increased between 1920 and 1933, union membership *declined* from five million to fewer than three million. Like the present, the 1920s were years of friendship between business and government, the administrations of Harding, Coolidge, and Hoover; they were the years of the "Red Scare," and of "welfare capitalism," which, taken together, effectively crippled the significant socialist movement of the time, and reduced the ranks of organized labor. That reduction was assisted by the "American Plan," an open-shop—*nonunion* shop—program. Its nature was epitomized by Mr. Dooley, the journalistic creation of Peter Finley Dunne, in a dialogue with his friend Hennessy: "But," says Hennessy, "these open shop min ye menshun say they are f'r unions if properly conducted." "Sure," says Mr. Dooley, "if properly conducted. An' there we are; an' how would they have thim conducted? No strikes, no rules, no contracts, no scales, hardly iny wages and damn few members."

In 1929 the depression took hold. The prestige and power of the business community suffered. They had taken credit for all that was great in the United States; now they had somehow to explain how their talents had brought 25 percent unemployment, falling incomes, bankruptcies, and the remaining broad range of disasters of the 1930s. Their explanation, which either blamed excessively high wages for workers, or, as with President Hoover, placed the cause in Europe, did not find a receptive audience.

Not a few leaders of the largest corporations had for decades seen the advantages of trade unionism, with effects both before and during World

War I. But the largest number of businessmen were not in agreement, and in the euphoric 1920s even the "enlightened" leaders had changed their minds. In the depression, the attitudes seeing trade unions as useful for business revived once more in small but influential circles, but unionism's principal strength came from the general unrest and the organizing drives of angry and desperate workers. Congress led the State toward a significant response.

Weak legislation favoring unionism was made a part of the same law that created the National Recovery Administration in 1933 (see Chapter 3). Its inadequacies centered on the lack of provisions outlawing business practices warring against unionism, or that would enforce even the weak law. These were substantially remedied by the Wagner (National Labor Relations) Act of 1935.

After its passage the number of organized workers rose rapidly—from the low of 2.9 million in 1933, to 4 million in 1936, 7.3 million in 1938, 9.5 million in 1942, 13 million in 1946, and about 18 million in 1960, after which the rate of growth slowed down, and then was reversed. The percentage of union members in the labor force peaked at 35 percent as World War II ended, dropped to 25 percent in the late 1970s, and is about half that today. Although the labor force has risen from about 70 million to almost 125 million from 1960 to 1991, there are fewer union members today than in 1960. That substantial decline has more than one reason behind it, but the role of the State has been vital, and that will be examined in Chapter 8.

One could interpret the rise of unionism of the 1930s and subsequently as having been *caused* by the Wagner Act of 1935, and indeed it was helpful. It is perhaps more worthy of comment that unionism was held back *until* the 1930s. The development of mass production industries, the steady growth of the labor force, the virtual cessation of immigration after 1920, the loss of prestige by business after 1929, and the widespread social unrest of the depression all must be given full weight, as must the unending and costly struggles of workers in virtually all industries over the decades. The Wagner Act removed obstacles to the formation of effective unionism, but it did not *create* unions: the fight for union recognition and security was the major cause of industrial disputes *after* the Wagner Act, and many of these were both bitter and bloody.[41]

As we have noted above, especially in the years during and after World War II, the ranks of organized labor grew rapidly, more than tripling in the decade after 1933, and doubling again by 1960. Along with that quantitative growth went an expansion of the larger meaning of trade unionism, as more than higher wages, shorter hours, and safer working conditions improved: from the 1960s on, very much facilitated by the sustained and substantial economic expansion underway, trade unions were able to bargain successfully for paid vacations, health care, pensions, and sometimes supplementary (to State) unemployment benefits. This accompanied, and significantly stimulated, State programs moving in the same directions, benefitting the nonunion labor force as well.

Although business opposition to unions and their demands never ceased, it was very much muted in the era of the 1960s. Economic expansion, combined with concentrated market power, meant that business could pay for all this along with *rising* after-tax profits, for demand for their products grew rapidly even as they passed on higher costs as higher prices. When the crisis of the 1970s began to emerge, the easy years of unionism came to be tested by growing corporate opposition. Soon this was translated into a harsher State—most obviously and vividly in 1981, when President Reagan broke the Air Controllers's strike.

As one looks back on the previous decade or so, the period in which union numbers, prestige, and political strength have all dwindled to a dangerously low point, the question arises, what happened? The import of the question is not to ask why there was increased business determination to cut costs by weakening unions, to move its production abroad to cheaper labor areas, and to seek and get support from the State against unions. All those developments could be taken for granted. The question really is, even so, why was U.S. trade unionism so easy to push toward its present weakness?

Part of the answer was suggested earlier, when the undemocratic nature of many unions was noted, a defect that contributes to apathy on the part of the rank and file member of unions, as it does for citizens in the larger body politic—which, of course, tends to weaken further what democracy there has been. Also, the very successes of unions, and the progressive social legislation of the 1960s, could and did lead who knows how many workers to conclude that they had it made, and who needs a union anyhow? The level of material well-being of the industrial worker, those most heavily-organized, had risen greatly in the twenty or so years after 1955. They, the most powerful of workers, were well off. For them, what's to struggle? For the rest, those with little or no organized power, the political path was virtually closed off.

The closing words of Marx and Engels's *Communist Manifesto* were "Workers of the world Unite! You have nothing to lose but your chains!" The best-off and politically strongest workers of the United States, who had never been more than intermittently involved in class, as distinct from "pork-chops," struggles, and least of all after the 1950s, believed they *did* have something other than chains to lose: cars, TV, homes, etc. And given the socialization processes of the United States, when the effort of holding onto those things and their jobs began to be increasingly difficult, there had been little political preparation for coming to grips with it. Indeed, something like the opposite of preparation for political effort has been the lot of the workers in the United States. All too many have been induced to work politically against their own interests; or through disgust have become effectively nonpolitical.

Each for Himself...

We in the United States pride ourselves on being a country in which *individualism* thrives, and within that, clearly it is *economic* individualism that dominates. Interestingly and importantly, when we find ourselves as part of a group—in athletics, politics, education, or, for present purposes, as members of a union—the individualism carries over: the group is used to serve our pride or our selfishness. All that is natural and normal enough, also outside the U.S.; but there, unlike here, workers' energies do not let it go at that.

Thus, it is not that unions fight for their own particular interests, but that they do so *individualistically*. There have been exceptions, but they have been rare and temporary. An example from 1948 that was true to form and that set the tone for most other unions in the years following is provided by the contract made by the United Auto Workers' Union (UAW) and General Motors. It was a time of anticipated inflation, and the then leader of the union, the charismatic and socially-minded Walter Reuther, first sought an agreement which, along with increased wages would provide for *no* price increase for GM. Ultimately, the UAW (after a membership vote) and GM agreed on a wage packet that would provide for an annual cost of living adjustment (COLA). That left the union in good shape for inflation, as it also put GM in a good position for passing on wage increases.

What has happened more recently is that COLAs have been reduced or abandoned as real wages and jobs have declined, and even what were once very strong unions seem to be unable to resist effectively, if at all. This is another way of raising once more the distinction between a trade union movement and a labor movement, a difference that is by no means merely semantic. As was noted earlier, trade unions do and must fight for decent wages, working conditions, pensions, and, not least, their own continuity (that is, union security). When they cease to do so, general deterioration on all matters takes place, as indeed has marked the last few years. If workers are to gain a decent living from their work, they must be able to have effective control over the market for their labor: that is what an effective union provides. It is not much different from the market control achieved by business monopolies—except that there is a very large difference between that which makes possible a decent livelihood and that which might make property owners richer.

And there is also a very large difference between the successes achieved by trade unions and the creation of an enduring political environment by labor in which such successes can be defended and enhanced. Without trade unions of course there could be no labor movement, for the former is the basis of the latter's membership and strength. A labor movement is by definition a *political* body, in the deepest sense of the term: it seeks to gain State power, and seeks to gain it by creating or by being part of a socialist movement. Trade unionism in the United States has had its political periods, to be examined briefly below, but they have been few and intermittent; and now they fade into memory.

In the last decades of the nineteenth century, before modern industrialism had taken a strong hold, workers and farmers, whether or not struggling to form unions, fought over the banking system, against monopolies, against the manner of electing senators, and over other issues affecting the people in general, not only themselves in particular. It was necessary to fight in that way then, and obviously so. It is necessary to do so today, also; but not so obviously. Trade unions then had little basis for national efforts (the railway unions were among the exceptions), nor were there many powerful *national* corporations. Urban workers cooperated with the angry farmers of the period to bring about, finally, the Populist Movement, which for many years had a radical wing.[42]

In the years leading up to and through World War I, a significant socialist movement took hold in the United States, centering not only in the major centers such as New York, Chicago, and San Francisco, but also in many smaller towns and cities in the middle states of the country. Often, but not always, the socialist movement was associated with then existing trade unions, and that was particularly the case of the railway unions, the leader of one of which, Eugene V. Debs, also became the head of the American Socialist Party—and was jailed for his and its strong opposition to the U.S. participation in World War I.[43]

In the 1930s, the CIO worked closely with what it hoped would be a continuing and ever-more liberal New Deal, and a social context favorable to the needs of working people. Since the 1960s, trade unions have remained political, but in an always narrowing sense. At the leadership level this has more often than not meant working *with* not against the interests of corporate power, and especially those part of the military-industrial complex. With few exceptions, labor leadership has long functioned within the context of a rigid bureaucratic structure, which it is to the leaders' narrow interests to exploit and maintain—very much as in any other bureaucracy. The best means for them to do that has been to concentrate the efforts of the union on "wage-only" types of issues, quite apart from what that might mean, in fact has meant, in abdicating any influence whatsoever in the larger and determining political context.

Like others who have climbed from a lower to a higher level of income and status, labor leaders too have been co-optable. The clear tendency of the corporate world has been to make it evident that it will only "do business" with business minded unions—except when conditions warrant an attempt to weaken or destroy them. They do this by coming down with overwhelming power—their own and the power they can muster in the media and the State—against those labor leaders and unions that seek to broaden labor's agenda and demands.[44] Only those leaders and unions that find ways of working *within* the business system have found survival and success feasible; more recently, not even that kind of conservatism assures either success or survival. Samuel Gompers, the first and longtime ruler of the AFL, spread the slogan "reward our friends and punish our enemies" as *the* political standard for unionism. Business has coopted that useful strategy in its dealings with organized labor also; although in the 1980s, the rewards have almost completely disappeared and the punishments—plant closures, reduced benefits and wages, and the like—have increased, as unionism's ability to resist has dwindled.

Because in the United States the main means labor has sought to protect and enhance itself has been through *business* unionism, it has also perforce adopted much the same aims and means as their business opponents. Thus, not only have unions attempted to control the supply of labor and to use the strike as their principal weapon—both essential means—but, like business, they have also resorted to gangsters, racketeers, and physical violence for both offensive and defensive purposes, against rival union organizers as well as against business firms. It needs to be added that the record in all these cases shows not only that the tactics of labor find their counterparts in the tactics of business, but also that business used each of these tactics first and/or simultaneously. In the absence of a prolonged and deep commitment to fundamental social change on the part of labor—a labor movement—the corruption and violence that has not always but often been associated with trade unionism should come as no surprise.[45]

None of the foregoing should be construed to suggest that labor's efforts to organize or their uses of strength have been either unnecessary or damaging from the viewpoint of *all* workers. Quite the contrary. Unorganized workers have gained from the successes of the organized; the organized themselves have gained even more, and have also learned organizational discipline which has been and can once more be of fundamental importance for political efforts. Nor would it be wise to overlook the difference between the functioning of the top bureaucracy of labor and of the frequently quite different functioning of *local* leaders, and the intermittent militancy and often broader focus of rank and file union members.

By and large, for the past several years, much that has been positive about trade unionism in the United States has diminished, and understandably so, given the downward economic pressures since the 1970s. At the same time, it must be noted that the rightward political movement of the United States that is characterized as Reaganism has been politically supported by a significant portion of the ordinary working people of this country, in and out of unions. That is an outcome of our larger history, a history that teaches us to believe that in looking out for ourselves, we have done all that is necessary.[46]

Much more than that and something much different from that is necessary if the people of this country are to have a decent economic, political, and social existence. When trade unions do not participate in building the appropriate sociopolitical efforts, the prospects for beneficial social change in this country are seriously, perhaps fatally, diminished. It is not only that trade unions, when they have succeeded, have done so in an individualistic, "pork-chops" manner that has held them back from a broader view; it is also the degree to which both organized and unorganized workers participate in the patterns of racial and sexual discrimination and fear that so much characterize our society.[47] In discussing this matter, we are looking at the Achilles heel of labor's actual and potential strength in the United States; it has already been crippling, and the nature and scope of present tendencies are ominous indeed. Further examination of this matter is here in order.

All Against All

We must go back to the 1880s at the very latest to connect labor history with the more general social history of the United States. Although immigration had been increasing since the 1850s, it was during the 1880s that the great waves of migration from the poorer parts of Europe and from Asia became strong. By 1910 over one million immigrants a year were arriving, mostly from southern and southeastern Europe (over 200,000 Italians alone came in that year). This was the period when industrialization was moving strongly and when the conditions of factories and of the cities were becoming increasingly ugly. From the viewpoint of those already "settled" (themselves, of course, immigrants of an earlier period—from the "better" areas of northern Europe such as England and Germany) these newcomers were also "increasingly ugly." Their language, their religion, their appearance—strange, different, "swarthy," Catholic, Jewish, Confucian—set their predecessors against them. The latter tended overwhelmingly to be white and (except for the Irish) Protestant and, by the late nineteenth century, reasonably well-fixed.[48]

The people of the United States had been well-schooled to transform all of this into divisions and hostility that were many-faceted. They had been schooled not least by our long-standing habituation to oppressing and even exterminating red, black, brown, and yellow peoples. The Populist Movement of the 1890s, which saw unprecedented political cooperation between poor whites and blacks, became the occasion for an intensification of racism. From the mid-1890s on, Jim Crow laws spread and deepened, and lynching became so common that it went unnoticed in the press (there were as many as a thousand a year officially record-ed).[49]

The prior and continuing oppression of Native Americans joined with stepped-up oppression of black people and a rapid growth of U.S. nationalism, religious bigotry and attitudes of cultural superiority. Nor were the processes of racism lessened by our participation in the Spanish-Cuban-American War, and especially in the Philippine Islands. Savage developments in the eastern half of the country were followed by savage developments in the western half, as Spanish-speaking and Asian immigrants were mistreated and killed. The lynching of Chinese, occasioned by local trade unions, was common in San Francisco at the turn of the century, their reward for doing the dirty work of building railroads, digging mines, working in the fields, and sweating in the factories of the time.[50]

Racial oppression and ethnic and religious hatreds did not of course begin in the United States nor, unfortunately, have they ended here, in either sense of the word *ended*. But the competitive and combative atmosphere of the United States, taken together with the well-entrenched Puritan work ethic and its corollary of economic individualism, made it easy for bigots and unscrupulous businessmen and politicians to exploit those always pervasive inclinations. Given the enormous power and prestige of business in this country, workers would have had difficulty under the best of circumstances in forming unions or developing a labor movement. But workers accepted and developed internalized obstacles in their thinking and behavior, obstacles to thinking of themselves in terms of class solidarity—or even, in this predominantly Christian society, in terms of social morality.

The "Wobblies," although never very influential in U.S. labor or politics, lived by the slogan "an injury to one is an injury to all." But the socioeconomic development of the United States has allowed all too many to see injuries to some as helpful to their own well-being—or even as desirable in and of themselves. Solidarity is a precious but delicate plant; it can scarcely grow or survive in a desert windstorm. It would be stupid to posit some inherent defect in the character of our people as a means to explain the depth and pervasiveness of racism and sexism in our society, just as stupid as it would be to ignore their existence elsewhere. But it is not foolish to note how these characteristics have become nourished, accentuated, and institutionalized by capitalism in the United States. It is reasonable to argue that if we are to avoid an accelerated social deterioration, let alone to sensibly hope for a decent future, we *must* find ways to reduce and eliminate these practices and attitudes throughout the society.

Racism is one of the two leading social cancers that lead many human beings to view others as being less than human; the other is sexism.

black, brown, red, and yellow people, and women of all colors including "white" have been systematically deprived of basic human rights, have been systematically discriminated against in the kinds and levels of education normally available, have been systematically denied access to "good jobs" and the higher levels of work, and have been paid less for the same jobs when they could get them, some of which is shown in Table 5.9.[51]

The movements in the foregoing relationships over the years indicate significant change upward for "nonwhites" from 1950 until the end of the 1960s, and then an essentially unchanging relationship between whites and nonwhites. A closer look shows a marked difference between the changes for males and females, the former rising from .54 to into the low .60s and staying there, but the incomes for nonwhite females rising from .49 to over .90. The explanation for this great difference is to be found largely in what happened to *black* men as compared with *black* women. Black men's incomes rose principally as they became blue-collar workers in the unionized industries (autos, steel, etc.) which have severely cut back on jobs since the 1970s; black women, exactly half of whom had been domestic servants in the 1950s were able to become employed, like most white women, in clerical, sales, and similar occupations.[52]

A good four-fifths of our population have since the 1970s endured stagnant or falling incomes, and those afflicted by racism and sexism have been able to earn only in the range of 60-70 percent of those incomes—as those at the top have soared. As it was for the notion of "prosperity" in the 1920s, the belief that the United States in recent years has been an "affluent" society is more of a cruel joke than a description of social realities for most of our people.

When we consider that half of the population is female and about a quarter not "white," and that the percentage of women working has risen rapidly and steadily since World War II, now exceeding well over half of all women, the data on racial and sexual discrimination take on a rather large dimension. The increased proportion of women working—regardless of age levels, marital status, and race—has been due to necessity not, as prejudicial jokes would have it, to allow women to buy more cosmetics or just to get out of the house. Real wages have been falling since the 1970s, as noted earlier; in order for families to keep their purchasing power from declining proportionately, it has been necessary as a tendency for the whole family to work: the slow rise in family income between 1979 and 1989, 7.5 percent, is due almost entirely to

Table 5.9
Median Earnings of Full-time Male and Female Workers

Year	Female as Percent of Male
1955	64
1965	60
1975	59
1983	64
1988	66

Median Weekly Earnings of Full-time Men and Women Workers, 15 Years Old and Over, by Occupation, March 1981

Earnings	Ratio of Women's to Men's
Professional and Technical	0.66
Managers and Administrators	0.55
Sales	0.49
Clerical	0.60
Operatives	0.60
All Occupations	0.60

Ratio of Nonwhite to White Median Income, United States, Selected Years

Years	Families	Males	Females
1950	0.54	0.54	0.49
1959	0.52	0.47	0.62
1969	0.63	0.59	0.85
1979	0.61	0.65	0.94
1983	0.62	0.63	0.90[53]

mothers entering the labor force.[54] Among the ills that continue to grow in our society, certainly this necessity for the family and the home to become yoked to (generally low-paying) jobs, is at least a contributing cause to the larger social breakdown, as measured in child delinquency, educational deficiencies, widespread drug use, and the like. There must be and there are alternatives to this unfolding social disaster.

The decline and fall of the Roman Empire has been cited innumerable times by critics of modern western society, as though what happened there and then could happen here and now. It cannot, because the societies have considerably more important differences than similarities. Some of the similarities are nonetheless worth pondering. One of the most respected historians of Rome, in a chapter entitled "The Disorganization of Public Service," wrote (in 1898) a condemnation of late Roman society that brought together the interaction of poverty, inequality of income and wealth, overweening power and rampant greed which, with only minor adjustments, might have been written of the United States today:

> It will be seen that in a society in which poverty is almost branded with infamy, poverty is steadily increasing and wealth becoming more insolent and aggressive; that the disinherited, in the face of an omnipotent government, are carrying brigandage even up to the gates of Rome; that parents are selling their children into slavery; that public buildings are falling into decay; that the service on the great post roads is becoming disorganized... [F]raud and greed are everywhere triumphant, ...the rich are growing richer and more powerful, while the poor are becoming poorer and more helpless...
>
> The overwhelming tragedy of that age was the result not of violent and sudden calamities; it was prepared by the slow, merciless action of social and economic laws, and deepened by the perverse energy of government, and the cupidity and cruelty of the rich and highly placed.[55]

Reading Suggestions

A useful analytical introduction to the structures of income and wealth is in Edwards, et al., *The Capitalist System*, Chapter 6, "Class and Inequality," as are the following two chapters on "Male Dominance" and "Racism," noted earlier in the text. Lars Osberg, *Economic Inequality in the United States* (Armonk, N.Y.: M.E. Sharpe, 1984) and Ben Seligman, *Permanent Poverty: An American Syndrome* (New York: Quadrangle, 1968) are excellent for both breadth and depth. More theoretical is David

M. Gordon, *Theories of Poverty and Under-Employment* (Boston: D.C. Heath & Co., 1972) and Dale Tussing, *Poverty in a Dual Economy** (New York: St. Martin's Press, 1975). The historical data on income and wealth distribution in the United States have been relatively skimpy until recently, and much of what does exist for the eighteenth and nineteenth centuries raises great difficulties about comparability. In their *American Inequality: A Macroeconomic History* (New York: Academic Press, 1980), Jeffrey G. Williamson and Peter H. Lindert, working both with the data and contemporary statistical techniques, have done about as much as can be to construct an orderly history and analysis. For those untrained in economics, parts of the book would be very hard sledding, but for the most part it is readable and the best study available going back into the colonial period. In his *The Pursuit of Inequality* (Oxford: Martin Robertson, 1981), Philip Green examines and criticizes the rationalizations that find the reasons for inequality in the characteristics of those at the bottom, rather than the behavior and power of those at the top. His work is philosophical, political, and historical, eminently readable, and most important.

We tend to think of poverty as an urban condition, which it surely is. But see Arthur M. Ford, *Political Economics of Rural Poverty in the South* (Cambridge, MA: Ballinger, 1973).

Because the meaning of *class* is generally neglected in U.S. discussions of these matters, it is worth mentioning a number of helpful studies, both broad and specific in nature. For viewpoints going beyond the very brief discussions I have provided (from Chapter 1 on) see T.B. Bottomore, *Classes in Modern Society** (New York: Vintage, 1966), R.H. Tawney, *Equality** (New York: Capricorn, 1961; originally published in 1929), C. Wright Mills, *The Power Elite** (New York: Oxford University Press, 1959), G. William Domhoff, *Who Rules America?** (Englewood Cliffs, N.J.: Prentice-Hall, Spectrum, 1967) and his *The Higher Circles** (New York: Vintage, 1971). Irving Louis Horowitz, ed., *Power, Politics, and People: The Collected Essays of C. Wright Mills** (New York: Oxford University Press, 1963), contains many essays on class, power, ideology, education, and other issues most relevant to much of this book. A careful and strong analysis is Erik Olin Wright, *Class Structure and Income Determination* (New York: Academic Press, 1979).

See also the penetrating studies of Richard Sennett and Jonathan Cobb, *The Hidden Injuries of Class** (New York: Knopf, 1972) and of F. Piven and R. Cloward, *Regulating the Poor: The Functions of Public Welfare**

(New York: Vintage, 1971). See also R. Cloward's later work, *The New Class War: Reagan's Attack on the Welfare State and its Consequences** (New York: Pantheon, 1982) and the fine collection of Pamela Roby, *The Poverty Establishment*, noted earlier. Harold Vatter and Robert E. Will, eds., *Poverty in Affluence** (New York: Harcourt Brace Jovanovich, 1970) is a useful book of readings covering a broad range of problems, analytical and factual. Charles H. Anderson, *The Political Economy of Social Class* (Englewood Cliffs, N.J.: Prentice-Hall, 1974) is a valuable and comprehensive analytical survey of an immense literature by a radical sociologist. Barbara Ehrenreich, in *Fear of Falling: The Inner Life of the Middle Class** (New York: Harper Perennial, 1990), as its title indicates, is an analysis of the kind of "social nervousness" that comes from living in a society simultaneously materialistic, economically stagnant, and contemptuous of those who have "fallen" or who have never risen.

A compelling work on inequality and the context in which it is created, which is at the same time an effort to show the ideological and mythological fog within which attitudes toward the poor exist, is William Ryan, *Blaming the Victim** (New York: Vintage, 1971). And see Richard H. de Lone, *Small Futures: Children, Inequality and the Limits of Liberal Reform* (New York: Harcourt Brace Jovanovich, 1979). See also Thomas Byrne Edsall, *The New Politics of Inequality* (New York: Norton, 1984) and his and Mary Edsall's essay "Race" cited in Chapter 1. Lester Thurow, in an important and long article in *Scientific American*, May, 1987, was among the first to see and to analyze the rapidly worsening distribution of income in the United States, in his "A Surge in Inequality."

The history of labor has been treated only superficially in the text. Those wishing to gain a more adequate basis for understanding will find no shortage of books; and of course no one book regarding such a controversial area can stand as sufficient. The classic source book and compendium is John R. Commons, et al., *History of Labor in the United States*, 4 vols. (New York: Macmillan, 1918–1935). A more selective look is provided by Len De Caux, *Labor Radicals** (Boston: Beacon Press, 1970), which takes the story from the Wobblies up to the 1960s, by one who was a part of it. The definitive study of the Wobblies is Melvyn Dubofsky, *We Shall Be All** (Chicago: Quadrangle, 1969), and a convenient survey is that of Patrick Renshaw, *The Wobblies** (New York: Doubleday; Anchor Books, 1968). The drama and vitality of the Wobblies—to whom I give this much attention because they combined an intense belief in personal freedom with an equally intense desire to organize a society in which ordinary working people would govern themselves—is caught best in the anthology by Joyce L. Kornbluh, *Rebel Voices** (Ann Arbor: University of Michigan Press, 1964). Also see Sidney Lens, *The Labor Wars** (New York: Anchor, 1974) and the deservedly popular *Labor's Untold Story** by Richard Boyer and Herbert Morais (New York: United Electrical, Radio, and Machine Workers of America, 1974). A new and lively history, essentially of the period since World War II, written by a lawyer who worked with the mineworkers', steelworkers', and teamsters' unions (always with dissident rank-filers), is Thomas Geoghegan, *Which Side Are You On?** (New York: Farrar, Straus & Giroux, 1991). An intensive study of one of those industries is provided by David Brody, *Steelworkers in America: The Non-Union Era* (Cambridge, MA: Harvard University Press, 1960). And see the revealing book by Jeremy Brecher, *Strike!* (Boston, MA: South End Press, 1979). Harry Braverman's *Labor and Monopoly Capital* was noted in Chapter 2. It is a powerful and profound study of—as his subtitle says—"the degradation of labor" in this century; that is, not only inadequate wages and poor to dangerous working conditions, but also the stripping away of any power whatsoever in the doing of work: the achievement by employers of "foolproof" technologies, and the like. Richard C. Edwards, *Contested Terrain: The Transformation of the Workplace in the Twentieth Century* (New York: Basic Books, 1979), and David M. Gordon, Richard Edwards, and Michael Reich, *Segmented Work, Divided Workers. The Historical Transformation of Labor in the U.S.* (New York: Cambridge University Press, 1982) take these matters further, and examine the struggles over that development.

Now we turn to a sampling of the literature on racism and sexism which, is fortunately, abundant. A useful starting point is Jacobs, Landau, and Pell, eds., *To Serve the Devil*, noted in Chapter 2, which provides analysis and materials regarding almost all those racially oppressed in the United States, going back to the colonial period. Herbert Aptheker, ed., *A Documentary History of the Negro People in the United States* (New York: Citadel, 1973) and W.E.B. DuBois, *The Souls of Black Folk* (New York: Fawcett, 1961, originally published early in the century) are both important, in their different ways. Gerda Lerner, ed., *Black Women in White America* (New York: Random House, 1973) brings two forms of oppression together. An excellent analysis of urban blacks' economic situation is William K. Tabb, *The Political Economy of the Black Ghetto* * (New York: Norton, 1970), and, with a broader framework, also analytically excellent is Raymond S. Franklin and Solomon Resnik, *The Political Economy of Racism* * (New York: Harper & Row, 1973). Robert L. Allen, *Black Awakening in Capitalist America* * (New York: Doubleday; Anchor Books, 1970) is a powerful critique, as is Patricia Cayo Sexton's *Spanish Harlem* * (New York: Harper & Row, 1965). G. Osofsky, *Harlem: The Making of A Ghetto* * (New York: Harper & Row, 1966) examines the history of black people in New York City from the early 19th century up to about 1930; in doing so he reveals how pressures and policies have worked to create and to maintain patterns of discrimination from our earliest years. One can learn much from the life and work of Malcolm X, about that remarkable man and the conditions against which he rebelled. See his *Malcolm X Speaks* * (New York: Meret, 1965). Also see Ralph Ellison's *Invisible Man*, noted in the preceding chapter, and Richard Wright's autobiographical *Black Boy* (New York: Harper & Row, 1937) and his *Native Son* (New York: Harper & Row, 1989, originally published 1940).

The literature on the conditions and the oppression of women did not by any means begin in recent years, but it has very much multiplied since the 1960s. An early book of readings makes a good starting-place: Robin Morgan, ed., *Sisterhood is Powerful* * (New York: Random House, 1970). The economic aspects of sexism were explored by Margaret Benston, "The Political Economy of Women's Liberation," in *Monthly Review* (September 1969); M. and J. Roundtree, "More on the Political Economy...," *Monthly Review* (January 1970); Peggy Morton, "A Woman's Work is Never Done," *Leviathan* (May 1970); and URPE in its RRPE, vol. 4, No. 3 (July 1972), devoted an issue, *The Political Economy of Women*, to this question, in about twenty essays, and did so again in vol. 8, No. 1 (Spring 1976), *Women and the Economy*. See also Cynthia Lloyd and Beth Neimi, *The Economics of Sex Differentials* (New York: Columbia University Press, 1979), Rosalyn Baxandall, et al., eds., *America's Working Women* (New York: Random House, 1976), and Barbara C. Garson, *All the Livelong Day: The Meaning and Demeaning of Routine Work* * (New York: Penguin Books, 1977). See also Gerda Lerner, *The Female Experience: An American Documentary* (Indianapolis: Bobbs-Merrill, 1977), and William Chafe, *Women and Equality: Changing Patterns in American Culture* (New York: Oxford University Press, 1977).

Three books worth reading, especially in conjunction with each other provide a penetrating set of analyses of the roots and conditions of poverty for women, the causes and cruelties of spreading homelessness —worse for women than for men, and particularly so for black women —and the recent and current ways in which various elements of U.S. society have sought to reverse what limited progress women had achieved for themselves before the 1980s: Rochelle Lefkowitz and Ann Withorn (eds.), *For Crying Out Loud: Women and Poverty in the United States* (New York: Pilgrim Press, 1986); Stephanie Golden, *The Women Outside: Meanings and Myths of Homelessness* (Berkeley: Univ. of California Press, 1992); and Susan Faludi, *Backlash: The Undeclared War Against American Women* (New York: Crown Publishers, 1991).

And last, an informed guess on a most unAmerican future, based on an analysis of current tendencies: Frank Levy and Richard C. Michel, *The Economic Future of American Families: Income and Wealth Trends* (New York: Urban Institute Press, 1991), which shows the widening inequality both between the present younger generation and its parents, and within that younger generation itself.

Notes

1. Carl Sandburg, from *The People, Yes,* by Carl Sandburg, copyright 1936 by Harcourt Brace Jovanovitch, Inc.; copyright 1964 by Carl Sandburg. Reprinted by permission of the publishers.

2. That literally reactionary movement took hold first in Britain in 1979, under Prime Minister Thatcher, and in the United States in the Reagan years. Of its several enabling causes, one was the lessening of both the quantitative and qualitative strength of unions in the United States and of the Left in Europe—resulting in important part from the improved well-being of the majority after 1960. In thinking about the economic gains of middle- and lower-income groups one may distinguish between income and transfers, where the distinction for present purposes rests on the difference between what is received as interest, profits, rents, wages and salaries, on the one hand, and what is received as transfer payments in money or in kind, such as pensions, subsidized health care, housing, etc. All forms of income, including average real wages, increased in the United States in the 1960s, and transfers increasing real income grew at the same time; but since the late 1970s the overall pattern of inequality has steadily reasserted itself, for reasons that will appear shortly. In other countries, Austria and Sweden, for example, there was

a substantial redistribution of real income downward in the decades after World War II. In those two countries, and others in Europe, although there is good reason to believe prewar patterns will not be fully reasserted, recently there has been a significant tendency in that direction.

3. In 1990, for example, it was noted that the average annual income of physicians in the United States was $119,000.

4. *Income* is a flow of money and purchasing power over time; *wealth* is a stock of things owned that have market value. Money income includes wages and salaries, social security benefits, dividends, interest and rents received, pensions, alimony received, net income from self-employment, and other periodic receipts. Some of the foregoing are for contributions to current production, the others are transfers, as indicated earlier. Wealth includes autos and homes as well as trucks and mines and corporate stocks; but for analytical purposes the ownership of productive—that is, income-producing—assets is the vital factor, and our reference when we measure it below.

5. We shall treat the nineteenth century in a summary manner. For a more extended treatment, see Alfred Conrad's essay "Income Growth and Structural Change," in Alfred Conrad and John R. Meyer, *The Economics of Slavery* (Chicago: Aldine, 1964), especially pp. 168–177.

6. The terms light and heavy when applied to industry refer to relative "weight" of capital equipment compared with labor. Thus, the typical light, labor-intensive, industry in the nineteenth century was the textile industry, for which the equipment had to be "manned" by numerous workers—when one compares the equipment/labor ratio in the steel industry, for example. Today, textiles are in large measure synthetic, using chemical equipment more and labor less, per unit of output. Despite all the complaints about low productivity in industry, the fact is that labor productivity has continued to rise substantially throughout the industrializing period, including the productivity of the U.S. industrial worker. The productivity problem in U.S. industry, as compared with that of Japan, for example, may be understood as being due to two major factors: lower investment in the United States and excessive managerial and supervisorial personnel—a ratio of seven managers to one, compared with Japan, is normal.

7. By the 1970s this had become so important and so common that the term "tax expenditure" came into effect. It means that the tax exemptions or privileges granted particular industries, individuals, or other groups, function as a lever to raise the taxes of everyone else, just as though the

government had increased its expenditures. These "tax expenditures," in the range of $20 billion annually in the 1970s, now exceed $100 billion.

8. Kolko, *Main Currents*, op. cit., p. 340. One rather substantial form of understatement came to light in the 1970s when it was learned that the computers of the Internal Revenue Service were not programmed to record annual incomes in excess of $100,000—that is, the incomes of a rather substantial number of very rich people. For a systematic discussion of some of the limitations of the data, see Herman P. Miller, *Rich Man, Poor Man* (New York: Thomas Y. Crowell, 1964), Appendix. Miller worked with the Census Bureau for fifteen years. The data to be presented in this chapter will often refer to "tenths," or "fifths," as well as "top 5" or "top 1" percent. The custom in the Census Bureau's reports is to divide the population in that manner: the 20 percent ("fifth") receiving the highest or lowest share of a given year's "personal income" for the nation. These are incomes before income taxes. "Disposable personal income" is after-tax income, and includes money transfers. Our intent is to show which category is used on each occasion.

9. The data and the end quotation are from Frank Levy, *Dollars and Dreams: The Changing American Income Distribution* (New York: W.W. Norton, 1988), pp. 24–25. He provides a thorough discussion of the problems and procedures surrounding the collection and the use of data discussed in this chapter in his Appendices A–E, pp. 215–29.

10. The figures given are official. Nongovernmental studies show higher rates, as in a report from the Joint Center for Political and Economic Studies, in September 1991. The reporting group was headed up by the widely respected Professor William Julius Wilson. It defined the poverty level as 50 percent of the median income for all households with heads age 20 to 55. They found that the rate for the United States was 18.1 percent—compared with 13.9 percent in Canada, 12.5 percent in Britain, 9.9 percent in France, 8.6 percent in Sweden, 7.6 percent in the Netherlands, and 6.8 percent in West Germany. The figures are for the late 1980s, after many years in which the levels of unemployment were lower and growth rates higher in the United States than in those countries with *lower* poverty rates.

The official measure of poverty will be analyzed shortly; suffice it to say here that it is a gross understatement in both quantitative and qualitative terms. The report was summarized in the *Washington Post*, September 20, 1991.

11. Herman P. Miller, op. cit., p. 29. The figure for 1991 was put forth

by the Census Bureau in a report of September 3, 1992.

12. *Historical Statistics of the United States*, p. 301.

13. The "median" family income is in the middle of all family incomes; that is, there are just as many families with incomes below as above that figure. It is one of several terms used for "average," the most common of which is the arithmetic mean, where the aggregate number (say, GNP) is divided by the total population, to give us average or per capita income—an average that is as often misleading as it is informative, concealing, as it does, the situation at the extremes of very rich and very poor, understating the incomes of the former and the numbers of the latter. An average is just that; it tells us nothing about the *distribution* of income or wealth, for which percentage shares are needed.

14. Levy, op. cit., p. 17.

15. Mishel and Frankel, *The State of Working America, 1990–1991*, pp. 18–19. Shortly we shall see that for those at the very top and the very bottom, those seemingly small changes are very large when expressed in dollar terms at the very top, or worsened living conditions at the very bottom.

16. Joseph Pechman, *Tax Reform*, p. 20. These figures are derived from Internal Revenue Service data, and include capital gains income. The difference between these and the census data that have been used in our other tables (unless otherwise specified) is substantial. Thus, census data for 1967 show the Top 5 percent receiving 15.2 percent, whereas IRS data show 19.6 percent, in excess of 25 percent in addition. Pechman's data do not go beyond 1986; it would be reasonable to expect that the share of the Top 5 percent in 1989 shown as 17.2 percent in census data would be closer to 30 percent when capital gains are included, given that in 1986 their share was 26.6 percent and unlikely to fall in the next three years.

17. Ibid. Pechman also shows that the next 13 percent after the top 2 percent increased their share of total income from 21 percent in 1951 to 27 percent in 1986. These are principally "the professional people (doctors, lawyers, engineers, accountants, college professors, etc.) as well as the highest-paid members of the skilled labor force and white-collar workers.

18. Derived from Table C in the review essay of Andrew Hacker, "Class Dismissed," *New York Review of Books*, March 7, 1991. His data are taken from Internal Revenue Service reports. His review encompasses two quite different but equally absorbing studies, Benjamin DeMott, *The*

Imperial Middle: Why Americans Can't Think Straight About Class, (New York: Morrow, 1990), and *Money Income and Poverty Status in the United States 1989: Advance Data from the March 1990 Current Population Survey, Bureau of the Census* (Washington, D.C.: U.S. Government Printing Office, 1990). Much of the data in this chapter have been derived directly or indirectly from the latter report.

19. From "The Shift in the Distribution of Income, 1980–1990," an as yet unpublished essay by James Cypher, who has granted me permission to use his data. He goes on to point out one meaning of the increased inequality of the 1980s: Had it not increased, the bottom 80 percent of the population would have had an additional $152 billion of income to share in the year 1989 alone—which, instead, the top 20 percent (meaning mostly the top 5-10 percent) in fact had.

20. "Full employment," like so many other important concepts of measurement, is a controversial term; and as it is used in mainstream academia, media, and politics, it has come to be an always rising number: 3 percent in the years after World War II, 4 percent in the 1960s, 5 percent in the 1970s, and edging 6 percent at present. The Employment Act of 1946, which requires among other matters that the President give an annual "Economic Report" to the Congress, was called the "Full Employment Act of 1946" originally; even that was too much of a red flag, and its name was changed. The definition of "full employment" is political: it depends upon who is speaking. For labor, it means a situation where labor markets are buoyant, thus increasing the bargaining power of wage earners; and precisely for that reason, the employing class wishes to have a concept of full employment—nowadays 6 per-cent—which keeps wage pressures low. Usually the latter position is put forth not as a way to keep wages low, but to avoid inflation. And inflation is usually analyzed as being caused by wage increases—even under conditions where prices advance before wages. Normally, and with rare exceptions, workers, unionized or not, are playing "catch-up."

21. This process was part and parcel of the global process that came to be called "restructuring," to be examined carefully in Chapter 7.

22. Karl Marx, *Wage-Labour and Capital** (New York: International Publishers, 1933; originally published 1849), p. 33.

23. Philip M. Stern has written two books showing the facts, proce-dures, winners and losers, and bases of our tax system, which works very much the opposite of its presumed intent: *The Great Treasury Raid** (New York: Signet, 1965), and *The Rape of the Taxpayer* (New York:

Random House, 1973). Though written some years ago, the validity of both books has, if anything, been strengthened rather than weakened by the passage of time. Congress makes our federal tax laws of course. Given that their annual income is $125,000, which places them in the top 5 percent, and that all have sources of income beyond that (from legal practice, etc.—nine-tenths of them being lawyers), it is understandable, indeed predictable that, apart from any other reason, they would be opposed to seriously effective progressive tax legislation. And there are other reasons as well, of course, not least among them the steady and heavy pressure of lobbying groups. Veblen considered the attempts to bribe such people as acts of "supererogation"—that is, unnecessary.

24. Mishel and Frankel, op. cit., p. 152. "Net Worth" includes both financial assets (money in the bank, stock shares, etc.) and tangible assets (auto, home, etc.). The figures for the bottom 90 percent require qualification: 20 percent of those families had a zero or negative net worth; 54 percent had a zero or negative net value of financial assets.

25. Op. cit., p. 153. In the same discussion, the authors point out that "...the typical black family with a given income has a tiny fraction of the wealth of a white family with the same income." Shortly we shall examine further the relationships between race and gender and income.

26. Of course the rich do spend a very great deal, which leaves still a very great amount unspent. One of the curious but explicable consequences of the upward redistribution of income is its impact on, among other areas, automobile production. That industry has of course been in deep trouble for some time—but not in its luxury car division. "Luxury-car makers are holding their own because the typical household-income range for luxury-car buyers is $75,000 or more. Last year, there were more than eight million households in that bracket, compared with just one million in 1980." *New York Times*, April 14, 1991. In addition to the books already cited for data and analysis on income and wealth, see the readable and easily available book of Ferdinand Lundberg, *The Rich and the Super-Rich** (New York: Lyle Stuart, 1968).

27. The *Business Week* essays are those of April 1, June 17, and August 5, 1972.

28. In his *The Other America** (Baltimore: Penguin, 1962). Interestingly, the book would quite probably not have received the attention it ultimately did had it not been for a very long discussion of it by Dwight MacDonald in the *New Yorker*—a magazine of and for the well-off, composed more of ads for very expensive products than of essays and

cartoons, but with a history of socially responsible essays. It was when Harrington's book was brought to the attention of the new President Johnson in 1963, after Kennedy's death, that he declared his "war on poverty."

29. Clair Wilcox, *Toward Social Welfare* (Homewood, Ill.: Irwin, 1969), pp. 26–27. Italics mine. Moreover: the "emergency use diet" was first concocted by the Office of Civil Defense for a post–nuclear attack period. Learning of such tenuous and distorting procedures, from President to CEA to SSA to OCD and back to the President and on to us, and knowing that much the same basis for estimating is used to this day, makes one's normally fragile faith in government figures and figuring approach the breaking point—and to wonder, now that a post–nuclear attack period is less likely than ever to exist, what new basis would be concocted if a new basis were to be concocted.

30. The foregoing paragraph is based largely on a fine article in *Dollars & Sense*, September 1990, "Being Poor Isn't Enough," by Tim Wise, which discusses, among other matters, Patricia Ruggles' important study, *Alternative Poverty Measures and Their Implications for Public Policy* (Washington, D.C.: Urban Institute Press, 1990).

31. "The Uses of Poverty: The Poor Pay All," in *Social Policy*, (July/ August 1971), by Professor Herbert Gans, of M.I.T.

32. Howard Wachtel, "Capitalism and Poverty in America: Paradox or Contradiction?" *Monthly Review*, June 1972. That issue also contains two supporting articles by David Gordon and Barry Bluestone, and all these have been reproduced, along with others, in an excellent collection by Pamela Roby, ed., *The Poverty Establishment** (Englewood Cliffs, N.J.: Prentice–Hall, 1972). A further causal factor has to do with the number of single-parent families with small children (not so common when Wachtel wrote), where the absence of publicly-funded child care facilities means that mothers must pay child-care costs that eat up most of their wages.

33. For an extended discussion of the general role of education in maintaining class distinctions and poverty in the United States, see the important book by Samuel Bowles and Herb Gintis, *Schooling in Capitalist America* (New York: Basic Books, 1976), and two books by Miriam Wasserman, *The School Fix, NYC, USA** (New York: Simon and Schuster, 1870) and *Demystifying School** (New York, Praeger, 1974), an anthology of many enlightening essays edited by Wasserman.

34. Of course, we use the term "class" frequently in the United States,

264 – U.S. CAPITALIST DEVELOPMENT SINCE 1776

but its reference is principally as regards income categories. A moment's reflection will remind that when we hear the term "lower class" we mean someone who is poor or almost so, with almost always an implicit suggestion of deficiencies of character and style. The "middle class," to which almost all people in the United States see themselves as belonging, has come to mean those neither in the top nor the bottom categories of income—say the "middle" 80 percent. And normally we categorize the very rich not as "upper class," but as "very rich." A useful and extended discussion of this matter may be found in the DeMott book cited earlier, *The Imperial Middle....* But also see the suggestions at the end of this chapter.

35. Gabriel Kolko, "The Decline of American Radicalism in the Twentieth Century," in James Weinstein and David W. Eakins, eds., *For a New America** (New York: Vintage, 1970), p. 208.

36. Quoted in Selsam, et al., *Dynamics of Social Change*, p. 136. (Emphasis in original.)

37. The foregoing characterization is of the unions and of their leadership. Like so much else in our society, the trade union form is democratic, but the practice is more often than not oligarchic—and that has often been an important factor in the apathy of many union members toward their own union, and unionism in general. Workers in general, either today or earlier, have not always been politically conservative, as Andrew Levinson makes clear in his *The Working Class Majority* (New York: Coward, McCann, Geoghegan, 1974), as does Sidney Peck, in *The Rank-and-File Leader** (New Haven: College & University Press, 1963).

38. I have analyzed this matter more fully in the essay "A Comparative Analysis of Economic Development in the American West and South," included in Harry Scheiber, ed., *U.S. Economic History: Selected Readings** (New York: Knopf, 1964), a generally useful collection of analytical studies.

39. For an overall survey, see Handlin, *The Uprooted*, cited earlier.

40. In the Reading Suggestions at the end of the chapter, numerous references to useful studies of labor history will be made, but here it is worth noting two recent books that help to explain the relative conservatism and weakness of U.S. labor, by comparison with other capitalist societies, Patricia Cayo Sexton, *The War on Labor and the Left: Understanding America's Unique Conservatism* (Boulder: Westview Press, 1991), and David R. Roediger, *The Wages of Whiteness: Race and the Making of the American Working Class** (London: Verso, 1991).

41. For a comprehensive treatment of the interwar years, see Irving Bernstein, *The Lean Years: A History of the American Worker 1920–1933* (Boston: Houghton Mifflin, 1960), and *The Turbulent Years...1933–1941*, cited earlier.

42. The most comprehensive history of labor's efforts in the United States is Philip Foner, *A History of the Labor Movement in the United States*, 4 vols. (New York: International Publishers, 1947–1964. Despite its title, the history is principally of *trade unionism.* There have been many studies of the Populist Movement; the most astute, in my judgment, have been those of C. Vann Woodward. See *Tom Watson: Agrarian Rebel** (New York: Oxford University Press, 1963), and the essay "The Populist Heritage and the Intellectual," in his fine collection *The Burden of Southern History** (New York: Random House, 1961). An article as important as its contents are surprising is Jack Abramowitz, "The Negro in the Populist Movement," *Journal of Negro History*, vol. 38, no. 3 (July 1953). What it shows of black-white political cooperation in the South in the 1880s and 1890s, is on the one hand encouraging but, given the savage reaction to it, taking the form of the Jim Crow laws and iron-clad segregation, it is also a terrible episode in U.S. history—fully recounted in Woodward's *The Strange Career of Jim Crow** (New York: Oxford University Press, 1966).

43. See James Weinstein, *Decline of Socialism** (New York: Random House, Vintage, 1969), for a fine analysis of the rise and decline of the socialist movement after 1912 in the United States.

44. A clear instance of this was in the attempt of the Waterfront Employers Association (San Francisco) to have the leader of the longshore union, Harry Bridges, deported. Six trials occurred, beginning in the 1930s after the essentially successful 1934 general strike, called by the longshore union. The charge against Bridges, an Australian by birth, was that he was a member of the Communist Party and therefore deportable. The employers had the constant cooperation of the Immigration and Naturalization Service and what was subsequently shown to be a stable of governmentally paid informers. By the time of the sixth trial, well after World War II, the *employers* moved to end the process—then being carried on enthusiastically by the State in the midst of the Cold War—having found that the union was a stabilizing influence on the waterfront. The "stabilization" amounted to a trade-off between employers and the union, whereby new and greatly labor-saving technology would be used, a portion of the workers would continue to

266 - U.S. CAPITALIST DEVELOPMENT SINCE 1776

receive good wages, and the work force as a whole would be, as it has been, substantially reduced. For the larger process of which this was but one instance, see Sexton's *The War on Labor and the Left*, cited earlier.

45. An analysis and history of these matters (up to the early 1930s) is provided by Louis Adamic, *Dynamite** (New York: Viking, 1934). An early study of the nature and probabilities of labor bureaucracy, which was all too prophetic was provided by C. Wright Mills, *New Men of Power* (New York: Harcourt Brace Jovanovich, 1948).

46. See Sidney Peck, *The Rank-and-File Leader*, cited earlier, and Stanley Aronowitz, *False Promises** (New York: McGraw-Hill, 1974), both of whom express the hopes and fears just raised, and in their different ways show the reasons for both, and the possibilities for a labor movement in the United States. Both write from their experience as workers, although they are now academics.

47. Which is not to overlook the many often successful efforts made by and within trade unions throughout their history in fighting against racial barriers, whether those of the Communist-led unions of the 1930s or the more generally organized efforts against racial and sexual discrimination—"equal pay for equal work"—in recent years. Whether self-interested or not, such efforts have been noteworthy, not least because unions were almost alone in pursuing them. There have also been significant instances of some unions attempting to maintain barriers, of course.

48. The Irish were themselves treated very badly, largely because of their Catholicism. It was common in Boston to see signs saying "Dogs and Micks not allowed." That nasty history has not prevented those of Irish descent today, nor those descended from those presently under discussion, from participating in the varieties of prejudice, discrimination, and hatred aimed at blacks, Hispanics, and Asians. Given the fact that virtually the entire population of the United States is descended from "foreigners" it would have been reasonable to expect that this country would have become the most tolerant of all. Some may remember the song from "South Pacific," "You've gotta be taught to hate." We have been, and although the process of "teaching" has been informal, it has been all the more effective for that.

49. See Woodward, *The Strange History of Jim Crow*, cited earlier.

50. It is sad to note that in prosperous Germany, where for a whole generation new workers have been brought in, also from southern and eastern Europe, to do the "dirty work"—quite literally the work that

"Germans" won't do—they are now under not only political but physical attack. The same has been true in one degree or another in Italy, France, Belgium, and elsewhere. By the 1970s it is estimated that one out of seven workers in Western Europe had come from the south of Europe, the Balkans, Turkey, and North Africa.

51. There is at least one important difference between racism and sexism that gives the former a stronger *economic* meaning than the latter. It is that women share the status and the class of their fathers and husbands, generally. That is, of course, one of the meanings of sexism. But it has meant that there are fewer women as a percentage of all women who are *poor*, say, than blacks as a percentage of all blacks. *Within* a given class or racial category, however, women are worse off than men, as measured by jobs available to them, pay for the same jobs, etc. Edwards, et al., in *The Capitalist System*, cited earlier, provide two substantial and comprehensive chapters combining analysis with statistical data, Chapter 7, "Male Dominance," and Chapter 8, "Racism," pp. 248-311. The term "nonwhite" is an official category, and is in itself a racist phenomenon—referring to people by what they are *not*. That the very term "race" should be used is dubious; but we cannot pursue such matters here.

52. Edwards, et al., pp. 258, 285, 287. The 1988 figures for male ratios are from U.S. Bureau of the Census, *Statistical Abstract of the United States, 1990* (Washington, D.C.: U.S. Government Printing Office, 1990) p. 411.

53. The data in the foregoing paragraph for 1988 are taken from U.S. Department of Labor, Bureau of Labor Statistics, *Handbook of Labor Statistics* (Washington, D.C.: U.S. Government Printing Office, 1989) p. 162; the data following comparing black men's with black women's incomes is from a summary of a Census Bureau release of September 20, 1991, *International Herald Tribune*, September 21–22, 1991.

54. Mishel and Frankel, op. cit., pp. 39–41.

55. Samuel Dill, *Roman Society in the Last Century of the Western Empire** (New York: Meridian, 1958), pp. 228–29, 244.

– 6 –

Nature and Nurture; Country and City; Waste and Destruction

Black spruce and Norway pine
Douglas fir and Red cedar,
Scarlet oak and Shagbark hickory.
We built a hundred cities and a thousand towns—
But at what a cost!
We cut the top off the Alleghenies and sent it down the river.
We cut the top off Minnesota and sent it down the river.
We cut the top off Wisconsin and sent it down the river.
We left the mountains and the hills slashed and burned,
And moved on.[1]

They are herding our hearts down freeways.
The architects of America say
This is how it will be in another century:
We will join with armies of geese
In the cities of weeds,
Living on grass, in love with our own dung.[2]

The problems now facing our cities, our society, our world, and our natural environment are problems of whole systems in dynamic imbalance. In the United States the roots of all these go back to our early years as a nation. They are simultaneously physical and social, economic and political, psychological, historical, and ideological in their origins and continuation, and in their worsening over time. Can conventional economics (and related social sciences) successfully grapple with such matters?

From previous discussions, we recall that conventional economics is highly abstract; it is concerned with purely quantitative *market* relationships; it takes both nature and historical time as "given," as it does also with technology; it has both a limited and a baseless view of our psychology; and, ideological both in its development and in its impact, it effectively ignores ideological and developmental matters. Such an economics can provide little understanding of either the nature or the origins of what now reaches the crisis stage. Indeed, it is precisely what economists consider most necessary and most desirable —that is, maximization—which in our history accounts for much of what has "gone wrong." Those who have exploited our natural resources, whether farmers or mineral and timber companies, or whatever, and those who have both developed and ravaged our cities, have been businessmen or have moved in tandem with them. To provide a society dominated by such motivations with a market economics of maximization is like providing an alcoholic with directions to the nearest bar.

Awareness of social and natural deterioration in the United States did not begin in recent decades. In the nineteenth and the first part of the twentieth century there was already a serious awareness of both environmental and urban problems, and movements for relevant reforms emerged to affect both: what were called "the conservation movement" and "the progressive movement." In neither case did their views as to the nature or the resolution of the problems lead them to examine fundamental institutions or to question the processes arising from them. They were reformers who, though often idealistic, were concerned with the economic and social *inefficiency* of rapacious resource use and of teeming, unhealthy, often dangerous, and unsightly cities. In short, they were concerned with making the existing system work better, more efficiently, less turbulently.[3]

The conservationists and urban progressives, often the same people, sought to bring order out of the growing chaos induced by rapid and pervasive industrialization and sprawling urbanization in the early twentieth century. Their contemporary counterparts are the liberal ecologists and urban planners. That viewpoint was and remains important, but it was and remains only partially valid. The attempt to eliminate dangerous and destructive resource utilization, and to remedy some of the deep inadecies of urban existence, is, of course, an aim entirely praiseworthy. But the liberal view sees these problems as *extrinsic* to the present socioeconomic system. Quite correctly, it is assumed that U.S. capitalism does not *need* blighted cities, polluted air, cut-over land, and wasted resources; what is overlooked is that for capitalist development to proceed satisfactorily in its own—as distinct from human—terms, the economy cannot be sufficiently constrained so as to *forestall* blighted cities, polluted air, and the rest.

There have, of course, been many laws and regulations and private/public efforts to effectuate environmental and urban constraints. That is not remarkable, given the sordid and frightening realities. What *is* worthy of remark is that accompanying all these actions has been a worsening of all the problems. Where there has been demonstrable achievement, and there has been much of it, its best result has been measured by a reduction of the rate of *increase* of deterioration, not by its decrease. The fault lies in an analytical failure, itself an outcome of a conscious or unconscious political/ideological position; and this leads to liberal policy recommendations that are invariably inadequate and can be damaging. The problem of the inaccurate compass being worse than none at all, once more. To repeat a vital point: a main reason for the *economic* dynamism of U.S. capitalism has been precisely that it has been *socially*, and here we add *environmentally* unconstrained. Now, when discussion is no longer about problems, as earlier in the century, but about crises, the universe of discourse must alter to meet our sense that time is running out.[4]

Economists and other social scientists, once in the background of such discussions, have today moved more to the fore. Whether they will have anything much to contribute depends upon whether or not economics moves toward the dynamic perspective of political economy. If it does so, and as it does so, it will have to be informed by some firm idea of the continuity of our development, of what brought us to where we are today, and of the manner in which business impulses have meshed with social and political developments to push us ever more rapidly to our critical present. Building on previous chapters, we continue our story with farmers in the United States, and their much idealized "way of life."

Farming as a Way of Business

The United States is among the very most *industrial* of all societies. Yet, our social nature remains inexplicable if we ignore the dominating role played by *farmers* in the shaping of our entire history and outlook, and our domestic and foreign policies. The first European settlers came here for many reasons, but they soon found themselves exploiting the land, while pushing aside or killing its original inhabitants. Up to the end of the nineteenth century, and despite the surge of industrialization that began around 1850, the numbers, the prestige, the economic importance, and the social perspective of farmers continued to take a leading role in setting the tone of U.S. life; was businesslike, and it was expansionist.

It had begun that way. Farming is, of course, a "way of life," as its proponents so often say. But U.S. agriculture has been given its qualities and direction by those who are best at making money from the cultivation of and speculation in land. Less than a decade after the first English settlers set foot at what became Jamestown, Virginia, their livelihood was dependent upon tobacco exports to England. So intense was their concentration on the marketing of tobacco that the Governor of Virginia (in 1616) had to *require* that each colonist plant at least two acres of corn for himself and each male servant, to avoid starvation.[5]

There were, of course, great differences in the agriculture and lives of the northern and southern regions of the colonies. But the differences were in the meanness or generosity of climate and soil, not in farmers' intentions. For those who set the tone in farming, the intention was to make money, not subsistence, from the land.

The South was by far the most productive region, with its rich soils and long growing season. Beginning with tobacco in the seventeenth century, the South went on to raise indigo (for dyeing), rice, cotton, and sugar. Slaves were used in tobacco cultivation; but large-scale slavery awaited large-scale cultivation: plantations. The latter began with rice and indigo, but became most characteristic with sugar and, of course, cotton. Cotton became king as three developments merged: the English industrial revolution (whose leading sector was cotton textiles), competition from Mexican long-staple cotton, and the invention of the cotton gin in 1793 (which made practicable the use of short-staple cotton, the variety best-suited to the southern colonies). The entire range of southern agriculture was commercialized, and dependent upon expanding foreign mar-kets—entirely dependent before the American Revolution, and critically so thereafter. A key factor in that equation was debt, that long ago.

The economics of southern farming held both the plantation owner and the small farmer in a pattern of rising debt, as they responded to market conditions and to the unfavorable bargaining terms set by powerful brokers, shippers, and financiers (usually) in London. The indebtedness combined with the rapid exhaustion of the soil, especially in tobacco and cotton cultivation, to make the southern agriculturist an expansionist in two ways: he had to keep moving westward in search of more fertile lands, and his marketing focus was essentially international.

In the North, nature was less generous than in the South, but still very generous indeed by comparison with, say, much of Europe. The "middle" colonies of New York, Pennsylvania, and New Jersey raised grains and livestock for domestic but also for export sale, mostly to Caribbean and Mediterranean markets. The harsher climate and rocky soils of New England made its settlers into part-time farmers, and into part-time loggers, handicraftsmen, fishermen, and whalers, until commerce and small manufactures took hold enough to create urban markets for their diversified farms. But like their counterparts in the Middle Colonies and in the South, New England farmers always looked west, and were tied into foreign markets for their well-being, directly or indirectly.

There was always a multiplicity of reasons for westward expansion from all the colonies, and there continued to be after independence—one of whose burning issues was who was going to have access to and control of western lands. Tied to the many reasons for the expansion—exhausted soils, excessive competition, a simple restless itch to move on—was one constant: land speculation. We cannot know the degree to which the westward movement would have been slowed without land speculation, but we may be sure it would have been a significant reduction quantitatively and that the whole quality of the process would have been very much altered—and, perhaps, have been less ruthless. On that score, there is little disagreement among historians. Veblen put it in his own way:

> Habitually and with singular uniformity the American farmers have aimed to acquire real estate at the same time that they have worked at their trade as husbandmen.... They have habitually "carried" valuable real estate at the same time that they have worked the soil of so much of their land as they could take care of, in as effectual a manner as they could under these circumstances. They have been cultivators of the main chance as well as of the fertile land.[6]

Farmers, Politics, and Power

The passion for always more land, in a country predominantly agricultural in its functions and outlook, meant that the political issues roiling life in the colonies and the new United States would center on the land, its value, and its uses.

Land policy—the accessibility, the size, and the price of western lands—persisted as a tempestuous issue. And, because the ownership of lands always required access to money and credit, monetary policy and control over banking were also destined to be a continuous source of political controversy. Because the market value of land was in important part a function of its earning power, and because that in turn was vitally dependent upon the foreign trade of the nation, tariff policy was also a key political issue. Finally, to enhance and realize the possibilities of real estate speculation and the marketing of commodities, an adequate transportation network—canals and railroads—was essential. It was around all these issues that power struggles took place in the century before the Civil War. They contributed to the War for Independence and they were decisive for the outbreak of the Civil War. The farmers won their way on all of them; or so it seemed.

In 1763, the British "drew a line in the sand" the length of the Appalachian range—"the Proclamation Line"—beyond which the colonists were forbidden to invest, trap, or farm. Probably no single act of the British was more unanimously opposed throughout the Colonies than this. It brought together northern and southern farmers, merchants, frontiersmen, and financiers, and revealed to the colonists that a century and a half of westward movement would, for them, have to be halted. This in turn meant that their economic hopes and even their solvency were doomed, to the advantage of British capitalists.

The resistance of agriculturists to that "line" found its more positive counterparts after the Revolution—in the Land Ordinances of 1785 and 1787 establishing the procedures for settling the West; in their steady pressure to reduce the minimum size of land purchase, and the cost per acre; in their pressure on local, state, and federal agencies to build canals and railroads; in the successful battle (in Jackson's presidency) to destroy the credit-controlling Second Bank of the United States;[7] in the movement toward free trade of the 1840s; and in the ability of northern industrialists and financiers to persuade western farmers to join in the political conflict and subsequent war against the southerners. This last was with the inducement of a more generous land and transportation policy, along with the fear that unless southern power could be displaced, western lands would fall under an unfavorable political dispensation.

Farmers seemed to be winning all these battles, but after midcentury they were doing so increasingly as unwitting tools of what Veblen calls "the massive vested interests" of the rising industrial nation. Farmers found themselves after the Civil War faced with sharply falling prices, with monopolistic railroads and commission merchants, and with monetary and tariff policies cut to the needs not of farmers but of industrialists and financiers. In short, the farmers were becoming an internal colony of the United States—they who had been the ideal, the presumably incontrovertible source of "American virtue."

Before the Civil War, farmers had been political but, because of their pervasive strength, loosely so. After the war, they began to organize. The last quarter of the century was dominated by the political struggle that ensued. The manner in which the farmers both won and lost had consequences reaching far beyond anything they sought or, except in an occasional nightmare, might have dreamed. The farmers sought only to maintain and expand the value of their lands and an ever-expanding market for their livestock and their crops. To gain those limited ends, they wittingly and unwittingly greased the skids for a vicious speedup in racism, for what became an overseas empire, and for an agriculture ruled less by farmers than corporations, what has come to be called "agribusiness."[8]

More Corn, More Hell

It will be recalled that the several decades after the Civil War were marked by worldwide industrialization, great improvements in technology, transportation, and communications, by pervasive national and international trade and competition, and by a tidal wave of economic imperialism. Of the innumerable consequences of those many processes, one was falling prices for all commodities, whose obverse side was rising production. The bushel price of wheat in 1871 was $1.24; in 1894 it was 49 cents. The production of wheat rose from 173 million bushels in 1859 to 468 million bushels in 1884. But *all* production and *all* prices were moving along such lines: the wholesale price index for *all* commodities fell from 135 in 1872 to 69 in 1896.[9]

In that context, the classic rule of U.S. economic life kept its hold: survival of the fittest. The "fittest" in farming were those who could enlarge their landholdings, whose technology could improve, and whose marketing and financial arrangements could be arranged most efficiently and least expensively. Whether large or small, however, the farmers joined in a campaign from the late 1860s until the end of the century to alter the setting in which that contest would be fought out. This era of agrarian discontent took shape first as a national movement, with the founding of The Patrons of Husbandry ("The Grange"), in 1867. Soon one farm woman coined the slogan by which the movement came to be identified: "Raise less corn and more Hell." The farmers raised more of both.

Along with the falling prices that began in the early 1870s, the result of impersonal forces working in both the national and the world economy, there were developments that were by no means impersonal, and the farmers fought for or against all of them. In 1873, silver had been "demonetized." The legislation doing that, passed by the then powerful Republican Party, meant that the United States went on a gold standard, that its supply of circulating money was reduced—thus exacerbating already severe deflationary trends. "Remonetization" of silver emerged as a searing issue, uniting farmers with urban workers; and it joined easily with anti-big business, antirailroad, antitariff, and comparable issues. Sitting at the center of all this, however, was an effort on the part of farmers to find "a new frontier" which could compensate for the slowing down of westward expansion[10] and the deterioration of prices—always a problem of some importance for debtors, which farmers are, always. In the decades before the mid-1890s, farmers sought solutions in an expanding *foreign* trade, applying pressure for lowered tariffs, cheaper and better transportation, and a "return to silver." Later, as these measures proved inadequate, farmers generally encouraged and supported the overseas imperialist ventures of the United States, in the hope that their purposes would thus be served.

In the first stage of those overseas developments, farmers received aid and comfort due to conditions entirely out of their range of influence: agricultural hardships in Europe, brought about by the spread of disease and a long period of unfavorable weather. In the midst of the unprecedented and severe depression that began in 1873, exports of crude foodstuffs began to increase spectacularly, strengthening the entire economy.[11] It was then that the U.S. trade balance shifted decisively from being "unfavorable," (an excess of imports over exports), to "favorable."[12]

If the meaning of those years—when the United States was lifted out of depression and into a new balance of trade status—was not lost on the farmers, neither was it lost on the industrialists. The United States had from its very first years depended on foreign markets for its economic health and expansion; now it was dependent on them for resolving what became a recurring problem: excess productive capacity, both agricultural and industrial. The 1870s were in an important sense an introductory lesson for both the United States and Europe concerning what all would understand fully in not so many years to come: "The United States," as Williams put it, "was rapidly becoming the most powerful nation on earth" (op. cit, p. 22.).

When the agricultural crisis of Europe subsided, the Europeans, for the first but by no means the last time, saw that they would have to raise barriers and find alternatives to the U.S. export invasion—the felt need and temptation to do which today is of course aimed at the Japanese by both the United States and Europe. In the 1880s and 1890s, alternative sources of supply in Argentina, in Russia, Egypt, and in India were encouraged (for grains, meat, and fibers, particularly), all under the direct or indirect control of the European imperial powers; and, especially in France and Germany, the path toward effective tariff barriers on both agricultural and industrial products was pursued with increasing haste and effect. By 1892, the French had climbed their first big steps along that path, with the famous Méline Tariff; the Germans had arrived a few years earlier, with the Prussian-inspired and politically most effective "rye and steel" tariff program.

With slight variations after those years, the course of European tariff policy remained protective up into World War II, a vital component of it always to protect against U.S., especially agricultural, exports. A central part of the design of the U.S. Marshall Plan (1948–1952) was to find expanded markets for U.S. exports, not least agricultural exports. In addition to drawing U.S. farmers once more into support for an expansionist foreign policy, this development has helped to make farm products the hard core of protectionism still, in the Common Market (European Community) countries. And what is true of farmers in the United States and Europe is also true of their counterparts in Japan. In all cases, restrictive trade policies and, often, expansionist foreign policies are supported by farmers, in the vain or successful hope that thereby they can protect their own incomes. That is a justifiable position to take; but as will be argued in our last chapter, the ways of the past and present are not the best ways for the farmers, and they are very much the worst ways for the present and future of the earth's people, wherever they might be—and worst of all for the world's poorest people.[13] But let us return to the farmers' efforts to protect themselves over the past century or so.

The System Joined

It is customary to point out that after 1896 the farmers' revolt subsided, to be replaced in this century by farmers' pressure groups, the key transforming development being the rise of farm prices after 1896, especially in the years of World War I. But this neglects an important matter, given short shrift in most histories of the United States: the whys and wherefores of the U.S. turn toward overseas imperialism at the turn of the century. Farmers were very much a part of that development, and among its conscious beneficiaries.

The discontent of farmers beginning to be voiced in the late 1860s developed into the Populist Movement, and the People's Party, by 1892—combining in the process urban worker with rural discontent, as well as active cooperation between small black and white farmers. It was the first vigorous coalition of that sort in the United States, and apart from some small labor and socialist groupings in earlier years, the first, and perhaps unwitting, attempt to find an *internal* rather than an *external* resolution of our economic and social problems.

The response of northern business and southern white leaders was to mount vigorous antiliberal, antileft, and contrived racist programs. Undercut by internal divisions and external pressures, Populism shifted to the right and dissolved, and both racism and overseas expansion were thereby strengthened.

In the heyday of nineteenth-century Populism, almost all farmers and their allies were ranged *against* big business; today, the dominating elements in agriculture *are* big business. The rural and urban contingents of Populism sought to bend State power to the needs of the common people; today, Big Agriculture and Big Labor work with Big Business and Big Government to defend themselves *against* the common people.

In 1892, Populism stood for a broad range of social and economic issues; by the election of 1896 most of its leaders could be satisfied with the promise of rising prices and land values and expanding foreign markets, even if that meant finding allies among previous business enemies and embarking upon a new form of colonialism. As Williams says,

The farmers who were quasi-colonials in the domestic economy thus became anti-colonial imperialists in foreign affairs, as a strategy of becoming equals at home.[14]

Already in 1895 the farmers were agitating to have the United States support the Cuban struggle against Spain, and then to guarantee that they would have enlarged access to Cuban markets, investment possibilities, and the like. Although U.S. farmers had no similar interest in Asia at the time, they found it possible to support the logic of those who did—the processors of cotton, meat, and flour, and the manufacturers who had visions of an endless Asian market.[15] Nor were they indifferent to the meaning of an isthmian canal—initially to be dug out of Nicaragua, but ultimately placed in Panama (a "nation" created forcibly by the United States out of Colombia for that purpose).

Like the years that produced the farmers' revolt, the mid-1890s were years of serious depression. The response laid down then has served as a template for U.S. foreign policy ever since:

The economic impact of the depression, and its effect in producing a real fear of extensive social unrest or even revolution, had completed the long and gradual acceptance by metropolitan leaders of the traditional farm emphasis on overseas market expansion as the strategic solution to the nation's economic and social problems.[16]

Farmers did not *want* war in 1898, nor did they expect it; they did not want war in the repetitive years of military intervention and gunboat diplomacy in the Caribbean, Central America, and Asia that carried us up and into World War I. But farmers did want expanding markets and agricultural prosperity. From the very beginning, when anything stood in the way of such economic aims—whether it was the rights or the lives of Native or African-Americans, or the possibilities of peace—it was relegated to a secondary consideration by most white farmers.

It should go without saying that the farmers of the United States invented neither U.S. racism nor U.S. imperialism. But at a critical moment in U.S. history, the last years of the nineteenth century, farmers lent their great prestige and their political numbers to the forces that were moving along those lines. It was a turning point for U.S. history, as much as it was for U.S. farmers. The indifferent slaughter of buffaloes and of Native Americans became a habit easily applied to the indifferent slaughter of Filipinos, Koreans, Vietnamese, Iraqis....[17]

The agricultural sector of the United States lost what life it could call its own as the twentieth century moved on; but the idealized picture and many of the ways of the farmer persist. It is these that are often called to mind when the standards of "the silent majority"—"the real Americans"—are invoked. Not all that is thereby suggested is good and not all of it bad. Much of what our people value, and much of how they calculate, is derived from the fact or the myth of the farm and the country town that was the social, political, and economic center of the farmer's life when not tilling the soil. As Veblen, who grew up on farms in Wisconsin and Minnesota, pointed out:

> It has come to be recognized that the country town situation of the nineteenth century is now by way of being left behind; and so it is now recognized, or at least acted on, that the salvation of twentieth-century democracy is best to be worked out by making the world safe for Big Business and then let Big Business take care of the interests of the retail trade and the country town, together with much else. But it should not be overlooked that in and through all this it is the soul of the country town that goes marching on.[18]

The "country town" mentality Veblen refers to has always been well-represented in the leading political personalities of our history, for better and for worse; also very recently: Harry Truman, Eisenhower, Nixon, George Wallace, LBJ, McGovern, Ford, Carter, Strom Thurmond, and, of course Reagan and Quayle. Saying so, this suggests that there is and has been a division of thinking and values among farmers, as well as the rest of us, throughout our history. Those who have won out have become part of the system of calculation and expansion that is the warp and woof of U.S. history. There were and are others: farmers who love the land and what it grows, and the pleasures of living on it; farmers who helped to swell the anti-imperialist and socialist movement led by Eugene Debs; farmers who are black and brown and yellow; and so on. Since the collapse of the People's Party in the mid-1890s, that other side of farmers has been moved far from the levers of agricultural power and influence, plays only a minor part in overall farm production, and even less than that in the larger life of the nation. Grant McConnell closes his study of *The Decline of Agrarian Democracy* with these somber words, worth quoting at length:

Perhaps the central political belief of nineteenth-century agrarianism was that power must be circumscribed and limited. The belief was not peculiar to the agrarians; others shared this characteristically American view of democracy.... From the time of Thomas Jefferson and John Taylor down to the era of the Populists, farm movements were preoccupied with the problem of the system of power emerging from capitalist organization. In our time not only has this historic cause been abandoned, but an entirely new structure of power has been built within agriculture itself. This is the greatest change of all.... We could view the rise of this structure of power in agriculture with equanimity if there were alternative structures open to those for whom it has no part or place. The pluralism of American society is one of its greatest political virtues.   Yet for this to continue as virtue presupposes that the means of power shall not be made the property of the few. This presupposition has failed in agriculture.

Herein lies the condition which the agrarian program of limited power was designed to prevent. Its existence today is the measure of the change that has come about. Agrarian democracy is gone from our scene. The loss is agriculture's—and the nation's.[19]

Agriculture and Agribusiness

Throughout the nineteenth century, the farmers were socially, politically, and statistically a predominating force; by the end of the century they were losing out in all but the statistics. The numbers of farms and farmers continued to increase up to 1935 in absolute terms, while falling in relative terms as the economy came to depend increasingly on industrial production and the growth of services (finance, distribution, education, health care, etc.). After 1935, farming and farms went into an absolute decline. Long before those numbers began to turn downward, the role of farming had undergone a transformation in the U.S. political economy.

The last great effort of farmers to affect broad United States policies was embodied in their impact on foreign policy around the turn of the century. Afterwards, although farmers intermittently and diversely joined in national political movements, their principal political activities were as a particular interest pressure group, lobbying for farm price supports, output controls, favorable tariff policies, and government-subsidized research. The decline in their numbers tells part of the story why; their success as a pressure group did much to facilitate that decline.

In 1870, over half of the people in the United States were engaged in agriculture. By 1930, fewer than a quarter were. By 1975 the percentage was just over 4 percent; today it is less than 2 percent. There were about one-and-a-half million farms in 1850. The number rose to four million by 1890, and reached its high point in 1935, with about seven million farms. By 1940, the number had dropped below six million; by 1975 to something over two-and-a-half million. Today there are barely two million farms, the smallest number in over a century.

Agricultural technology in all its dimensions has of course altered spectacularly over the entire period, and the long-term trend of agricultural production has been just as spectacularly upward by any measure: per farm, per acre, per capita, etc. Associated with all the foregoing has, of course, been an increase in the size of the average farm, as the number of farms has declined. Nowadays, fewer than 10 percent of all farms produce well over half of all agricultural output. In 1972, fewer than 1 percent of all farms, mostly corporations, produced 25 percent of total farm output. In 1987, about 50 percent of farms with an annual value of sales of $10,000 or less—the small farmer—sold 2.5 percent of total farm sales; 0.5 percent of farms with annual sales of $1 million or more sold about 28 percent of the total. As elsewhere in the U.S. economy, there is a "dual economy" in agriculture, with over a million very small and poor farmers at one end of the pole, and a few hundred thousand large or very large corporate farms at the other.[20]

The effectiveness of farmers as a narrow pressure group first took hold in the 1920s, and especially in the Hoover administration. Those first steps led directly to the present close cooperation between large farms, government, and agricultural colleges, and to the industrialization of agriculture. It was in agriculture that the first major advances in technology were made in the United States, with the mechanization of harvesting in the 1830s.[21] Since then agricultural technology has kept up or exceeded that in industry. Since 1950, for example, farm productivity has risen twice that of manufacturing industry, the gains going to the very largest farms—for the investments necessary have become formidable —while the small and idealized farmer has been squeezed out of farming and into the factories and the cities.

In the long history of farming in the United States, to have been a tenant farmer was not a sign of failure but of first steps toward ownership. After World War I, however, as agriculture industrialized in the midst of widespread overcapacity, farm tenancy and sharecropping (the latter always an accompaniment of poverty) tended to become indistinguishable: tenancy had become the way *down* or out.

The mass exodus from farming was accelerated by the 1930s depression and by the Dust Bowl tragedies of the same years; the exodus was pushed toward completion by the great step up in electrification, mechanization, and chemicalization in farming during and after World War II. Millions of farmers went bankrupt and were "tractored out" in the 1930s, and became part of a migratory labor force or of the unemployed. The military and production needs of World War II came just in time—or, for many, just too late.[22]

Present-day farm policies began in 1928, under President Hoover. The policies have evolved to prevent low farm prices and market instability for a broad range of farm products—keeping prices up through government purchases and loans, and supply down through production controls and quotas. The largest farms are by far the prime beneficiaries of the programs for the simple reason that benefits are tied to output; and often the small farmer's output is too small to bring any benefit whatsoever—though the need is great. We may make some comparisons, for 1967 and 1987. In the earlier year, the poorest *20 percent* of farmers received *1.1 percent* of government payments to farmers; the richest *5 percent* received 42.4 percent. Total government payments in 1967 were $3 billion. In 1987, the poorest 13.5 percent received 0.5 percent of total payments, totaling $49 million for them, at an average of $482 per farm; the richest 5.0 percent received 31.3% of the total, amounting to over $3 billion, for an average of $79,000 per farm.[23] The data clearly show that, although farm policies have been and still are carried out in the name of preserving the small family farm, the largest, usually corporate, farms are those that are "preserved."[24]

We may both close our discussion of farming and provide a bridge to the problems of our cities and of the environment by examining a further dimension of farm policies, little known to the public but of great importance in agriculture, especially now to the largest farms; namely, governmental programs financed by federal and state funds that undertake research on the whole range of matters affecting agricultural productivity. The latter have done much over the years to stimulate and improve mechanization, seeds, soil management, and the like; they have also been prime movers in the almost universal chemicalization, and not least the "petrochemicalization," of farming. Though it has doubtless had a significant effect in raising the productivity of farm lands, it has had an equally significant impact on the destruction of the environment, and not a few human beings. The case of DDT is only the best known of a long list of chemicals that have poisoned the soil, the waters, and surrounding foliage in such fashion as to unhinge the balance of nature, a balance that depends upon insects, birds, and small animals—all for some years now having been in the process of being poisoned, some moving toward extinction.[25]

Contemporary ecological imbalances are tipped most drastically in dangerous directions by *industrial* production and the use of industrial products, most especially the automobile and petroleum products (including petrochemicals in farming). But in the contemporary agricultural pattern there is a specially disturbing aspect of the problem, for agriculture provides our food. That our food is provided in ways that poison as well as sustain us, and that it is produced in ways that destroy as well as replenish natural forces is frightening; that all this is the direct result of government subsidies for research in the Department of Agriculture and in the land-grant universities is disturbing, to say the least. At a U.S. Senate hearing in the summer of 1972, the nature and status of those relationships was aptly summarized as

> a land-grant complex, a system composed of Federal research agencies and big universities in each state created in the last century with endowments of public lands or their monetary equivalent..., whose research was originally intended to serve consumers as well as rural communities, [but is] now focused largely on the development of big machines for vast farming enterprises, the breeding of crops for mechanized harvests and studies of chemicals for big corporations and big producers... with little regard for the quality or safety of products for the consumer or the small farmer. One result... has been to drive farmers and workers off the land and into the crowded cities.[26]

A good three-fourths of all U.S. families now live in small or large cities, and the problems afflicting us today show themselves mostly there. Poverty, pollution, racism, violence, transportation mess, urban sprawl, health and housing and educational deprivation, all these and more dance around in tight and deadly embrace in our increasingly forlorn cities; and they are all explicable in their current as in their historical conditions as "by-products" of a process of social development in which profit and power—not natural or social balance, not human needs and possibilities —were the guiding standards. The deterioration of nature has been a quiet, almost hidden process, and it must be studied and read about to be known about; quite the opposite is true of the deterioration of life in our cities: one can't help but know of it. But the two sets of looming disasters have entered our lives hand in hand. That the damage to *all* of nature would accompany the damage to its human component was seen by Marx over a century ago:

> In modern agriculture, as in the urban industries, the increased productiveness and quantity of the labor set in motion are bought at the cost of laying waste and consuming by disease labor-power itself. Moreover, all progress in capitalistic agriculture is a progress in the art, not only of robbing the laborer, but of robbing the soil; all progress in increasing the fertility of the soil for a given time, is a progress towards ruining the lasting sources of that fertility. The more a country starts its development on the foundation of modern industry, like the United States, for example, the more rapid is this process of destruction. Capitalist production, therefore, develops technology, and the combining together of various processes into a social whole, only by sapping the original sources of all wealth—the soil and the laborer.[27]

The great and rich land space of the continental United States was swept over and conquered in a process so swift and violent that it has been called "the rape of the land." Heedless of the delicate balances of nature, human or otherwise, the exploiters of the land moved for greed more than need, for power more than satisfaction. So it has been also with the ways our cities have grown and changed and deteriorated, in one wave after another. So too with the poisoning of our air and water. What land speculators were to farming, real estate and urban development interests were and are to our cities; as in farming, the entrance of the State into the picture in this century has meant not a mitigation but an intensification of a long-standing process of social recklessness. The more rapid and more pervasive economic expansion of this century has brought with it more misuse of the land, more deadly cities, and environmental destruction and deterioration that is as appalling as it is frightening.

The Jeffersonian dream of an agrarian democracy is barely remembered these days; the nightmare of urban decay and suffocation has become the reality. How did our cities get that way, and how do they now change?

Civilization and Its Discontents

Not so long ago, there was a firmly held notion that cities were the repository of all that is most precious in western social development. If that belief was held too carelessly, there is even less to support the one that now spreads and grows: the cities embody all that is to be avoided. Furthermore, as this view spreads, it becomes a self-fulfilling prophecy.

The cities of the United States at their best were never fit places to live for a large percentage of their inhabitants, whether in the nineteenth or this century. But apart from a small handful of people who can find ways to experiment with rural living, mostly young and/or well-off, the alternative to *making* our cities fit places to live is quite probably the disintegration of what we mean by civilization—whose Latin root *means* city. That we have done so little to rescue our cities and have done it so badly, testifies to how very fragile the civilized base has been for our social development.

A careful analysis of how our cities came to be, how they have changed over time, and how they have fallen into their current desperate state, if combined with an analysis of how all that related to our overall socioeconomic development, would quite probably also tell us that a substantial reorganization of our cities *and* our society is necessary to make either livable or, in an acceptable sense of the term, *civilized* for all its inhabitants.[28]

Recorded history begins with cities, when social development had reached the stage when production and productivity were advanced enough to allow a significant number of the population to be sustained even though they did not produce their own food; when a relatively complicated division of labor had emerged, requiring government and writing—of, among other things, history.[29]

All this, and much else besides, appears to have come forth a millennium or two before Christ in the rich river valleys of the Indus, the Tigris and Euphrates, and the Nile. In the ancient period, cities of course served commercial purposes; but their religious, military, and administrative functions were dominant. During the medieval period, cities emerged and grew primarily because of their strategic locations which, leading them to become both military and religious centers, favored the development of commerce. In the capitalist era, cities have arisen, expanded, and decayed almost entirely in response to economic needs and possibilities—whatever their earlier origins.[30]

In the United States, the cities of the eastern seaboard—most notably Boston, New York, Philadelphia, Baltimore, Charleston, and Atlanta —waxed or waned as the changing patterns of agriculture, manufacture, foreign and domestic trade, finance, and transportation altered. They, and the cities that grew up in the trans-Appalachian West, fought strenuously and self-consciously to place roads, canals, and railroads in such a manner as to become magnets for the trade, the industry, and the finance that could not otherwise flourish. In the early nineteenth century the competition between towns and cities for public favor and finance for such purposes was intense. If the emergence of Manhattan from a small town to becoming the nation's most populous city is to be understood, for example, the story must begin with its advantages as a trading center: it was on the very edge of the Atlantic, connected to the interior by the Erie Canal, and favorably located between New England and the South.

In diverse combinations, much the same factors affected the other cities throughout the United States: Chicago, Omaha, Cincinnati (long known as "Porkopolis"), New Orleans, St. Louis, Detroit, San Francisco, Los Angeles, or Seattle. Transportation advantages, due to location near water routes, or emergence as a railroad center, made towns into commercial centers; then they emerged as centers of industry and finance, and in the process, came to be large population centers.

The reasons why the cities grew give important clues as to the criteria both utilized and neglected along the way, regarding the quantity and quality of what we now call human services: housing, transportation, health, educational, and cultural-recreational facilities. These services came into being as responses to essentially market rather than human criteria, the sole exception being, in some cities, cultural facilities.[31]

The medieval European city often tended to develop in "rings," moving outward from the initial walled city to "suburbs," one ring after another; or, it was controlled in a more quadratic design from the beginning, as were many Central European cities, particularly in the eastern regions of Germany (where such planned cities go back as far as the twelfth century). By comparison, the spatial development of U.S. cities was haphazard. As the structure of the economy changed, nationally and locally, new patterns of production and new inflows of people ensued. What began as commercial districts became industrial and financial; initially residential districts became commercial or industrial; initially suburban areas became part of the "central city." Perhaps the most vivid example of the latter development is Harlem, once a village separated from the bustle of Manhattan by long stretches of "country."[32]

Cities and Suburbs; Sprawl and Decay

Urban development in the United States may be viewed as having three reasonably clear-cut stages: (1) most of the nineteenth century, (2) the forty years or so ending just before World War II, and (3) from World War II to the present. The earliest period covers the growth of cities proper, the second sees the emergence of malignant growth including the significant expansion of suburbs, and the latest brings us the megalopolis, urban sprawl, and the dying city—dying both because of and despite the vigorous commercial construction—especially of financial towers and hotels in city centers—that characterized the years of the 1960s and subsequently.

Throughout the nineteenth century, U.S. cities multiplied and grew, but it was in some kind of rhythmic balance with the growing economy. Immigration became a river and then a torrent after 1850, as we have seen; agriculture was becoming relatively less important (although it was producing more and more, with its rising productivity); and industrialization became the prime mover of urbanization. It was not until the turn of the century, however, that the kinds of urban problems now so familiar to us began to become obvious and pressing—widespread slums, rampant health problems, poverty, blatant corruption, street crime, and the like. What Lincoln Steffens had to say about St. Louis at the time of its World's Fair (1904) might for the most part have been written yesterday:

> The visitor is told of the wealth of the residents, of the financial strength of the banks, and of the growing importance of the industries, yet he sees poorly paved, refuse-burdened streets and dusty or mud-covered alleys; he passes a ramshackle fire-trap,

crowded with the sick, and learns that it is the City Hospital....
Finally, he turns a tap in the hotel, to see liquid mud flow into
wash basin or bath tub.[33]

Immigration and industrialization were both rapid after 1900, and net
migration from rural to urban locations became a constant. In 1920, for
the first time, there were more people in our cities than in the countryside.[34] The cities that grew fastest were those already the largest. Into
these rapidly expanding metropoli in every region of the country streamed
people who took up the lowest-paying and dirtiest jobs. They had come
from the poorer areas of Europe and Asia before World War I; later they
were African-American and Spanish-speaking Americans moving from
country to city. Their cheap labor was very much desired, but attitudes
toward them were marked by contempt, or worse; the quality of their
lives was beyond the consideration of the "WASP" power structures that
ruled almost all cities in the United States. They were despised as
Catholics or Jews, as poor, as black, brown, yellow, red, or "swarthy"; for
them, the cities, never well-planned and only partially attractive and
pleasant, were sink-holes.
   Much sentimental nonsense has been written about how the poor and
oppressed of the cities after the turn of the century were "taken care of"
by the political bosses and machines then dominant; even today respectable opinion not infrequently lauds a Mayor Daley (the elder) as the last
of an unfortunately vanishing breed. The machines did have a function,
of course, much like that which a bandage has for a running sore. There
is reason for nostalgia among "respectable people" today concerning our
cities before World War I and into the 1930s, but it is not because most
of them were comfortable, decent, and safe for most of their inhabitants.
Rather, it is because the cities then *seemed* tractable, manageable; they
were still growing, still serving indispensable economic functions. Today,
all too much of the growth is cancerous, serving an economic system
whose main flows are more financial and speculative than productive.
   Today, it is megalopoli, not cities, that grow. Many of the functions
performed in and by cities are now taken care of in once suburban
residential areas that are now also "suburban" *industrial* areas; and the
cities have been filled by a forced migration of rural people—and, more
recently, economic and political refugees from Asia and Latin America
—who are predominantly black, brown, and yellow. This process has
been occurring as fewer and fewer industrial jobs are to be found; with

fewer jobs of *any* kind to be found. In order to be manageable today, the cities would have to be managed in critical part *for* and *by* the despised poor people of color, residents who constitute a large, tending toward the largest percentage of the central cities' population. Such a politics would go against the grain of the United States; it has never happened, and its necessary politics and funding—at least at present, as racism and hatred and fear of the poor rises—becomes always more implausible.

A few suburbs developed in conjunction with the steam railroad after 1850. But the first significant suburban development went along with the electric urban, interurban, and suburban railway, as this century began. What continental railroad developers were to westward expansion, electric railway and subway developers and their real-estate cohorts were to urban-suburban development.

In the years just before World War I, automobiles began to be mass-produced, and that brought about the next major suburban movement. The possibilities associated with the electric railway and the automobile were fairly well exhausted before World War II, especially under the negative impact of the depression. Since 1945, however, population has risen more than 110 million; there has been (into the 1970s) a full generation of rising real income; the automobile has become an almost universal possession; and the nation's industrialization, urbanization, and suburbanization have moved to levels of apparent saturation. In the process, both the causes and the consequences of suburbanization have altered greatly.

Suburban development before the 1930s was made possible by transportation facilities that were taken advantage of by predominantly upper-income families. The suburb then, typically, was separated from the city by open stretches of country, and provided an opportunity to combine the advantages of the city with country life. The suburban railway made its few stops, and provided a leisurely and even a pleasant interlude; and some very few drove to work and back. There were no "freeways."[35]

All that began to change as we moved into and out of World War II. The most striking changes were earliest to be seen in and around Los Angeles, which already by the 1930s was a forbidding look into the future of our cities. Los Angeles drew people in from all over the nation, but especially from the Midwest and the South, as its oil wells, its aircraft production, its light and cheap labor manufactures, its warm climate near the ocean, and its Hollywood glamour provided both jobs and dreams.

The model it established for the rest of the country was well-captured by Mumford, over thirty years ago:

> Los Angeles has now become an undifferentiated mass of houses, walled off into sectors by many-laned expressways, with ramps and viaducts that create special bottlenecks of their own. These expressways move but a small fraction of the traffic per hour once carried by public transportation, at a much lower speed, in an environment befouled by smog, itself produced by the lethal exhaust of the technologically backward motor cars. More than a third of the Los Angeles area is consumed by these grotesque transportation facilities; *two-thirds* of central Los Angeles are occupied by streets, freeways, parking facilities, and garages. This is space-eating with a vengeance. The last stage of the process already beckons truly progressive minds—to evict the remaining inhabitants and turn the entire area over to automatically propelled vehicles, completely emancipated from any rational human purpose.[36]

How the horror portrayed by Mumford came to be was explained before a U.S. Senate Committee in 1974 by Bradford Snell, who added some details of his own:

> Thirty-five years ago Los Angeles was a beautiful city of lush palm trees, fragrant orange groves and ocean-clean air. It was served then by the world's largest electric railway network. In the late 1930s General Motors and allied highway interests acquired the local transit companies, scrapped their pollution-free electric trains, tore down their power transmission lines, ripped up their tracks, and placed GM buses on already congested Los Angeles streets. The noisy, foul-smelling buses turned earlier patrons of the high-speed rail system away from public transit and, in effect, sold millions of private automobiles. Largely as a result, this city is today an ecological wasteland: the palm trees are dying of petrochemical smog; the orange groves have been paved over by 300 miles of freeways; the air is a septic tank into which four million cars, half of them built by General Motors, pump 13,000 tons of pollutants daily. Furthermore, a shortage of

motor vehicle fuel and an absence of adequate public transport now threatens to disrupt the entire auto-dependent region.[37]

There are still some few cities that do not fit that model; but most that do not are racing to catch up. Greater Boston, Greater New York, Greater Cleveland, Greater Atlanta, Greater Houston, and, of course, Greatest Los Angeles, all vie with each other for growth, come what may. The San Francisco Bay Area, thought by many as recently as the 1960s to be exempt from such deterioration was at that very moment coming to be perhaps a pluperfect example of how very strong the drives are to catch up in the mad race of "development."

The Bay, enormous and convolute, ringed by hills in turn sloping into graceful valleys, has been shrinking and dying as a body of water. Over 40 percent of the water area of the Bay has been filled in during this century (and it is these filled in areas that are most vulnerable in the region's intermittent earthquakes). Steadily increasing amounts of effluent from the U.S. Navy (based in the Bay), private industry, and residences, have combined with frequent oil spills to kill off much of the underwater life of the Bay—"Fisherman's Wharf" exists now as a place of bad food and expensive trinkets for tourists—and to render its waters dangerous to humans.

In addition, its once lovely valleys have seen orchards replaced by residential and industrial sprawl, all suffocating beneath a permanent layer of smog. That this will never be enough was suggested by a recent two-page ad in the *New York Times* by the boosters of San José (50 miles south of San Francisco), whose population, 40,000 in 1940, is now over 750,000 and rising. The ad boasted of San Jose's "runaway construction," its numerous airline passengers, its new car sales, its "progress," and asked for business readers to help swell the progression toward its becoming "the Los Angeles of the North." Which it already is.

The personal automobile has almost entirely replaced the systematically neglected and now dilapidated and expensive interurban railway; the suburbs have developed their own ghettoes,[38] their own smog, indeed their own suburbs. Industry has accompanied the automobile to the suburb, and the city has lost its ability to provide a decent livelihood for an already high and always growing percentage of its residents, nor is it able or willing to pay for its needed social services—education, health, child care, etc. And where now is this growing surplus population to go? All major U.S. cities now lurch from one fiscal crisis to the next, each successive crisis more intractable and more painful to more people than its predecessor—as the federal government continually reduces the grants upon which states and localities had by necessity become dependent, and which had come from their residents' federal taxes. The daily news announces school closings today, cessation of bus service the week after; firemen, policemen, refuse collectors, teachers, and hospital workers organize and (usually without much positive effect) strike for better incomes and working conditions, attempt to stave off the city's or state's slashes, their rising taxes, and the rising cost of living. And the sad waltz goes on.

All major cities have been and are in deep and growing trouble; but perhaps New York City's plight is worth a moment's particular attention, because of its symbolic as well as its real importance in the nation's life—and, it may be added, in the role it plays in the image held of the United States by those in other countries. Since the mid-1970s, New York has been trembling on or over the edge of disaster. The view from Washington, D.C. usually blames the turbulent plight of New York on iniquity, perversity, corruption, stupidity, and self-indulgence—as though such characteristics could not be found more easily in the national government than New York. But "the City's" troubles arose principally out of what most of those who rule this nation consider to be the considerable triumphs of the post-World War II era: massive building and highway projects—and the associated disruption of whole chunks of the city (leading to loss of jobs and fewer taxpayers)—plus New York's share of the costs and wastes of U.S. militarism. If there was one group that could be identified as having continuing great power in New York in the postwar years, it would be the "construction complex"—the banks, the builders and associated unions, the autonomous agencies, the federal and state bureaucracies, the politicians getting and dispensing patronage in the late twentieth-century version of "the Great Barbecue."[39] New York City narrowly averted formal bankruptcy in the 1970s, and the price paid to do so was the deterioration of the city even more. Today, New York stares at possible bankruptcy once more—and asks the question as to what remedies remain for a patient down to skin and bones, in a local and national economy considerably less resilient than even that of the mid-1970s.

Meanwhile, other cities have moved in tandem with New York, if also a bit behind—lagging, not because of greater fiscal rectitude in the past but because New York has had certain special characteristics which, if anything, should have occasioned pride more than castigation: it has been more alert to the educational, cultural, and basic economic needs of its denizens than the other cities of the United States, in part because of the vitality of its demographic mix, in part because it has been amongst the least undemocratic of cities in the United States.

The Agony of the Cities: Nothing Fails Like Success

The listing of the urban afflictions of the United States has become a persisting drone in the background of daily life, like the whine of mosquitoes. We have already been bitten often, and we must fear that more than mosquito bites are on their way. The items on the list are all too familiar: housing problems that regularly combine insane, ugly, and costly urban construction with a steady worsening of a century-long housing shortage; maddeningly inadequate public transportation which, although here and there it increases, is generally on the decline both quantitatively and qualitatively, as it also costs always more to use; schools bursting with tensions while the hope of learning, even of competence, drains away; widespread drug addiction, most terribly among the young; crime and police brutality marching together in a horrifying procession; rapidly increasing costs for always less available medical care; mounting homelessness and welfare needs that are met by "workfare" laws and falling welfare budgets, as the cost of living endlessly rises; rising unemployment along with declining unemployment compensation benefits both in duration and amount; a steady increase in those officially classified as poor, most tragically among children; and smog, and power blackouts, and....

The crisis of our cities is another way of describing a serious deterioration in the way our citizenry lives. More than three-quarters of us work, reside, go to school, get addicted, are arrested, pushed around, become ill and neglected, in a city somewhere.[40] Many of the states are shuddering on the brink of fiscal disaster or, like California, with its and the nation's largest state deficit ever (over $11 billion in 1991), falling over the edge: and having to close more schools, let more bridges become dangerous, reduce health services even more—and build more prisons. But the problems of the states derive from two principal sources: the growing needs of the cities and the declining funds from the federal government. The situation has become so ferocious, and its political repercussions on mayors and governors so dire, that recently some of the latter have even begun to say things that could not have passed their lips as recently as two years ago: "Perhaps our problems would not be so grave if we spent less on the military and more on our society?" After all, military expenditures (in the always understated government account,) were $16 billion in 1946, doubled by 1951, doubled again by 1966, and again by 1979, and then once more doubled, to $259 billion in 1985, rising toward $300 billion as the 1980s ended, where they now seem to be stuck, come heaven or low water. (*Economic Report of the President, 1991*, current dollars.)

The rash of emergency announcements of these days suggest that the living and fiscal conditions of our urban life have come unstuck, and they are accurate. But the inadequacy of city life in the United States is by no means new. It would be difficult to match the squalor and brutality found in 1900 Chicago, as depicted by Upton Sinclair in *The Jungle*, or their continuation in James T. Farrell's *Studs Lonigan* or, for that matter, the Chicago after World War II found in Nelson Algren's *Man with The Golden Arm*. The inadequacies have been there all along. But the new emigrants who filled the cities before World War I, and the internal migrants up through World War II and for a while after, put up with what in these days is not always tolerated; and what was put up with earlier could be camouflaged or pacified by one kind of handout or another, or hidden from view in ways no longer possible. The toleration diminishes, as do the "handouts," and the camouflage has peeled away. Belief in the basic beneficence of the system, even worse, hope for the future, have shriveled: the system no longer delivers enough of either to the growing numbers of desperate people in a growing number of cities.

Has it been the quantitative failure of the system that is responsible for this series of qualitative defeats? If by quantitative one means GNP, and other major "indicators" that are put forth as meaningful, the answer is no. It is in what lies behind the well-known numbers that the defeats live, and not least in the most important but not most publicized numbers of income and wealth distribution, where the present shortfalls and future apprehensions of people of color, of women, of the young, and of children are found:[41] taken together, where a healthy—or unhealthy—majority of the people are found, almost all living in cities that smother body and soul.

Withal, the economic system has been at its very best in the one way that is counted in our system as most important: it has done what it is designed to do, which is to produce goods—any old goods—and to yield profits and luxurious living to those within the top 10 percent of the population. Although they may have difficulty in breathing or paying their medical bills or getting to work and back, the next 10-20 percent, moreover, have done better than that *many* people have ever done in other times or places. The system *has* succeeded, if only in the sense that it can do no better: GNP, after all, is over $6 trillion, and that ain't hay. Is it?

The problems of the cities are now acute not only for those who live and work in them and, less directly, those who live in the larger metropolitan areas surrounding them, but also for those who own city real estate, and whose plants, offices, and stores are still located in the cities. Industrial and commercial firms may move to the suburbs (or Asia or some place) as fast as decorum and costs will allow, but there are certain limits to that process, as there are limits to the exodus of middle-income homeowners to the already troubled suburbs. Quite apart from consider-ations of human misery, in other words, there are hundreds of billions of dollars to be lost if the cities are not saved. Which by no means assures that they will be, in fact, "saved."

This threat has placed the urban crisis on and off the front pages now for many years, and has been made all the more vivid by the turbulence seen almost daily on those same front pages. The Urban Coalition some years ago sought to enlist the voluntary cooperation of businesses in bringing new life to the cities. The federal government joined with local and state governments to renew and redevelop the decayed central cities. These and other programs have done both a lot and a little. Some slums have been wiped out and replaced by shiny new towers—office buildings, department stores, middle- and high-income apartment houses and hotels. And while old slums continue to fester, as in the South Bronx, new ones are created, as when "gentrification" pushes people out of decaying areas and into areas previously almost tolerable that then become not so. Urban renewal has come to be called urban removal—to still other slums—for the former residents of the slums, thus increasing rents while compressing the population.

The intensity and spread of the urban problem guarantees that its existence is known to all; its social, political, and economic dangers to those at the top of the society have guaranteed that all levels of business and government have initiated or become part of innumerable programs with the stated intentions of eliminating poverty, slums, mess, and sprawl. Many of the programs die on paper. Those that are implemented are not infrequently followed by a worsening of the very problems they have sought to cure, sometimes because of the programs, sometimes despite them. Why?

Surely a key part of the answer to what goes wrong must begin with a fundamental reality: remedial programs are almost always designed, run, and administered by those who, by their interests and their outlook, have been responsible for a large part of the processes that created the problems they seek to cure—not in intention, of course, only in practice. The programs are run by those at the top—the top of federal, state, or local governments, of the appropriate bureaus; the top of the economy, or their accepted political representatives on the national, regional, and local levels. Whether the reference is to work training programs where resistant unions as well as businesses have a say; to urban development and renewal where real estate developers, banks, and construction companies move into decision-making positions; or to transportation and environmental reform where *all* power groups move in—whether in these or other instances, "the vested interests" have the largest say: the foxes preside over the chicken coop.

Take urban renewal. In the shaping of federal urban housing and renewal programs, the process normally begins with what appear to be the best of intentions, in or out of Congress. Immediately a variety of pressures comes to bear: to place administration and control of programs on the local level, which means under the control of those in power, which means those already with power in the city, not those with the need; *not* to allocate adequate funds; *not* to compete with existing housing. Quite probably the most promising efforts along these lines were made in the late 1960s—when at least efforts were *being* made. But a convincing study sums up the results of that time as follows:

> Our survey has shown that the men and women who make basic public housing policy at the local level are in no sense represen- tative of the client group the programs are intended to serve. A substantial proportion of the commissioners do not favor adding to the stock of publicly subsidized housing, nor use of newer forms of public housing, nor many of the "liberalization" trends, including increased tenant participation.... [The authority] inserts, at a critical level of internal decision-making, an interven- ing layer of part-time, lay commissioners who act as a brake on the program by failing to keep abreast of new trends and

techniques and by representing a microcosm of middle-class white views about the poor, their housing, and the responsibilities of government.[42]

Unfortunately, urban renewal has seldom made the cities a better place to live for their residents, whose housing deteriorates and becomes more expensive, who find decent jobs increasingly difficult to get, and so on. But urban renewal almost *always* helps the developers, the banks, the construction and real estate industries—at least for a while. It does so by building high-rise office buildings, shopping centers, and freeways cutting through the residential areas of the very people who are supposed to be its beneficiaries. Scandals of corrupted financing and flimsy construction have been and remain the stuff of which the "development of our cities" has been and is made; it is the way of that world.

The essentially private power structure that built our cities in the past, in response to speculative and market stimuli, is now a complex private-public structure that "rebuilds" our cities, still in response to the lure of profits, still buttressed by "cooperative" politicians at all levels. The process is not new; what gives it the stench of scandal is that it is carried out in the name of those who are in fact harmed by it. But there's little new there, either, as the history of our farm policies (among others) shows.

Meanwhile, and with the opposite of improvement in view, the mosquito drone intensifies. Intense concern with the urban crisis began in the Kennedy Administration and continued in the Johnson Administration. As the Vietnam war deepened and continued, the War on Poverty and against Urban Blight devolved into skirmishes. Under President Nixon, the rhetoric of urban rescue found its principle in presumably liberal Daniel Moynihan's notion of "benign neglect"—which, though the neglect turned out not to be benign at all, at least had the small virtue of bringing rhetoric and reality closer together. With the economic crises of the 1970s, the cause of decent cities was lost; with the 1980s, Reagan, grinning, snoozing, and deceiving all along the way, was able to turn both rhetoric and reality against most of the people of the cities. That he succeeded in that is less of a comment on his being a "great communicator" than on the steady diminution of good sense and decency in the United States.

The Effluent Society

So go the cities and cityfolk of the United States, as so have gone its farms and farmers. Standing off at an analytical distance sufficient to allow the two social areas to be placed in the same focus, we may be able to understand that the present condition and unpromising future of both our countryside and our cities, our agriculture and industry, our farmers and workers—that is, of our society—are the outcome of a set of systematic historical processes that have bound them together economically, politically, and socially.

What city and country have in common that has carried both to the troubled present is a social process that has combined individual cupidity with social stupidity, creating a historical development that has led to immense waste, misuse, spoliation, and destruction of resources, both human and nonhuman. Nor have either the causes or the consequences of these processes been limited to the United States: the agriculture and the industry of all the industrial capitalist nations, and those of the non-capitalist economies, have moved to much the same commands, have displayed much the same environmental recklessness, and have wasted and spoiled in much the same ways, if not always to the same degree.[43] And the poorest people of the world have had the least to say, receive the least—if any—of the benefits, and pay the highest costs.

In his inaugural address in 1933, President Franklin Delano Roosevelt spoke of "one-third of the nation" as "ill-clothed, ill-fed, and ill-housed." And he went on, at the very lowest point of the depression, to admonish a weary and shocked nation that "the only thing we have to fear is fear itself—nameless, unreasoning, unjustified terror which paralyzes needed efforts...." It is by no means an exaggeration to say that despite all the changes of almost sixty years, one-third of our people still have insufficient income to eat or to be housed decently, even if sufficient clothing is a much lesser problem. But today fear is not the main paralyzing factor that prevents movement toward needed social policies: it is rather some combination of ideology and a continuing flow of misinformation, on the one hand, and a perverse form of individualism that nourishes a willful mindlessness and heartlessness, on the other. And if it is a good one-third of our own people who live miserable, desperate, even dangerous lives, it is a good four-fifths of the world's population that lives so. Less than a billion people live at one level or another of the sphere of production and consumption that is the best the world has to offer: that billion or so, except for their poor, in North America, in the nineteen nations of what in 1993 will become the European Economic Area, plus the Japanese, the Australians, and perhaps a few more million at the top of the "newly industrializing countries," and other bits and pieces of Africa, Asia, Latin America, and the Middle East. That leaves well over four billion people who go without adequate food, clothing, shelter, medical care, or education; whose lives are cruelly and needlessly shortened, cramped, and miserable; and at least ten million who quite simply die of starvation, every year.

In passing, between the lines, and sometimes explicitly in this and foregoing chapters, I have suggested or pointed to various forms of waste and environmental damage, and have seen them as organically related to the historical impulses and needs of modern capitalism: exploitation, expansion, and oligarchic rule. Now it is analytically appropriate to knit together the several strands of previous pages in order to explain the resulting coexistence of enormous economic waste with deep and unmet human and social needs, of extraordinary productive efficiency with equally extraordinary socioeconomic inefficiency, of always more rapidly improving areas and levels of science and technology moving alongside processes that have already extinguished much life, human and otherwise, and that threaten calamities so terrible as to be virtually unimaginable.

If all this had been unavoidable, it would simply constitute a profound historical tragedy. But it was not inevitable; it has been and remains a product of human decisions made in the context of historically created institutions that may and must now be seen as having at best played themselves out or, more probably, as having always been misguided. That the world was heading this way long ago was seen by Veblen on the eve of World War I. After underscoring needs and pointing to social changes that might fulfill them, he went on to warn,

> But history records more frequent and more spectacular instances of the triumph of imbecile institutions over life and culture than of peoples who have by force of instinctive insight saved themselves alive out of a desperately precarious institutional situation, such, for instance, as now faces the people of Christendom.[44]

What we have wasted are our natural resources, the productive capacities we have developed to make them resources, and the already developed talents and considerably greater human potentialities that could have been and could now put our needs and our possibilities together. We waste and destroy not just in what we do, but also in what we fail to do. And, quite apart from anything else, because we now waste so much—probably *half* of what we do or could produce, as will be argued below—we also damage and destroy much more than we would if we were to waste much less.[45]

Where to begin to tell this appalling story is an arbitrary decision, for it is chicken and egg, egg and chicken. We begin by saying that what strikes most as a new development — this coincidence of great wealth and great want, terrible waste and terrible destruction—is at least as old as the joining together of capitalism and nationalism and imperialism and industrialism, the four horsemen of what could well become our apocalypse.

The More Things Change...

The stark contrast between what is and what could be has existed often before. Each time it recurs it does so at a higher level of divergence between the harsh realities and the beckoning possibilities; each time, also, there has been an ensuing catastrophe more devastating than its predecessors. The modern era began that way, as R.H. Tawney noted sardonically (in 1926):

> Nourished by the growth of peaceful commerce, the financial capitalism of the age fared not less sumptuously, if more dangerously at the courts of princes. Mankind, it seems, hates nothing so much as its own prosperity. Menaced with an accession of riches which would lighten its toil, it makes haste to redouble its labors, and to pour away the perilous stuff, which might deprive of plausibility the complaint that it is poor. Applied to the arts of peace, the new resources commanded by Europe during the first half of the 16th century might have done something to exorcise the spectres of pestilence and famine, and to raise the material fabric of civilization to undreamed-of heights. Its rulers, secular and ecclesiastical alike, thought otherwise. When

pestilence and famine were ceasing to be necessities imposed by nature, they re-established them by political art. The sluice which they opened to drain away each new accession of superfluous wealth was war.[46]

Since then, the bloody sluice has been open more than shut: in the seventeenth century there were only four years *without* war; fighting seldom stopped in the eighteenth century, which crossed over into the nineteenth with the great bloodbath of the Napoleonic Wars, the completion of which began the "century of peace" (1815–1914)— peaceful only in the sense that the Great Powers fought much more against "the lesser peoples" for empire, rather than each other. And then, in 1914, history's largest and most destructive war began, to be followed by a seemingly endless chain of always longer and more destructive civil and international wars, up to the present. The kinds and degrees of human, social, and natural destruction thus entailed defy description.

But honors for massive waste and destruction of resources, equipment, and lives do not go only to war. The surrounding socioeconomic system when it has been "at peace," itself a somewhat murky notion, is also responsible for enormous waste and destruction. Capitalism has been simultaneously the most efficient *and* the most wasteful production system in history; and, like wars and preparations for wars, the productive system becomes always more efficient *and* always more wasteful and destructive. This is so even setting aside the considerable contribution capitalism and its associated nationalism and imperialism have made to the outbreak of wars: through competition for markets, resources, investment outlets, strategic locations and, since World War II, military and paramilitary attempts to prevent, stifle, and subvert basic change over the globe.

Even in this bloody century there may have been more waste and accompanying human and environmental damage in what have been called periods of peace than in those of war. How is that possible? It is because of the systematic and ubiquitous restriction of production in both agriculture and industry, *and* the waste of labor and materials and equipment in the promotion, packaging, and selling of commodities, *and* the pervasive practices of "deliberate obsolescence" in durable consumer goods, *and* the enormous amount of unused capacity and unemployed and underemployed labor that have characterized this century—more than just "waste" to those unemployed and underemployed, of course—*and*, to bring the dirty laundry list to an abrupt end at its most wasteful activity, global military production and practices. To wrap in one package environmental damage, destruction, and waste, we may note simply that the Pentagon is the eighth largest user of petroleum in the world, exceeding all but seven nations.

In all these and still other ways, to degrees unimagined even by otherwise well-informed people, economies everywhere, led by the capitalist economies—with ours leading theirs—have become increasingly ingenious at finding means to use resources wastefully or to underuse them. That in the absence of substantial social change such would be the ever-growing tendency was posited by Veblen as early as 1904, when he observed that

> wasteful expenditure on a scale adequate to offset the surplus productivity of modern industry is nearly out of the question. Private initiative cannot carry the waste of goods and services to nearly the point required by the business situation.... Private waste is no doubt large.... but something more to the point can be done and indeed is being done, by the civilized governments in the way of effectual waste. Armaments, public edifices, courtly and diplomatic establishments, and the like, are almost altogether wasteful... [and] they have the additional advantage that the public securities which represent this waste serve as attractive investment securities for private savings.... But however extraordinary this public waste of substance latterly has been, it is apparently altogether inadequate to offset the surplus productivity of the machine industry, particularly when this productivity is seconded by the great facility which the modern business organization affords for the accumulation of savings in relatively few hands.... So long as industry remains at its present level of efficiency, and especially so long as incomes continue to be distributed somewhat after the present scheme, waste cannot be expected to overtake production, and can therefore not check the untoward tendency toward depression. But if the balance cannot be maintained by accelerating wasteful consumption, it may be maintained by curtailing and regulating the output of goods.[47]

What underlies this seemingly insane "political economy"? We can often begin to answer such a question by assuming that results usually flow from aims; and the results of these intersecting private and public policies have been the maintenance of market stability and profitability and social peace—not totally, of course, w...h would be impossible, but surprisingly much, considering the great p..mps of change at work in the modern world.[48]

A Litany of Waste

Because the notion of waste implies an opposed notion of usefulness, it is, of course, impossible to settle upon a definition that would find universal agreement. Like most other works concerned with this dimension of our economic life, what follows adopts a conservative notion of waste, meant deliberately to avoid exaggeration of the realities created by our history. Even understated, however, the figures are staggering in themselves and unsettling in their implications.

For present purposes, I accept the conclusion that "useful output in the U.S. economy could have been $1.2 trillion higher in 1980 than it actually was...; 49.6 percent higher than its 1980 level." Among other reasons for viewing this as a conservative understatement is that its authors count about 70 percent of military output as "useful."[49]

To say that "capitalism has been simultaneously the most efficient *and* the most wasteful productive system in history" is to point to the contrast between the great efficiency with which a particular modern factory produces a product, such as toothpaste, and the contrived and massive inefficiency of an economic system that has people pay for toothpaste a price over 90 percent of which is owed to its packaging and marketing, rather than its production. So toothpaste is trivial. Automobiles are not. Until recently, it was assumed that about 15 percent of all jobs were directly or indirectly connected with the production and the use of the automobile: "What's Good for GM Is Good for America." In a Federal Trade Commission Inquiry of 1939, General Motors presented figures showing that a Chevrolet with a market price of $950 had production costs of about $150. The rest was for advertising, distribution, and profits—and the production costs included the useless appearance changes that, it has been estimated, amount to at least one-third of production costs over time. To this it may be added that between 1928 and 1939, years encompassing the worst depression in history, GM's return to net worth *averaged* 35 percent.[50]

It should be noted that in 1939 the sales effort was just beginning to master the art of waste, by comparison with the more recent past and present. What is true for toothpaste and autos is of course true for virtually all consumer goods as well as a small but rising percentage of capital goods—for example, in the realm of computers.

The processes within which all these products are produced and sold become always more efficient and, at the same time, always more costly to the society—and to nature: nowadays, not just planned obsolescence, but use-and-throw-away products, normally made of plastic, which add to already substantial amounts of destructive waste.

The foregoing is suggestive of a much broader and deeper process of waste—so broad and deep and in its various elements so thoroughly mixed together, that here the processes can be discussed only in very general terms. This will be done by touching on the various ways and means of waste in two (artificially separated) "sectors": industry and the military, understanding that there is considerable overlap in all respects. After that, a closely connected but analytically distinguishable and always more worrisome problem will be examined, that of "destructive wastes," the wastes that contaminate the environment and poison or threaten the processes of life.[51]

Waste in Industry

At the center of the structure of waste in industry is "the sales effort." That comprises advertising, sales promotion, trivial product change, and, not least, the shaping of social mentality. As Paul Baran put it decades ago, "people steeped in the culture of monopoly capitalism do not want what they need, and do not need what they want."[52] We in the United States badly *need* better health care, housing, education, and transportation, for example; but the people have been led to *want* more and newer autos, TVs, fast food, artificial stimulants, and so forth. And the public accepts (much of it with enthusiasm) extraordinary military expenditures as it also accepts policies that have reduced the provision of what is needed and that have very much worsened the lives of a substantial percentage of the population—including many who have supported those policies.[53]

That such processes go on and accelerate is not due to nature but to a defiance of its laws by the power and the needs of those who possess economic and political strength. What the latter have needed and created is a society dependent upon consumerism and militarization, which in turn have required a successful process of mind management—whether its intentions have been defensible or malign, whether for selling products, ideology, or politicians. It has been costly in money, skills, and resources, at the same time that it has steadily robbed the society of a decent future.

The role of advertising has been central in bringing about these conditions. It is an activity that increases rapidly over time, both in its quantities and its skills. "Companies devoted 2 percent of the GNP in 1980 to advertising expenditures. If they had spent as little—in real dollars per capita—as they did in 1948, we would have saved...1.2 percent of actual GNP."[54] Going beyond these simple numbers, we must point to the foolishness of continuous real or imagined product changes that are *being* advertised, whether for razors, or beer, or autos, or deodorants, etc.

But there are more important matters involved. Only one among them has to do with the poisoning of food. In the past few decades the food industry has been almost completely revolutionized in terms of its *scope*, from largely local to national and multinational, its *products*, from largely natural to largely processed, and the degree to which all foods are in small or large degree dependent upon additives, such as nitrates, or artificial substances, such as cyclamates, few of them entirely safe, and some of them very dangerous.

Much more than advertising has been part of this evolution, of course, but it could not have happened without advertising and its ramifications.

Impossible to quantify, but at least as important, is that advertising has even larger costs hidden in the processes that are at its heart, without which it would not exist in its present kind or degree: it is an industry whose purpose is the reshaping and the creation of needs for the purposes of profit, and the manipulation of political thought and behavior, irrespective of the consequences to society, nature, and people.[55]

Let us now turn to *output restriction* in industry. Industries vary according to product and technique, but in general the optimum rate of capacity utilization is around 85 percent. Output restriction means producing at less than optimum, that is, inefficiently. It is a practice that can only persist to the degree that an industry is noncompetitive in structure. Its purpose is to keep price from falling or to support its increase; and it cannot work unless the entire industry follows suit. In a competitively structured industry (and in the absence of government intervention to keep prices from falling, as in agriculture) the natural tendency is to increase production when prices are tending to fall, as a means of maintaining sales and income. But it is difficult to find an industry that is competitively structured; instead, as we have seen in Chapter 3, they are typically *oligopolistic*, that is, with few sellers, and a very few dominant sellers—as in autos, steel, aluminum, beer, detergents, cigarettes, etc.—so that it is both desirable and possible to achieve effective collusion, illegal though it is.

Although the appearances and the rhetoric of most markets are those of competition, the reality is one of "administered prices" (as economists put it). Sometimes the normal becomes obvious, as with the dramatic price rises for oil in the 1970s. Since then, surely everyone has learned that the level of oil prices (and therefore gasoline, fuel oil, and many other prices) is determined not by "natural reasons" (although price fixing is very natural indeed), but by whether or not OPEC is able to put oil in short supply with agreed-upon output restrictions. But what is true for oil is true in general for all industries for the same reasons, and the output restriction and price "stability" are accomplished in much the same manner, though considerably less obviously. Thus, and only by way of example, when in 1974–75 the U.S. economy was hit by a severe recession, the automobile industry cut back production, laid off about one-third of its workers, and *raised* prices by 10 percent.

More broadly, it may be assumed that on the average, industrial output could be at least 5 percent higher than is normal, were "spoiling the market" not a common and realistic fear. That is a lot of waste, even if the foregoing estimates are off a point or two (and they may well be an understatement).

The foregoing refers to waste in what is *not* produced. The waste in what *is* produced is also important. Much of what is produced is designed *not* to last beyond a certain length of time, determined not by engineering or physical criteria but by demand and market saturation. The auto industry is a prime instance of this, but by no means unique. If, in order to use its capacity profitably, the auto industry must have an average buyer hold on to a new car for only three years and then buy another new one, it then becomes auto *industry* practice to build cars that begin to run up substantial repair bills after three years, at the same time as advertising and style changes are building desire. Thus the used car market becomes an integral part of the auto industry. What is more, the car makers make

308 — U.S. CAPITALIST DEVELOPMENT SINCE 1776

a goodly share of their profits from the sale of parts, and their sales are increasingly to rental fleets (some owned by the producers) that after a year or so sell off the fleet cars as used. It may or may not make business sense, but it surely doesn't make economic sense.[56]

And then there is the enormous and increasing waste of human energy and skills, the waste of labor in industry. It may be measured in several ways: (1) unemployment and underemployment, (2) the productive efficiency of those who work full-time, and (3) the allocation of labor between productive and nonproductive jobs.

Unemployment and Underemployment

Unemployment in the United States since 1900, excluding the years of the two world wars, has averaged 6.9 percent—just about what it was early in the recession that began in mid-1990. This says nothing about people who are working half-time or less, and need and wish to work full-time, or those who are trained steel or auto workers but now can only find work in jobs requiring few or no skills; nor does it tell us about how many who, because they have unsuccessfully sought jobs for so long, have ceased to look—the "hard-core" or "discouraged" unemployed—and are thus not counted as unemployed, for one is "not in the labor force" unless one either has a job or is known to be looking for one. It is generally estimated that a figure for the rate of unemployment that took account of involuntarily part-time and discouraged workers would be at least 50 percent higher than the official rate.[57]

It is worth pondering how much more could have been produced with all that unused labor (and unused industrial and agricultural capacity) in this century, or even in the past two or three years. One could come up with a number for that, however controversial it might be; one could not come up with a number for the qualitative, and in the long run more important side of all this unused and underutilized labor, that is, the education and training and morale that could have been, had there been a society seeking to use and develop, rather than simply to use, its human resources.

Efficiency of Full-Time Workers

Anyone who has ever worked in a factory, an office, a store, even a hospital or a school, knows of the extensive and virtually systematic "soldiering on the job" that characterizes almost all jobs—when the boss isn't looking—despite all the supervisory personnel and equipment paid to "look." This is so for two major reasons: morale and fear. The fear comes from the widespread and usually correct belief that working faster will mean working oneself out of a job: insecurity about continuing employment is endemic for virtually all wageworkers. The morale problem relates to workers' commitment to their job, employer, and/or product. Workers are seldom treated as full human beings—in terms of rights, intelligence, feelings—on the job, and the less so when the enterprise is huge. Workers know that what they work with is designed to be "foolproof" and that they are the presumed fools. And they know well before the consumer does if the product they are producing is shoddy, or ill-designed, or *designed* to fall apart at some early time. Workers may or may not believe they are being exploited, but they know they are being used and that, like some of their products, they are destined for rapid discard. Only genuine fools would be able to maintain their morale under such conditions. Worker ownership and/or control within the capitalist system can do and has done much to lessen this widespread alienation where it exists; but its existence is fragmentary and unlikely to spread. Worker discontent is another form of waste; even more, it has serious negative effects in the social and political realm.[58]

Allocation of Labor

The distinction between productive and nonproductive work is both obvious and subtle: productive labor is that which produces goods and services for sale and use, nonproductive labor produces nothing, it exists to manage and supervise the productive workers. In the United States in 1980, managerial and supervisorial personnel constituted 10.8 percent of total nonagricultural employment. The figure for Sweden was 2.4 percent, for Germany 3.0 percent, and for Japan 4.4 percent. It cannot be argued that in that period the U.S. economy grew more rapidly than the other three, or that our productive efficiency was higher, or that the economy—or its workers' morale—was healthier.

Military Waste

The examination of industrial and agricultural waste, whether in what is done or what is withheld, locates certain areas of waste in what is in larger part *not* waste. The reverse is true for military production. The reference here is not to $150 screwdrivers or $700 toilet seats; those are mere symbols for an immense and scandalous and shocking reality, constructed by the mafia of the main corporate beneficiaries, the military brass, a long-standing and crowded assembly of petty and great politicians, and a population all too willing to be made fools of, the latter on the mistaken notion that such economic misdeeds are necessary for their jobs—and their nation's glory—to continue: waste, and want not.[59]

The realities of military expenditures are too complex to be more than touched upon here, although we can go beyond the amusing and petty symbols: it consists in part of the costs in dollars, in the processes of planned obsolescence brought to high art (aided and abetted by cost-plus pricing), and, perhaps most important of all, in its long-run social and economic consequences.

The place to begin is with the word *military*. Almost everyone refers to military spending as *defense* spending. It sounds necessary, even useful, put that way. The wording connects with an important terminological change of 1947. It was, as we shall see in the next chapter, the very year in which what has determined so much of the world's destiny since then was given a big shove. Among other changes, the Department of War, as it had been called since 1789, has been renamed the Department of Defense. This was done by the same people and at much the same time that the Central Intelligence Agency (CIA) was being given a new, different, and much more liberally financed life (it had been the Office of Strategic Services during World War II), and when the National Security Council (which became Oliver North's base of operations) was born. The military draft, or selective service, was then reinstituted, although we were not at war. It was argued that the defense of the United States had to extend to anywhere and everywhere in the world where developments threatening, even worrisome to the United States were taking place, or *might* take place. At the height of the Cold War, the United States had over 2,000 military bases overseas. The War Department had fought very few wars; the Defense Department would be hard put to find a twelve-month period in which it was not overseeing a war somewhere, acknowledged or not, declared or not.

So be it. But even if we do spend a lot on the military, it's only a small fraction of GNP, right? Wrong. Like so much else in contemporary government, what numbers *are* is determined by definitions, and who is to make them for a nation but its government? As we saw in Chapter 4 (note 7), the manner in which the government classifies military expenditures (omitting the $100 billion or so cost of interest on the military share of the debt—now the largest budget item—for example), and has redefined what does and does not go into the budget (most importantly, Social Security), vastly understates how much and what share of government expenditures are military in nature and purpose. It is reasonable to assume at least half of all federal expenditures as being directly or indirectly military-related. Earlier, we showed that since 1946, even by official count, we have spent at least $5 trillion on the military.[60]

The waste in the midst of all that is quite simply mind-boggling. It takes various forms. *Item*: the antiballistic missile (ABM) complex in North Dakota cost $6 billion, when it was completed in 1975. It was closed, permanently, 48 days later. *Item*: it is in the very nature of military production that when it is used, it is used up very rapidly; mostly (and fortunately) it is never used. Frequently, probably as frequently as possible, military "goods" are rendered obsolete by the weapons manufacturers—or, less frequently, by foreign developments. *Item*: whether used or not, they are produced almost entirely (90 percent) within "cost-plus"—that is, profit-guaranteed—contracts. Average final cost overruns are 320 percent of the winning estimate originally submitted. And if the costs are three times greater, so are the profits: an attractive incentive for inefficient production, if one were seeking such. Nor do companies lose their privileged status if what they have produced and sold does not work according to promises or specifications; if they did, the military-industrial complex would be riddled by bankrupt companies.[61] *Item*: quite apart from anything else, can anyone who has ever spent time in the army, navy, marine corps, air force, or the Pentagon please give an estimate of how much time was spent doing nonwork, or no work?

All this costs about $300 billion a year, and those who gain from it, or think they do, are the most stubbornly effective opponents of the slightest degree or kind of change away from its long and wasteful life.

So granted all that, the reasonably well-informed working person thinks, at least it creates needed jobs, doesn't it? There the answer is more complex. Military expenditures certainly took us out of the depression of the 1930s; and *because* of military expenditures it surely was easier (and politically wise) to have those other forms of social expenditure (see Chapters 4 and 8) that have kept us from serious depression, if not recession, since World War II. But only, it seems, up to the late 1960s. At that time, some academic and congressional studies, doubtless given an impetus by politicians dubious about the Vietnam war, and one trade union (the machinists') study, all came to the conclusion briefly noted earlier: *if* the level of government expenditures were to remain the same, and *if* military expenditures were replaced by expenditures on schools, housing, education, and the like, the jobs per government dollar would be anywhere from one-third to over one-half greater. As time has passed since the 1960s, that percentage has risen, for the reason that it was originally correct: since the 1960s the kinds of things that are meant by military expenditures are increasingly high-tech. A few hundred B-52s dropped more bombs on Vietnam than tens of thousands of bombers did in Europe and Asia during World War II; one hydrogen bomb could itself outdo all of those. A nuclear submarine carries enough firepower to destroy many cities on one mission. As General Electric, one of the largest of the producers of military stuff, likes to say, "Progress Is Our Most Important Product."

A tiny number of very large corporations produce all these things—planes, submarines, bombs—and they use relatively few highly trained workers (technicians, scientists, engineers). They all do very well, but they are a small percentage of the millions who worked at making weapons during World War II. In 1941, Roosevelt asked for "50,000 planes," and helped to end the depression. Reagan asked for $1.6 trillion to be spent in five years, got it, and may well have helped to bring us toward the "silent depression" of the 1990s.

What does it mean to say "a few" corporations get most of the military contracts? During and since World War II, one hundred corporations have regularly received about two-thirds of all prime contracts (parts of which they subcontract, increasing their already great power); the top thirty-three receive 50 percent; almost all of this is awarded in five industries: aircraft, electronics and telecommunications, shipbuilding and repairing, vehicles, and oil; about 90 percent of prime contracts are negotiated rather than won through competitive bidding—the exception, instead of the rule it is supposed to be; and, unsurprisingly, the profit rates of the top ten military contractors (in 1984) were 25 percent, twice that of manufacturing corporations in general that year.[62]

Finally, there is another important contrast between the meanings of military and social expenditures: The high-tech that greatly and increasingly characterizes military production means that half as much in *wages* but 20 percent more outlay in *salaries* result from a given dollar of government expenditure, compared with the average social expenditure. This is another element tending to increase the inequality of income distribution. "So," concludes Reich, "military spending is easily expandable, is highly profitable, and benefits the major corporations in the economy."[63]

It is the military's job to protect us from enemies by threatening to destroy them, one way or another. They have done a lot of that, but the larger destruction created by "our way of life" is more persistently and—absent nuclear war—more pervasively and permanently destructive. Some of that is due to sheer thoughtlessness or recklessnesss—comparable to the way in which we harm ourselves with tobacco, alcohol, and other stimuli and drugs. Much of it, probably much more of it, is in the area of destructive wastes: we waste so much, and so much of the consequence of that is destructive.

Mother Nature in the Gunsight: Destructive Wastes

Human beings are one part of nature, of course, along with other animals, the seas, the forests, the land. But we are the only part that can change the rest of nature, often irreversibly; and we are the only part that can and does change itself in the process, for better or for worse. Earthquakes destroy, as do floods; beavers chew down trees and dam up creeks; lightning sets forests on fire. But the damage done in these and all other instances of natural alteration is soon absorbed or reversed; in any case, it is local.

Not so for us. In being the most creative and constructive of nature's elements, people are at the same time the most careless and destructive—careless of their own well-being and destructive of their environment and, through wars and other violence, their fellow human beings. Even more, as is now a commonplace, people are moving toward a transformation of nature so substantial as to be irreversible and damaging on what is still an unimaginable scale: as with the ozone layer, the warming of the earth, the poisoning of the earth's air and waters, etc. Just one sad but instructive *Item*: as the forests of the Amazon Basin disappear, in consequence of an accelerating and spreading exploitation, so do the oxygen supply and the bird population of the Northern Hemisphere disappear, proportionately. These disappearances are connected with each other and are also connected with the larger processes of economic and social obliviousness characterizing our world.

How does all this connect with capitalism? Is it not merely an outcome of otherwise benign industrialism, a set of processes one neither wishes to nor has the ability to alter substantially? As so often in these pages regarding complex matters, we can only point to the basics, and hope the reader will turn to additional reading. As for capitalism, we look once more to the heart of the matter: expansion.

Throughout its history, expansion has been like an all-powerful magnet pulling the economic process ever faster through time and space; it, and the profit seeking that energizes the capitalist process, have always been and are still heedless of the consequences to all but "the bottom line." Indeed, Milton Friedman, the most effective ideologue of "market capitalism" in the past several decades, has insisted that the capitalist has a duty *not* to think of anything but profits and that which supports them—which does not, for him, include Mother Nature; and the society has a duty *not* to interfere with the capitalist—a parody of Adam Smith, but much listened to these days. (Friedman also believes that *everything* should be privately owned and operated for profit: schools, parks, jails, the military, hospitals, and... everything. And recently, especially in the United States and Great Britain, the capitalist process has been going his way.)

Until one thinks about it, it sounds like a good idea. When one does think about it, one discovers that although the capitalist takes the gain from this process, everyone else, including by now Mother Nature, pays the costs. When economists first began to think about such matters, they used the term *external diseconomies*. But what they had in mind was minimal compared to the natural disasters the public now lives with, to say nothing of those that are just appearing over the horizon. And even at their best, those earlier economists did not realize that as corporate power grew, and as it compared the profit possibilities from the status quo and the threat of alternatives environmentally less dangerous, the corporations would use their immense economic *and* political power *and* public relations campaigns to "counter, suppress, and eliminate" those other alternatives.[64]

Wastefulness and the destructive wastes they increase did not await this century to begin; it is rather that their amounts and their types taken together have made what was once at most a passing problem into a major threat. Thus, if an industrial plant dumps chemicals into a large river at the rate of X units/day, the river can cleanse itself. If ten more plants on the same river do the same, the problem is altered. If both banks of the river become dotted with such plants *and* if their effluents are of a higher form of toxicity, the river will be destroyed as a living process, and what has depended upon it—for drinking, for agriculture, for industry—will be faced with a major problem. As the rate and spread of economic expansion and industrialization have grown in this century, the process of natural destruction has become ubiquitous—of the air, the water (bays, rivers, lakes, even oceans) and the soil—and in turn has of course found its way into food chains on the land and in the seas. We are crowding nature out of existence, with always more of too much poison of too many kinds in too many places all at once. For what?

A rich country like the United States has no need for further growth in the *level* of real gross national product. What *is* needed, and badly, is a substantial change in the *composition* of production, in what is and is not produced and in what relative magnitudes. To put it simply, we need fewer weapons and more food, fewer autos and more public transportation, fewer financial services and more health services. But it must be understood that a change in the structure of production involves a change in the structure of consumption; that, in turn, requires a change in the real distribution of income—itself unimaginable without a change in the decision-making procedures, that is, a change in the structure of power. For the capitalist system as it now stands, it is quantitative improvement that is seen by its decision makers as vital; but for the population, it is the reverse: qualitative change is necessary if there are to be quantitative adequacies or improvement.[65]

Road Map to Disaster

The scope and spread of industrialism in the United States and elsewhere have been hailed as the totems of successful achievement. The existence now of widespread and growing environmental damage has been viewed until quite recently much as a drunken hangover might be—the unfortunate by-product of a great spree. But hangovers go away, normally; ecological imbalance worsens dynamically. "What is at stake in the ecological crisis we face today," said Murray Bookchin over twenty years ago,

> ...is the very capacity of the earth to sustain advanced forms of life. The crisis is being drawn together by massive increases in "typical" forms of air and water pollution; by a mounting accumulation of nondegradable wastes, lead residues, pesticide

residues and toxic additives in food; by the expansion of cities into vast urban belts; by increasing stresses due to congestion, noise and mass living; by the wanton scarring of the earth as a result of mining operations, lumbering, and real estate speculation. The result of all this is that the earth within a few decades has been despoiled on a scale that is unprecedented in the entire history of human habitation on the planet.[66]

It should be obvious from the preceding pages that the manner in which the history and present processes of our society have performed has brought us to a situation in which our present *economic* means and ends have placed us on a *social* path increasingly troubling, dangerous, and costly—quite the opposite of the promises of industrial capitalism as usually viewed. Equally obvious is that the relevant processes are numerous, complicated, and intertwined. We cannot pursue all or even most of them adequately here; perhaps none at all, in a full sense. But by narrowing ourselves down to a few matters closest to our own daily lives, perhaps light may be shed that will illuminate some of the rest of the terrain. In what follows and concludes this chapter we shall look briefly at the powerful relationships between autos and petroleum, with a passing glance at "the energy crisis" and petrochemicals—all connected, all growing daily in their uses and destructive effects.

Referring to the auto-petroleum complex, Barry Weisberg put the problem succinctly:

No other factor has exercised such a predominant influence upon the direction and definition of the American industrial empire. In terms of capital formation, patterns of employment, the extent of marketing penetration, transportation, urbanization, energy, ecological imbalance and American foreign policy, they are unrivaled in influence. The impact of their economic priorities upon the public policy of the United States is unsurpassed by any other lobby or combination of lobbies. The network of subsidiaries, affiliates, and joint ventures runs into the tens of thousands and affects the political economy of virtually every nation. Automobiles and petroleum determine the political composition of governments and the chemical composition of the atmosphere.[67]

We have already said much about this giant in our midst, in earlier pages and chapters. There is more to say. Dependence upon this pattern of production, jobs, consumption, transportation—and submission to its associated politics—first became an addiction in our society, as it is becoming so in others. The people of this country never decided that this should be such a dominating characteristic in our lives, or that private transport should so fully displace public transport; nor is it likely that given the opportunity the people would have decided to afflict themselves in such a manner:

> If in 1910, one asked, "A new form of individualized transportation—the automobile—has been devised. It is terribly convenient, but within 60 years it will directly kill 60,000 people each year and injure millions of others. Untold millions will suffer from heart and lung diseases that it causes; and because of it our cities will fall into decay, perpetuating and exacerbating racial and other social antagonisms, etc. Would you prefer an automobile-based transportation system to a public transportation system that does not have these noxious side effects?" it is inconceivable that many would have answered affirmatively. It is not a matter of lack of foresight; no mechanism existed for allowing any foresight to affect the decision about urban transportation.[68]

And what would a sensible transportation system look like? It would stress a combination of safety, convenience, comfort, speed, and the efficient and safe use of resources. A transportation engineer asked to design a system to meet such standards in engineering, rather than profit terms (and after distinguishing between cargo and passengers) would have us fly very long distances, go by rail between city and suburb and between cities only two or three hundred miles apart, use public transportation systems within cities (electrified underground and surface rail systems), and private or rented automobiles for recreational and some few other purposes. Instead, we go by private car everywhere, every day, except when flying (and then we generally drive to the airport). Cargo is carried in almost as foolish a pattern, using trucks and, even when there is no hurry, air, instead of rail. All this, flying in the face of well-established facts showing the tremendous, social, and human costs of the current reality, which *displaced* something very much like the ideal system noted above.

The wastefulness and dangers of the transportation system are in a real sense the Siamese twins of the same problems in the energy system—although the latter has problems of its own, not least those connected with nuclear energy production and its deadly wastes. The largest oil companies in the world are those of the United States, and they are the largest energy companies as well, controlling or owning the major natural gas, coal, and uranium companies. The oil companies began to be energy companies before the oil crisis of the 1970s; then their long-term tendencies sped up. Now, no matter *what* happens that might cause a shortage or price increase for any source of energy, it is beneficial to the major oil companies, the biggest of which is EXXON. It has been asserted that they cooperated with more than resisted the OPEC increases of the 1970s; if they didn't they would have been poor businessmen.[69]

There has been a series of energy *crises* in the past twenty years or so; but there has never been a *shortage* of oil. The crises have been created. Their meaning depends very much upon the viewer: from the standpoint of the general public, it is the latest and most spectacular instance of the use of concentrated economic and politic power; from the viewpoint of the oil companies, the origins of the crises have been an ongoing and substantial oversupply of oil combined with growing environmentalist pressures. The oil crises serve very well the purpose of lessening any political pressures that might interfere with the best interests of the oil companies, as they see them—and as they have taught the public to see them. As James Ridgeway pointed out in 1973,

> These companies know, as the average citizen does not, that the energy crisis could be the most important political and economic issue of the last quarter of the twentieth century. Not only does the production, distribution, and use of energy underlie the entire environmental movement, but also energy is the foundation of the modern industrial state.[70]

The waste in the energy industry is the stuff of which fables are made. The pattern of land ownership and use in the United States has led to "competitive drilling" for crude oil, as compared with the "unit field system" in, say, the Middle East. What might cost upwards of $15 a barrel to extract in Texas costs at most $2 a barrel in the Middle East (whatever the market price might be). Our pattern of extraction means that about two-thirds of the oil is left in the ground or can be taken out only at even higher costs. (Instead of being blown out by natural gas pressure, as elsewhere, it must be pumped out.) And about half of underground coal never gets out of the mine. (To say nothing of the tens of billions of dollars spent on nonweapons nuclear energy plants, that have never opened and—one hopes—never will.) All this sets aside wastes of distribution, conversion, use. We are told daily of the precariousness of our energy supplies, the authors of which daily participate in throwing those supplies to the winds.[71]

Nor should we leave a discussion of autos, petroleum, and destructive wastes without at least a brief glance at the petrochemical/plastics industrial complex, a blood brother to the auto/petroleum complex in both social and resource terms.

Through every day and night, everyone in the leading industrial countries, and a growing percentage of others in the world, is eating something, wearing something, cleaning a car or house with something, sleeping on something, surrounded by products made from oil: petrochemicals and their numberless products and offshoots. They have taken the place of something natural, or organic—cotton or wool, steel or copper or wood, animal wastes (for fertilizer)—or they are put into otherwise natural products to preserve them or make them more attractive, such as additives in foods and other products.

As one of several manifestations of the so-called chemical revolution of this century, this trend began in Germany before World War I, when it developed coal tar derivatives for its explosives industry and as a substitute for its lack of key resources, including oil. That unpleasant beginning now has an unpleasant middle and threatens a considerably more unpleasant end.

Nature cannot handle synthetics, chemically synthesized artificial products: detergents in the rivers, bays, and oceans quite simply never disappear; plastic containers do not rot, nor do those aluminum cans in their billions; pesticides kill some insects, allow others to multiply, and at the same time poison the soil; synthetic fertilizers are at best questionable in their effects on food. (And as we shall see in Chapter 7, they, and the "Green Revolution" have created additional economic and political problems for the governments and farming peoples of the nonindustrial countries.) An as yet unknown but probably very high percentage of these synthetic products is toxic, virtually all of them are nonbiodegradable, and some of them are destroying our protective ozone layer. Their residues, when they don't rise destructively into the atmosphere, must be carried away, be buried, be sunk, be hidden, something. One of the developing fights these days is: in whose backyard? (The answer, naturally, is of those with the least or no power, adding injury to insult.)

It is easy to believe what we are led to believe, that modern society has created this demon by reverse serendipity; that is, an unstoppable technological process of undeniable goodness has somehow become at best problematic. But that is only a good cover story. The truth is that *all* these products, produced almost always by giant companies, are quite simply more profitable to produce and sell than their natural predecessors. And if it turns out that they are all more dangerous, or at the very least more troublesome, to people, to society, to nature—and that is how it has turned out—well, after all, who lives forever? Got a smoke?

For Whom the Bell Tolls

Setting modern war aside, one cannot imagine a more effective system for destroying life than the socioeconomic system within which the world now functions—except, of course, we cannot set war aside. The latter grows from very much the same social matrix as the warping of agriculture, the lingering death of our cities, our mountains of waste, and the damage to nature. The main difference is that the destruction by war is deliberate whereas that coming from our economic system is a "spillover." But the social outlook guiding both disasters is the same, as is the technology: growth for its own sake, production for its own sake, consumption for its own sake, power for its own sake and for the sake of continuing the rest—these are the drives that have shaped the contemporary world, whose leader is still the United States.

Such lamentations could be endless, and connect with all aspects of our present life processes—as they become more like death processes. A social system as thoroughly imbued from top to bottom with the dynamic of expansion as ours, in its economics, its politics, and in its culture, has much to learn and to unlearn if the foolishness, the waste, the deterioration, and the dangers are to be replaced by processes that might provide us with what we need and cherish, and to do so within a framework of safety and decency. Political battles have been and are being fought, and here and there, now and again, there seems to have been a victory. But of what kind? There is no city better off today than ten, twenty, or thirty years ago. The meaning of farming is defined always less and less in its traditional "way of life" terms, and more and more in the terms and the realities of agribusiness, as more and more the practices of agriculture become restrictive, and the word "bountiful" becomes a dim memory. The environmental battles have at their best reduced the rate of *increase* of deterioration and poisoning and waste and destruction. We all need victories better than those.

But we shall not achieve them within either the economic or the political status quo. It used to be said that although China has been invaded innumerable times over the centuries, it has swallowed its invaders, made them Chinese. The same may be said of the attempted reforms of the recent past: they have been swallowed by a status quo of economic and political power that resists their entrance into the system and has the power to coopt, to alter, even to reverse the meaning of such reforms. The reforms have been pushed through the legislative processes of government at all levels; and they have been compromised within the framework of those same governments. How and why and when we shall try to understand in Chapter 8.

Next, the United States and the world economy, the arena whose numerous processes and relationships have always been vital and often positive in our history, but whose vitality and meaning now include seemingly menacing changes.

Reading Suggestions

A very large number of books and articles have been referred to in this long chapter. What follows can, therefore, be relatively brief, with the hope that what has gone before will be kept in mind. Matters connected with agriculture and food will be taken up again in the next chapter, where more reading suggestions will be found.

A few more suggestions for reading about our cities. Theodore Lowi, writing in the heyday of liberal policies, his focus especially on urban reforms, was able to show the deep inadequacies of those policies and related politics, in his *The End of Liberalism* (New York: Norton, 1969), a book all the more effective in that Lowi speaks as a liberal. Among Lewis Mumford's many searching studies, for present purposes his *The Highway and the City* (New York: Harcourt Brace Jovanovich, 1958) was uncomfortably prescient, and still helpful.

Included in the problems of the cities are their governments. Two studies commend themselves, the first easier reading than the second, but both worthwhile: Mike Royko, *Boss** (New York: New American Library, 1971), a knowing look at one-time (and longtime) Chicago Mayor Daley's empire, and Edward C. Hayes, *Power Structure and Urban Policy: Who Rules in Oakland** (New York: McGraw-Hill, 1972). A book of readings, broad both in focus and viewpoint, is Joe R. Feagin, ed., *The Urban Scene** (New York: Random House, 1973). Lincoln Steffens, whose quote about the St. Louis World's Fair is found above, was one of the so-called "Muckrakers" at the turn of the century. Harvey Swados, ed., in his *Years of Conscience: The Muckrakers* (New York: World, 1962) has constructed a fine anthology of their works—critical attacks on poverty, corruption, monopoly, etc.—which includes an essay by Steffens. The flight from city to suburb has been both disruptive and disturbing in its results and social implications. Richard Sennett sees that flight as having created a major sociopolitical problem for the society in his *The Uses of Disorder* (New York: Random House, 1970).

In 1981–82, a serious recession took hold, during and after which conservative and reactionary policies came to be increasingly common, not least as they affected cities (and not only in the United States). Two books that treat of the early and current consequences of those years are Ivan Szelenyi, ed., *Cities in Recession: Critical Responses to the Urban Policies of the New Right* (Beverly Hills, CA: Sage Publications, 1984), which treats of more than the United States, and Christopher Jencks and Paul E. Peterson, eds., *The Urban Underclass* (Washington, D.C.: Brookings Institution, 1991), concerned only with the United States, with a large number of tables and graphs and a broad variety of essays concerning the contemporary situation of U.S. cities.

Early in this chapter, Bradford Snell's testimony to Congress on the deliberate reduction of U.S. public transportation by private purchase was quoted. His analysis along with a program for a sensible system may be found in his *American Ground Transport: A Proposal for Restructuring the Automobile, Truck, Bus, and Rail Industries* (Washington, D.C.: USGPO, 1972).

In addition to Barry Commoner's *The Closing Circle*, noted earlier, important and useful information may be found in his *The Poverty of Power: Energy and the Economic Crisis* (New York: Knopf, 1976) and in his *The Politics of Energy** (New York: Knopf, 1979), where he shows how totally unnecessary either a food or an energy shortage is, among many other matters. Robert L. Heilbroner, in *The Human Prospect* (New York: Norton, 1974) has put forth a careful, clear, and deeply gloomy analysis of past, present, and future that one can only hope is wrong. Finally, mention of a new journal, *Capitalism, Nature, Socialism*, whose first issue was in 1988. It is a radical approach to ecology, broadly and deeply defined. The principal editor is Prof. James O'Connor, University of California, Santa Cruz. Associated with the journal is the Center for Ecological Socialism. Its CES/CNS Pamphlet 3, *Atmospheric Destruction and Human Survival*, by Kenneth Neill Cameron (1992) presents a set of realistic proposals for reversing our present fatal course. Available through: CES/CNS, P.O. Box 8467, Santa Cruz, CA 95061.

Notes

1. Pare Lorentz, from the soundtrack of the film *The River*, from *A New Anthology of Modern Poetry*, Selden Rodman, ed. Reprinted by permission of Stackpole Books.

2. Floyce Alexander, *Los Angeles*. Reprinted with permission of the author.

3. See Faulkner, op. cit., Chapter 15 ("The Era of Reform"), and also his *Quest for Social Justice* (New York: Macmillan, 1931), a social history of the progressive period. The best treatment of the conservation movement is Samuel P. Hays, *Conservation and the Gospel of Efficiency* (Cambridge: Harvard University Press, 1959). James Ridgeway, *The Politics of Ecology* (New York: Dutton, 1971), traces the development back to the English industrial revolution, through the pre–World War I years, and up to 1970.

4. So it is that people in high places, whether corporate or public, feel impelled to speak in urgent terms of urban and environmental pressures. So it is that President Bush calls attention to himself as "the education president" *and* "the environmental president," as he quietly reduces the federal funding of cities and states (which in turn must therefore cut their education budgets) and promotes oil drilling in environmentally fragile areas.

5. These indentured servants were before long outnumbered by African slaves. A useful overall history of U.S. agriculture is U.S. Department of Agriculture, *Farmers in a Changing World* (Washington: USGPO, 1940), especially the first three hundred pages or so. Like many governmental studies written in the 1930s, this book is remarkably objective, not so easy to say of governmental documents today.

6. *Absentee Ownership*, p. 135.

7. The "Second Bank" was the rough equivalent of the Federal Reserve System of today. Jackson's success in eviscerating the bank's powers led to almost a century in which the United States was alone in the industrial world in not having a central bank (of which, more in Chapter 8).

8. Grant McConnell's *The Decline of Agrarian Democracy* (Berkeley: University of California Press, 1953) has become the classic analysis of the political path so briefly traced out in the preceding paragraphs, beginning with the broad efforts of the last years of the nineteenth century and closing with the domination by the Farm Bureau—that is, the largest "farmers" by the 1940s. Woodward's books, noted earlier, detail the participation of the farmers in the growing racism of the same period, and William Appleman Williams' *Roots of the Modern American Empire*, cited earlier, traces out the role of farmers in supporting U.S. overseas imperialism.

9. See Shannon's *Farmer's Last Frontier*, cited earlier, for such economic data, and for the larger political and social history of agriculture in the post–Civil War period.

10. New lands were, of course, still being settled in the 1870s and 1880s, but the slowing down process was troublesome both quantitatively and qualitatively. In 1890 the Census Bureau literally announced "the closing of the frontier," a recognition that the prior deceleration of available land had virtually ground to a halt. Qualitatively, the problem for farmers was bound up with the fact that lands opening up in the last quarter of the century were relatively arid and more suited to large grazing than to small cultivated tracts. The Homestead Act of 1862 (whose stated intention was to encourage small-scale settlement and ownership: in effect, 160 acres of land free with five years of settlement and cultivation) had come to benefit large timber, mineral, and railroad corporations almost exclusively. As has been and will again be suggested in this book, original stated intentions, after repeated legislative amendments and revisions, often become reversed in practice: thus it has been with the progressive income tax, with social security, farm benefit programs, etc. We live in a democracy, but democracy is government by pressure, and the most effective and lasting pressures come from those with existing strengths.

11. Exports of crude foodstuffs: 1875, $79 million; 1876, $94 million; 1877, $155 million; 1880, $266 million; 1881, $242 million.

Exports of manufactured foodstuffs: 1875, $110 million; 1877, $150 million; 1880, $193 million; 1881, $226 million. Williams, *Roots of the Modern American Empire*, p. 20.

12. From 1873 on U.S. exports exceeded imports in an always stronger trend, with only slight interruption—until 1971, when the trend was just as strongly reversed. The U.S. trade and payments processes will be discussed and analyzed more fully in the next chapter.

13. There are about 5.5 billion people in the world. UNICEF has estimated that at least 500 million are permanently and dangerously hungry, and especially so, children: In the mid-1970s, it was estimated that 10 million children die every year from hunger and malnutrition-related diseases; by 1986 that figure had risen to 14 million (= 40,000 a day) (*International Herald Tribune*, December 16, 1986). The nature of this problem will be examined in some detail in the next chapter. Meanwhile, the reader is referred to the powerful study of Susan George, *How the Other Half Dies: The Real Reasons for World Hunger** (Harmondsworth, England: Penguin Books, 1976).

14. Op. cit., p. 25. "Anticolonial imperialism" as a political stance for farmers in practice meant (1) opposition to colonialism, which in turn meant (2) contesting for power in colonial areas against European nations (e.g., Spain in the Caribbean and the Pacific), and seeking (3) to gain equal access to all markets in the world on a basis of free competition. In the event, given the technological superiority of both U.S. industry and agriculture, this meant a growing *economic* empire for the United States, without the customary *political* institutions of colonialism. Thus, "anticolonial imperialism."

15. That such "visions" were largely groundless, and given their force by a vigorous nationalist-expansionist drive, is well-argued by Marilyn Blatt Young, "American Expansion, 1870–1890: The Far East," in *Towards a New Past*, cited earlier.

16. Williams, op. cit., p. 41.

17. For a description and documentation of the political and military events accompanying the war in Cuba and the Philippines, see Zinn, op. cit., Chapter 1.

18. *Absentee Ownership*, pp. 152–53. And see Sinclair Lewis, *Main Street*, for vivid portrayal of Veblen's position.

19. Op. cit., pp. 180–81. Those words were written in 1953, when the structure of political power within agriculture was, by comparison with today, relatively democratic—as, indeed, the national political

structure was, by comparison with today's.

20. The foregoing data are derived from *Historical Statistics of the United States*, and *Statistical Abstract of the United States, 1990*, both cited previously. Two examples of what this duality means in terms of farm incomes: (1) when farm income rose over 20 percent between 1972 and 1973, in connection with rapidly rising food prices, 90 percent of the increase went to just 200,000 giant farms, less than 10 percent of the then total; (2) in 1986, 29,000 large farms, a little over 1 percent of the total, gained 46 percent of all farm profits.

21. The major exception was the invention of Eli Whitney that created the techniques for producing interchangeable parts in the manufacture of muskets, prompted by the needs of the army in the War of 1812. This became a critical element in mass production technology. But of course Whitney is better known for his prior invention of the cotton gin, no exception at all to our generalization concerning agriculture and technology.

22. Although there are not many left to squeeze out of the farm population anymore, the process continues, causing people to become part of the "migrant" labor force in the East for a while, thence to settle in the northern slums—the last of the tenant farmers. The "Dust Bowl" was a product of the misuse of the arid lands west of the Mississippi, which should never have been used, as they were, for grain or cotton cultivation. See the important article by Paul W. Gates, "The Homestead Law in an Incongruous Land System," reprinted in Scheiber, *United States Economic History*, cited previously, in Chapter 10, which shows the misuse of the land and the manner in which a law presumably designed to foster widespread ownership did much to deliver the vast public domain to large corporations, who control it still. Steinbeck's *Grapes of Wrath* is an unforgettable portrait of the depression/Dust Bowl exodus of the small farmer, a tragedy that went well beyond its economic dimensions.

23. *Historical Statistics* and *Statistical Abstract*. The data just provided are organized differently in the sources for the different years; but the picture thus presented is clear in any case.

24. The inequities of farm policies within the agricultural sector are plain enough. Also inequitable is the manner in which city dwellers, that is, the main purchasers of food, are inequitably dealt with in terms of the costs (taxes) and benefits of the programs. See Edward Higbee, *Farms and Farmers in an Urban Age** (New York: Twentieth Century Fund, 1963).

25. Rachel Carson's *Silent Spring** (Boston: Houghton Mifflin, 1987; originally published 1962) awakened many in the United States to environmental deterioration in much the same way as Michael Harrington's *The Other America* (also 1962) did for poverty. Barry Commoner, an eminent biologist, was one of the first scientists to raise the alarm about environmental destruction, in his *The Closing Circle* (New York: Knopf, 1971). The "silence" of Carson's book refers to a rapidly developing absence of birds, as insects, their main food supply, are wiped out by pesticides.

26. Reported in the *New York Times*, June 20, 1972. Among the most diligent in these regards has been the University of California at Davis. Among its many accomplishments in recent years has been the chemicalization of tomatoes to provide longer "shelf life" and what may be called premature redness (suggesting ripeness, though the tomatoes are far from it), and as well tomatoes that come off the vine in the shape of cubes, so as to be more efficiently transportable—in vast quantities, of course. The problem is, they are tasteless (and also nutritionless?). So the most recent development from the scientists of UCD has been to inject still another chemical in the tomato to give it the *taste* of a tomato. Side effects have not yet been reported.

27. *Capital*, vol. I, pp. 506–07.

28. An excellent place to begin to find such understanding is the classic study of Lewis Mumford, *The City in History** (New York: Harcourt Brace Jovanovich, 1961). Mumford ranges far back in time and broadly over space, but the United States is an important part of his focus. A narrower, stimulating, and controversial analysis is Jane Jacobs, *The Economy of Cities** (New York: Random House, 1965).

29. Two marvelous, wonderfully readable histories that take one from the prehistoric to the modern period are by the late and eminent archaeologist/anthropologist/historian V. Gordon Childe, *What Happened in History** (Harmondsworth, England: Penguin, 1985; originally published 1948), and *Man Makes Himself** (New York: New American Library, 1951).

30. In the United States, the principal, perhaps only, exception to the last generalization would be Washington, D.C., which was, however, a quite minor southern city until the political economy of the United States around the turn of the century required an explicitly strong central government.

31. The latter responded to the "market" also; but museums, concert

halls, libraries, parks, private colleges and universities were more often created for nonmarket reasons: the tastes or interests of the rich; the complicated social and/or religious convictions of, for example, the steel magnate Andrew Carnegie, who financed innumerable public libraries in the United States; the strong European influences on the United States, which diluted the otherwise pure fluid of U.S. commercialism.

32. Osofsky's book, *Harlem: The Making of a Ghetto*, cited earlier, in tracing out the longstanding oppression of black people in New York, along the way provides a very useful view of the process of urban development, from Manhattan's earliest years up to the 1930s. See also Robert G. Albion, *The Rise of New York Port* (New York: Scribner's, 1939), and, for a more general history, Taylor, *Transportation Revolution*, cited earlier, whose scope goes well beyond its title.

33. If it had not been written yesterday, there is reason to believe it could be written tomorrow—except for the "liquid mud." The book is Steffens' *Shame of the Cities** (New York: McClure, 1904), p. 31. Even earlier conditions are described by Jacob Riis, *How the Other Half Lives** (New York: Hill and Wang, 1962; originally published 1890). On these and related matters, see the excellent essay by Stephen Thernstrom, "Urbanization, Migration, and Social Mobility in Late Nineteenth-Century America," in Barton Bernstein, ed., *Towards a New Past*, cited earlier.

34. For the data and the related processes, see Faulkner, *Decline of Laissez-faire*, cited earlier, especially Chapter 5.

35. Except as rare phenomena, such as the Bronx River Parkway, connecting the then richest county in the nation, Westchester, with the most populous city, New York. See Sweezy, *Cars and Cities*, cited earlier.

36. *The City in History*, p. 510. For three fictional treatments, but all close to the bone of truth, see Upton Sinclair's *Oil!*, which treats of more than its title suggests regarding Los Angeles, Nathaniel West's *The Day of the Locust*, which, written in 1940 and centered on the ways and means of Hollywood, evokes not just the "L.A. Life," but, insofar as that city has often been the leader of the U.S. sociocultural parade, was uncomfortably prescient of what the U.S. has become. The novel ends suddenly, with a race riot at a movie premiere. The fairly recent film "Chinatown" (starring Jack Nicholson and Faye Dunaway) tells the story of how, in the 1920s, gangsterism and civic corruption combined with greed to provide waterless Los Angeles with abundant supplies of cheap water, taken—in effect, stolen—from the people and the areas surround-

ing and to the north of the rapidly expanding city. As for the speed of urban automotive transportation, note this: In 1907, horsedrawn vehicles in New York City moved at an average speed of 11.5 miles per hour; nowadays, autos, taxis, and buses move about 5 miles per hour, unless the traffic is heavy.

37. Bradford Snell, "American Ground Transport," in *Hearings* before the Subcommittee on Antitrust and Monopoly, 93rd Cong., 2nd Sess. U.S. Senate (Washington, D.C.: USGPO, 1974), pp. A–2 and A–3. Just preceding that quotation, Snell argued that "GM has both the power and the economic incentive to maximize profits by suppressing rail and bus transportation. The economics are obvious: one bus can eliminate 35 automobiles; one streetcar, subway or rail transit vehicle can supplant 50 passenger cars; one train can displace 1,000 cars or a fleet of 150 cargo-laden trucks. The result was inevitable: a drive by GM to sell cars and trucks by displacing rail and bus systems." He then goes on to posit "GM's role in the destruction of more than 100 electric surface rail systems in 45 cities, including New York, Philadelphia, Baltimore, St. Louis, Oakland, Salt Lake City and Los Angeles" (p. A–2). When the San Francisco Bay Bridge opened in 1939, on one level there ran a comfortable, safe, and inexpensive electric railway. This was bought up by National City Lines (a creation of GM) in the early 1950s; by the mid-1950s, no trains, just (GM) buses and cars, and the bridge became a constant home for massive traffic jams. The BART system, opened in the 1970s at the cost of many billions, tunneled under the bay to serve the purposes of the destroyed train system. And always more autos go inching always more slowly over the bridge. The proverbial Man from Mars, had he watched all this from afar, might have wondered how such a dumb species had managed to survive so long.

38. Westchester County of New York State, still one of the richest counties in the United States, also has the highest percentage of welfare poor per capita in the nation.

39. For a fine discussion of the crisis of New York in the 1970s, and how it has worsened and deepened since then, see the essays by Jason Epstein, "The Last Days of New York," and "The Tragical History of New York," in *New York Review of Books*, February 19, 1976, and April 9, 1992 respectively. For a thorough study of the "construction complex" and associated matters, see Robert A. Caro, *The Power Broker: Robert Moses and the Fall of New York** (New York: Random House, 1975). A government analysis that counters the banalities of the White House

and shows the larger spread of the problem is *New York City's Financial Crisis*,* "A Study Prepared for the Use of the Joint Economic Committee," 94th Cong., lst Sess. (USGPO, 1975).

40. The role of the contemporary State regarding these matters will be the focus of Chapter 8. Here it is appropriate to note just three real, as distinct from election-inspired, "points of light" that suggest much beyond themselves: "For a long time," said Dr. David W. Baker, "we have assumed in this country that if someone really needs health care they can get it, at least in the emergency departments. These studies show that is just not true." The studies, in which Baker participated, were done at over 280 hospitals in the U.S.A. They showed that "overcrowding of emergency rooms has become so severe that substantial numbers of seriously ill people are simply giving up and leaving before they are seen by a doctor...." *New York Times*, August 27, 1991. But we are at least slowing down drugs and crime with our always growing federal spending against them? "Questioning the Bush administration's strategy in the war on drugs, the chief investigative agency of Congress said that anti-smuggling efforts costing billions of dollars had failed to reduce the flow of cocaine into the United States." *International Herald Tribune*, September 28, 1991. $2.2 billion was allocated for this effort in 1989. CBS news reported on October 25, 1991 that the Columbian "drug kings" are now having poppies (for heroin) grown in addition to coca in the same areas. So perhaps we haven't been jailing enough criminals? "The prison population has more than doubled, from 329,821 in 1980, to 703,687 at the close of 1989...[and is expected to be] over 1.1 million inmates by 1994." James Austin, *NCCD* Focus, December 1990, p. 1. NCCD is The National Council on Crime and Delinquency.

41. Children are the most rapidly rising group of those officially classified as poor, and they are increasingly the children of families headed by a single female (irrespective of color); and the wages of a young male high school graduate, which have been falling since 1971, were, in 1987, just 18 percent less than that for the equivalent worker in 1979. See Mishel and Frankel, op. cit., pp. 175–76 for children in poverty, and pp. 217–19 for incomes of young males (25–37 years old).

42. Chester Hartman and Gregg Carr, "Housing Authorities Reconsidered," *Journal of the American Institute of Planners* (January 1969). Quoted in David Gordon, *Problems in Political Economy: An Urban Perspective** (Lexington, MA: D.C. Heath and Company, 1971), p. 361. Gordon's book contains many valuable readings, ranging through urban

employment, education, poverty, crime, health, housing, transportation, and environmental problems, written from a variety of perspectives, most of them critical. Though some of the essays were written as descriptive of the conditions of the 1960s, most of them retain validity to the present—or even more so, because their analyses have held up through many changes. For an equally critical but conservative viewpoint, see Martin Anderson, *The Federal Bulldozer** (Cambridge: M.I.T. Press, 1964).

43. The quality of social life in recent decades has varied greatly between, say, Sweden and Greece, or the United States and Germany, as regards the cost and availability of human services; but all have "protected" agriculture in ways that in the long run have been damaging both to most producers and most consumers; and the same has been true of industry, as regards waste in production, environmental damage, etc. Sweden, for example, now among the most enlightened socially, has high military expenditures and is among the most dependent upon nuclear plants for its energy. And, quite apart from the dangers of the plants themselves, neither the Swedes nor anyone else has found a way to dispose of nuclear wastes. Nor are the noncapitalist countries much different in results, however different the causes may be. For various reasons, they have suffered from both productive *and* social inefficiency, and their environmental damage has been, if anything, worse than that of the great damages done by the capitalist countries. It must be noted that the noncapitalist countries and, as well, the nonindustrial countries, quite irrespective of their substantial institutional, ideological, and other differences, have sought and/or been forced to pursue the same paths of economic growth as the capitalist powers of the world. This matter will be discussed further in the next two chapters.

44. *The Instinct of Workmanship*, p. 25. Except that now it is not only the "peoples of Christendom" but almost all of who and what live on the planet. The imbecile institutions won out in 1914, shortly after Veblen wrote, and at least 10 million died in that war and at least another 60 million in the next one, and who knows how many others between those two wars and since—to say nothing of the other terrors and misery that have accompanied the convulsions and chaos of this century.

45. Suppose, for example, that we had a sensible transportation system, depending much less on the private automobile and much more on various forms of public transportation. As will be suggested shortly, the reduction of environmental damage simply from the production and

use of fewer automobiles—and less petroleum, etc.—would alone significantly reduce the rate of increase of environmental damage, while also releasing resources for more desirable purposes.

46. R.H. Tawney, *Religion and the Rise of Capitalism*, cited earlier, p. 76. Writing after World War I, in which he was a soldier, Tawney, like so many at the time, was in a state of mind combining outrage with shock—and for good reason, considering the optimism about the human condition that had preceded the war. The kind of slaughter that horrified so many in, say, the Vietnam and the Gulf wars (appearing first in the U.S. Civil War, the first industrial war), was the norm for the four years of World War I. A most evocative study of the processes both of the war and the shock is Paul Fussell, *The Great War and Modern Memory* (London: Oxford University Press, 1975). Fictionally, the U.S. poet E.E. Cummings conveyed the nature of that war in his *The Enormous Room*, as, for Germany, did Erich Maria Remarque, in his influential *All Quiet on the Western Front*. In this section I am covering much the same ground in much the same ways as in Chapter 4 of my *Waste of Nations*, cited earlier, and will again later.

47. *The Theory of Business Enterprise*, pp. 245–258. When Veblen refers to how "extraordinary this public waste...has latterly been," he has in mind the first steps of the United States (in the Caribbean and the Pacific) into the overseas imperialist contests then beginning to heat up to what became World War I.

48. It may be useful here to comment on these processes in noncapitalist societies, such as the Soviet Union, China, and Cuba. Military expenditures are also substantial in *all* such countries, and inefficiency and waste are also widespread. There are at least two points to be made about such facts: (1) Much of the military expenditures—not all—are a consequence of long years of "containment" and may reasonably be seen as defensive. (Washington has made no secret of the fact that one of its aims was to weaken the Soviet economy by an intense arms race.) In any case, such expenditures are *never* for the purpose of using up excess productive capacity or maintaining industrial profitability; and (2) apart from the ways in which these countries copy the capitalist countries in wasteful products, such as auto design, their waste is due to weaknesses in their system, rather than a way to absorb "unprofitable" strength. Be that as it may; there is nothing for us to do with respect to countries outside our framework. This book is written for those inside.

49. The understatement is added to when we consider that unques-

tionably the decade of the 1980s took us to even higher levels of waste. Other reasons for seeing this as understatement include the fact that their estimate took no account of restricted production in industry or agriculture (such as unutilized acreage and equipment and labor) or the waste in what is produced (e.g., in deliberate obsolescence) or destroyed deliberately (as with coffee) or by rotting (as with stored grains and dairy products)—all told, a large amount of added waste. The data are taken from Edwards, et al., *The Capitalist System*, p. 331, which is quoting the important book by Samuel Bowles, David M. Gordon, and Thomas E. Weisskopf, *Beyond the Waste Land: A Democratic Alternative to Economic Decline* (New York: Anchor Doubleday, 1983). This is part of Chapter 9, "Waste and Irrationality," of the Edwards book, already referred to several times in earlier pages.

50. Federal Trade Commission, *Report on the Automotive Industry* (Washington, D.C.: USGPO, 1940).

51. We have already examined agricultural waste above, and will again in Chapter 7. Pioneer analytical work regarding the socially wasteful processes of capitalism was put forth in K. William Kapp, *The Social Costs of Private Enterprise* (Cambridge: Harvard University Press, 1950). See also Commoner, *The Closing Circle*, cited above, and, for a more general and theoretical approach, see Edward N. Wolff, *Growth, Accumulation, and Unproductive Activity* (Cambridge, England: Cambridge University Press, 1987).

52. Paul A. Baran, *The Longer View* (New York: Monthly Review Press, 1969), p. 101. This is a collection of Baran's essays. The quote is from an essay published in October 1959 in *Monthly Review*, "Marxism and Psychoanalysis."

53. It has been conservatively estimated that "approximately 50 million people still live in the deteriorated and socially dysfunctional areas called slums." See "Slums and Poverty," by Gary Knox, Chapter 9 of a very useful collection, *Social Costs in Modern Society*, edited by John E. Ullmann (Westport, Conn.: Quorum Books, 1983). Therein reference is made to S. Walter and P. Choate, *America in Ruins* (Washington, D.C.: Council of State Planning Agencies, 1981), and its estimate that the total bill for infrastructural renewal would come to $3 trillion (Ullman, p. 277). And then came Reagan and Bush, and then Bush and (gulp!) Quayle.

54. Edwards, et al., *Capitalist System*, p. 330. GNP in the United States is about $6 trillion. Two percent of that would be about $120

billion, and of course advertising has increased noticeably since 1980. The unemployment compensation President Bush vetoed in 1991 would have cost about $20 billion, and helped over 8 million desperate people. The reader is referred again to Stuart Ewen's *Advertising and the Social Roots of the Consumer Culture,* cited earlier. Given the central importance of TV in shaping our minds for both business and political purposes, it is worth studying that part of the advertising world in itself. Two excellent books are Jerry Mander, *Four Arguments for the Elimination of Television* (New York: Morrow, 1978), and Rose Goldsen, *The Show and Tell Machine* (New York: Dial Press, 1977). For the larger role of the media, see Robert Cirino, *Don't Blame the People* (New York: Random House, 1971) and James Aronson, *The Press and the Cold War* (Indianapolis: Bobbs-Merrill, 1970).

55. It would be interesting to know what percentage of those who do the advertising for cigarettes, for example, are themselves convinced that it is substantially dangerous, and who have themselves ceased to smoke for that reason. But we do know something else just as interesting, if also more distressing. In 1991 a private poll taken of about 100 (anonymous) scientists who work for the American Tobacco Institute—which puts forth an almost continuous flow of statements denying any dangers whatsoever connected with smoking—showed that a good two-thirds of those scientists believe in the dangers as real.

56. And Detroit discovered it didn't make business sense either, when the Japanese (especially) began to take sales away from the Big Three in the U.S. market, as the U.S. public slowly but surely discovered they could get a cheaper, well-designed, *and* more durable car from foreign car makers. By the time Detroit awakened—and they have yet to awaken fully—the share of imports had risen beyond the alarming point, and, market analysts believe, permanently. The Japanese alone now have over 31 percent of the U.S. market, and a goodly portion of people under forty have never driven a GM, Ford, or Chrysler car and probably never will.

57. The costs of unemployment must be measured in several ways: the loss of goods and services not produced, the loss of purchasing power that would stimulate the economy, and, not least, the anxiety and demoralization of those who need and want work. Estimates of the narrowest of these dimensions, lost purchasing power, are made by John Innes, in Chapter 7 of Ullman, *Social Costs.* Calculating conservatively for 1976, when the official jobless rate was 7.7 percent, Innes placed the loss between $54 and $70 billion (pp. 114–18). Today's figure would be

at least double that of 1976 for the economy and official unemployment.

58. For a profound analysis of just what and just how much the industrial worker has lost as this century has unfolded, see Braverman, *Labor and Monopoly Capital*, cited earlier. As for social and political consequences of demoralization, one might hope or even expect that angry or frustrated workers would seek to change the society toward something more meaningful, and under their control. Marx thought so; Veblen expected that the frustration would be taken out in conspicuous consumption, patriotism, and the like.

59. Studs Terkel, in his *Hard Times*, noted earlier, interviewed hundreds of people on their experiences during the 1930s depression, and the almost universal attitude was "Never again." Which helps to explain why so many have been so easy to fool.

60. More importantly, military expenditures should be viewed in terms of what economists call "opportunity costs"—that is, what *could* have been produced with the same set of resources, etc., had they *not* been used for the military, as well as the higher number of jobs from nonmilitary production, for the same government expenditure. John E. Ullman shows that the cost of two B-1 bombers (obsolete before they became operational, but still being built) would take care of rebuilding Cleveland's water supply system; that the Navy's F-18 fighter program costs the same (in 1983 dollars) as the amount it would take to modernize the U.S. machine-tool stock to bring it to the average level of Japan's; and that every $1 billion spent on the B-1 and creating 58,000 jobs would have meant 83,000 jobs in mass transit construction, 118,000 jobs in education, and so on. See *Social Costs*, Chapter 15, for these and other related data. It may surprise some to learn that it was President Eisenhower who said, in 1953: "Every gun that is made, every warship launched, every rocket fired signifies in the final sense a theft from those who hunger and are not fed, those who are cold and not clothed. This world in arms is not spending money alone. It is spending the sweat of its laborers, the genius of its scientists, the hopes of its children" (ibid., p. 227). Eisenhower, and/or his speech writer, knew what opportunity costs are.

61. "Of thirteen major aircraft and missile programs since 1955 which cost $40 billion, only four (costing $5 billion) performed at as much as 75 percent of the design specifications. Yet the companies with the poorest performance records reported the highest profits." Michael Reich, in Edwards, et al., *The Capitalist System*, p. 335.

62. Ibid., pp. 334–35.

63. Ibid.

64. The quoted words are from Edwards, et al., op. cit., p. 350. It is also important to note that even when, as is almost always true, the costs of precautions and alternatives are passed on to the consumer (and even profitably so, as in the case of auto seatbelts, a matter not of the environment but of safety), companies almost always resist to the end: the reason being that they want *no* decision-making but their own, about anything, anytime. They agree with Friedman about their duty; better, he agrees with them. Friedman calls these kinds of problems "spillover effects." Our cup runneth over.

65. For the nonindustrial countries both quantitative and qualitative change are needed even more drastically than in countries such as ours. But what can happen in those countries, as matters now stand, is very much connected with what happens in the richer countries, and how the latter move with respect to changes in the poorer countries. This question is part of the focus of the next chapter.

66. "Towards an Ecological Solution," *Ramparts*, May 1970, reprinted in part in Edwards, et al., *Capitalist System*, p. 388–92.

67. *Beyond Repair: The Ecology of Capitalism*, cited earlier, p. 98.

68. Larry Sawers, "Urban Form and Mode of Production," *RRPE*, vol. 7, no. 1 (Spring 1975). Sawers concerns himself mostly with the formation of U.S. cities in this valuable essay.

69. See Michael Tanzer, *The Energy Crisis: World Struggle for Power and Wealth* (New York: Monthly Review Press, 1974). For a conservative economist whose specialty is the oil market, and who denies the existence of a real or a probable oil shortage, see M.A. Adelman, *The World Petroleum Market* (Baltimore: Johns Hopkins Press, 1975). While others were having difficulties during the Gulf war of 1990–91, the oil companies were seeing their profits rise by 100 percent and much more.

70. James Ridgeway, *The Last Play: The Struggle to Monopolize the World's Energy Resources* (New York: Dutton, 1973), p. 3.

71. An excellent discussion of matters concerning transportation, energy, petrochemicals, and related economic and political processes is Michael H. Best and William E. Connolly, *The Politicized Economy* (Lexington, MA: D.C. Heath, 1976). It is easy to see that if imported oil rises to over $15, it becomes profitable to pump oil from the ground in the United States—one of several reasons why the large oil companies have welcomed the OPEC moves of the past twenty years or so.

– 7 –

World Economy and Imperialism

While this America settles in the mould of its vulgarity,
heavily thickening to empire,
And protest, only a bubble in the molten mass, pops and
sighs out, and the mass hardens,

I sadly remember that the flower fades to make fruit,
the fruit rots to make earth.
Out of the mother; and through the spring exultances,
ripeness and decadence; and home to the mother.[1]

For the capitalist developmental process to have begun, to flourish, and to persist, there has always been and must always be vibrant interaction within and between the national and world economies. And the process has always been something like a circus tightrope act: when strong, the capitalist system has moved through time dynamically, from crisis to crisis, balance achieved and lost and regained, always at higher levels of technology, organization, production, and real incomes.

To prosper, even to survive, it has been emphasized that this system must satisfy its strongest imperative: it must expand through capital accumulation ("vertically") within each *national* economy, and it must expand through trade and investment ("horizontally") in a buoyant *world* economy. The need for these interconnected processes of expansion is primary to the *system*; the needs of each country's people must be, have been, and remain subordinated to the needs of capital—for better and for worse.

The capital accumulation and the exports of each nation have in common that (1) the production of neither is purchased by consumers *within* the national economy, but (2) both are required to maintain levels of profitability in each capitalist economy. Either accumulation or exports can lead to higher levels of consumption and have, of course, done so, but that is neither their purpose nor their functional consequence.

An important difference between capital accumulation and exports is that the former leads directly to increased productive capacity in new or old products and often to improved productivity, and therefore to the need to find new outlets for consumption, *and/or* exports, *and/or* further investment, *and/or*, as has been vital since World War II, to higher levels of government spending in order to cheapen and to support the accumulation process.[2] Exports, in contrast, constitute a use of existing productive capacity having no necessary connection with any further national economic developments, except insofar as the economy becomes habitually structured to supply an export market. If this export market declines, serious national economic problems arise. This is not an insubstantial exception, considering the harsh realities of shrinking industries such as autos and steel.

It is also important to note that just as investment is directed by and for the class of owners and controllers of capital, exports/imports are either for use in production—raw materials, machinery, etc.—or mostly for the consumption of the higher-income population in the importing nation. Thus, both capital accumulation and exports/imports, both investment and world trade, are accomplished by and for a small fraction of the world's people.[3]

The world economy therefore represents a kind of safety valve for what would otherwise be each nation's excess productive capacity; but the world economy is much more than that. Without it the contemporary national economies and their potential excess capacities quite simply would not exist. From its earliest beginnings, capitalism as a system has depended upon the existence of a growing and always more integrated global economy. The interchanges of capital and consumer goods, raw materials and foodstuffs, technology and services, and finance and labor in the global economy have served as the principal source of the dynamic and constructive imbalance that characterizes capitalism as a social, economic, and political system. And when the world economy has faltered and weakened, all the capitalist world, individually and collectively, has been in jeopardy.

The foregoing has emphasized the importance of the *processes* of capital accumulation and world trade. Those processes take place within sets of *structures*, national and international. The structures of the world economy are unsurprisingly very similar to those of the national capitalist societies that participate in it: they are characterized by functionally vital inequalities of income, wealth, and power.

We have seen that capitalist society is normally democratic in many of its political institutions, but simultaneously lives within a framework of oligarchic rule, the latter a consequence of the great inequality of wealth and income, and therefore of power. This pattern is essentially repeated, in somewhat different form, in the world economy. There we may see a three-tiered structure of power: Tier I is occupied by the unchallengeable economic and military power of the "hegemonic" nation of the world; Tier II's members are the other industrial or industrializing powers; and Tier III is made up of the nonindustrial, colonial, neocolonial, dependent—in short, imperialized—countries.[4]

There has been trade among peoples since prehistoric times. But there have only been two functioning *world economies*, as those words are used here: that which took hold in the mid-nineteenth century, its Tier I "hegemon" being Great Britain, and that which emerged after World War II, with the United States as the unchallengeable power.

The industrial and financial strengths of the dominant nation's economy nourish the growing strength of the world economy and, at least for a while, add to that nation's own power, in every way. But the dominant nation does more than extend its economic strength: it creates the basic structures and shapes the main processes of the world economy. Most important of all, it disciplines the always-volatile competitive and nationalistic tendencies of the member economies, whether those countries are relatively powerful or weak. The chaotic interregnum of 1914–45 resulted from the breakdown of the world system of Britain, and the complicated inability of what became the U.S.-dominated system to emerge.

Within this three-tiered structure, the prime beneficiary is the lone occupant of Tier I. The Tier II countries benefit substantially in economic terms, but those enlarging benefits are paid for by a certain loss of sovereignty. The Tier III societies, apart from appearances and a very small percentage of their people, gain nothing and lose almost everything—economically, politically, socially, and culturally—from their normally coerced membership in the world economy. The hegemonic power rules with "carrots and sticks": mostly carrots for Tier II and mostly sticks for Tier III countries.

That mainstream social scientists and politicians do not see the foregoing structures and outcomes in this way, and least of all the disastrous outcomes for Tier III peoples; instead they speak of "partners in progress," or "fostering the development of the less-developed," should occasion no surprise. But such views are necessarily misleading, if only to their audiences in Tiers I and II. As will be emphasized in later pages, both the positive and the negative roles played by all three tiers have been essential to what is normally seen as the healthful functioning of the world economy. If, as seems likely, the United States economy continues to weaken in its position of relative unchallengeability, the question then arises as to what the "next structure" could or would look like. That will be speculated on at the conclusion of this chapter.

The structure just described is that of a world economy that is at the same time an imperialized world. The members of the top two tiers were or are all, in one degree or another, imperialist nations: Britain most of all, in its heyday before World War I, but also the others: Belgium, France, Germany, Italy, Japan, the Netherlands, Russia, and the United States.[5] Since World War II, we shall see that the United States has presided over an empire even grander than that of Britain's, and that the Tier II countries have been all those noted above (but also including Great Britain and, since 1917, excluding Russia), plus a few newcomers.

Until recently, most of the people of the United States would have found it hard to believe that this country's well-being is now, let alone always has been, vitally dependent upon its participation in the world economy; and still today, almost all would repudiate the notion that the United States is or has been an imperialist nation, let alone the most successful imperialist nation of all. Our history in both these respects will be examined in detail after the origins and functioning of the capitalist world economy have been analyzed; but here it probably is helpful to speak briefly to those misgivings.[6]

By comparison with other nations we have been, of course, *relatively* self-sufficient—not surprising, given our uniquely abundant quantity and quality of natural resources. Much closer to the normal pattern for modern industrial societies, Great Britain has had to import half of its food and close to four-fifths of its raw materials for at least a century. Before World War II, U.S. foreign trade seldom approached even 5 percent of our GNP (except the unusual moment of World War I), and it hovered around 5 percent up through the 1950s. Since the 1960s that has changed notably, until by the mid-1980s our exports were about 9 percent and our imports close to 12 percent of our GNP.

In this as in other social relationships, however, quantitative measures taken alone are misleading. From the very beginning, our economic development has been critically dependent upon our foreign economic relationships. In the past century that dependence has steadily increased, and especially in recent decades—until now the U.S. economy is dependent not just for its health (and many of its troubles) but for its very functioning on its exports of goods and services, its resource imports, its foreign investments, and, since the 1980s, on its heavy borrowing from abroad.[7] The dependence, and both the benefits and the problems arising from it, grew along with the expansion of the U.S. empire.

Nobody would dispute that we were dependent on external economic relationships in our colonial period; all colonies are. But when we achieved our independence it was the terms not the importance of those relationships that changed. U.S. foreign economic relationships and policies have been in a state of constant flux from the colonial period to the present; both ends and means have changed—a necessity for a nation whose economic structure is changing rapidly, in a rapidly changing world. But the one constant in that history has been the dependence of this country's well-being on its ties with the rest of the world.

Those who have thought otherwise have been transfixed by the natural wealth and great size of the United States—the first "continental-sized" modern economy in the world—which has set it apart from all other nations. What has made us *like* other capitalist nations is that we have been a *capitalist* society, and like those others, almost all our history has been written and seen as *national* history, abetted by patriotic sentiments, education and entertainment, and the sheer availability of such historical materials. And most history, others' and our own, has been as superficial concerning capitalism as a system as it has been concerning the global setting within which national capitalist economies have functioned.

As for imperialism, the people of the United States quite generally see us as the leading "free world" power, and take pride in our status as Number One. But very few people in the United States see it as being imperialist *at all*, let alone as the world's leading imperialist nation. Yet we are that nation, and have become so in the very processes that made it possible and necessary for the United States to organize the integrated world economy of the last few decades—in the absence of which, it is fair to say, the history of those decades (and, of course, of capitalism itself) would have been vastly different—if unknowably so.

One reason our people so quickly deny the imperial status of the United States is the almost universal lack of understanding of what imperialism is and does. Preceding chapters have sought to shed light on the meaning of capitalism; now we must explore the development and the nature of imperialism.

Like capitalism, imperialism is a historical process. To attempt a one-line definition of it is to promote more confusion than enlightenment. Our attempt to clarify the concept and the reality will move analytically and historically within the framework of several related questions: *When* and *why* does a society expand its influence and control over other areas? *Where* is it able and likely to do so? *What* does the relationship mean to the imperialist and to the imperialized societies? *How* are the relationships developed and maintained, and *how* and *why* do they change in nature and in meaning over time? *Who* benefits and who pays, at either end of the relationship? In seeking to answer these questions, we shall first set forth a very general statement, and then explore the specific historical developments preceding and accompanying the emergence of the United States as the great power it became.[8]

Imperialism: Becoming and Being

The seeds of both capitalism and nationalism are to be found in the medieval trading cities, such as Florence, Milan, and Venice, London, Bruges, and Cologne. So are the seeds of mercantilism and *modern* imperialism, sometimes called "the new mercantilism."

"Buy cheap and sell dear" was the slogan emblazoned on the medieval merchant's escutcheon. The implementation of that policy abroad had two sides to it: *protection* and *privilege*. Internally for the towns it required a third policy, what the great historian of mercantilism Eli Heckscher called *provisioning*.[9] "Mercantilism," he adds, "is medieval town policy writ large." In an important sense, that is so; it is also useful to say that modern imperialism is "mercantilism writ large." But there are many important differences between town economy, mercantilism, and imperialism —and of the varying meanings of protection, privilege, and provisioning for each—differences given by the development of capitalism and its accompanying industrialism. The similarities and the differences both deserve comment.

The medieval trading town functioned very much as a unit in facing the external world. Surrounding it was the countryside, the source of its foodstuffs and sometimes of its fibers and ores, used in medieval industry and trade. The provisioning policy of the towns had as its aim the guarantee of a steady and cheap supply of what the towns needed to consume and produce, an aim that placed the ruling merchant class in conflict with the surrounding feudal nobility, and that ultimately brought the merchant into alliance with the rising monarchs who were increasingly at odds with the feudal nobility. When merchant-king alliances were effective, the modern nation-state was the result.

The merchants sought a united front in their dealings with other medieval traders in far-flung towns: Italians, Germans, and Flemings dealing with England, for example. The Italians and Flemings in the twelfth, thirteenth, and fourteenth centuries were most powerful, and could function effectively in a pattern resembling "free trade." In the fourteenth century, the individually weaker North German towns banded together in the Hanseatic League, a grouping of about seventy towns acting as a powerful unit in their trading activities over the face of Northern Europe and England.

In their own towns the merchants sought price and wage policies providing stability and a supply of exportable products at costs that would allow profits. The famous "just wage and just price" policies of the medieval towns were "just" up to the point only where the ruling merchants could flourish in their interregional activities. Much that was "bought cheap" was a result of exploitative relationships outside and within the towns; and what was "sold dear" was a function of the strength of the merchants elsewhere, and that strength was enhanced whenever and wherever possible by trading privileges and by both economic and military protection. By the fourteenth and fifteenth centuries, the degree to which the necessary protection and privileges were forthcoming was becoming a matter of national or quasi-national power at both ends of the relationship.

As the early modern period began and nation-states began to replace trading cities as the focus of commerce and industry, the aims of foreign policy remained much the same, although means could and had to change: the scope of affairs had enlarged, and so had the power of the contestants. Provisioning policy now meant the assurance of domestic and external sources of food and raw materials; in turn this led to a colonial policy whose aim was to control the trade and resources flowing from the colonies, and to prevent rival states from having access to those same areas. There were great gains to be made from success and great losses to be suffered from the success of others—losses measured in profits, and in national economic and military strength. The medieval town policy of "buy cheap and sell dear" became a national policy, the slogan in the process changing to "beggar thy neighbor." One nation's strength was seen as inversely related to the strength of the others: at the very moment that access to an ever-expanding world of economic possibilities and virtually limitless resources was unfolding as never before, the universal social outlook assumed the world was like a pie—fixed in size, your slice making my slice smaller. And the wars over the slices became always larger, always more numerous.

This was all preindustrial, in the fetal period of capitalism from the sixteenth into the eighteenth century termed "primitive accumulation" by Marx. As the eighteenth became the nineteenth century, means changed. Both needs and possibilities were stronger, and the developing changes were reflected in a new meaning for provisioning, protection, and privilege. Summed up, the new meanings created modern imperialism. At this point it is necessary to draw some distinctions between mercantilism and imperialism.

Capitalism in the mercantilist period was commercial rather than industrial in its dynamic. Colonial policies tended to have seaports and coastlines as their geographic locus. The great gains in trade were typically made from high-value/low bulk commodities: pepper and tea, sugar and slaves, gold and silver. This might be expected in an era of long, slow, and dangerous voyages. As modern industry developed, the patterns changed. Steamships and railroads tied continents together, allowing and requiring hinterlands to be penetrated. Bulkier, lower-value commodities were needed to supply growing industry and industrial populations with raw materials and foodstuffs. The relatively short-term commercial investments of the earlier period were added to by necessary long-term investments—in expanded harbor facilities, in railroads, in mines, and in plantations. The political impact of *mercantilist* colonial policy was typically manifested in effective relationships with *local*, often tribal, rulers and the regulation of privileged and protected trade between colony and metropolis. The new *imperialism* required,

as the colonial system of earlier centuries did not, a large measure of political control over the *internal* relations and structure of the colonial economy. This is required, not merely to "protect property" and to ensure that the profit of the investment is not offset by political risks, but actually to create the essential conditions for the profitable investment of capital. Among these conditions is the existence of a proletariat sufficient to provide a plentiful and cheap labour-supply; and where this does not exist, suitable modifications of pre-existent social forms will need to be enforced (of which the reduction of tribal land-reserves and the introduction of differential taxation on natives living in the tribal reserve in East and South Africa are examples).

Thus the "political logic of imperialism" is

> to graduate from "economic penetration" to "spheres of influence," from "spheres of influence" to protectorates or indirect control, and from protectorates *via* military occupation to annexation.[10]

There has been much discussion of which comes first, political/military or economic expansion: Does trade follow the flag, or does the flag follow trade? Both have happened, and they have also walked hand in hand from the beginning. The gains and rivalries associated with mercantilism and imperialism were handmaidens of colonial and imperial *strategies*—for instance, control of seaports and coaling stations, the development of naval stations for refueling and battle readiness—if for no other reasons than to keep them from rivals. There was a graceful interaction: strategic considerations facilitated economic advance; economic advance required strategic considerations. Chickens and eggs.

The late nineteenth century wave of imperialism swept the globe; the sun never set on the British flag; next door, in some contiguous colony, European flags also waved in the sun. Imperialism became direct, and control became direct. Colonial governments were *colonial*, and their "legal" masters were in the metropoli. Thus did the nineteenth century end and the twentieth begin.

After World War I, the colonial seams began to give; after World War II they tore apart. Earlier, mercantilism had given way to imperialism; after World War II, imperialism gave way to *neocolonialism*, sometimes called "welfare imperialism." The strain on traditional imperial ties—those of England and France, of Holland and Italy, Germany and Japan—had first appeared after World War I, in conjunction with the strains developing *within* these major capitalist powers. The depression of the 1930s transformed strains into various forms of deep struggle; and World War II gave the *coup de grace* to traditional imperialism. The older imperialist powers lacked the financial and military resources necessary to hold on to their territories, whether they knew it or not. Britain, bled dry by three decades of depression and wars, knew it better than some others; it loosed its hold on India and most of its other colonies without a fight. France was less prudent. It spent much of its wealth and let the blood of the French and the peoples of North Africa and Indochina flow for years before it let go, almost splitting apart as a nation in the process.

The United States stood waiting, and prodded the process along. As the only major power strengthened by World War II, the United States was able and eager to move into the "vacua" created by European and Japanese collapse. Our always more aggressive involvement was heralded as preserving freedom and promoting economic development. With these slogans on our banner, we strode forth to create the largest, the most profitable, and the most costly imperialist network in world history, as befitted the most powerful nation in world history. Our style was not to control ports or nations directly, as in days of yore; we sought to control only the finances, the economies, the military, and "the hearts and minds" of our neocolonial empire—ways we had begun to learn in our prep school days early in this century.

U.S. expansion overseas after World War II was not confined to previously colonial areas. Our hegemony was global: inroads into Europe, Canada, Central and South America, the Caribbean, the Middle East, South and Southeast Asia and Japan, and steel rings around the USSR and China. But our impact on the world was substantially diverse, depending upon whether the affected area was developed industrially or not when we took a strong hand. In Western Europe, Canada, and Japan, our strength helped to rescue and to speed up what had already been advanced economies; in the nonindustrial part of the capitalist world, our impact continued that of the earlier pattern: we deepened its *underdevelopment.*[11]

As has been briefly noted earlier and will be discussed again later, this new order of neocolonialism has become quite turbulent and undergone numerous changes since the 1960s, in consequence both of internal resistance and the growing power of multinational/transnational corporations. It is by no means clear what these changes mean for the present, and of course the future is even more murky—not only for the largest part of the world's peoples whose societies have been "neocolonialized," but, given the critical role played by Tier III in the functioning of Tiers I and II, for all of us as well.

Up to here, we have put forth a string of very broad generalizations intended only to begin answers to our questions regarding the when, why, what, etc., of imperialism. The when and the why move in terms of needs and possibilities; the where in terms of what is useful and necessary and possible, the what points to profit and power and enhanced development for the strong, exploitation and underdevelopment for the vulnerable. But all these arguments require further support and elaboration if they are not to stand as mere assertions. We commence that process with another and central question: does capitalism *require* imperialism? And a somewhat different question: where there has been imperialism, has there always been capitalism?

Capitalism and Imperialism

Empires litter the pages of history—Persian, Phoenician, Greek, Roman, Carthaginian, Byzantine, Holy Roman, to mention only a few. Although commercialism was an important part of the lives of some of these societies, only by totally misusing the term could we classify any of them as capitalist. And, on the other hand, the modern Swiss are surely capitalist, but, internationalist though they and their innumerable connections are, it would distort the term to see them as imperialist. Still, as a world economic system capitalism has *always* been imperialist; or such, at least, is our argument. How and why is this so?

The most persuasive argument stating that capitalism does *not* require imperialism—indeed, that capitalism and imperialism are *opposed* in their general features—was that put forth by Schumpeter, among the most learned of economists. His definition of imperialism, one of those troublesome one-liners, helps to obscure the problem from the beginning. "Imperialism," he says, "is the objectless disposition on the part of a state to unlimited forcible expansion." By "objectless" Schumpeter means expansion for its own sake, and he observes that "objectless tendencies toward forcible expansion, without definite utilitarian limits—that is, non-rational and irrational, purely instinctual inclinations toward war and conquest—play a very large role in the history of mankind."[12] Probably that happened in the past, and doubtless such inclinations persist in the present. What is at issue, however, is whether and when such inclinations become "object*ful*" and useful, indeed necessary, for the maintenance of a social system such as capitalism, quite apart from whatever role expansionism might have played when and where *not* necessary. On this, O'Connor is pertinent. "In connection with economic expansionism," he says,

> pre-capitalist and capitalist societies differ in five general ways: First, in pre-capitalist societies economic expansion was irregular, unsystematic, not integral to normal economic activity. In capitalist societies, foreign trade and investment are rightly considered to be the "engines of growth." ...Second, in pre-capitalist societies the economic gains from expansion were windfall gains, frequently taking the form of sporadic plunder. In capitalist societies, profits from overseas trade and investment are an integral part of national income, and considered in a matter-of-fact manner. Third, in pre-capitalist societies plunder...was often consumed in the field by the conquering armies...In capitalist societies, exploited territories are fragmented and integrated into the structure of the metropolitan economy...Fourth, in pre-capitalist societies debates within the ruling class ordinarily revolved around the question whether or not to expand. In capitalist societies, ruling-class debates normally turn on the issue of what is the best way to expand. Last, in relation to colonialism...land seizure, colonist settlement, or both was the only mode of control which the metropolitan power could effectively exercise over the satellite region...; capitalist societies have developed alternative, indirect, and more complex forms of control.[13]

A basic reason for the inability or refusal of Schumpeter and other mainstream social analysts to see the connection between capitalism and imperialism is their inability or refusal to see the role played by expansion and exploitation in capitalist development; or, perhaps to put it more accurately, their belief that the necessary expansion will take place under benign circumstances. For Schumpeter, expansion abroad is necessary, but it takes place through the "rational" mode of free trade; expansion at home takes place through the turbulent but effective impact of technological development on the growth and the institutions of capitalism. But capitalism's entire history has been characterized by obstacles placed in the way of free trade, apart from the exceptional (almost solely for Britain) decades of the late nineteenth century, which were decades also of raging imperialist expansion. Technological development, far from breaking down monopolies through Schumpeter's hoped-for "gales of creative destruction," facilitated their entrenchment in each particular industry after the "gale" had passed.

Growth and development within a country are socially difficult to initiate and to sustain: they require expanding markets and resources and a docile labor force; they entail change throughout the society, not just in its economic institutions. In comparison, markets, resources, and cheap labor are readily obtainable abroad, most particularly, of course, in the Tier III societies. What might take decades and much civil conflict to achieve at home can be achieved abroad more quickly, with less or no domestic conflict. Granted that it has been a relatively common matter for the populations of the powerful societies to become excited over foreign dangers and possibilities, real or imagined. But *why* do they become excited? What induces them to pay taxes, to make sacrifices, even of their blood? Whatever may be said of the precapitalist world, and whatever may be said of the "common man's" inclination to "go West," what may and must be said of the modern capitalist world is that business sees the butter for its bread, and sometimes the bread itself, in what have become the colonial and neocolonial areas of the world. That the major share of profits and trade derive from relationships among and between the *developed* countries seems to contradict this assertion, but only if we fail to see the capitalist system as a *global* division of labor, and the crucial role played by the natural resources—in this century, especially oil—in the underdeveloped countries.

In Great Britain and the United States, the two leading capitalist and imperialist powers of the past two centuries, the principal voice shaping public policy both at home and abroad, whether directly or through the channels of public opinion, has been that of business. As Veblen said,

Representative government means, chiefly, representation of business interests. The government commonly works in the interest of the business man with a fairly consistent singleness of purpose. And in its solicitude for the business man's interests it is borne out by current public sentiment, for there is a naive unquestioning persuasion abroad among the body of the people to the effect that, in some occult way, the material interests of the populace coincide with the pecuniary interests of those business men...It seldoms happens, if at all, that the government of a civilized nation will persist in a course of action detrimental or not ostensibly subservient to the interests of the more conspicuous body of the community's business men.[14]

But even assuming that the imperializing process has been at the behest—or at the very least with the acquiescence—of business, has it been necessary, *required*? There is no way of finding an unequivocal answer to that question; we can only point to constant associations and explain why the associations have occurred, still leaving open whether or not they *had* to occur. Perhaps, for example, capitalism could have existed without poverty; it has not, so we must explain why poverty exists in the midst of riches. Similarly (although it is much to be doubted) capitalism *might* have grown and been sustained without overseas expansion and control and force and violence; but just what would have taken the place of the stimuli and gains from that expansion and control has never been explained. Kemp has put this point exactly:

To claim that "imperialism" was not a necessary stage in capitalist development is to imagine that the colossal development of the productive forces which took place in the nineteenth century could have proceeded without the bringing into being of a world-wide economy dominated by the leading capitalist powers. It is to imagine that somehow the characteristics of early industrial capitalism could have become permanent, without the growth of combines and monopolies, as an atomized collection of owner-financed firms. It is to assert that there was no relation between the politics of states and the dominant economic interests within them. It is to assume that the powerful economic forces released by capitalism were kept in tow by old-line statesmen, demagogues and ideologues. It is to argue, with Schumpeter, the most clear-sighted and consistent representative of this school, that the characteristics of "imperialism" were atavistic survivals foreign to the true nature of capitalism, adopted by the bourgeoisie only as a result of betrayal.[15]

Some readers will have been persuaded of the hand-in-glove relationship between capitalism and imperialism by now; some others never could be. Let us conclude this general part of the discussion with an observation of Harry Magdoff's on the same question:

Imperialism...is so intertwined with the history and the resulting structures of modern capitalist society—with its economics, politics, and ruling ideas—that this kind of question is in the same category as, for example, "Is it necessary for the United States to keep Texas and New Mexico?" We could, after all, return these territories to the Mexican people and still maintain a high-production and high-standard-of-living economy...Or one might ask, "Is Manhattan necessary for the United States?" It would surely be equitable to return land obtained from the Indians in a sharp deal...Such a move to wipe out a terrible blot on the conscience of white America could be socially useful. Moreover, a new financial headquarters of the United States (and the capitalist world) could be designed to avoid slums, smog, pollution, and traffic crises....

The relevant question is not whether imperialism is necessary for the United States, but to discover the rationality of the historic process itself; why the United States and other leading capitalist nations persistently and recurringly acted in the imperialist fashion for at least three-quarters of a century.[16]

Now we move from this attempt to provide a skeletal framework for understanding imperialism in general, to a fleshing out of it with a historical discussion.

The Baton of Economic Power

Capitalism and nationalism emerged together in history, and induced comparable and compatible attitudes and behavior. Economic individualism and competition have their counterpart in nationalism and national rivalries. It would be foolish to believe that any one merchant, industrialist, or financier could attribute his economic successes entirely, or even mostly, to his own doings, independent of the larger socioeconomic context within which he makes his gains; similarly, it would be foolish to attribute the economic successes of a particular nation to *its* own doings, independent of the world economy. In recent centuries, there has always been one country in the lead. It has been economically strongest and supreme in technology, and it has dominated the patterns of trade, finance, and production of the time. And it has had its way in shaping and using the political and military forms of the time.[17]

In the embryonic years of capitalism and nationalism, before either existed as such, the territorial states (not nations) of Venice and Florence carried the baton of economic leadership. In the late medieval and early renaissance periods, Venice ruled the eastern Mediterranean; Florence, not a naval power, drew its strength from its transalpine trading and financial relationships. Florentine capital and trade stimulated what became the more dynamic northern rim of Europe—principally Antwerp, Holland, and later England—at the cost, finally, of Florentine decay and collapse.

Economic advance in the medieval period was principally a result of growing interregional trade, which in turn stimulated and required urban (premodern) industry and finance. The dynamic process that has characterized world economic history ever since worked slowly but inexorably even then: the leading area benefited from its dominant relationships with lesser trading partners; the latter, transformed in the process, ultimately took over the lead. The nature of that process persists in the present; it is the scope and content that have changed: national/international in scope, industrial in content.

The sixteenth century brought rapid overseas expansion, newly found resources, and the need for expensive military forces on both land and sea. Traditional political and social patterns broke down, giving way chaotically to the emergence of new nations, new religious institutions, and the beginnings of capitalism. The Italians had brought Western Europe to that point; for centuries the Italians did not go beyond it, but the earlier "backward areas" did.

Beginning as cities, the Venetians, Milanese, Florentines, and Genoese grew into territorial states, and spent much of their time and resources fighting each other while extending their economic relationships to the east, west, and north. The scope of these relationships required an alteration in the traditional medieval pattern of interregional politics, a pattern given its nature and its sweep by the "universal" Roman Catholic Church. In the fifteenth century, the Italian city-states invented diplomacy, as a means of undertaking and securing their negotiations abroad, mostly outside of Italy. In doing so, they hastened the birth of the nation-states that came to exist in strength in the sixteenth century, and whose rivalries produced the massive and enduring conflicts that brought us to the present. A new world was being born. As Mattingly has said,

> Our modern notion of an international society composed of a heterogeneous collection of fictitious entities called states, all

supposed to be equal, sovereign, and completely independent, would have shocked both the idealism and the common sense of the fifteenth century. Such a society would have seemed to philosophers a repulsive anarchy...; and the concept would have been equally uncomfortable to practical statesmen.[18]

The transformation from medieval to modern economies took centuries, and longest of all for the Italians. Benefiting for so long from their optimal location in the Mediterranean, the world's greatest trading highway linking the rich Near East with the emerging transalpine North, the Italians had little inclination to seek greener pastures. Columbus was hired by Spain; Cabot, also an Italian, was hired by England. The hinge on which the door opened for modern economies—that is, larger in scope, industrial in production—was the exploration and exploitation of overseas territories. Marx put it vividly:

The discovery of gold and silver in America, the extirpation, enslavement and entombment in mines of the aboriginal population, the beginning of the conquest and looting of the East Indies, the turning of Africa into a warren for the commercial hunting of black-skins, signalised the rosy dawn of the era of capitalist production. These idyllic proceedings are the chief momenta of primitive accumulation. On their heels treads the commercial war of the European nations, with the globe for a theatre. It begins with the revolt of the Netherlands from Spain, assumes giant dimensions in England's anti-jacobin war, and is still going on in the opium wars against China, etc.[19]

In the fifteenth and sixteenth centuries, Portugal and Spain swept over the Far East and the New World. Their social and economic institutions were anachronistic; their gains drained away into Northern Europe, and especially into the hands of those who busied themselves in Antwerp—"a center of unbridled capitalism." Antwerp's location was central to the sea and overland trade of the North; it was granted a monopoly over the Portuguese spice trade first, and of the Spanish trade later (under Charles V). It was a glorious period, and a short one; it ended when Spanish largesse became Spanish destruction. Antwerp's typical figure, Tawney remarks, "was the international financier," serving the hustling merchants and princes who fattened on this enlarged world.[20]

Trade War, War of Trade

The fall of Antwerp after the mid-sixteenth century, due to religious and civil strife and the depredations of the Hapsburgs, was followed by the rise, not of a city—which for centuries had been the centers of economic strength—but of a region: the United Provinces, with Holland at their lead, and Amsterdam at the center of Holland. It was the first approximation to an economically viable *national* unit. Though tiny in population, perhaps two million, and bereft of the normal run of soils, minerals, timber, and the like (and with most of its "soil," the so-called "polders," built up out of the sea and protected by dikes), the Dutch rose to heights never before reached economically. Industry, trade, and finance combined with an enormous fleet to allow the Dutch to dominate the world in the seventeenth century, and to remain financially strong throughout the eighteenth century. France and England struggled in that century to wrest the baton from the Dutch, and from each other.[21]

Until the seventeenth century, the colonization of the world was in the hands of the Portuguese and the Spanish, while the Italians continued their hold on the Mediterranean—against rising competition from both English and French merchants. In the seventeenth century, the Dutch gained control over whole areas, as in the East Indies, or unique trading privileges, as in Japan. Their trade branched out from Holland to Scandinavia, to Africa, to all of the Americas, and to Asia. The Dutch East India Company was quite probably the most powerful single lay organization the world had seen up to that time, the General Motors of its day, only more so. Holland's intra-Asian trade was more profitable than its Asian-European trade, which was very profitable indeed. Some idea of the relative economic strength of the Dutch, as well as of "mercantilist" thinking, is given by a famous argument of Colbert (first minister of King Louis XIV of France) in 1669:

> Commerce is carried on by 20,000 vessels and that number cannot be increased. Each nation strives to have its fair share and to get ahead of the others. The Dutch now fight this war [of trade] with 15,000 to 16,000 vessels, the English with 3,000 to 4,000 and the French with 500 to 600. The last two countries can improve their commerce only by increasing the number of their vessels and can increase the number only by paring away from the 15,000 to 16,000 Dutch ships.... It must be added that trade causes perpetual strife both in time of war

and in time of peace between all the nations of Europe to decide which of them shall have the greatest share.[22]

The Dutch—much like the Japanese today, in this respect—lacking natural resources of their own, imported them from all over the world, processed them, and sold the higher-value product, once more, all over the world. They had begun to do that in the medieval period, with fish from the North Sea and the Baltic. That led to shipbuilding; to enhanced trade; to industries processing the grain (into gin, as well as flour), the cocoa, the coffee, the tobacco, the diamonds, the fibers, etc. From it all, the tiny nation of the Dutch, constructing an empire located on all the continents in the process, became the leading trading, financial, industrial, and shipping nation. In finding its way to that eminence, the Dutch, like the Italians before them, opened up and stimulated other areas. And having done so, they fell into decline.

The other areas included France and England, both larger in population and richer in natural resources than the Dutch. Both were able also to copy, or to reproduce, the economic sources of Dutch strength. The English became much better at it than the French, although, at the opening of the eighteenth century if there seemed to be a serious rival for Dutch power, it was the French. As the eighteenth century wore on, it increasingly became the scene of an Anglo-French struggle on land and sea, in Asia (especially India), in the Caribbean and North America, and on the Continent. When the French were finally defeated at Waterloo, the underlying economic strength of the British was the decisive factor.

British economic strength was given its critical edge over the French by the trading proclivities and abilities of the British, derided by the French as "a nation of shopkeepers." In the eighteenth century, France was by far the richer of the two nations—but only for a small fraction of its people. It had twice the population of Britain and was blessed with the best and broadest agricultural resources of any European nation. But in the emerging capitalist world where trade was vital, the natural riches of France, requiring little foreign trade, turned out to be dynamic disadvantages. Recall Colbert's calculation of the numbers of French and English vessels: England with its much smaller population had five times as many ships as the French. Ships, shipbuilding, and sailors strengthened fighting as well as trading capacities, of course.

France, rich and the dominant military power of Europe, was continually involved in continental warfare. The splendor of its Court had another side to it: its power, its corruption, and its taxes bled France dry, and influenced the pattern of French production toward the elegant and the military. The economic power of the future lay with those who moved toward the mass production of the mundane. While France was moving toward cultural and military supremacy in the seventeenth and eighteenth centuries, England was ridding itself of outworn feudal and monarchical institutions, spreading its trade, and improving its technology in agriculture and industry. In England, there was a bourgeois revolution in the seventeenth century, and an industrial revolution toward the end of the eighteenth century; in France, the consolidation of absolute monarchy in the seventeenth century, and a weak bourgeois revolution at the close of the eighteenth century. In England, Adam Smith; in France, Napoleon.

Rule Britannia

The nineteenth century belonged to Great Britain. The Dutch, although economically supreme in the seventeenth century, presided over a string quartet by comparison with the symphony orchestrated by Great Britain in the nineteenth century. The Dutch scrambled continuously, in and between wars; the strength of Britain achieved the *Pax Britannica*. Industrialism and modern technology made the difference: it was a difference in scale, scope, and penetration, entailing differences in all aspects of social existence—while laying the foundations for the even greater enlargement of all these once more, in our own period. The sixteenth through the eighteenth centuries were given their dynamism by trade, and overseas relationships were mercantilist; the nineteenth century was industrial in its dynamic, and imperialist overseas. These contrasts require further elaboration.

Industrialism means many things. England, as the first industrial nation, was characterized by increasing specialization within the economy and the sharp decline of its prior agricultural sufficiency; increasing use of coal and iron in production and for transportation; increasingly capital-intensive production—that is the use of machinery, with high fixed costs—and the consequent need for mass markets; and attempts to assure that no part of this increasingly interdependent system would break loose and bring it all down. For England especially, the new industrialism meant the need to import the major portion of its foodstuffs and raw materials. These were not produced, generally, at ports or coastal strips, but in the hinterland. The iron steamship made it possible to carry bulky and low-priced commodities more cheaply and more reliably than sailing ships; the railroad made it possible to penetrate whole continents. The process of realizing these needs and possibilities led to the annexation of whole territories. In addition to privileged trade, there was privileged investment; instead of colonial outposts, an empire; instead of forts, occupying armies; instead of dots on a map, whole areas colored pink: "The sun never sets on the Brtitish flag."[23]

The British were not alone, either in need or in possibility. But they were the strongest in both. The last part of the century saw them in growing competition with the other "Great Powers"—being part of that competition was what *made* a nation a "Great Power"—and, by its very end, with Japan and the United States. In turn, control over overseas areas was necessary to keep others out, as well as to make what gains there were from getting in, oneself. Control of the high seas was sufficient to this end in the nineteenth century, for sea power played the role that air power and nuclear missiles now do. To say that the nineteenth century was the century of the *Pax Britannica* is to say that Britain's navy was without peer—so strong, it didn't have to be used. There was not even a close second to Britain's role as world ruler until the 1890s. The umbrella of control was based on a virtual monopoly of naval and mercantile sea power; under that umbrella, British business thrived overseas, and a period of the freest international trade and most unified international monetary system in history had been created. Nor is it unimportant that the peace established by Britain allowed U.S. development to proceed unhampered by foreign violence or the necessity to sustain a significant army and navy. As will be seen later, U.S. hegemony after World War II created a similar worldwide condition for the capitalist system—but with something Britain did not have: on the one hand, an ideological power struggle, and on the other, a mounting economic struggle with those of the same ideology.[24]

Britain's economic well-being in the nineteenth century depended squarely on buying, selling, and investing all over the world. The relationships developed with the United States and with Germany are most informative in showing how the very process of British success in these economic activities meant the creation of rivals even mightier than itself, as had been the case earlier for those who had once carried the baton of greatest power.

Britain's two principal customers for consumer and capital goods and loans were Germany and the United States. In return, Britain took in foodstuffs and raw materials, gold, commissions, profits, and interest. But the importation of goods and capital for the United States and Germany meant an enhanced ability to develop their own economies, a stepped-up process of industrialization. Doubtless the British relationship was more necessary for Germany than for the much richer United States; in both cases, however, Britain was creating rivals in trade, industry, and finance, as well as for imperial space. In the 1890s, voices were already being raised in England to curb its free trading policies in favor of protection and to anticipate an open conflict with Germany, which was expanding its technologically more advanced navy, competing with increasing effectiveness in world markets, and seeking to catch up in the race for empire.[25]

Like Father, Like Son

Before the colonies broke loose from the British, their foreign trade moved within a complicated and extensive system of restrictions, prohibitions, requirements, and subsidies, all designed to enhance British profits and power. Initially this model of mercantilist policy worked to the mutual benefit of Britain and the colonists; by the mid-eighteenth century, the same system constrained the colonists so as to benefit the British.

British colonial policy for North America in the seventeenth century had two main aims: to strengthen British trade and shipping at the expense of the Dutch, and to strengthen the colonies, through subsidies and guaranteed markets, as potentially strong economic and strategic assets. It was classic mercantilism, and the colonists had almost two centuries of habituation to such policies before their onerousness led them to a violent break from Britain.[26]

Among our very first steps after Independence was the creation of our own mercantilist system. Alexander Hamilton was the most productive and influential economic thinker of the new nation, issuing one *Report* after another. His *Report on Manufactures* (1791), revolving around the need to develop industry and to protect it in its "infant" stages, set the stage for a coherent and tight protectionist trading policy, with subsidies mixed in where needed. Like the European experience on which it was modeled, U.S. protectionism recognized the importance of foreign trade: protectionism was designed not to reduce its volume, but, through selectivity, to minimize its costs and enhance its gains. The mercantilism of Hamilton has appeared and reappeared in our history, interspersed with movements seemingly going in the opposite direction; and it continues today.

It is instructive to take a brief look at Daniel Webster's four decades of governmental service in these respects, which involved a complete turnaround on foreign economic policy—justified for Webster by the changing economic situation of the New England region he represented. As a Representative from New Hampshire (1813–17), and Massachusetts (1823–27), Webster represented the trading center of the United States, and as such he was an ardent free trader, opposed to any form of protectionism. Later, as a Senator from Massachusetts and U.S. Secretary of State (both in the 1840s), Webster used his orator's talents on behalf of protectionism, for by then New England was the principal home of the "infant industries" of the nation. In the 1820s, he was an opponent of protectionist Henry Clay, whose "American system" was designed to give U.S. farmers a "home market" composed of buyers earning incomes from manufactures in the United States; a decade or so later, Webster and Clay were protectionist allies, leaders of the "Whigs," a party whose explicit business concerns foreshadowed the Republican Party that emerged just before the Civil War.

After the deaths of Clay and Webster, both in 1852, the Whig Party disappeared; it had been split earlier over the question of tariffs and, as well, over the extension of slavery to the new states: the Northern Whigs supported tariffs while the Southerners (exporters of raw materials and importers of manufactures) pushed for freer trade. The latter won out in 1846 with the Walker Tariff, which reduced protective tariffs while seeking to increase revenues through high tariffs on goods not produced in the United States ("revenue tariffs"—such as on coffee). Those who opposed the Walker Tariff favored increasing trade also, so long as the trade that took place did not injure U.S. industry.

Nobody then doubted the critical importance of U.S. foreign economic relationships which, in that early period, involved borrowing steadily from Britain, and paying back through the rising exports of (almost entirely) agricultural products—and most of all, cotton. When the conflict between the northern and southern interests brought the nation to the edge of civil war, the South assumed that the importance of the relationship between cotton exports and British textiles was such that Britain would actively and effectively intervene on the South's side. That Britain did not do so testifies to the less evident but nonetheless more powerful relationships already existing for trade and investments in the North; however, the South's assumption testifies to the acknowledged importance of trade in the United States at that time. Its importance accelerated in subsequent decades.

From Youth to Maturity to...?

The United States, as the first colony to be exploited in a modern way and the first to rebel, had very early on begun to view the Western Hemisphere as its backyard, a habit not yet broken. We could not expel the British from Canada; but from the rest of North America, the Spanish, the French, the Russians, the Dutch, and the English were bought out or pushed out. The Monroe Doctrine set the tone as early as 1823: there would be *no* further European colonization or attempts to implant monarchy in this hemisphere; the United States would not meddle with existing colonies nor in internal European affairs. However, in much less than a century we had begun to meddle in others' colonies; both during and after World War I our military, our capital, and our policies took a hand in European affairs.

The Republican victory that brought Lincoln to the presidency also set the stage for a set of foreign economic policies suited to emerging industrialism. Strong protective tariffs were passed in 1862, and immigration was stepped up through the revival of indentured labor. In 1873, with what the farmers called the "Crime of '73," silver was demonetized (in favor of gold and deflation) so as to integrate the U.S. economy with the emerging British-run international gold standard. And, as we saw in Chapter 6, U.S. exports of unfinished and processed agricultural commodities expanded substantially in the late 1870s, deepening a dependence on agricultural exports that continues to the present.[27]

As with agriculture, so with the international financial, trading, and industrial relationships of the United States after the Civil War. The U.S. economy was transformed from one that was relatively passive and dependent for its health upon foreign economic relationships to an increasingly aggressive economy upon whose health the rest of the world slowly but surely became dependent. That transformation was well on its way by the 1920s, even in the context of a collapsing world economy; by the 1950s, in the aftermath of many years of depression and war that was catastrophic for the rest of the world, the United States was indisputably some mixed-metaphorical combination of an economic Red Cross and saviour, the linchpin, and the locomotive of the world economy and capitalism. The data that follow suggest some of the quantitative signs of the process.

Up until the 1870s, the United States was in the textbook category of an "immature debtor" nation: it owed other countries, on net balance, and it imported more than it exported. It was in the 1870s that the status was changed to "mature debtor"—still in debt, on balance, but now exporting more than importing, due in largest part to the upsurge in agricultural exports. But when Europe's agricultural crisis ended our exports continued to exceed our imports for an entire century, except for three years (1888, 1889, and 1893). Then, in 1971–72, the balance reversed, for the first time in a century; and except for two years (1973 and 1975) it has risen to spectacularly "unfavorable" levels since—of which, more later.

In the midst of World War I, we became an "immature *creditor*" country, as our rising export of capital, combined with our strong trade position (both processes speeded up by the war, but on their way in any case), brought us to where we were *owed* by the world on net balance, but we continued to export more than we imported. A "mature creditor" nation by definition imports more than it exports, and pays for it with earnings over and above those from merchandise exports—from investments, shipping and other services, etc.). When our imports began to exceed our exports in 1971, we became a mature creditor nation; accompanied by a widespread feeling of uneasiness already then. As the 1980s unrolled, that uneasiness became panic in the minds of many, in the United States and elsewhere—not because of the numbers themselves, but because of their reasons for being. When Britain became a mature creditor nation, in the nineteenth century, its excess of imports over exports was easily paid for by its earnings from its foreign investments, not, as has become our case by borrowing. A new category now needs to be invented to categorize the situation of the United States: Reckless Born-Again Debtor Nation?

Now we shall examine some of the tendencies underlying and bringing about these qualitative changes in the position of the United States in the world economy, with the help of some figures.

Our transition from immature to mature debtor in the 1870s was accompanied by our growing productive powers, and thus our growing exporting powers; this in turn meant a changing economic structure. From being an exporter chiefly of crude raw materials and foodstuffs, such as cotton and wheat, we became an exporter *also* of semifinished and finished manufactures, such as steel and machinery. Table 7.1 shows how the absolute amounts grew over time, and how their relative positions changed. (Distortions in the numbers from inflation were not significant in terms of the years compared and our purposes here.)

Table 7.1
U.S. Exports and Imports, Selected Years, 1850-1970
(million $)

Year	Finished Manufactures		Crude Materials	
	Exports	Imports	Exports	Imports
1850	17	95	84	13
1870	58	174	214	57
1890	133	231	309	180
1910	499	368	574	578
1930	1,898	757	829	1,002
1950	5,741	1,504	1,886	2,465
1970	26,001	22,463	4,492	3,474

Source: Adapted from *Historical Statistics of the U.S.*, Part 2, p. 839.

Note that between 1890 and 1910 the United States had changed from a net importer to a net exporter of finished manufactures; and in the same period it changed from being a net exporter to a net importer of crude materials. More recently, as the figures for 1970 show, there was been a tendency toward balance in exports and imports, for both manufactures and crude materials.

Table 7.2 shows the rising importance of the United States in total world exports of manufactures up to the mid-1950s, and its relative decline since then.

The above data, and more to follow later, must be read with important background movements in mind. The great change upward in the decades from the nineteenth into this century reflect the always increasing productive complexity and strength of the U.S. economy.

Table 7.2 *Percentage of U.S. Exports of Manufactures as a* *Percentage of World Exports of Manufactures*[28]	
1899	11.6
1913	13.0
1929	20.4
1950	26.6
1966	17.5
1984	14.0

But there is one important reservation to be made concerning our sharp rise around 1950—namely, that the rest of the industrial world had been devastated by the war—and another about our relative decline from about 1960 on—namely, that the increased strengths of the other economies in the world meant that our relative loss was accompanying a very large absolute gain in our production, exports, and real incomes. That is true until the 1980s, when our relative decline measured the decreased ability of the United States to compete with many of the manufactures of Germany and Japan (especially), our increased dependence upon oil imports, and, among other matters to be discussed later in this chapter, the ways in which the rise of the multinational (or transnational) corporation led to diverse effects upon our national production and exports.[29]

The notion that the United States has had, or has, a slight dependency on its foreign economic relationships stems directly from the percentage that exports and imports have borne to our GNP. The mentality regarding this question in this century was shaped in the long period before 1960 when, except for war years (and as noted earlier), our exports or imports were always below 5 percent of our GNP. The figures began to approach 10 percent by the late 1970s and 15 percent by the late 1980s, placing us in something like the same qualitative position as many of the other industrial nations of the world—although quantitatively it is useful to keep in mind that the United States is still by far the largest economy in the world, producing about one-fourth of the entire world's

GNP. As the other countries well know, what happens to our 12–15 percent of GNP that goes to exports or imports is of vital importance to all those who buy from or sell to us. We are the bull in the China shop of the world economy, for better and for worse.

Perhaps it would be more accurate to say that we are the very largest bull in that shop, surrounded by another half dozen or so also large animals: Britain, Germany, Japan, France, Italy, and Canada (now, with the United States, "The Group of Seven"), along with the Low Countries and the Scandinavians. This handful of countries is responsible for about 90 percent of world industrial production of the capitalist countries—the United States still producing more than twice that of Japan, three times that of Germany, and higher multiples for France, Britain, Italy, or Canada. The countries just named are each others' best customers for commodities and investment, as they have been since the industrialization movement took hold, long ago. Naturally, one may add: and just as "naturally" as in the internal relationships of each capitalist country, those at the bottom, whether depressed income groups or depressed nations, see the gap between themselves and the rich steadily widening over time. The dual economy phenomenon is pervasive, internationally as well as nationally.[30]

Adolescent Giant

As World War I ended, the United States had emerged as the industrial, commercial, and financial center of the world, and Britain, without acknowledging it for many years (if, for many of the British, ever), slipped into economic stagnation and a secondary world status. Nor was there much in the way of rhetorical or realistic recognition of the new state of affairs in the United States—except in the failed global hopes of Woodrow Wilson. For better or for worse, the nature, obligations, and possibilities of the leading position of the United States in the world economy was not matched by a suitable or a coherent foreign policy for several decades. When, after World War II, that policy fell into shape—again, for better or for worse—its very successes would come to be our undoing, the usual "failures of success." The "immature creditor" status of the United States after 1918, in short, was more than an economist's dry classification; it well describes our state of mind, and the immature policies with which we related to the rest of the world.

A creditor nation is a net exporter of capital, a net lender to private parties and governments abroad. Debtor nations can only maintain a healthy balance in *their* external relationships if they can sell in the markets of the lending countries (and earn foreign exchange)—as, for example, the United States could when, in the nineteenth century, it was able to export increasing amounts of production to Britain and other creditors (and as the underdeveloped countries today cannot, in the same ways or appropriate quantities). From the Civil War on, the United States was a high protective tariff nation, with only an occasional and minor deviation. That was perhaps understandable up to World War I; from then on it stood in conflict with our creditor position. Nonetheless, our tariffs rose again in the 1920s, and were jacked up to their highest levels ever in 1930.[31]

If the free trade policies of Great Britain in the nineteenth century were taken as the proper standard for the world leader, the United States was breaking the rules of the game. In the fragile world economy after World War I, for the economic leader to break the rules meant that the game would be lost by everyone—including the president of the club.[32]

But Great Britain could *not* be taken as the standard for foreign economic policy after World War I, nor was it by the United States, despite the entreaties of liberal economists from 1920 on. Why not?

First, when Britain began to rule the world economy, there were no other significantly industrialized economies. A free trade policy maximized both exports and imports, and the imports did not constitute a threat to British industry: they were increasingly needed imports of raw materials and foodstuffs. Ricardo had advocated free trade thirty years before Britain adopted it; it made sense for that economy in that world. Subsequently, economists transformed Ricardian notions into eternal verities, good for all times and places; Ricardo had been concerned with one time and one place, and he could and did assume away foreign competition. When the United States moved into dominance after World War I, it faced Great Britain, Germany, Japan, and a handful of lesser industrial countries as competitors. All were hungry for markets, all were bristling with protective devices.

Second, when Britain forged its international policies, the major powers had been and would remain at peace with each other. Britain ruled the sea lanes, as both merchant and naval power. The United States came into supremacy in the midst of World War I, itself a result of great instability and conflict. The years after that war were merely a resting period—an "armistice"—until World War II. In that period, the world was rocked by revolution, and outbreaks of revolutionary and counterrevolutionary developments in the fragments of the dismembered Hapsburg empire; by a frenzied inflation in Germany, where prices rose an incredible 4 *trillion* times between 1918 and 1923; by fascism in Italy and then in Japan and Germany (and Portugal, and Spain, and elsewhere); by a severe and endless worldwide depression; and by the collapse of colonial economies. Had the United States sought to behave like a "mature creditor nation" from 1920 on, some of these developments *might* have been averted or softened; however, most of them would have been untouched by anything the United States could do. It was no longer the nineteenth century. Different trading policies were needed; different policies to run an empire were needed, also. Indeed, a much-modified capitalism was needed *within* the major national economies if there was to be, also, a much-modified and workable world economy. The United States *after* World War II—as always, for better and for worse—was both able and inclined to create the framework within which such changed policies could be developed. They will be discussed and analyzed shortly.

Something else made our possibilities quite different from those of Great Britain in the nineteenth century: the internal balance of power and the social outlook in the United States concerning power and influence. The United States could not reproduce the experience or adopt the principles of nineteenth-century Great Britain simply because we had become dominant in the world economy; in addition to the differences between the two periods, there was the difference in the social and political currents of the two nations. In part because our independence as a nation was won through war, the United States—despite its perennial dependence on the world economy—was and is nationalist in its mood and in its policies; always, and now as a nationalistic empire.[33]

From the Embargo Act of 1807, through the "Buy American" campaigns of the 1830s, 1890s and the 1930s (and perhaps the 1990s?); from the geographic expansion that has characterized our history from its first moments up to the present, the United States—in moods varying from buoyant to desperate to generous to arrogant—has shaped its internal and external policies on the steady assumption that this country has special qualities that give it special rights. Other countries also use their power to advance their national interest, of course. The United States, however, has assumed that *its* national interests, after all is said and done, are to the interests of other countries; and if that is less clear to others than to those in the United States, so much the worse for them.

In the 1920s and 1930s, the world broke out with a rash of economic nationalism, marked by import quotas, export subsidies, rising tariffs, competitive currency devaluations, foreign exchange controls, and the like, to the accompaniment of a steadily falling volume of world trade and rising international hostility. The United States, far from acting to slow or reverse these suicidal tendencies, participated in them, not least with the tariff of 1930. Perhaps worse, in 1933 a "World Economic Conference" was convened, in the hope that the mutual throat-cutting accompanying the worsening depression could be halted. The key nation in strength and influence was of course the United States, but newly installed President Roosevelt, "after a brief interval in which it seemed he would throw his force into the World Economic Conference, abandoned international responsibility, even disparaged it, by fostering nationalist devices, though not without the face-saving afterthought that a prosperous America would do most to produce a prosperous world."[34]

New Frontiers: The Muscles Flex

In 1846, Britain, once thoroughly mercantilist, moved to full free trade, quite simply removing *all* obstacles—knowing it had nothing to lose and much to gain by doing so. After the Walker Tariff Act reductions of that same year, the United States never again made such a fulsome move toward free trade, not even in its own period of dominance. In 1934 we took a small step in that direction, with the Reciprocal Trade Agreements Act (RTAA) and the Export-Import Bank; other steps of the same sort have been taken in subsequent years—most notably in the creation of the General Agreement on Tariffs and Trade (GATT) after World War II—but nothing resembling Britain's "1846." Our conscious needs for expanded foreign markets, taken together with confidence in the ability of our production to compete effectively in an open market—the basis for our "Open Door" policy for China, many decades earlier—made for the institutionalization of a new world trade doctrine, hesitantly in the 1930s, vigorously in the 1940s and later. But, as will be seen, what was sought and achieved—most fully under Kennedy—was trade *expansion* for the world economy, not the total removal of obstacles to imports.

It is sometimes said that the United States has finally abandoned its long "isolationist" stance for a new "internationalism." It is more appropriate to see our earlier position as nationalism with an inferiority complex, and our developing position since the 1930s, and especially since the end of World War II, as nationalism with a superiority complex. Be that as it may, the RTAA was designed to increase trade through negotiated, bilateral, mutual tariff reductions, between the United States and one nation at a time; the Eximbank was aimed at increasing exports to Latin America (mostly), through loans to governments for the financing of purchases from U.S. companies. In the context of the depressed 1930s, neither of these measures had much effect; the effects have been more substantial in the considerably more buoyant economies since World War II (as also for domestic New Deal measures, as we saw in Chapter 4).

When World War II began, it abruptly shoved aside the depression and transformed the context within which foreign economic policies would or could be made. But the war did not prevent plans from being thought of and proposed, some of them aired in the late 1930s, and all aimed at market expansion abroad. The nature of the problem was stated clearly by Dean Acheson in 1944 when, as Assistant Secretary of State, he told a congressional hearing:

> We cannot go through another ten years like the ten years at the end of the twenties and the beginning of the thirties, without having the most far-reaching consequences upon our economic and social system. When we look at that problem, we may say it is a problem of markets...We have got to see that what the country produces is used and sold under financial arrangements which make its production possible...You must look to foreign markets.

But couldn't the United States consume everything it produces?

> That would completely change our Constitution, our relations to property, human liberty, our very conceptions of law. And nobody contemplates that. Therefore, you find you must look to other markets and those markets are abroad.[35]

Soon an impressive collection of men from the world of corporate industry and finance (as Acheson was) began to construct programs that mixed economic expansion with what came to be the political economy of the Cold War. Their names became very familiar in the ensuing years: John Foster Dulles, Averell Harriman, James Forrestal, John J. McCloy, A.A. Berle, Jr., Robert Lovett, Douglas Dillon, Dean Rusk, Christian

Herter, George Ball.... Most of these were associated with both the Council on Foreign Relations and the State Department, the Department of Defense, and the CIA, moving back and forth between corporate offices, the Council, and governmental positions with ease: truly "a circulating elite." The journal of the Council, *Foreign Affairs*, is generally conceded to be the most influential journal of its kind.[36]

After World War II the United States became the effective, determined, and self-conscious architect of and ruler over a new capitalist world economy—and much more. When in 1944 at Bretton Woods (N.H.) we undertook to exercise leadership openly, the United States was uniquely strong. All the other once-powerful nations were economically, socially, and physically damaged or ruined, their imperial possessions going or gone, tens of millions of their people wounded, killed and/or homeless. Everywhere but in the United States, capitalism was terribly weak and on the defensive.

In sharp contrast, and apart from its relatively low war casualties and total absence of war damage, the United States was blessed in every way by World War II, as earlier by World War I. We had been rescued from severe and seemingly endless depression (unemployment over 17 percent in 1939, still over 10 percent in 1941), and we had been modernized and strengthened both absolutely and relative to all others—economically, militarily, and politically. The military and big business, both viewed with suspicion or hostility as the war began in Europe in 1939, had attained new heights of admiration and acceptance as it ended, aided in no little part by the maturing commercial and political skills of Madison Avenue (and the cinematic heroism of the Ronald Reagans and John Waynes). After 1945, neither U.S. capitalism nor its military was effectively challengeable. It was well understood in the higher circles of the United States and, grudgingly, elsewhere that the survival of world capitalism depended upon U.S. initiative and power. And given the fact that the Soviet Union was probably the *most* severely damaged of all nations by World War II, the threat to capitalism was not via military expansion by the Soviet Union but through the continuing socioeconomic collapse of the main structures of capitalism.[37]

Uncle Hegemon

Beginning in 1941 with the Atlantic Charter, put together by Churchill and Roosevelt, and coming to fruition in the Dumbarton Oaks and

Bretton Woods conferences of 1944, both with widespread international participation, the United States used its power to shape the new international organizations that were institutionalized in 1945 and 1946: the United Nations, the International Monetary Fund (IMF, or Fund), and the International Bank for Reconstruction and Development (IBRD, or World Bank). All these organizations were to be dominated by the lopsided economic, military, and political power and prestige of the United States in the postwar world.

The IMF was designed to stabilize the international monetary situation over time, in effect to function as a substitute for Britain's "automatic gold standard," which had played much the same role before 1914. The IBRD was designed to lend for capital projects. The assets of both institutions were dominantly those of the U.S. from the beginning, and the United States has been the prime decision-making power in both organizations, as it later came to be in the Inter-American Development Bank.[38]

In the decade following 1945, the United States created a whole new framework within which its (and others') entire foreign policy would move. Unlike the UN, the IMF, and the IBRD, which were all international in their construction, albeit much-dominated by the United States, the next steps were devised by and for the United States. The first public offering of the drama opened in Fulton, Missouri (President Truman's stomping grounds), with Churchill's famous "Iron Curtain" speech, in 1946. In 1947 a whirlwind of institutional innovations took shape:

1947   *The Truman (Greece-Turkey) Doctrine.* Truman asked for and received $400 million from Congress "to help free peoples to maintain... their national integrity against aggressive movements that seek to impose upon them totalitarian regimes." Control of the Balkan area before World War II had been in British hands, now too weak to continue.

       The National Security Act. Created the "National Military Establishment," incorporating the preexisting Department of the Navy with the new Department of the Air Force and Department of the Army under the Department of War, whose name was then changed to Defense. The Act also created the CIA and the National Security Council, which swiftly became, as it remains, the pivotal center of foreign policy-making.

1948 *The Marshall Plan.* At a commencement address at Harvard in June 1947, General George Marshall, then Secretary of State, proposed what became in 1948 the European Recovery Program. In its four years of operation, the program gave $13 billion (then a very large sum) to eighteen Western European nations for a broad variety of investment projects. Over 70 percent of the amount was spent for U.S. goods. The program was sold to Congress on those grounds, and as a means of "rolling back the tide of communism."[39]

Organization of American States (OAS). All nations but Canada in this hemisphere were charter members. Its stated purpose is to protect the hemisphere from "the interventionist and aggressive designs of international communism."

Selective Service Act. The United States had had a military draft only during the Civil War, World War I, and beginning in 1940, for World War II. This new Act built the draft into our postwar history.

1949 *North Atlantic Treaty Organization (NATO).* The military counterpart of the Marshall Plan.

Point Four Program. Announced in Truman's inaugural address in 1949—the fourth point in his speech— it was a program of technical assistance to "underdeveloped areas." It has continued in various forms since then.

1950 *Subversive Activities Control Board.* Created by the (Senator) McCarran Internal Security Act, aimed at controlling and restricting "domestic communism." In the same year, the University of California obliged its faculty to sign a "loyalty oath" (swearing "not now or ever" a member of the Communist Party), Senator Joe McCarthy began his battle against the U.S. State Department, as infiltrated by "over 200 Communists" (nobody ever shown to be so), and the Korean War—called a "police action" —began, creating symmetry between domestic and foreign affairs.

American Military Assistance Advisory Group (MAAG). Created to assist and advise the French in their Indochina War. In 1951 we began to assist France in financing the war; by 1952 we were paying three-quarters of the bill. When the French were defeated at Dien Bien Phu in 1954, and withdrew, the United States entered the continuing civil war, first as a financier and advisor to a series of feeble Saigon governments, then slowly but surely, beginning with unacknowledged Green Beret soldiers ("advisors"), becoming fully involved in the war, up through 1975. In that long period, over 3.5 million U.S. military personnel served time in Indochina, and about 60,000 of them died there.

1951 *Japanese-American Treaty.* A mutual security pact, one of whose provisions allowed the United States to "administer" Okinawa, still one of our major military bases in Asia. The treaty was renewed in 1960 and subsequently, and although the United States has agreed to phase itself out of Okinawa, the military bases remain, despite substantial protest over many years by the Okinawans.

1954 *Southeast Asia Treaty Organization (SEATO).* The Asian counterpart of NATO.

1955 *Middle East Treaty Organization.* Another NATO counterpart, made up originally of Iraq, Iran, Turkey, Pakistan, and Great Britain, with a participating U.S. military mission. In subsequent years, with great turbulence in the Middle East, that organization has changed from METO to CENTO (*Central Treaty Organization*) to a memory.

Thus, in a very few years, the United States jumped headlong into the international arena, armed with economic, military, and political supremacy. There was some very vocal opposition in the first few years, both from conservatives such as Senator Robert A. Taft, and from the liberal-left, whose numbers peaked in the period surrounding the 1948 election.

It is worthwhile to note the role of U.S. trade unionism in this process of dramatic internationalization and militarization of the United States. The AFL and the CIO, which had been separate organizations until 1955, then merged. They provided both opposition to and support for growing U.S. intervention around the world: opposition from left-wing unions in the CIO—all of which were expelled in 1949 and 1950—and substantial and growing support from the rest of the CIO and the entire AFL.[40]

In 1947, when the Marshall Plan was first under discussion, organized labor was skeptical; at its convention in 1948, the CIO endorsed it. In 1949, both the AFL and the CIO cooperated in the explicitly Anti-Communist International Confederation of Free Trade Unions; in the 1950s labor officials were secretly accepting funds from the CIA for working against foreign left unions abroad.

Thus did the web of cooperation between organized labor, the cold warriors of Washington, and corporate leaders become tighter and tighter until, in 1966, George Meany, then president of the AFL-CIO, could proclaim that criticism of the war in Vietnam "can only pollute and poison the bloodstream of our democracy."

In sum, a plethora of programs and activities, always increasing, spreading, and deepening in their meaning for a good quarter of a century after 1945. All that, plus the blandishment, the threats, the force, and the enormous expenditures at home and abroad—most of all in Germany and Japan, contributing significantly to their subsequent economic strength—whatever else it meant, created a buoyant, compliant, and disciplined world economy.

It is worth adding that to the degree that the United States succeeded in its conscious efforts to diminish *national* capitalism in Europe, as in its promotion of the European Community, it also diminished the political power of the European Left: one of the several meanings of the "Americanization" of the world. Now we turn to how it all worked out—so well in the 1950s and 1960s, and so troublesomely, in one way and another, since then.[41]

Dollar Shortage to Dollar Glut

The election of 1952 brought General Eisenhower and Richard Nixon to the White House. The old-fashioned "isolationist wing" of the Republican Party had been suppressed, and a working consensus on anticommunism abroad and at home had been created between the GOP and the Democratic Party, by whatever means—including McCarthyism—necessary. Organized labor and agriculture worked in harmony with organized business at the highest levels; the gains made from arms production and rising exports assured that almost any conflict could be ironed out with minimal trouble—at least for those at the top of the Big Four of agriculture, business, government, and labor.

The Korean War was brought to an end by Eisenhower. Foreign economic affairs approached the euphoric for the United States. The U.S. economy was finding or creating expanding markets abroad for its extraordinary productive capacity, and additional outlets for capital. In the early 1950s, the U.S. produced nine of every ten new autos in the world, and accounted for a little under a third of world exports. By the mid-1950s, as the world began its real recovery from the ravaged years before, those percentages of course fell. But in those years just after 1945, with the world desperately short of productive capacity of all kinds, there emerged what was called "a dollar shortage": quite simply, the rest of the world needed and wanted more from us than could be produced and sold to the dollar area (mostly the United States, but also Canada and much of Latin America). But as suggested earlier, the economic and political framework created in those same years made it possible for economic strength elsewhere to recover and grow, along with our own. Today, as Germany and Japan lead the parade of our competitors, and there is a "yen shortage," there are grounds for at least wry smiles.

But already in the Truman years, one matter in addition to markets and investment outlets had come to be seen as vital: the increasing dependence of the United States on imports of raw materials: small quantities of strategic materials such as tungsten, chromium, columbium, and the like, and, looming in the near future, large quantities of petroleum, iron ore, and similar materials.

Thus in 1951, the International Development Advisory Board's *Partners in Progress* ("The Rockefeller Report") made the connection between raw materials dependency and foreign policy explicit. In 1952, the President's Materials Policy Commission issued a five-volume report ("The Paley

Commission Report") entitled *Resources for Freedom*. In the report, past, present, and future supplies of raw materials were studied, evaluated, and measured against new demands and technology. The conclusion was twofold: by the 1970s, the United States would be vitally dependent upon imported raw materials, quantitatively and qualitatively; and its foreign policies must reflect and fulfill that need. They were right about their predictions, and their recommendations for a vigorous foreign policy, becoming a reality even before they wrote, were more than realized in the years to follow. The means adopted turned on U.S. investments in the countries possessing the needed resources, and on political/military arrangements suited to assuring secure flows of both raw materials and profits for themselves. The geographic framework entailed was imperial in its scope; the policies were imperialist—or, better, "neocolonialist"—in their nature. The Cold War provided the rationale for those policies, in the name of defending the entire "Free World" from Communist aggression.[42]

The fifteen years or so following 1945 were of course marked by upsets large and small, at home and abroad: the Chinese and Cuban revolutions, a Cold War that didn't always sail smoothly, and the semi-defeat in Korea; and there were four recessions between 1948 and 1961, despite the enormous amounts of production going into arms and exports. But in general, those were years of growing optimism and confidence, indeed of complacency—the students of the 1950s were called "the silent generation"—regarding U.S. economic and military strength. Problems arose and would continue to do so; but with most of the world seeking U.S. consumer and capital goods and accepting our political and military leadership, even adopting elements of our popular culture, what's to worry?

Troubles for the Pax Americana

When the 1960s began, the United States seemed unchallengeable in the world, and few indeed were challenging the U.S. system at home. By the end of the 1960s and continuing into the early 1970s, doubts and turbulence at home had become widespread, due to racial unrest, poverty, the Indochina War and the draft, and a growing malaise and alienation: "Can't Get No Satisfaction" was a very popular song among the young (and some not so young). In the same years, power grew elsewhere: the other industrial capitalist countries had gone beyond recovery to bursting strength. Tier III countries were finding ways to resist and to show independence—Tanzania and Vietnam in their ways, Peru and Chile in theirs, the oil exporting countries, through OPEC, in theirs. If, as emperor, the United States was by no means naked, neither were its clothes of the latest cut.

As earlier in history, the great strength and power of the dominant nation, while simultaneously providing a high and rising demand for its own production and stability and economic growth, also assured the renewed and increased strength of the preexisting industrial economies while accelerating the processes of social change in the dependent nonindustrial economies in Asia, the Middle East, Africa, and Latin America. By the mid-1960s the consequences of all these changes were appearing: economically in the worsening of the U.S. balance of trade and payments; politically and militarily in the softening of our alliances and, most notably, in the disaster of the Indochina War. The first postwar administration to sense the implications of these difficulties was that of John F. Kennedy.

Kennedy's advisors knew the U.S. empire was already well along by 1960; they also knew it could not function in the same terms as its British predecessor, whether economically, politically, or militarily. For us to adopt the status of "mature creditor nation," different means were necessary; as they were also if we were to hold down challenges to existing and vital patterns of dependency. Some contrasts between Britain in its heyday and the threats and possibilities facing the United States were noted above; some elaboration is now appropriate.

In Britain's day, "internationalism" could and did mean free trade. Britain's competition did not appear until the end of the nineteenth century, and then as *newly* industrialized nations. The United States came to eminence in the midst of already extant industrialized and highly nationalistic societies. By 1960, as a result of U.S. policies of investment and encouragement, these other nations—most of all Germany and Japan—were becoming technologically competitive or superior to us, in ways not so in 1934, the year of the RTAA. U.S. loans and investments facilitated the modernization of foreign industries, and as a condition of Marshall Plan aid we pushed the Europeans into patterns of cooperation which strengthened the separate economies and enabled them ultimately to stand against us in a united front relating to, say, tariffs. Comparable steps stimulated the Japanese economy. And both the Japanese and Germans were given great stimuli to their economies by the enormous military expenditures made by the United States *in* their economies (among other such important matters) over many years: consider the stimuli to the German economy from U.S. military housing, eating, recreation, etc., for over 300,000 U.S. troops for decades.

Our export surplus rose to $7 billion in 1964, and then began to fall. It became negative in 1971, as noted earlier, for the first time in this century, and shortly thereafter began to take on gigantic proportions. The Trade Expansion Act of 1962, the legislation heading Kennedy's list of priorities, had aimed to *prevent* that from happening. It was designed to encourage the necessary expansion of European and Japanese exports, but *only* insofar as our own exports could expand at least as fast, thereby maintaining and increasing our export surplus. But not even the Number One power is omnipotent, let alone able to eat its cake and have it too. As was discussed in Chapter 4, the very developments that expanded production, investment, and trade, and that so stimulated the U.S. economy after World War II, also produced our main competitors. The process of global economic expansion *had* to slow down, then as in the past. When that happened, after 1973, the policies of the New U.S. Empire had begun to sputter.

In 1975, there seemed to be something more than a respite, when the U.S. ran a large trade surplus of over $11 billion. But it was due to temporary energy and food shortages in Europe. The U.S. recovered from the serious 1974–75 recession, but its giant trading partners did not. Ever since then, and except for Japan, they have all had unemployment and/or inflation rates ranging from serious to worrisome—the average jobless rate vacillating around 9 percent in the European Community, including Germany—despite what has otherwise often seemed to be "prosperity."[43]

The changing and deteriorating place of the United States in the world economy fits in with what might be expected, when we recall the relative decline of Britain before World War I. But if the fall from the once unchallengeable supremacy of the United States was unavoidable on a general level, it has also had a set of causes and consequences that did not and could not exist in any earlier period. These include the role of contemporary technology and business organization (especially the multinational/transnational/supranational—MNCs/TNCs/SNCs— corporations), to be examined separately in the following section of this chapter; but of at least equal weight have been the militarization of the U.S. economy and of its foreign policy, and the accompanying growth of the foreign investment of the MNCs of the United States—which taken together were critical in creating the rapidly expanding world economy of the 1960s. And then, the troubles that began in the 1970s and never resolved either by the United States or others, were given a very strong push toward an always more intractable crisis by the monetary, fiscal, and military policies that took hold as the 1980s began.

Taken together, the policies of the past twenty years accelerated the transformation of the U.S. economy from having been exceptionally strong to becoming always more fragile, and from the world economy's largest creditor to its largest debtor country—a process whose next steps are at best problematic. A closer look at those transforming years is needed here.[44]

The economic nationalism that with brief exceptions had characterized our history reappeared explosively in 1971, when President Nixon, confronted with the first modern trade deficit, responded by "going it alone": although the United States had created the liberal trade and investment provisions of Bretton Woods in 1944, in 1971 we were also the first to violate those agreements. From then on, if it hasn't been one thing, it's been another. In tracing through what made for our transformation, it is useful to keep in mind that what gave the U.S. economy its real and its apparent strength was ultimately the source of its undoing.

What led Nixon, as much an "internationalist" as any U.S. president has ever been, to change direction? On the surface, it was the trade deficit of 1971. But behind that were longer-run and more abiding processes, at the heart of which were our foreign investment and military activities. Both constitute a demand for foreign currencies, much as though the United States were importing the labor and materials going into plant and barracks construction, etc., overseas. As the world economy was expanding in the 1960s, so were those expenditures abroad[45]—and in doing so, not only contributing to the strengthening of other economies but also constituting a growing negative development for our balances of trade and payments.

The military side of this, already quite substantial by the mid-1960s, was much aggravated by the war in Indochina which, by 1966, had become greatly and increasingly expensive in both dollars and lives—so much so, as noted earlier, that President Johnson felt the need to lie both to the public and his own budget chief about the dollar expenses (while promising that "the boys will be home by Christmas").

Meanwhile, in keeping with Bretton Woods agreements, the U.S. dollar was the key currency in the world economy, and the United States backed the value of the dollar with gold at a fixed amount ($35 an ounce). As U.S. dollars began to pile up in foreign central banks during the 1960s—and especially that of Germany—pressure began to build from abroad for the United States to end the war and, failing that, foreigners in the late 1960s responded by exchanging their surplus dollars for gold. Du Boff's description of what then happened is apt (pp. 157 –58):

Richard Nixon's own answer was not long in coming: when you're losing, change the rules of the game. On August 15, 1971, with no advance warning to any government, friendly or otherwise, he unilaterally slammed shut the U.S. gold window against foreign central banks, terminating dollar convertibility into gold and unhinging the exchange-parity rate of the monetary unit that had been the world's sole international reserve currency since the Bretton Woods agreement of 1944. Not only did [he] overturn the existing international monetary system. Equally fateful was his decision to impose a temporary surtax of 10 percent on imports, a signal that from now on the United States would discard free trade whenever its usefulness seemed outmoded for American purposes.

The 1970s were beset by many untoward developments in addition to the foregoing: the oil price shocks of 1973–74 and then again in 1978–79, the recession of 1974–75, and the rising inflation of the decade, peaking in 1979–80, with then another short recession. Moreover, in addition to emerging excess capacity in key industries—autos, steel, chemicals, textiles, machinery, and many others—and responding to that, the U.S. banks began avidly to seek borrowers in Tier III, both because real investment borrowing in the United States was a dwindling category (because of those excess capacities) and because of the very high rates of interest able to be squeezed from the nonindustrial countries—or so it was thought, until the defaults that began in 1982 (of which more later). And in some of those countries, which came to be called Newly Industrializing Countries ("NICs"), worldwide excess capacities were being added to—autos and shipbuilding in South Korea, electronics in Taiwan, etc. And then came Reaganomics.

Despite all the troubles before 1980, and given that most other major economies were also in crisis, the U.S. economy remained not only the largest but the strongest in the world. Although our trade balances were negative, when petroleum imports are excluded our exports and imports were more or less in balance up through 1981:

Table 7.3		
	Nonagricultural exports	Nonpetroleum imports
1972-73	$ 46.7	$ 56.6
1980-81	187.6	178.9[46]

But if we examine those same relationships for the mid-1980s, we find that exports were $191.9 versus imports of $311.1 billion (ibid.). What had happened?

The short recession of 1980 (January through July) was over by the time Reagan took office in early 1981, but the worst inflation in our modern history continued. In the summer of 1981, recession struck again, the most severe since the depression of the 1930s, as measured by unemployment (10.7 percent) and capacity utilization (68.8 percent), with other measures also either the worst or close to the worst since 1939. That the recession was deliberately created in order to end the inflation is almost universally accepted. Whether, as some believe, the credit or blame is to be given solely to the head of the Federal Reserve, Paul Volcker, or shared with the Reagan Administration, is the only major point in dispute.[47]

What became the focal point of the trouble for U.S. exports in the 1980s was the policy of raising interest rates, and the connections between that, the value of the dollar in world trade, and our trade balance. By late 1981 the average prime rate was caused to rise toward 19 percent (in late 1991 it was around 7 percent, for purposes of comparison)—which meant that directly and indirectly the abilities of businesses and consumers to borrow were severely inhibited. Other countries facing inflation raised their rates also, but when the United States allowed its rates to begin to fall, others did not follow all the way: one of many signs by then that the discipline of the world economy was slackening. What this meant in turn was that the value of the dollar rose in relation to other currencies (DuBoff, p. 161). Specifically:

From 1980 through early 1985 the trade-weighted value of the dollar on foreign exchange markets rose by about 60 percent; [that is,]...it took 60 percent more foreign currency of the major U.S. trading partners to buy a dollar. The effect was to make U.S. exports much more expensive and imports cheaper.

By 1983, the Reagan Administration was going full steam ahead on its vastly expanded program of military expenditures. Although, as we have seen, Reagan came into office promising to balance the budget and to toss Keynesian deficit spending into the wastebasket, he promptly began the biggest deficit spending spree in history, and filled out the meaning of "military Keynesianism." The economy of the United States promptly began to emerge from recession, and continued to expand for the rest of the decade—as what economy wouldn't, with a tripling of its national debt: from about $1 trillion when Reagan took office, to over $3 trillion when he waved us all bye-bye.[48]

The other major economies grew much less rapidly than we in the 1980s, and what growth they had was owed in significant part to huge exports to the United States: "the locomotive of the world economy." As Du Boff points out, "during the recovery years of the mid-1980s, increases in American GNP accounted for 70 percent of world demand growth in industrial nations, nearly twice as much as in previous postwar recoveries" (ibid.).

In Chapter 4 we sought to show the illusory quality of the 1980s expansion; when we see it in the framework of the world economy, that appears even more clearly. The enormous boom in U.S. imports allowed foreign manufacturers not just to get their foot in our door, but to move permanently into the buying habits of both consumers and businesses—whether for automobiles and electronics, metals or machinery. At the same time, and adding to the effects, those years did little to break the habits of U.S. businesses in terms of production or pricing: when, after 1985, the United States was able to get the Group of Seven to cooperate in lowering the value of the dollar—thereby reversing the earlier process that had "priced U.S. goods out of world markets"—the tendency of the majority of U.S. businesses was to keep or push their prices up as foreign prices (in dollar terms) also rose. The consequence was that, quite apart from quality considerations, the opportunity to win back customers was forgone for what was shortsightedly seen as a way of increasing profits. Meanwhile, other important processes continued to grind away at the strength of the United States in the world economy, whether measured in terms of trade and payments accounts, competitive strengths, or technological progress.

The stepped-up militarization of the U.S. economy promulgated by Reagan must be faulted heavily in this regard: it was, in the old saying, gilding the lily. Well before 1981, voices had begun to be raised questioning either the need or the advisability of the United States spending so much of its resources, skills, equipment, and taxpayers' dollars on the military. We shall turn to some of that criticism in discussing the role of the State in the next chapter, but here it is relevant to ponder the costs simply in terms of the balance of trade and payments, implied by some of the figures as they stood as early as 1970:

In addition to the 600,000 military men in Southeast Asia, there are 300,000 U.S. Ground and Air Forces stationed in Europe and South Korea. Tens of thousands of Americans serve in warships on the high seas. There are over 1,200,000 U.S. fighting men stationed overseas at 2,270 locations in 119 countries. Additional divisions, air forces, and fleets stand by in the continental United States prepared to execute numerous contingency plans for every area in the world deemed to be of interest to the defense and welfare of the United States and its allies.[49]

The militarization of the United States, at home and abroad, was a source of increasing economic and political strength in the decades after 1945, but only for a while. Looked at economically, it was a terrible hemorrhage of national wealth and a further plunge into social inefficiency, in what already by the 1960s had become a highly competitive world economy. It stimulated the economy, even kept it from collapse—but, as Reagan was fond of saying, "there's no such thing as a free lunch." (Except, evidently, for Reagan?)

But there were other processes at work in the same period which also, although initially beneficial to the economy, over time came to intensify the problems just discussed. By the 1960s, the most important of these were connected to the growth of the multinational, transnational, "supranational" corporation. That growth, discussed from a different standpoint in Chapter 3, has an always more complex set of effects on the functioning of the U.S. economy at home and abroad, and it deserves closer examination.

Much Bigger than a Breadbox

The twentieth century is social earthquake country: war, revolution, vast changes in social behavior, wildly contrasting periods of economic expansion and contraction, an always widening gap between rich and poor, and a constant reshuffling of socioeconomic/political forms all over the globe—north, south, east, and west. This extraordinary social turbulence recalls the seventeenth century, except that the kinds, the pace, and the spread of change in this era have been considerably more substantial, in both their constructive and destructive dimensions. Into this highly unstable world entered the MNC, the most powerful business institution ever.[50]

For a good quarter of a century now, the MNC has swarmed all over the globe—"nestling everywhere, settling everywhere, establishing connections everywhere"—seeking out the most favorable combinations of labor, resource, marketing, tax, and financial conditions. There is a great irony involved in that process: the MNC has been able and inclined to move and act as it has because of the national and global political economy of monopoly capitalism—not least the multidimensional role of the State in creating and maintaining a context favorable for capital accumulation at home and all over the world. But it is unquestionably true that the MNCs, while continuing to rely on the State for help with matters of taxes, labor, research subsidization, and foreign policy, etc., have become increasingly independent of that same State—reminding one of maturing and strengthening young people who continue to depend on their parents for this and that, but who go their own way as they do so.

The impact of this transformation has been striking, so much so that many observers now see "global monopoly capitalism" as being replaced by "global capitalism."[51] Among the most important meanings of that difference is the change in the conditions of labor: monopoly capitalism in the industrial countries meant a substantial improvement in workers' conditions—regarding their money and social wages, job security, and the like—whereas "global capitalism" has brought with it and has had as one of its principal aims a return to the labor conditions of an earlier era—a decline in material levels of life for workers in the already industrialized countries, accompanied by increased use and exploitation of workers in the rest of the world—and, of course, increased profits.[52]

Whether the MNC will function over the long term so as to strengthen world capitalism or the power of any given nation within the world structure, or tend to make things come unstuck, is presently impossible to know. The fate and the meaning of the MNC will be determined by the swirling currents of world economic and political life over the next decade or so; but what can be said already is that the MNCs constitute a major force of that "swirling." They are already the most dynamic institution at work in the world economy. They are the big business organization *par excellence*; and their strengths have been so great as to be directly responsible for the most important process shaping the world economy in the past two decades. It is the process called "restructuring." Only part of that process was looked at briefly in Chapter 3, when we noted the "hollowing out" of the U.S. corporation. Its larger significance and what accompanies it reverberates throughout each national economy, as it simultaneously transforms the functioning, even the meaning of the measures, of world economic behavior, as will now be seen.

What has been occurring through the growth and spread and strengthening of MNCs in the world may be seen as a global replaying of what happened in the U.S. economy with the rise of the giant national corporation. In the United States in this century, the main dynamics of both economic and political life have been provided by the emerging supercorporation. Much of what has happened has been in consequence of their direct needs and desires; and very little has happened that they saw as incompatible with their own interests. Labor policy, monetary and trade policies, tax and resource policies, have all changed in complicated ways throughout this century, but as they have changed they have never veered very far, for very long, from the ways found acceptable to Big Business. Is it likely that the consequences of monopoly/oligopoly in a national economy will be reproduced on a global scale by MNCs from the United States, Japan, Germany, Great Britain, and elsewhere? As of this moment, the answer would seem to be both yes and no.

Of necessity, because the scope *is* global, there are and will be important differences; but because the powers of the MNC are great and concentrated and capitalist, there have been and will be important similarities. One very important difference between the dynamics of domestic and of global concentrated economic power has already become evident: the rise of monopoly capitalism within nations carried with it the great expansion of the powers of the State, whereas the rise of "global capitalism" *transforms* the already great powers of the State, in the process reducing some of its activities (those concerned with social as distinct from corporate well-being). Furthermore, as the power of the

MNC has grown and spread the global economy, like so much of the national economies, is becoming "privatized" in its relationships: for example, as private multinational banks take the place of governmental lending, and private multinational weapons producers *sell* what was once given as "military assistance" in the Tier III nations.

The implications of these and other developments moving in the same direction are several and vital, not least those that point to increased international economic instability, and to the probability that the people of the involved nations will have an always decreasing say concerning the global role of their nation's economy, or the several meanings of that to the national economy. Limited though that role is and has always been, the people do have the *formal* political right to influence their government's policies, but no such right to affect the policies of private companies.[53]

The MNCs movement toward relative autonomy in the world economy has many sides to it, a good part of which can be discussed under the heading of "restructuring."

Item: The MNC is the ultimate in business flexibility, and its flexibility is labor's weakness. The MNC moves in and out of areas, products, and techniques with an ease hitherto unknown. Labor's greatest strength has always been the striking union. MNCs can and do reduce, redistribute, or entirely relocate production in the face of a strike, or as has been common, as a means of reducing the costs of their domestic labor force. It has become common for unions to grant concessions to the company in order to maintain jobs, and then to lose the jobs anyhow.

Item: Whether or not tariffs should be raised or lowered is a controversial matter, even with the best of intentions of all parties. With the MNCs power, however, the legitimate elements of the controversy become irrelevant. Tariffs lose their meaning when production by an MNC takes place *within* another nation's boundaries, a development that was among the stimuli to the initial growth of the MNC, especially in Europe. The only way to curb that tendency would be to erect barriers to the international flow of *capital*, something so unlikely that it has barely been discussed, let alone proposed. Organized labor, if it is to have any say at all in this or the previous matter can only hope to gain it by *organizing* internationally, at the moment a dim prospect.

Item: How do the pervasive MNCs affect the national trade and payments positions for their own countries? The MNCs, as was noted earlier, of course include virtually all the very largest corporations in the world. They are giant producers, with annual sales mounting in the trillions of dollars (GM's sales alone in 1990 were over $125 *billion*). They must constantly shuttle investment and working capital from nation to nation, and they can and must, as rational businesses, *speculate*. As financial expert Hugh Stephenson put it,

> International corporations may at any moment have an overall balance sheet in a dozen or more currencies. This gives them both the commercial *need* and the commercial *means* to protect their interests by "speculating," or (more politely) "taking positions" in the foreign exchange markets.[54]

Among the most active and largest of the MNCs are the oil companies, of course. Stephenson goes on to quote an oil company treasurer as saying "When I write a cheque, it is the bank that bounces."

A final *Item*: although probably not among the initial motivations of the forming MNCs, one of their main practices has become the evasion of their national responsibilities—not least in importance, their taxes—by their ability to conceal and/or manipulate the business activities that are *internal* to the company but *external* to its nation, through what is called "intrafirm trade." As Joyce Kolko points out,

> The growth of intrafirm trade, or foreign trade between branches of one company, is a structural feature that makes obsolete or irrelevant whole categories in international trade. In order to exploit beneficial tax arrangements, firms notoriously distort the price structure; one result is that the trade figures used to guide government policy are unreliable at best. And this form of trade is increasingly dominant: 27 percent of all U.S. exports were to subsidiaries, and 56 percent of the total imports were from affiliates in 1982, most of them representing intrafirm trade. The so-called increasing dependence of the U.S. economy on foreign trade, reported to be 25 percent in 1980, double the 1970 level, really therefore reflects transfers within U.S. MNCs.[55]

We saw in Table 7.2 that the percentage share of the United States in world exports of manufactured goods in 1984 had fallen sharply from its level in the 1950s, down to 14 percent, and that the 1984 share of U.S. MNCs in the world total was 18.1 percent, noticeably greater than that of their nation.[56] That kind of difference in itself is suggestive of the immense changes underway in today's national and global economies. Leaving much undiscussed in this area, we now pursue one further dimension of the meaning of the MNCs in the world economy, as we focus on the societies of Tier III. What does the great and growing strength of the MNC, U.S. and otherwise, mean to the relationships between the leading capitalist nations and the dependent economies of Tier III, and within the latter? Earlier, we examined some of the meanings of mercantilism, colonialism, and imperialism to the weaker societies. As we turn to the contemporary period, the focus will be on neocolonialism, and the role played in it by the MNCs, a role that has intensified the retrogressive developmental process that has been the lot of the weaker societies. By now, after all this discussion on the world economy, to say nothing of imperialism, with more still to come, it is not inappropriate for the reader to wonder "what has all this got to do with the economic history of the United States?" To which the answer has already been given, and will be given once more: the United States has dominated the world economy for the past half-century and dominates it still, despite all; and it has been and remains the principal influence in the Tier III societies, both because of its predominance among the world's MNCs and because of the influence of U.S. foreign policy in the rest of the world. We begin with some statements of the World Bank, virtually created by and still under the dominance of, the United States.

Backward into Underdevelopment

More than once in previous pages it has been argued that the structures of income, wealth, and power within capitalist nations are reproduced in the structures of rich and poor nations and peoples in the world economy. Another similarity resides in the ways in which "poverty" is defined in both the rich nations and for the poor nations (by the economists of the rich nations, usually).

The World Bank, formed in 1944 by and for the purposes of what had been and would again become among the world's most powerful nations, in its most recent report on poverty in the "developing world," after noting various instances of "enormous economic progress," finds it "staggering—and all the more shameful—that more than one billion people in the developing world are living in poverty."[57] The report goes on to define those living in poverty as having *less than $370 a year*. It is generally accepted that finding dollar and level-of-life equivalents from

nation to nation and culture to culture can at best be a rough approximation: However! Five or more times $370 would still be an annual sum
suggesting poverty, even by official U.S. measurements.[58]

There is no "developing country" in the world where the largest part of
the population does *not* live in poverty. If, as seems reasonable enough,
one means by poverty that condition where food, clothing, shelter,
medical care, and education are all absolutely and relatively terribly short
in supply, then one need merely visit any developing country to *see* the
poverty—sometimes surrounding its glistening buildings, governmental
or MNC in ownership—unless, as in Mexico City, for example, the poor
are arrested if found in the areas where visitors shop and look.

In another report accompanying that on poverty, the World Bank states:

During the past forty years many developing countries have achieved
progress at an impressive pace...[R]apid and sustained development
is no hopeless dream, but an achievable reality. Nonetheless, many
countries have done poorly, and in some living standards have
actually fallen during the past thirty years.[59]

Both the quoted statements were authored by informed and reasonable
people with good intentions, and they read that way. Both statements
could also have been made, with appropriate changes, about the United
States in the 1980s. And both were made within an outlook and an
analysis that stops short of asking some of the most important questions.
Not all will be asked here, either, but we must pause for a few. Why,
after "forty years of development" are there still—taking their figures as
valid—a billion people seeking to live on less than $370 a year? And
why only forty years? The rich nations have been assisting these areas
toward development for at least five centuries—from Columbus and the
soldiers, merchants, and priests accompanying or following him, to the
British carrying their "White Man's Burden" and the French their
"civilizing mission," to ourselves in the Philippines, where "our little
brown brothers" were "unfit for self-government [and so] there was
nothing left for us to do but to take them all [the islands] and to educate
the Filipinos, and uplift and civilize and Christianize them, and by God's
grace do the very best we could by them, as our fellow men for whom
Christ also died. And then I went to bed and went to sleep and slept
soundly."[60]

There was never an intention on the part of the outsiders to seek means for making the "host" societies stronger; quite the contrary, the aims were of course to strengthen the individuals and/or the nations of the outsiders, no matter what. And where there was any kind of concern for the peoples of Asia, Africa, Latin America, or the Middle East on the part of the Spanish, the British, the Germans, the Japanese, or, among others, ourselves, it was in the spirit of the missionary: to make them over in their own image—religiously, politically, ideologically, culturally, whatever. Nowadays, sometimes the missionary spirit continues, but less and less so over time, as the representative of the MNC replaces the true missionary, the politician, the ideologue, whomever.

A vast literature on the overseas activities of the major powers has emerged in the past century (to go back no further). An interesting aspect of that literature is that it almost always views the relationship between the powerful and the weak societies from the standpoint of the powerful, with little or no inquiry into what even *happens* in the "host" country. Beginning with J.A. Hobson's influential *Imperialism*, and going to Veblen's *The Nature of Peace* and Lenin's *Imperialism*, the focus was on the whys and wherefores of imperialism for the metropolis —Hobson seeing "the taproot of imperialism" as "the unequal distribution of income" in the industrial nation (Britain, for him), Veblen seeing it in much the same way, as an outcome of excess productive capacity and the need to use it somehow or another to maintain profits and power, and Lenin, much influenced by Hobson (even though the latter was not even a radical, let alone a revolutionary) seeing imperialism as "the highest stage of capitalism," wherein monopoly, financialization, and international competition for colonial areas' resources and investment outlets combined to push the major powers toward world war.[61]

Except for an occasional study emanating from someone from the colonized areas (e.g., R. Palme Dutt, in India), it was not until after World War II, and in the context of the growing and strong push for independence from the imperialized nations, on the one hand, and the developing movement of neocolonialism, on the other, that a literature began to develop that places the analysis in the countries of Tier III, and examines just that, and/or the relationships between the two sets of nations, with the emphasis on the weaker country. Included in such works have been important studies seeking to understand the socio-pscychological and political responses of imperialized peoples, such as Frantz Fanon's important *Wretched of the Earth*. But our attention must be confined to the political economy of the processes in general, and then, more specifically, with two fundamental, worsening, and illuminating crises of the Tier III countries: hunger and debt.

The Political Economy of Underdevelopment

Among the most enlightening of the post-World War II analyses have been those of Paul Baran, André Gunder Frank, and Samir Amin. Baran, writing in the 1950s, although his focus was on the imperializing powers and most specifically on the United States, developed an analysis that shed important new light on the meaning of that imperialization on the "host" countries: a disruptive and forced push into *under*development. Frank, having lived in Latin America most of his life, carried Baran's work further, and went beyond it to develop "dependency theory." And Samir Amin, an Egyptian, brought these and other works together while pushing ahead further with his own analysis of "unequal development."[62] We shall content ourselves below with a summary of Frank's analysis of dependency—the main link between the powerful and the weak societies that helps to explain the origins, persistence, and almost constant deterioration of their weak economies and powerless societies.

Frank's elucidation of the great and systematically growing gap between rich and poor nations moves within several hypotheses: *First,* "in contrast to the development of the world metropolis, which is no one's satellite, the development of the national and other subordinate metropoles is limited by their satellite status." The latter are the underdeveloped countries. *Second,* "the satellites experience their greatest economic development and their most classically capitalist industrial development if and when their ties to the metropolis are weakest." (As, for example, during the depression of the 1930s, or during the two world wars.) When the ties regain their strength, Frank argues, *under*development once more ensues. *Third,* "the regions which are the most underdeveloped and feudal-seeming today are the ones that had the closest ties to the metropolis in the past." Related to these hypotheses are two more: *Fourth,* what are thought of as latifundia or haciendas today (the "feudal-seeming" plantations) were born as *commercial* enterprises in the dim past; and, *fifth,* the decline of these plantations as viable institutions is due to a decline in the demand for their products. Summing up, Frank concludes that the economies and the societies of Tier III (especially those of Latin America, his main focus) have undergone a process of deterioration and distortion because of their coerced relationships with the developed countries. They have gone backward into underdevelopment. Whatever else that process has meant, it has transformed by far the largest part of the Tier III countries (1) from being societies with relatively low per capita incomes to dependent nations whose people are mostly impoverished, undernourished, hungry, or starving; and (2) from independent groups of people classified not by their "nationality" but by their clan, tribe, culture, etc., into "nations," that are not only dependent in the senses of Frank's analysis, but, as the latest stage in that condition of dependency, choked by debt—whose total in 1989 "...seems to have stabilized at $1.3 trillion, about 50 percent [of third world] GNP. Adjusted for inflation, it is about 25 percent larger than it was in 1982."[63]

Too Many People?

In this world of crowded cities, clogged streets, and long lines for rock concert tickets, it is easy to be persuaded that such problems or irritations would vanish if there were fewer people. Such notions are transformed into angry convictions when we read of the five billion or more people, all too many of them already hungry or starving, who will soon be seven and then ten and then fifteen billion people—most of them, of course, in Asia, Africa, and Latin America. So what if they are hungry? Wasn't Malthus right? Isn't it their own fault, after all? At the limit, as mathematicians might say, such ideas are correct: if there were *no* people, there would be no problems. But here we all are; and despite the wishes of some to the contrary (those with the best seats), we are all in the same boat.

So even if those angry ideas were right, and we'll try to show they are not, the problems would remain, and would *have* to be resolved. It is important to understand at the outset that if our problems *were* caused by "too many people" they would be impossible to resolve—even by genocidal tactics going utterly beyond anything possible: such ideas, in short, are a message of despair, easily translatable into a message of hate and fear. Fortunately, there are positive and mutually beneficial steps that can be taken; and they are compatible with our sense of morality, if also at odds with contemporary practices.

Whether it's crowded streets and long lines or those "more than 14 million children [who] are now dying every year"[64] from starvation or diseases whose origin is malnutrition, in all cases mentioned and others like them, the problems are a function of social institutions that are neither necessary nor, in their relevant respects, desirable. "Certainly there are too many people in some parts of the world," says economist and Nobel laureate Robert Solow, "but there is hardly any doubt that modern technology could make it possible for all of them to be adequately fed."[65]

Without further ado, I shall proceed to assert that the tragedy of world hunger, growing always worse, amounts to a vast social crime, and no less so because, like manslaughter, it is unintended. World hunger is unnecessary, the consequence of interacting individuals, groups, companies, and governments which, seeking one form or another of private or public advantage (profits, national or foreign political gain, etc.) have transformed an abundant nature into a human and social disaster. This assertion will first be supported by a simple listing and summary quotation from some of the "twelve myths" of world hunger, as put forth and analyzed in the valuable book of Frances Moore Lappé and Joseph Collins.[66]

1. "There's Simply Not Enough Food." But abundance, not scarcity, best describes the supply of food in the world today. Increases in food production since about 1960 have outstripped the world's unprecedented population growth by about 16 percent. Even though enough food exists, the poor are not able to purchase it. Even in the richest nation of all, the United States, at least 20 million people cannot afford a healthy diet and more than an eighth of the poor children are stunted by malnutrition. But who can argue that not enough food is produced? Surely not U.S. farmers; overproduction is their most persistent headache. Nor the U.S. government, which has to store enough surplus cheese, milk, and butter to provide every citizen with almost 50 pounds, and enough surplus wheat to bake nearly seven loaves of bread for every human being on earth.

2. "Nature's To Blame." It is convenient to believe that droughts and other events "beyond human control" cause famine. Rather, it is human-made forces that make people increasingly vulnerable to nature's vagaries. Pushed onto marginal lands or deprived of land altogether, in debt to usurers who claim most of their harvests, so poorly paid that nothing is left to fall back on, and weakened by chronic hunger, millions die. Natural events are not the cause. They are the final blow, often accompanied, as in mid-19th century Ireland, by inhuman policies—"Am I right to harbor the thought that only Victorian England could let the Irish starve with the comforting thought that it was for their own good?"

asks Solow,[67] in the review noted earlier—or by war, civil war, or a punishing State, as in Ethiopia.

3. "Too Many Mouths To Feed." Must we slow population growth before we can hope to alleviate hunger? This is not the same question as, "Is it desirable to slow population growth?" The answer to the latter question for many reasons, large and small, is a very firm "yes," but to the first question, "no." Surveying the globe, there is in fact *no* correlation between population density and hunger. For every Bangladesh, a densely populated and hungry country, we find a Brazil or a Senegal, where significant food resources per capita coexist with intense hunger. Or we find a densely populated country like the Netherlands, where very little land per person has not prevented it from eliminating hunger and becoming a large net *exporter* of food. Since there is not a correlation between population density and hunger, it may be argued that hunger and rapid population growth occur together because they have a common cause. The common cause is the powerlessness of the poor.[68]

4. "It's Food *versus* the Environment." Unquestionably, crop and livestock production has been and is being pushed into marginal, erosion-prone lands, and has torn down age-old rain forests, while the environment is also being poisoned by pesticides. But neither the principal motivation behind these activities nor any significant part of their results has been to alleviate world hunger. If such harmful activities occurred in the course of a policy aimed squarely at reducing world hunger, environmentally damaging actions—including, incidentally the much praised "Green Revolution"[69]—would be slowed substantially or halted entirely as failures. Instead of blaming the hungry for wrecking the environment, we should seek to answer questions such as: "Why are peasants denied productive agricultural land and forced onto lands that should not be farmed or resettled in rain forests?" "Why are big operators allowed—and even publicly subsidized—to tear down tropical rain forests?" "Why do most farmers who use chemical fertilizers and pesticides think they cannot afford the risk of shifting to less chemical-intensive methods?" "If desertified areas are helped to regenerate, who will control the process, who will benefit, and who will lose?" "Why are environmentally sound alternatives for food production little known and even suppressed rather than fostered?" "Can humanity afford to treat food and the resources to produce it just like any other commodity?"

5. "It's Justice *versus* Production." One of the outcomes of industrialism has been a cult of bigness: bigger means more efficient. That is

wrong, as also the opposite is wrong. In industry and in agriculture (among other areas) bigness works well for this, but not for that; here, but not there. Studies of both sectors have shown this time and again. Looking here only at food production, it is well-known that the biggest landowners, especially (but not only) in Tier III societies, cultivate only a small percentage of their arable land—for example, only 14 percent in Central America. That is high inefficiency in itself. But even comparing productivity between large and small farms in terms of the land actually cultivated (rather than all that is owned), the small farm is significantly more (or at least as) efficient—whether in Tier III or in the United States. Still, it is natural to believe, don't those large farms *really* function more efficiently in terms of dollars invested, even if not in per acre yields? Not if you take into account, especially in the United States, the preferential access of agribusiness to credit, irrigation, chemical fertilizers, pesticides, technical assistance, and marketing services, much of that being paid for by taxpayers (including the taxes of the smaller farmer). The smaller farms tend to have higher productivity because they are worked largely by their owners, who literally put in more and better time than hired labor.

6. "The Free Market Can End Hunger." That was the comforting (and enforced) thought of the British in the deadly Irish famine of the 1840s. Not to believe that does not imply that one believes "the unfree market can end hunger." It is to recognize that there is not and has not been a free agricultural market in memory. The only question is in which of the many ways the market is interfered with, by whom, and for whom, and with what consequences. In our preceding chapter concerning U.S. agricultural policy, it was related that the free market was interfered with at its root with land policy, and then transportation policy, and monetary policy, and trade policy, and finally—when all that taken together wouldn't do it for the farmers—with farm policy: all at the behest of agricultural business, which otherwise believes in the free market. And so it is still, also for Western Europe and Japan and *all* the Tier III nations. After interference with the basics is accomplished, "individual preferences" take over: purchasing power takes over. And we're back where we were some paragraphs ago: poverty, powerlessness, and hunger.

To bring this to a close, a few generalizations, made in the hope that the reader will continue to pursue the abundant literature. First, by now it should be clear that the connection between rising production and lowering world hunger does not exist, any more than it did for rising

GNP in the United States in the 1980s, as poverty and lowered incomes also increased. What matters is who controls the production and its technology, who does the work, and who gets the rewards. Secondly, even when reforms take place, land reforms among them, unless they are accompanied by an increase in the purchasing power of the poorest, hunger will be unabated. Thirdly, in the words of Susan George,

The only available choices are self-reliance or dependency. If governments of poor nations continue to walk the road of food aid, the MNCs or the World Bank, they do so in the full knowledge that solutions offered for their problems will continue to be technocratic and exploitative and that all the strings will be pulled by outsiders. Doubtless for such governing élites even total loss of dignity and national self-hood is preferable to loss of power and of a comfortable life. Others have learned that there is honour in austerity, that charity is no substitute for justice and that nothing can equal the people's strength when their leaders have the courage to speak a single word to their would-be masters: No.[70]

Too Much Debt

It was noted earlier that there has been a "privatization" process for Tier III debt. In the years after World War II, as the United States and, in time, other industrialized countries "assisted in the development" of the Tier III countries, there was also a rising tide of government grants and subsidized (low-interest) intergovernmental loans. This went on in substantial quantities up through the 1960s, aided and abetted competitively as the Soviet Union was doing something similar in its bloc of countries. But as was also noted earlier, by the close of the 1960s excess productive capacity was becoming pervasive in the industrial capitalist world, and in the 1970s it was a serious problem: the stagnation half of stagflation.

Thus, beginning in the late 1960s, mostly at first in the United States, bankers' pressures were placed upon governments to reduce their grants and loans in order to make room for private banks to do the lending—at considerably higher interest rates. As the "petrodollars" resulting from oil price increases in the early and late 1970s piled up in banks, the pressures continually increased—until they were no longer necessary.[71]

For those who are borrowers—almost everyone—it takes a mental effort to understand that bankers become desperate when they run short of those to whom they can lend. Their main source of income is, of course, the interest payments they receive on loans; excess reserves for banks are like excess capacity for industry. As the crisis of the 1970s emerged and continued, the banks could not put money out at interest in adequate amounts in their own countries; consequently, they became eager hustlers of credit to most of the Tier III and to some of the noncapitalist countries, such as Poland and Cuba.

Interest rates initially, though high in nominal terms were not so in real terms, that is, after adjustment for inflation. But as the 1970s went on, the Tier III countries were undone by the fact that the interest rates had been contracted for as being variable to move up with inflation—an inflation that continually worsened beyond expectations. Real rates for the borrowing countries became murderously high as inflation mounted and moved toward catastrophe when the dollar began to soar (especially for the oil importing Tier III countries)—for all oil sales and most Tier III loans are denominated in dollars. In the 1980s, the dollar, inflation, oil prices, and interest rates all declined, but so did the export prices (and usually the exports) of Tier III, so they were helped not at all.

What the increase in debt and the cost of servicing the debt came down to for the Tier III countries was a blow to their already weak economies. Although almost everyone believes that the Tier I and II countries export capital to Tier III, and thereby "assist" in their development, the statistics show an increasing "negative transfer," a flow of capital from poor to the rich nations. That outflow, which was already great, at about $38 billion in 1987, jumped to over $50 billion in 1988, leading one World Bank official to see, in his own words, that "the situation in the Third World is getting worse, not better."[72]

The outstanding debt of Tier III, noted above, is something over $1.3 trillion. A good share of that debt is "manageable," perhaps half of it. The rest varies from problematic to insoluble. The hard-core is about half a trillion, four-fifths of which is owed by Mexico, Argentina, Brazil, and Venezuela, and two-thirds of that is owed to private banks, mostly in the United States. Mexico went into default in 1982, only the first of many, all for the same set of reasons: as the demand and prices for their production have fallen in the world economy, the debtor countries earn less and owe more and borrow just to make interest payments; they are on a treadmill that takes them ever faster toward financial and economic, perhaps political, collapse.

To make matters worse, the uses to which the massive loans were put rarely yielded projects that enhanced the economic life of the debtor country or its ability to repay:

For the most part, the loans financed...pharaonic construction projects, the military budgets of repressive governments, high living by the Third World elites, capital flight—i.e., investment in wealthy-country assets by Third World elites—and especially, the payment of interest and principal on the debt itself.[73]

It sounds a bit like what has been going on in the process that transformed the United States from a creditor to a debtor country—consumer and military binges, lots of corruption and lots of interest to pay. The recklessness that attended the search for borrowers in Tier III was matched in the United States by the recklessness of the borrowers: the U.S. government, a very large number of junk-bond selling corporations and, of course, "creditworthy" consumers borrowing to shop 'til they dropped.

Fortunately for the people of the United States—as matters now stand—we are the Tier I nation, and we can borrow without what has come to be called "conditionality"—that is, the conditions set, mostly by or through the IMF, that must be met for gaining more credit for staying or getting out of default. It all surfaced with Mexico in 1982, and has come to be called "debt restructuring" —a delicate euphemism for default. Debt restructuring means that the point of default has been passed, and that formal default—which in the banking world is in the same category as patricide—is postponed by placing an indefinite moratorium on the repayment of principal, usually a limited moratorium on interest payments, and/or a special loan for the payment of interest and to keep the debtor country's economy functioning. This is accompanied by "conditions": an austerity program that lowers social expenditures and/or imports and/or consumption, while allowing unemployment to rise: all this in societies with already desperately low levels of life and desperately high levels of unemployment. And it leaves untouched the heedlessness of all concerned, those at the top at both ends, and forces those at the bottom to shoulder the human and social costs.

Already by 1985 it was clear that the opposite of progress was taking place, and Reagan's Treasury Secretary put forth the "Baker Plan," meant to "swap" debt for a variety of other presumably more attractive financial assets, but which never got off the ground. By 1989 the results of private and public policies were clearly doing little to prevent an explosive economic and political situation exacerbated by Tier III debt. So Bush's Treasury Secretary put forth the "Brady Plan," for the gradual reduction of debt principal and debt interest—in effect, an admission that the debt could never be paid off, and that Tier III and the rest of the world would be in more trouble if they had to pay all the interest than if they didn't.

The Brady Plan, as a step toward realism, was an improvement over its predecessor. Like the former, it was widely acclaimed. At the most optimistic it was hoped that the program might begin to have beneficial effects within a few years—depending, as it does, on the cooperation of private banks (who must write off assets and mark down income), central banks, and governments.

Some of that began to happen in 1990, until interrupted by the recession that began in the United States in the summer of 1990, and in most of the world economy a bit before or soon after. Naturally the recession has hit the Tier III countries harder than the rich nations. So their needs for what the Brady Plan proposed have multiplied at the same time that what some think of as the "generosity" of the rich nations has virtually disappeared. "An end to the debt crisis remains elusive," said the World Bank in December 1988. It seems even more so now.[74]

We'll All Go Together When We Go

Comprehension of the afflictions of the Tier III countries leads some concerned people to shrug and turn away from what seems to be an impossibly tangled and hopeless situation. Others seek solutions that depend upon the good will of the rich countries or revolution in the poor countries. All these and more have been done, while the problems deepen and innumerable lives remain and always more become "nasty, brutish, and short." Is there no good way out of this immense disaster?

A way out can be specified, and some of its bare elements will be momentarily. Clearly, and unfortunately, any hopeful set of processes for Tier III countries requires at the very least the recognition and acceptance of what has been seen as *fact* in the foregoing pages: the relationships between the rich and the poor nations have not only been entirely to the advantage of the former and the detriment of the latter, they would not have been created and endured otherwise. The processes we have been discussing are systematic, and even though their disastrous outcomes have not been *willed*, the ways and means that created them have been "normal," persistent, and ubiquitous. Quite simply, the rest of the world has been seen as ripe for exploitation of one sort or another, in one way or another, in one place or another, for many centuries. The capitalist world economy has heedlessly functioned so as to ruin and distort the Tier III societies, bringing malnutrition and starvation to their people, and also, a final point, to contribute decisively to their militarization. This deserves a brief elaboration, not just because it has been so harmful, but it is also among the easier of the deadly processes to end. And that will also end this chapter.

We have dwelt much on the military in preceding pages. The Tier III nations, because they have not been independent politically until recently, and because they remain dependent economically, have been roiled for all the post-World War II years (at least) by internal movements seeking basic change, and by the "carrots and sticks" thrust at, usually imposed upon, them by the major actors in the Cold War. Their rulers and their governments have ineluctably been shaped by those processes. And all too many of them have wasted precious resources on military expenditures and activity. "Them" means who? The ordinary people of such countries? No, it means their governments, as often as not corrupted and authoritarian, also explicable by their histories as colonies. Be that as it may, of the $1 trillion of military expenditures in the world every year, at least a third of that is made by Tier III countries. They have been given their arms through the Cold War, and they have also bought them on their own.

Although, and in part because, the Cold War is over, arms sales to Tier III countries continue and, if the sellers have their way, will expand. "It's mainly Middle East purchases that are giving U.S. arms manufacturers a boost," says *Business Week*, in its story (November 25, 1991) "A New World Order for U.S. Arms Makers," but "mainly" leaves not only the purchasers but users in much of Latin America, Africa, and Asia. Most of the weaponry in the Tier III societies is purchased not for war with others, but to keep the peace at home—and to buttress the incomes and power of the military elites.[75] If the United States cannot afford the waste entailed by military expenditures, even less can those of Tier III countries, some appearances to the contrary notwithstanding.

The central point remains that what goes on in Tier III takes place on a stage created by Tiers I and II, over the centuries. Some of the lines spoken might have occurred without colonialism, imperialism, and neocolonialism—but not many, and not the most devastating. Whether it is hunger, or debt, or military expenditures, or distorted economies and ruined environments, the main lines have been written and directed by the main powers. The biggest "assistance" that can be given to the Tier III societies is to be left alone—or, more usefully, for virtually none want to be left entirely alone, to be left to their own devices, to receive only what they ask for, and when, and how, and why. If there is aid given by the rich, it should be administered through agencies clearly dominated by poor countries; and hopefully such agencies might have as one guiding criterion that the countries receiving aid be seeking greater self-reliance within an always more democratic society, involving, if that were so, their own poor in the decision-making process. With economic self-reliance and increased democracy, decreased militarization could and should follow (or precede). This in turn means that the Tier III countries need to alter the relationships between *themselves* in at least two ways: they must search for ways to diminish whatever hostilities and differences they have between them, over boundaries and other matters; and they must learn to cooperate economically, to build "common markets," share facilities, etc., so as to reduce dependence upon their historical exploiters.[76]

Of course, all that is "idealistic," "unrealistic," out of the question, etc. Probably. But could this suggestion be any less realistic than the belief—what C. Wright Mills called "crackpot realism"—that the institutions and attitudes that have brought the world to its present condition could, with modest changes, commence to have acceptable rather than their customary and long-standing devastating consequences? One would not wish to bet one's life on it.

Whatever the future will bring, the State will have been in the midst of its delivery, either as obstacle or helpmate—and most likely as some combination of both. We next turn to an examination of that complex beast.

Reading Suggestions

A good place to begin on the world economy is William Ashworth, *A Short History of the World Economy Since 1850* (London: Longmans, 1987), an unexciting but comprehensive summary of the main developments of the past 150 years or more. In addition to the many readings already cited, a clear and readable study of the rise and slowing of U.S.

power in the world economy is Walter Russell Mead, *Mortal Splendor: The American Empire in Transition* (Boston: Houghton Mifflin, 1987). William A. Williams examines the first and continuing steps of the United States into overseas imperialism in his influential *The Tragedy of American Diplomacy** (New York: Dell, 1962), and Herbert Feis, *The Diplomacy of the Dollar, 1919–1932** (Baltimore: Johns Hopkins University Press, 1950; Norton paperback, 1966) is a useful study of that brief period when the United States first put its feet in the waters of world economic dominance. In *The Limits of Power: The World and United States Foreign Policy, 1945–1954** (New York: Harper & Row, 1972), Joyce and Gabriel Kolko provide an intense analysis of those crucial years for essentially the same matters.

The foreign policies of the United States in the Cold War years have been many sided—geographically, economically, politically, etc. Some useful studies on those complexities are Carl Oglesby and Richard Shaull, *Containment and Change** (New York: Macmillan, 1967), which traces the Cold War back to 1917; Walter LaFeber, *America, Russia, and the Cold War* (New York: John Wiley and Sons, 1967) and also his *Inevitable Revolutions* (New York: W. W. Norton, 1984), concerned with Central America; James J. Petras, et al., *Latin America: Bankers, Generals, and the Struggle for Social Justice* (Totawa, N.J.: Rowman and Allenheld, 1986). As the war in Indochina became central to the United States, Noam Chomsky, a noted linguist at M.I.T., turned his attention more and more to U.S. foreign policy. Among his many important and illuminating critiques are *American Power and the New Mandarins* (New York: Vintage, 1969), *For Reasons of State* (New York: Vintage, 1973), and among many other books by himself and with Edward S. Herman, *The Washington Connection and Third World Fascism* (Boston: South End Press, 1979), and (cited earlier) *Manufacturing Consent*. See also Herman's *Beyond Hypocrisy: Decoding the News in an Age of Propaganda** (Boston: Smith End Press, 1992), concerned largely but not entirely with foreign affairs.

Vital to the functioning of the world economy for the entire century, but especially in its last half, has been the control of oil. I note four books, all useful, but with varying viewpoints: Michael Tanzer, *The Political Economy of International Oil and the Underdeveloped Countries** (Boston: Beacon Press, 1969), Robert Engler, *The Politics of Oil** (Chicago: University of Chicago Press, 1961), Anthony Sampson, *The Seven Sisters** (New York: Viking, 1875), and M.A. Adelman, *The*

World Petroleum Market, noted earlier. The international oil companies, the "seven sisters" among them, are of course among the most important MNCs in the world economy. R.J. Barnet and Ronald Muller, in their *Global Reach: The Power of the Multinational Corporations* (New York: Simon & Schuster, 1975) have provided a broad survey and analysis that shows how, on balance, the MNCs are damaging to the Tier III societies, whatever their mixed effects "at home."

Joyce Kolko, in her *America and the Crisis of World Capitalism* (Boston: Beacon Press, 1974) is helpful on the MNC, and even more so in her perceptions of the developing crisis of the 1970s—which led her subsequently to write the important *Restructuring,* noted earlier. Among the many enlightening studies of the various elements of that crisis, I note the following: Susan Strange and Roger Tooze, eds., *The International Politics of Surplus Capacity* (London: Allen & Unwin, 1981), and her *Casino Capitalism,* noted earlier; Chris C. Carvounis, *The United States Trade Deficit of the 1980s: Origins, Meanings, and Policy Responses* (New York: Quorum Books, 1983); Yann Fit, Alexandre Faire, and Jean-Pierre Vigier, *The World Economic Crisis* (London: Zed Press, 1976); and the important work of Stephen Marris, *Dollars and Deficits* (Washington, D.C.: International Economic Institute, 1985) and his follow-up, *Deficits and the Dollar Revisited: August 1987* (same publisher, 1987). Observing these matters more from the political than the economic viewpoint is David Calleo, *Beyond Hegemony: The Future of the Western Alliance* (New York: Basic Books, 1987).

A few more books on hunger: Jon Bennett, *The Hunger Machine: The Politics of Food* (New York: Blackwell, 1987), Susan George, *Feeding the Few: Corporate Control of Food,* and her *Ill Fares the Land: Essays on Food, Hunger, and Power* (both Washington, D.C.: Institute for Policy Studies, 1979 and 1984, respectively), and Michael Franklin, *Rich Man's Farming: The Crisis in Agriculture* (London: Routledge, 1988).

For further reading on Tier III debt (among some other connected matters), see Howard M. Wachtel, *The Money Mandarins* (New York: Pantheon, 1986), Martin Mayer, *The Money Bazaars* (New York: E.P. Dutton, 1984), Peter Korner, et al., *The IMF and the Debt Crisis: A Guide to the Third World's Dilemma* (London: Zed Books, 1986), Teresa Hayter and Cathy Watson, *Aid: Rhetoric and Reality* (London: Pluto Press, 1985), Cheryl Payer, *The Debt Trap: The IMF and the Third World* and *The World Bank: A Critical Analysis* (New York: Monthly Review Press, 1975 and 1982, respectively).

Finally, the literature on colonialism and its variations up to the present is enormous. The bibliography of Stavrianos, *Global Rift*, is probably the most comprehensive and useful for consultation. Meanwhile, a few suggestions on its theory and practices. A wonderful book, written by a man who was killed in Cambodia, is Malcolm Caldwell, *The Wealth of Some Nations** (London: Zed Press, 1977). In addition to Kemp, *Theories of Imperialism*, cited earlier, see R. Owen and B. Sutcliffe, eds., *Studies in the Theory of Imperialism* (London: Longman, 1972), Arghiri Emmanuel, *Unequal Exchange: A Study of the Imperialism of Trade** (New York: Monthly Review Press, 1972).

Slave trading and sugar cultivation both predate the capitalist period, of course, but it may be said that their coming together in the dawning years of capitalism was comparable to the "critical mass" in nuclear fission: from then on, the two took on an explosive development as clearly shown in Sidney W. Mintz, *Sweetness and Power: The Place of Sugar in Modern History*, noted earlier. For a narrow and penetrating study of those developments in a principal area, see R.B. Sheridan, *Sugar and Slavery: An Economic History of The British West Indies, 1623–1775* (Baltimore: Johns Hopkins University Press, 1974). On Africa, an excellent way to begin is with Walter Rodney, *How Europe Underdeveloped Africa* (Washington, D.C.: Howard University Press, 1974). Gunnar Myrdal, *Asian Drama: An Inquiry into the Poverty of Nations,** 3 vols. (New York: Pantheon Press, 1968) has deservedly become the classic work.

Those who started the whole overseas expansion into Africa and Asia were the Portuguese, and the process is well-examined in C.R. Boxer, *The Portuguese Seaborne Empire, 1415–1825* (New York: Alfred A. Knopf, 1969). Celso Furtado, *Economic Development of Latin America: A Survey from Colonial Times to the Cuban Revolution* (Cambridge: Cambridge University Press, 1970) is the best starting-point for understanding that long and continuing history.

For insights into a vital aspect of neocolonialism, see Herbert I. Schiller, *Mass Communications and American Empire* (Boston: Beacon Press, 1971) and *Communications and Cultural Domination* (White Plains, N.Y.: International Arts and Sciences Press, 1976).

And last, for an understanding of the terrible role played by the United States in the unauthorized war in Cambodia, see William Shawcross, *Sideshow: Kissinger, Nixon, and the Destruction of Cambodia** (New York: Simon & Schuster, 1979).

Notes

1. Robinson Jeffers, *Shine, Perishing Republic,* from *Selected Poems* by Robinson Jeffers. Copyright 1925 and renewed 1953 by Robinson Jeffers. Reprinted by permission of Random House, Inc.

2. Accumulation is made less expensive for business by the State when it subsidizes research, industrial parks, training, etc.; it otherwise supports accumulation directly and indirectly by providing markets for both consumer and capital goods and services. See O'Connor, *Fiscal Crisis of the State,* cited earlier, especially Chapters 1, 4, and 5.

3. See Edwards, et al., *Capitalist System,* pp. 99–118 for a useful general discussion of these points.

4. This characterization may be confusing for those familiar with the notions of "First, Second, and Third World nations." That terminology grew out of the Bandung Conference of Nonaligned Nations in the 1950s. The "First World" were the capitalist, the "Second" the communist, and the "Third World" were the nonaligned nations. In the ensuing decades that terminology has come to be used for a variety of purposes; in any case, it does not serve the same purposes as the classification used here. What does overlap is the system used by Wallerstein, op. cit., who speaks of "core, semi-periphery, and peripheral" societies. The first would include my Tiers I and II, and the others would be mostly Tier III. The nations that have presumed to function outside the capitalist orbit—such as China, Cuba, what has been the Soviet Union, etc.—are not included in the three tiers. This does not mean they have not been at all affected by the capitalist world economy; it does mean that they have not been *integrated* into that economy, that their participation has been very much residual, partial, and quite frequently against their will—also negatively, as in the embargoed countries of Cuba and Vietnam. All this may or may not be changing in the near future.

5. The Scandinavians were Tier II, industrial without empires (except in the deep past), and the Spanish and Portuguese were imperial without (until quite recently) much industry, neither Tier II nor Tier III. Classification systems can be all-inclusive perhaps, as in botany, but that is not seen as necessary or desirable for present purposes.

6. And to recall the works of Van Alstyne and W.A. Williams, noted earlier.

7. As will be seen, heavy borrowing is not new to us in the world economy; it was characteristic, necessary, and fruitful throughout the

nineteenth century. But then we were a rapidly expanding and improving economy, and the borrowing was to finance accumulation and development. In the more recent period, the heavy foreign borrowing has been accompanied by heavy domestic borrowing, the sum and substance of both to finance military and consumer expenditures. Here as so often, whether or not figures lie, they seldom by themselves provide understanding.

8. A fine brief introduction to this complicated subject is James O'Connor, "The Meaning of Economic Imperialism," in a collection of his essays, *The Corporations and the State** (New York: Harper & Row, 1974). A recent and powerful book that explores both the theoretical and the practical, the historical and the contemporary functioning of the capitalist world economy in ways both similar to and quite different from my own presentation is Joyce Kolko, *Restructuring the World Economy** (New York: Pantheon, 1988). Further reference to this fine study will be made when the period since the 1970s is examined, but it would be worthwhile now for the reader to consult the "Introduction," pp. 3–15 for an overview.

9. Eli Heckscher, *Mercantilism* (London: Allen & Unwin, 1935), 2 vols., is the basic work. But see his brief discussion in the *Encyclopaedia of the Social Sciences*. Perry Anderson's *Lineages of the Absolute State*, cited earlier, is indispensable for these developments.

10. Maurice Dobb, *Political Economy and Capitalism* (London: Routledge, 1973), pp. 239–40.

11. Following André Gunder Frank, whose work will be utilized later in this chapter, we shall argue that capitalist control of what became colonial/imperialist areas transformed *un*development into *under*development—that is, a relatively stable into a retrogressive process, areas with low levels of self-sufficiency into poverty-stricken lands.

12. Joseph A. Schumpeter, *Imperialism and Social Classes* (New York: Kelley, 1951), pp. 7, 83. Edited and with an introduction by Paul M. Sweezy. (Originally written in 1919.)

13. O'Connor, "The Meaning of Economic Imperialism," pp. 155–56.

14. *The Theory of Business Enterprise*, pp. 286–87. Veblen's attention to such matters is most sustained and intense in his *An Inquiry Into the Nature of Peace** (New York: Macmillan, 1917).

15. Tom Kemp, *Theories of Imperialism* (London: Dobson, 1967), pp. 165–66. As a survey of various theories of imperialism, this is by far the very best book of its kind.

16. *Social Policy* (September/October 1970). The quote is from Magdoff's part of an exchange between himself and S.M. Miller, Roy Bennett, and Cyril Alapatt, "Does the U.S. Economy Require Imperialism?" Magdoff's part is also reproduced in *Monthly Review* (October and November 1970), as "The Logic of Imperialism."

17. Spain in the sixteenth and France in the eighteenth century constitute seeming exceptions to this generalization: compared to either the Dutch or the British economies, both were institutionally and technologically retarded. Yet each in its time was seemingly "the leader," and that by the virtue of military prowess—at the cost, however, in both cases, of distorting what would in the longer run be more rewarding economic relationships. And both achieved their power before capitalism had become a powerful and irreversible process.

18. Garrett Mattingly, *Renaissance Diplomacy** (London: Cape, 1955; Penguin, 1965), p. 24. Up until about 1400, he points out, the West "still thought of itself as one society. Christendom was torn by the gravest internal conflicts, by religious schism, doctrinal dispute, and the endemic warfare of class against class.... But Latin Christendom knew itself to be one" (p. 16).

19. *Capital*, vol. I, p. 751.

20. *Religion and the Rise of Capitalism*, p. 67. In the long quote concerning destruction in our preceding chapter that begins "Nourished by the growth of peaceful commerce...." and goes on to the pestilence and famine "re-established by political art," it is Antwerp Tawney has been discussing.

21. Excellent histories of the period of Iberian and Dutch dominance are J.H. Parry, *The Spanish Seaborne Empire* (New York: Knopf, 1966) and C.R. Boxer, *The Dutch Seaborne Empire* (New York: Knopf, 1965). Toward the end of the eighteenth century and in the beginning of the nineteenth, the Dutch, while remaining rich, maintained their wealth and income through finance (lending abroad, especially to rising Britain) and their colonial possessions, particularly the Netherlands East Indies, most of which became Indonesia, in 1948. But in that same period of decline mixed with wealth, the Dutch also allowed unemployment and poverty to become serious and persistent. Those interested in painting will also know that Flemish and Dutch painting flourished along with the periods of economic strength, and for some time after.

22. So, "beggar thy neighbor." Quoted in Heckscher, *Mercantilism*, vol. 2, pp. 26–27.

23. This was a proud slogan of the British; in the late nineteenth century for the Germans, the counterpart slogan was to find "a place in the sun."

24. A most illuminating approach to the relationships between economic and military power has been provided by Frederic C. Lane, the great economic historian of (especially) the Mediterranean world, in the four essays that comprise Part Three of his *Venice and History: The Collected Papers of Frederic C. Lane* (Baltimore: Johns Hopkins Press, 1966). The leading concept in Lane's analysis is "protection rents and costs," where rent (as used by economists) is a return to monopoly—in this case the monopoly of organized violence—and the costs are those of military supremacy. His analysis fits the processes of the growing and lessening strength of the United States very closely, although he did not write with that as an evident focus.

25. See Ross J.S. Hoffman, *Great Britain and the German Trade Rivalry, 1875–1914* (Philadelphia: University of Pennsylvania, 1933), Alfred E. Kahn, *Great Britain in the World Economy*, and Albert Imlah, *Economic Elements in the Pax Britannica* (Cambridge: Harvard University Press, 1958). The classic work describing and analyzing the overall financial network is Herbert Feis, *Europe: The World's Banker** (New Haven: Yale University Press, 1930).

26. The nature and intensity of the rivalry between the Dutch and the British is definitively described and analyzed by Charles Wilson, *Profit and Power* (New York: Macmillan, 1957).

27. The pattern also continues to change. As a percentage of value added in agriculture, exports doubled, from 12 percent to 25 percent, between 1850 and 1900. In that same period, while per capita domestic consumption of food, feed grains and livestock was stable, production rose rapidly, the difference being accounted for by exports. In this century, usually about one-sixth of farm income has depended upon exports, and that percentage rose to an average of about one-quarter in the 1970s, as the United States pursued an aggressive export sales program. As both the European and Japanese markets have been protected and the Tier III countries have suffered from falling incomes, farm exports have fallen into a decline—and farmers in the same period have become among the most vigorous supporters of subsidized exports to the noncapitalist world—despite a world-view that would seem to suggest a different politics. For figures, see Du Boff, op. cit., pp. 143–44 and 163–64, and the annual *Economic Report of the President*.

28. The figures up to 1950 are taken from A. Maizels, *Industrial Growth and World Trade* (Cambridge: Cambridge University Press, 1965), pp. 426–27 and 434, and for subsequent years from Du Boff, op. cit., p. 155.

29. Thus, although U.S. manufactured exports as a percent of world manufactured exports was 14 percent in 1984, the percentage of U.S. multinational corporations' exports to that same world total was 18.1 percent, of which more than half was done by foreign affiliates of U.S. multinationals. This was all fine for the companies, but not so fine for the U.S. economy, even after taking the whole complex of relationships into account, as will be discussed soon below. On a different note, one important element to be noted in our negative trade balance is the role of oil. For more than half of this century, the U.S. was a large exporter of oil. By the 1960s we had begun to import oil, but in relatively small quantities, never exceeding $3 billion annually. By 1973, before the OPEC price increases, the figure had risen to over $8 billion, in 1980 to almost $80 billion, and by 1987, when prices had dropped substantially, to $43 billion. Even if we imported no oil, our trade balance would almost always have been negative, but the oil imports make a difficult situation more so.

30. The bases for the generalizations regarding world trade were first developed by Folke Hilgerdt, in two studies for the League of Nations, *The Network of World Trade* (1942) and *Industrialization and World Trade* (1946). His studies were extended in the massive work of Maizels, cited earlier. Ingvar Svennilson, *Growth and Stagnation in Europe* (Geneva: United Nations, 1954) contains much additional data. It also offers an at least partially effective analysis of the stagnation of European economies between the two world wars, the principal focus of the book.

31. As will be seen a bit later, although the United States has changed its rhetoric and some of its practices regarding protected trade quite substantially in our period of hegemony, it remains a high tariff country in general. Most revealingly, in the Reagan years of great insistence on worldwide free trade, U.S. tariffs and other less obvious but perhaps more effective obstacles on the average rose, only the best-known of which is VER, the "voluntary" export restraint of Japanese autos to the U.S.

32. U.S. policies and the relevant economic data for the 1920s and 1930s are thoroughly examined in Hal Lary, et al., *The United States in the World Economy** (Washington, D.C.: Department of Commerce, 1943). The study was in effect a call for the United States to grow up,

essentially along earlier British lines. As such, it has a quaint ring to it.

33. There have been noticeable and significant differences in the manner and content of rule as between England and the United States: the English relatively cohesive, self-assured, and haughty; the United States relatively undisciplined, self-righteous, combative, and more inclined "to go it alone"; the English with little or no respect for others, seen as permanently beyond the Pale, we believing others should want to be and can be *like* us, and puzzled or angry when that is not so. A historian of U.S. intellectual history has put it this way: "In countless ways Americans know in their gut—the only place myths can live—that we have been Chosen to lead the world in public morality and to instruct it in public virtue." Loren Baritz, *Backfire: Vietnam—The Myths that Made Us Fight, the Illusions that Helped Us to Lose, The Legacy that Haunts Us Today** (New York: Ballantine Books, 1985), p. 11. This is from the chapter entitled "God's Country and American Know-How."

34. Broadus Mitchell, *Depression Decade*, p. 57.

35. Quoted by William A. Williams, "The Large Corporation and American Foreign Policy," in David Horowitz, ed., *The Corporations and the Cold War** (New York: Monthly Review Press, 1969), pp. 95–96. Lloyd C. Gardner's essay in the same book, "The New Deal, New Frontiers, and the Cold War," is very useful, as is his book *Economic Aspects of New Deal Diplomacy* (Madison: University of Wisconsin Press, 1964).

36. For an extended discussion of this matter, see G. William Domhoff, "Who Made American Foreign Policy, 1945–1963," in the Horowitz book cited in note 35.

37. The United Nations has estimated that the United States lost 450,000 military personnel during the war and effectively no civilians, and the Soviet Union lost 28 million military plus civilian personnel. See Gregory Frumkin, *Population Changes in Europe Since 1939* (Geneva: United Nations, 1954). Given that military threat is connected to economic strength in some functional manner, it is also relevant, in considering the limits of any Soviet military threat from 1945 to 1950—the years in which the threat was made the basis for the Cold War—that of all economies, the Soviet economy was among the very weakest, and the United States' of course the very strongest.

38. One of the signs of the relative decrease in power of the United States in recent years is that increasingly, it has had to consult, rather than merely to inform, its fellow board members.

39. And it was sold to the people as just more of the milk of U.S. kindness. But it was closer to oil than milk, and a shrewd use of economic and State power. As Tanzer writes, "Since war-torn Europe and Japan were heavily dependent upon U.S. assistance for reconstruction, the [U.S.] oil companies and the U.S. government used this opportunity to virtually ram American-controlled oil down the throats of the world to replace coal. Thus, Walter Levy, head of the Marshall Plan's oil division, and previously an economist for Mobil, noted in 1949 that 'without ECA (the Marshall Plan) American oil business in Europe would already have been shot to pieces,' and commented that 'ECA does not believe that Europe should save dollars or even foreign exchange by driving American oil from the European market.' Approximately $2 billion of total Marshall Plan assistance of $13 billion was for oil imports, while the Marshall Plan blocked projects for European crude oil production and helped American oil companies to gain control of Europe's refineries." Tanzer, op. cit., pp. 17–18. Twenty years later Exxon (Standard Oil of New Jersey) had 35,000 service stations in Europe.

40. The unions expelled were the United Electrical Workers, the Mine, Mill, and Smelter Workers, the Fur and Leather Workers, the Food, Tobacco and Allied Workers, the Marine Cooks and Stewards, the Fishermen, the International Longshoremen's and Warehousemen's Union, and the American Communications Association. See Ronald Radosh, *American Labor and United States Foreign Policy** (New York: Random House; Vintage, 1969), pp. 435–36. The quote from George Meany, occurring a few sentences later in the text, is from p. 4; pp. 3–29 and 435–52 provide a summary and an evaluation of organized labor's contribution to the Cold War, including its secret cooperation with the CIA.

41. See Fred Block's clear and excellent study, *Origins of International Economic Disorder* (Berkeley: University of California Press, 1977), Michael Moffitt, *The World's Money* (London: Michael Joseph, 1983), and David P. Calleo, *The Imperious Economy* (Cambridge: Harvard University Press, 1982), all of whom, in different ways, examine the main elements constituting the emergence of the new world economy and some of the beginnings of its decline. As for the diminution of *national* capitalism: the latter will last as long as capitalism does, for reasons that don't require discussion at this point. But the "national" part of that system has lost much of its force recently for two reasons. First is that the United States has usurped important elements of the sovereignty of

both Tier II and Tier III nations, as was necessary if the capitalist world economy was to function effectively. Second, within that framework, and given our times, technology, and organizations, the giant international supercorporations—MNCs or TNCs—both can and in some sense must function to an important degree independently of their own and their host nations, come what may. We shall give explicit attention to these companies shortly.

42. See Harry Magdoff, *The Age of Imperialism: The Economics of U.S. Foreign Policy** (New York: Monthly Review Press, 1969). His data on the importance of foreign trade and raw materials, in his Chapter 2, are an excellent example of how what seem to be insignificant quantities are in fact qualitatively critical.

43. Not only the Japanese economy, but also most of the West European economies—and especially the German—have been strong in a real sense since the crisis of the 1970s began, but that strength has been accompanied by persistent high unemployment. How can the two coexist? It is because the "social accord" achieved in European countries in the 1960s not only keeps the social peace, it also prevents any sharp decline of purchasing power. In effect, social expenditures help to keep the economy strong, and the strong economy pays for the social expenditures. Germany, for example, which has been the largest exporter in the world economy for most of the past decade (except for one year when the United States was), also collects 38 percent of GNP in taxes—compared with 30 percent in the United States. For an illuminating study of this point, and comparisons between the United States and Europe, see the fine (though not completed) book by the late Andrew Shonfield, *The Use of Public Power* (Oxford: Oxford University Press, 1982), including the Foreword by Sir John Hicks. Briefer by far, but incisive, is the excellent essay by Louis Ferleger and Jay R. Mandle "American's Hostility to Taxes," *Challenge*, July–August, 1991, pp. 53–55. It shows, among other matters, that "the United States compared with other comparably developed countries, is undertaxed, and the taxes which it does collect are less progressive in their source than is the case for any other nation." (p. 55)

44. Because it is both inclusive and excellent, I shall follow the story as put forth by Du Boff, op. cit., pp. 153–63, in his chapter entitled "To Hegemony and Back." Where I quote him directly, the page numbers will be indicated in the text. Reference will also be made to a prescient and lucid essay by James M. Cypher, "Militarism, Monetarism, and

Markets: Reagan's Response to the Structural Crisis," *Merip Reports*, November–December 1984.

45. U.S. foreign investment rose from $30 billion in 1960 to $76 billion in 1970, to $216 billion in 1980; and profits from those investments as a percentage of total corporate profits rose from 12 percent in 1960 to 23 percent in 1980. In the same years, the foreign assets of U.S. banks as a percentage of total bank assets rose from 1.5 percent to 26 percent. Cypher, op. cit., p. 10.

46. Adapted from Du Boff, op. cit., p. 161. Figures are in billions of dollars. A caution on the figures for imports is in order, especially from the 1970s on: as will be seen when we look more closely at the activities of the multinational corporations, much of their "intrafirm" trade, always growing, causes official trade figures to be an inadequate guide to trade realities.

47. William Greider, *The Secrets of the Temple*, is a readable and important analysis of the Federal Reserve System, which puts it all at the door of Volcker. Others, myself included—with the help of David Stockman—conclude that the White House wanted a recession not just to end inflation but also to aid in the disciplining of organized labor and to support a rise in military expenditures. See Stockman's *Triumph of Politics*, cited earlier.

48. "...Ronald Reagan's pledge to balance the budget in his first three years in office and create a surplus in his fourth [was] probably the single most wildly inaccurate presidential forecast in U.S. economic history." Haynes Johnson, *International Herald Tribune*, November 25, 1991, in an article entitled "A Promise That Bush has Broken" (to create 30 million jobs during eight years in office). Having lost jobs instead of creating them, he may be unable to have the whole eight years to keep his promise, even though his deficit added another $1 trillion to the national debt, 1989–92.

49. Colonel James A. Donovan, *Militarism, U.S.A.** (New York: Scribner's, 1970), p. 2. Colonel Donovan is now retired from the U.S. Marine Corps.

50. As noted earlier, such corporations are called "trans-" and "supra-" as well as "multi-". We shall use MNC to mean all three, even though there are slight differentiations among them.

51. Very much worth consulting is Robert J.S. Ross and Kent C. Trachte, *Global Capitalism: The New Leviathan* (Albany: The State University of New York Press, 1990), a strong combination of description

and theory, which also provides a valuable survey of the relevant literature.

52. Such processes had an earlier *internal* life in the United States. Toward the end of the nineteenth century, and gaining new speed in the 1920s, the textile companies of New England, facing unionization, tax, and other challenges, moved their productive facilities to the South. There, locating themselves in lightly populated areas, they created company towns, paid "dirt wages" to otherwise unemployed poor whites, received favorable tax provisions (and were in some cases subsidized by states or localities)—and, in the process, not unimportantly, provided work for an all-white industrial labor force that might otherwise have become politically troublesome. I have discussed this as an instance of colonization of the South by northern capital in my "Comparative Economic Development of the American West and the South," reprinted in Scheiber, op. cit. For the same processes, also see C. Vann Woodward, *Origins of the New South, 1877–1913* (Baton Rouge: Louisiana State University Press, 1951).

53. The "privatization" of lending to Tier III countries was already well advanced by the mid-1970s. It was described and commented on insightfully by Emma Rothschild in her "Banks: The Politics of Debt," a two-part essay in *New York Review of Books*, May 27 and June 24, 1976. In those essays, she anticipated the problems this would raise for both ends of the relationship—placing both the banks (and their nations) and the poorer countries in a dangerous position.

54. Hugh Stephenson, *The Coming Clash: The Impact of Multinational Corporations on National States* (New York: Saturday Review Press, 1972), p. 123. When he wrote this, Stephenson was editor of the London *Times Business News*. Since he wrote, speculation has become the principal dynamic in the international financial system: it was estimated by *Barron's* in 1987 that of the *daily* global financial transactions of $150 billion, 90 percent are speculative, the rest for trade and investment. However, that was for 1987. In its very long and very informative essay, "Fear of Finance: A Survey of the World Economy," *The Economist* (of London), Sept. 19, 1992, states that "a central bank survey estimated net daily turnover of foreign exchange at $650 billion" for the year 1989, and put the 1992 figure at $900 billion per day. It's time for the Marx Brothers to return and put some sanity into the global financial system.

55. *Restructuring the World Economy*, p. 215.

56. Du Boff, op. cit., p. 155.

57. *World Development Report, 1990: Poverty* (New York: Oxford University Press, 1991), p. 1.

58. In an acute critique of the World Bank reports mentioned in the text, Paul Burkett helps us to comprehend that $370 figure by elaborating on it: "Suppose you are one of three children in a household in which your father works 50 hours per week (with no holidays) ... and whose wage is, say, $1300 per year (i.e., 50 cents an hour). Your mother earns $600 per year by working as a domestic servant.... The total household income is thus $1900 per year, or $380 for each of the household members. According to the World Bank, this household is not among the one billion poor people in the world." (Because its income is above $370 per person.) "Poverty Crisis in the Third World: The Contradictions of World Bank Policy," *Monthly Review*, December, 1990. Fifty cents an hour sounds impossibly low, but it is not unusual for, say, Mexican workers in the factories just across the U.S. border; and Nike shoes are produced in Indonesia at fifteen cents an hour.

59. *World Development Report, 1991: The Challenge of Development* (Oxford: Oxford University Press, 1991), p. 1.

60. Thus President McKinley recounting to some ministers how he came to his decision to enter the war in the Philippines. Subsequently, at least 300,000 Filipinos, under the leadership of *their* George Washington, Aguinaldo, were killed by our soldiers. Quoted in Zinn, op. cit., pp.16–17. Along with that quote is a running commentary from those representing agricultural and commercial interests, whose aims were more down to earth. For a most useful, comprehensive, and illuminating analysis of those "five centuries of assistance," see the unique book by L.S. Stavrianos, *Global Rift: The Third World Comes of Age* (New York: William Morrow, 1981). Stavrianos begins the history in 1400 and takes it to 1980, covering the whole world in the process. His "Third World" is neither the same as my Tier III (an economic classification for the 19th to 20th century), nor the political usage that appeared in the 1950s. For him, "...the Third World was born in the 15th century in Eastern Europe, for the phrase 'Third World' connotes those countries or regions that participated on unequal terms in what eventually became the global market economy" (p. 32). The reference to Eastern Europe has to do with the German movement eastward in medieval times. Among the many virtues of this book is its comprehensive bibliography.

61. Hobson's *Imperialism* (London: Allen & Unwin, 1902), Veblen's *Nature of Peace*, cited earlier, and Lenin's *Imperialism* (New York:

International Publishers, 1939) are the works noted. See also Rosa Luxemburg's *Accumulation of Capital* (London: Routledge & Kegan Paul, 1951), where the explanation is, like Hobson's, basically "underconsumptionist."

62. Baran's seminal work is *The Political Economy of Growth** (New York: Monthly Review Press, 1957). For Frank, see a summary essay, "The Development of Underdevelopment," in Robert I. Rhodes, ed., *Imperialism and Underdevelopment: A Reader** (New York: Monthly Review Press, 1970), Chapter 1, also as Chapter 1 in his own *Latin America: Under-Development or Revolution** (New York: Monthly Review Press, 1969), and again in James D. Cockroft, André Gunder Frank and Dale L. Johnson, *Dependence and Underdevelopment** (New York: Doubleday; Anchor, 1972). Frank has been a prolific writer in this area, and his other works support his main theory. The quotations from him that follow in the text are to be found in all three of the works above. Samir Amin's massive two-volume analytical-historical study, *Accumulation on a World Scale: A Critique of the Theory of Underdevelopment* (New York: Monthly Review Press, 1974), concludes by arguing that "everything in this field still remains to be done." Some of it he did himself in his subsequent *Unequal Development* (New York: Monthly Review Press, 1976).

63. Edward R. Fried and Philip H. Trezise, eds., *Third World Debt: The Next Phase* (Washington, D.C.: Brookings Institution, 1989), p. 5.

64. From the UNICEF Report of 1986, cited in the previous chapter.

65. "How to Stop Hunger," *New York Review of Books*, December 5, 1991. Solow, who teaches at MIT, makes this statement in the course of reviewing an important book by Jean Dréze and Amartya Sen, *Hunger and Public Action* (Oxford: Oxford University Press, 1991). What follows in the text will indicate that Solow's position—"hardly any doubt"—is very much an understatement of what can be done.

66. Frances Moore Lappé and Joseph Collins, *World Hunger: Twelve Myths** (New York: Grove Press, 1986; a Food First Book). I shall quote directly or paraphrase from their listing, without referring to all twelve. The interested reader is encouraged to read the whole book, and to write to the Institute for Food and Development Policy: Food First, 145-9th Street, San Francisco, CA, 94103 for further reading and research.

67. Unfortunately, Prof. Solow may not be right about that. Although, for example, the IMF and its personnel do not *wish* anyone to starve, it is probable that the constraints their loans impose (that allow unemploy-

ment to rise as social expenditures fall)—in the name of long-term growth and development—have reduced the level of life in many countries in at least the short-term, and insofar as that level for many has already been precariously low, it may be assumed that malnutrition has been worsened, and deaths resulted. It needs reminding that the IMF policy has its roots in the laissez-faire ideology of mid-nineteenth century England. (To be discussed further in the next section, concerning Tier III debt.)

68. The authors' arguments for this position must be read to make it more than an assertion. See pp. 23–32. But also see Josué de Castro, *The Geopolitics of Hunger* (New York: Monthly Review Press, 1977; first published as *The Geography of Hunger*, 1952), a book concerned entirely with the connections between population growth, poverty, and hunger. The author is a Brazilian biologist.

69. The authors argue well and at length, pp. 47–66, that the "green revolution" benefits those who are exacerbating the problem of world hunger, rather than its victims. See also Bernhard Glaeser, ed., *The Green Revolution Revisited: Critiques and Alternatives* (London: Allen and Unwin, 1987), for a thorough history and analysis, and, as well, Chapter 5 of Susan George's *How the Other Half Dies* (cited earlier), and the entire book on the larger question of world hunger.

70. *How the Other Half Dies*, p. 286.

71. Nor, by the late 1970s, were governments—especially the leaders of this process, the United Kingdom and the United States—as easily able or inclined to make grants, given their nations' own problems and growing taxpayer revolts.

72. "Poor 'Pay' $50 billion to Rich," *International Herald Tribune*, September 6–7, 1989. "The outflow of $50.1 billion from all developing countries in 1988 represented the difference between new lending of $92.3 billion and repayments of principal and interest of $142.4 billion" (ibid.).

73. "The Abyss of Third World Debt," by Robert Pollin, in *Monthly Review*, March 1989. This essay is a review of two excellent books, Susan George, *A Fate Worse Than Debt: The World Financial Crisis and the Poor* (New York: Grove Press, 1988), and Sue Branford and Bernardo Kucinski, *The Debt Squads: The U.S., the Banks, and Latin America* (New Jersey: Zed Books Limited, 1988). Pollin also points out that the major banks whose reckless lending was a vital part of the cause of the disaster, have mostly flourished through the crisis years. Quoting George, he shows that "between 1982 and 1985, profits rose at Bankers Trust by

66 percent, at Chase Manhattan by 84 percent, at Chemical Bank by 61 percent..." and so on.

74. "Borrowing Ebbs, But World Debt Crisis Remains," *International Herald Tribune*, December 19, 1988.

75. See Saadet Deger, *Military Expenditures in Third World Countries*, the annual reports of R.L. Sivard, *World Military and Social Expenditures*, and also Michael Klare, *American Arms Supermarket* (Austin: University of Texas Press, 1985) and, with Cynthia Aronson, *Supplying Repression: U.S. Support for Authoritarian Regimes Abroad* (Washington, D.C.: Institute for Policy Studies, 1984).

76. Much has been proposed by many along these and other lines. See Stavrianos, op. cit., and also his own "Common Vision," pp. 807–14, and also a powerful new collection of critical essays, *The Development Dictionary: A Guide to Knowledge as Power*, Wolfgang Sachs, ed., London, Zed Books, 1992. Put together by a brilliant—and largely unknown—group of economists, sociologists, philosophers, and the like from all over the world, it is a devastating critique of the very *idea* of development—not only because of its already devastating consequences over the past decades, but finally in its ultimate meaning for life on this earth. It is not just that in recent decades the material gap between rich and poor has always deepened and widened, but that the developmental goal—whatever else that might mean—aims to Westernize and homogenize all of the globe, all of humanity. They, and I, think that would be a terrible tragedy.

– 8 –

The State

Was it for this our fathers kept the law?
This crown shall crown their struggle and their ruth?
Are we the eagle nation Milton saw
Mewing its mighty youth,
Soon to possess the mountain winds of truth,
And be a swift familiar of the sun
Where aye before God's face his trumpets run?
Or have we but the talons and the maw,
And for the abject likeness of our heart
Shall some less lordly bird be set apart?
Some gross-billed wader where the swamps are fat?
Some gorger in the sun? Some prowler with the bat? [1]

All agree that what the State has or has not done has been of great
importance in the social and economic development of modern societies.
But beyond that simple statement, disagreement sets in and soon becomes
sharp. When has the State's role been beneficial and when harmful?
When vital and when of small consequence? How does one measure the
State's importance, and within what temporal and functional framework?
How does the State relate to private groups, at any time and over time?

Asking these and other questions places an examination of the role
of the State in a context of ideological and theoretical dispute. It also
raises still another question: to what degree and in what ways does the
relationship of the State to economic development manifest and in what
ways does it conceal the changing structure and functions of *power* in
modern capitalist societies?[2]

The activities of governments have been much studied by historians, but very much as though "government" and "State" are the same entities. The larger and more decisive meaning of the State and, therefore, the role of *power*, remains a vast *terra incognita*. It is power that informs and is informed by the complex relationships between public and private institutions; at the center of that complex will be found the State system, supported by and maintaining the political and social system over which it rules. To explore and map out the ground that comprehends power, socioeconomic stability or change, and the State is slippery work; if we are to understand our past and have any say whatsoever in our future, that effort is essential.[3]

Simple and Sweet

Historians and social scientists of the mainstream who have dealt with the government, the State, and power in capitalist society customarily have been motivated by a particular tension and have operated with a particular assumption; and, just as customarily, neither the tension nor the assumption has been explicit. The tension has been between those who thought it desirable to minimize the role of the government and those who wished to see its powers broadened; the assumption has been the *pluralist* notion that government in capitalist societies, like the parallel assumption concerning the economy, is guided by the forces of (voter) competition. Some elaboration of both of these points is necessary.

Great Britain is thus seen to have had a "weak State" in the nineteenth century, Germany a strong one. The terms of the historical discussion have almost always been confined to easily discernible, hotly debated, and explicit policies: statutes, regulations, fiscal, monetary, and trade policies, subsidies, and the like. Seldom is there an analysis of what governments did *not* do, or what *ceased* to be done—for example, in the way of social and human protection—let alone what the State was responsible for that did not appear in specific actions, or that did not "appear" at all.

This last-mentioned role of the State, what we may call its nonactions, is by its nature the most obscure. When examined carefully it is also among the most revealing of the relationships between private power, governmental activities, and social conditions. Put together with the more obvious manifestations of power, this aspect of social existence allows a long step to be taken toward an understanding of the State. An absence of such understanding encourages the following kind of misleading observation concerning social conditions in industrializing Britain. The statement was made, it should be noted, by a respected economic historian who has done more than others to study "the State":

> ...in the age of laissez-faire the role of government in economic affairs was largely a passive one...The social evils in town and countryside that followed in the wake of the Industrial Revolution might have been alleviated at an earlier date if the governing classes had been better informed about the great changes that were taking place in the mines and factories...The government was inactive because it saw no good reason why it should do anything.[4]

"The governing classes," it may be assumed, contained men who were the creators and beneficiaries of the very conditions of which the author thinks they were ignorant, ready in a trice to employ the coercive power of the State to subdue those who sought to change these conditions, the same coercive power that had been used to abolish social protections at "an earlier date" (as was discussed above, in Chapter 2). The "social evils" mentioned by Professor Henderson were due to the absence of social controls at the time, as the "self-regulating market economy" held full sway. Given the earlier abolition of such controls, their continuing absence can be explained in good part by "non-decision making," a phenomenon analyzed explicitly and usefully as follows:

> ...nondecision making is a means by which demands for change in the existing allocation of benefits and privileges in the community can be suffocated before they are even voiced; or kept covert; or killed before they gain access to the relevant decision-making arena; or, failing all those things, maimed or destroyed in the decision-implementing stage of the policy process.[5]

This is close to the "negative selection" analysis of the German sociologist Claus Offe, which seeks to show how "anticapitalist" interests, whether or not self-consciously, are systematically rebuffed or excluded from the processes and policies of the State.[6] Those who have been involved in political activities to try to make the United States a less unkind and less harsh society in recent decades have experienced all these deflecting techniques in full measure; indeed, it is the success of such techniques in maintaining (or worsening) the status quo that adds to our need to study the nature and workings of power.

Nondecision making is one of the major means of preventing or slowing down social change, of steering unavoidable change in directions harmless to the main structures of the society. It is the "oligopoly" of those who hold great power; while those who are deflected, ignored, suffocated, and whose proposals are "maimed or destroyed" are those with much less or no power.

In capitalist democracies the guiding assumption of conventional social analysts, the assumption upon which their "theory of the State" is based, is *pluralism*. The pervasiveness of this assumption, and the confusions surrounding it, require that it be looked at critically. After doing so, we shall attempt an abbreviated analysis of the origins and uses of power and the role of the State in U.S. history, in the distant and more recent past.

Few economists have anything approximating a "theory of the State," or are even conscious of the need or relevance of one. In the fragmentation characteristic of contemporary social science, economists who might feel that need can, so it is believed, turn to the political scientists. The latter would be much offended at the suggestions above that the State has been neglected as an object of analysis. They have a theory of the State: pluralism. The only thing wrong with it is that it takes for granted the very matter most requiring examination: power. In this neglect, the political scientists have matched their economist counterparts who take private property and basic capitalist institutions for granted. But, as Ralph Miliband has pointed out,

A theory of the state is also a theory of society and of the distribution of power in that society. But most Western "students of politics" tend to start, judging from their work, with the assumption that power, in Western societies, is competitive, fragmented and diffused: everybody, directly or through organized groups, has some power and nobody has or can have too much of it. In these societies, citizens enjoy universal suffrage, free and regular elections, representative institutions, effective citizen rights, including the right of free speech, association and opposition; and both individuals and groups take ample advantage of these rights, under the protection of the law, an independent judiciary and a free political culture.

As a result, the argument goes, no government, acting on behalf of the state, can fail, in the not very long run, to respond to the wishes and demands of competing interests. In the end, everybody, including those at the end of the queue, gets served.[7]

Pluralism as the basis for thinking about the State assumes that sovereignty resides in the voter and that political outcomes depend upon competition among those vying for those votes. Neoclassical economics, the body of theory that guides most economists' thinking, has its parallel assumptions. The consumer, like the voter, is sovereign; business firms vie with each other for the consumer's vote—that is, the consumer's dollar. Economic demand determines economic supply; political demand determines political supply. It is a sweetly comforting set of beliefs for those who accept it, and no further thought is needed; all that is ignored are the underlying social structures and institutions that make some considerably more equal than others. All that is ignored, that is, is power—how it is distributed, how it is gained, how it is lost, how it is used. A theory of the State without a theory of power is, in the old saying, like Hamlet without the Dane.

Power, Power, Who Has the Power?

What *is* power? It is the ability to act effectively, to make things go one's way, and to keep them so. The Latin root for the noun *power* and the verb *to be able* is the same. Power is the ability, for present purposes, to make or to influence decisions and nondecisions. Where does it come from? Most simply, power is held by those who control what is most valued in their society; what has been valued; what is coming to be valued. What is valued may be *tangible*, like productive assets or weaponry, or *intangible*, like the ability to formulate or represent cherished beliefs or aspirations. And there is likely to be a dynamic interaction between the two.

Control over the means of material survival places its possessors at the center of power in any society, although the forms and functions associated with such control have differed quite substantially in history —a priesthood in Ancient Egypt, the Church and its warriors in medieval Europe, for example. Control over productive wealth in a capitalist

424 - U.S. CAPITALIST DEVELOPMENT SINCE 1776

society as *a source* of power comes closest to being *the* source of power. This characteristic is one way of defining capitalism; it also helps to explain the great dynamism of capitalist economic development.

Still, complexity in the structures of power exists in a capitalist as in any other kind of society. This complexity is substantial and upon reflection obvious. Power derives from different areas of society—economic, political, military, religious, cultural, social—and functions at different levels—local, national, international. Nonetheless, out of this patterned and dynamic complexity, order may be discerned: we may think of *structures* of power.

Visually, we may think of a manysided pyramid, its sides representing the diverse sources of power, and its shape, narrowing to a peak, representing the concentration of power. Power changes hands over time, which suggests that this visual image be thought of as a film, rather than as a diagram. Nor should it be forgotten that those who have power at lower levels of the pyramid—those who control local education, medical facilities, or the police, for example—have power that for some purposes can be just as vital, just as much a matter of life and death, as that wielded at the top.

Thus, for example, power in the medieval world was in the hands of those who ruled over religious and military affairs; they also controlled the productive land (then the principal form of wealth). Which came first, the chicken—religious and military power—or the egg—control of the land, need not detain us here; there were both tangibles and intangibles involved. And for the medieval serf, the locally held power was decisive in determining the conditions of life.

Something concerning the chicken and egg argument does seem worth noting here. A view held by some Marxists would argue that the "egg"—control over the land—came first; a more complicated view, held by some other Marxists, would see the long and militarized anarchy of the so-called Dark Ages as having its unifying factor in the Roman Catholic Church and its stabilizing factor in unremitting military activities. Church functionaries were often fighters; together the "cross and the sword" comprised the aristocracy of medieval Europe; and the serfs supported them by their labor on the land. The "middle class" was virtually nonexistent in the early Middle Ages; as it became more prominent through its expanding mercantile activities, it was leaned on and/or fought against increasingly by the feudal military and clerical nobility; and the structure of power was changing in the process.[8]

The consequences of the successful discharge of the feudal military function included an increase in political stability and thus in trade and industry; the unifying role of the Church began to break down, and to seem a hindrance. The Reformation of the sixteenth century had many sides to it, in as many areas; central to that struggle was a challenge that denied the fiscal and political prerogatives the Church had long possessed. In what had been an epoch whose deep attachment to religious belief is almost unintelligible to moderns, any major struggle for power had to revolve around the control of religious institutions and translate itself in important part into religious categories: the confessional, the role of the priest, faith and works, and the like.

When the Church lost its hegemony in Europe, its place was taken by the descendants of those militarists who once walked hand in glove with the Church; as secular dynasties they now ruled over nations in a time of substantially larger and more expensive conflict. Merchants and financiers were quite frequently indispensable for this transition. They were needed to finance the once feudal/hereditary but now mercenary fighting forces; and their trade and industry gave strength to the new nations.[9]

The stage was set for still another struggle for power. From the viewpoint of capitalist development, its most decisive manifestation was in seventeenth-century England: a struggle between what has been called "the divine right of kings" and "the divine right of capital." It was not a clear-cut struggle to its participants, nor would the struggle's eventual outcome—laissez-faire capitalism—be entirely clear for over a century after the dust settled. (And it may be added that many on "the winning side" would have then been appalled by what they had made possible, a not uncommon happenstance.) That age was still very much a religious one: thus, "the Puritan Revolution." It was also the age of mercantilism, and of a class of merchants and financiers whose strength had increased along with England's: thus, "the bourgeois revolution."

The English Civil War began in 1640 and ended in 1688. The motives of those involved were mixed, and any one of a particular religious, business, or military status might well have been found on either side. But the bourgeois mentality was the most viable. By the close of the century, the bourgeoisie had begun to move toward parity with the aristocracy (monarchy and hereditary peerage), even with the Established Church playing a subsidiary and supporting role to the latter. Thus the dynamic new economic forces and the more traditional political and social values came into an uneasy but workable balance, a balance that has yet to disappear totally in England. The structure of power had been decisively altered by the turbulence of the seventeenth century; the nation of shopkeepers had been born; capitalist control over production soon came to be valued *most* in the nexus of power.[10]

The State as a System of Power

Who most valued this control over production? Not, surely, the simple folk who found themselves with increasing speed and ruthlessness swept off the land and into the brutal conditions of the towns, the mines, mills, and factories; nor the women and children who pulled coal carts deep in the mines or tended cotton spindles in the "satanic mills" for twelve or more hours a day. What is valued and why does not tell us much about the *acquisition* of power; the *who* is always important, the who and their location in the structure of power as society moves through time.

Except for revolutionary periods, alterations in the structure of power are brought about by those already sitting fairly high on the pyramid; the alterations allow them to move up higher. The Tudor and Stuart dynasties that led England toward the civil war that in turn reduced the power of the Crown did *not* value economic matters above all else; that honor was reserved for their own presumably noble attributes. But of necessity the monarchs did value rising economic strength in England, without which England would have been subdued by the feisty rivalries of the sixteenth and seventeenth centuries. So men of trade, industry, and finance rose slowly but surely into positions of influence and importance, each step making the next easier.[11] Politics and opinion, education and literature, paid both increasing homage and criticism to the new men of affairs; religious standards subtly but steadily altered in their favor—as Tawney shows brilliantly in his long essay introducing *The Discourse Upon Usury* (cited earlier). The English Civil War signified that the mixture of new and old structures was no longer viable; existing political institutions, the formal structure within which power works, had to be revised. A new State system was needed, a system suited to the needs and possibilities of surging capitalism.

The modern capitalist State system, as Ralph Miliband sees it, has many components: government; administration and bureaucracy; military, paramilitary, and security forces; the judiciary; lesser (local and state) governments; and legislative assemblies (federal and other). But Nicos

Poulantzas, another of the most creative of recent Marxian theorists of the State, goes beyond Miliband's definition of the State system as follows:

> The system of the State is composed of *several apparatuses* or *institutions* of which certain have a principally repressive role, in the strong sense, and others a principally ideological role. The former constitute the repressive apparatus of the State..., in the classic Marxist sense of the term (government, army, police, tribunals, and administration). The latter constitute the *ideological apparatuses of the State*, such as the Church, the political parties, the unions (with the exception, of course, of the *revolutionary* party or trade union organizations), the schools, the mass media..., and, from a certain point of view, the family. This is so whether they are *public or private*...This position is in a certain sense that of Gramsci himself, although one he did not sufficiently found and develop.[12]

Miliband's response to this analytical alteration is itself an important contribution, both to his own and the general understanding of the State. He says, in direct reply,

> I am extremely dubious about this.... [Just] as it is necessary to show that the institutions mentioned...*are* part of a system of power, and that they are, as Poulantzas says, increasingly linked to and buttressed by the state, so is it important not to blur the fact that they are not, in bourgeois democracies, part of the state but of the political system. These institutions *are* increasingly subject to a process of "statization"; and... that process is likely to be enhanced by the fact that the state must, in the conditions of permanent crisis of advanced capitalism, assume ever greater responsibility for political indoctrination and mystification.[13]

The debate between these two theorists, and the numerous other differences among nonmainstream analysts concerning the State, are of great importance both analytically and politically—one must, after all, understand the State, if it is to be altered in its structures and functions, either in minor or major degree. We cannot attempt either to pursue further or to settle those vital controversies; we can only emphasize the need to examine them and work through them and around them carefully.

As will be seen, my own understanding is a synthesis of the positions stated above.

Underlying the foregoing disagreements is the epigrammatic Marxian view expressed in the *Communist Manifesto*: "The executive of the modern state is but a committee for managing the common affairs of the whole bourgeoisie." Whether that is construed to mean that the State system responds directly or indirectly to the capitalist class ("instrumentally," as for Miliband, or "structurally," as for Poulantzas, or in terms of "consciousness and ideology," as in a Hegelian-Marxian view) or in some complex that puts them together, is a matter for further work and observation.[14] Here we may at least state with great firmness that however that debate proceeds, it has already made the notions of "pluralism" seem almost comic in their cheerful banalities.

The State system, whether defined narrowly or broadly, is the system through which power flows; within it power grows, for use within and outside the State system itself. That system, like the larger social system it represents, is oligarchic and pyramidal in structure: a powerful few at the top and people of some but not much power in the middle; the mass of participants in the State, as in the economic system, functioning as mere hirelings. Within each of Miliband's six categories (to be discussed below) the pyramidal structure is reproduced. As between the categories there is a difference between higher and lower: top federal government positions are usually in the State elite; top local positions usually are not, for example.[15]

The *sources* of power are diverse, with control over the means of production the most decisive. The framework through which power is *used* to steer the State system is that of the political system. The forms or institutions of politics, like the sources of power, are diverse: power is applied through *pressure*—in and through political parties, and directly on or in the agencies of the State through lobbies—whether industrial, agricultural, financial, labor, religious, or professional lobbies (such as the American Medical Association), "senior citizens," and the like. And of course the most powerful interested groups can directly fill the top layers of the State, and entrench their representatives there—in the president's cabinet, for example. However, as Poulantzas states, "...the *direct* participation of members of the capitalist class in the State apparatus and in the government, even where it exists, is not the important side of the matter."[16] A capitalist democracy is one in which government is determined by *pressure*, to be sure; but the pressure of a very few can literally move mountains, while pressure from the rest of us is barely felt, if at all.

The component parts of the political system are constantly seeking to bend the State system to their wills; they are also among the legitimators of that system and the larger society over which it presides. We now examine in more detail these elements of State power.

Competition among the Few

In the State system of the United States, the *government* is the executive branch: the president, the cabinet, and his top aides. The government is not the State, but the government does speak for the State. As Miliband puts it,

> the state...is a nebulous entity; and while men may choose to give their allegiance to it, it is to the government that they are required to give their obedience. A defiance of its orders is a defiance of the state, in whose name the government alone may speak and for whose actions it must assume ultimate responsibility.[17]

Electoral contests for control of the government are contests for who shall interpret and represent the interests of the State. Except in revolutionary or counterrevolutionary periods, however, these contests take place within narrow limits—narrow enough, usually, that the expression "Tweedledee and Tweedledum" has come to characterize them more often than not. However, in periods of rapid social change, contests for power *within* the system, reflecting divisions of opinion between the most substantial groups, have led to more important electoral choices. Ours have been such times.[18]

The next sector of the State system, *administration* and *bureaucracy*, includes the numerous public and semipublic agencies (such as the public Federal Trade Commission, and the semipublic Federal Reserve System [the "Fed"]). These agencies are presumed to work in harmony with government, and usually do. Whether they do or not is not a matter of statute; they are not necessarily responsible to the executive. Their heads are frequently appointed for periods that extend beyond the government of one term. (The seven directors of the Fed, for instance, are appointed for fourteen years, staggered over time.) The largest number of the working members of such agencies are civil servants, subject neither to appointment nor election. Although presumably devoid of "political" inclinations, in fact (and especially at the top levels), their political leanings tend to be strong, and tend to become well-known when they come into conflict with the executive—a fairly frequent occurrence, especially with the head of the Fed. The main tendency for these administrators, as for virtually everyone at the top levels of the State system, is to be conservative, and to be drawn from the top business or professional levels of the society.

The *military, paramilitary,* and *security forces* of the State will receive a separate treatment when, later, we seek to evaluate the role of the Pentagon, the National Security Council, the FBI, and the CIA in the current State system; here they will merely be characterized. As principal coercive elements of the State, they serve the government of the day and its foreign and domestic policies, although they are independent of executive control with regard to appointments for all but the very top positions. In the past half century or so, this coercive force has grown considerably more than the rest of the State system. Again, Miliband:

> Nowhere has the inflation of the military establishment been more marked since the second world war than in the United States, a country which had previously been highly civilian-oriented. And much the same kind of inflation has also occurred in the forces of "internal security," not only in the United States; it is probably the case that never before in any capitalist country, save in Fascist Italy and Nazi Germany, has such a large proportion of people been employed on repressive duties of one kind or another.[19]

The *judicial* sector of the State system is presumed to be independent of the interests of the government, though not of the State; it is presumed to deal with continuity and adherence to established law. The top federal judges are appointed for life by the presidents; such appointments are among the juiciest plums in the large orchard of patronage that enhances the power of the presidency. Presidents are often in conflict with one or another of Supreme Court and other federal judges; an additional reason presidents cherish their right to appoint. Viewed over the long run, however, the range of conflict is narrow, especially as regards the arena of political economy. The memory of man knoweth not the appointment of a federal judge who questioned the fundaments of the U.S. capitalist

system, least of all the sanctity of private property. Veblen put it wryly: "In the nature of the case the [property] owner alone has any standing in court. All of which argues that there are probably very few courts that are in any degree corrupt or biased.... Efforts to corrupt them would be a work of supererogation, besides being immoral."[20]

What Miliband calls "subcentral government"—that is, in the United States, local, county, and state governments—is a bewildering array that reproduces in form and function most of the State system, but at a lower level of power and, usually, of importance. For day-to-day questions of life, however, and as was noted above, the lower-level system may be and usually is critical. This welter of governments is, in fact, the prime channel through which much of power of the State runs; it is also the primary channel through which the voice of local and regional interests is conveyed to the State élite. They are, as Miliband remarks, "power structures in their own right" (p. 53).

The final segment of the State system is the *legislative assembly*: the two branches of Congress, and their counterparts in states and localities. Historically, Congress has provided both conflict and cooperation for the executive, although always within the narrowly defined limits that characterize the behavior of the other elements of the State system. In this century, there has been a marked tendency toward concentration and centralization in the economy, as we have seen, and that tendency has had its counterpart in the same patterns in the State system. The power of the federal government vis-à-vis the separate states has grown to a disproportion that would have seemed incredible to people at the turn of the century; and this is equally so as regards the power of the presidency vis-à-vis Congress—so much so that the term "imperial presidency," first used to characterize the Nixon era, is now seen to apply to the powers that have accumulated for that office, irrespective of its holder.

These developments toward concentration and centralization in the economy and the State system are both cause and result of the internationalization and militarization of the United States. Already in the 1930s influential voices were expressing alarm at how "dangerously slow and inefficient" the processes of representative government are when considerations of foreign policy are at stake. By 1952, when Eisenhower won the office, "consensus" on foreign policy had been achieved between the two major parties; consensus on foreign and military policy thenceforth came to mean that the executive branch would decide first and convince, intimidate, or trick Congress to go through the formalities of granting what became—effectively—automatic appropriations afterward.

It was in the first years of this century that the path that led us to our present deplorable condition began to be cut through the foliage of what was by comparison a relatively democratic nation; and the path was very much smoothed by the accumulating powers of the State system and its education of and growing experience with the processes of *legitimation*, now to be examined. Each step "ahead" was made easier by those preceding; and each step made reversal of the process more difficult. Just as the rich, because of their wealth, grow richer, so do the powerful grow more powerful, most especially in the absence of a concerned electorate.[21]

It's All Right...

Modern societies all use coercive devices of one sort or another to one degree or another; by far more important than coercion are the practices that bring about voluntary acquiescence.[22] These practices have come to be called *legitimation*. Taken together with the public and private institutions that they legitimate, the ways in which acquiescence is achieved make a grim joke of pluralistic notions of political competition, just as oligopolistic economic power and modern advertising make a mockery of notions of textbook competition. Whether or not the processes to be described constitute conscious *deception* to achieve their results is not important; indeed, the high probability that what the "legitimators" do comes out of principled conviction rather than guile—although there is more than enough of that to go around, of course—makes their impact that much more powerful.

Politically we grow up within a universe of discourse in which certain matters are taken for granted and others lie beyond the Pale. We are socialized to be deaf and blind and dumb on a broad range of matters, the more so the more basic they are to the society's functioning. The process is not much different in its results from that which affects our tastes in food. Certain foods, enjoyed in other countries—snails or horsemeat in France—are seen as repulsive or as nonfoods here; and so it is with political questions—socialized health care in Sweden, for example.

Of course *anything* can be and is discussed. Whether or not an audience will assemble, listen, or watch, or, if it does, will do so with "an open mind," is a matter of who is saying what to whom. At any time there is an informal, undesigned apparatus that sustains the largest elements of the status quo. The constituent elements of that apparatus vary from time to time and place to place, of course. They include: the major political parties; the media; the educational system; religious institutions; popular cultural life (including TV, organized athletics, and film); public relations and advertising; the family—in short, much of what Poulantzas refers to as the *ideological apparatus* of the State. From cradle to grave, we are enclosed within certain options and views presented as reasonable, as "common sense"; contrary options and views are easily dismissed as "idealistic," "foolish," "foreign," "juvenile," or "dangerous" with regard to job, to security, to virtue, to almost anything. Legitimation is one side of a conservative process whose other side is socialization —the larger educational process.

Those who are heard most clearly and most frequently in and from the apparatus just noted are those at the top of its parts: political leaders; the major commentators in the media; the establishment in the schools and universities; religious leaders; celebrities; the largest corporations; and, although diminishing swiftly over time in influence, parents (themselves part of an ongoing socialization process). Social leaders rise to the top because they function effectively within the existing system. Few people ever come to doubt a system that carries them to high levels of income and status; most, indeed, find such a system totally praiseworthy for recognizing their special talents. They are believers when they begin, and true believers as they rise. By comparison, dissenters are seen as failures, as scruffy, as inexplicably angry, distraught, shrill, something awful. All this is pretty obvious; let us look at the news media for illustration.

The "Pentagon Papers" of the early 1970s informed us of the conscious deception practiced by several presidencies on both the media and the public concerning the war in Indochina.[23] But those Papers tell us nothing of the systematic bias of the news media in presenting what they know regarding controversies over foreign policy, labor struggles, protest groups, and the like.

As was noted in Chapter 3, the media too have been part of the process of concentration and centralization, with most of us getting our ideas (insofar as they come through the media) from a relative handful of sources—one "local" newspaper, and three national TV networks. The media are of course owned and controlled by big businesses, who are of course in it for money, and naturally disinclined from rocking what is in part their boat. If that is not always true of the journalists who work for the distinctly conservative publishers and network executives, the pressure is great for it to become so—or to remain concealed. News that smells of criticism is modified, truncated, or, more frequently, not presented at all. Reporters who would make their way do not make it by filing unprinted stories. As is well-known, if their "beat" is the White House, they lose their access if they are seen to be critics. Advertisers complain; readers and viewers complain; presidents and vice presidents complain. Reporters shape up or ship out. The news takes on all the qualities of a rooting-section at a football game, with the newspeople rooting for our side—in effect, the status quo. Our generals are grave, resourceful, even humane and funny; theirs are sneaky, treacherous, cruel. Businessmen are responsible citizens; strike leaders are reckless of the interests of the economy and even of their rank and file. The police are brave, beleaguered, patient; protestors are violent, amoral, wild-eyed.[24] Doubtless this systematic dichotomy in adjectives is for some commentators a matter of playing the game; for most it is a matter of developed conviction. The road to the top is a finishing school.[25]

Turning to the more general process of legitimation, there can be little doubt that the most insistent and respected voice in the United States—except on matters connected with war—is the voice of business. That is only partly because most "professionals"—doctors, lawyers, publishers, entertainers, and athletes—have a high regard for making money, whatever else they may take seriously. Mainly, it is because, as noted in Chapter 3, a capitalist society depends for its health on a healthily functioning business sector. Policies that might militate against that would cause a "loss of confidence" among businessmen. For most people in the United States there is no lively awareness of or interest in an alternative to the status quo; the possibility of such a loss of confidence is tantamount to the possibility of unspeakable economic disaster. In short, business has the open respect of the entire society, except for the few who criticize business, and who usually forfeit respect in the process.

The pressures brought to bear on the State system are therefore most effectively those of business people or business-minded people; the people who occupy the top and middle posts of the State system are almost entirely people from the middle or upper social brackets. Prior education, aspiration, and function prepare those who are called to be deserving of their responsibilities. The U.S. Senate, once known as a "rich man's club," still deserves that description for all but a very small number; and so does the rest of the top drawer of the State system.[26]

From States to State to Super-State

The foregoing discussion applies as a sketch outline of the State system in the United States today. The nineteenth-century conditions were different in content, form and process. An examination of three of the conflicts marking that century will serve the twofold function of highlighting the differences while at the same time revealing the central role of power in the process of social change: (1) the so-called Bank War; (2) the Civil War; and (3) the Populist uprising. These conflicts represent, respectively, the successful struggle to move toward laissez-faire capitalism; the triumph of industry and finance over agriculture and commerce as the dynamic center of U.S. capitalism; and the last gasp of Jeffersonian democracy as either ideal or reality. Each struggle was an effort to alter the State system, and, as well, in the case of Populism, to restore an idealized past.

Bank War

One of the first achievements of the triumphant English bourgeoisie after their Glorious Revolution was the creation of the Bank of England. The First Bank of the United States, chartered for twenty years in 1791, was designed to serve much the same purposes for the United States. Both were "central banks"; that is, bankers' banks, endowed with the responsibility of influencing the supply of money and the rate on borrowed money in terms of "the public interest"—as defined by bankers.

Mercantilist in their origins, central banks have become a key feature of all modern capitalist economies. The United States is unique in having created, allowed to lapse, recreated, and then destroyed its central bank, all that in less than fifty years. From the 1830s until the creation in 1913 of the Fed, our present central bank, the United States was the only major capitalist economy without a central bank, ours having been destroyed in the middle of Andrew Jackson's two terms as president.

The charter of the First Bank of the U.S. lapsed, amidst controversy, in 1811. The monetary chaos that followed led to the chartering of the Second Bank of the U.S. (1816–36). One-fifth of the Bank's stock was owned by the federal government; the rest was in private hands. The Bank served as a repository for federal funds, most important of which were payments for public lands and customs collections. In that period, the latter amounted to about 90 percent of all government revenues.

If you examine your paper money (currency) you will see that either the U.S. Treasury or the Fed "promises to pay to the bearer on demand" the amount of "money"—$10, $20, etc.—on the paper. (If you are foolish enough to insist, you will receive other paper money in exchange, it being defined as "legal tender.") Such money is still called a "bank note." In the period of the Second Bank, bank notes were promises to pay in *specie* (gold or silver) to the bearer of the note. The issuing banks were private (which they cannot be since 1934 in the United States), chartered by state governments; and the Second Bank issued its own notes, the soundest of the time.

When a Kentucky bank transmitted, say, $1,000 to the federal government for some Kentuckian's land purchase, or when a New York bank turned over $1,000 in customs collections for an importer to the government, those private banks were placing their notes—their "IOUs"—in the hands of the Second Bank. The Bank became their creditor; it could demand specie in return for the note. The notes of the various banks came into existence in response to loans to their customers, very much as deposits do today when you borrow from a bank. The banks, creditors to their customers, were debtors to the Second Bank. The latter's ability to demand specie was in fact its power to curtail the lending (and earning) capacities of the banking community: and that meant the Bank had critical control over the uses of the economic surplus. Then as now, power over the extension of credit is the power in some degree to influence the nature and direction of economic activity, and the degree was greater then. Then as now, such power is among the most important political powers; then as now, that power rests in mostly private hands, or in the hands of those congenial to the banking world.[27]

The Bank itself made loans, its principal business. It was a profitmaking institution, as well as having a public function. Quite naturally, other banks saw the Bank as a competitor, and one with extraordinary power. The Bank's directors and owners tended to represent the older and more powerful mercantile and financial interests of the new nation, and especially those in Philadelphia. By the 1920s, New York City was rising in strength, Baltimore was seeking to do so, and the West was opening up rapidly. The bankers, land speculators, and merchants in those and comparable areas saw the Bank as "the monster of Chestnut Street." Andrew Jackson, a westerner, vowing to destroy the Bank, made it the central issue of his reelection campaign in 1832.[28]

Jackson, who had risen to the presidency because of his military exploits as "the hero of New Orleans" (1815) and his murderous campaigns against the Native American tribes of the Southeast, was a planter and friend of the larger propertied interests in Tennessee. He was, and still is, thought to speak for "the common man." In his fight against Biddle and the Second Bank, Jackson's most numerous supporters were the western farmers and the urban workers of the East. Standing less noticeably behind them, however, were the bankers, merchants, manufacturers, and land speculators who saw the credit-restraining powers of the Bank as the last remaining obstacle to rapid increases in their fortunes. Jackson won reelection in 1832; the Second Bank, although its charter had four years left to run, was rendered ineffectual until its charter ended. The relatively concentrated financial and mercantile structure of power was displaced, pushed aside by a rapacious and rugged laissez-faire capitalism. Politically, this meant that the jealousies of the individual states as against the federal government were institutionalized: the era of effective "states' rights" accelerated. In practice this meant that raw economic power was the almost pure representation of State power for the rest of the century. "The great barbecue" began soon thereafter.[29]

Civil War

The forces unleashed by the destruction of the Second Bank led to a great stepup in all forms of economic expansion: banks multiplied rapidly (there were over 10,000 banks issuing bank notes by the 1850s); trade and industry spread from the Atlantic seaboard out to the Mississippi Valley; canals and railroads tied the broad lands together; soils, minerals, and forests were exploited with abandon. A new economic structure was taking shape; but the political structure lagged behind.

We need summarize only briefly what was discussed earlier concerning the South: by the 1820s it was the leading sector in the U.S. economy, with its King Cotton. Its economic needs and its social system gave it a viewpoint on matters of the State profoundly different from that coming to be held by the manufacturers, merchants, and financiers of the North. But up to the Civil War, the South on balance held the largest part of the strategic posts in the State system: Supreme Court justices, heads of congressional committees, cabinet posts, and the presidency.

The South used its nature-given rivers and coasts for the bulk of its transportation needs; the North had to build canals and railroads. The South exported its cotton, and imported manufacturers; the North wanted protection (especially from British competition) for its growing industries. The South had a labor supply over which it was both economically and politically unchallenged; the North was faced with labor short in supply and politically free. The South's needs for westward expansion, though pressing, were modest as compared with the temptations and needs facing the North and West. In short, the South wanted a State system that was suited to planter capitalism; the North needed a State system that would enhance industrial capitalism and rapid westward expansion. The pressures and conflicts were rumbling underground by the 1840s; by the 1850s they were ready to erupt.

Slavery was, of course, the major *public* issue of the Civil War. Whether it was the most important causal issue is another matter.[30] We can do little to reconstruct the inner motivation of those in the past. But, and as was noted earlier in a different connection, one can gain useful insights into what those involved in a struggle wanted most by seeing what those who won did with their enhanced power. The slaves were freed, of course. But within a few years, the promises of "forty acres and a mule" were discreetly shelved; more important and at least as revealing, arrangements were made between the triumphant North and the defeated South to allow the latter to regain full sway over its *internal* (including its racial) politics in exchange for northern control of the federal government and easy access to the investment possibilities of the resource-rich South—in railroads, timber, land speculation, minerals, and the like.[31]

The new State system rapidly removed all obstacles to the full realization of industrial capitalism in the United States. All obstacles, perhaps, but one; that one, the lingering belief in the promises of the United States as a Jeffersonian democracy—a society of independent small holders—underlay the Populist struggle toward the end of the century.

Vox Populi

The Populist struggle, perhaps because it contained so much of the hopes and fears of so many in the United States, has been misrepresented in histories from its own day (the 1890s) until now. It is seen generally as having its center in the Middle West; actually, the South, and especially the Deep South, was its stronghold. It is viewed as centering on money fanaticism, which may have represented its midwestern supporters, but did not represent Populism. It is viewed as being inextricably mixed with racism; in fact, the Populist movement in the South brought the only years—and they were few—in which racial egalitarianism was practiced, and in which poor whites and blacks fought shoulder to shoulder, politically and physically.[32]

The distinction must be made between populist tendencies and Populism. The former is a collection of conflicting notions that more often reflects the biases of those who recount them than it does the nature of Populism. The latter was a movement based on the dire needs of its main participants and a nostalgic and hopeful view of what could be and was "supposed to be." It sought to reassert the hegemony of ordinary people, while not doubting the desirability of basic capitalist institutions. Small farmers, small businessmen, and workers were seen as the true heart and muscle of the United States; the State should be *their* instrument and *their* protector—against Big Business, Big Banks, Big Railroads, and the misuse of government. Those were the Populists' wishes; the subsequent uglier realities were the source of their anger and their politics.

They found themselves faced with ruinously falling prices for their crops and a shortage of credit; with extortionate rail rates and commission charges; with manipulated commodity exchanges; with state and even more federal legislatures, and especially the Senate (whose members were not then directly elected), that responded to the direct pressures of the most powerful. By 1896 they also found that the movement leadership had come under the domination of a distorted view of their aims—"free silver"—and a Nebraskan, William Jennings Bryan. He represented not only what was slightest in Populism but worst in the United States. Whether Bryan revealed his inner essence when he became an aggressive Secretary of State under Wilson or the born-again prosecutor of Scopes in the famous "monkey trial" is a matter of dispute; but that essence lay somewhere other than in the central position of the Populists.

Populism was moribund well before the election of 1896 gave it the final blow. Taking no chances, the massive GOP campaign of 1896 was the first truly modern political campaign. Master minded by Marcus Hanna, a Cleveland shipping, banking, transportation, and newspaper magnate, the campaign made regular assessments on businesses, engaged in widely publicized scare tactics, and effectively scattered the opponents of big-business rule, the "communists" of the day. In the South the same period saw a new and more intensified set of segregation ("Jim Crow") laws, accompanied by a tidal wave of lynchings—as many as a thousand in one year. By then the heart of Populism was barely beating, its racial egalitarianism had been replaced by confusion and hatred, and its social and political goals had given way to narrow economic criteria, soon to be measured by the level of farm prices.

The removal of Populism from the political scene sped up even more the consolidation of economic power that Populism alone had resisted: the State system moved toward "political capitalism," as the economy moved toward monopoly capitalism. Institutionalized racism came to be as much a part of the urban North as slavery had been in the South;[33] white people went about their business and looked the other way. And, already in 1897, the drums of overseas imperialism had begun to sound for those who would soon march to them, over and over again. The present act of the drama of the United States had opened; the mass of the citizenry became a background chorus to it, mixing laughs with screams, cheers with anger. Most stood silently, hoping for the best, with their eye on the main chance—some seeking the big bonanza, most just trying to get along.

Lost Democracy

The opening years of this century for many in the United States seemed very much like our own times seem to us; it was an age of dislocation:

> The decline of political democracy and the rise of monopolies were not the only dark aspects of American civilization. Among those which called for remedy were the gross inequality of wealth, wide existence of poverty, racial inequality, the domination by big business of politics, religion, education, and the courts, the selfish and stupid waste of natural resources, carelessness of human life, exploitation of women and children....America's new rulers were the "robber barons" and her new God, Financial Success.[34]

The accompanying hue and cry of social criticism was begun by writers and reformers, conscious things were getting out of joint; the policies that ultimately ensued were shaped and controlled by businessmen and the politicians who suited them. Reformers awakened business to the chaos of the time; a genuine threat to "business as usual."

Able to organize their own kind, and powerful enough to move others, big business brought some order out of that chaos. It was order cut to the needs and aims of industrial capitalism. Thus the Progressive Movement, frequently seen as an antibusiness reformist movement, resulted in a set of far-reaching changes that strengthened the hold of business on the United States. And the Progressives' "respectable reforms" also did much to take the steam out of popular discontent—a preview on a relatively small scale of what would happen as the New Deal became institutionalized after World War II. For all that to happen, the hold of business criteria had to extend itself deeply and consciously into the State system, which in turn had to be expanded and strengthened to insure domestic and international order.[35]

In the days just before the Nazi seizure of power, a respected German economist noted:

> The animosity of German capitalism against the state does not rest upon fundamental theoretical foundations, but upon purely opportunistic considerations. It is opposed to the state when control is in the hands of a political majority whose permanent good will it doubts. German capitalism, which would like to be freed of the power of the state, and which seeks to push back state intervention as far as possible, is constructed exclusively upon the most thorough intervention of the state.[36]

German capitalists had worked steadily to devise a State system suited to their needs throughout much of the nineteenth century. U.S. businessmen, operating in a less stringent social and natural context, needed only to be left alone: laissez-faire (plus tariffs, control of labor, and gifts) was just right. The rapid and pervasive industrial development that swept the United States at the end of the century, however, created a set of problems that individual businesses, no matter how large, could not resolve by themselves: they needed help from State institutions, an "executive committee to manage their common affairs...," to provide the requisite scope. Advanced industrial capitalism, even in the United States, requires social institutions that will prevent its precarious and fruitful interdependencies from becoming a source of breakdown, whether economic, social, or political. In short, *rationalization* becomes a necessity.

The term rationalization is manysided in its meaning, for it is designed to cope with diverse problems. Brady, in his massive study of the German rationalization movement of the 1920s—the first such in the world—comments:

> ...rationalization was begun, and largely carried through, at a time when forces were converging to undermine the institutional framework of German capitalism. As the rationalization movement developed, it became increasingly clear that its progress was to be conditioned by the solution of numerous issues directly related to the radical and far-reaching changes that were taking place in the political, economic, and social institutions of the country. The drift to the two extreme wings, and the politicization of nearly the whole range of economic problems, meant that these issues were to be resolved, if at all, in an atmosphere of bitterness, struggle, and drawn compromise.[37]

Although both the timing and the content of the German movement were different from the comparable (but lesser) movement in the United States, the impulses were very much alike. In the United States, their beginnings were in the Progressive Movement, in the decade or so preceding World War I. As Kolko notes:

> Progressivism was initially a movement for the political rationalization of business and industrial conditions, a movement that operated on the assumption that the general welfare of the community could be best served by satisfying the concrete needs of business. But the regulation itself was invariably controlled by leaders of the regulated industry, and directed toward ends they deemed acceptable or desirable. In part this came about because the regulatory movements were usually initiated by the dominant businesses to be regulated, but it also resulted from the nearly universal belief among political leaders in the basic justice of private property relations as they essentially existed, a belief that set the ultimate limits on the leaders' possible actions.[38]

The Burdens of Success

The problems that led to the new political needs ranged through the whole society. The absence of a central bank and other control institutions in the economy allowed normal business fluctuations to translate into severe panics and depressions. The depression of the 1890s was unprecedentedly deep; the "Panic of 1907" was a panic in more than name. The giant corporations that emerged from the immense combination movement of 1897–1904 behaved with no more recklessness than businesses always had; by then, however, they were no longer mice but bulls in a china shop. National markets for interdependent industries meant pervasive and deeper crises. Business competition had always been alarming to the businesses competed with; the heavy industrialization of the new century made alarm an inadequate reaction. Financial manipulation was a popular business sport throughout the nineteenth century; in the twentieth century it brought Wall Street and a host of other financial enclaves intermittently crashing down. Business could no longer afford to cavort heedlessly; it had to settle down and grow up.

Much the same was true of the exploitation of our natural resources, as was noted earlier. Mining the soil, cutting over timber lands, and the spoliation of mineral resources had brought great profits; if continued in the same way and in greater amounts, such exploitation would dry up its sources, kill the goose. Resource management was necessary: resource management by business. Nor were human resources in a totally different category, at least analytically. Housing, labor conditions, and welfare had never been a matter of keen concern for those who "developed" the cities and hired the workers, of course, but the scope of such activities had never been as great as they suddenly appeared to be in the new century. Urban housing and welfare reform and some mitigation of harsh labor conditions were put forth as desirable. They would not stop the running sores, but they might at least hide them. Mostly, not even that happened.

From the Spanish-Cuban-American War up through World War I, the presidency passed from McKinley to Roosevelt to Taft to Wilson. They were different types of men, and their reputations in history books emphasize those differences. But they had at least one characteristic in common: they provided continuity in the creation of the new "political capitalism." The solidifying developments within the State system took place in the first administration of Woodrow Wilson. The "New Nationalism" of Teddy Roosevelt translated easily into the "New Freedom" of Wilson. All four presidents found themselves occupied with foreign affairs more than any president since Jefferson: McKinley agonized the United States into the Spanish war; Roosevelt created

Panama and its (or our) canal; Taft served as the first U.S. governor of the Philippine Islands; Wilson, promising to keep us out of war, sent U.S. troops first into Mexico and then into World War I. From then on, public relations and manipulation developed into a high art—as was fitting and necessary.[39]

The continuity manifested itself in domestic as well as in imperial policies; all busied themselves with conservation, with urban reform, with "trustbusting," and with financial and industrial reforms. They were the obstetricians of "political capitalism," born around 1900, growing ever since—albeit with some seeming interruptions.

Those who have come to social awareness since World War II are likely to take the ways and means of political capitalism as the "natural" state of affairs; those whose consciousness was formed in earlier decades will remember that the normal condition for U.S. capitalist society was assumed to be one in which the State was unobtrusive in economic and other matters. The State has always operated so as to provide an acceptable and favorable context for capitalist development. In the nineteenth century it did so largely through "nondecisions," that is unobtrusively—except for generous railroad subsidies, protective tariffs, and the like. But in this century the State's role became obtrusive and explicit. The political outlets and institutions of the State had to and came to be used to attain the desired conditions of stability, predictability, and security. Characterizing this development, Kolko says:

> *Stability* is the elimination of internecine competition and erratic fluctuations in the economy. *Predictability* is the ability, on the basis of politically stabilized and secured means, to plan future economic action on the basis of fairly calculable expectations. By *security* I mean protection from the political attacks latent in any formally democratic structure.[40]

There were many conflicts along the way, of course: between various aspects of the business world; between labor and business; between local and national politicians; between socialists, anti-business reformers, and those who represented business interests; between anti-imperialists and imperialists. There are always conflicts; more to the point is who wins out, and how; and one must remember that alongside those who seek what they get are those who, seeking something else, unwittingly assist those who win out.

Business standards won out in these conflicts, but the standards were those of *giant* business, not of all businesses. As the century began, the giants represented the most intense gathering of power in the society, and because it was economic power it was easily transformed into State power. These were the new monopolists; their breeding ground was the old competition. One of the consequences of the State system created in those years was that the movement from small to large to giant firm came to be more under control than in the previous century. The new laws and regulatory agencies put a curb on the rapacious behavior within industries, much as Great Powers do with Lesser Powers in the world of Statesmanship, making the giants more secure against interlopers. It also meant a loss of whatever benefits the public may have derived from the uncontrolled warfare of business—for example, lower prices. The invisible hand that presumably transforms naked self-interest into society's well-being would have to find a different strength than price competition. The antitrust laws of the 1890s began by forbidding collusion and the "intent to monopolize." By the 1930s, amendments made it *illegal* to engage in price competition. By the 1960s, with rare exceptions, competition took the form of "non-price competition," the technique that had begun to spread in the 1920s—and which causes prices to rise rather than to fall. Taken together with economic expansion, the institutionalization of nonprice rivalry made the laws against price competition unnecessary.[41] In an economic world where advertising, sales promotion, research and development, product variation, and lobbying became the chief means for enhancing corporate strength and profits, the battle, of course, went to the already strong, even more than earlier.

One of the closest students of the early period of Progressive reforms, in intending to characterize the beneficial qualities of the period, says:

> By 1917 a change appeared evident in the entrepreneurial spirit and conduct of private business. The flush days of the "robber barons" had passed; leaders of business and of the larger institutions had begun to show some of the characteristics which distinguish them today [1951]. Risk and profit had become less important than security and power....[42]

But when the robber barons of feudal times passed from the scene, it was because their territories had come under the control of a count, a duke, a prince, or a king, with the financial assistance of the merchants upon whom the barons had preyed. The analogy therefore breaks down. In the United States the robber barons *became* the counts, dukes, and princes, and the king largely bent to their will. And, although the search for security and power is certainly what the "larger institutions" sought, they reduced their risks and increased their profits as a result.

The areas encompassed by these efforts cut through the entire economy, producing new laws and a new bureaucracy. Some examples of these are:

Labor. The Clayton Antitrust Act (1914) exempted unions from the antitrust laws, which up to then had been applied against them more than against business combinations. Since 1914 that exemption has been steadily narrowed. The relevant parts of the Act were overeffusively seen as "labor's Magna Carta," a term used again with more reason for the Wagner Act (1935). In 1916, the Adamson Act provided for an eight-hour day for railway workers (the first such federal law), the most powerful of all unions at that time; and in 1926, the Railway Labor Act provided for labor protections that were generalized in the Wagner Act.

Banking. The Glass-Owen Currency (Federal Reserve) Act of 1913 recreated a central bank for the United States, a minimal step to stave off the habitual panics and financial collapse of the preceding decades. The only banking "system" the United States had after Jackson was created by the National Bank Act of 1863—created to help finance the Civil War—whose nature was such as to intensify panics once they had begun. That the new "Fed" was itself weak and badly organized was revealed in the 1920s, when its actions (and nonactions) helped to make 1929 worse than it might otherwise have been. It was strengthened in the New Deal legislation of the mid-1930s.

Taxation. The 16th Amendment was ratified in 1913, providing for a progressive income tax. Although it was never very progressive, it was more so initially than now: incomes below $4000/year were exempt, and in 1913 that was a "middle-level" income. Of taxation, more later.

Conservation. The Newlands Act of 1902 provided for the "reclamation" of arid lands through irrigation. What this meant was a financial boon for irrigation companies in gaining easy and cheap access to the shrinking public domain, most of which had been arid for many years. President Teddy Roosevelt was an ardent conservationist—and hunter.[43]

Consumer Protection. Roosevelt was also an ardent supporter of good eating. Much impressed by Upton Sinclair's *The Jungle* (an exposé of the meat-packing industry, among other matters), he joined reformers by creating the Pure Food and Drug Administration, and signing the Meat Inspection Act (both 1906).

Business Regulation. The Federal Trade Act of 1914 added the Federal Trade Commission to the enforcing agency of the Justice Department, which also includes the Antitrust Division for enforcing the Sherman Act. The courts first used the latter Act against business, in the Northern Securities Case (1904). In 1911, it was used to break Standard Oil into seven separate companies (of Ohio, New Jersey, California, Indiana, etc.), although the Rockefeller family was not required to divest itself of its dominating ownership in the new structure. Most authorities agree that the stepup in antitrust enforcement led not to more competition but to oligopoly—the modern form of monopoly. The Hepburn Act of 1906 and the Mann-Elkins Act of 1910 gave new powers to the Interstate Commerce Commission (created in 1886) for railroad regulation. The long-run effect has been that railroads, though presumably in continuing and rising competition with other transportation industries (truck, air, bus) have continually raised rates and maintained profitability while reducing service both quantitatively and qualitatively.

Foreign Trade. The Webb-Pomerene Export Trade Act (1916) allowed companies involved in foreign trade to form selling cartels for achieving uniform sales policies, thus exempting them from the antitrust laws—this to sharpen the already sharp edges of U.S. competition in the world economy.

In the Catbird Seat

Efforts by corporate liberals and their supporters to create a new State system after 1900 were halting, contradictory, and controversial; the onset of World War I speeded up the development, gave it more coherence, and greatly lessened controversy. The impact of the war on the U.S. economy was so beneficial, however, that in contributing to the upper echelon prosperity of the 1920s it also allowed a reemergence of laissez-faire as the dominant business mood.

The economic gains of the United States from the war need no further discussion here; the institutional changes accompanying the sustained upsurge in production were equally significant. Businessmen, and especially those from the industries most closely connected with war production—metals, fuels, vehicles—were drawn into the councils of government as never before. They were predominantly from the large corporations. As occurred with even greater strength in World War II, the government sought to maximize production and minimize conflict in the economy. This entailed active and close cooperation between representatives of industry, agriculture, and labor, with industry as the dominant member. The Council of National Defense and the War Industries Board were the key agencies. Their leading personnel were those who had also led in the creation of the new State system in the years leading up to the war.[44]

Subtly and firmly the easy use of State power by business became unchallengeable. The political habits of those who used that power and those who acquiesced in it were transformed. Those who might think differently were largely those who opposed both the war and the system that presided over it: the Socialists, led by Eugene Debs (imprisoned for over a year). As has happened more than once, before and since, a general opposition to U.S. involvement in war was transformed into enthusiastic support once the guns began to fire. The opposition was crushed, its leaders vilified and jailed.[45] The larger outcome was that it made easier the repression of the entire Left in the years after the war, through the "Palmer Raids" of 1919–20 and the "Red Scare" that ensued—whose most famous instance was the Sacco-Vanzetti case.[46]

In those years, as again after World War II, a major consequence of anti-Left campaigns was to remove whatever influence radical ideas might have had on the trade union movement, leaving the latter weak and docile. The "consensus" on foreign policy in the Cold War had its earlier tryout and counterpart in a "consensus" on domestic policy in the 1920s, both aided and abetted by repressive and scare tactics.

The mood of business could be laissez-faire in the 1920s because the reality was so firmly under their control as to require little in the way of explicit governmental assistance. The decade opened with Harding as president, followed by Coolidge and Hoover. If Harding had any distinction at all in the office, it was that he was a close competitor to

Buchanan and Polk as the most mediocre of presidents (up to that time); although as far as we know the others lived on a somewhat higher "moral" level. Calvin Coolidge precisely signified the temper of the times for those on top. He gained the prominence he needed for "presidential stature" by helping to break a strike when he was governor of Massachusetts. He was famous for saying little: "Silent Cal" was his nickname. What little he said was telling, however: "The business of America," he pronounced, "is business." And: "The man who builds a factory builds a temple, the man who works there worships there, and to each is due not scorn and blame, but reverence and praise." Hard to beat that.[47]

As F. L. Allen notes in his entertaining evocation of the spirit of the 1920s, *Only Yesterday* (noted earlier), "The great god business was supreme in the land and Calvin Coolidge was fortunate enough to become almost a demi-god by doing discreet obeisance before the altar" (p. 211). By some, the relationship between divinity and business was pushed explicitly. Bruce Barton, founder of one of the largest advertising agencies (BBD&O) wrote in 1924 what became immediately number 1 on the best-seller list, *The Man Nobody Knows: A Discovery of the Real Jesus*. Jesus, it appears, was "the founder of modern business":

> He picked up twelve men from the bottom ranks of business and forged them into an organization that conquered the world.... Nowhere is there such a startling example of executive success as the way in which that organization was brought together.[48]

The God that Failed

Harding and Coolidge, by comparison with Hoover, were simpletons. Hoover's critical view of the evolving State system has been misunderstood or neglected, largely because his reputation become bound up so tightly with the 1930s depression, which began in his term. Hoover was a committed adherent of capitalism, but he opposed the direct use of the State to advance the interests of capitalists. He knew, as president, that what he opposed was already a prominent feature of the U.S. capitalist system. He believed in self-reliance, in voluntary cooperation with others having the same needs. W.A. Williams states Hoover's position:

> ...Hoover feared that the corporation leaders would produce an American form of fascism. If labor became predominant, on the

other hand, the result would be socialism or some willy-nilly variation thereof.... If each broad interest group in the economy continued in its evolving attitude of viewing the governnment as a marketplace in which to compete for its share of the gross wealth, then the system would ultimately be dominated by a state bureaucracy which would lack even the distinguishing character-istic of a positive ideology. And wars engendered by struggles for predominance in the world marketplace threatened to produce a tyranny of even graver proportions because of the increased role and influence of the military.[49]

What Hoover feared from business was in place before he won office in 1928. Whatever cogency his ideas might have had was buried, as he was, by the avalanche of the Great Depression. The collapse of the economy was inaccurately blamed on those who had inaccurately taken credit for its exaggerated achievements—some wry justice in that—as everyone increasingly began to look to the State for succor.

Sophisticated though "corporate liberals" were by comparison with small businessmen before World War I, they were not yet sophisticated enough to create a State system that would give any significant access to that system by those *not* in business: "the business of America," after all, "is business." Their slight inclination to think otherwise was lessened to zero by the roaring confidence of the 1920s.

The fall from grace of business in the 1930s allowed some degree of balance, however minimal, to be achieved, over the howls of betrayal —FDR as "traitor to his class"—of most of those in business, as the State became explicitly interventionist in matters of the business cycle, monetary and fiscal policies, protection for labor and the aged, agricul-ture, and foreign trade. Never very much, never anything like enough, but far too much for those steeped in the traditional ideology. However much the New Deal was responsible for turning red ink to black in the accounts of business, finally, it never ceased to seem an intruding monster to the largest part of the business world.

There had been precedents for all the developments of what came to be the New Deal, both in the United States and other capitalist countries. The New Deal put them together in a different balance, designed to suit the 1930s and the United States. That until after our entrance into World War II it all added up to too little to end the depression, let alone to lift most of that "one-third...ill-clothed, ill-fed, ill-housed" up from their depths, is testimony to just how tight the hold of ideology is, just how different "common sense" is from "good sense."

Largely ineffectually, leaders of the New Deal in the mid- and late-1930s tried to reeducate corporate leaders to what they had first begun to learn and apply three decades earlier. The education that took was World War II and the Cold War, which showed them and others just how valuable that education could be when measured in profits, in social stability, in domestic peace and world power. The growth and developmental aspects of the years after World War II were examined in Chapter 4. The stabilizing and tension-promoting aspects of the new State system will occupy the remainder of this chapter.

The Best Laid Plans...

The decade of the 1950s comprised the years of the "great celebration," of the "silent generation," and of the avuncular Ike. The upsurge of left-wing attitudes and organizations from the 1930s and 1940s had been squashed by spy scares, McCarthyism and the repression that gave it teeth, and by the often enthusiastic cooperation in these endeavors by intellectual and labor leaders. Marx became a four-letter word, Veblen a barely-known freak. The influence and power of the United States expanded all over the globe, capitalism in Europe and Japan arose from what had seemed to be its grave, and flourished as never before in the United States.

In the midst of this quiet and complacency, the sociologist C. Wright Mills wrote his *Power Elite* (cited earlier), a biting appraisal of the State system of the time. Leading liberals in the United States, meanwhile were beginning to write of the "end of ideology," and opining that "the fundamental political problems of the industrial revolution have been solved...."[50]

Mills was the first U.S. academic social scientist after World War II to recognize the extraordinary role then being played by foreign policy and militarization in the entire life of the United States and its foreign satellites. The original and controversial quality of his argument led to an immediate reaction from "liberal, radical, and highbrow critics." Almost all of the reaction was scornful.[51]

As Mills saw it, "the power élite" has three components: "the corporate rich," "the political directorate," and "the warlords." For him, as in my earlier discussion of the State system, the first two components overlap: the political directorate holds the top posts of the State system; those who occupy those posts are from the highest levels of business—in fact, in spirit, or in association (for instance, corporate lawyers). That is, the power élite reduces itself to two segments, corporate rulers and the Pentagon. How much power the Pentagon has and the degree of autonomy with which it has or could use that power is now a matter of substantial controversy; when Mills first made his argument about the military, it was dismissed out of hand from all quarters, for varying reasons.

The final test of greatness for an analytical contribution does not depend upon its being indubitably "correct," but on whether or not it leads to substantial questioning, further research, and improved understanding. *The Power Elite* qualifies as such a work. The way in which Mills made his case stimulated many others to their own hypotheses and studies, which were stimulated as well by the increasingly *obvious* growth of the State system and its military component then and later. Much of the discussion has moved along lines that oversimplify and distort the real problems suggested by Mills; it has taken place largely within the *liberal* universe of discourse and analysis. There are other, more radical analyses as well, both more penetrating and more ominous in their import. Seymour Melman's work is representative of the former at its best, as James O'Connors's is of the latter. We now examine each in turn.[52]

Warfare State?

A professor of industrial management at Columbia University, Seymour Melman emerged in the 1960s as the foremost liberal academic critic of the self-destructive tendencies of the United States, as it continually built up its destructive weaponry. As one of the most intensive students of the military-industrial complex in the United States and a critic of military-related waste and the misuse of our entire range of resources, Melman also became a critic of the war in Indochina. The opening words of his influential *Pentagon Capitalism* define his position clearly:

An industrial management has been installed in the federal government, under the Secretary of Defense, to control the nation's largest network of industrial enterprises. With the characteristic managerial propensity for extending its power, limited only by its allocated share of the national product, the new state-management combines peak economic, political, and military decision-making.[53]

In 1974 Melman produced still another book in what has become a series, *The Permanent War Economy: American Capitalism in Decline* (New York: Simon and Schuster). There he "delineates the workings of a new economy...in the firm and in the aggregate—that has been spawned by the military system, and that has resulted finally in a military form of state capitalism" (p. 12). Melman is quite clearly antimilitarist, and just as clearly he is *not* anticapitalist. Indeed, side by side with his very strong attitudes against war is his fervent belief that the multi-dimensional consequences of "a permanent war economy" will bring U.S. capitalism down:

In the experience of many people during the thirty years after World War II, especially in the upper middle class and in the technical and administrative occupations, the expectation that war spending brings prosperity was borne out. What went unrecognized was that war economy produces other, unforeseen, effects with long-term destructive consequences. These include the formation of a new state managed economy, deterioration of the productive competence of many industries, and finally, inflation— the destruction of the dollar as a reliable store of value.... [The] $1,500 billion spent on the military since World War II produced no economically useful products for the society.

And, somewhat later:

The permanent war economy, far from solving problems of capital and labor surplus in American economy, as suggested by the conventional wisdom, will be shown to perform as a prime generator of uninvestable capital, unemployable labor, and industrial inefficiency... [and] to be a prime cause of the American inflation of the 1970s, a development that is inexplicable to those trained in contemporary economics that classifies military outlays as just another species of government spending.[54]

The data confronting Melman and all other students of the role of military production in the U.S. economy make such characterizations plausible; and, given the intensification of developments toward both militarization and economic decline since 1974, not only plausible but compelling. The figures by themselves already then, to say nothing of later, were substantially worrisome:

In the United States, 10 percent of our personal income and 20 percent of our manufacturing output are derived from this war industry. Indirectly, the livelihood of twelve to fourteen million Americans, including two-thirds to three-fourths of our scientists, now depends on this industry. The defense sector has had the fastest rate of growth of any area in the economy, and it accounts for more than half the research done in this country since the Cold War began.[55]

To which may be added, as Melman points out in *Permanent War Economy*, "...the military element in 1971 was 73 percent of the $97 billion of total federal purchases for all uses...[;] the assets of the U.S. military establishment [in 1970] were 38 percent as much as the assets of all U.S. industry [$544 billion]" (p. 23).

But. The key to understanding is in finding what questions to ask, and then going to work (from which still more—and "better"—questions usually arise). In our earlier discussion of imperialism, we quoted some liberal social scientists whose question was "Does the U.S. economy require imperialism?" And their answer was, of course, "No." Melman, concerned with the militarization of the U.S. economy, asks the same kind of question. The concluding chapter of *Permanent War Economy* is headed "Does American Capitalism Need a War Economy?" And the whole chapter is an extended "No!" regarding not only U.S. capitalism but capitalism in general—when he shows, for example, that military spending as a percent of GNP is many times higher in the United States than in Germany or Japan—where, however, there has been an enormous amount of *U.S.* military spending, as noted earlier—but that their growth rates have generally been notably higher than ours. In the conclusion to the book, Melman proposes ways and means for the United States to "exit" from its condition of "permanent war economy." His alternatives are unquestionably attractive, eloquently summarized, and very much worth pondering and working for (p. 299):

...instead of military nonproductive activity dominating public budgets, a concentration of public funds on reconstructing vital areas of public economic responsibility; instead of operating on the assumption of a permanent war economy, thoughtful planning for conversion to other work; ...instead of economic neglect and social decay for 30 million Americans, an effort to end poverty and economic underdevelopment....

These proposals and others of their kind will be discussed, and in one way or another both supported and criticized in the next chapter; here we shall approach the arguments of Melman concerning militarization analytically rather than programmatically. The place to begin is to note that there is more than one argument involved, quite apart from what one thinks of militarism and militarization. Is the U.S. economy in a process of decline, and if so, why? Has its productivity, both recently and for the long term been damaged and reduced? Would there have been a more viable economy, higher real incomes, greater economic strength and a more viable and enduring *capitalism* in the absence of militarization? Have we wasted our engineering, scientific, and skilled labor talents by diverting so much of them to military production and services, directly and indirectly?

These and other questions of their sort that could be raised concern a set of complex social processes, of course, by no means confined to their economic content. More than anything else necessary to begin to find appropriate answers is the need to come to grips with a very large question indeed: In the absence of the Cold War and all that it has meant in domestic and international global economic and political process-es—much of which has been discussed in earlier pages—where would the U.S. and the world economy be now? And our politics? Our minds?

It would be absurd to try to answer such questions with anything more than broad guesses based on arbitrary hypotheses as to a very large number of very important matters. What can be said, however, is this: (1) The probabilities are very high indeed that "military Keynesianism" has been fundamental in sustaining acceptable levels of production, jobs, and profits in the United States and the other leading capitalist econo-mies—especially the two strongest, Japan and Germany. (2) Although the U.S. economy is surely in a process of decline relative to its principal competitors, that, as has been suggested earlier, is an unavoidable consequence of a successfully functioning world economy, as the experience of Britain suggested (as did, in a lesser way, that of the Dutch in the seventeenth century): as Veblen said, "it is the penalty of taking the lead." (3) This is not to suggest that the U.S. economy does not have serious and worsening absolute weaknesses, that any or all of them were inevitable, nor that militarization has not been responsible for some of the most important of them—for example, most of the horrendous national debt and a significant part of our balance of payments deficit (because of military expenditures abroad). But it must be understood that the most dynamic parts of the U.S. economy in the past several decades have been an organic outcome of militarization, and that the sector most involved, manufacturing, has maintained its productivity increases over the appropriate time period. Indeed, the areas in which the United States initially took the lead technologically—transistors, and nuclear energy, among other areas—had their origins in projects organized, paid for, and inspired by the military.[56] As for the waste of scientific and other talent, (4) anyone familiar with universities for the past half century will also know how, as Cypher puts it, "...under the stimulus of a variety of government subsidies, the science and engineering departments of universities [generated] an increased supply, and even an oversupply of qualified labor power."[57]

Unlike so many in the universities, Prof. Melman was never taken in by what may be seen as the propaganda of the Cold War; but in none of his many important books and articles does he see the *creative* connections between "the corporations and the Cold War," and the maintenance and the flourishing of capitalism—as such things are measured in our society. There was and is a high consciousness among the corporate leaders who served in or as advisors to the State as to what the alternatives were as between "an American Century," necessarily undergirded by militarization to an important degree, or, failing that, "radical readjustments in our entire economic structure..., changes which could hardly be made under our democratic free enterprise system."[58]

But there is a larger argument to be made concerning militarization and the period since World War II. It concerns the mutually supportive relationships between (1) the militarization of the economy and society, and (2) the substantial increases in the real and social wages of at least two-thirds of the U.S. population—and, given the central role of the United States in the *world* economy, also in the other rich countries. The larger argument will be that without both, neither would have been possible—"under our democratic free enterprise system."[59]

Warfare/Welfare State

The major political tendencies in a society such as ours cannot be evaluated without an analysis that centers on the power, the needs, and the modes of conduct of giant national and multinational corporations. Baran and Sweezy's *Monopoly Capital* (1966, cited earlier) sought to provide an analytical framework within which the key processes and relationships could be investigated and understood. The theoretical center of their analysis is "the tendency of the surplus to rise." What is the "surplus" and why does it tend to rise?

> The economic surplus... is the difference between what a society produces and the costs of producing it. The size of the surplus is an index of productivity and wealth, of how much freedom a society has to accomplish whatever goals it may set for itself. The composition of the surplus shows how it uses that freedom: how much it invests in expanding its productive capacity, how much it consumes in various forms, how much it wastes and in what ways.[60]

Baran and Sweezy see the surplus as rising from just under 29 percent of GNP in 1929 to something close to 60 percent in the early 1960s, with the State (on all levels) absorbing over half of the present postwar surplus. Clearly an analysis of the State becomes critical for understanding the behavior of society, whether or not one fully accepts the foregoing conceptual apparatus and its estimates.

Keynes, in his *General Theory of Employment, Interest, and Money* made it clear that the State had to intervene for there to be a level of "effective demand" that would support general profitability and acceptable levels of jobs and incomes. Baran and Sweezy, as Marxists, took that analysis further. Their treatment of the economic surplus argues that an economic surplus that is not *absorbed* (by some combination of investment, consumer, export, and government demand) will decline—that is, the economy will contract, until the magnitude of the surplus *can* be absorbed. A surplus that is not absorbed will not be generated, nor will its accompanying sales and incomes. Seen in this way, the accomplishments of modern industrial capitalism—its great productivity and production—become also the source of its major problem—failure of the accumulation process. To save capitalism, the State—seen as problem, not saviour, in classical and neoclassical economic thought—*must* intervene. Thus the characteristic feature of *all* modern industrial capitalist nations is not only that they are concentrated in their economic structures but that the State has become central to their life processes. James O'Connor, much stimulated by the work of Baran and Sweezy, has been foremost among U.S. economists in seeking to explain this modern "political economy." What follows depends very much on his contributions.[61]

O'Connor posits three sectors in the economy: (1) the monopolistic sector, (2) the competitive sector, and (3) the State sector. He assumes the economy to be marked by surplus capital and surplus labor. It is the interaction of all of the foregoing that gives the economy and the State their quality and direction. The quality is that of a monopoly capital warfare/welfare State; the direction has combined imperialism, militarization, racism and sexism to bring us to our present condition; and the future direction (as he saw it in 1973) is problematic.

The monopolistic sector is the pride of the U.S. economy. It is where productivity, high profits and the highest wages are found. It is the world of the giant corporation, the "household names"—GE, GM, EXXON, IBM, ITT—and of the strongest unions (the teamsters and construction unions being notable exceptions). It is where the greatest concentration of business and labor exists, and where productive capacity is (except for agriculture) most obviously in surplus.

The competitive sector is where most businesses, and as many workers as in the monopolistic sector, function. Unlike the monopolistic sector, productivity is relatively low and technology nondynamic; profits are low; wages do not allow a decent livelihood; and labor is in surplus. This sector comprises small retailers and producers, and their like. Competitive businesses often have substantial power on *local* issues; their power on the national level is confined to their limited influence on the two major political parties.

The State sector (federal, state, and local) is responsible for State expenditures and activities. The nature and importance of that responsibility is well-clarified by James O'Connor, and warrants lengthy quotation (pp. 6–7):

State expenditures have a twofold character corresponding to the capitalist state's two basic functions [accumulation and legitimation]: social capital and social expenses. *Social capital* is expenditures required for profitable accumulation; it is indirectly productive.... There are two kinds of social capital: social investment and social consumption.... *Social investment* consists of projects and services that increase the productivity of a given amount of labor-power and, other factors being equal, increase the rate of profit. A good example is state-financed industrial-development parks. *Social Consumption* consists of projects and services that lower the reproduction costs of labor and, other factors being equal, increase the rate of profit. An example of this is social insurance, which expands the reproductive powers of the work force while simultaneously lowering labor costs. The second category, *social expenses*, consists of projects and services which are required to maintain social harmony—to fulfill the state's "legitimization" function. They are not even indirectly productive.... The best example is the welfare system, which is designed chiefly to keep social peace among unemployed workers.

In the process, the State indirectly generates as well as absorbs and redirects a growing part of the economic surplus. It is the most rapidly growing of the three sectors. Although its function is to provide economic stimuli and social stability it has been both the source as well as the mitigator of the tensions accompanying the socioeconomic crisis O'Connor saw coming in 1973. Its ways of doing both have deepened *and* contained the crisis.

Surplus capital is a way of characterizing the excess productive capacity and the corollary supply of investment funds which, in the absence of the State sector, would have brought U.S. capitalism to the bursting point some time ago. The key role of the State has been to use up and to create outlets for capital—in the military, in nonmilitary goods and services, and abroad. Given that fundamental development, U.S. business has been able through advertising and sales promotion to develop the "consumerism" that propels our people (and increasingly, others) to spend more than they earn whenever possible, on almost anything—until they lose or fear to lose their jobs, if and when the State's functions no longer suffice, or as in recent years, when its policies become perverse.

Surplus labor in a capitalist economy is the other side of surplus productive capacity. In a rational society there would be neither; in a society where marketability and profitability are the criteria of production and of employment, there must be both. Surplus labor was seen as a "problem" in vivid terms in the 1930s. One of the most widely read writers of the time was Walter B. Pitkin, author of the best-selling *Life Begins at Forty*, in which he was speaking to middle-income groups. In another book, *Let's Get What We Want* (1935), Pitkin, then very popular in business circles, proclaimed:

> ...most well-mannered debaters carry on with the White Lie of Democracy; and thus reach worthless conclusions. A land swarming with tens of millions of morons, perverts, culls, outcasts, criminals, and lesser breeds of low-grade humans cannot escape the evils all such cause.... So long as we have an underworld of 4,000,000 or more scoundrels willing to do anything for a price, and a twilight world of fully 40,000,000 people of profound stupidity and ignorance, or indifference, and a population of nearly 70,000,000 who cannot support themselves entirely and hence must think first of cost, whenever they buy things, we shall have a nasty mess on our hands.[62]

Contemporary liberal and radical critics of the United States in the Cold War period have usually joined in one major error: they have assumed that military spending has risen to astronomical levels, which is true, but that nonmilitary spending has increased only slightly; not true. The basis for that error is not simply a nonreading of the data but an assumption that social sophistication is totally absent among the corporate élite. Put differently, it is a failure to understand that strong impulses toward "liberalism" in recent decades have come from many of the largest corporations, the counterpart of what was so in the Progressive period before World War I. Before looking at some of the relevant data on this side of State spending, the view of David Rockefeller, head of Chase Manhattan Bank when (in 1971) he took the following position, can serve as a *leitmotiv*:

> In view of the emerging demands for revision of the social contract, a passive response on the part of the business community could be dangerous. Any adaptation of our system to the changing environment is more likely to be workable if those who understand the system's problems share in designing the solutions. So it is up to businessmen to make common cause with

other reformers... to prevent the unwise adoption of extreme and emotional remedies, but on the contrary to initiate necessary reforms that will make it possible for businessmen to continue to function in a new climate.... By acting promptly, business can assure itself a voice in deciding the form and content of the new social contract.[63]

The "new social contract" referred to by Rockefeller was a step beyond the then well-formed warfare/welfare State, a step in the direction of the West European "social accords," an attempt (in O'Connor's terms) to transform social expenses into social capital: to the so-called "military-industrial complex" Rockefeller would have added a "social-industrial complex." Put into effect on a broad scale, his proposals might well have softened and shortened the crisis just beginning to take hold as he spoke; but because that crisis *was* emerging, his ideas, put forth to an audience of businessmen, fell on deaf ears. Had there been at that time in the United States something approximating the Left forces in Western Europe, his message would have been forthcoming from them.

Even so, to speak of a warfare/welfare State is to suggest that some meaningful, if limited, steps in that direction had already been taken; but as we shall see, the very factors making for that progress are now serving to obstruct its further movement. To build the warfare state was not difficult, for the attitudes necessary for it had a long history in the United States: but those same attitudes were part of a mix that stood in opposition to the politics necessary for the construction of a welfare state in this country. Especially is that so when our long love affair with what may be seen as a naive individualism is taken into account. Violence and raw patriotism run deep in the grain of our history; concern for social balance has at best been a veneer. Building the U.S. empire has been like rolling off a log; the other task set by the corporate élite, to say nothing of that offered by Rockefeller, is like trying to roll that log up a steep slope. By today, the slope has become almost vertical, clifflike. When the effort was being made seriously, in the twenty years or so that ended in the 1970s, the energy behind it combined the power of corporate leaders with that of the surplus population of the State and competitive sectors; and the resistance to it came largely from small business and organized labor in the competitive sector and some of the powerful in the State sector. If only, a Rockefeller might think, if only those who have resisted would try to understand what O'Connor makes clear:

...both welfare spending and warfare spending have a two-fold nature: the welfare system not only politically contains the surplus population but also expands demand and domestic markets. And the warfare system not only keeps foreign rivals at bay and inhibits development of world revolution (thus keeping laborpower, raw materials, and markets in the capitalist orbit) but also helps to stave off economic stagnation at home.[64]

Herewith some representative data representing this development: Total government spending (federal plus state and local) was 8 percent of GNP in 1890; by 1960 it was approaching 30 percent; by the end of the 1980s it was approaching 40 percent. Military spending, except for the two world wars, was unsubstantial until after World War II—it was less than that spent on the postoffice in the 1920s; in the past decade and more, as noted earlier, it amounts to over half of federal spending. State and local spending, almost entirely nonmilitary, increased over seventyfold in this century. Local and state spending is in the area of social capital (transportation, education, health), income maintenance (such as welfare), and fire and police forces. But the federal government also spends on social capital (highways, education, housing and community development—although decreasingly as the 1980s began), on income maintenance, and various other forms of social consumption (food stamps, etc.). All categories of State spending began to rise rapidly in the 1960s, for both "guns and butter": in the 1960s alone, for example, military spending rose by 75 percent, while income maintenance outlays rose by 100 percent, and local and state spending classifiable under welfare rose even more.[65]

The State thus accomplishes many vital functions for maintaining U.S. capitalism: (1) the social capital provides facilities and skills that reduce the costs and increase the profits of business; (2) the social capital that takes the form of income maintenance enhances purchasing power; (3) military and paramilitary forces abroad and at home create and maintain a framework within which orderly business can be transacted; (4) the research and development associated with military production, an important part of social capital, enhances productivity in at least some areas and subsidizes investment in the monopoly sector; (5) jobs are provided both outside and within the State sector: since the 1960s something over 25 percent of the work force has owed its jobs directly or indirectly to State payrolls and contracts.

Of the many factors making the recession that began in 1990 so stubborn and severe, one is that the reduction of social expenditures, accomplished in critical degree by the lowering of federal grants-in-aid to cities and states—the main locale for such expenditures—has naturally meant the direct loss of thousands of State jobs, and indirectly a further loss through the consequent decline of purchasing power. It is not unimportant to note that those for whom State jobs have been most decisive in getting or staying out of poverty have been those most benefited by the earlier expansion of State jobs—African-Americans, Asian-Americans, Hispanic-Americans and women irrespective of color—not least because discrimination is more difficult to accomplish in public than in private enterprises.[66]

This development toward State stringency is but one part of what O'Connor anticipated (in 1973) in his *Fiscal Crisis*. That "crisis" may be summed up as the tendency for *necessary* State expenditures to outrun *politically feasible* revenues. It all has to be paid for, through taxation of all kinds on all levels. The so-called "tax revolt" that emerged in the 1970s—symbolized by "Prop 13" (1978) in California—arose not from careless construction or administration of the new State system, but from the very features that made the system necessary and that once made it possible. Veblen would say that the system had the defects of its virtues; Marx would see it as the culminating set of the inherent contradictions of capitalism—except that in the nineteenth-century capitalism of Marx there was no room for the modern State system.

The underlying cause that made it necessary in capitalist terms to begin (in the 1970s) to shrink the welfare side of the warfare/welfare State, as was noted in Chapter 4, was the faltering of the accumulation process, and the inflation that accompanied it: stagflation. Thus it was in the 1970s that the domestic politics of the United States came to turn away from what had been the New Deal/Fair Deal/New Frontier/Great Society programs and toward the relative conservatism of Nixon, Ford, and Carter, thence to be hurled into the cruel Malthusianism of the Reagan and Bush years.

That set of strengthening tendencies toward the political Right is not to be explained principally in terms of the personalities involved; rather, such personalities and their policies became acceptable, even enthusiastically so, to a population that has learned to be mindless, careless, heartless. As was discussed in preceding pages, the new monopoly capitalist system that made "consumerism" along with spectacular personal, business, and State debt accumulation and the "social accord" possible was the rapid rate of expansion that took hold after the 1950s. That in turn depended on the Cold War and the expanding and linked national and world economies.

So long as the whole system was interacting smoothly, guns and butter were not in competition with each other. But because it had to be financed by taxation, and taxation could only be painless so long as incomes were rising faster than taxes, the stage was set for major troubles. The troubles would take the form, as O'Connor pointed out, of politically-encouraged conflict between the "lesser peoples" of the competitive sector (where also dwelt the beneficiaries of the "kinder and gentler society" that was created in the 1960s) and those higher up on the scale—most importantly, the blue- and white-collar workers of the monopoly sector. The latter were taught by the racist, militarist, and ideological politics that thrust Reagan into power that their inability any longer to buy as much as they wished, while also trying to pay for earlier purchased cars and houses and rising taxes, could be blamed on "welfare cheats"—not on decades of military expenditures, excess productive capacity, massive waste, falling real wages, etc. The brutal message fell on receptive ears.

Shine, Perishing Republic

The State system has exfoliated in all its parts, but some parts have grown considerably more than others. They are the parts most satisfying and least controversial among those at the top and middle levels of power, and those of the underlying population—at this time a sizeable and growing percentage—who have found the rhetoric of the latter persuasive. They are the parts that hue most closely to our nation's long-standing love affair with money-making and expansion, by any means necessary.

The fuel of U.S. dynamism has been the combination—these days rather weak—of investment directed by profit and the work ethic accepted by the people. The accompanying dualism in the economy has had its corollary in the State system. The nonmilitary segment grew, but could not keep up with the natural, normal, and powerful tendencies to create and maintain inequality in the distribution of income and wealth, aided directly and indirectly by militarization. As we saw in Chapter 5, nonmilitary policy initiatives in the 1960s halved the percentage of our people living in poverty; but in the 1980s, as Reaganomics more than doubled the income of the top 1 percent of the population, the income of those in the bottom 80 percent stagnated at best, while poverty rose rapidly. The military side of the State system was "sold" in a manner effective enough to sell refrigerators in the Arctic; social expenditures were, so to speak, brought in through the side door—most effectively in the Johnson years, the very years in which our militarism in Vietnam became so costly in lives and wealth.

Overseas imperialism as a way of life for the United States is now just about a century along. In the decades since World War II, almost imperceptibly, militarization of our economy, our politics, of our society joined the parade of a militarized foreign policy. In my view and in those of many others cited above (Oglesby, Kolko, Cypher, Magdoff, Williams, Klare, Sweezy, O'Connor, et al.) our militarization has not been a reasoned response to external military threats to our national safety; instead it has been a conscious and deliberate attempt to underpin economically and geographically expansionist policies, as outlined in Chapters 4 and 7. To achieve that, given the widespread *anti*militarist attitudes prevalent in the United States in the 1920s and 1930s, a massive propaganda effort was essential. Doubtless some of the propagandists, high and low in power and prestige, *believed* there was a real threat; doubtless some still do.

There was, of course, an important threat of sorts, as World War II ended, but it was neither military nor economic—as how could it have been, with the United States possessing the most powerful combination of air, land, and seapower, plus a monopoly on atomic weapons, and the only strong economy in the world, and the strongest in history? Not only were all the other major capitalist nations and the Soviet Union physically and economically flattened from the long years of war, but the even longer period that comprised fascism and depression had put capitalist rule in Europe very much on the defensive *politically*. At the same time—and quite apart from anything having to do with the Soviet Union—the parties and arguments of the Left and its record as the principal political and military opposition to fascism (*partigiani* in Italy, *maquis* in France) made it seem quite reasonable that socialism was likely to spread all over Europe—without a gun being aimed, let alone fired. Once the Cold War began and the Soviet Union had begun to recover from the devastation of the war and many years later developed its own nuclear arsenal, a military contest became something more than a rhetorical possibility. But by then the plans and programs of the United States for Europe, Japan, and the world economy were firmly in place, and had commenced to be so when the Soviet Union was still in desperate straits.

Moving into the geographic and economic soft spots allowed by the weakening of all the other capitalist powers, the United States gained two additional bonuses after World War II: the stimuli from military production and a virtual end to domestic dissent—until the 1960s. And during the 1960s, it should be remembered, the dissent took hold in largely noneconomic realms: civil rights and connected antipoverty movements, the draft and the war in Indochina. With the passage of civil rights legislation, a "war on poverty" (both under Johnson), rising incomes, a de facto end to the draft (under Nixon) and, finally, an end to the war, the voices of dissent in the United States, though never stilled, had lost their effectiveness—and most especially when their insistence was on economic and racial matters.

Capitalism—or as it has come to be called "the free market system"—and freedom had become synonymous, dissenters at home were dupes or worse, opposition abroad part of an international conspiracy (communist and/or "terrorist") to overrun the world.[67] Attitudes toward public policies that might promote opportunities, jobs, and the amenities of life to the lower two-fifths of the population—that is, that would provide for social stability and higher overall productivity, to say nothing of a modicum of social decency, the function of the welfare state—became suspect, lowering substantially what had in any case been the low norms of the United States.

Slowly and quite surely for the past twenty years or so, both the universe of acceptable and effective political discourse and the kind of person who could rise to high political levels shifted toward conservatism and reaction. Richard M. Nixon's political career exemplifies the process all too well. He first won a seat in the House in 1946 (by vilifying his mildly liberal opponent as a Communist) and became known almost entirely for his work on the House Un-American Activities Committee; that made it possible for him to win a seat in the Senate (again vilifying his opponent, also mildly liberal, as a Communist); then campaigned for vice president as Ike's bully boy, characterizing staunchly conservative Adlai Stevenson as "Adlai the appeaser..., a Ph.D. graduate of Dean Acheson's cowardly college of Communist containment" (Acheson was one of the architects of the Cold War, as it happens, and a noted Wall Street lawyer); then had to resign from the presidency (shortly after the resignation of *his* vice president, Spiro Agnew, *his* bully boy, implicated in corruption from when he had been governor of Maryland)—saying "I am not a crook!"—because of Watergate. The point of this historical discussion is two-fold: Nixon showed just how successful a career built on innuendo, lies, sentimentality, and negativism could become; secondly, Nixon, seen as a right-winger in the 1950s and 1960s is now looked back upon as having been a pragmatic conservative, even, in domestic policy, as a liberal. In sum, a person and policies once classified as on the Right have, without changing, shifted to the Center: he who was once widely called "Tricky Dick" is now listened to as an elder statesman, and, by many who once derided him, as a president of quality.

What now is seen as "conservative" is what earlier was seen as reactionary, or even, in some of its representatives and policies, fascist. What has changed fundamentally have not been the persons or the policies but the nation and its people.[68]

How and why could the United States descend to these lower depths of sense and decency? Education and popular discussion in the United States has done little to generate substantial answers to such questions, for in general our interest in social analysis has been limited, and our tendency to personalize historical processes: we credit Roosevelt for this, blame Reagan for that, and so on. Of course, personalities are relevant; but more to the point is how and when particular personalities are able to rise to positions of power.

From the late 1940s on, the people of the United States underwent a complicated series of changes in attitudes and behavior. For reasons made explicit (and sometimes left implicit) above, some of those attitudes and patterns of behavior survived and strengthened, others weakened or disappeared. Understandably, the "winners" were those connected with the ideas and aspirations of the powerful: "the ruling ideas of any era are the ideas of its ruling class."

In changing so, our people came to value more what earlier they had found less valuable, or entirely valueless; and, perhaps even worse, to place in a black hole much of what had once been socially laudable and praised. It was not all a matter of ideas and fear-filled rhetoric, of course. A very high percentage of the people had come to be dependent upon the militarized empire for their jobs and profits; or so they came to believe. As things have been, of course, the belief was not entirely foolish, even though as things *now* stand real income and jobs are in trouble in some critical degree *because* of our addiction to empire and militarization. From being the cutting edge of what was seen as our prosperity, the imperial/military basis of U.S. production has become a two-edged sword: our external and militarized relationships in becoming vital to the United States, now that they have run into a period of complicated troubles and change, have become the cutting edge of worsening economic and political problems. Let us cite a few examples of this process:

The greatest surge of economic militarization—adding much gilt to an already very gilded lily—began in 1982–83 with Reagan. When Reagan took office, the national debt was around $1 trillion; when he left it was around $3 trillion; now it is over $4 trillion. Reagan asked for a $6 trillion military spending program for the 1980s, and got a very large part of it. Just what this experience by itself meant, an experience given the nation by the strongest budget-balancing rhetoric it had ever heard from a presidential candidate or sitting president, can be gleaned from a few figures:

• As a percent of GNP, in the twenty years after 1950, the total national deficit averaged about 0.6 percent; in the 1970s it was about 1.8 percent; in 1980–84 it averaged 4.3 percent; from 1985 to date it has always been above 5 percent. Despite *his* rhetoric, and that of Congress, the deficits of Bush's years (fiscal 1990 and 1991) have easily broken the earlier record set by Reagan.[69]

• Interest payments on that debt never went above 1.3 percent of GNP until 1980, but they have been well over 3 percent since 1985 (3.8 percent in 1990). Those interest payments, about $290 billion in 1992, go almost entirely to the top tenth of income receivers, and are one more means of redistributing income upward (and, in Keynesian terms, thus lowering the propensity to consume from a given level of GNP) and intensifying stagnation tendencies.[70]

• If we view the growth of the modern State system as a means of resolving a combination of domestic and international problems and possibilities, economic and otherwise, and most especially see the uses of the State since the mid-1970s as a means of combating actual and developing crises, then we must agree with O'Connor when he says,

In economic terms..., the "solution" adopted by capital and the
state in postwar USA to historical crises of overproduction of
capital slowly but inexorably created a crisis of underproduction
of capital defined in terms of insufficient amounts of surplus
value produced and unproductive utilization of the surplus value
which was produced. In sociological terms..., the working class
and salariat, large-scale capital and new forms of capitalist
competition, and the state, i.e., the structure of modern U.S.
society, increasingly, albeit blindly, became social barriers to
capitalist accumulation.[71]

And it is O'Connor's important insight that "'solutions' to past crises
became 'problems' during succeeding ones" (p. 55).

It is quite probably true that nobody in the halls of power *ever*
contemplated at the beginning (say, in the late 1940s) that the
militarization and consumerization of U.S. society would, or even could,
go as far as it has, quantitatively or qualitatively. Had they, it is also
improbable that they would have foreseen the sociopolitical consequences
of such processes—producing at the same time levels of opulence and of
poverty that standing alone would have been striking, but when taken
together become not only shocking but explosive. What is one to make
of a people divided (for purposes of discussion) into three groups,
composed (1) of those who have more than they need and continue not
only to shop insistently for more and more but seek also by whatever
means to enhance their already satisfactory or enormous incomes, as they
scorn and fear (2) a very much larger group composed of those who are
without adequate means of life, let alone comfort and decency, some
growing *millions* of whom are "homeless," all in this group more victims
than propagators of petty crime (and crimes of violence), trapped in the
vicious circles of poverty (that the 1960s taught us *can* be reduced in
circumference, where the social will exists), their children doomed in
large numbers to ill-health, maleducation, drugs, and the rest, and both of
the foregoing two groups surrounded by (3) the largest group of all, the
upper rings of which hope to find their way to number 1, and the largest
number of which have a deadly fear of becoming members of the scorned
and feared number 2—as in recent years, indeed, many have.[72]

The dirge could go on all too much longer. Let us end it with one
of the larger scandals of this nation, uniquely blessed with the quality and

quantity of its resources, its diverse peoples, its social *possibilities*, as compared with all other societies. How does one measure the accomplishments of a society? Doubtless there are many ways, each with its own validity. For present purposes, the measure will not be how high the GNP, how many cars and Olympic medals, or the like, but with what happens to the people of the society, and most particularly those most vulnerable: the children and the old. A collection of examples may make the point better than an extended argument:

Item: "After government programs are counted, the poverty rate of 10.9 percent for the American elderly was nearly four times the average in the other countries. The poverty rate of 20.4 percent for American children was about three times as high."[73] For a nation where the family is enshrined by praise and sentiment from on high and low, how is that explained?

Item: Ten children are killed by guns every day. Three children die from child abuse every day. Seventeen thousand children die from poverty every year. One out of every seven teenagers attempts suicide; every day six succeed. The United States ranks number 19 in infant mortality in the world, number 22 in mortality rates for children under 5 years, number 19 in the number of school children per teacher, number 8 in childhood poverty. Virtually alone among industrial nations, the United States does *not* provide the following: medical care and financial assistance to all pregnant women; a family allowance to workers and their children; paid maternity/paternity leave.[74]

If the United States were only a well-off nation (like Italy, for example) such conditions would be unacceptable; but although the United States is a very rich nation, as things now stand steps to *end* such conditions are unacceptable. Better than others elsewhere, we have been taught to blame the victims and turn the other way—usually toward a shopping mall.

If It's Broke, Fix It

One of the many charms of the United States has been its joking ways of dealing with serious matters: "There's no such thing as a free lunch," when criticizing social expenditures; and "If it ain't broke, don't fix it," when deregulating banks. Both of these have been staples of our political diet for at least the past fifteen years. But as the foregoing chapters and pages have sought to make clear, there *is* a free lunch if you're lucky

THE STATE — 471

enough to be sitting at the right table, the one with power marking the places; and the U.S. system *is* broken, by any measure of workability, viability, and, not least, social decency. But it wasn't broken by others or by bad luck; quite the contrary. It took a lot of doing, for at least two centuries, to take the possibilities of the new nation and transform them into the ongoing uglinesses of its history. The doing was composed of an ideology of self-seeking—not especially admirable but at least defensible —that over time became greed and inanity; an explicable hunger for geographic expansion over a relatively empty continent that swiftly became an unslakeable lust and that trampled everything and everyone in its way, and then kept going beyond the continent, and let the devil take the hindmost; a need to be armed in order to gain freedom, transformed over the centuries into a readiness to use arms, as individuals and as a nation, on the very flimsiest of pretexts;[75] a nation which, if it was to fill up with a population that might use its abundant resources, had to become "a melting pot" of the world's peoples and which, as it did so, steadily melted out the cultures and traditions of the peoples who became our citizens, and just as steadily developed a culture of racism that seems to know no end.

So here we are, as of this writing, with a president whose prior claim to fame was as head of the Central Intelligence Agency: How would we view the head of another country who had been its chief of spies? Although Bush seems fairly alert by comparison with his predecessor, like his Reagan, he seems to be captive of an ideology which, whatever might have been said of it a century or so ago, has been made outmoded by our history and, in practice, by people like himself. Bush presides over the largest and most active State system in our history; but again, like Reagan, he goes on and on about free markets (although his own wealth was accumulated in the oil industry, anything but a free market), while seeing to it that the remaining largesse of the U.S. economy is made available to, as he likes to put it, "his kind of guy," regarding the environment, capital gains tax reductions, and the like.

Anyone who has lived out of the United States for any length of time knows that "furriners" are of mixed minds about our nation and our people. They really like most "Americans"—the style, the music, the clothes, the "feel," the presumably relaxed nature of our existence. At the same time, they can't believe much of the content of our life: our leaders (Reagan was not to be believed!), our poverty in the midst of plenty, our carelessness with food and family, our treatment of each other, our quick turn to violent means to solve complicated problems.

All countries are rife with imperfections, and their peoples generally know it; what is difficult for outsiders to understand is how and why the United States should have the kinds and the degrees of "imperfections" *we* have—we are so rich, so democratic, so full of possibilities: we have far fewer natural and historical "excuses" for our many ills.

It is justly believed that the United States can and should—must—do better; and it is hard to believe that we so painfully continue to waste our resources, our possibilities, our people's actual and potential abilities. The time is well overdue for the people of the United States to understand, to feel, and to act on that set of judgments. But first we must take our history seriously, must understand what we have been and are, and why; we must, to repeat Lincoln's words, "disenthrall ourselves."

The last chapter will put forward some of the ways and means under discussion in the United States to change our society for the better, for beginning to meet our already severe and always greater needs, and to move toward the realization of our wonderful possibilities. Of necessity, such proposals must be tentative; the fondest hope accompanying them is that they might become part of an always expanding and deepening political discussion.

Reading Suggestions

Pluralism as an explanation of the sources and uses of power in the United States is examined within a broad analytical spectrum in Richard Gillam, ed., *Power in Postwar America: Interdisciplinary Perspectives on a Historical Problem* (Boston: Little Brown, 1971), including essays by Sweezy, Mills, Kolko, and a leading pluralist, Dahl. Evidence for the validity of pluralism seems to be provided by the various dimensions of electoral contests in the United States. That appearances are belied by realities is made clear by many studies, among them Walter Karp, *Indispensable Enemies: The Politics of Misrule in America* (New York: Saturday Review Press, 1973), which shows the conscious and cynical cooperation between the two parties that has both persisted and grown in this century, processes that find their counterpart in the presumed hostility between Congress and the Executive. Thomas Ferguson and J. Rogers also delve beneath the surface in two of their works, *The Hidden Election: Politics and Economics in the 1980 Presidential Campaign* (New York: Pantheon, 1981) and *Right Turn: The Decline of the*

Democrats and the Future of American Politics (New York: Hill and Wang, 1986). Probing even more deeply are Erik Wright, in his *Class, Crisis, and the State* (London: Verso, 1979), and Ira Katznelson and Mark Kesslman, *The Politics of Power** (New York: Harcourt Brace Jovanovich, 1975). And see Ralph Miliband's latest book on the State: *Divided Societies: Class Struggle in Contemporary Capitalism* (Oxford: Oxford University Press, 1990).

Maurice Zeitlin, *American Society, Inc.* (Chicago: Markham, 1970) and Morton Mintz and Jerry S. Cohen, *America, Inc.** (New York: Dell, 1971) bring together economic with noneconomic factors to examine power, the latter in a lighter fashion than the former. Alan Wolfe has shed light on the State often in recent years; in addition to previous citations to his work, see *The Limits of Legitimacy: Political Contradictions of Advanced Capitalism* (New York: Free Press, 1980), which nicely complements O'Connor's analysis.

In the examination of the relationship between the Cold War, the State, and the political economy many suggestions have already been made; and here are a few more: Because of its excellence, I repeat the reference to Lawrence Wittner, *Cold War America*, and add C. Solberg's *Riding High in the Cold War* (New York: Mason & Lipscomb, 1973), both of which examine the internal sources and consequences of the Cold War in enlightening ways. See also Jerry Sanders, *Peddlers of Crisis: The Committee on the Present Danger and the Politics of Containment* (Boston: South End Press, 1983) and Hugh G. Mosley, *The Arms Race: Economic and Social Consequences* (Lexington, MA: D.C. Heath, 1985), and the earlier, still relevant book of readings by Herbert I. Schiller and Joseph D. Phillips, eds., *SuperState: Readings in the Military Industrial Complex** (Urbana: University of Illinois Press, 1872). Useful both for analysis and data is James L. Clayton, *On the Brink: Defense, Deficits, and Welfare Spending* (New York: Ramapo Press, 1984).

The Cold War was, of course, a global process, and it has been studied as such very usefully in M. Shaw, ed., *War, State, and Society* (London: Macmillan, 1984); one of its best essays is that of Michael Cox, "Western Capitalism and the Cold War System," pp. 136-94. For some of the story of how Japan's economy was affected beneficially by its defeat and the subsequent processes of the Cold War, see Theodore Cohen, *Remaking Japan: The American Occupation as New Deal* (Glencoe, Ill.: Free Press, 1987). And an excellent final reminder of the unnecessary and terrible economic and political costs paid in the past decades is Mary Kaldor, *The Imaginary War: Understanding the East-West Conflict* (London: Blackwell, 1990).

For those who might wonder why Bush should be denigrated (at least in part) because he was once head of the CIA a knowledge of that institution is necessary: See Steven Emerson, *Secret Warriors: Inside the Covert Military Operations of the Reagan Era* (New York: G.P. Putnam's Sons, 1988), John Prados, *Presidents' Secret Wars: CIA and Pentagon Covert Operations Since World War II* (New York: Morrow, 1986), Morton Halperin, Jerry Berman, Robert Borosage, and Christine Marwick, *The Lawless State** (New York: Penguin, 1978), Landau's *The Dangerous Doctrine*, cited earlier, Edward S. Herman and Noam Chomsky, *The Washington Connection and Third World Fascism* (Boston: South End Press, 1979), Tom Gervasi, *The Myth of Soviet Military Supremacy* (New York: Harper & Row, 1986), Jonathan Marshall, Peter Dale Scott, and Jane Hunter, *The Iran-Contra Connection: Secret Teams and Covert Operations in the Reagan Era* (Boston: South End Press, 1987), and, for a onetime insider's view, Philip Agee, *Inside the Company: CIA Diary** (Hamondsworth, Engl.: Penguin, 1975).

For a number of analyses of what in terms of human needs has always been insufficient and that under the malignly neglectful influence of Reaganism became drastically more so, see Frank Ackerman, *Hazardous to Our Wealth: Economic Policies in the 1980s* (Boston: South End Press, 1984), Robert Lekachman, *Greed Is Not Enough: Reaganomics* (New York: Pantheon, 1982), the excellent collection of essays by Colin Greer and Frank Riesman, *What Reagan Is Doing to Us* (New York: Harper & Row, 1982), Fred Block, et al., *The Mean Season: The Attack on the Welfare State* (New York: Pantheon, 1987), F. Piven and R. Cloward, *The New Class War: Reagan's Attack on the Welfare State and Its Consequences* (New York: Pantheon, 1982), Michael B. Katz, *The Undeserving Poor: From the War on Poverty to the War on Welfare* (New York: Pantheon, 1989), and, for just one example of one of the innumerable ways in which the Pentagon contributes to massive waste and corruption, see Nick Kotz, *Wild Blue Yonder: Money, Politics, and the B-1 Bomber* (New York: Pantheon, 1987).

Education and health care have been among the main casualties of these recent years. That inadequate education did not, of course, begin under Reagan (indeed it seems to have begun with his own) is made clear in Jonathan Kozol, *Death at an Early Age: The Destruction of the Hearts and Minds of Negro School Children in the Boston Public Schools*

(Boston: Houghton Mifflin, 1967); that it worsened is shown in his more recent *Illiterate America* (Garden City, N.Y.: Anchor Press/Doubleday, 1985). And that there is an alternative path that was tried, succeeded (with the children), and was stopped in its tracks is shown in George Dennison's eloquent *The Lives of Children* (New York: Random House, 1969). As for health care, it has been made clear in many countries for many years that health care can be provided more equitably, more satisfactorily, and more cheaply than in the United States. For three studies that provide comparative analyses, see Gosta Esping-Andersen, *The Three Worlds of Welfare Capitalism* (Oxford: Polity/Blackwell, 1990), Arnold J. Heidenheimer, Hugh Heclo, and Carolyn Teich Adams, *Comparative Public Policy: The Politics of Social Choice in Europe and America* (New York: St. Martin's Press, 1983), and Andrew Shonfield, *The Use of Public Power*, cited earlier. That a substantial improvement in health care is of course possible also in the United States is discussed in one modest version by Rashi Fein, *Medical Care, Medical Costs* (Cambridge, MA: Harvard University Press, 1986). The same is so as regards our scandalous housing conditions, as shown in Chester Hartman, *America's Housing Crisis: What Is to be Done?* (London: Methuen, 1983).

Because Reagan and Reaganomics have added so much weight to the burdens the majority carries for the benefit of an always slimmer minority, it is worth taking time to see just how big a shell game the people have been putting up with (and cheering); that is, it is worth taking a long look at Reagan and how he got to where he did. The two journalists best-informed on Reagan as person and president are probably Haynes Johnson, *Sleepwalking Through History: America in the Reagan Years* (New York: W.W. Norton, 1991), and Lou Cannon, *President Reagan: The Role of a Lifetime* (New York: Simon & Schuster, 1991). The portrait that emerges is one of a man who combines incompetence with guile and nastiness, while managing to convince virtually everyone he is Mr. Nice Guy. That the people of the United States have had such a grand love affair with such a person is a fact of stupefying proportions.

And that takes us, finally, to an excellent book of a different sort. Bertram Gross, a lawyer who literally wrote the "Full Employment Act of 1946" for the Congress (for whom the use of the word "full" was seen as dangerous, so the bill's name was changed to "Employment...."), has since become a professor and written a foreboding and all too plausible book, *Friendly Fascism: The New Face of Power in America* (New York:

M. Evans, 1980). Gross uses the term "friendly" not because he believes fascism—sometimes called "capitalism with the gloves off"—has been or ever could be anything but horrible, but to suggest something also horrible: in the United States, unlike, say, Germany, fascism—meaning, in this case, an absence of a functioning political (to say nothing of economic and social) democracy, combined with falling living standards for the largest part of the population, and the continuing militarization of society—could become a full-fledged reality slowly, surely, undramatically, and without any but individual and small group resistance. In other countries where fascism has come to power there was an organized Left and a reasonably (or potentially) strong socialist movement, neither of which exists in the United States—although it is conceivable that racism could be used in the United States just as fear of revolution has been elsewhere. Gross's book was written before Reagan was elected president, and he thought then the United States might be halfway there—fascism, like a thief in the night, with one foot in the door. It is a calm, careful, and persuasive analysis, not so much the work of a doomsayer as one who warns and proposes constructive change. In some ways the book is reminiscent of Sinclair Lewis's novel of the 1930s, *It Can't Happen Here.*

Notes

1. William Vaughn Moody, "An Ode in Time of Hesitation," from his *Poems and Plays.* Reprinted by permission of Houghton Mifflin, Inc.

2. A good part of these introductory pages follows closely my analysis in "The State, Power, and the Industrial Revolution, 1750–1914," *URPE Occasional Paper, No. 4* (Spring 1971), largely concerned with Great Britain, France, and Germany.

3. In the past three decades or so there has been a major upsurge of effort to this end among those on the analytical Left in Western Europe and North America. A good part of that is summarized, evaluated, and used as a starting-point for further work in an excellent two-part essay by David A. Gold, Clarence Y.H. Lo, and Erik Olin Wright, "Recent Developments in Marxist Theories of the State," *Monthly Review* (October and November 1975).

4. W.O. Henderson, *The State and the Industrial Revolution in Prussia, 1740–1870* (Liverpool: University Press, 1958), pp. xii–xiv. The reference in the quote is to Great Britain.

5. Peter Bachrach and Morton S. Baratz, *Power and Poverty: Theory and Practice** (New York: Oxford University Press, 1970), p. 44.

6. Offe is one of those whose creative theoretical work is reviewed succinctly and well in the Gold et al. essay just noted, Part 2. References to Offe's and others' works are usefully collected in that essay.

7. Ralph Miliband, *The State in Capitalist Society* (New York: Basic Books, 1969), p. 2. Harold J. Laski, *The State in Theory and Practice* (New York: Viking, 1935) is an earlier and still relevant attempt by a Marxian political philosopher to understand the modern State. A most useful critique of "liberal" theories of the State is C.B. MacPherson, "Politics: Post–Liberal Democracy," in Robin Blackburn, ed., *Ideology in Social Science*, cited earlier.

8. For the origins of feudalism and serfdom, see F.L. Ganshof, *Feudalism* (London: Longmans, 1952). For the definitive study of the complexities of the period see Marc Bloch, *Feudal Society*, noted earlier. A simpler Marxian view is well-put in Marion Gibbs, *Feudal Order* (London: Cobbett Press, 1949). This study only covers English society, which helps to explain what I take to be the undue simplicity of the analysis. For a detailed and absorbing study of the intricate patterns relating the Church elite to the lay nobility and the peasantry in medieval Tuscany, see George W. Dameron, *Episcopal Power and Florentine Society, 1000–1320* (Cambridge: Harvard University Press, 1991). Perry Anderson's two volumes and Immanuel Wallerstein's *Modern World System*, both noted in Chapter 2, are helpful for understanding the transformation of medieval and the emergence of early modern social formations.

9. The classic process, on which there were many variations, had merchants and incipient monarchs working together against a feudal nobility. Where that did not occur, or where it faltered, the nation-state did not arise until centuries later. See, for example, G. Barraclough, *The Origins of Modern Germany* (New York: Putnam, 1963; originally 1949), esp. Part Four.

10. The evolution of power structures was quite different elsewhere. In the United States, the capitalist class, though its base and its composition changed continually, started out on top, with no competitors from the past (monarchy or Church, for example) and the ability to sweep potential competitors aside or into its net. Our Civil War, which some might see as a major exception to the foregoing generalization, whatever else it may have represented, was a struggle between two kinds of capital: planter

and mercantile–industrial. See Louis M. Hacker, *The Triumph of American Capitalism* (New York: Columbia University Press, 1940), for a strong argument on this matter. Increasingly, as the nineteenth century proceeded, the U.S. businessman was largely able both to create and to control the political and social ("normative") sources of power: the system of government, the political system, and religious and educational institutions all accepted the directions and values established by business to a degree unmatched elsewhere. It is thus that we became "the business society par excellence." The historically evolved patterns in Germany, Italy, Japan, and France were different from each other, as well as from Britain and the United States. See Barrington Moore, cited earlier, for some of the appropriate analysis of those differences, and my own essay "The State, Power...," cited above. For the English Civil War and its complexities, see Christopher Hill, *Reformation to Industrial Revolution*, cited earlier, and Michael Walzer, *The Revolution of the Saints* (New York: Atheneum, 1968).

11. An important and illuminating analysis of this process is Henri Pirenne, "The Stages in the Social History of Capitalism," *American Historical Review*, vol. XIX, no. 3 (April 1914), pp. 494–515.

12. Italics in original. The structure elucidated by Miliband is found in Chapter 2 of his *The State*, and it is much elaborated upon in Chapters 4 and 8. (What I call "lesser governments" Miliband, who is British, classifies as "subcentral.") The quotation of Poulantzas is taken from the important debate between him and Miliband in Blackburn, *Ideology in Social Science*, cited earlier, pp. 238–62, in which Poulantzas, in keeping with his own major study, *Political Power and Social Classes* (London: New Left Books, 1973) furnishes a searching (and friendly) critique of Miliband's *The State*, and the latter replies. Some of this is well-discussed in Gold, et al., noted above. It may be noted that Poulantzas raises the name of Antonio Gramsci, whose ideas have become influential for many on the Left both in Europe and North America, and concerning which we shall have more to say below.

13. Ibid., pp. 261–62. (His emphasis.)

14. See Part 1 of Gold, et al., for these distinctions and a clear discussion centering on them.

15. What is meant by "a powerful few at the top"? It would be foolish to try to settle on a number: 2,000 or 100,000 or 1,000,000. But even if we were to settle on the last, a million, we would be speaking of less than half of 1 percent of the population of the United States—where

we mostly go blithely through our political thinking with the pluralistic notion, commonly put as "one man, one vote," interpreted to mean one person's power is no greater than another's. Nobody could really believe that upon even a moment's reflection; the historical-ideological magic has been to reduce the moments in which we reflect upon such matters.

16. In Blackburn, op. cit., p. 245. (His emphasis.) The reasoning of Poulantzas on this matter is subsequently agreed with by Miliband, in a complicated fashion. See ibid., pp. 258–59.

17. *The State in Capitalist Society*, p. 50.

18. Poulantzas is useful on this point when he refers to "...fractions of the capitalist class... [and] existent differences and relations under imperialism between comprador monopoly capital, national monopoly capital, non-monopoly capital, industrial capital, [and] financial capital...," in Blackburn, op. cit., p. 244. "Comprador monopoly capital" refers to interests in an underdeveloped country's capitalist class, simultaneously a *dependent* and an *exploitive* group in the world-economic system.

19. Ibid., p. 52. That was written in 1969. In those days such statements about the scope of "internal security" forces—that is, the CIA and the FBI, principally, although there are many other agencies that keep dossiers on the public—were pooh-poohed by the stalwarts of the mainstream. Little did we know, then, how very much more extensive, "illegal," unconstitutional, and repressive these forces have been—and remain, as an almost continuous flow of appropriate congressional inquiries since the mid-1970s have divulged: with little dampening effect, it is clear, as, for example, the Iran-*contra* activities, more serious in their techniques, purposes, and effects than Watergate, suggest. Congress lacks some combination of ability and resolve to ask even the appropriate questions in their inquiries, very possibly because some of their answers might come too close to the activities of the inquirers. For a brief, comprehensive, and clear study, see Saul Landau, *The Dangerous Doctrine: National Security and U.S. Foreign Policy** (Boulder, Colo.: Westview Press, 1988). A massively detailed and probably the definitive study of the various crimes and misdemeanors committed at all levels and in all areas of the State system in the *Iran-contra* affair is Theodore Draper, *A Very Thin Line: The Iran-Contra Affairs* (New York: Hill and Wang, 1991).

20. *Theory of Business Enterprise*, p. 282n.

21. It may be recalled that in Chapter 4 we noted the process of

"legitimation" in a different context, with a somewhat different meaning: the reference, depending upon James O'Connor's analysis in his *Fiscal Crisis of the State*, was to the manner in which State expenditures support capital accumulation and, especially through social expenditures that reduce the harshness of the capitalist process, help to "legitimate" the system. Our focus there was, so to speak, on the hardware, whereas in what follows it will be on "software."

22. The relevant processes and relationships comprise and create what Gramsci called "the hegemony of the bourgeoisie." I shall discuss Gramsci at some length in the next chapter; until then it may be helpful to point to an excellent and brief introduction to his principal contributions: Eugene Genovese, "On Antonio Gramsci," in his *In Red and Black*, cited earlier. Gramsci led the Italian Communist Party until he was imprisoned by Mussolini in 1926. He wrote profusely while in prison; eleven years later, as he was dying, he was allowed to leave prison. His political starting-point was to explain why fascism took power in Italy even though the socialists were numerous and well-organized—more so than elsewhere in Europe, at the time. His analytical starting-point was Marx's epigram: "The ruling ideas of any era are the ideas of its ruling class."

23. It was Daniel Ellsberg, a onetime U.S. Marine Corps officer who served in Vietnam, and later had a high-ranking position on the National Security Council (for which the Pentagon Papers were produced, at the behest of Secretary of Defense McNamara) who, with his children, Xerox'd the papers and furnished them to the *New York Times*. There have been many published editions of them. Perhaps more useful for our focus here is Ellsberg's own book, *Papers on the War** (New York: Simon & Schuster, 1972), which opens up the jungle of the government in showing how far from the "American Dream" it strayed as it took and sought to keep the nation into and through what Ellsberg properly calls a criminal war. A different kind of insider, David Halberstam (of the *New York Times*), in his *Best and Brightest* (New York: Random House, 1972), provides an extraordinarily detailed account of the personalities and policies of the 1960s, and provides a good surface account of how our getting stuck in what he calls the "quagmire" of Vietnam was a consequence of sustained dishonesty, arrogance, confusion, and ideology, rather than anything having to do with the interests of the people of the United States—let alone those of Indochina, millions of whom were killed, maimed, and had their lives ruined. One of the questions that

comes to mind as one reads Halberstam is why he waited so long to tell his story, a story he had in his possession for many years in which his truth might have helped to bring a quicker end to the war.

24. The uproar over the savage beating of the black driver in Los Angeles in 1990, accepted as real only because videotaped, considering the fact that such incidents—without the film—happen almost daily, was a confirmation of just how removed from social reality the average citizen is.

25. In addition to previous citations, an excellent survey of "How the news media use bias, distortion and censorship to manipulate public opinion" is Robert Cirino, *Don't Blame the People** (New York: Random House, Vintage, 1971). An earlier and beautifully written collection of (*New Yorker*) essays that is deeply revealing of the same matters is A.J. Liebling, *The Press** (New York: Ballantine Books, 1961). And see also James Aronson, *The Press and the Cold War**, cited earlier.

26. C. Wright Mills, in his *Power Elite*, cited earlier, in his *White Collar** (New York: Oxford University Press, 1951), and in his *New Men of Power: America's Labor Leaders*, cited earlier, analyzes all this generally and with specific application to business, the professions, and labor. G. William Domhoff, following in Mill's footsteps, relates these matters to the social and political setting in several of his books, including *Who Rules America?*, cited earlier, and *The Higher Circles** (New York: Random House; Vintage, 1971).

27. A major difference between the earlier and the present system is that the First and Second Banks were *creditors* of the private banks, but the Fed is a *debtor*. Member banks must keep an amount equal to a certain percentage of their deposits (their liabilities) on reserve in the Fed (*its* liabilities). The latter exercises its influence on the supply of money and credit and the interest rate through means that alter the amount of reserves or the amount required. See any introductory economics text for a fuller explanation. Those who are appointed to the Board of the Fed are from the banking community, or acceptable to it.

28. The Bank was located on Chestnut Street, in Philadelphia. Its head by the late 1820s was Nicholas Biddle, an astute and strong-minded banker in his own right. The best and most comprehensive discussion of the relevant issues—and a fine piece of historical writing in itself—is Bray Hammond, *Banks and Politics in America From the Revolution to the Civil War* (Princeton: Princeton University Press, 1957). Probably

the most popular book written on the subject is Arthur Schlesinger, Jr., *The Age of Jackson* (Boston: Little, Brown, 1946). It is a model of intensive scholarship combined with unsupportable interpretation, as Hammond shows explicitly, dominated by Schlesinger's attempt to find justification for various elements of the New Deal. Hammond's own book is very much dominated by *his* contemporary concerns; namely, to support a strong Federal Reserve System. History—including this one—is seldom written by people without serious interests in their own present: a virtue, not a vice. But it is well for both the historians and their readers to be conscious of those interests.

29. The expression is Vernon L. Parrington's in his *Main Currents in American Thought**, 3 vols. (Norman: University of Oklahoma Press, 1977; originally 1927–30), which is a critical analysis of literary and other intellectual thought from the Colonial period up to 1920, written very much from a Jeffersonian standpoint.

30. For an informative and succinct analysis of this point, see Barrington Moore, "The American Civil War: The Last Capitalist Revolution," Chapter III of his *Social Origins*, cited earlier.

31. C. Vann Woodward, *Reunion and Reaction** (New York: Doubleday; Anchor, 1956) provides the definitive interpretation of the sordid "Compromise of 1877 and the End of Reconstruction," the consequences of which included the conservative-racist coalition still central to our social existence.

32. C. Vann Woodward has been cited earlier regarding certain of these matters. For a direct statement consistent with the position just put forth, see his "The Populist Heritage and the Intellectual," in the collection of his fine essays, *The Burden of Southern History** cited earlier, and also Chapters 8 and 9 of his *Origins of the New South*, cited earlier. For black/white cooperation, see Jack Abramowitz, "The Negro in the Populist Movement," cited earlier.

33. Not without a firm foundation in the pre–Civil War past, however, as Osofsky, cited earlier, and Leon F. Litwack, *North of Slavery: The Negro in the Free States, 1790–1860** (Chicago: University of Chicago Press, 1961) both make clear.

34. Faulkner, *Decline of Laissez Faire*, pp. 368–69. And that from a mainstream historian.

35. These generalizations, and others to follow, depend upon the important historical revisions about the period developed by Gabriel Kolko in *The Triumph of Conservatism* and by James Weinstein in *The*

Corporate Ideal in the Liberal State, 1900–1918, both cited earlier. Probably without intending to do so, Robert H. Wiebe, *Businessmen and Reform** (Chicago: Quadrangle, 1968) presents information that allows the same conclusions. Kolko centers on the ability of the large corporations to use the State to curb uncontrolled competition and reduce instability; Weinstein emphasizes the role of the large corporations and their National Civic Federation in conscious displacement of laissez-faire, over the opposition of smaller businesses and their National Association of Manufacturers.

36. All of which might as easily be said of business attitudes and conditions in the United States since World War II. The analysis, quoted by Robert A. Brady, *Business as a System of Power*, p. 294, is that of M.J. Bonn, *Das Schicksal des deutschen Kapitalismus* (1903).

37. Robert A. Brady, *The Rationalization Movement in German Industry* (Berkeley: University of California Press, 1933), p. xiv. The two "extreme wings" were socialism and fascism. That movement in Germany combined business with political and engineering criteria, yielding cartels, interindustry and State coordination, and complementary plant locations (coke near steel near machinery production, for example)—called "combinats"—the next step beyond which would have been national economic planning. Indeed the first Soviet five-year plan (1928) saw the German combinats as a model. Among capitalist nations the Japanese have most closely approximated the rationalization movement in Germany; the steps in the United States have been considerably more modest.

38. Kolko, *Triumph*, pp. 2–3. In his study *Railroads and Regulation*, cited earlier, Kolko documents these generalizations about regulation for an industry interpreted quite differently in previous studies. Kolko's main point is that though the impulses for regulation may arise outside the industry to be regulated (farmers, in the case of the railroads), the industry comes to see the regulation as something that can be shaped to its own interests—as they see them. That conclusion, in the light of the history of regulated industries, seems inescapable. However, most conventional observers, seeing each reaffirming instance as an aberration, have let the conclusion slip through their flimsy analytical nets.

39. The media were blunter in those early days than they have been since. By the time the United States had "pacified" the Filipinos (at the end of Taft's governorship, 1901–04, from which he went on to be Secretary of War and President), several hundred thousand Filipinos had

been slaughtered—not without the substantial encouragement of the then leading San Francisco weekly, *The Argonaut*, as exemplified in this editorial of 1902: "There has been too much hypocrisy about this Philippine business—too much snivel—too much cant. Let us all be frank. WE DO NOT WANT THE FILIPINOS. WE WANT THE PHILIPPINES. All our troubles in this annexation matter have been caused by the presence in the Philippine islands of the Filipinos.... Touched by the wand of American enterprise, fertilized by American capital, these islands would speedily become richer than Golconda was of old. But, unfortunately, they are infested by Filipinos.... They are indolent...; and they occupy land which might be utilized to much better advantage by Americans. Therefore the more of them killed, the better...." The whole editorial is reproduced in Jacobs, et al., *To Serve the Devil*, vol. 2 (cited earlier), pp. 335–37. (Full caps in original.)

40. Kolko, *Triumph*, p. 3 (Italics in original.)

41. Laws forbidding price competition, such as the "Resale Price Maintenance Act" of 1937, most generally called "fair trade laws," emerged after the National Industrial Recovery Act was declared unconstitutional in 1935. The National Recovery Administration (NRA), a form of self-government in business, gave the power to fix prices to industry trade associations, and violators were punishable by law. The similarities between the NRA and those for "self-management in industry" under the Nazis are both striking and unsurprising—given that a Nazi delegation came to the United States in 1934 to study the institution. See Robert A. Brady, *The Spirit and Structure of German Fascism* (New York: Viking, 1937). A major difference is that the German laws were not declared unconstitutional.

42. Faulkner, *Decline*, p. 379.

43. Reminding me of Veblen's comment: "Sportsmen—hunters and anglers—[speak of]...a love of nature...as the incentive to their favorite pastime..., which could be more readily and fully satisfied without the accompaniment of a systematic effort to take the life of those creatures that make up an essential feature of that "nature" that is beloved by sportsmen" (*Theory of the Leisure Class*, p. 257).

44. See Soule, *Prosperity Decade*, Chapters I, II, and III.

45. Even when, as in the case of the IWW, it took no stand against the war. For the cooperation of the trade unions, the opposition of the Socialist Party, and the curious position of the IWW, see James Weinstein, *Decline of Socialism*, cited earlier, pp. 47–53.

46. Wilson's Attorney General, A. Mitchell Palmer, organized raids on homes and offices of "suspected Communists." Thousands were arrested, hundreds jailed and deported. The socialist movement was still strong, the Russian Revolution was publicized as a direct threat to the United States, immigration was still high, and strikes were numerous. Foreign-born people were most noticed among the "troublemakers," and aliens could be deported if the Secretary of Labor found them to be "radical." Sacco and Vanzetti were anarchist labor organizers accused and convicted in 1921 of a payroll murder in what was and remains widely considered to have been a frame-up. They were electrocuted in 1927.

47. Quoted in James W. Prothro, *Dollar Decade: Business Ideas in the 1920s* (Baton Rouge: Louisiana State University Press, 1954), p. 224. This is an excellent and revealing study of what businessmen thought at a time when they had the confidence to be candid about their social philosophy. Some of what is revealed is frightening, some of it funny.

48. Also quoted in Prothro, pp. 29–30. Judas Iscariot is viewed in that connection as being a bit overzealous, an early Oliver North of sorts, but of good spirit.

49. Williams, *The Great Evasion*, cited earlier, p. 155. The reference to "corporate leaders" producing "an American form of fascism" has its reference in the role played by Italian fascism, often called "the corporate state." See Carl T. Schmidt, *The Corporate State in Action* (New York: Viking, 1939), concerned with the rise and nature of Italian fascism.

50. Daniel Bell, *The End of Ideology** (New York: Free Press, 1960), S.M. Lipset, *Political Man** (Garden City, N.Y.: Doubleday, 1960), p. 406. The ideas leading to these conclusions were put forth earlier in the British journal of elegant liberal opinion, *Encounter*, which was financed in important part by CIA funds—first denied, then admitted and apologized for. Bell and Lipset are among the most noted pluralists. As some readers will have been reminded, just as ideology "ended" in the late 1950s, we were told by a U. S. State Department intellectual that history "ended" in the 1980s.

51. The classifications are those of G. William Domhoff and Hoyt B. Ballard, eds., *C. Wright Mills and the Power Elite** (Boston: Beacon Press, 1961), a very useful collection of the criticisms and of Mills's response to some of them. Miliband's book on the State, cited earlier, is dedicated to Mills. Although among the most prolific and creative of U.S. sociologists, Mills never rose above the rank of associate professor; nor, it may be added, did Veblen. I sought to find the basic similarities

and differences between the two in my essay, "Veblen, Mills, and the Decline of Criticism," in *Dissent*, Winter 1964.

52. A collection of essays comprising both viewpoints may be found in "Special Issue: Militarism and the U.S. Economy," *Economic Forum*, Summer 1982, vol. XIII, no. 1. Included are the important essay by James M. Cypher, "Ideological Hegemony and Modern Militarism: The Origins and Limits of Military Keynesianism," Michael T. Klare's "The Political Economy of Arms Sales," Linda Hunter's "The Economic Effects of Military Expenditures in the Third World," Seymour Melman's "Arms Race: Economic Drain," and my own "Militarized Economy, Brutalized Society."

53. Seymour Melman, *Pentagon Capitalism** (New York: McGraw-Hill, 1970), p. 1. See also the book of readings edited by him, *The War Economy of the United States** (New York: St. Martin's Press, 1971). His first book in this area, in which his central position began to appear, is *Our Depleted Society** (New York: Holt, Rinehart, and Winston, 1965). More recently he has published *Profits Without Production** (Philadelphia: University of Pennsylvania Press, 1983). In that book Melman examines the main structures and processes of the U.S. economy, and in explaining what he sees as its decline finds the root cause in the militarization of the economy. What is declining, for Melman is not just U.S. economic strength but capitalism as the center of that strength. Even those who have argued that Melman has missed the main point of what he has so exhaustively explored—the integral role of imperialism and militarization in contemporary capitalism—praise him as one of a very small handful of honorable and humane academics in a university establishment that normally works hand-in-glove with the military-industrial complex.

54. Pages 19 and 24. Melman's figure of $1,500 billion is a conservatively calculated understatement, appalling though it is as it stands. See the earlier discussion in Chapter 4 for an explanation of the calculations, and the figure including expenditures since then, which brings us closer to, or beyond, $6 trillion.

55. James L. Clayton, ed., *The Economic Impact of the Cold War** (New York: Harcourt Brace Jovanovich, 1970), p. 281. Those are the words of the editor. It will be noted that they were written in 1970, and known that since then the tendencies affecting all such figures have been up, not down. The many essays in this collection are very informative on various aspects of the development.

56. James M. Cypher has been among the most industrious in arguing the position just suggested. It is clear from his writings that they are not inspired by an attraction to military ends and means but are a critique of the way capitalism meets its needs and goals. In addition to essays of his noted earlier, see "The Liberals Discover Militarism," in *Government in the American Economy*, ed., Robert Carson (Lexington: D.C. Heath, 1973), and "A Prop Not a Burden," in *Dollars & Sense* (January, 1984). As was pointed out earlier in another connection (in Chapter 6) the first major technological advance in the United States, which led to the system of interchangeable parts production (arguably *the* major U.S. technological contribution), was invented by Eli Whitney, for the purpose of producing military muskets.

57. *Journal of Economic Issues*, March 1987, "Military Spending," cited earlier, p. 37.

58. The argument is that of Will Clayton, out of Wall Street to vice president of the Export-Import Bank, to Assistant Secretary of Commerce, to Undersecretary for Economic Affairs in the State Department during the Roosevelt and Truman Administrations. He was a key figure in the Committee for Economic Development, the organization that has played the same role as that played by the National Civic Federation before World War I. The quotation is from an important essay by David W. Eakins, "Business Planners and America's Postwar Expansion," in *Corporations and the Cold War*, cited earlier, p. 168.

59. And points to a question to be examined in the next chapter: without a Cold War, and with falling purchasing power induced by corporate and State policies, what does the future hold for capitalism?

60. *Monopoly Capital*, pp. 9–10. In an appendix to the book, Prof. Joseph D. Phillips's made analytical and statistical estimates of the components and behavior of the economic surplus, pp. 369ff. The major components of the surplus are property income, the wastes of distribution, advertising, and selling, the incomes of those in the financial/legal sector, and, largest of all, government expenditures. These are all defined as such in the sense that the incomes and expenditures involved are not necessary to maintain current levels of production and life. As we shall see momentarily, James O'Connor modifies this conception, showing the government to be a generator as well as an absorber of the surplus. In an important and clarifying recent essay, "The Tendency of the Surplus to Rise, 1963–1988," Michael Dawson and John Bellamy Foster, working with an improvement over Phillips's statistical methodology (and

updating his statistical tables), conclude that the "law of the tendency of the surplus to rise" has been found to be fairly consistent, that "the entire rise in surplus as a percentage of GNP...can be accounted for by the growth of...net interest, surplus employee compensation (i.e., finance, insurance, real estate, and legal services), advertising costs, and the profit element in corporate officer compensation," and, like Phillips, they find the percentage of the surplus to GNP to be in excess of 50%. They end by quoting a 1990 statement of Paul Sweezy to the effect that "[t]here's no way the capitalist class can now manage the vast amount of surplus the economy is capable of producing." I have tried to clarify the applicability of the concept of the economic surplus to contemporary political concerns in "Social Commitment and Social Analysis: The contribution of Paul Baran," *Politics & Society*, vol. 5, no. 2 (1975).

61. Earlier we have referred to his *Fiscal Crisis of the State*, which is the source of the main argument to follow. But his collection of essays, *The Corporations and the State*, also referred to earlier, is valuable in several connections, as are his subsequent major works that continue the main thread of *Fiscal Crisis*, namely, *Accumulation Crisis* and *The Meaning of Crisis* (New York: Blackwell, 1984 and 1987, respectively). Also, in the early 1970s, O'Connor was instrumental in the establishing of an international journal exploring the various dimensions of the State: *Kapitalistate*, difficult to find, but worth the effort. Robert A. Brady's *Business as a System of Power*, cited earlier, was the first study to show the similarity of tendencies among all leading capitalist economies, leading toward both monopoly and "political capitalism" and, where necessary, fascism. Andrew Shonfield, *Modern Capitalism*, cited earlier, covers much of the same ground for the years since World War II, though less critically.

62. Quoted in Brady, *Business as a System of Power*, p. 266n. Brady also quotes Pitkin in his *Spirit and Structure of German Fascism*, to show that the Nazis were not alone in their views in the capitalist world. The U.S. population in 1935 was about 126 million. Adding Pitkins's figures of more or less dispensable people, we get 114 million, leaving only 12 million high-grade humans not having to think of cost whenever they buy things. Many are called, few are chosen.

63. *Wall Street Journal*, December 21, 1971. Quoted in O'Connor, *Fiscal Crisis*, p. 227.

64. *Fiscal Crisis*, pp. 150–51.

65. O'Connor, op. cit., Chapter 4 for data through the 1960s. See

Economic Report of the President, 1991 for subsequent years. Of course a rise of 75 percent in military spending meant more absolutely than a doubling of social expenditures, considering their relative starting points: spending on what the government calls "human resources" in 1960 was a bit more than half of that on the military—if one includes social security (which one shouldn't) and doesn't include veterans' payments, and other items that are military (which one should).

66. That this particular consequence was not pure happenstance is but one more instance of the decline of social decency in the United States, a decline whose way has been paved principally by racism. In addition to the many references to appropriate works in earlier pages, see the recent book of Thomas and Mary Edsall, *Chain Reaction: The Impact of Race, Rights and Taxes on American Politics** (New York: Norton, 1991) which treats the racism of those who practice it eagerly in politics and the timidity of those (largely in the Democratic Party) who fear its electoral backlash if they don't. When this combined with the greed of consumerism, falling real incomes, and what were seen as high taxes in the late 1970s and 1980s, it became an awesome and awful political force.

67. Just how the term "terrorism" has come to have considerably more ideological than factual content and is the monopoly only of designated enemies of the United States, irrespective of the behavior of designated friends and of the United States itself (e.g., in mining the harbors of Nicaragua), is thoroughly and convincingly examined in Edward S. Herman and Gerry O'Sullivan, *The Terrorism Industry: The Experts and Institutions That Shape Our View of Terror* (New York: Pantheon, 1989). Also of importance in this and broader matters is Herman's book with Noam Chomsky, *Manufacturing Consent: The Political Economy of the Mass Media* (New York: Pantheon, 1988). Both books are massively documented and finally irrefutable in their findings—but neither has been given more than minimal attention despite the eminence of the authors (Herman a leading financial economist, Chomsky perhaps the major figure in the area of linguistics).

68. My essay "Militarized Economy, Brutalized Society," noted earlier, is largely concerned with that devolution.

69. The figures to follow, taken from *Budget of the United States Government: Fiscal Year 1992* (Washington, D.C.: U.S. Government Printing Office, 1991) are systematically understated: among other matters, count the tens of billions of dollars for the S&L bailout as "off-

budget," and don't take account of other tens of billions "borrowed" from the Social Security Trust Fund. Be that as it may, Reagan's highest official deficit (1986) was $208 billion. Fiscal 1990's was $278 and 1991's is estimated to be $400 billion. Without the understating factors, the figure for fiscal 1991 (ended September 30, 1991) would be *at least* $450 billion. Lots more debt, lots more interest, lots more reason to keep social expenditures down, lots more reason to hold back from using fiscal policy to end the slump. Not so incidentally, although the media frequently note that Bush will seek ways to turn the recession around because of the 1992 election, in my reading I have seen no comment on there being a rather large responsibility to do something quite apart from an election.

70. Thus increasing the need for increased real investment, government spending, and/or exports. The source of the data on deficits and interest is Henry Cavanna, ed., *Public Sector Deficits in OECD Countries: Causes, Consequences and Remedies* (London: Macmillan Press, 1988), p. 52, from the essay on the United States by Rudolph G. Penner, Director of the Congressional Budget Office. His figures include both on- and off-budget data (the most relevant procedure), which is why the interest cost is higher than I have cited earlier, using the *Economic Report of the President.*

71. James O'Connor, *Accumulation Crisis*, cited earlier, pp. 55–56. "Surplus value" in this connection may be taken as roughly equivalent to the "economic surplus" discussed above. O'Connor's reference to underproduction of capital and unproductive utilization of the produced surplus overlap with my earlier discussions of financialization, consumerism, and waste, governmental and otherwise.

72. The reader is referred to an earlier reference, Barbara Ehrenreich's *Fear of Falling.*

73. "The High U.S. Poverty Rate: A Product of Deliberate Choice?" *International Herald Tribune*, October 30, 1991. The report summarizes two academic studies which both conclude that "America has high poverty rates not because it must but because it chooses to." The "other countries" noted in the text are Australia, Sweden, Germany, the Netherlands, France, and Britain.

74. From a "Report of the State of California Social Services Advisory Board," September 25, 1990. These and similar data are ultimately based on UNICEF and similar sources. As is well-known, the United States and the Union of South Africa are the only two rich nations

without a national health care program. The United States ranks high in its medical schools and is quite probably most advanced in medical technology; and we spend more than others as a nation, absolutely and per capita. At the same time, at least 35 million are without any health insurance, as noted earlier emergency rooms and public clinics are criminally understaffed and overcrowded, and then there are the data just put forth in the text—a small sample. Why all this? Only part of it is that medicine is a moneymaking business—nowhere else are there incorporated businesses whose names are "Hospitals for Profit," one of the stronger sets of stocks in the market. But, as the *New England Journal of Medicine* pointed out in 1991, 24 cents of each U.S. health-care dollar goes to paperwork. That money would be more than enough to underwrite the 35 million who have no health insurance. Again, why so much paperwork? There are 1,500 private insurers of health care in the United States. Canada, for example, has one: the government. Some day, it may be believed, the United States will have a national health insurance program. And after it has been established, will there be a study telling us how many lives could have been saved or improved had we done it decades earlier? Meanwhile, the phenomenon of "job lock" affects a good 30 percent of our people: mostly middle-income people who don't change jobs *only* because they fear to lose their health-care benefits. The data on paperwork are quoted in *U.S. News & World Report*, May 13, 1991, on "job lock" in *International Herald Tribune*, August 23, 1991.

75. It may be noted in passing that if ever there was a war that the United States clearly should have fought, it was that against Hitler. But between September 1939 and the end of 1941, as the Nazis marched through Poland, the Low Countries and France, bombed the British and invaded Russia, the United States—except for loans and trades—stayed out. Only after the Japanese attacked us and we then declared war against them, and Germany declared war against us, did the United States enter the European war. And it may also be noted that in the military files—including my own—of those who in the 1930s had sought to alert the people of the United States to the fascism of Germany, Italy, Japan, and Spain, there was stamped "prematurely antifascist."

- 9 -

Needs and Possibilities

These are transitional years and the dues will be heavy.
Change is quick but revolution will take a while.
America has not even begun as yet.
This continent is seed.[1]

Neither knowledge of history nor of social analysis can tell us what the future holds; taken together, at best and at most they can tell us how we got to where we are, something of what to look for in the unfolding present, and some of the questions most needing study. In some sense, we cannot even know where we are until after this present has become part of our past. Are we now on the threshold of a promising future, more bountiful for more people than ever before, or, as is just as plausible—or more so?—are we slipping into an indefinitely long period combining stagnant or falling real incomes for those in the industrialized countries, with something much worse for ourselves and everyone else?—remembering that "worse" neither begins nor ends with solely economic considerations.

It is probably true that every era, if it has been thought about in this way at all, has been seen in its time as exceptional in one way or another. Our period, the past half-century or so, may be seen as especially so because of its novel, numerous, and important combinations and contrasts, and because of the degree of awareness of ongoing processes and relationships. All historical periods are different, which is why we think of them as "periods." But it is not inane to see the years approaching the twenty-first century as being quite different from any other—because of those "combinations and contrasts," and that "awareness."

Whether or not one chooses to call it progress it is a fact that today's world, and the United States within and still dominating it, is caught up in a complex of interacting economic/political/cultural/technological processes and relationships that make our lives simultaneously more threatening and more promising than ever *could* have occurred before. We are able to create and ruin, construct and destroy, more rapidly and more pervasively than others ever could at any previous time. Depending upon what is done in the next generation or so, this power will become our glory or our shameful tragedy: as of now, it is both.

The historically unique strengths of the post-World War II society we have been calling global monopoly capitalism are that it has created what might be termed "both and" rather than "either or" sets of realities—a generalization obviously requiring elaboration, and through which, in the foregoing chapters, we have been weaving the historical process in and around. We have done so when we have pointed to (1) the always more pervasive and deeper hold of controlled (oligopolistic-monopolistic) markets *and* the always greater rivalry between business giants; (2) the always stronger and more obtrusive State (irrespective of the political rhetoric that claims another direction) *and* an always freer hand for (at least) supercorporate business; (3) always greater national and personal wealth and higher real incomes *and* always more destitution, hunger, homelessness, and misery; (4) rising numbers of jobs *and* sustained high levels of unemployment in all three tiers; (5) more democratic institutions and political participation *and* more centralized political control and "management"; (6) more personal and social security *and* more personal and social fears and insecurity; (7) more political and personal independence *and* more economic, political, and personal dependence; (8) more production and productivity *and* more waste and inefficiency; (9) more market scarcities *and* more excess productive capacity; (10) continuous talk of peace, *and* continuous bloodshed.

All these contrasts and simultaneities, and others that might be noted, taken together with one other set—more access to education and information (through formal and informal channels) *and* more ignorance and confusion—have created a world throbbing with tension, puzzlement, fear, and anger, *and* with more apathy *and* with more hope than ever: Dickens's "best of times and worst of times," once more, cubed.[2]

In the midst of an earlier time of rapid and violent change, the mid-nineteenth century, a time when those riding the rising waves of industrialism and technological accomplishment had begun to think within the naive optimism of "the idea of progress," Marx observed, in a famous passage,

> Men make their own history, but they do not make it just as they please; they do not make it under circumstances chosen by themselves, but under circumstances directly encountered, given and transmitted from the past. The tradition of all the dead generations weighs like a nightmare on the brain of the living.[3]

In this last chapter, as the focus shifts from what has been and is to what in my view could and should be, we cannot allow ourselves to ignore or forget the great weight of *our* ways and means, the "traditions" of the United States, and the "nightmare" they constitute for extricating ourselves from a social process that seems as likely as not to make an already ominous reality become something considerably worse—whether the reference is to broad political and cultural and environmental probabilities or, more narrowly (but very broad in itself, as well), to what may well be a long-term stagnant economic process for the United States and therefore probably for the rest of the world.

The constituent elements of our nightmare partake of all the dimensions of that gloomy outlook. And it can never be forgotten, either, that the United States—despite and because of its current economic weaknesses—remains the single most influential nation in the world; that if we fail to renovate our society to make it simultaneously less destructive to nature and people, less wasteful of precious natural and technological resources, less careless of its social needs, then though the rest of the world may seek ways to do those things without us (and if so, with our probable opposition), its way will be much more difficult. It is not mere rhetoric to see ourselves as living in "one world"; and the United States is the major force to be reckoned with in that world, come what may.[4]

To be desperately brief in clarifying what is meant by "nightmare" in this connection, I shall point to only two characteristics of the United States—which, however, reach into every nook and cranny of our social existence. I refer to the particular evolutions of individualism and of racism in the United States, and their many ramifications and interactions. Their meaning and their existence—and the continuing deformation of the former and the deepening and spread of the latter—constitute a formidable barrier to the realization of any program that aims at social renovation and social decency—*both* of which are not only desirable but necessary, if there is to be either.

In earlier discussions it has been emphasized more than once that any critique of either individualism or racism can neither begin nor end with the existence and history of the United States. We are part and parcel of the world that produced us—a capitalist, colonialist, racist world; but we have gone farther with all of those traits than others, taken either separately or together. That generalization would seem quite outrageous to almost all the people of this country; outside the United States it would seem reasonable to many or most, and to more than a few here at home, not because it has been taught but because it has been learned.

The problem concerning individualism is not simply, perhaps not even mostly, that it has been transformed so widely into inordinate greed; it is that in moving so far in that direction we have developed what Veblen called "a trained incapacity" to see ourselves as *social* beings, and therefore we have at least temporarily lost our ability as a people to search for or accept social solutions for social problems—except more police and jails for more crime.

Such an individualism both intensifies our ingrained racism and further stifles the possibilities for social improvement: those who oppose *any* social policy that might increase the well-being of the bottom layers of our population have always used racism to deflect the attention and smother the intelligence of those who would be among the direct and indirect beneficiaries of such policies—and the efficacy of that strategy is rising.

Consequently, in trying to think through the elements of a future that would increasingly meet our personal and social needs we must also find ways to undo the paralyzing legacies of our past. We must both learn and unlearn, lest our quagmire become a deadly quicksand. In other words, before beginning to specify sets of policies that might serve the future of ourselves and our society, we must think through how to achieve a *politics* that could make the implementation of such a program more than a fond hope.

Learning and Unlearning

If this century has taught nothing else, it is that there are no easy solutions to social problems, even to those that seem utterly simple—for example, like insuring health and safety on the job. We have seen that even when such a policy is legislated and put in place, those who find it threatening to their profits or their power can see to it that it is not allowed to function in an effective manner. The social resolutions desired by the already powerful can be slipped in through the side door of the State system, "at night and by cloud," as Veblen put it; but the broad range of policies needed by the rest of us requires an evolving politics of genuine democracy—which means open and widespread information, discussion, and political participation to open the front doors of our government to the needs of the entire society and its diverse segments.[5]

Merely to raise these points is to open a can of worms. From the time that human beings began to record their thoughts and actions such matters have been under debate and discussion—going back to Hammurabi and Hillel in Babylonia, Aristotle and Plato in Ancient Greece—and in the few pages we can allot to such matters obviously we could not attempt an adequate brief summary even of those I find attractive, let alone of all the major points of view.[6] Because of their pertinence and wisdom I shall make my discussion of some fundamental political questions begin mostly with the ideas of Gramsci and of the lesser-known contemporary historian/philosopher, Michael Ignatieff.

Concerning Gramsci, who has been briefly noted earlier, I shall confine myself to one of his many contributions, wherein he analyzes the immense difficulties entailed in bringing about genuine and lasting social change; the discussion of Ignatieff—who treats of questions of human solidarity and need—will, like his work itself, be less broad in scope but not therefore unimportant, as I hope will become clear. First, Gramsci.

Before he became prominent as the leader of the Italian Communist Party, Gramsci was a teacher. In the years encompassing and following World War I in which he rose to political leadership, the Italian Left, growing in strength and influence, was seen as among the most promising (or threatening) in the world, because of its substantial organizational strength in both agriculture and industry, its ability to call and to win many strikes, and its influence in Italian cultural life. Its activities and strengths peaked as the 1920s began; but by 1922 Italy had not a socialist but the first fascist government in the world, led by Mussolini—as a person, almost the polar opposite of Gramsci. All of this is recounted because it played such a role in that thought of Gramsci which can be of importance to us in the United States today, different though his and Italy's experience were from our own.

A political prisoner for eleven years (at the end of which he died), Gramsci pondered the question, "What went wrong?" Why fascism, instead of socialism, for Italy? And why so easily? The key to his explanation is found in the analytical concept of "ideological hegemony":

> ...an order in which a certain way of life and thought is dominant, in which one concept of reality is diffused throughout society in all its institutional and private manifestations, informing with its spirit all taste, morality, customs, religious and political principles, and all social relations, particularly in their intellectual and moral connotations.[7]

Gramsci was a Marxist, one who saw the need and had the substantial ability to broaden and deepen Marxian thought, most especially as regards the political and cultural realms. The embryonic notion of hegemony is found in the Marxian epigram we have noted earlier: "The ruling ideas of any era are the ideas of its ruling class." Gramsci made that notion the starting-point for his attempt to understand the great power of capitalism over "the hearts and minds" of the people, and the consequent need for the elements of a new hegemony, a new social vision, to be developed—a different, coherent, and comprehensive view of the needs and possibilities of human beings in society, modifying and changing the capitalist view of economics, politics, culture, and morality. In Gramsci's view, social power and a different State system cannot be achieved by "smashing the State," or any such abrupt or violent process; instead a long and broad process of clearing a jungle and building a city is needed.[8]

This takes us to the question of *force*. Gramsci's notion of hegemony has close links with the function of "leadership" in the social process: the class that has or could have hegemony in society is the class for whose leadership there is or could be effective and pervasive support, ranging from enthusiasm to passive acquiescence; naked force plays a minor, and usually an implicit, role. As Boggs, writing of Gramsci, says,

> The traditional Marxist theory of the State—including Lenin's own concept of hegemony—was, according to Gramsci, limited in the exclusive attention it paid to the role of force as the basis of ruling class domination; there was no understanding of the subtle but pervasive forms of ideological control, manipulation, and domina-

tion... a crippling legacy that led to the impoverishment of revolutionary strategy in virtually every socialist movement. No regime, regardless of how coercive or authoritarian it might be, could sustain itself through organized state power alone, for in the long run its scope of popular support or "legitimacy" was bound to be crucial, particularly in moments of crisis. In differentiating these two types of control, Gramsci contrasted the functions of "domination" (direct political coercion) with those of "hegemony" or "direction" (consent, ideological control) ...correspond[ing] roughly to the ... distinction between state and civil society. It was obvious to Gramsci that Marxism, as an expression of the vast majority of the people, would have to take account of both spheres of control in order to press its claim as a viable political force.[9]

It would be difficult to find an industrial capitalist nation in which the "hegemony" of the capitalist class is as thoroughgoing in its spread and depth as in the United States. As the nation continues its way through an ever more painful socioeconomic crisis, it is that hegemony which allows the rule of those who brought us there to continue without serious challenge; but if and as that crisis continues to deepen in the absence of a developing alternative vision, the resort to continued militarization, combined with falling living standards, will be accompanied by the settling in of our form of "capitalism with the gloves off": in the place of an always more feeble democracy, an always more centralized oligarchy. How the social peace would be kept cannot be said; but it can be said that one way is likely to be by disturbing the peace elsewhere.

As the U.S. economy writhes in the first stages of what threatens to be a prolonged recession/stagnation, there are many who believe and hope that such hard times by themselves will bring the population to political life. That mistaken judgment has been made before—most disastrously during the very hardest times of all for Germany, 1929–1933, which, however, brought Hitler to power. That is, the hegemony of the ruling oligarchy is not simply economic, nor simply anything. It is the consenting acceptance of the main elements of social existence by the mass of the population. That hegemony will not be effectively displaced by an economic crisis alone; quite the contrary, in the absence of a strong popular movement toward social sense and decency, an economic crisis tends to intensify hate, fear, and the attraction of irrational politics.[10]

Among the "main elements of our social existence" that the majority of the people of the United States consentingly accept are the wretched miseries of at least a third of our population, an acceptance aided and abetted by our now almost innate tendency to "blame the victim," especially if the blamer is white and the victim is not: perhaps the most triumphant and poisonous consequence of the combination of racism with ideology. Any serious and hopeful steps toward a saner, safer, stabler, more abundant, more decent—more satisfying—social process in the United States must begin by understanding and seeking to overcome the deadly and stultifying grip of racism; but it cannot do that unless it begins very much at the same time with the manner in which we have allowed our ideology to demean us as human beings. A good place, among others, to begin with that vital task is to compare what our ideology has taught us with what we need to know, in particular about our actual and desirable relationships with each other in society.

It is with this in mind that I now turn to the thought of Michael Ignatieff. In illuminating the intricacies of this question—those surrounding "our need for fraternity, social solidarity, for civic belonging"—Ignatieff shows us how much that is precious we stand to lose (including life itself) if we fail to deal adequately with this need. At the same time he identifies the towering obstacles that obstruct the path for our doing so—not least among them that we do not now possess even a "language of need." Gramsci saw the realization of our deep needs prevented by thickly encrusted social habits and attitudes, by the hold of ideology. Writing while caged in a fascist prison, he lived by the philosophy he thought necessary for all who would change society from its deadly ways: "Pessimism of the intellect, optimism of the will." Ignatieff, in a different but complementary fashion, sees our history as having emptied us of once-existent and humanly vital attitudes and activities. Also intellectually pessimistic, the optimism of his will is manifested in his book.

"We Must Love One Another or Die"

Those words,[11] written as Europe began another round of mutual slaughter, could not have meant that if we *do* love one another we shall become immortal. The death was of a different kind, the death of our humanity.[12] It is this that occupies Ignatieff in his *The Needs of Strangers.*[13]

In the preceding chapter, reference was frequently made to "the welfare state." The immediate precapitalist origins of such relationships in western civilization are to be found in medieval Europe, in the social and moral order ruled over by the Roman Catholic Church, an order overturned by the emergence of dynamically interacting capitalism and nationalism. The next emergence of such a state of affairs was in Bismarck's Germany. Given that some significant aspects of post–World War II welfare states, both in Western Europe and North America, were adaptations of the Iron Chancellor's social policies, some light is shed on the many shortcomings of today's "welfare" institutions: Bismarck's aim was to maintain social peace by "welfare" that would blunt the cutting edge—angry desperation—of social unrest; there was no hint of human solidarity, no hint of "loving one another" in his schemes of social insurance.[14] Not quite right things were done for not quite right reasons—except for Bismarck and his circle. The purpose of this side excursion has not been to fault Bismarck, but to help us find our way through the thickets of confusion surrounding what in his time was called "the social question."

Perhaps a place to begin is to understand just how much has changed in western society in the past two centuries or so. We live in "nations" today, but that is a very new, artificial, and—as we know from, say, the bloodletting in what was Yugoslavia—a very unstable, even volatile institution. For our purposes, with needs as the focus, what the nation lacks is what was provided for it in the long and habituating history of our species—in tribes, clans, one form or another of "family," that is, in some *small* group, its members rarely moving more than a few miles away from "home," all knowing each other—and, more to the point, knowingly dependent upon each other. That they were living at a level and in ways none of us would willingly adopt is of course true; that early history is noted here to emphasize not only that our species survived that way, but also that its survival was clearly dependent upon a solidaristic mode of existence.

Explicably, our society lacks anything like that sense of solidarity, *and* we are virtually without consciousness of the need for something like it. The mentalities and values of our ancestors were shaped by the material hardships of their history; we moderns are shaped by the realities and possibilities of material abundance.

But our history, in addition to bringing a large number of us to levels of material well-being unimaginable in the dim past of our ancestors (even were we to confine the content of well-being to food, clothing, and shelter) has made us vulnerable to and victim of *unnecessary* personal and social ills, as we have overwhelmingly accepted an ideology that says the market is a satisfactory substitute for, among other matters, democratic rule and solidarity: not a perfect world but, as Adam Smith thought it would be, the best of all possible worlds, given our inability as a species to trust, or to be trusted by—or to care for—others.

In losing our ability to think of ourselves as social beings, we lose the ability to think of ourselves and others as having *needs* other than those we can "satisfy" in the market, or, those grudgingly supplied through a cold State apparatus (or private charities).[15] It is what does and does not happen in those conditions that Ignatieff seeks to understand.

> Modern welfare may not be generous by any standard other than a comparison with the nineteenth-century workhouse, but it does attempt to satisfy a wide range of basic needs for food, shelter, clothing, warmth and medical care. The question is whether that is all a human being needs. When we talk about needs we mean something more than just the basic necessities of human survival. We also use the word to describe what a person needs in order to live to their full potential. What we need in order to survive, and what we need in order to flourish are two different things. The aged poor on my street get just enough to survive. The question is whether they get what they need in order to live a human life (pp. 10-11).

Ignatieff goes on to wonder when it is right to speak for the needs of strangers; whether it is possible to define what human beings need in order to flourish; and to point out that "the administrative good conscience of our time seems to consist in respecting individuals' rights while demeaning them as persons" (p. 13). To pursue this argument, I believe I can do no better than to offer a string of consecutive quotations in the author's own words. His argument is at once delicate and strong.

> The distinction I want to make is...one between needs which can be specified in a language of political and social rights and those which cannot. Most arguments in politics these days are about the first sort of needs, for food, shelter, clothing, education and employment. The conservative counter-attack on the welfare state

is above all an attack on the idea that these needs make rights. ...[which] puts into question the very notion of a society as a moral community (pp. 12–13).

It is because money cannot buy the human gestures which confer respect, nor rights guarantee them as entitlements, that any decent society requires a public discourse about the needs of the human person. It is because fraternity, love, belonging, dignity and respect cannot be specified as rights that we ought to specify them as needs and seek, with the blunt institutional measures at our disposal, to make their satisfaction a routine human practice. At the very least, if we had a language of needs at our disposal, we would be in a better position to understand the difference between granting people their rights and giving people what they need.... [A] decent and humane society requires a shared language of the good. The one our society lives by—a language of rights—has no terms for those dimensions of the human good which require acts of virtue unspecifiable as a legal or civil obligation (pp. 13–14).

In the end, a theory of human needs has to be premised on some set of choices about what humans need in order to be human; not what they need to be happy or free, since these are subsidiary goals.... There cannot be any eternally valid account of what it means to be human. All we have to go on is the historical record of what men have valued most in human life. There does exist a set of words for these needs—love, respect, honour, dignity, solidarity with others. The problem is that their meanings have been worn out with casual over-use in politics (p. 15).

Giving the aged poor their pension and providing them with medical care may be a necessary condition for their self-respect and their dignity, but it is not a sufficient condition. It is the manner of giving that counts and the moral basis on which it is given...whether entitlements are understood to be a matter of right, a matter of deserving, or a matter of charity. In many Western welfare states, entitlements are still perceived both by the giver and the receiver, as gifts. To be in need, to be in receipt of welfare, is still...a source of shame (p. 16).

In the United States one does not need to be told these things, only to be reminded of them. It would be hard to find a society in which shame is greater over unemployment, poverty, hunger, poor housing or homelessness, even over old age, disability, and illness; or one in which the attitudes toward those in basic need are more scornful, insulting, hateful, and, as well, fearful. And when, as is happening in rising numbers as these words are written, many who were recently in the scorning category find themselves placed among the scorned by unemployment and in the long lines for assistance where dignity is shredded, the psychological consequences are of course devastating, and sometimes fatal.[16]

I have not mentioned that Ignatieff has his inquiry depart from the fate of Shakespeare's *King Lear*—a profound allegory of profound tragedy. Lear's personal tragedy, remanded by his daughters to the "satisfaction" of his basic needs in a state of dishonor and indignity, is a terrifying glimpse into current realities for numberless millions, and the looming probabilities for who knows how many more—in this the richest nation in the world's history (as Lear's kingdom was also rich). And Ignatieff, learning from Shakespeare, teaches us that the

> allegiances that make the human world human must be beaten into our heads. We never know a thing till we have paid to know it, never know how much is enough until we have had much less than enough, never know what we need till we have been dispossessed. We [like Lear] must be blinded before we can see. Our education in the art of necessity cannot avoid tragedy (p. 50).

But how much more tragedy can be endured in our nation and world before reaching a point of no return? Being beaten over the head can awaken one; it can also make one senseless. If all those not yet consciously and seriously afflicted by the callous social institutions of U.S. capitalism must be so afflicted before they take steps to regain a lost humanity, we may have to pass through a disaster that would be the social equivalent of Hiroshima. We cannot take that chance, for we cannot afford such damage.

Taken together, Gramsci and Ignatieff have defined a vital portion of the political problem that must be dealt with if our society's dangerous shortcomings are to be overcome. That the numbers of people in the United States able and inclined to take steps in the necessary direction is now vastly less than what is needed goes without saying; that the numbers would probably become much greater than now seems possible, were an embracing movement with a humanly promising and clearly sensible program to develop, does *not* go without saying, but there have already been such welcome surprises in our recent past (in civil rights and anti-Vietnam efforts, for example), and it can happen again. It is more than whistling past the graveyard to remind ourselves that while there's life, there's hope. But suppose that social doom is our fate no matter what we do—something we cannot know for sure—is there some dignified way to spend our time that does not include resistance and striving?

Before turning to the content and complexities of a synthesis of current proposals, the main thrust of the Gramsci/Ignatieff discussion must be emphasized: no program for desirable social change in the United States can make headway or endure unless it is recognized just how strong the hold of capitalist ideology has been and is on the "hearts and minds" of our people—*and* ourselves. The civil rights and antiwar efforts of the past were just noted as successes. In a larger sense, they were also failures. Important rights were won by those to whom they had been previously denied; and the war in Vietnam was restrained from becoming nuclear—the only way the U.S.A. could have "won"—and finally it ended. But racism continues and deepens, and the mentality and the policies that took us into Vietnam thrive still: that is what he meant when Bush proclaimed the Gulf War as showing that "the Vietnam syndrome" had been conquered. The ultimate weaknesses of those and of other social efforts in the United States were caused by the ideological grip Gramsci knew must be loosened. Not least of the meaning of that grip for us, here and now, is that those of us in liberal/radical politics, like our conservative and rightwing opponents, also tend to be competitive and combative among ourselves; we too tend to be individualistic, to take ego trips, to have a hunger for power, or status, or something that convinces our natural allies to turn away; we too, not always but all too often, see the satisfaction of the needs of those who cannot sufficiently help themselves to be acts of kindness, or as gifts, not as an act of fraternity, of human solidarity. Not just others, but all of us have to learn and to unlearn—and considerably more than has been suggested above.

So, if, as, and when we all go to work seeking to get our heads screwed on straight, how should we then proceed, with what principles, goals, means, programs?

What and Who and When and Where?

In the explanation of capitalism in Chapter 2, we quoted Tawney's criticism of its debasing principles. The words are worth keeping in mind as we think ahead to a safer, saner, more humanly rewarding society:

> It is obvious, indeed, that no change of system or machinery can avert those causes of social *malaise* which consist in the egoism, greed, or quarrelsomeness of human nature. What it can do is to create an environment in which those are not the qualities which are encouraged. It cannot secure that men live up to their principles. What it can do is establish their social order upon principles to which, if they please, they can live up and not live down.[17]

Principles

Our principles inform our ends and means; they are what we take to be of highest and enduring importance. As has been implicit in earlier pages and will be made explicit now, our movement should be toward (and the maximum practice of at any moment on the way) economic and political and social *democracy*, social *equality*,[18] personal *freedom*, and *peace*. All more or less familiar, of course, but considerably more often than not as empty or deceitful rhetoric. If such principles are even to be approached in practice, we must take explicit account of what has to be offset and *undone*: economic autocracy and political oligarchy, institutionalized racism and sexism in all quarters of our lives, numerous de facto and legal constraints on the freedom of individuals to live as they choose even when such freedoms would be harmless to others, the leukemia of militarism and violence in our society, and a broad range of encrusted and supportive attitudes toward all these matters. To the "learning and unlearning" discussed earlier, a political movement toward a healthy society must add "doing and undoing."

One means of preventing lofty goals from being abstractions usable by all political types is to apply them to specific programs. A first step in that direction is to insist that democracy, equality, and freedom imply maximizing the *decentralization* of power and the *debureaucratization* of administrative functions throughout the society—in the economy and the government, in education, health care, and the informative and cultural functions of the media—everywhere.

An immediate set of objections to the foregoing goals would circle around the presumed intractability of human nature; that is, the assumption that if present realities are dangerous and ugly that is due to something innate in human beings rather than required and rewarded by the present socioeconomic system. The needs and functions of the capitalist system encourage and solidify such beliefs. Even those in our society who see much wrong in it can thus believe that it makes little or no difference what they do or don't do. So why bother? That gloomy set of attitudes, like our attitudes toward consumerism and militarism, suit the existing system just fine; but they and what has given rise to them can be changed. The first critical set of possible and necessary changes has to do with our connected economic, political and social structures.

Structures

The structures of *production* and *employment*, of *consumption* and *foreign* trade, and of *income, wealth*, and *power* are in continuous, dynamic and mutually supportive interaction. As each now stands, it must be changed substantially, but none can be without concomitant changes in all the others. Furthermore, although the foregoing refer to structures of the economy, they also intermingle with and act to shape political, social, and cultural relationships and processes, which would and must change reciprocally to some degree with those of the economy.

Clearly, the pattern of production relates closely to the pattern of employment, especially when we include the technologies utilized. Also, however, what is produced, and by whom, and how, is also the principal set of determinants of what and how much can be exported/imported, invested, and consumed, and by whom; and in turn, that is all directly and indirectly set by those with the wealth and the connected power to make the commanding decisions.

Out of this tangle of connections and interdependencies we may extract from earlier chapters a few key generalizations which, in describing present realities, reveal abundant opportunities for social changes that would supply our needs and improve our society: (1) there is an enormous amount of waste and inefficiency; (2) a major contribution to that waste and inefficiency has been our military use of resources, equipment, and labor, with also a large share of the responsibility owed to the means used to control excess capacity by restricted production, and to enlarge sales through wasteful nonprice competition; and (3) there has been a shocking misuse and underuse of the labor force, whether employed, underemployed, or unemployed.

In this moment of great need for public policies to lift the level of material well-being for dozens of millions of our people, to rescue our infrastructure, to lessen unemployment, to provide adequate health care, and more, the common governmental and private position[19] is that "we cannot afford..." this, that, or the other thing, usually citing debts and deficits as the reason. It should be plain that such an answer arises from ideology, ignorance, or indifference, and usually some combination of all of them. We have the economic capacities to meet all our existing needs and to go well beyond them; our problem is not economic, but ideological and political.

Here it is important to inject a related but different and important point: most of the discussion of our present recession (or stagnation) assumes that the rate of increase of GNP is inadequate, and must but cannot now be heightened (because *private* investment and consumption are insufficient). Neither the first nor the second part of the assertion is correct. We do not need to increase the *rate*, but we do need to change the *composition* of GNP. We can do that, and if we choose we can also increase the rate of expansion through *public* policy (without troublesome inflation). These generalizations will be supported later; the emphasis here is that it is our *structure* of production, not its *level* (or changing level) that is vital.

Thus: We produce too much of certain *commodities*—such as automobiles and weapons—and too little of certain others—such as mass transit facilities and housing. We have too many of certain types of *services*—advertising, finance, and the military, and too few in health care and education. It goes back to Baran's epigram: "We are taught to want what we don't need, and not to want what we do."

We can teach ourselves to want more sensibly; but it will take political work for that to become manifest in our economic and social structures. Earlier we have discussed our always substantial unemployment, easily but not fully comprehended when it is understood that the *minimum* level of unemployment sought by public policy is 5 to 6 percent—that is, something over seven *million* people seeking but unable to find jobs.

At present (August 1992) the official rate hovers near 8 percent, and we may say that the real rate is a good 50 percent higher than that (as explained in Chapter 4). In short, it is by no means an exaggeration to say that many more than 10 million potentially productive people are without the full-time work they need and wish. This does not take account of an even greater number who, though working, are producing a good or a service that is useless or—in being harmful—worse than useless.

Thus, a fundamental material argument for change is that an altered structure of production and something approximating genuine full employment[20] would not only eliminate the enormous *waste* of our economy, it would at the same time increase the real per capita income of the population—and considerably more than, say, the longed-for 3 to 4 percent increase of GNP (which is at least twice what can be expected under present conditions)—although using presently unused labor would by itself also increase GNP significantly. This sort of point could be made in many different ways, but all of them would reveal the *economic* shortcomings of this system that prides itself first and foremost on its economic accomplishments and its "rationality."

None of this, or anything like it, is possible regarding economic structures so long as the decision-making authority remains in the hands of those who control and benefit from the existing patterns of production, consumption, income, and wealth: the hidden bottom of the iceberg that so often sinks reforms. To change the patterns of production and consumption requires a lasting change in the structure of power; and that will only happen through the formation of a broad and continuing political movement that changes the manner in which the State system operates, and for whom.

It is my view that a definitive change of the necessary sort requires an equally definitive change in the structures of ownership and control, moving in the direction of democratic socialism. But it is clear that such a political movement in the United States is embryonic, at most. That being so now, it is also my judgment that it is politically necessary for the foreseeable future to seek changes significantly modifying but still acting within the capitalist framework, there being no realistic alternative but to acquiesce in an always more brutal status quo.

Just now, with the dramatic events that are making the Cold War a bad memory, the most sensible and the most promising area within which immediately to make a substantial political effort is that having to do with military expenditures. If we cannot now organize the politics to unseat *that* aged and enfeebled monster, it is hard to see when and with respect to what we ever could.

Swords to Ploughshares

Talk of a "peace dividend" began in the early 1950s, when Eisenhower was president. There has never been one. No matter how the Cold War went, there was always a clutch of reasons given for *increasing* military expenditures. The reason most frequently pressed was that the Soviet Union's military strength was at least equal and soon would be greater than ours, in this or that area: "the missile gap" of Kennedy's day was perhaps the favorite, and even after "the gap" was officially shown to be in our favor, expenditures "to close the gap" continued to rise.

There have always been, and still are, those who believe in military expenditures for military reasons; but they are superfluous except as a background chorus, given the great power and numbers of those who have encouraged and supported military expenditures for economic reasons: profits and jobs.

The Bush presidency began in 1989, just as there could no longer be a question that the Cold War, if not already over, was disintegrating rapidly. Under growing pressure for acknowledging that large fact—at the same time that budget and deficit problems were thickening the air—the Bush administration moved in revealing ways: it announced a large-scale closing of military bases.

What was revealing is that the savings from such changes would be a tiny percentage of annual military expenditures, but that those small savings would amount to large losses for those civilians who worked on the bases and the small businesses in surrounding communities: that is, the resulting political pressures would be in the direction of halting further cuts in *any* military expenditures.[21]

Now that the Soviet Union no longer exists, arguments for *increasing* military expenditures have become fanciful for all but certifiable lunatics; but it does not follow that military expenditures will be made to *decrease* significantly without considerable political pressure from the population. Both the executive and the legislative branches tend strongly toward *minimizing* cuts, and even those in Congress who ask for larger cuts are still speaking in terms of, say, 15 percent over five years, versus 5 percent over the same period. Quite apart from the substantial influence over members of Congress by corporate interests, there is the great fear of losing elections through the defections of voters who have been "cold-warriorized."

Arithmetic and Life and Death

In an earlier chapter we stated that about $1 trillion is spent annually in the world for the military—roughly $300 billion of that in Tier III, about the same in the United States, and the rest by the Soviet Union and Tier II countries (most heavily, Britain and France).[22] We shall have occasion to raise the question of Tier III expenditures in a later section; suffice it to repeat here that already, as weapons manufacturers in the world have sought adjustment to the disappearing Cold War, they have stepped up their efforts to sell to Tier III countries, particularly in the Middle East and South Asia.

The military expenditures in what was the Soviet Union are undergoing a rapid decrease, and there have been substantial cuts announced there (perhaps ironically) as a "peace dividend." We propose a reduction of U.S. military expenditures of one-third, about $100 billion, as soon as practicable, with a longer-term goal of at least twice that. Assume a total federal budget of around $1 trillion. A $100 billion cut, assuming no other decreases in federal spending, would increase federal *social* spending capacities more than the apparent 10 percent,[23] and our excessive military strengths would not be reduced so much as they would cease to increase—not least because the military budget is not only chronically overweight but also padded.

It has been shown that far from this entailing a loss of jobs—or profits[24]—such changes, accomplished within the framework of what has long been called "conversion," promise more jobs, as well as more commodities and services serving a necessary social function: in short, a higher level of material well-being than that provided by the Cold War. As noted in the preceding chapter, Seymour Melman has taken the lead in making such proposals in the books and articles of his we have listed; and as one whose life's work has been the study of industrial management, he may be expected to know both the difficulties and the possibilities of industrial conversion.

Before passing on to how the resources freed by conversion could be well-used, it is worth pointing out that groups pressing for conversion have existed for some time in many communities—including those, like the Silicon Valley area in California, where military expenditures are the bread and butterof the local economy—so the political work need not start from scratch.

Conversion may be seen as a bridge making it relatively easy to cross from this toward a better society. Those who doubt such conversion of military facilities is within the realm of economic possibility (setting political obstacles aside), may think back to the years just after World War II, and wonder what became of all those plants that produced tanks, machine guns, military aircraft, and, among other things, machinery and clothing and food for the military (in 1943, more than half of GNP was purchased by the government for the war). They became, in the same order, trucks and cars, typewriters and similar products, civilian aircraft, mass transit vehicles, and machinery, clothing, and food for the nonmilitary.

Of course there are difficulties for conversion, as there are for life itself. But the difficulties—retraining both blue- and white-collar staff and modifying machinery and plants, for example, all of which should be assisted by federal funds—should be seen as opportunities rather than difficulties, if the will is there; just as reducing the armed forces by a third or a half need not be seen as more unemployment, but as more available labor—in a society learning how to use its human resources in more constructive ways (and, not unimportant, giving skilled military personnel a chance to do something more promising with their lives). That all this would cost us is obvious; less obvious is that all this would add to real incomes, purchasing power, and the tax base considerably more than it would cost. To live differently and better, we must learn to think differently and better. Cold War thought, like its aims and means, was and remains destructive, always easier to achieve than the complications of constructive thought and activity.

Having identified one major source for *paying* for a better society, we now turn to some of the nuts and bolts of a program for socioeconomic change, beginning with the area of services which, as will be seen, also includes desirable types of employment.

If We Can Put Men on the Moon...

Why can't we have a health-care system that is not mostly a way of making money? One answer, of course, is that they wouldn't have been put on the moon if the projectile that got them there hadn't been produced in the military-industrial complex, and funded for principally military purposes. We have never taken health care that seriously as a *social* matter; although, of course, each of us has been fairly serious about our own family's health, more or less. We have this vision of ourselves as a people: generous, but also hard-headed; soft-hearted but not fools. When one looks at what we spend on health care and the "bottom line," it seems we should change our self-image: in 1992 it was expected that $817 billion, 14 percent of GNP, would be spent privately and publicly in the United States, more than anywhere else in the world, absolutely or relatively; and in recent years those expenditures have been rising more than twice as fast as GNP.[25] Withal, it is (under) estimated that about 35 million of our citizens have no health insurance, and therefore very little if any health care. And those who do have insurance—as many reading these words can attest from their own experience—do not get adequate health care, and must pay a lot in addition to get what little they can.

Why is this so? Part of the answer has to do with those 1,500 separate insuring companies noted earlier; and all the paperwork and profits involved, which requires not just paper, but work, time, money. And some has to do with the high tech of U.S. medical care, a good part of it serving no function other than medical people scratching each others' backs with mutual references of patients, or fending off malpractice suits by having all possible (high-tech) examinations made. And part of it has to do with the high cost of prescription drugs.[26] That the population is aging is also important, but it is aging in *all* the industrialized countries, and their health care costs much less, per capita, or as a portion of GNP. And then: the *average* care is considerably better in Britain, France, Germany, Italy, Sweden, etc., than it is in the United States, where not everyone gets even some care. And then again: those whose decisions have shaped health care in the United States are themselves getting much better than average care.

The problem in the United States is that health care is seen as a commodity.[27] Not all, but most doctors become so in the anticipation of having very high incomes. The average doctor in 1990 received as medical fees something like $120,000. (And if he was incorporated, as so many doctors now are, he paid lower taxes on his fees and investments, as well.) Many years ago, a good percentage of doctors—family doctors, they were called; or country doctors—*seemed* to be doctors because they felt the work to be both important and interesting. Practicing medicine these days in the United States is one way of being a capitalist; for some doctors, just another way. Believe it or not, it is not that common elsewhere; nor is it unknown, just as it is not unknown in the United

514 — U.S. CAPITALIST DEVELOPMENT SINCE 1776

States for there to be doctors who have become so because they still think the work is important and interesting.

Interestingly, and importantly in terms of useful changes, nurses seem generally to be much the opposite in motivation. Almost always terribly underpaid and overworked, they also do much of what is vital in bringing patients back to health or keeping them alive—and feeling human.[28] In an improved health-care system in the United States, the powers and incomes of nurses would rise, and those of doctors decline.

A fundamental means for understanding what is wrong in the United States regarding health care (among other matters of social need) is that it has been commodified: it is something one buys or sells, like one's labor, clothing, skis, or video games. The United States, like all other industrial societies to one degree or another, has of course moved away from treating such care in purely commodified terms: thus, for example, "public health" systems,[29] emergency clinics, and, of course, Medicare. But all these are reluctant and underfunded exceptions to the general rule: you get what you can pay for.

But it is absurd—indeed, in social terms, also some combination of obscene and unbalanced—to see health needs in anything like the same terms as, for example, the desire for a new TV set. In the welfare—and capitalist—societies of Western Europe, such as Germany, France, Italy, Britain, the Low Countries and Scandinavia, the social services have been de-commodified to one important degree or another. What happens to one when ill, or out of work, or old or disabled, is not a private but a social responsibility: the need, as in Ignatieff, has become a right.[30]

We must move swiftly to create a national health-care system for the United States, one in which anyone, irrespective of age, gender, color, income, anything,[31] will have guaranteed and trouble-free, dignified access to the needed health care, from prenatal to preventive to intensive—"from womb to tomb," as the saying went in Britain when its program was begun under the Labor Government in the late 1940s. And that reminds: there was much talk in Britain in those first years about the great shortage of dentists, because of the enormous numbers of new patients going "just because it was free." It wasn't too long before good sense overcame ideology, and it was realized that none but masochists would writhe in a dentist's chair "just because it was free." Before World War II, Britain had long been known as a nation of people with bad teeth—which, of course, hurt.[32]

Along with what we normally mean by health care, we easily can and we must provide child care for working parents, paid maternity-paternity leaves, and make whatever other provisions are necessary to see to it that our people have the right to be healthy, for no other reason than that they exist: as though each of us were mother, father, brother, sister, son, or daughter and friend to the other—as, in some finally valid sense, though strangers, we are.

Down the Tubes

We extended that right to education long ago, but the need was the political economy's and the principle closer to obligation than to right: one *must* go to school. (That's what truant officers were for. Are there still truant officers?) The law began with a grade school requirement in the late nineteenth century, as industrialization took hold and it was discovered that workers had to be able to read and count in order to work properly in most industrial jobs. That could be taken care of by completing grammar school (note the term "grammar school," which could as easily have been "arithmetic school") before World War I. High school became the requirement in the ensuing decades. Nowadays college is the practical, though not, of course, the legal requirement.[33]

From the first years when public education was made available and required in the United States, there have been two educational "tracks," roughly determined by class; and there are still.[34] One track was meant to provide at least some education, the other to provide almost entirely training. The first has always been meant to develop the minds of those who might go on to college and perhaps the seats of power; the second has been for those who will work in the factories, the shops, the offices. For the first, Choate and then Harvard; for the second, P.S. 132 and then some job; or by the 1930s, if you were bright and diligent, maybe CCNY.[35]

There was a lot wrong with that system in the first half of this century, but in its own terms it worked reasonably well. In the last quarter of this century it has ceased to work well in anybody's terms: the educational system in the United States has become dysfunctional. Not always, but all too often, it resembles in some of its parts a play pen for the reasonably well off, in others a disciplinary barracks for all concerned. What went wrong?

Something was wrong from the beginning, as has been suggested above when its "practical" purposes were noted. Practical purposes are all well and good, but the principle purpose of an educational system, from preschool through adulthood, must be to nourish, strengthen, and expand our creative and constructive possibilities, and enable us to understand and to appreciate nature, our society, our culture, ourselves.

The educational system, as is always and everywhere true, both serves and mirrors the social system of which it is a part. Naturally. As the larger system changes, for the worse or the better, so does its educational sector, leading and lagging, being changed by and contributing to the change of the larger system (most obviously, though not necessarily most valuably, through its technological and scientific elements). There was much that was positive in our educational system in the first half of the century; there still is, but it has diminished and continues to do so rapidly at all levels. Why?

There cannot be a simple answer to such a question, but we may be sure that there will be no change for the better in education (through vouchers or exhortation or "education presidents") unless there is an improved social system; and vice versa. But something else may also be asserted with surety: the deterioration of education is the result of the always more prominent role played in our development by our society's defects: its racism, its deformed individualism, its consumerism, its militarism—not in that or any other order: they are all tangled in one knot.

Thus, racism has meant not two but something like three educational tracks, despite the various policies of the 1960s whose stated intent was to undo the third: most notably, school busing. And, because the racism of those on the non-élite track is thickened and heated by job and sexual torments, the ongoing result now for decades has been for those who can manage it (through riches or sacrifice) to send their children to private schools, and for the remaining and very large majority of students (and their parents) to live in apprehension, fear, and resentment—the very worst atmosphere for learning and teaching. To add another poison to this stew, it is now a rising trend that when local or state governments (as required by law) ask voters to pay increased taxes to improve, maintain, or even keep open their schools, the voters choose instead to keep the money and shop, even some of those with children.

But what has militarism got to do with this? Looking back at our discussion of the State system, we recall and note that military spending as a portion of the budget, connected deficits that frighten and intimidate both lawmakers and citizens, and the cutting back of federal grants-in-aid to localities and states (a main financial support for education in the past) have combined to assure that when, on top of all else, the school system runs out of money, all hell will literally break loose—as indeed it has. As for deformed individualism, it is the flip side of consumerism as well as an important part of the impulse that has parents sending their children to private schools instead of joining with others to save the public school system.

The foregoing has to do with grammar schools and high schools. But colleges and universities are, of course, sinking in the same swamp. Anyone who has taught for many years in our colleges and universities, from the worst to the best, knows that what has fallen apart below can no longer support any part of what should be above. The best private schools are now doing something near to what the best public schools used to do, but no more; and most students at today's colleges and universities did not go to private schools.

A noticeable percentage of them do not read, perhaps do not wish to read (except textbooks and exams), know close to nothing of their society's history (and couldn't care less), and take a pragmatic, income-oriented, view of learning, at best.

These and other afflictions and attitudes are not self-inflicted by the young, who can but work with what their elders have presented them; their generation has from birth had to inhale air both physically and socially fouled. If the young and this society are to have a future worth the effort to get there, the educational system must be rescued. And, like the rest of what is needed, it can be.

Anchors Aweigh

Assuming that appropriate attitudes toward education can become effective, among the primary aims must be a thorough house-cleaning of the educational establishment. Our health care is corrupted by a "health empire" whose powers are used more to make money than to preserve health; our educational system is just as corrupt, but it is power more than money that has been the corrupting agent. That the power sought and gained is often petty only worsens matters, for those who seek and gain petty power hold on to it more grimly than those at the very top.

The focus here is and must be our schools, not our colleges and universities. This is not to exempt the latter from any such charges. It is to say that unless we transform the first dozen or so years of formal education into what they can and must be, what happens in "the higher learning" won't count for much.

"Debureaucratization" was posited as a necessity pages ago. Among the leading candidates for that process are the primary and secondary schools themselves, but even more, their controlling administrative systems. Those who rise to the levels of decision-making in the school system are seldom if ever those who are interested in education; they are interested in their own situation. Petty though their power may be in the society as a whole, it looms large as a destructive force in education—as so many teachers and students have discovered. Those who decide to become teachers (like those who decide to become nurses) more often than not have the appropriate purposes in mind: to teach (to heal). One does not become a grade or high school principal, let alone a system bureaucrat, for love of education or teaching: indeed it often seems that scorn, rather than love, for the young is dominant. The evident motive is power. Bureaucracies are stifling wherever they exist; when they act to stifle the minds of children, it is akin to manslaughter.

In the grade and high schools, what books and teaching practices are used are some bureaucrat's choice, not some teacher's, with rare exceptions. That is bad enough; worse is what is chosen. Again, exceptions exist, but need it be stressed that convention and conservatism (and, where relevant, puritanism) are the rule? Intriguing books, mind-opening ideas, innovative ways of teaching, all these must be snuck through the border guards of education, smuggled into the classroom like the contraband they are. Here and there a cheery and livening teacher, whether in the 2nd or the 11th grade; here and there a teacher who, despite all the soporific books (written to be sold on a mass and very profitable basis for just this enormous and noneducating market), manages to awaken the minds and delight the hearts of children. But mostly, school, which could and should be a place to rush to and to remember with gratitude, is rushed from and remembered as some mixture of the comic and the oppressive. Education as a big bore. As tragedy.

Of course, it must be understood that an educational system living by the standards put forth as principles above—creativity, and the like—would function as a very subversive element in this (or any other) society; and if the powers that be had to choose between the harmful and dying system we now have and one that would enrich the mental and emotional lives of the young, can there be any doubt how they would choose?[36] The powers that be are quite happy with the "subversive" consequences of science and technology, which they can bend to their own purposes. They either don't know or don't care that also that is kept below its possibilities by an educational system trapped and sinking from the weight of dullness, desperation, and fear.

What can we do? What must we do? Any proposals for change must take into account how very imposing the bureaucratic structure of the educational establishment is, how impenetrable the minds that occupy its seats of power, how habituated the teachers to the ruts in which they have been placed, how very resistant the financing governmental bodies at all levels to change of any kind. The educational system is not crippled by a broken leg, it is beset by cancer. It may or may not be curable, but like the health care system, the literal and figurative loss of life means that every effort must be made to lift our society and ourselves out of its murderous swamps. The effort must be begun or, as in some cases, continued, as much and as rapidly as possible. What might its elements be?[37]

First, debureaucratization, which means very much increasing the control of parents, teachers, students and other interested citizenry, while very much decreasing the control of any and all educational bureaucracies. If the will and the politics are there, some interim ways and means can be found to bridge the present to the future, as personnel and policies undergo change. Second, assuming we the people begin to have a significant say in educational policies, what should be said? A lot.

Classes should always be smaller rather than larger. That means more teachers. Not all who teach need be credentialed, for two reasons: (1) the credentials are won from that band of bureaucrats, and do not have much to do with teaching and learning (ask any teacher what he or she learned about teaching in so-called "education courses"); (2) there are lots of things to be done in classrooms up through high school that require understanding, concern, and liveliness first, and professional characteristics next or not at all. Parents, after all, are not credentialed, but do a lot of teaching that is important.

The development of skills should, of course, be a part of the educational process, at all levels, but not the largest part of it. The largest part should seek to encourage creativity and curiosity, self-reliance and independence, and cooperation rather than competition. There are many occasions in which teachers and students can and should change roles, and at the very least classrooms should be places where discussion is common rather than rare. Teachers should have authority in the classroom (but never be authoritarian) if their knowledge and ability endow them with it; otherwise they should not be in the classroom at all.

Emphasis should not be on grades but on growth. The hierarchical structure of administrator, teacher, and student should be eliminated—perhaps most easily by eliminating the largest part of the administration. (A favorite remedy of Veblen,[38] and not at all shocking after one concentrates on what it is that administrators really do.) Education should be seen as a lifelong activity, schools as places with revolving doors, day and night, and in all seasons. (The summer three months' vacation, after all, was designed for the need for "hands" at harvest time, in an agricultural society.) And the curriculum at all levels should contain materials that will help the young *not* to learn what the rest of us have to unlearn: those habits of mind that support racism, sexism, and militarism, first and foremost.

Recently, however, there has been an increasingly effective conservative/right-wing movement going strongly in the opposite direction. It attacks what it calls "political correctness" and "multiculturalism" in the schools and universities. It has succeeded in placing on the defensive that small percentage of teachers who seek to present the scarce and ever more necessary materials that help to break down the walls of ignorance, fear, scorn, and hate—and the bullying and terrible harm they allow. The impression these latest descendants of the despicable Senator Joe McCarthy have intended to create—already with considerable success—is that those who present such materials have both the intention and the power to intimidate and oppress those who teach traditionally and in presumably value-free ways.[39] Their false alarms have succeeded in filling newspapers and magazines with a rising number of calls for the authorities to put out the fire said to be sweeping the nation. Bah and humbug.

Were this not so ominous, it would be absurd. Except for those few universities where there are so-called women's or black studies (or the like) departments, in which all or a majority of the faculty members might reasonably be assumed to concern themselves principally with the past, present, and future of those represented in their departments' titles, one will look far, wide, and almost always uselessly if one hopes to find in the other thousands of community colleges, colleges, and universities in the United States even one faculty member who openly departs from the mainstream attitudes of the nation regarding color, class, gender, or foreign policy.[40] One may assume and hope that there are innumerable teachers at all levels who would like to join the few who openly teach the materials now under attack—but who dare not do so, and would be dismissed were they to try.

The movement against those who do seek to help the students "unlearn," is using the very same tactics as Joe McCarthy when he attacked the State Department for being infiltrated by "200 members of the Communist Party," and never provided one name, or any evidence.[41] But it worked for him, and it is working for those using smear and innuendo today—revealing, among other things, just how much *more* must be unlearned.

Perhaps, one day in a future not yet discernible, the recognition will have dawned, because it will have been learned the hard way, just how valuable and indispensable the contributions of the peoples and cultures of Africa, Asia, and Latin America have been to the life and vitality of this country; as it also may have been learned how much women have been and are oppressed, and how much they have contributed (largely unbeknownst to men, including professors) to our development and survival in the dim and recent past. That the few teachers who seek to do this now are mocked and their jobs (as always) threatened, adds to our country's many disgraces.

Before turning to changes having to do with production (as distinct from services), one further area needs discussion: incomes. Just as neither health nor education should be seen as a commodity, neither, of course, should life itself. There are many who, because they are old or, for a variety of reasons unable to work (disability or dependent children, mostly), cannot live decently or, in some cases, at all, without the establishment of what is often called "an income floor."[42] In the past, much of what must be provided by such a "floor" was provided in such people's families (and in many countries still is). In the United States, such provision steadily vanishes, as public supports—that very frayed "safety net"—also fall.

It would be pointless here to say what the floor should be in dollars or purchasing power; but it may be qualitatively defined. Everyone should have the *right* to have enough to eat, a decent place to live, sufficient clothing, and the ability to live, not just survive. The latter means their needs should be met without impinging on their dignity, and that their lives should not be confined to gazing at four walls (or a TV). To meet those goals, and others congruent with them, would require not just incomes for those in need, but also for those who would help to make their lives comfortable, pleasant, and dignified. Some of that could and should mean seeking and finding ways for those in need themselves to remain or become consciously *useful* (teaching, learning, providing certain services to those in their own "group")—a very strong need for all of us. More than that could be said here, but need it be?

Waste Not, Want Not

What has been proposed in the preceding sections for health, education, and "income floors" would of course have costs, big ones: in labor, resources, equipment, almost everything. Those costs could be paid in substantial part by demilitarization; the rest could be paid for, with lots left over, by reducing the wastes of production and of nonproduction outside the militarized sectors (many of which are both—autos and electronics, for example). That means using productive facilities in different ways, and it also means using available labor both more fully and more usefully. Many programs and details along these lines have been put forth in recent years, it is encouraging to note, and they will be referred to in the Reading Suggestions (or have been earlier, or as we now go along). Here we trace out some of the essentials.

First: All those who are doing (or expect to be doing) some job where your service or product is humanly useless (which doesn't mean it isn't profitable), raise your right hand: one million, two million, three million.... To say, as was done in Chapter 5, that about half of all U.S. productive capacity is wasted (by production and nonproduction) is to say that about half of all labor is wasted. Let's assume that is a large exaggeration (but it isn't), that only about a quarter of all labor is wasted: that is, the labor of more than 30 million working people—white-collar, blue-collar, agricultural, industrial, service, whatever—is socially useless. Suppose the society began to change by trying to reduce that to only about one-eighth of all labor wasted by the end of ten years. Right there we have added more than 15 million working people, able to work with some of the best technology in the world—in industry, in agriculture, in services, etc. But what in the world would they produce, not being produced now? And how would it be paid for, and by whom?

Well, what do we need? We need lots more food in the world, and also at home (concerning which, more in a moment). Lots more shelter here in the United States, that is, built for people at the bottom not those at the top. We need lots more (public) hospitals—even though most private hospitals now are half empty (at $750/day, the current average, that's easy to understand), just as those dentists' chairs in Britain were half empty in the 1930s. We need more school buildings. We need to rebuild our bridges (New York City alone has over 100 bridges in dangerous condition, and counting). Our cities' streets have become famous for their potholes. We need to rebuild our water systems and our sewers, before we literally slide into serious danger. We need, in short, to rebuild our infrastructure, estimated to cost about $3 trillion, just about half of our GNP in a good year, all by itself.[43]

Just think of all the really good jobs that would be involved in all that production, building, and rebuilding. And the incomes and purchasing power. And therefore all the other jobs increased by that increased purchasing power. It looks so good, as they say, there must be something wrong with it. There is. The people who now have the power to move in those directions don't have any intention of doing so, or any recognition that it's in *their* interests, not just us others. They will have to be forced by political power to move in directions consonant with their own interests.

But they're not really completely wrong, or dumb. If the society were to move in the directions noted in this chapter, it would do so only because the structure of power—who makes what decisions—would have changed: it would have to, or the other changes couldn't happen. And once that precious structure begins to change, those on the top murmur to themselves (albeit unconsciously, for many or most), "who knows where it would all end?" Who knows, indeed? But the direction would certainly be away from the capitalism so dear to the hearts of those on top, even if it were good for their bottom lines—that capitalism wherein the rights of capital are neither challenged nor challengeable. So we are back to where we began in this chapter: our politics. More of that in our concluding pages. Now we turn to the agriculture of all three "tiers," and the connections between other matters afflicting Tier III and ourselves.

Those Whom the Gods Would Destroy
They First Make Mad

Throughout this book much attention has been given to two starkly opposing conditions: excess productive capacity in almost everything, and desperately little for life's needs almost everywhere. This particular coexistence of too much and too little is madness: especially unnecessary and especially devastating for food. We have noted earlier the official reports of at least 500 million who are always hungry, the 10 to 20 million who starve every year, the 14 million or so children who die of malnutrition-related causes every year—and have left it to the imagination to wonder about the additional hundreds of millions who are just plain miserable all the time, as they seek food, worry about food, never ever have enough food. But surely, our habits of mind tell us, it is because there are too many people and too little of the good earth to feed everyone. Perhaps that common thought wasn't adequately buried and covered over in Chapter 6. So, we begin again with the way the growing of food is organized, by whom, and for what purposes—this time from a slightly different standpoint.

Ever since the Common Market became a reality, in the late 1950s, there has been a bone of contention between the Europeans and the United States (and now also Japan) that has made it difficult for a long list of otherwise easily manageable trade conflicts to be resolved: agriculture. Strange, that as between these highly industrialized and rich nations such a bone would exist, let alone have such importance. The problem has two sides to it: (1) in all the countries involved there is, and for a good half century has been, a significant voting bloc made up of farmers (some of them, especially in the United States not "farmers" but big agricultural companies), with substantial political clout and very much concerned that (2) in none of their countries can their farms' products be sold profitably without government intervention. There is excess capacity, and lots of it: for dairy products, grains, fruits and vegetables, poultry and meat. And, as was pointed out earlier, the problem is exacerbated by the exported food production of Tier III, almost entirely owned and controlled by Tier I and II companies.

And how do the governments intervene? They pay farmers not to produce and require them to restrict production in order to be so paid, they keep prices up by buying surpluses and storing them (while they cost and rot), they subsidize exports that could thus be sold at lower prices elsewhere, except that barriers to prevent that are erected, they participate in programs to hold good acreage fallow; and when all else fails, bury or burn.[44]

The main thing wrong with these policies is not the conflicts they cause between rich nations, or that the "problem" ("excess" capacity) continues and deepens with the years, it is rather a problem whose two sides are that the real farmers (not the agribusinesses) have lost their dignity and, slowly but surely their farms as well, while at least a couple of billion people are not eating as much as they need, and the rest of us are paying a lot more than real costs—not because of nature, or "economics," but politics. That's good, because we can do something more easily about politics than we can about nature and "economics."

What can we do? Like so much else, it is not the problem that is complicated, nor therefore its solution. What stands in the way is habit, and ideology, and power. What should be done has already in part been done—and undone. We begin with the farmers. There has been and there is and there could be even more of a farmer's "way of life." Like the rest of us, farmers like to make money, but they like most to do that by putting in a good crop, harvesting it, and selling it at a reasonable profit, over the years. Farmers really do *not* like to be paid for not planting, for not harvesting, and most of all they do not like to destroy or see destroyed what they have planted and harvested, or to hear of its rotting away in a warehouse. Just ask them.

There was a plan to let farmers "just farm away" in the United States, made by (Truman's) Secretary of Agriculture Brannan. It was never adopted here, but its twin still functions in Sweden and also was adopted by the Labor government and worked in Great Britain, but had to be stopped when they entered the Common Market. The plan called for farmers to produce as much as their reason dictated, letting "the laws of supply and demand" (hear that, free marketeers?) determine both output and price. This would naturally mean rising output (on account of improving technology, if nothing else). If the resulting prices were to leave farmers with inadequate incomes, the difference would be made up with an *income* subsidy. Something like what goes on now, just as a horse is something like a rat: both have four legs. What farmers in the United States, Europe, and Japan get now is a *price* subsidy. The overall consequence is restricted production and higher prices, and it has become like a drug addiction for farmers and governments, always more on the habit: but the people of the world, well-off or desperate, pay the main costs.[45]

Perhaps better programs could be devised than variations on the Brannan Plan; but it's so much more sane and beneficial than current (and worsening) realities that we needn't stretch our minds trying to work another one out. The big farmers—the big agribusinesses—object to an *income* support program for a very good reason: any ceiling on incomes would leave them off to one side, very quickly. But many of the real farmers also objected in 1949, because their pride makes it difficult to swallow "income support." But not incomes through price supports? That politics can be worked through and the dignity that farmers have already lost can be regained: and many more people would have much more food. One might think that would make farmers happier than lining up for checks for not planting.

One more note needs attention in this respect: in Tier III, as was suggested in Chapter 6, there really *must* be a set of changes that gets the big foreign agricultural corporations out and lets the onetime farming people back on their lands so they can grow a good share of the food they need. They were pushed off their lands in the first place, and the corporations can be pulled off now. How? Through political means, taking away the taxpayer/military/political-supported policies emanating from Tiers I and II that have pushed the always difficult lives of the peoples of Africa, Asia, and Latin America toward genocide.[46]

The fundamental problem of the peoples of Africa, Asia, and Latin America has nothing to do with too many people or a stingy nature. That nature is the opposite of stingy is why the major powers have moved into those areas over the centuries; nor was there ever even an appearance of "too many people" until the policies of colonialism and imperialism had their long-run effects of simultaneously diminishing age-old economic support structures while increasing the rate of population growth.

We, the major powers, are their problem. It is not that we view them as "strangers," as we do those with unmet needs in our own society; we don't see them as human beings at all, unless cheap labor is seeing people as human. To the exploitive possibilities of cheap labor and abundant resources, the recent years have given the major powers additional stimuli, the two biggest-ticket items being good markets for high-interest loans and for weapons sales.[47] Those the causes, these the effects: billions of people caught up in the vicious circles of underdevelopment which, besides starvation and misery and short lives for them, for our nations means a (reverse) capital flow, markets to dump dangerous wastes and to sell products either increasingly difficult or illegal to sell in the rich countries—from weapons to dangerous baby foods to pesticides (which come back to us as tomatoes, etc.), and a rising number of other products.

And if that were not enough, we place land mines in their roads to a better future. Quite apart from the inclination of the peoples of some of those countries to accept or support tyrannical governments without our "help," when they do seek to replace such governments with something more promising, you may be sure that the CIA (or its like) will be in on arrangements to create or support some military dictatorship, lest a worse fate—in its definition—befall.

This Land is Our Land

Or it could be, if we worked away at it. To make it the land of all the people, instead of one that's owned and controlled by a tiny fraction, much has to be changed. Much that needs to be changed is basic, close to the bones of the system, out of our reach, as of now. We have to have a politics based on the understanding that we are in it for life, that we must change what we can now step by connected step, and build for more and more necessary and possible changes, as our strength grows.

The structural changes discussed earlier were concerned with domestic production and services. But any serious movement along those lines would require changing our position in the world economy: depending less upon imports, exports, and foreign investments—either by us elsewhere, or by others in the United States. Neither we nor any other industrial country can or should seek to be totally independent of the world economy; but there is room for a much lessened dependence, and we need to use that room if we are to be able to arrange our domestic economy in desirable ways. As a capitalist society we have quite naturally become "hooked" on foreign trade and investment; it goes with the territory. If we are to develop a healthy society we have to kick that habit.

Here we cannot go very far in terms of detail, but basic elements of what seems appropriate can be pointed to. First, we must reduce our *exploitation* of the Tier III peoples. That will not happen easily or quickly, but it can be lessened, just as exploitation in the rich industrial countries was lessened in the evolution of "capital-labor" and "social" accords. Of course that was done in a process that went along with increasing exploitation in Tier III.

But just as what in fact happened in Tiers I and II in the 1960s and subsequently would not have been seen as possible earlier, what is not seen as possible now for the relations between all three tiers could happen. It would take an appropriate politics to do it; such a politics is necessary and possible. Its consequences would include genuine economic development for Tier III countries, rather than a continuation and deepening of dependency, developments that could be healthy for the rich, as well as the now poor nations.

It would take thought and at least some sense of solidarity, rather than guns to move in that direction. A necessary first step toward making such changes possible would be a politics that was effectively anti-militaristic at home: it would be interesting to see just how far the exploitation of other countries could be carried *without* the use or the threat of guns. As was pointed out in Chapter 7, by far the largest share of the trade and investment in the world economy takes place between the rich countries, and serves the function of absorbing what otherwise would be excess capacities. That such excess capacities exist and grow anyway is another indication of how difficult it is for a capitalist society to absorb its always growing production and productivity. That could be made a lot less difficult if a rising share of production were to go to human and social needs (like those specified earlier).

We saw earlier that the main bone of contention between the rich nations in trade discussions has to do with agriculture. The main bone of contention between the United States and Japan is our automobile imports. But the real problem is not that we import Japanese cars in great quantities, and that they buy so few of ours,[48] but that we buy so many autos of any origin, and use so many of our resources for our own production and the use of all of them, and slowly kill ourselves in the process. Mad as hatters.

And if we improved our transportation system, made it more public and less private, we'd use less fuel, and import less oil—and have less reason to bloody others and ourselves in the Middle East, for example. That reasoning is applicable to a broad range of imports; just as a broad range of our exports could be slimmed down if, for example, we ate more of our own food, used more of our own steel for construction of housing and schools, more of our machinery for making needed products—etc.

We had a long ride as Uncle Hegemon. It's hard to find what good it did anybody, but easy to do a body count of our own and especially of other peoples. The old boss of Time, Inc., Henry Luce, wanted "an American century." That would have cost the world and us more than could have been borne; half a century has been more than enough. Have we intruded somewhere—in Africa, Asia (which includes the Middle East), Latin America—where it could be said that those societies or their peoples have been made demonstrably better off, as compared with demonstrably worse off?

And in almost gaining almost the whole world, how profiteth the people of the United States? Whatever was wrong with the United States when our "century" began, and there was plenty wrong, it was nonetheless then a society with a dynamic and a spirit that had considerably more promise, contained considerably more hope, than now. That it was also full of threats, soon to become a developing reality, this book has sought to show.

But now we live in what is becoming a shambles of a society—jittery, fearful, cynical, jaded, and angry in spirit, with an economy shot full of holes—a society facing for the first time in its whole history the prospect, more likely the probability, of continuing an already long period of falling real incomes for the average. We have seen that the process in fact began in the mid-1970s, but was hidden by the means we took to try to counter it: the whole family going to work, and plunging into debt, among other means.

Perhaps more to the point, we now live in a society that *cannot* continue on the path begun in the late 1940s, that cannot find a means of replicating that long ride. The world has changed, in big part because we changed it. Like Britain as this century began, our easy ride is over. Unlike Britain, there is no equal of the United States to create a new and flourishing capitalist world economy with a convenient Cold War to grease the ways.

We must come to grips with our real needs and, happily, with our real possibilities. We have to begin to be genuinely political people, aiming to put the power of this nation where it belongs, and where alone it can be safe, in the hands of ordinary human beings. We must build a political movement that comprehends our needs, understanding that we have been many peoples with many different needs. Many need a decent chance to catch up, having been held back by a national history that has institutionalized prejudice and discrimination and repression, by color and gender. And we all need a society that views education and health and old age and poverty and disability and difference in ways almost upside-down from our habit. And so much more, only some of which has been argued for earlier.

Those who are angry can build such a movement; those who hate cannot build anything. Committed men and women are indispensable; zealots are sand in the gears, as well as a pain in the neck. Thought, analysis, and reflection are essential; dogmatism is poison.

"America," the midwestern poet Carl Sandburg wrote more than half a century ago, "was promises." Decency, sanity, safety, the love of life itself, require that those promises be redeemed. With effort, patience and impatience, and love, they can be.

Reading Suggestions

What follows will fall into two parts, roughly. First, suggestions that will assist the processes of rethinking our society, our ways of analyzing, and our politics; the second will be books either entirely or substantially programmatic—and some combine the two, as this book does.

Alan Wolfe's works have been noted in other connections. Here his recent *Whose Keeper?: Social Science and Moral Obligation* (Berkeley: University of California Press, 1990), is challenging. His earlier, *America's Impasse: The Rise and Fall of the Politics of Growth* (Boston: South End Press, 1981), is useful both analytically and programmatically. Howard Zinn's recent *Declarations of Independence: Cross-Examining American Ideology* (New York: Harper Colins, 1990), is very helpful in showing how dissent is stifled. More technical but nevertheless important and readable for the nonprofessional is Fred Block, *PostIndustrial Possibilities: A Critique of Economic Discourse** (Berkeley: University of California Press, 1990), a penetrating study of how outworn our concepts (etc.) are for understanding and dealing with current needs and possibilities. Useful analyses of the shortcomings of economics and proposals for change are found in Charles K. Wilbur and Kenneth P. Jameson, *Beyond Reaganomics: A Further Inquiry into the Poverty of Economics* (South Bend: Notre Dame University Press, 1990). On racism, Bob Blauner, *Black Lives, White Lives: Three Decades of Race Relations in America** (Berkeley: University of California Press, 1989), explains the limitations of policy since the 1960s.

On a different level, the historian Philip Slater, who has concerned himself with the roots of consumerism in his earlier work, pushes further in *A Dream Deferred: America's Discontent and the Search for a New Democratic Ideal*, (Boston: Beacon Press, 1991). The errors of omission and commission of the U.S. Left, as well as its past achievements and current needs are examined well by the sociologist Richard Flacks, in *Making History: The American Left and the American Mind** (New York: Columbia University Press, 1989).

Of programs there is practically no end, it is good to know. Here we note but a few, which very much overlap with each other, as well as with my own proposals. For a more extended discussion of my own, see Chapter 5 of *Waste of Nations*. The book by Bowles, Gordon, and Weisskopf, *Beyond the Wasteland* (1983), has been noted earlier, and it remains valuable. They have taken another and longer look, in *After the Wasteland: A Democratic Economics for the Year 2000* (Armonk: M.E. Sharpe, 1990). Older, and still valuable, is Martin Carnoy, Derek Shearer, and Russell Rumberger, *A New Social Contract: The Economy and the Government after Reagan* (New York: Harper & Row, 1983). See also Ronald E. Muller, *Revitalizing America* (New York: Simon & Schuster, 1980), Gar Alperovitz and Jeff Faux, *Rebuilding America* (New York: Simon & Schuster, 1981), and Walter Mead, *Mortal Splendor*, noted earlier, who puts forth a general framework for change in both domestic and foreign policies. Richard Sandbrook, *The Politics of Basic Needs: Urban Aspects of Assaulting Poverty in Africa* (London: Heinemann, 1982), is helpful in cricitizing what has been done and proposing alternatives. Marcus Raskin is very useful in his *The Common Good: Its Politics, Policies, and Philosophy* (New York: Routledge & Kegan Paul, 1986), as is Chester Hartman in his *Winning America: Ideas and Leadership for the 1990s* (Boston: South End Press, 1988), a book that ranges from family policy and health care to military and foreign policy.

Finally, two books. The first sets the record a bit straighter about the role of public policy, which has been so much denigrated of late: John E. Schwartz, *America's Hidden Success: A Reassessment of Twenty Years of Public Policy* (New York: Norton, 1983); and the second is an old book, "hopelessly idealistic" but very much worth reading book by an anomaly if ever there was one, a Buddhist economist, the late E.F. Schumacher: *Small is Beautiful* (New York: Perennial Press, 1974).

Notes

1. Diane di Prima, *Revolutionary Letter #10*. Copyright 1971, 1974 by Diane di Prima. Reprinted by permission of City Lights Books.

2. Especially when the events in the noncapitalist world are also taken into account. What has just been summarized has been meant to refer to global capitalism. But of course good parts of it have been true for the socialist/communist world as well; and as most of that world breaks into pieces and its system of rule crumbles, both the hopes and the fears are doubtless higher there than in our more stable—but also very precariously situated—system.

3. This is part of the opening statement of *The Eighteenth Brumaire of Louis Bonaparte*, a short work concerned with the seizure of power by one who would become Napoleon III. It may be found in many editions; here we have used *Karl Marx and Friedrich Engels, Selected Works** (Moscow: Progress Publishers, 1968), pp. 97ff.

4. "Already…, we can just begin to feel our old attachments, our old citizenship, being emptied of its rationale. All the changes which impinge upon the politics of modern states are global in character: the market in which we trade, and in which our economic futures will be shaped, is global; the ecology in which we live and breathe is global." Michael Ignatieff, *The Needs of Strangers* (London: Chatto & Windus; Hogarth Press, 1984), p. 139.

5. Given the view of capitalism I have presented in earlier chapters, it may be understood that any "opening of the front door" neither could nor would come about on any large scale—on a dynamically promising and satisfactory scale—without substantial resistance and conflict from the powerful and their supporters. At this point that problem is set aside, to be discussed again later, with now the brief observation (1) that a long educational/political process is essential to take us to the point where we could generate such a program *or* the conflict that would meet it, and (2) were we to reach such a political area, we might then be able to continue to go ahead and through the resistance—assuming the procedures of democracy still to exist.

6. Although it is pertinent to quote from Rabbi Hillel, who lived at about the same time as Christ. He raised a question central in the Judaic social ethic and for what follows: "If I am not for myself, who will be for me? And if I think of myself only, what am I? And if not now, when?"

7. Gwynn Williams, quoted in John M. Cammett, *Antonio Gramsci and the Origins of Italian Communism** (Stanford: Stanford University Press, 1967), p. 204. This book is most helpful for an understanding of Gramsci and of his ideas. See also the excellent brief book by Carl Boggs, *Gramsci's Marxism* (London: Pluto Press, 1976). Gramsci's own writings are easily available. See his *The Modern Prince and Other Writings** (New York: New World Paperbacks, 1967) and the larger and well-annotated selection in Quintin Hoare and G.N. Smith, eds., *Selections from the Prison Notebooks of Antonio Gramsci** (London: Lawrence & Wishart, 1971).

8. Of course, Gramsci's aim was a socialist society, and what will be put forward programmatically by me in later pages will not be, although

I earlier expressed my view that a democratic socialist society is the appropriate long term goal. But the way from here to there in the United States cannot be made by one great leap either in language or politics. As the poem that opened this chapter states, "This continent is seed," and we must learn how and where to plant and nourish those seeds before planning how we shall organize our garden parties.

9. Carl Boggs, "Gramsci's Prison Notebooks," in *Socialist Revolution*, no. 11 (1972), p. 97. The distinction between "state" and "civil society" is as follows in Gramsci: "In Russia the State was everything, civil society was primordial and gelatinous; in the West there was a proper relation...[between them]...and when the State trembled a sturdy structure of civil society was at once revealed. The State was only an outer ditch, behind which there stood a powerful system of fortresses and earthworks...." From the *Prison Notebooks*, cited above, p. 238. For our purposes, "civil society" is the realm of economic behavior, ideology, politics, and religion, that of the State the realm of coercion and repression.

10. Again, Gramsci: "It may be ruled out that immediate economic crises of themselves produce fundamental historical events; they can simply create a terrain more favorable to the dissemination of certain modes of thought and certain ways of posing and resolving questions involving the entire subsequent development of national life" (*Prison Notebooks*, p. 184).

11. From "September 1, 1939," *Collected Works of W.H. Auden: Complete Poetry* (Princeton: Princeton University Press, 1989).

12. Nor was the "love" by any means to be confined to what is normally called "romantic love." Erich Fromm, in his *The Art of Loving** (New York: Harper & Row, 1956) is very much concerned with this same point, when, as a psychoanalyst, he speaks of the varieties of love—romantic, family, solidaristic—and of love as an attitude and set of feelings dependent upon and generating concern, understanding, and respect, not just for those around one, but for those whom one does not know: for "strangers," as Ignatieff would have it. Fromm's first book in this general area, *Escape from Freedom** (New York: Avon Books, 1982, originally 1941) was an attempt to explain in sociopsychological terms why the Germans so enthusiastically embraced the irrationalities and horrors of Nazism. A more recent book, *To Have or To Be?** (London: Jonathan Cape, 1978) seeks to relate our nature and possibilities as human beings to the "pathologies" of modern society that presently

lead to what he calls "technocratic fascism," and the needs and resources we have to avoid that fate.

13. The book is under 150 pages, but its economy of thought and language allows the author to pursue his questions in the company of St. Augustine, Adam Smith, Rousseau, Marx, and, among many others, Freud, without sacrifice of depth or clarity. Of the hundreds of books I have cited, this is one of the two or three most compelling for our "needs and possibilities." Although in this section I shall not always acknowledge it in the text, my thoughts on this question are indebted to his, and I hope not to have distorted his arguments. After direct quotes I shall give the page numbers in parentheses in the text.

14. Thus at the same time that what we would call social security was being provided, voting rights for the working class were being denied: wisely so, from Bismarck's standpoint, for when those rights were gained, what grew most rapidly was the socialist vote, giving Germany the largest socialist party in the world by 1914—which, however, enthusiastically voted to support the war. See W.O. Henderson, *The Industrial Revolution in Europe, 1815–1914* and Veblen's *Imperial Germany and the Industrial Revolution*, both cited earlier.

15. Whose benefits fall principally into the laps of the rich. See Teresa Odendahl, *Charity Begins at Home: Generosity and Self-Interest Among the Philanthropic Elite* (New York: Basic Books, 1990).

16. For the ugly details of the welfare system in the United States, see F. Piven and R. Cloward, *Regulating the Poor*, cited earlier, vividly supported by the novel of Sol Yurick, *The Bag*, concerning the system in New York City. Yurick wrote from his own experience as a social worker.

17. R.H. Tawney, *The Acquisitive Society*, p. 180.

18. Because the word "equality," like so many other fine words has also become debased, a comment here seems worthwhile. The equality to be sought is first and foremost that of life opportunities and treatment by others. Some of course are physically stronger and/or more intelligent than others. But the differences in our lives are not determined by those characteristics so much as by social institutions and attitudes—toward color, gender, religion, etc.—matters that *should* have no bearing on our life opportunities or treatment by others. Nor here is the meaning of equality to be found in exalting "sameness," which in any case does not and cannot exist among us. It is to be found in justice, in the venerable principle of "doing unto others as you would have them do unto you."

A fine study of this question, and related matters, is R.H. Tawney, *Equality* (New York: Capricorn Books, 1961; originally 1931).

19. Including most but not all mainstream economists, important exceptions being Robert Eisner (recently head of the American Economics Association), Lester Thurow, Robert Heilbroner and, although both he and Heilbroner would resist classification as mainstream (with some reason), J.K. Galbraith.

20. "Genuine" full employment would be something under 3 percent, so-called "frictional unemployment," where workers are between jobs. Even that percentage could be lowered significantly in a society with an agency designed to do so—easy as pie, were there the will to create it.

21. With a useful twist, in that the largest percentage of closings was in districts represented by Democrats in the House, which of course put them in a difficult position, no matter what. The Bush people have shown themselves to be masters of such Machiavellian ways, not least in causing the Democratic-dominated Senate Judiciary Committee to vote for a strongly right-wing black in the Supreme Court.

22. Much of what follows is a modification of similar arguments made in my *Waste of Nations*, cited earlier, pp. 102 ff.

23. Because only about one-third of the total budget covers "social expenditures": social insurance, aid to farmers and small business, transportation, health, education. The rest goes to military and paramilitary ("national security") programs, and "government operations" (close to $300 billion of which is for interest on the debt). That is, the savings from a reduction of military spending equaling one-tenth of the total budget could increase social spending by one-third—or more, if agricultural support programs were made less necessary by other output- and demand-increasing changes we shall propose below.

24. Although, as has been noted earlier, profits on military contracts are a good twice those of civilian production, and that extra largesse from the taxpayers would disappear.

25. The data are from the Department of Commerce, as reported in *International Herald Tribune*, December 21, 1991–January 1, 1992, "High-Tech Cures and Aging Patients Push U.S. Health Spending Off the Chart."

26. It is not unusual for the major pharmaceutical companies, among the very most profitable of all companies, to make profits of 1,000 percent on their products. The justification they give is their putative cost of research, although as often as not the cost has not been borne by them

and enters arbitrarily into pricing. A genuine and large cost of the pharmaceutical companies is attributable to their many salespeople, constant visitors in doctors' offices, their purpose to provide various inducements to doctors to recommend their own rather than some other company's product. It is a fact that numerous people in need of prescription drugs *stay* in need because they cannot pay their high prices. It is also a fact that "generic" drugs, exactly the same as "brand name" drugs, are seldom prescribed by doctors, though available in pharmacies. Pharmaceuticals should not be hawked like beer, not when what is being bought and sold is someone's right to live. And one would like to think that the Hippocratic Oath would keep doctors from recommending medications because of some salesman's hype.

27. And it was both made and is kept that way through the American Medical Association, hospital associations, equipment manufacturers, and the major pharmaceutical companies. For an earlier but still accurate analysis of the major and linked elements of the (that is, our) problem, see Barbara and John Ehrenreich, *The American Health Empire** (New York: Random House, Vintage, 1971).

28. That generalization comes from when I worked as an orderly in surgery in San Francisco County (now General) Hospital. One experience was telling for the matter at hand: A student during the day, I worked the late night shift, when we did only emergency or very long operations. When an ambulance arrived with siren open, I would go to Emergency to take the patient to surgery. But first there was an interview. One could not be a patient if one had financial assets of $300 or more. One night, a man screaming in pain with a ruptured appendix was led to state that he had some $400 in savings. He was placed back in the ambulance and taken to a private hospital. And a few days later, appropriately broke, he was back at S.F. County. He might have died in the financially caused delay, of course. But one can't make exceptions, lest....

29. Which have their modern origin in mid-nineteenth century London, when its respectable residents found that the inadequate sewage systems spreading cholera were unable to distinguish between poor and rich. The principle underlying public health applies to much else in today's world, but those with power either have limited horizons and/or intelligence, are closet murderers or suicidal types, or, perhaps, all of the above.

30. For an analytical discussion, and factual comparisons among and between 18 capitalist countries in Europe and North America, see Gosta

Esping-Anderson, *The Three Worlds of Welfare Capitalism*, cited earlier. His many tables, which show the United States at the farthest remove from de-commodification, would come as a surprise to most in the United States; and the historical and analytical chapters are most illuminating. The beginnings of commodification of land and labor in the Britain of the Industrial Revolution, and then of all else, is examined with great power and intensity in Polanyi, *The Great Transformation*, cited in Chapter 1.

31. That medical care has been and is unevenly and unfairly distributed also for reasons other than income is well documented. See for example, Charlotte F. Muller, *Health Care and Gender* (New York: Russell Sage Foundation, 1990). Though not always for the best of reasons, but helpful as a first step, many businesses, the largest in particular, are now becoming supporters of a national health care system, because of the rapidly rising and utterly ridiculous costs of the present system. That being so, it is now becoming less dangerous for those in Congress to support changes. But if and when a national health care system *is* legislated, unless there is substantial political input by ordinary people it may be expected that the resulting system will be shaped as a compromise between general business interests and the business of those in the health care system, which will still leave good health for much of the population out of reach.

32. It is generally agreed that ex-Prime Minister Thatcher caused her own downfall because of the popular belief that her next step toward the free market was to privatize health care in some important degree, or entirely.

33. And it is so largely in terms of job preparation—computer training most obviously (today's reading and counting equivalent). There were fewer students finishing high school before World War I than now finish college, relatively as well as absolutely. And just as now in Italy, for example, those with a good high school (*liceo*) education are normally better educated than those with an average college education in the United States, a good U.S. high school education before World War I was also considerably more of an education than it—or a college tour—is likely to be today. Interestingly, Britain was behind the United States in providing what we call public education; and it only began to do so by finding the funds in the late 1890s by an addendum to an arms appropriation, passed to modernize the British navy in anticipation of a struggle with Germany. See R.J.S. Hoffman, *Great Britain and the German Trade Rivalry*, cited earlier.

34. Sometimes the two tracks meant different schools; more often, the two tracks were in the same school, involving different curricula, one that assumed high school was the end of formal education, the other seeing it as preparation for college. This usually meant two different social sets, brought together only for athletic events or, painfully, and as immortalized in James Dean's "Rebel Without a Cause," in emotional relationships.

35. That is, for New York City, whose enormous population and demographic mix and relatively democratic politics required and provided a degree of accessibility not available in most of the rest of the nation until after World War II. Thus, the Bronx School of Science both before and after World War II, a high school, had students that many a university professor would love to see in their classes today. The western states took the lead in developing public ("land-grant") universities, funded by the federal government as a by-product of railroad development; and California in the 1930s added numerous "junior colleges" (now all over the country, as "community colleges") for going beyond high school for two years. For an acute and comprehensive discussion of the class divisions organizing education, see Samuel Bowles and Herbert Gintis, *Schooling in Capitalist America*, cited earlier.

36. When Reagan was governor of California, he certainly had no doubt. He was so bent on suppressing what little life there was in the educational system he had to be restrained by the business world. They reminded him (or taught him for the first time) that it is in the educational system that workers are trained, technology is developed—all that sort of thing—at the taxpayers' expense. Wake up, Mr. Governor!

37. The reader is referred once more to the writings of Dennison, Kozol, Wasserman, and others mentioned earlier.

38. See his *The Higher Learning in America: A Memorandum on Conduct of Universities by Businessmen** (New York: Sagamore Press, 1957, originally 1918): "...except for a stubborn prejudice to the contrary, the fact should readily be seen that the [governing boards] are of no material use in any connection; their sole effectual function being to interfere...." (p. 48). Veblen's direct focus in the foregoing was the university, but his point of view was relative to the whole educational system. The original subtitle of this book, disallowed by the publisher, was "A Study in Total Degradation."

39. Doubtless there are some authoritarian personalities among the teachers of these valuable materials who have such an intention (but not

such power), and that is to be regretted. But they are a small minority, and the very large majority are in fact fervent believers in both academic freedom and democracy: quite apart from anything else, those in a minority must so believe, for practical reasons. Meanwhile, those who attack the whole effort of the multiculturalist, anti-racist, and anti-sexist teachers are blinded by the large motes in their own eyes. See note 40 for one example.

40. Mostly the programs under attack are found in Ivy League universities such as Columbia, Cornell, Dartmouth, etc., and their counterparts elsewhere, such as Stanford and Berkeley, as well as at a small number of state colleges. Such programs began only in the very late 1960s, and have been diminishing since the mid-1970s, in funding and staffs. Cornell's (then called) Black Studies program began in 1970, following a series of events that started in 1966. Then, when there were only four black (student) faces on the campus (which had 15,000 students), three of them from Africa, a program for recruiting such students began. By 1968 there were about 200 black students. They believed, accurately, that some of their educational needs were not being met. In that year, after meeting for several weeks with a faculty group (of which I was one member), they petitioned to have two courses, one on Black Literature, the other on urban economic conditions. I was also on the Dean's committee for approving all new courses. Another member of that committee, now a dean at another Ivy League university and a prominent voice of this new McCarthyism, voted first against having the course in Black Literature (which was to be taught by a white—there being no black—member of the faculty), and made it clear that it was his opinion that no such courses were then or would be needed. (The course was nonetheless approved.)

Meanwhile, life went on in 1968. Martin Luther King, Jr. was assassinated, and that night *white* students attacked the living quarters of the *black* students, burning crosses in front, throwing excrement on the doors, and other such acts. In 1969 the black students, using the old southern slogan—that sometimes to get a mule's attention one must hit him on the nose with a stick—occupied a building. White students with guns tried to take the building, and were stopped (by other whites, it is good to say). The black students then had guns passed into them. The campus was ringed by over 400 armed sheriffs and deputies brought from all over New York State. A disaster was narrowly averted, when the vice president (the president was in hiding) signed an agreement for, among other things, a Black Studies Program. When the faculty met to discuss this, later, a strong majority was against *any* agreement—but not, presumably, against any disaster. (I well remember in 1968, a year earlier, one colleague in the History Department who, with but four black students in a class of over sixty students, carried a revolver in his brief case (or so he told me) when he went to class, his reason being that the students were asking angry questions.) Our vines have bitter grapes. I take the space to tell these—incredible?—things to provide a bit of light on the hypocrisy of at least some of these who claim to be rescuing the universities from barbarians.

41. Nor has the question been raised, suppose there had been members of the Communist Party of the United States—a legal political party—working in the State Department? What harm would or could such persons do, at all—but especially when compared with the demonstrable harm to the nation of all those years of witch-hunting? Beginning some years before the current effusions, was the (still successful) denigration of "liberals," the nation having run out of "Communists." Were these trends to continue—and who can say they won't?—it will become unsafe to be anything but a couch potato.

42. In a reasonable society, we might come to speak also of income ceilings, not just because *seeking* to go beyond a certain level of income—say, just for the hell of it, $1 million a year—should seem crazy rather than admirable and shouldn't be encouraged, nor because one who earns a comfortable income of $50,000 certainly does not do work less than 1/20th in usefulness of *anyone* else, but because anything in excess of that should be taxed away and used for social purposes. One notes that in the same year Time Warner Inc. was laying off 600 of its employees, its chair, Steven J. Ross, received $74.9 million in cash under two bonus programs, plus $3.3 million in salary; and that in 1990, Lee Iacocca, head of the failing Chrysler Corporation, took in $4.6 million ($20.5 million in 1986), while his counterpart at GM, Mr. Sempel, whose company announced layoffs of 74,000 people in 1991 (as GM expected to lose about $2.5 *billion*) and whose income was over $2 million in 1990, had it increased in 1991. The Japanese have commented that such people would be fired if they did so badly in Japan, and also that instead of firing production workers the highly paid and over-staffed managerial component should have its incomes and numbers reduced. Equivalent executives in Japan receive about one-sixth the income and face an income tax rate more than twice as high: 65 percent. Sounds like unfair

competition. (Readers may wonder if decimal points have been misplaced. No. See "Robber Barons are Back, and No One's Up in Arms," September 27, 1991, and "A Metaphor for Failure, January 6, 1992, *International Herald Tribune*.) Mr. Ross could give his $3.3 million to the 600 he fired ($5,000 apiece) to help them pay their rent, and still have $74.9 million left over for shopping. Such examples could be cited at great length, and the list lengthens as the recession lengthens. Ah! Wilderness.

43. See S. Walter and P. Choate, *America in Ruins*, cited earlier, as quoted in Ullman, *Social Costs*, cited earlier, p. 277. The Walter-Choate estimate (made for the Council on State Planning Agencies) was for 1981. The following decade of Reagan follies clearly raised that cost by a substantial percentage. As for housing: in 1983, it was estimated that "approximately 50 million people live in the deteriorated and socially dysfunctional areas called slums." See Ullman, Chapter 9.

44. During the 1930s, near Tulare, California, I remember seeing oranges being burned in great piles, which required pouring kerosene on them to get them going. That was when lots of people in California could have used an orange, or, for that matter, the kerosene. One of the bitter criticisms of agricultural policies in the same years had a slogan about "killing baby pigs and burying them, while people starve."

45. See Edward Higbee, *Farmers in an Urban Age*, cited earlier, and Murray Benedict, *Farm Policies of the United States, 1750–1950* (New York: Twentieth Century Fund, 1953). *U.S. News and World Report,* May 23, 1988 noted that "In 1986, European storage facilities held beef stocks equal to nearly one third of the global meat trade; U.S. silos bulged with stock totaling two years' worth of world grain exports.... The developed world now spends $150 billion a year subsidizing bumper crops." The Department of Agriculture reported on May 19, 1988 that "U.S. farmers will leave 76 million acres of farmland unplanted this year," an amount of land equal in area to the entire states of Illinois and Iowa, *San Francisco Chronicle*, May 20, 1988. That farmers, especially small farmers, are not the beneficiaries of high food prices is well shown in Nick Eberstadt, "Myths of the Food Crisis," *New York Review of Books*, February 19, 1976. In 1982, when the Reagan steamroller got going, "cutting 900,000 households off welfare rolls and reducing benefits to 70 percent of all food stamp recipients, $2.2 billion [was spent]... just to keep certain dairy products off the market; some 13.8 *billion* pounds of milk... had to be bought by the government. Some $400 million must

be spent on storage and interest on the money paid for the 1 million tons of commodities that are involved." From Chapter 13, "Food," in Ullman, *Social Costs*, cited earlier, p. 215. Crazy, man.

46. The discussion and reading suggestions of Chapter 6 regarding agriculture and food are basic for judgments in this area.

47. That the Tier III countries have incurred debt not by or for their own people, as distinct from corrupt and dictatorial governments, is widely acknowledged. But it is the taxes, and the lost possibilities of economic well-being, that are paid for by the people as a whole. That forcing those debts to be paid in customary ways, in IMF ways, or at all is both unjust and counter-productive is slowly dawning on authorities in Tiers I and II, but optimism is not yet appropriate. For further discussion and reading see my *Waste of Nations*, op. cit., Chapter 5.

48. That they buy so few of ours is due to many factors, but certainly one of the stupidest of them is that U.S. auto manufacturers try to sell cars with the driver on the left side, whereas the Japanese sit on the right—and drive on the left. *They* send *us* cars with the steering wheel on the left, of course. More unfair competition. Ford, which shares a plant with Mazda in Japan, is the sole exception, and then only with the cars produced in the Hiroshima plant.

Name Index

Subject Index

DOUGLAS DOWD did his undergraduate and graduate work in economics and philosophy at the University of California, Berkeley, and received his Ph.D. in 1951. He joined the faculty there in 1950. In 1953 he moved to the Cornell Department of Economics, where he taught until 1971, having also served as its Chair. While at Cornell he was awarded a Guggenheim Fellowship and also became a Fulbright Fellow, both for his research on and teaching in Italy. He resigned from Cornell University to return to the San Francisco Bay Area, where he taught again several times at Berkeley, at the University of California at Santa Cruz, at California State University at San Francisco, and for many years at San Jose, from which he retired in 1992. In 1986 Professor Dowd began to divide his time working both in San Jose and Bologna, Italy. He continues to teach in Bologna as Professorial Lecturer in International Economics at the School for Advanced International Studies of Johns Hopkins University.

Professor Dowd has published numerous essays and reviews in the professional journals germane to his interests as well as in critical periodicals such as *Monthly Review, Politics and Society, The Nation*, and *Dissent*, along with essays in periodicals of opinion such as *The Yale Review* and *Challenge*. He has published two books concerning the U.S. economist Thorstein Veblen, as well as *Modern Economic Problems in Historical Perspective, The Twisted Dream: Capitalist Development in the United States Since 1776*, and *The Waste of Nations: Dysfunction in the World Economy*. Among others of his books is *Step by Step*, written with Mary Nichols, concerned with their and others' experiences in the civil rights struggles in the South in 1964.

He and his wife Anna divide their time between San Francisco and Bologna, Italy.

Clinical Laboratory Science Review:
A Bottom Line Approach
Third Edition

Patsy C. Jarreau, MHS, CLS(NCA), MT(ASCP)
Associate Professor, Department of Clinical Laboratory Sciences
LSU Health Sciences Center; New Orleans, Louisiana

CHAPTER AUTHORS

Larry Broussard, PhD, DABCC
Professor, Department of Clinical Laboratory Sciences
LSU Health Sciences Center at New Orleans

Angela Foley, MS, CLS(NCA), MT(ASCP)SH
Associate Professor, Department of Clinical Laboratory Sciences
LSU Health Sciences Center at New Orleans

Daniel Haun, BS, MT(ASCP)H
Director for Client Services
Medical Center of Louisiana

Marcia Firmani, PhD, MT(ASCP)
Assistant Professor, Department of Clinical Laboratory Sciences
LSU Health Sciences Center at New Orleans

Louann Lawrence, DrPH, CLS(NCA), MT(ASCP)SH
Professor, Department of Clinical Laboratory Sciences
LSU Health Sciences Center at New Orleans

Mary Lux, PhD, CLS(NCA), MT(ASCP)
Professor, Department of Medical Technology
University of Southern Mississippi

Mary Muslow, MHS,MT(ASCP)SC
Corporate Laboratory Director
Willis Knighton Health Systems

Elizabeth Williams, MHS, CLS(NCA), MT(ASCP)SBB
Associate Professor, Department of Clinical Laboratory Sciences
LSU Health Sciences Center at New Orleans

Michele Zitzmann, MHS, CLS(NCA), MT(ASCP)
Associate Professor, Department of Clinical Laboratory Sciences
LSU Health Sciences Center at New Orleans

D0022348

Discarded Date FEB 1 2 2024

Asheville-Buncombe
Technical Community College
Library
340 Victoria Road
Asheville NC 28801

the Foundation

LSU HEALTH SCIENCES CENTER
New Orleans, Louisiana

Graphics and Layout: *MASON Communications;*
Shreveport and New Orleans, LA; kesm@bellsouth.net
Illustrations: *Ky E.S. Mason, Mitchel Rubin, and Paulette Gaudry*

Louisiana State University Health Sciences Center Foundation
c/o Department of Clinical Laboratory Sciences
1900 Gravier Street
New Orleans, Louisiana 70112
Phone: 504-568-4276

Any procedure or practice described in this book should be applied by the clinical laboratorian under appropriate supervision in accordance with professional standards of practice. Care has been taken to confirm the accuracy of information presented and to describe generally accepted practices. However, the authors, editors and publisher cannot accept any responsibility for errors or omissions, or for consequences from application of the information in this book, and make no warranty, expressed or implied, with respect to the contents of this book. This book is written to be used as a review book for national and state certification exams. It is not intended for use as a primary resource for procedures or to serve as a complete textbook for clinical laboratory science. Copies of this book may be obtained directly from LSU Health Sciences Center Foundation.

ISBN 0-9670434-1-7
Library of Congress Catalogue Card Number 2004116444

Printed in the United States of America

CONTRIBUTORS

Mary Hebert, BS, MT(ASCP)
Microbiology Technologist
Rapides General Hospital, Alexandria

Libby Spence, PhD, CLS(NCA), MT(ASCP)
Professor, Department of Clinical Laboratory Sciences
University of Mississippi Medical Center

ACKNOWLEDGMENTS

We would like to acknowledge the chapter authors for their dedication to the future of clinical laboratory science, and their generous cooperation in the production of this edition.

We would also like to thank Sylvia Rayfield, who donated publication rights for this work to Louisiana State University Health Sciences Center in honor and memory of Betty Lynne Theriot, the original author whose professional and personal life brought tremendous enlightenment to so many of us.

We gratefully recognize the continual support of the School of Allied Health Professions and the Foundation of the LSU Health Sciences Center.

— **The Department of Clinical Laboratory Sciences**
LSU Health Sciences Center
New Orleans, LA

DEDICATION

Betty Lynne Theriot
1954-1997

This book is dedicated to Betty Lynne Theriot whose creativity and inspiration made this, the third edition, and the previous editions possible. As president and founder of Creative Educators, she developed instructional methods in clinical laboratory science and allied health and presented extensively at local, regional and national conferences. She was co-author and editor of several books published by Creative Educators including Clinical Laboratory Science Review: A Bottom Line Approach, Clinical Instruction in Blood Banking, and Clinical Instruction in Parasitology.

Betty Lynne was very active in professional organizations and was honored as Louisiana Society for Clinical Laboratory Science Member of the Year in 1997, Educator of the Year in 1994, and recipient of the American Society for Clinical Laboratory Science Sherwood Medical Professional Achievement Award in Education in 1997.

Her loss has had a profound effect on the profession of clinical laboratory science. She was the ultimate educator persistently seeking new information and using innovative methods to make learning fun and more effective. She stimulated creativity and was an inspiration and mentor to her students and colleagues. Her willingness to provide assistance to other professionals was recognized nationally. Betty Lynne's energy, vitality, and infectious enthusiasm will remain forever with those who knew her.

Proceeds from the sales of the second edition were used to fund annual scholarships for students in clinical laboratory science. In 2004 the Betty Lynne Theriot Distinguished Professorship was established in the LSU Health Sciences Center Department of Clinical Laboratory Sciences. We look forward to funding more scholarships and other worthy projects to benefit the profession through continued sales of this book.

PREFACE

This book is intended for all students of clinical laboratory science as a review reference as well as a course supplement. It is also relevant for medical students and other allied health students who are responsible for knowledge of the many clinical laboratory tests currently performed on patients. Educators in allied health, nursing and other medical careers will benefit from the many "memory tools" which simplify educational concepts.

INTRODUCTION

Welcome to the unique study experience we offer in this book. Because of our clinical and academic backgrounds, we've been able to streamline the thousands of details in the clinical laboratory science profession to determine the "bottom line".

To HELP you remember this bottom line, we've created graphics, stories, acronyms and mnemonics.

Handy test alerts *(for concepts frequently tested)*

Easy format *(concise outlines, charts and cross-referenced index)*

Learning tools *(to jog your memory)*

Practice questions *(with answers and rationale)*

Good luck on the exams and in your career!

REMEMBER!

It's Not What You Know, But What You Remember That Counts!

TABLE OF CONTENTS

IMMUNOHEMATOLOGY

by Elizabeth F. Williams

Donor Selection and Blood Collection

COLLECTION OF DONOR BLOOD

1. Follows registration, medical history, and physical examination *(See Danny Donor)*

2. Preparation of venipuncture site - proper scrub, iodophor compound *(PVP-iodine polymeriodine)* complex, aseptic technique

3. Scrub site for minimum 30 seconds

GENERAL INFORMATION

1. Maximum collection — no more than 10.5 mL of whole blood per kilogram of body weight, including samples

2. Medications must be evaluated by MD; platelets from donors who have taken medication within 36 hours that irreversibly affects platelet function *(i.e., aspirin)* must not be used as the <u>only</u> source for platelets *(can be part of a pool of platelets)*

Criteria for Donor Selection

• Age	17 yrs. (min) - no max - (evaluate by M.D.)
• Temperature (oral)	≤37.5°C or ≤ 99.5°F
• Blood Pressure	≤180 systolic ≤100 diastolic
• Hb	≥12.5g%
• Hct	≥38%
• Pulse	50 - 100 beats/min
• Weight	minimum 110 lb / 50 kg

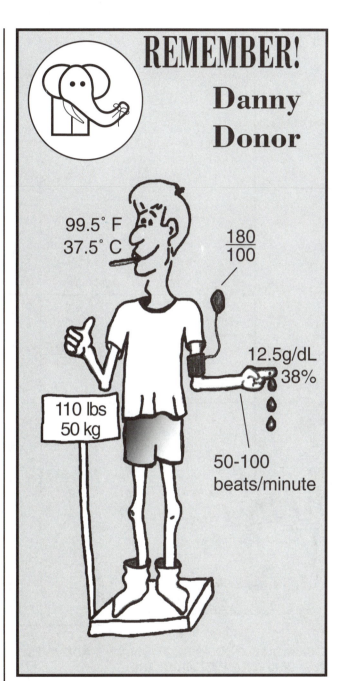

REMEMBER! Danny Donor

99.5°F 37.5°C — 180/100 — 12.5g/dL 38% — 50-100 beats/minute — 110 lbs 50 kg

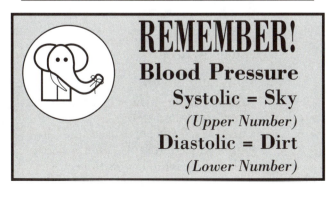

REMEMBER!
Blood Pressure
Systolic = Sky
(Upper Number)
Diastolic = Dirt
(Lower Number)

TEST Alert!
Evaluate Suitability of Potential Donor

1 YEAR: *Possible exposure to hepatitis, HIV or malaria;*	• Hepatitis B Immune Globulin • Possible exposure to hepatitis, HIV & malaria • Recipient of blood/blood products • Tattoo • Mucous membrane exposure to blood • Skin penetration with instruments contaminated with blood/body fluid • Sexual contact with individual symptomatic for any viral hepatitis, confirmed + for HBsAg / HIV or in high risk category • From completion of therapy for syphilis or gonorrhea or reactive STS • Traveled to endemic area for malaria with or without antimalarial drugs**, and were free of malarial symptoms during that time • *> 72 hours in a correctional institution* ** Plasma preparations without red cells are exempt from these restrictions-malarial parasites are intracellular *(in red cells)*

3 YEAR:
Possible exposure to malaria
	• Asymptomatic during the time
	  - Visitor/immigrant from area endemic for malaria
	  - Previously diagnosed with malaria
	  ** Plasma preparations without red cells are exempt from these restrictions-malarial parasites are intracellular *(in red cells)*

INDEFINITE *Definite disease or habits strongly associated with bloodborne pathogens*	**VIRAL DISEASES:** • Viral hepatitis after age 11 • + confirmatory test for HBsAg • Repeatedly reactive test for anti-HBc • Donated only unit to recipient who developed post transfusion hepatitis, HIV, or HTLV • Present/Past infection of HCV, HTLV, or HIV • Evidence of parenteral drug use **OTHER DISEASES:** • Received dura mater or pituitary growth hormone of human origin; family history of CJD or risk of vCJC • History of Chagas' disease, babesiosis

TEST Alert!

Donor Deferrals:
Focus on Bloodborne
Pathogens

COMMON BLOOD ANTICOAGULANTS, ADDITIVES AND REJUVENATING SOLUTIONS

1. CPD - anticoagulant
   a. Citrate, phosphate, dextrose
   b. 21-day expiration

2. CPDA-1 - anticoagulant
   a. Adenine added
   b. 35-day expiration

3. Additive solutions
   a. Contain dextrose, adenine, sodium chloride and other substances

   b. Added to enhance red cell survival; 42-day expiration

4. Rejuvenating solutions
   a. Contain pyruvate, inosine, phosphate and adenine
   b. Restores 2, 3-DPG and ATP
   c. Added during storage or up to 3 days after expiration date
   d. Can freeze unit or, if used in 24 hrs., can be stored at 1-6C *(must wash cells before transfusion to remove solution)*

Knowledge of Anticoagulants/Rejuvenating Solutions & Expiration Times

AUTOLOGOUS DONATIONS

1. Donations for self; no age limit

2. Hct - 33%; Hgb - 11 g/dL

3. No bacteremia

4. Preoperative collection must be labeled "for autologous use only" and used only for this patient

5. Autologous units — segregate from allogeneic units

6. Low volume collections
   a. Use regular blood bags; volume drawn <10.5 mL/kg body weight for minimum weight (450 + 45 mL plus testing samples)
   b. If 300-404 mL drawn, label as Red Blood Cells Low Volume (components may not be made from these units)
   c. If < 300 mL drawn, use proportionately less anticoagulant (see below)

Volume to draw: *(example: 90 lb. donor)*

$\frac{90 \text{ lb.}}{110 \text{ lb.}}$ x 450 ml *(standard donation)* = 368 ml

If donor weight is given in kg, divide donor weight by 50, then multiply by 450
$\frac{(\text{donor wt in kg} \times 450)}{50}$

Amount of anticoagulant to use:
a. 368 x 14% = amt of anticoagulant
b. 368 x .14 = 51.5 = 52 ml of anticoagulant needed

Amount of anticoagulant to remove:
63-52 = 11ml; remove 11ml of anticoagulant from primary bag into attached satellite bag prior to draw

Appropriate Use of Autologous and "Salvaged" Units

7. Inoperative collections, "salvaged" blood collected during surgery, washed "on-site" and returned to patient during procedure

HEMAPHERESIS/APHERESIS COLLECTION

1. Donor criteria same as for whole blood

2. Must wait 48 hours after apheresis procedure to donate whole blood

3. FDA limits to 500 mL/ collection (or 600 mL if weight > 175 pounds)

4. Limits number of donor exposures

5. Methods
   a. By centrifugation — withdrawal of whole blood, removing selected fraction and reinfusion of the remaining components into the donor
   b. Filtration – removal of only plasma through a membrane for normal plasma collection or for therapeutic purposes
   c. Adsorption — removal of only a selected constituent of plasma with reinfusion of plasma after constituent removed

Terms Associated with Apheresis

	SEPARATION & COLLECTION OF:
Cytapheresis	cells
Plasmapheresis	plasma
Plateletpheresis	platelets
Leukapheresis/ Granulocytapheresis	leukocytes/granulocytes

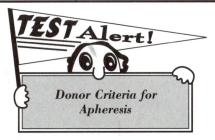

Donor Criteria for Apheresis

HEMATOPOIETIC PROGENITOR AND STEM CELL COLLECTION

1. Used to reconstitute bone marrow post chemotherapy/irradiation or to replace abnormal marrow cells with normal marrow cells *(congenital immune deficiencies, anemias, malignant*

4

disorders of bone marrow, red cell disorders, etc.)

2. Cells obtained from bone marrow, umbilical cord blood and peripheral blood *(apheresis)*

3. Allogeneic marrow — HLA-identical match lowers GVHD risk; ABO compatibility not required

Donor Blood Processing

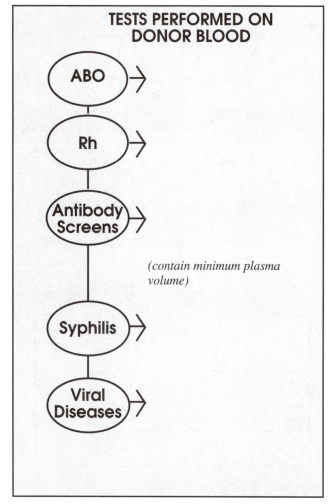

TESTS PERFORMED ON DONOR BLOOD

ABO →

Rh →

Antibody Screens →

(contain minimum plasma volume)

Syphilis →

Viral Diseases →

Components/Transfusion Practice

WHOLE BLOOD

1. Given in cases of severe shock *(blood loss ≥ 25% blood volume)* needing rbc's for oxygen and plasma for volume

2. Rarely used due to increased use and availability of components

RED BLOOD CELLS (Packed Cells)

1. Red cells with plasma removed by sedimentation, centrifugation or washing

2. Provides same oxygen carrying capacity as whole blood with less volume

3. <80% hct *(indicates sufficient plasma removal)*; 55-65% hct if additive solution used

4. 1 unit raises hemoglobin *(hb)* 1g or hematocrit *(hct)* 3%

WASHED RED CELL

1. Plasma removed by successive saline washes *(automated instrument)*

2. Prevents allergic response to plasma proteins and anaphylactic shock in IgA deficient patients with anti-IgA *(IgA is in normal plasma)*

3. Expires 24 hours after seal of original unit broken

LEUKOCYTE REDUCED RED CELLS

1. 85% of red cells retained

2. Final wbc count < 5 x 10⁶ to prevent febrile nonhemolytic reactions and for other uses *(ex. to prevent CMV transmission)*

3. Preparaton by filtration preferred
   a. Washing will remove leukocytes also

4. Used primarily for patients with repeated febrile nonhemolytic *(FNH)* reactions; usually due to presence of cytokines released from white cells or alloimmunization to HLA or leukocyte antigens

FROZEN CELLS

1. Cells protected from ultra low temperatures by cryoprotective agent *(glycerol)*

2. Must be thawed at 37C and glycerol removed prior to transfusion

3. 80% original red cells must be recovered

4. Used for storage of autologous units and "rare" units; expires in 10 years

5. Stored at -65C or colder; 1-6C for 24 hours after deglycerolizing

FRESH FROZEN PLASMA (FFP)

1. Prepared by separating cells and plasma by centrifugation and freezing plasma within 8 hours of collection

2. Expires 1 year from date of collection when stored at ≤ -18C or colder or 7 years stored at ≤ -65C

3. Once thawed *(between 30-37C)*, expires in 24 hours if kept at 1-6C

4. Must be ABO compatible with recipient cells; not necessarily ABO identical

5. Used for multiple coagulation deficiencies, factor XI deficiency, and other congenital deficiencies for which no concentrate is available

FFP:
Determine compatibility and storage requirements

CRYOPRECIPITATE
(cryoprecipitated antihemophilic factor)

1. When FFP frozen within 8 hours of whole blood collection is thawed at 1-6C, a cold insoluble portion of plasma forms — CRYO

2. CRYO is separated from thawed FFP and refrozen immediately

3. Must contain ≥150 mg of fibrinogen and ≥80 IU/bag of factor VIII

4. Also contains Factor VIII:C and von Willebrand factor of Factor VIII molecule and Factor XIII

5. Store at ≤ -18C for 1 year from date of phlebotomy; 1-6C after thawing

6. Transfuse within 6 hours of thawing; 4 hours after pooling

7. Used for:
   a. Fibrinogen and Factor XIII deficiencies
   b. Severe von Willebrand disease (some Factor VIII concentrates contain vWF)
   c. Topical fibrin sealant
   d. Seldom used for hemophilia because of Factor VIII concentrates which have little or no risk of viral infection transmission (use DDAVP for mild hemophilia A)

Cryoprecipitate: Expiration and Amount of Fibrinogen Contained

FACTOR CONCENTRATES

1. Recombinant products are prepared from plasma pools; plasma pool is processed to purify and concentrate the proteins and inactivate viruses

2. ↑ levels of specific factors with minimal volume compared to FFP

3. Hemophilia A – treat severe with Factor VIII and mild with DDAVP *(stimulates endogenous Factor VIII release)*

4. Hemophilia B – treat with Factor IX *(better than Factor IX complex which can lead to thrombosis)*

5. Inhibitors to Factor VIII – treat with porcine Factor VIII *(low cross-reactivity)* or Factor IX complex *(bypass Factor VIII in cascade)*

6. von Willebrand disease – treat with Factor VIII concentrates that have vWF; mild cases treat with DDAVP

Identify Factor Deficiencies and Select Appropriate Component for Transfusion

☞ (See coagulation section if you need refreshing!)

PLATELETS

1. Prepared from whole blood *(stored at 20-24C prior to processing)*
   a. First a light spin *(to remove red cells)* followed by heavy centrifugation *(to spin down platelets and white cells)*
   b. Supernatent plasma is expressed into another bag and may be frozen *(FFP)*
   c. Remaining plasma, platelets and white cells = platelet concentrate

6

2. Conditions
   a. For severe thrombocytopenia and platelet dysfunction
   b. Prophylactic use of platelets when platelet count is low is controversial *(threshold depends on patient's risk of bleeding)*
   c. Contraindicated in TTP and heparin-induced thrombocytopenia

3. Platelets from donors who are within 36 hours of taking drugs *(i.e., aspirin)* that impair platelet function should not be used as a "single source" *(apheresis product or single unit for a newborn)*

4. Platelet refractoriness *(lack of expected response)*
   a. Antibodies to HLA class I antigens
   b. Platelet antibodies or neutrophil/lymphocyte antibodies

5. Transfusion
   a. 1 unit of platelets should raise platelet count 5,000 – 10,000 in average sized adult
   b. Do NOT transfuse through a microaggregate filter
   c. Only one ABO type/pool; expires 4 hours after pooling

6. QC
   a. pH ≥6.2 at end of storage; stored in volume of plasma necessary to maintain pH, usually 30 – 70 cc
   b. 5.5×10^{10} platelets/unit or $> 3 \times 10^{11}$ platelets/plateletpheresis in 90% of units tested
   c. Store continuously rotating at 20 – 24C *(room temp)*
   d. Outdate depends on type of bag used
   e. Individual leukoreduced platelets - $<8.3 \times 10^{5}$ leukocytes; leukoreduced pooled platelets or plateletpheresis product - $<5 \times 10^{6}$ leukocytes
   f. Must be checked for bacteria before issuing

7. Transfuse ABO compatible to infants

Platelet Collection, Preparation, and QC

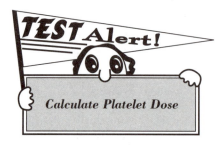

Calculate Platelet Dose

GRANULOCYTES

1. Usually obtained by apheresis

2. Decline in use due to new antibiotics, recombinant growth factors and adverse effects from granulocyte transfusion *(acute lung injury)*

3. Used for neutropenic patients with documented gram negative sepsis who have not responded to antibiotics

4. Can transmit CMV, induce HLA immunization, and cause GVHD, if not irradiated

5. Stored without agitation at 20 – 24 C for up to 24 hours, but should be transfused ASAP

6. ABO-compatible with recipient

IRRADIATED BLOOD AND COMPONENTS

1. Prevents graft *(donor lymphocytes)* vs. host *(recipient lymphocytes)* disease *(GVHD)* by inactivating donor lymphocytes

2. Recommended for fetus receiving intrauterine transfusion; immuno-supressed or immunocompromised patients, recipients of units etc.

3. Minimum of 25 Gy *(2500 cGy)*

4. RBCs expired on original outdate or 28 days after irradiation, whichever is first

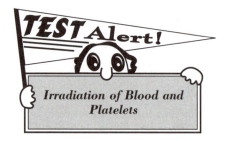

Irradiation of Blood and Platelets

MISCELLANEOUS

1. 63 ml of anticoagulant/bag

2. Expiration based on expectation of 75% of transfused cells will be in circulation 24 hours after transfusion

3. Changes in plasma during storage *(1-6C)*

NH_4 ↑   pH ↓
K^+ Na+

4. Transporting blood and components
   a. Red cells kept at 1 - 10C
   b. Platelets and granulocytes kept at 20-24C
   c. Frozen components kept frozen

5. Expiration of blood/components when seal is broken *(packing cells or pooling components)*:
   a. Products stored at 1-6C = 24 hrs
   b. Products stored at 20-24C = 4 hours

6. Pooling components:
   a. If red cells visible in pooled product, component plasma antibodies should be compatible with those red cells

Blood Transport Temperature

b. Expiration of pooled components
   ❖ *Platelets - 4 hours (open system)*
   ❖ *Cryoprecipitate - 4 hours (open system)*

7. Unit of blood cannot be returned and reissued if >10°C *(room temperature 15-30 minutes)* or if seal disturbed

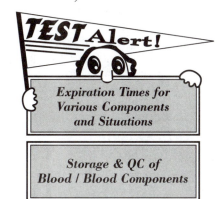

Expiration Times for Various Components and Situations

Storage & QC of Blood / Blood Components

Component Quality Control

COMPONENT	STANDARDS	STORAGE
Red Blood Cells *(Packed Cells)*	Hct 80% *(Maximum)*	1-6°C *(Closed System)*, 21 Days *(CPD)*, 35 Days *(CPDA-1)*, 42 Days *(Additive)*; 1-6°C *(Open System)*, 24 Hours
Leukocyte Reduced Cells	85% of Original Cells, < 5x10^6 Leukocytes in 95% Units Tested	1-6°C, Same as Red Cells
Frozen Red Cells	>80% of Original Red Cells, Adequate Removal of Cryoprotective Agent	10 Years, -65°C or Colder *(40% Glycerol)*; -120°C *(20% Glycerol)*; 24 Hours Once Deglycerolized
Fresh Frozen Plasma	Frozen to ≤ –18°C or ≤ –65°C within 6-8 hours *(Depends on Anticoagulant)*	12 months, ≤ –18°C
Cryoprecipitated AHF	≥80 IU/Unit x Number of Components in Pool; ≥150mg Fibrinogen	12 Months, ≤ -18°C
Platelets, Single Donor *(Closed System)*	≥5.5 x 10^{10} plt/unit in 90% of Units Tested; pH 6.2 or Greater in 90% Units Tested at Maximum Storage Time	3/5 Days, *(Depends on Collection Bag)*, 20-24°C with Constant Agitation
Platelets, Pooled *(Open System)*		4 Hours, 20-24°C with Agitation
Platelets, Leukocyte-Reduced	≥ 5.5 x 10^{10} Platelets in 90% of Units Tested; < 8.3 x 10^5 Leukocytes in 95% of Units Tested; <5 x 10^6 in Pooled Platelets	Same as Platelets
Platelets, pheresis	≥ 3.0 x 10^{11} plt/unit in 90% of Units Tested pH 6.2 or Greater at Maximum Storage Time	5 Days, 20-24°C with Constant Agitation 24 Hours *(Open System)*
Granulocytes, pheresis	≥ 1.0 x 10^{10} Granulocytes in 75% of Units Tested	24 Hours, 20-24°C

8

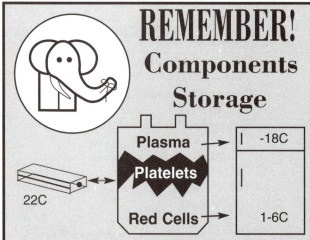

REMEMBER!
Components Storage

Plasma → | -18C

Platelets

22C

Red Cells → | 1-6C

To help you remember storage temperatures for the basic components: Think of a unit of whole blood sitting by a refrigerator. The **plasma** goes straight across to the freezer and is stored at **-18C** or colder. The **red cells** go across into the bottom of the refrigerator and are stored at **1-6C**. Like plates in your home are stored on a shelf at room temperature, **platelets** are stored on a rotating shelf at **22C**.

Component Therapy

WHAT WOULD YOU DO IF . . .

1. An O negative patient needs 6 units of platelets. Only O positive platelets are available. What needs to be considered in this case?

Ans.   The platelets once pooled have an expiration of 4 hours. Since the patient is O negative, the physician may want to consider RhIG. This will depend on the patient (*Female of childbearing age? Elderly? Diagnosis? Probability of getting more platelets, etc.*)

2. A unit of red cells was issued to the OR at 2:00 a.m. It was returned at 2:45 am unentered. It was kept at 2C in a blood bank monitored cooler. Can this unit be accepted for reissue to another patient?

Ans.   Yes, a unit of RBCs can be reissued if it was not entered and was maintained between 1 - 10C during storage and transportation. There should be at least 1 segment still attached to the donor bag.

3. A patient with a mild case of vonWillebrand's disease suffered minor cuts and bruises in a car accident. What should the physician consider as the treatment of choice in this situation?

Ans.   Patients with mild vonWillebrand's disease can usually be treated with DDAVP. This drug causes release of vWF from endothelial cells causing the plasma level of vWF to increase. More serious cases usually require Factor VIII concentrates (*some are available with vWF*) or cryoprecipitate.

4. What is the component of choice for a patient in DIC with a low fibrinogen level?

Ans.   Cryoprecipitate is used because of the high concentration of fibrinogen. FFP can be used to restore the depleted coagulation factors, but the volume needed to restore fibrinogen is usually too large.

5. A 95 pound female with a hemoglobin level of 11.0 g/dL wants to donate an autologous unit for upcoming surgery. Based on this information, can she donate? If so, how much can be drawn and how much anticoagulant should be removed?

Ans.   Her hemoglobin level is acceptable for autologous donation. Her weight is under 110 lbs., so you will need to calculate how much blood to draw and whether any anticoagulant needs to be removed from the primary bag prior to collection.

$$\frac{95}{110} \times 450 = 389 \text{ ml to draw}$$

As little as 300 ml can be drawn without reducing the anticoagulant. Units between 300 and 404 must be labeled "Red Blood Cells Low Volume Unit." Components may NOT be made from this unit.

6. A 33 kg autologous donor has completed the pre-donation screening. How much blood can be drawn from this individual and how much anticoagulant must be removed?

Ans.   Volume to draw: $\frac{33}{50} \times 450 = 297$ ml

Amount of anticoagulant:
297 x 14% = 42 ml

Amount of anticoagulant to remove:
63 - 42 = 21 ml

ABO System

ANTIGENS OF ABO SYSTEM

1. Chains of sugar molecules in which specificity is determined by immunodominant sugar

2. Genetic pathway

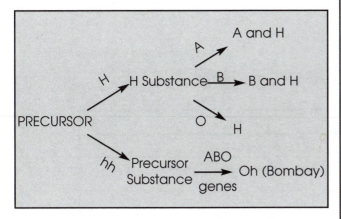

3. Subgroups of A
   a. A_1 and A_2
      ❖ *Principal subgroups of A*
      ❖ *Serological difference based on reactivity with anti-A_1 (Dolichos biflorus* or human anti-A_1). (*lectin - plant or seed extract diluted to agglutinate specific human blood group antigens)*
         ☞ A_1 cells are agglutinated
         ☞ A_2 cells are NOT agglutinated

CELL	ANTI-A1
A_1	pos
A_2	neg
A_3	neg

Fundamental Characteristics of Lectins

   b. Other subgroups (A3, Ax, etc) contain less A antigen and more H antigen

RELATIONSHIP OF ABO, H, SE, AND LE

1. Lack of H is genetically hh *(Bombay phenotype)*
   a. hh has no fucose which is needed for attachment of A or B sugars *(Bombay therefore forwards as an O)*
   b. Anti-H *(Ulex europaeus)* will NOT agglutinate Bombay cells *(hh)* but will agglutinate O cells

2. Se *(secretor)* gene allows expression of A, B, H, and Le^b in saliva

3. Le antigens are plasma antigens which adsorb onto red cells as individual matures
   a. Individual with Le gene *(and NOT Se gene)* will have Le^a on red cells and in saliva *(Se not needed for presence of Le^a in saliva)*
   b. Individual with H and Le genes will have H and Le^a on red cells and Le^a only in saliva *(Se not needed for presence of Le^a in saliva, but it is for H)*
   c. Individual who has the H, Se and Le genes will have H and Le^b on red cells *(H and Le have added appropriate fucose molecules to precursor substance)* and very little Le^a is detectable *(however in saliva, H, Le^a and Le^b will all be detectable)*

CELL GROUPING (FORWARD GROUPING)

1. Reagent anti-A and -B are designed so testing is performed at room temperature

REAGENT ANTI-A	REAGENT ANTI-B	INTERPRETATION
+	0	Group A Cells
0	+	Group B Cells
+	+	Group AB Cells
0	0	Group O Cells

2. Unknown cells + antisera = NO agglutination *(cells lack antigen to which antisera [reagent antibody] corresponds)*

3. Unknown cells + antisera = agglutination *(cells possess antigen to which antisera corresponds)*

SERUM GROUPING (REVERSE GROUPING)

1. Testing is performed at room temperature with saline suspended known group A_1

and B red cells; optimum reactivity of serum anti-A and -B is 4C

A1 CELL	B CELL	ANTIBODY IN SERUM	INTERPRETATION
0	+	Anti-B	A
+	0	Anti-A	B
0	0	None	AB
+	+	Both	O

a. Unknown serum + reagent red cells = NO agglutination *(serum lacks antibody to antigen on red cell)*
b. Unknown serum + reagent red cells = agglutination *(serum has antibody to antigen on red cells)*

Discrepancies in ABO Grouping

Problems with Red Cells:	Resolution Techniques
• Rouleaux — Failure to Wash Cells	Repeat with Saline Washed Cells
• Mixture of Cell Types — Example: A or B Transfused with O Cells	Check Transfusion History
• Subgroups *(Example: A_2 with or without anti-A_1)*	Test with Anti-A_1 for A Subgroups
• Unusual Genotypes *(Example: Bombay)*	Test with Anti-H for Bombay *(Bombay Lacks H Antigen and Cells will not Agglutinate with Anti-H; Bombay Serum will Agglutinate A_1 & B Cells as well as Group O Screening Cells)*
• Disease Processes — Example: Leukemia or Bacteria *(Acquired B Phenomenon)*	Check Patient Diagnosis; ID Beyond Scope of This Review
Problems with Serum:	
• Rouleaux — Due to Increased Serum Proteins *(Example: Waldenstrom's or Multiple Myeloma)*	Saline Replacement
• Room Temperature or Cold Reacting Antibody *(H, I, M, N, P1, or Lewis, or anti-A1 in an A2 or A2B Individual)* Reacting with their Corresponding Antigens on Reverse Cells	"Mini" Cold Screen or Panel *(Test at Lower Temperature)*
• Age — Elderly *(Antibody Production has Decreased)* or Newborn *(Antibody Production Has Not Reached Optimum Levels)*; Missing Antibodies	Check Patient Age; "Mini" Cold Panel *(May Enhance Serum Anti-A or Anti-B so Interpretation will Agree with Cell Grouping)*
• Compromised Immune System — Example: A/Hypogammaglobulinemia	Check Patient Diagnosis; "Mini" Cold Panel *(See above)*

☞ "MINI" COLD PANEL

Principle: Used to (1) Enhance serum anti-A and anti-B reactions when they are expected but are not demonstrable using room temperature readings, and (2) Identify "cold" antibodies reacting with other antigens on A_1 and B reagent red cells.

PATIENT SERUM TESTED WITH:				INTERPRETATION
A/B Cells	O Cells	O Cord Cell *(if available)*	Autocontrol	
+	+	0	+	Anti-I
+ or 0	+	+ or 0	0	Unexpected antibody reacting at colder temperatures *(anti-H, -M, -N, -P_1 and Lewis antibodies)*
+	0	0	0	Anti-A or Anti-B

☞ SALINE REPLACEMENT

Principle: Saline replacement can differentiate rouleaux from agglutination. Rouleaux is typically described as having a "stack of coins" appearance when observed with a microscope. When the serum in the test mixture is replaced with saline, the cells dissociate. In assessing rouleaux formation, knowledge of the patient's clinical diagnosis and his/her serum protein content and proportions is helpful. Rouleaux is associated with multiple myeloma and Waldenstrom's macroglobulinemia

Evaluate ABO grouping - Subgroups & Discrepancies

Select Reagents & Methods to Handle Rouleaux

Rh System

ANTIGENS

1. D, C, E, c, e

2. Presence of D is only antigen routinely tested

D GROUPING

1. D is most immunogenic of all blood group antigens

2. D grouping *(Rh type)* is based on presence or absence of D when tested with anti-D

3. Weak D
   a. D reactive at antiglobulin phase only
   b. Weak D is considered D positive
   c. Testing for weak D required on donors and OB patients

Testing and Interpretation of Weak D

Evaluate Positive D Control

4. Monoclonal / Polyclonal Anti-D
   a. Separate D control not necessary
   b. Control is a negative reaction with anti-A or -B in ABO cell grouping *(patient A and B cells not spontaneously agglutinating)*

c. If patient is AB positive, must use a 6-8% albumin control, autocontrol or DAT

5. D control *(used with high protein anti-D reagents)*
   a. Must be negative for D negative grouping to be valid; if positive, repeat with another type of anti-D *(monoclonal, chemically modified or saline)*
   b. Must contain same media as anti-D reagent without the anti-D *(use same manufacturer's control)*
   c. Ensures agglutination with anti-D reagent is due to presence of D antigen and NOT due to proteins in reagent or agglutination of in vivo antibody coated cells *(positive DAT)*
   d. Most common cause of a positive D control is a positive DAT

UNUSUAL PHENOTYPES

1. Rh null - no D, C, E, c or e antigens; cells have associated hemolytic anemia since Rh structure is integral part of rbc membrane

2. Deleted cells *(-D-)* - missing one or more of normal Rh alleles

RH ANTIBODIES

1. IgG clinically significant

2. May agglutinate at 37C as well as AHG

3. Anti-C, -c, -E, -e react stronger with enzyme-treated cells

	IgM Antibodies	**IgG Antibodies**	
REMEMBER!	anti-I, -H anti-M, -N anti-P1 anti-Lea, -Leb	anti-D anti-C, -c anti-E, -e anti-M (some)	anti-K, -k anti-Fya, Fyb anti-Jka, -Jkb

Other Blood Group Systems

LEWIS

1. Plasma antigens that adsorb onto RBCs; not alleles

2. Not on cord cells

3. Antibodies
   a. Do NOT cause HDN *(Lewis antigens are not on fetal cells and Lewis antibodies usually IgM)*
   b. IgM antibody
      ❖ *Can be hemolytic*
   c. Usually only seen in Le(a-b-) persons
   d. Often seen in pregnant women who may temporarily become Le(a-b-)

I, i

1. I - absent or weak on cord cells

2. i converts to I as infant matures due to branching of carbohydrate chains; not alleles
   a. Infants - i positive, I negative
   b. Adults - I positive, i negative

3. Antibodies
   a. Anti-I
      IgM cold antibody
      ❖ *Reacts with all adult cells (except rare i adult)*
      ❖ *May mask clinically significant alloantibody*
      ❖ *Remove anti-I to detect underlying antibodies by:*
         ☞ an autoadsorption (if not recently transfused) or allogeneic adsorption
         ☞ RESt adsorption
         ☞ prewarming serum and using IgG AHG instead of polyspecific

P

1. P_1 antigen strength deteriorates upon storage

2. Antibodies
   a. Anti-P_1
      ❖ *IgM cold antibody*
      ❖ *Anti-P_1 (NOT anti-P) can be neutralized to reveal other clinically significant alloantibodies (P_1 substance in hydatid cyst fluid)*
   b. Anti-P
      ❖ *Frequently the specificity of the biphasic Donath-Landsteiner antibody found in Paroxysmal Cold Hemoglobinuria*
      ❖ *Reacts with all P or P_1 positive cells*

MNSs

1. M and N are codominant alleles

2. Antibodies
   a. Anti-M and -N
      ❖ *Usually cold IgM; no HDN*
      ❖ *Often show dosage (property whereby antibody reacts strongest with cells having a homozygous expression of antigen as opposed to heterozygous cells)*
      ❖ *Will NOT react with enzyme-treated cells (M and N antigens are destroyed by enzymes)*
   b. Anti-M
      ❖ *Many examples are IgG and can cause HDN*
      ❖ *May require acidification of serum to identify*
   c. Anti-S and anti-s - IgG
   d. Anti-U - IgG
      ❖ *Formed by black individuals who lack S, s and U*

KELL

1. K and k *(cellano)* are codominant alleles
   a. K antigen is second most immunogenic *(next to D)*
   b. 91% are K negative

c. Antigens inactivated with 2-ME, DTT, or AET

2. Antibodies - IgG

KIDD

1. Jk^a and Jk^b are codominant alleles

2. Antibodies
   a. IgG
   b. React STRONGER with enzyme treated cells
   c. Titers rise and fall rapidly
   d. Associated with delayed transfusion reactions

DUFFY

1. Fy^a and Fy^b are codominant alleles
   a. 68% African Americans are Fy(a-b-)
   b. Antigens destroyed by enzymes
   c. Antigen typing – Fy(a+b-)
      ❖ *whites – homozygous for Fya (FyaFya)*
      ❖ *blacks – probably heterozygous for Fya (FyaFy-) – dosage problem*

2. Antibodies
   a. IgG
   b. Weak examples may show dosage
   c. Negative reaction with enzyme treated cells

Parentage Testing

ABOUT PATERNITY TESTING . . .

- Maternity is Assumed

- You may have problems that include ABO and/or D grouping

- In paternity testing, there is a chain of sample custody that must be adhered to in legal cases

- Molecular techniques are replacing serological methods

DIRECT AND INDIRECT TESTING

1. RBC blood groups with codominant alleles can be used for parentage testing along with HLA system and DNA analysis

2. Maternity is assumed

3. Direct exclusion – marker present in child, absent from father and mother

Direct Example:

	ANTI-K	ANTI-k
Alleged Father	+	0
Mother	+	0
Baby	+	+

4. Indirect exclusion – child lacks a marker that the alleged father must transmit

Indirect Example:

	ANTI-K	ANTI-k
Alleged Father	+	0
Mother	0	+
Baby	0	+

Question?

Is the alleged father, tested below, excluded?

Testing: Father: KK
            Mother: kk
            Baby: Kk

Answer:

The alleged father is NOT excluded.

Evaluate Serologic Reactions Used in Paternity Testing

Antibody Screening and Identification

SCREENING CELLS AND PANELS

1. Commercially prepared group O red cells with a specific distribution of blood group antigens (*screening cells contain 2-3 different cells; panels vary from approximately 10 - 20 different cells*)

2. Patient serum is added to the cells
   a. Serum-cell mixture is tested at various temperatures, with different enhancement media, and with antiglobulin reagent (*indirect antiglobulin test [IAT]*)
   b. Patient serum may also be tested against his own cells (*autocontrol*) to determine the presence of an autoantibody

Enhancement Media Chart

albumin (bovine)	↓ net negative surface charge; only ↑ antibody uptake if under low ionic conditions; Rh antibodies may show at 37°C
Low Ionic Strength Saline (LISS)	↑ antibody uptake which allows ↓ in incubation time
Enzymes (bromelin, ficin, papain, trypsin)	Removes sialic acid which ↓ negative surface charge and promotes cell agglutination, ↑ reactivity of Rh, Kidd and Lewis antibodies; usually ↑ warm and cold autoantibodies; destroys M, N, S. Fya, and Fyb antigens
Polybrene	↑ antibody activity, ↓ incubation time; causes reversible cell aggregation; if ag-ab reaction occurs during aggregation, this agglutination does not reverse
Polyethylene glycol (PEG)	↑ antibody uptake; removes water which ↑ antibody concentration which promotes antibody uptake

3. IAT
   a. Antibody attaches to corresponding antigen on red cells at 37C (may see hemolysis)
   b. Excess serum/antibody removed by saline washes (failure to adequately wash cells may cause a false negative – human globulins, i.e., antibodies, proteins, etc., not wash away will neutralize the AHG)
   c. Antiglobulin is added and will bind to antibody on the cells
   d. Positive reaction is indicated by agglutination or ↓ in size of button due to hemolysis at 37C
   e. Check cells (IgG sensitized cells) are added; these should be positive indicating AHG was actually added in the final step and was not neutralized

4. Notes
   a. Enzyme treated (ficin, papain, trypsin and bromelin) cells are available to compare with panel results of untreated cells
   b. Panel results
      ❖ *Compare enzyme-treated and untreated cells - enhanced: Kidd, I, and some Rh* (NOT D); *destroyed: Duffy, M, N, and S*
      ❖ *Dosage - Rh (other than D), M, N, Kidd (Jk^a and Jk^b) and Duffy (Fy^a and Fy^b)*
      ❖ *Strength of reaction may separate multiple antibodies* (Panel with 1+ and 3+ reactions may mean two different antibodies)
      ❖ *Phase of reactivity* (see chart: Antibody Characteristics)
      ❖ *Autocontrol - if positive, may indicate a delayed transfusion reaction; if positive along with all panel cells, autoantibody indicated*
   c. Prewarmed technique - After proving no clinically significant antibodies also present, eliminate reactions due to cold antibodies
      ❖ *Warm serum and cells separately to 37°C before mixing together*
      ❖ *Wash with warm saline prior to further testing (crossmatch, panel, etc.)*

5. Determine patient antigen status

REMEMBER!
Enzymes:
P.B. Ficin The Lumberjack

P.B. Ficin - The Lumberjack

Papain   **B**romelin   **F**icin   **T**rypsin

Antigens on branches are chopped down by enzymes.
Other antigens are exposed (ex., c, Jk^a and I).

Antigen Characteristics

DOSAGE	ENZYMES		CORD CELLS	
	Enhanced	Destroyed	Present	Absent
M, N, S	Kidd	Fya, Fyb	i	I
Rh (other than D)	Rh	M,N		Lewis
Kidd	Lewis	S,s (variable when		Sda
Duffy (weak example	I	using "in house)		
of the antibody may		treated cells)		
show dosage)				

Antibody Characteristics

Temperature	Media	Antibody Class	Specificity
4-22C	Saline	IgM	Anti-I Anti-H Anti-M Anti-N Anti-P1 Anti-Lea Anti-Leb
37C	LISS/Albumin	IgG	Rh Antibodies: Anti-D Anti-C Anti-c Anti-E Anti-e
		IgM	Cold Antibodies Reacting at a Higher Thermal Range
37C	AHG	IgG	Anti-D Anti-C Anti-c Anti-E Anti-e Anti-Kell Anti-Duffy Anti-Kidd Anti-M (some)
		IgM (Using Polyspecific)	Complement Binding Antibodies; Most Common: Anti-I Anti-Lea Anti-Leb

REMEMBER!
Dosage

Kid(d)s and Duffy the Monkey (Rh) eat lots of M&Ns

Kidds	=	anti-Jka, -Jkb
Duffy	=	anti-Fya, -Fyb
Monkey	=	Rh (other than D): anti-C, -c, -E., -e
M&Ns	=	anti-M, -N, -S, -s
Lots	=	dosage

REMEMBER!
Antibody Temperatures of Reactivity

Let's go on a journey to help you associate blood group antibodies and their temperatures of reactivity:

First, we are going to a place that is very cold. In your mind, see yourself putting on a fur parka, gloves and some very warm boots. Let's get in our kayak and start paddling. We paddle and paddle and just when you think you can't paddle one more stroke, we finally reach land.

Up ahead, we see an igloo and we know that it is very cold here because the thermometer on the igloo reads 4° C. Suddenly out of the igloo comes Lewis the Eskimo. We know he is a very friendly eskimo, because he says, "HI." This tells us the Lewis, H, and I antibodies react in the cold. Next, we see the most amazing sight. Out of that same igloo comes a penguin, the #1 penguin, and under his wing, he is carrying the biggest brown bag of M&Ns you have ever seen. This tells us the P_1, M & N antibodies also react in the cold. From our journey to the cold, we know that Lewis, H, I, P_1, M and N antibodies best react at 4° C.

To learn about antibodies that react at 37° C, we must travel to a different part of the world. Let's get in our kayak and paddle to jungle territory. We paddle for what seems like days. The sun is shining and it's getting warmer and warmer. We quickly shed our fur parka, gloves and boots. It must be at least 37° C!

Finally, we reach land and gaze at the jungle that lays before us. Up ahead, we see Jungle Jim reading a book about the Rhesus monkeys he sees in the jungle. This tells us Rh antibodies are **seen** at 37° C.

Jungle Jim tells us there are other things in this environment that cannot be seen unless you look very closely. He takes us to the middle of the jungle. We hack our way through vines and branches until we come to a clearing. In the middle of the clearing, we see 2 big huts and a very tiny hut. The big huts have the owners' names on them. One belongs to the Kells, and the other belongs to the Duffys, and the little one must be for their Kid(d)s.

So, from our visit with Jungle Jim, we know the Rh antibodies can be seen directly at 37° C, but to see the Kell, Dufy, and Kidd reactions, we must look further and we do this through antiglobulin testing.

QUICK REVIEW —
Take 3 minutes and repeat the story out loud! Okay, now state the optimum temperature at which the following antibodies react: P_1, Kell, Jk^b, M and Le^a. Congratulations! The story works!

Here's your chance to show how much you remember about panels. For Panels 1 and 2, state:
1. What antibody *(ies)* is *(are)* present?
2. What antibody *(ies)* is *(are)* not eliminated?
Turn to the end of the chapter for the answers when you are through.

Panel 1

Cell No.	D	C	E	c	e	M	N	S	s	P1	Lea	Leb	K	k	Fya	Fyb	Jka	Jkb	Sal IS	LISS 37C 10'	AHG (IgG)
1	O	+	O	+	+	+	+	+	O	+	+	O	O	+	+	+	+	+	O	1+	2+
2	+	+	O	O	+	O	+	O	+	+	O	+	O	+	+	O	O	+	O	O	O
3	+	+	O	O	+	+	O	+	O	O	+	O	O	+	O	+	+	O	O	O	O
4	+	O	+	+	O	+	+	O	+	+	O	O	+	+	O	O	+	+	O	2+	2+
5	O	O	+	+	+	+	+	O	+	+	+	O	O	+	+	+	+	+	O	1+	2+
6	O	O	O	+	+	+	O	O	+	+	O	+	O	+	+	O	+	+	O	1+	2+
7	O	O	O	+	+	+	+	+	+	+	O	+	+	+	O	+	O	+	O	1+	2+
8	O	O	O	+	+	+	+	O	+	+	+	O	O	+	+	+	+	O	O	1+	2+
9	O	O	O	+	+	+	O	+	O	+	+	O	O	+	+	+	O	+	O	1+	2+
10	O	O	O	+	+	+	+	O	+	O	O	+	O	+	+	O	+	+	O	1+	2+
11	O	+	O	+	+	O	+	+	+	+	O	O	O	+	+	+	+	O	O	1+	2+
AC																			O	O	O

Panel 2

Cell No.	Rh					MNSs				P	Lewis		Kell		Duffy		Kidd		LISS 37C 10'	AHG (IgG)	Enzyme 37C	Enzyme AHG (IgG)
	D	C	E	c	e	M	N	S	s	P1	Lea	Leb	K	k	Fya	Fyb	Jka	Jkb				
1	0	+	0	+	+	+	+	+	0	+	+	0	0	+	+	+	+	+	0	1+	0	0
2	+	+	0	0	+	0	+	0	+	+	0	+	0	+	+	0	+	+	0	1+	0	0
3	+	+	0	0	+	+	0	+	+	0	+	0	0	+	0	+	+	0	0	0	0	0
4	+	0	+	+	0	0	+	0	+	+	0	0	+	+	0	0	+	+	0	2+	0	2+
5	0	0	+	+	+	+	+	0	+	+	+	0	0	+	+	+	+	+	0	1+	0	0
6	0	0	0	+	+	+	0	0	+	+	0	+	0	+	+	0	+	+	0	1+	0	0
7	0	0	0	+	+	+	+	+	+	+	0	+	+	+	0	+	0	+	0	2+	0	2+
8	0	0	0	+	+	+	+	0	+	+	+	0	0	+	+	+	+	0	0	1+	0	0
9	0	0	0	+	+	+	0	+	0	+	+	0	0	+	+	+	0	+	0	1+	0	0
10	0	0	0	+	+	+	+	0	+	0	0	+	0	+	+	0	+	+	0	1+	0	0
11	0	+	0	+	+	0	+	+	+	+	0	+	0	+	0	+	+	0	0	0	0	0
AC																			0	0	0	0

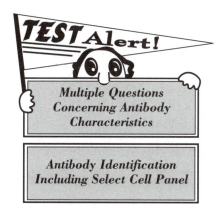

Multiple Questions Concerning Antibody Characteristics

Antibody Identification Including Select Cell Panel

DAT (Direct Antiglobulin Test)

1. Antiglobulin added to washed red cells

2. If cells coated in vivo, antiglobulin will react with the IgG antibody and/or complement *(depending on type of AHG used)*

3. EDTA sample is optimum; EDTA chelates CA++ preventing complement activation by plama antibody (causes a false positive DAT)

Sample Used for DAT

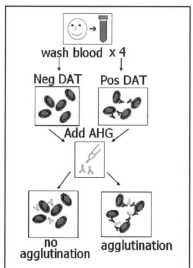

wash blood x 4

Neg DAT · Pos DAT

Add AHG

no agglutination · agglutination

• Reprinted with Permission from Jarreau P and Williams E. *The Uses of Direct Antiglobulin Testing. 2004 Event 2.* ASCP-API Educational Commentary. ASCP Press, 2004

4. Add check cells to all negative antiglobulin tests in antibody detection and compatibility testing

Positive DAT

IMMUNE HEMOLYTIC ANEMIAS		
Condition		Protein Coating Red Cell
AUTOIMMUNE HEMOLYTIC ANEMIA (AIHA)		
• Warm Autoantibodies (WAIHA)		IgG and/or Complement
• Cold Hemagglutinin Disease (CHD)		Complement
• Mixed Type AIHA		IgG and Complement
• Paroxysmal Cold Hemoglobinuria (PCH)		Complement
DRUG INDUCED HEMOLYTIC ANEMIA (DIHA)		IgG and/or Complement
ALLOIMMUNE HEMOLYTIC ANEMIA		
• Hemolytic Disease of the Newborn		IgG
• Transfusion Reaction		IgG

AHG Reagents *– monoclonal / polyclonal*

- Polyspecific (anti-IgG & anti-C3b or C3d)
- Anti-IgG
- Anti-complement

Avoid refrigerating a red top tube before performing DAT. Auto anti-I may attach to I antigen present on red cells and cause a FALSE POSITIVE DAT. This will also cause a FALSE NEGATIVE COLD AGGLUTININ TITER since that test measures the anti-I *(cold agglutinin)* in serum.

AHG REAGENTS

1. Can be polycolonal, monoclonal, or blends of monoclonal or monocolonal/polycolonal
   a. polycolonal- inject animals with purified IgG, IgA, IgM, C3, or C4
   b. monoclonal – hybridoma derived

2. Polyspecific– antibody to human IgG and C3d component of complement; other complement components may be present

3. Monospecific – antibody to IgG or to C3b, C3d

4. Perform DAT with polyspecific to screen and monospecific to characterize the globulin

5. Perform IAT with monospecific anti-IgG to avoid cold, complement-binding antibodies

6. Use check cells to confirm all negative antiglobulin tests in antibody detection and compatibility testing when using anti-IgG; confirms AHG added and not neutralized (insufficient removal of serum proteins prior to addition of AHG)

ELUTIONS

1. Principle based on breaking antigen-antibody bond, removing antibody from cell surface

2. Used to determine antibody specificity in cases of positive DAT due to IgG antibody(ies), i.e., HDN and transfusion reactions

3. Types
   a. Lui freeze-thaw and heat - ABO antibodies
   b. Low pH acid, digitonin-acid, cold-acid, and dichloromethane – all antibodies
   c. No single method best for all antibodies

4. Last wash control
   a. Prior to elution, red cells coated with antibody should be thoroughly washed to remove any residual serum antibody
   b. Test the "last wash" (supernatent) prior to testing eluate
   c. "Last wash" should show NO reactivity with reagent cells
   d. If positive, the coated cells must be washed additional times and a new eluate prepared
   e. Positive test results using "last wash" indicate serum antibody contamination of supernatent; may give false positive eluate results if further washing not performed

TEST Alert!

Interpret Eluate Results

Recognize Problems when Testing Eluate Last Wash

NEUTRALIZATION (INHIBITION) TESTS

1. Soluble antigen can bind with antibody to inhibit a reaction with RBCs; allow detection of alloantibodies "masked" by the following antibodies:
   a. Lewis substances – in saliva
   b. P1 substance– in hydatid cyst fluid

and pigeon egg whites
   c. Sda substance – most abundant in urine
   d. ABH sugars - inhibit anti-A, -B, -H
   e. Chido and Rogers substances – epitopes of C4 (complement)

INACTIVATION

1. Sulfhydryl reagents
   a. AET and DTT – destroy or weaken Kell system
   b. ZZAP – enzyme + DTT – Kell system and those destroyed by enzymes
   c. DTT and 2-ME – destroy or diminish activity of IgM antibodies

ADSORPTION

1. Used to:
   a. Separate multiple antibodies
   b. Remove autoantibody – reveal alloantibody "masked" by autoantibody
   c. Confirm antigen existence on RBC
   d. Confirm antibody specificity

2. Autologous adsorption (patients own serum and cells) can be used for patients not recently transfused

3. Allogeneic adsorptions (patients serum and other cells) can be used on patients recently transfused

Additional Technologies to Detect Antigen-Antibody Reactions

GEL TESTING

1. Perform serological work in special chamber with controlled centrifugation
   a. Gel acts as a filter - unagglutinated cell pass through gel; agglutinated cell cannot.
      ❖ *Negative reactions, the cells settle at the bottom;*
      ❖ *Positive reactions, the cells remain on the top or only partially travel through the gel depending on agglutinate size*
   b. Phenotype cells when reagent antisera (i.e., anti-A, -B, -D, etc.) is in the gel; cells agglutinate when exposed to antibody during centrifugation
   c. Antiserum/serum/plasma and cells can be added together in the upper chamber; sensitized cells agglutinate when exposed to the IgG in the gel

and cannot can not go through

d. DAT by gel - no washing needed; only RBCs go through gel and sensitized cells agglutinate when exposed to IgG in the gel

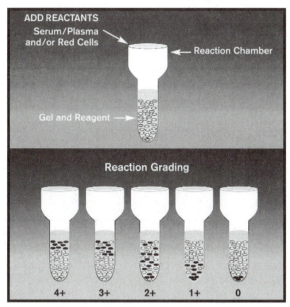

ADD REACTANTS
Serum/Plasma and/or Red Cells — Reaction Chamber
Gel and Reagent →

Reaction Grading

4+ 3+ 2+ 1+ 0

• Reprinted with Permission from Ortho-Clinical Diagnostics

SOLID PHASE

1. Antibody or antigen - fixed to a microwell plate
   a. Antibody fixed to plate
      ❖ *RBCs with the antigen are added*
      ❖ *Adhere to antibody on sides of microplate*
   b. Antigen fixed to plate
      ❖ *Plasma with the antibody is added*
      ❖ *Antibody will adhere to antigen on sides*
      ❖ *Wash; add check cells to attach to antibody*

2. Positive reactions have cells adhering to sides of microwell plate

3. Negative reactions have RBC pellet at bottom of plate since no attachment

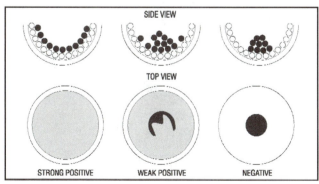

SIDE VIEW

TOP VIEW

STRONG POSITIVE   WEAK POSITIVE   NEGATIVE

• Photo courtesy of Immucor, Inc.

Pretransfusion Testing

1. Sample accompanying request

   a. Serum or plasma from intended recipient
   b. Labeled with 2 unique identifiers and date of collection
   c. Must have system to identify phlebotomist
   d. Retain for a minimum of 7 days after transfusion

2. Tests
   a. ABO and D grouping
   b. Antibody screens
   c. Crossmatch
   d. Autocontrol not required

3. Compare current results with prior testing

4. Crossmatch
   a. Patient serum reacted with donor RBCs
   b. Observe for agglutination or hemolysis
   c. Demonstrate ABO compatibility
   d. Carry through to 37C incubation with AHG if current antibody screen positive or prior history of clinically significant antibodies

5. Immediate spin or computer crossmatch if current antibody screen negative and no prior antibody history

   a. Only test for ABO required if no clinically significant antibodies currently or in history
   b. Computer
      ❖ *If validated system and other requirements met*
      ❖ *Two determinations of ABO group, one on current sample*
      ❖ *Donor confirmed for ABO and Rh (on negative units)*
      ❖ *System can verify correct data entry and contains logic to alert if mistakes made*

TEST Alert!

Evaluate Results of Incompatible Crossmatch

6. Antigen typing
   a. Patients with clinically significant antibodies should receive antigen negative units
   b. Confirm antigen negative status by reacting cells with commercial preparations of the antibody
   c. QC rarely used antisera on day of use
      ❖ *Positive control: heterozygous cell (ex. anti-K tested with a Kk cell rather than a KK cell)*
      ❖ *Negative control: cell without antigen (ex. anti-K tested with a kk cell)*

TEST Alert!

Select Appropriate Controls for Antigen Typing

7. Alternate blood groups
   a. O rbc's to any blood group
   b. AB may receive A, B and O rbc's
   c. D negative gets D positive in an emergency if no D negative available *(follow with RhIg, if possible)*

REMEMBER!
For Decisions Involving
- **Compatibility Testing Results**
- **Selection of Units for Transfusion when ABO Identical is NOT Available:**

Decide what ABO antibody (ies) is (are) in the patient's plasma. Any red cells lacking that (those) antigen(s) will be compatible.

REMEMBER! NO WHOLE BLOOD!

WHEN ABO IDENTICAL IS NOT AVAILABLE.
1. For RBCs
   a. Decide what antibody (ies) is (are) in the patient's plasma
   b. Transfused cells must lack corresponding antigens

2. For Plasma
   a. Decide what antigen(s) is (are) on the patient's RBCs
   b. Transfused plasma should lack the corresponding antibody (ies)

Donor		Recipient of RBCs				Donor		Recipient of Plasma			
		O	A	B	AB			O	A	B	AB
	O	x	x	x	x		O	x			
	A		x		x		A	x	x		
	B			x	x		B	x		x	
	AB				x		AB	x	x	x	x

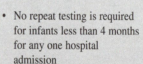

Special Considerations for the Neonatal Crossmatch (< 4 months)
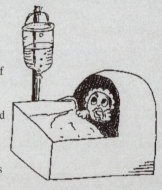

- Initial ABO and D Grouping
- ABO serum grouping is not required unless giving ABO type not compatible with mother
- No crossmatch is necessary if initial antibody screen negative using infant or maternal serum or plasma and group 'O' is given
- No repeat testing is required for infants less than 4 months for any one hospital admission
- Majority of institutions use 1 O neg unit for all neonates; aliquots are taken through a sterile docking device so expiration date is not altered
- For infants weighing < 1200 g at birth, blood products with reduced risk of CMV transmission should be used if the mother is CMV negative or CMV status is unknown

Transfusion Practice

WHAT WOULD YOU DO IF . . .

1. A group B patient needs blood, but ABO identical blood is unavailable. Which alternative group(s) may be used?
Ans. Group O since B individuals have anti-A and O units have no A antigens (or B antigens!)

2. A group AB patient needs blood, but ABO identical is unavailable. Which alternative group(s) may be used?
Ans. Any blood group red cells since AB individuals have no ABO antibodies.

3. A group O patient was crossmatched with group B red cells. Will this incompatibility be detected?

Ans. Yes, the patient serum contains anti-A, -B and -A,B and will show agglutination when added to the group B cells (probably a strong reaction at immediate spin).

4. A group B needs FFP. Which blood group(s) would be acceptable?

Ans. A group B patient has B antigens on his red cells. NO group with anti-B will be acceptable (therefore no A or O). Group B (has anti-A) or group AB (no ABO antibodies) will be fine.

5. A group B neg needs 3 units of red cells and 1 unit of FFP. No B neg RBCs or FFP are available. What would be the choice for both components?

Ans. O neg red cells is the appropriate ABO group to select. If this is an emergency and no B neg or O neg is available, B pos or O pos would be used. The FFP should be AB since group O and A contain anti-B.

6. Four units of O neg RBCs are issued on emergency release to the ER. Immediately after the blood is issued, a blood sample and a request for 4 more units is received. The 4 additional units of O neg RBCs are issued and the type and crossmatch is started. The patient turns out to be an A pos with a negative antibody screen. The crossmatches with the first 8 O neg units are compatible and the antibody screen is negative. The ER calls requesting 6 more units. What ABO/Rh group should these next 6 units be?

Ans. - The patient should be switched to D positive blood now. The question is whether the A units will be compatible with the passively transfused anti-A and anti-AB after receiving 8 units of O neg RBCs. CPDA-1 and additive units contain very little residual plasma, i.e., ABO antibodies. In transfusing a small number of units, there is little risk associated in switching the patient to A pos RBC except for a transient positive DAT. Even in transfusing 8 units, there may not be a problem unless the patient is a child or small adult. A new post transfusion sample can be requested and tested for ABO antibodies either with an immediate spin crossmatch or a crossmatch carried through to AHG to detect ABO antibodies.

Adverse Effects of Transfusion

INTRAVASCULAR HEMOLYTIC TRANSFUSION REACTION

1. Transfused RBCs react with preformed antibodies in the recipient as transfusion is occurring.

2. Uusually due to clerical error involving ABO system

3. Fever - most common symptom accompanied by chills, low back pain, anxiety

4. Physiological events
   a. Hemoglobinemia
   b. Hemoglobinuria
   c. Hyperbilirubinemia
   d. Can result in kidney failure and death

EXTRAVASCULAR HEMOLYTIC TRANSFUSION REACTION

1. Due to clinically significant antibodies such as Rh, Kell, Kidd and Duffy; usually occurs after transfusion completed

2. Delayed transfusion reactions
   a. Hours to days after transfusion
   b. Indicated by NO rise or a ↓ in hemoglobin after transfusion
   c. Positive DAT *(key characteristic)*
   d. Often due to Kidd antibodies

TEST Alert!

Evaluate Results of Possible Hemolytic Transfusion Reactions Including Delayed Reactions

URTICARIAL

1. Symptoms - itching and hives

2. If urticaria only symptom, give antihistamine and transfusion may continue

3. Caused by donor antibodies to soluble plasma antigens

FEBRILE NONHEMOLYTIC (FNH)

1. Temperature rise associated with transfusion

2. Due to:
   a. Recipient preformed antibodies reacting with donor lymphocytes, granulocytes, or platelets
   b. Infusion of cytokines in donor bag from storage
   c. Leukocyte-reduced blood components; pre-storage leukoreduction prevents cytokine buildup

ALLERGIC REACTIONS

1. Recipient pre-formed IgE antibodies to soluble substance in plasma

2. Mild - urticarial - hives with itching
   a. Give antihistamines and continue transfusion

3. Severe - anaphylaxis – systemic symptoms including hypotension, shock, sometimes death
   a. Classic anaphylaxis – IgA deficient patient with anti-IgA reacting with IgA in donor plasma
   b. Give washed cells or plasma components from IgA deficient donors

TRANSFUSION-RELATED ACUTE LUNG INJURY (TRALI)

1. Acute respiratory insufficiency and bilateral pulmonary edema by X-ray without cardiac failure; includes chills, fever, and hypotension

2. Donor antibodies to recipient HLA or neutrophil antigens; rarely, recipient antibodies to transfused granulocytes

TEST Alert!

Symptoms of Adverse Reaction Due to Granulocytes

TEST Alert!

Correlate Lab Data to Determine Type of Reaction and Treatment

Transfusion Reactions

TYPE	CAUSE
Hemolytic	Antibody to rbc antigens *(usually ABO)*
Febrile	Antibody to wbc/plt antigens/preferred cytokines
Urticarial	Antibody to soluble antigen in donor plasma
Anaphylactic	Anti-IgA
Transfusion-Related Acute Lung Injury	Donor antibody to recipient HLA or neutrophil antigens

Transfusion Reaction Workup

Clerical Check → Most hemolytic transfusion reactions result from administering blood to the incorrect patient

Visual Hemolysis → Compare with pre-transfusion sample (see below)

DAT → May be negative if all incompatible cells are destroyed; ABO antibodies rapidly activate complement leading to lysis

ABO → ABO on post sample

Other Tests → If error in any of above tests: perform ↓
- *Antibody screen pre/post samples*
- *Re-crossmatch pre/post samples*

Keep in Mind:
Positive hemolysis, negative DAT

- **Patient in sickle cell crisis**
- **Thalassemia or G6PD deficient patient**
- **Unit overheated/frozen**
- **All cells hemolyzed**

TRANSFUSION TRANSMITTED INFECTIONS

1. Bacterial contamination is now most common since currents tests detect most viruses
   a. All platelets must be tested for bacterial contamination before issue

2. Other diseases – HBV, HCV, HIV, HTLV, CMV, EBV, Babesiosis, Malaria, Chagas disease, West Nile virus

3. "Look Back" - Identification of individuals who have received seronegative or untested blood from a donor later found to be infected

4. Must have a mechanism to encourage reporting of possible transfusion-associated infections

Hemolytic Disease of the Newborn

ETIOLOGY

1. Infant inherits antigen from biological father

2. Mother has corresponding IgG antibody *(sensitized by previous pregnancies or transfusions)*

3. Maternal antibody crosses placenta and coats fetal cells

4. Coated cells removed from fetal circulation causing anemia and hyperbilirubinemia

5. Bilirubin has affinity for lipid rich layers of skin and brain and is a potent neurotoxin causing brain damage *(kernicterus)*

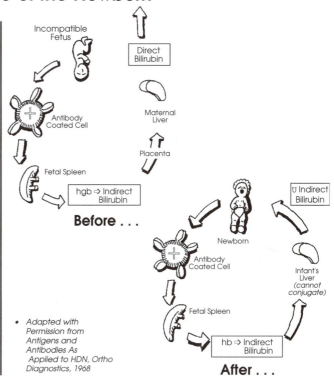

- *Adapted with Permission from Antigens and Antibodies As Applied to HDN, Ortho Diagnostics, 1968*

Comparison of HDN Due to ABO and Anti-D Antibodies

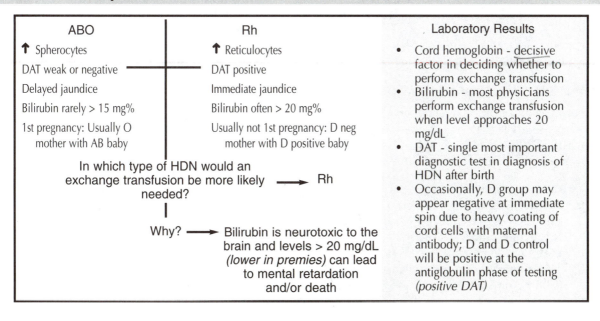

ABO	Rh	Laboratory Results
↑ Spherocytes	↑ Reticulocytes	• Cord hemoglobin - decisive factor in deciding whether to perform exchange transfusion
DAT weak or negative	DAT positive	• Bilirubin - most physicians perform exchange transfusion when level approaches 20 mg/dL
Delayed jaundice	Immediate jaundice	• DAT - single most important diagnostic test in diagnosis of HDN after birth
Bilirubin rarely > 15 mg%	Bilirubin often > 20 mg%	• Occasionally, D group may appear negative at immediate spin due to heavy coating of cord cells with maternal antibody; D and D control will be positive at the antiglobulin phase of testing *(positive DAT)*
1st pregnancy: Usually O mother with AB baby	Usually not 1st pregnancy: D neg mother with D positive baby	

In which type of HDN would an exchange transfusion be more likely needed? ⟶ Rh

Why? ⟶ Bilirubin is neurotoxic to the brain and levels > 20 mg/dL *(lower in premies)* can lead to mental retardation and/or death

INTRAUTERINE TRANSFUSION

1. Supplies antigen negative blood

2. Unit selection
   a. Group O, D negative
   b. Negative for antigen to which maternal antibody directed *(compatible with maternal antibody)*
   c. Must be irradiated
   d. Should be from CMV seronegative donor or a leukoreduced unit if mother status CMV negative or unknown
   e. Should be negative for hb S
   f. Should be very fresh; usually < 3 days old

EXCHANGE TRANSFUSION

1. Replaces antibody-coated cells (which would increase bilirubin levels if destroyed) with antigen negative cells

2. Reduces maternal antibody and bilirubin levels

3. Removes antibody-coated cells which would ↑ bilirubin levels when destroyed

4. Acceptable samples for crossmatch
   a. Maternal sample - highest concentration of maternal antibody
   b. Eluate from infant's cells
   c. Infant serum

5. Unit selection
   a. Group O, if ABO HDN; D negative, if Rh HDN
   b. Negative for antigen to which maternal antibody directed *(compatible with maternal antibody)*
   c. < 5 days old
   d. Should be negative for hbS
   e. Should be irradiated

RH IMMUNE GLOBULIN (CONCENTRATED ANTI-D)

1. Antepartum administration given at 28 weeks to all D negative women and again within 72 hours of delivery to D negative women with D positive infants

2. Two preparations of RhIg
   a. Intramuscular (IM) injection only - 1 vial (300 µg or 1500IU) neutralized 30 mL whole blood (15 mL RBCs) fetal-maternal hemorrhage (FMH)
   b. IM or intravenous preparation - 1 vial (300 ug or 1500 IU) neutralizes 17 mL RBCs

3. Must do a test on all RhIg candidates to determine if more than one vial necessary; rosette test usually used for screening

4. If rosette test positive, Kleihauer-Betke acid elution will quantitate fetal maternal bleed *(fetal cells resist acid elution and appear pink while adult cells are ghost cells)*

TEST Alert!
Given the Amount of FMH, Calculate RhIg dose

HLA System (Human Leukocyte Antigens)

1. Glycoprotein molecules on cells surfaces
   a. Class I – on platelets and nucleated cells (mature RBCs have very small amount)
   b. Class II – on B lymphs; monocyte/macrophages; T lymphs

2. Genes located on short arm of chromosome 6 *(major histocompatibility complex)*

3. Contribute to self/non-self recognition; immune responses; coordination of cellular and humoral responses

4. Second in importance only to ABO for long-term survival of transplanted solid organs and most important in hematopoietic progenitor cell transplantation

5. Plays a role in:
   a. Immune-mediated platelet refractoriness
   b. FNH-TR
   c. TRALI
   d. Posttransfusion graft-vs-host disease (GVHD)

6. Used for:
   a. Susceptibility to certain diseases
   b. Parentage testing
   c. Forensic investigations

7. Detection
   a. microlymphocytotoxicity — HLA-A, -B, -C, -DR, and -DQ
      ❖ *Principle similar to RBC typing only uses WBC's, rabbit complement, and a dye exclusion technique to determine cell viability /death*
   b. DNA-based Assays

General Knowledge of Genetics of HLA System

Quality Control

REAGENT QC

1. Reagents – each day of use
   a. Antihuman globulin
   b. Blood grouping reagents
   c. Antibody screening and reverse grouping cells

2. Results - compare with previous results; inactivity implies reagent deterioration

3. Antiglobulin Reagent
   a. No need for separate QC
   b. Requirement to add IgG sensitized cells to all negative antiglobulin tests in antibody detection and compatibility testing
   c. Negative tests imply:
      ❖ *Insufficient removal of serum proteins prior to addition of AHG (insufficient washing which allowed AHG to be neutralized by remaining serum)*
      ❖ *Omission of AHG from procedure*
      ❖ *Must repeat tests*

QC of Antiglobulin Reagent and Implications of Nonreactivity

EQUIPMENT QC

1. Hot blocks/waterbaths: 37C ± 2; observe temperature, day of use

2. Refrigerators: 1-6C *(as well as alarm activation checks)*

3. Serofuge/Cell Washer:
   a. Timer checks
   b. Speed
   c. Function - Are cell buttons clearly delineated, is supernatant clear, do cells resuspend with gentle agitation?

4. Component centrifuge

5. Thermometers – tested initially

Appropriate QC of Serofuge

PANEL 1 ANSWERS *(page 17)*	PANEL 2 ANSWERS *(page 18)*
1. Anti-c 2. Anti-E & -K	1. Anti-Fy^a & Anti-K 2. Anti-E & Anti-Jk^b *(not ruled out on original panel; eliminated by enzymes)*

IMMUNOHEMATOLOGY SAMPLE QUESTIONS

1. The following results were obtained when testing a sample from a 20 year old first time donor.

CELL GROUPING		SERUM GROUPING	
anti-A	anti-B	A1 Cell	B Cell
3+	neg	1+	3+

The most likely cause of this ABO discrepancy is
   A. Lack of immune response
   B. Loss of antigen due to disease
   C. Oh (Bombay)
   D. Subgroup of A

2. The serum in the panel below is from a patient transfused 5 months ago. The most probable antibody is
   A. Anti-c
   B. Anti-I
   C. Anti-k
   D. Autoantibody

3. Red blood cells which are to be tested with antiglobulin reagent are washed to
   A. Remove traces of bacterial proteins
   B. Wash away traces of free hemoglobin
   C. Remove unbound serum globulin
   D. Expose additional antigen sites

4. An antibody screen gave no reactions at immediate spin or 37C, but showed a 2+ reaction when antiglobulin reagent was added. The most likely antibody causing these results would be anti-
   A. I
   B. Jka
   C. Leb
   D. P₁

5. Which of the following would cause an individual to be rejected as a blood donor?
   A. Pulse of 95
   B. 13 g/dl hemoglobin
   C. Age 65
   D. Blood pressure of 185/120 mm of mercury

Cell No.	C	D	E	c	e	K	k	Fya	Fyb	Jka	Jkb	Lea	Leb	M	N	S	s	Sal IS	LISS 37C 10'	AHG (IgG)
1	+	0	0	+	+	0	+	+	0	0	+	0	+	+	+	+	0	0	0	2+
2	+	+	0	0	+	0	+	+	+	+	0	0	+	0	+	0	+	0	0	2+
3	+	+	0	0	+	+	+	0	+	+	0	+	0	0	+	0	+	0	0	2+
4	0	+	+	+	0	0	+	0	+	+	+	0	+	+	0	+	0	0	0	2+
5	0	0	+	+	+	0	+	0	+	0	+	+	0	0	+	0	+	0	0	2+
6	0	0	0	+	+	0	+	0	0	+	0	0	0	0	+	+	0	0	0	2+
7	0	0	0	+	+	0	+	+	+	+	+	0	+	+	0	0	+	0	0	2+
8	0	0	0	+	+	+	+	+	+	+	0	+	0	0	+	0	+	0	0	2+
AC																		0	0	2+

6. Over a two week period, the reactions of your QC antibody show a gradual decrease from 2+ to a very weak positive with your antibody detection cells (screening cells). These results most likely indicate
   A. Acceptable performance of reagents
   B. Inappropriate antibody specificity
   C. Inconsistent grading of reactions
   D. Deterioration of QC antibody

7. The following reactions were obtained on testing maternal serum and infant cord cells.

MATERNAL SAMPLE	INFANT CORD CELLS
O negative (D weak - mixed field)	A Positive
D Control: Negative	DAT: Negative
Antibody Screen: Negative	

The most likely explanation for these results is a/an
   A. ABO grouping error on infant
   B. Detection of antenatal Rh immune globulin
   C. Fetal-maternal hemorrhage
   D. False negative DAT

8. Based on the following results, select the best conclusion.
   Mother: MMR°R°
   Alleged Father: MMrr
   Child: MNR°r

The alleged father is
   A. Not excluded
   B. Excluded by his D antigen
   C. Excluded by his e antigen
   D. Excluded by his M antigen

9. A 24 year old A negative female was transfused with approximately 70 cc of an A positive RBC unit. How many vials of Rh Immune globulin should this woman receive?
   A. 0, she is not an RhIg candidate
   B. 2
   C. 3
   D. 4
   E. 5

10. The transfusion component of choice for a patient with a prolonged bleeding time, increased APTT, decreased levels of Factor VIII antigen and impaired aggregation of platelets in response to ristocetin would be
   A. Cryoprecipitate
   B. Factor VIII
   C. Fresh frozen plasma
   D. Platelets

11. An A negative mother with a high titer of anti-D delivers a jaundiced infant. The infant is A negative with a strongly positive (4+) DAT. The test most likely in error is
   A. Infant's DAT
   B. Infant's D type
   C. Mother's ABO type
   D. Mother's antibody identification

12. How many units of platelet concentrates would be needed to raise the platelet count 150,000/mm3 in an average sized adult?
   A. 4
   B. 8
   C. 12
   D. 15

13. A technologist inadvertently used a clotted sample that had been refrigerated overnight to perform a DAT. An erroneous result may occur because
   A. Clotted samples contain more complement
   B. Calcium and magnesium ions are present
   C. Complement may be activated at 4C
   D. IgG antibodies may dissociate from the cell surface

14. A patient has experienced febrile reactions following 2 red cell transfusions. The best component to use if subsequent transfusions are needed would be
   A. Neocytes
   B. Packed red cells
   C. Washed red cells.
   D. Leukocyte-reduced red cells

15. Cord bloods are wahed prior to ABO and Rh grouping to
   A. Expose A and B antigens
   B. Remove Wharton's jelly
   C. Eliminate infant's anti-i
   D. Prevent reagent neutralization

ANSWERS AND RATIONALE

1. D

This donor is a probable A2 subgroup with anti-A1. Option A is incorrect because the donor demonstrates anti-A and anti-B in his/her serum. Option B is incorrect because loss of B antigen is not explained by disease (loss of A antigen has been documented in some leukemias); blood donors are usually healthy. Option C is incorrect because a Bombay forwards as an O. They have no H antigen for transferases to attach A or B sugar molecules.

2. D

When serum demonstrates the same strength of reactivity with all cells tested including the autocontrol, an autoantibody is suspected. (This occurs in patients with warm autoimmune hemolytic anemia.) Option A is incorrect because cells 2 and 3 lack the c antigen but have reactivity with the serum tested. Option B is incorrect because most examples of anti-I would demonstrate activity at immediate spin/room temperature as opposed to strong reactions at the antiglobulin phase. Option C is incorrect because the autocontrol is positive and individuals forming anti-k would be k negative. (The previous transfusion was 5 months ago and no transfused cells would be in circulation at this time to explain the positive autocontrol.)

3. C

Antiglobulin reagent will react with any serum globulin whether it is in serum or coating red cells. Therefore, if all unbound serum is not removed, it will bind with the antiglobulin reagent and neutralize. Options A and B do not contain globulin. Option D describes the effect of enzymes on some red cell antigens.

4. B

Most examples of Anti-Jka react only at the antiglobulin phase of testing. Options A, C and D are antibodies that generally react at the immediate spin/room temperature phase of testing.

5. D

The systolic pressure should be no higher than 180 mm of mercury and the diastolic pressure should be no higher than 100 mm of mercury. Options A, B and C fall within acceptable donor criteria.

6. D

A steady decrease in reaction strength in reagent quality control signifies a loss of antigen or antibody potency. Option B would show consistent readings but at incorrect phases or with incorrect cells (QC antibody should react with all screening cells at the antiglobulin phase of testing). Option C would show a more erratic pattern of reactions (some days stronger, some days weaker).

7. C.

A positive D weak test in a post partum patient is usually due to a fetal maternal hemorrhage in which the fetal D positive cells have entered the maternal circulation at birth. Option A is incorrect as it is plausible for an O negative mother to have an A positive infant. Option B is incorrect since the maternal antibody screens are negative (RhIg = anti-D). Option D is incorrect since hemolytic disease of the newborn is not indicated.

8. D

In paternity testing maternity is assumed. The child's M antigen is inherited from the mother as she is homozygous for M (MM). The child's N antigen must be inherited from the biological father which this alleged father does not possess. Option B is incorrect since the father does not possess a D antigen (rr=dce/dce). Option C is incorrect since the child has e as does the father.

9. E

The female is of childbearing age and is an Rh immune globulin candidate. RhIg is expected to counteract 15 cc of RBCs. 70 cc / 15 cc = 4.66 vials. You would round up to 5 in this case as a baseline. Depending on hospital policy, you may give extra vials as a safety factor. In a fetal-maternal bleed the number of cc is divided by 30. This is because a fetus would bleed whole blood and a 30 cc whole blood bleed has approximately 15 cc of RBCs. If the IV form of RhIg is used, the number of cells it neutralizes is 17. 70 / 17 is 4.1 so you still round up to 5.

10. A

These laboratory data suggest a patient with von Willebrand Syndrome. Cryoprecipitate is the only component containing von Willebrand factor (vWF) as well as factor VIII. Both of these are deficient in these patients. It is the vWF that is responsible for the platelet aggregating effect of ristocetin.

11. B

The words "high titer" are a clue that there is sufficient anti-D in the mother's plasma to cross the placenta and possibly bind all D antigen sites in a D positive infant. The reagent anti-D used in D grouping will have no available D binding sites and will not demonstrate agglutination. These cells will appear to be D negative. (However, the D weak test and D control will be positive at the antiglobulin phase.) The positive DAT is due to the anti-D coated cells.

12. D

One unit of platelets theoretically increases the platelet count in an average sized adult 5,000 - 10,000/mm3.

13. C

Most adult serum contains some anti-I which reacts optimally at 4C. When placed in the refrigerator (4C), the anti-I will bind to the I antigen on the cells and activate complement. This in vivo coating of the red cells with complement will cause a positive DAT if polyspecific antiglobulin reagent is used in testing. (Anti-IgG antiglobulin testing would be negative and anti-complement antiglobulin testing would be positive, if performed.) Option A, B and D are correct statements but not the best rationale for the question.

14. D

Many febrile nonhemolytic transfusion (FNH) reactions are due to cytokines released from WBCs in the stored blood or to recipient antibodies to antigens on donor lymphocytes, granulocytes and platelets. Patients experiencing a FNH reaction for the first time do not always have a similar reaction with subsequent transfusions. Leukocyte-reduced products are recommended for patients who exhibit 2 or more FNH reactions.

15. B

If cord blood is not collected appropriately ("stripped" rather than aspirated from the umbilical cord), it may be contaminated with Wharton's jelly. This substance, if not removed through saline washes will cause red cells to mechanically "stick" together possibly causing false positive interpretations. Option A is incorrect because the A and B receptors on cord cells are exposed sufficiently for ABO and Rh grouping. Option C is incorrect because infant's do not have anti-i. (Cord cells have i antigen).

REMEMBER!

Do or Do Not.
There is no such thing as try.

— *Yoda*

IMMUNOLOGY AND SEROLOGY

by Patsy Jarreau

CHARACTERISTICS OF IMMUNOGENS

1. Large molecule *(molecular weight of at least 10,000)*
2. High complexity *(simple repeating units do not make good immunogens)*
3. Chemical composition *(proteins and polysaccharides are better than carbohydrates)*
4. Foreignness *(the more different from the host, the more immunogenic)*

TYPES OF IMMUNITY

Active vs. Passive

ACTIVE	PASSIVE
Individual Produces Antibody	Antibody Transferred to Individual
Follows Immunization or Infection	Example: Gamma Globulin Injections
Memory *(lasting)*	No Memory *(temporary)*

What type of immunity is associated with rubella immunization? ⟶ Active Immunity

What type of immunity is associated with neonatal (<4 months), syphilitic IgG antibody titers? ⟶ Passive Immunity

Natural vs. Adaptive

NATURAL *(Innate)*	ADAPTIVE *(Acquired)*
Non-Specific	Specific
No Memory	Memory
Examples: Exogenous *(Skin)*	Examples: T Cells *(cytokines)*
Endogenous *(Stomach Acid)*	B Cells *(antibodies)*
Phagocytosis *(PMNs)*	
NK *(Natural Killer Cells)*	

Adaptive: Cellular vs. Humoral

CELLULAR	HUMORAL
T Cell / Lymphokines	B Cell (Plasma Cell) / Antibody
Defense Against Viral / Fungal Infections (Intracellular Organisms)	Defense Against Bacterial Infections (Extracellular Organisms)
Delayed Hypersensitivity (Ex. Transplant Rejection)	Antibody Dependent Cellular Cytotoxicity (ADCC)

TEST Alert!

- *Type of Immunity Associated with Immunization*
- *Type of Cell Producing Antibody*
- *Immunity Associated with Viral Infections*
- *Immunity Associated with Bacterial Infections*

CLASSES OF IMMUNOGLOBULINS (Based on Heavy Chains)

1. IgG
   a. Greatest concentration in serum
   b. 4 subclasses
   c. Activates complement *(except for IgG4)*
   d. Crosses placenta
   e. 75% of total antibody concentration

34

2. IgM
   a. Largest antibody *(pentamer)*
   b. Fixes complement best
   c. Prominent in early immune response
   d. 5-10% of total antibody concentration

3. IgA
   a. Predominant antibody in body secretions *(tears, saliva, nasal mucosa)*
   b. Serum IgA *(monomer)* & secretory IgA *(dimer)*
   c. Primary defense against some local infections at mucosal surface
   d. Two subclasses

4. IgD
   a. Unknown function
   b. Present on B cell surface

5. IgE
   a. Allergy
   b. Triggers release of histamines from mast cells

Function of Immunoglobulins

REMEMBER!
Antibody Functions

Ig **G** - **G**reatest Plasma Concentration (70%); **G**oes Across Placenta

Ig **M** - **M**ega (largest immunoglobulin molecule); Activates Co**M**plement Easily

Ig **A** - s**A**liva, Te**A**rs (body secretions)

Ig **D** - **D**on't Know Function

Ig **E** - Allerg**EE** (allergy)

Immune Response Curve

1st Exposure to Antigen *Sensitizing Dose*

2nd Exposure to Antigen *Booster Dose*

Immune Response

LYMPHOCYTES IN THE IMMUNE RESPONSE

1. T cells
   a. Produced in thymus
   b. No immunoglobulin present on cell surface
   c. Possess T cell receptor *(TCR-1 or TCR-2)* - CD3+
   d. Rosette with sheep red blood cells *(SRBC)* - CD2+
   e. Comprise 80% of circulating lymphocytes
   f. Subsets
      ❖ *T helper cell*
      ❖ *T cytotoxic cell*
      ❖ *T suppressor cell*

g. After presented with antigen by Antigen Presenting Cell *(APC)*
   - ❖ *May become memory cell*
   - ❖ *May release lymphokines (T helper)*
   - ❖ *May be cytotoxic (T cytotoxic) - effector cell*
h. May interact with B cells
   - ❖ *T helper - CD4+*
   - ❖ *T suppressor - CD8+*

CD4 : CD8 Ratio in AIDS Patients

Characteristics of Lymphocytes

	T CELLS (80%)	B CELLS (5-15%)	NULL CELLS
Surface Receptor	T Cell Receptor *(TCR-1 or TCR-2)*	Surface Immunoglobulin *(IgD or IgM)* Complement Receptors	Neither
Surface Markers	CD2+ - Rosette with Sheep RBCs) CD3+ - T Cell Receptor CD4+ - Helper Cells CD8+ - Suppressor Cells, Cytotoxic Cells	CD19+ CD20+	CD16+ CD56+
Rosette with Sheep Red Blood Cells	Yes	No	No
Function	Become Memory Cell Release Lymphokines Become Cytotoxic *(CD8+)* Interact with B Cells *(CD4+ or CD8+)*	Evolve into Plasma Cells Which Secrete Antibody	Natural Killer Cells Killer Cells - *Antibody Dependent Cellular Cytotoxicity (ADCC)*

Normal T Cell : B Cell Ratio = 8:1
Normal T Helper : T Suppressor Ratio (CD4:CD8)= 2:1
AIDS Patients - Reverse T Helper : T Suppressor Ratio

Characteristics of T&B Lymphocytes

2. B cells
   a. Possess cell surface immunoglobulin *(IgD or IgM)*
   b. Evolve into plasma cells which secrete specific antibody into plasma
   c. Comprise 5-15% of circulating lymphocytes

3. Third population cells *(null cells)*
   a. No cell surface immunoglobulin or T cell receptor
   b. NK *(natural killer)*, K *(killer)* cells
   c. CD16+

EVALUATION OF T AND B CELLS

1. Rosette Test
   a. Incubate sheep red blood cells *(SRBC)* with known number of purified lymphocytes; SRBCs bind to E-rosette receptor *(CD2)* on T cells
   b. Count rosetted lymphocytes; percentage of T cells can be calculated
   c. Estimate of B cells: 100% minus calculated percentage of T cells
   d. Estimates of absolute counts: patient's total lymphocyte count multiplied by percentage of T or B cells

2. Monoclonal Antibodies
   a. Can be used to differentiate T and B cells by detecting cell surface markers *(CD markers)* with flow cytometry
   b. Produced by immunizing mouse with specific antigen, combining mouse spleen cells with myeloma cells *(plasma cells fuse with myeloma cells forming a hybridoma)*. Hybridoma can produce monoclonal antibodies for indefinite period of time.

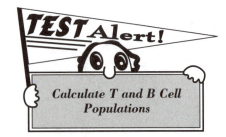

Calculate T and B Cell Populations

Complement Cascades

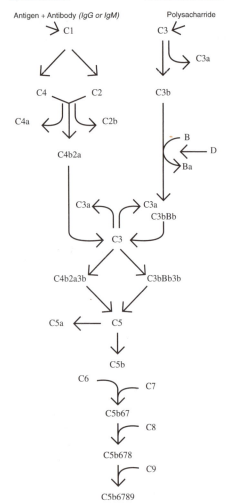

CLASSICAL   ALTERNATIVE

Antigen + Antibody *(IgG or IgM)*   Polysacharride

*Adapted with permission
from ASCLS, American Journal of Medical Technology
1982; 48:735*

COMPLEMENT

1. Approximately 21 chemically distinct proteins
   (14 effector, 7 control)

2. Functions to control inflammation
   a. Activates phagocytes *(chemotaxis)*
   b. Lyses target cell *(foreign organism)*
   c. Opsonization - attach to complement receptors on neutrophils, monocytes
   → enhance phagocytic binding

REMEMBER!
Complement Cascades

CLASSICAL
- Components
- Activated by Immune Complexes *(IgG, IgM)*
- Bind in Numerical Order Except at the Beginning *(C1, C4, C2, C3, etc.)*
- Usually "a" fragments go into plasma, "b" fragments attach to cell *(exception: C2a & C2b)*

ALTERNATIVE
- Factors
- Activated by Lipopolysaccharides, Polysaccharides
- Involves C3 at 2 Points in Cascade
- Involves Factors B & D

3. Cascades *(pathways)* - require calcium and magnesium
   a. Classical pathway
   b. Alternative pathway

4. Control proteins
   a. C1 esterase inhibitor
   b. C4 binding protein
   c. Factor I *(degrades C3b)*
   d. Factor H *(competes with Factor B)*

Characteristics of Hypersensitivity Reactions

TYPE	MECHANISM	EXAMPLES
Type I (anaphylactic, immediate)	IgE Mediated (antigen binds to IgE-sensitized Mast Cell ➤ Histamine Released)	Bee Sting Hay Fever Asthma
Type II (antibody dependent cytotoxicity)	Antibody Attaches to Cell Bearing Corresponding Antigen ➤ Cell Death	Transfusion Reaction AIHA (Autoimmune Hemolytic Anemia) Hashimoto Thyroiditis Goodpasture Disease
Type III (immune complex)	Formation of Large Immune Complexes Not Cleared by Mononuclear Phagocytic System	RA (Rheumatoid Arthritis) SLE (Sytemic Lupus Erythematosus) Serum Sickness
Type IV (delayed)	Sensitized T Cells Release IL; Monocyte and Lymphocyte Infiltration; > 12 hours to develop	Contact Dermititis (Poison Ivy, Chemicals) TB Leprosy GVHD (Graft vs. Host Disease)

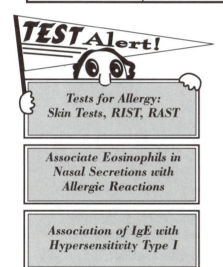

TEST Alert!

Tests for Allergy: Skin Tests, RIST, RAST

Associate Eosinophils in Nasal Secretions with Allergic Reactions

Association of IgE with Hypersensitivity Type I

Principles of Antigen-Antibody Reactions Used in Serologic Testing

PRECIPITATION

1. Principle
   a. Soluble antigen + antibody (in proper proportions) ➤ visible precipitate
   b. Lattice formation (antigen binds with Fab sites of two antibodies)

2. Examples
   a. Double diffusion (Ouchterlony)
   b. Single diffusion (radial immunodiffusion)
   c. Immunoelectrophoresis
   d. Immunofixation

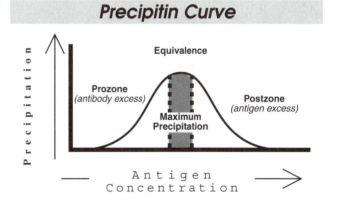

Precipitin Curve

REMEMBER!
Pros Have
Good Bodies

PRO

PROZONE = Anti*body* Excess

38

Definition of Prozone

AGGLUTINATION

1. Principle
   a. Particulate antigen + antibody ➤ clumping
   b. Lattice formation (*antigen binds with Fab sites of two antibodies forming bridges between antigens*)

2. Examples
   a. Direct agglutination (*Blood Bank*)
   b. Passive hemagglutination (*treat RBCs with tannic acid to allow adsorption of protein antigens*)
   c. Passive latex agglutination (*antigen attached to latex particle*)

INHIBITION OR NEUTRALIZATION REACTIONS

1. Similar in principle and interpretation of results

2. Antibody-binding
   a. Hemagglutination inhibition (*serum antibody reacts with known nonparticulate antigen ➤ binding occurs*)
   b. Neutralization (*antibody neutralizes toxin*)

3. After binding, antibody is not available to react in indicator system

4. Results:
   a. NO agglutination or NO hemolysis = positive reaction
   b. Agglutination or hemolysis = negative reaction (*antibody not bound in original reaction and is available to react with indicator cells*)

5. Generally, positive control samples used in inhibition or neutralization tests show no reaction and negative control samples show a reaction (*opposite of results in direct agglutination testing*)

6. Example of inhibition: hemagglutination inhibition test for rubella

7. Example of neutralization: antistreptolysin O test (*ASO*)

COMPLEMENT FIXATION (CF)

1. Antibody and antigen allowed to combine in presence of complement

2. If complement is fixed by specific antigen-antibody reaction, it will be unable to combine with indicator system

3. Precautions
   a. Serum *must* be heat inactivated
   b. Stored serum becomes anticomplementary
   c. Extensive QC/standardization required
   d. Only use for IgM antibodies

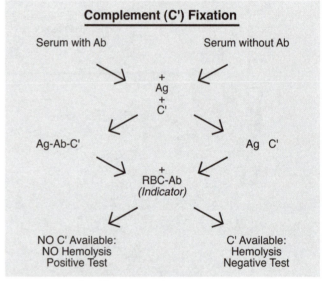

Complement (C') Fixation

Serum with Ab — Serum without Ab

+ Ag + C'

Ag-Ab-C' — Ag C'

+ RBC-Ab (Indicator)

NO C' Available: NO Hemolysis Positive Test — C' Available: Hemolysis Negative Test

RADIAL IMMUNODIFFUSION (RID), SINGLE IMMUNODIFFUSION

1. Principle: Unlimited antibody incorporated into agar + serum added to circular well in agar ➤ diffusion occurs

2. Methods
   a. Fahey (kinetic)
      ❖ *Read before ring reaches maximum size (6-12 hours)*
      ❖ *Logarithmic relationship between diameter of precipitin ring (d) and antigen concentration ➤ read from plotted standard curve*
   b. Mancini (end-point)
      ❖ *Read at maximum size (24-48 hours)*
      ❖ *Linear relationship between area of precipitin ring (d^2) and antigen concentration ➤ read from plotted standard curve*

DOUBLE DIFFUSION (OUCHTERLONY)

1. Used to determine relationships between antigens and antibodies

2. Place antigens and antibodies in adjacent wells cut in agar, diffusion results in visible precipitate, examine bands formed and read in relation to standard in adjacent well

3. Location of bands depends on concentration and rate of diffusion

4. Used to identify antibodies associated with autoimmune disorders

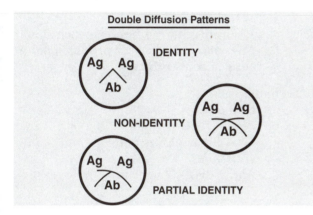

Double Diffusion Patterns

IMMUNOELECTROPHORESIS (IEP)

1. Gel diffusion + electrophoresis

2. Electrophorese serum proteins, fill trough in agar with antibody

3. Antigen and antibody diffuse through agar
   a. In equivalence zone, precipitation arc appears
   b. Size of arc determined by antigen concentration
   c. Abnormal contour of arc may indicate monoclonal gammopathy

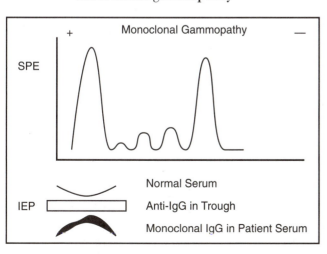

Monoclonal Gammopathy

Normal Serum
Anti-IgG in Trough
Monoclonal IgG in Patient Serum

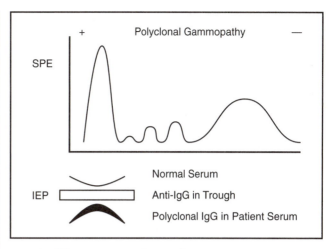

Polyclonal Gammopathy

Normal Serum
Anti-IgG in Trough
Polyclonal IgG in Patient Serum

4. Most commonly used
   a. Serum IEP: monoclonal gammopathies
   b. Urine IEP: Bence Jones protein

IMMUNOFIXATION

1. Protein electrophoresis + immunoprecipitation

2. Procedure
   a. Apply specimen to 6 positions on agarose plate
   b. Electrophorese to separate proteins
   c. Apply monospecific antisera to 5 patterns using the 6th for reference
   d. If antigen present, antigen-antibody complexes form and precipitate; wash, stain

3. Highly sensitive method, easy to read

4. Used to classify monoclonal gammopathies *(determine heavy and light chains involved)*

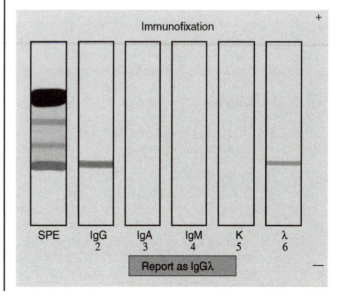

Immunofixation

SPE | IgG 2 | IgA 3 | IgM 4 | K 5 | λ 6

Report as IgGλ

ROCKET IMMUNOELECTROPHORESIS (LAURELL)

1. Similar to RID but electrophoresis used to speed formation of precipitate

2. Procedure
   a. Gel contains antibody
   b. Add antigen to well cut in gel
   c. Add standards to other wells
   d. Apply electric current to rapidly migrate antigen through gel
   e. A cone-shaped area of precipitation forms *(looks like a rocket)*
   f. Measure height of rocket and compare to standard curve

COUNTERCURRENT IMMUNOELECTROPHORESIS

1. Procedure
   a. Two rows of wells are cut in gel
   b. Add antigen to well in one row; add antibody to corresponding well in other row
   c. Apply electric current to gel
   d. Antigen and antibody migrate toward each other
   e. Precipitate forms if specific antigen for the antibody in the corresponding well is present in patient's serum

RADIOIMMUNOASSAY (RIA)

1. Very sensitive and specific

2. Can be used for detecting antigen or antibody *(explanation below detects antigen, but using known antigen to detect serum antibody is also possible)*

3. Competitive binding assay
   a. Patient antigen and labeled antigen are incubated with known amount of specific antibody *(unlabeled and labeled antigen compete for binding with antibody)*
   b. Wash to remove unbound antigen
   c. Radioactivity counted on a gamma counter; compare to standard curve
   d. Results
      ❖ *The lower the radioactive count, the higher the concentration of unlabeled antigen*

4. Examples
   a. Tests for hepatitis antigens and antibodies
   b. Radioimmunosorbent Test (RIST) - measures total IgE concentration
   c. Radioallergosorbent Test (RAST) - measures IgE to specific allergens

ENZYME IMMUNOASSAY (EIA/ELISA)

1. "Sandwich technique"
   a. Monoclonal or polyclonal antibody adsorbed on solid surface *(bead or microtiter plate)*
   b. Add patient serum; if antigen is present in serum, it binds to antibody coated bead or plate
   c. Add excess labeled antibody *(antibody conjugate)*; forms antigen-antibody-labeled antibody "sandwich" *(antibody in conjugate is directed against another epitope of antigen being tested)*
   d. Add substrate, incubate and read absorbance
   e. Washing required between each step
   f. Absorbance is directly proportional to antigen concentration

2. Examples:
   a. HIV testing
   b. Serum HCG *(pregnancy)*
   c. Tests for hepatitis antigens and antibodies
   d. Antibodies to bacteria

TEST Alert!

Properties of Conjugates Used in ELISA Procedures

ENZYME MULTIPLIED IMMUNOASSAY (EMIT)

1. Used to measure concentrations of small molecules such as drugs and hormones

2. Principle
   a. Add patient serum to an enzyme-drug conjugate; also add anti-drug antibody
   b. Add enzyme substrate and incubate
   c. Positive test
      ❖ *Color formation*
      ❖ *Drug in patient serum combined with anti-drug antibody; sites on the enzyme portion of the conjugate remain available to bind with substrate*
      ❖ *Color produced*
   c. Negative test
      ❖ *No color formation*
      ❖ *Anti-drug antibody attached to the drug in the enzyme-drug conjugate and blocks the active*

sites on the enzyme; substrate unable to bind to enzyme
- ❖ *No color produced*

NEPHELOMETRY

1. Procedure
   a. Serum substance reacts with specific antisera and forms insoluble complexes
   b. Light is passed through suspension
   c. Scattered *(reflected)* light is proportional to number of insoluble complexes; compare to standards

2. Examples:
   a. Complement component concentration
   b. Antibody concentration *(IgG, IgM, IgA, etc.)*

IMMUNOFLUORESCENCE

1. Direct — Add fluorescein-labeled antibody to patient tissue, wash & examine under fluorescent microscope

2. Indirect — Add patient serum to tissue containing known antigen, wash, add labeled antiglobulin, wash & examine under fluorescent microscope

3. Example
   a. Testing for Antinuclear Antibodies *(ANA)*
   b. Fluorescent Treponemal Antibody Test *(FTA-Abs)*

FLUORESCENCE POLARIZATION IMMUNOASSAY (FPIA)

1. Principle
   a. Add reagent antibody and fluorescent-tagged antigen to patient serum
   b. Positive test
      - ❖ *Antigen present in patient serum binds to reagent leaving most tagged antigen unbound*
      - ❖ *Unbound labeled antigens rotate quickly reducing amount of polarized light produced*
   b. Negative test
      - ❖ *If no antigen present in patient serum, tagged antigen binds to reagent antibody*
      - ❖ *Tagged antigen-antibody complexes rotate slowly giving off increased polarized light*

FLOW CYTOMETRY

1. Method of choice for T- and B-cell analysis *(lymphocyte phenotyping)*

2. Principle
   a. Incubate specimen with one or two monoclonal antibodies tagged with fluorochrome
   b. Single cells pass through incident light of instrument *(laser)* which excites fluorochrome and results in emitted light of different wavelength
   c. Intensity of fluorescence measured to detect cells possessing surface markers for the specific monoclonal antibodies that were employed
   d. Forward light scatter indicates cell size or volume
   e. 90° side-scattered light indicates granularity

3. Common Uses — DNA analysis, reticulocyte counts, leukemia/lymphoma classification

Principles of Antigen-Antibody Reactions Used in Serology

SERIAL DILUTIONS

1. Testing for infectious diseases is performed on acute and convalescent specimens *(about 2 weeks apart)*

2. Must see 4-fold or 2 tube rise in titer to be clinically significant

Serial Dilution Calculations

Compare Pre & Post Titers to Determine Diagnosis of Measles and Rubella

TERMS USED IN EVALUATING TEST METHODOLOGY

1. Sensitivity
   a. Analytical Sensitivity — Ability of a test to detect very small amounts of a substance
   b. Clinical Sensitivity — Ability of test to give positive result if patient has the disease (*no false negative results*)

2. Specificity
   a. Analytical Specificity — Ability of test to detect substance without interference from cross-reacting substances
   b. Clinical Specificity — Ability of test to give negative result if patient does not have disease (*no false positives*)

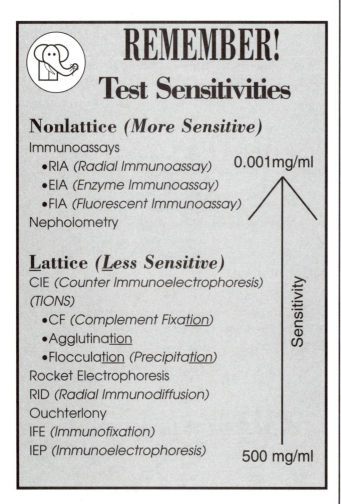

REMEMBER!
Test Sensitivities

Nonlattice (*More Sensitive*)
Immunoassays
- RIA (*Radial Immunoassay*)
- EIA (*Enzyme Immunoassay*)
- FIA (*Fluorescent Immunoassay*)
Nepholometry

0.001mg/ml

Lattice (*Less Sensitive*)
CIE (*Counter Immunoelectrophoresis*)
(TIONS)
- CF (*Complement Fixation*)
- Agglutination
- Flocculation (*Precipitation*)
Rocket Electrophoresis
RID (*Radial Immunodiffusion*)
Ouchterlony
IFE (*Immunofixation*)
IEP (*Immunoelectrophoresis*)

500 mg/ml

Sensitivity

Relative Sensitivities of Serologic Methods

Specific Disease States and Associated Laboratory Tests

SYPHILIS
1. Caused by *Treponema pallidum*
2. Course of disease: Primary, secondary, latent, tertiary; also congenital infections

TREPONEMAL TESTS
1. Darkfield microscopy - used to visualize motile organisms from primary & secondary lesions
2. Fluorescent treponemal antibody absorption test (*FTA-Abs*)
   a. Indirect immunofluorescence assay
   b. Remove nonspecific antibodies from serum by using sorbent
   c. React serum with Nichol's strain of *T. pallidum*
   d. Add fluorescein-labeled antihuman globulin and wash
   e. Read for fluorescence
3. *Treponema pallidum* Immobilization Test (*TPI*)
   a. Patient serum + live treponemes
   b. If antibody present, treponemes immobilized
   c. View using darkfield microscopy
   d. Expensive, seldom used
4. Microhemagglutination Assay for *T. pallidum* (*MHA-TP*)
   a. Patient serum + red cells sensitized with *T. pallidum*
   b. If antibody is present, agglutination occurs

NONTREPONEMAL TESTS (REAGIN TESTS)
1. Venereal Disease Research Laboratory (*VDRL*)
   a. Microflocculation (*microscopic*)
   b. Antigen = cardiolipin + lecithin
   c. Antibody (*reagin*) = IgM or IgG directed against damaged tissue or organism
   d. Serum requires heat inactivation
   e. Flocculation indicates reactive serum
   f. Test of choice for screening CSF
   g. False positives in malaria (*100% b.f.p.*), SLE, RA, hepatitis, pneumonia, aging and infectious mononucleosis
2. Rapid Plasma Reagin Test (*RPR*)
   a. Microflocculation and coagglutination of charcoal particles (*macroscopic*)

b. More sensitive, less specific than VDRL
c. Antigen = cardiolipin + charcoal particles
d. No heat inactivation necessary
e. Black clumps form in reactive test
f. False positives — same as VDRL

Sensitivity of Tests for Syphilis

PRIMARY STAGE

FTA-ABS
RPR
VDRL
} ↑ Sensitivity

SECONDARY STAGE
All Tests Equally Sensitive

LATE STAGE

FTA-ABS
MHA-TP
TPI
} Equal Sensitivity

Reagin Tests   Poor Sensitivity

FTA-ABS: *Most Sensitive in All Stages*

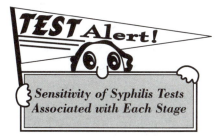

Sensitivity of Syphilis Tests Associated with Each Stage

RHEUMATOID ARTHRITIS (RA)

1. Production of IgM or IgG antibodies directed against IgG

2. Diagnosis requires radiologic and clinical findings

3. Affects joints & periarticular tissues

4. Laboratory findings
   a. High titers of rheumatoid factor (RF)
   b. Low titers of complement

5. RF titer does not correlate with intensity of disease

6. Lab test: particulate carrier *(latex or RBC)* attached to IgG; tests for serum IgM; read visible agglutination; run positive and negative controls

COLD AGGLUTININ DISEASE (CAD)

1. Characteristics
   a. Antibody agglutinates below 25C (best at 0 - 5C)
   b. IgM antibodies (beta or gamma-globulin); usually anti-I or anti-i
   c. Marked rise indicates *Mycoplasma pneumoniae* (atypical pneumonia)
   d. Lower titer elevations: influenzas or adenoviruses

2. Principle
   a. Add dilutions of patient serum to Group O RBCs
   b. Refrigerate for several hours
   c. Read for agglutination

REMEMBER!

Do NOT Refrigerate Specimen for Cold Agglutinin Assay

Antibody will bind to red cells leaving serum free of antibodies and result in a false negative or decreased cold agglutinin titer.

Blood Group Specificity of Cold Agglutinins

INFECTIOUS MONONUCLEOSIS (I.M.)

1. Causative agent: Epstein-Barr Virus *(EBV)*

2. Test for heterophile antibodies *(Rapid Differential Slide Test*
   a. Step I: Using two serum aliquots, absorb one with guinea pig or horse kidney cells and the other with beef erythrocytes
   b. Step II: React each aliquot with sheep or horse RBCs *(indicator)*
   c. Interpretation: Greater agglutination in kidney absorbed serum than in beef RBC absorbed serum ➤ positive for I.M.
   d. No heat inactivation required
   e. Run positive and negative controls
   f. Single titer not related to intensity of disease; but change in titer may be

44

used to monitor course of disease
   g. False positives: leukemia, CMV, Burkitt lymphoma, RA, viral hepatitis

3. EBV specific tests
   a. Immunofluorescent tests for IgM and IgG anti-viral capsid antigen *(VCA)*, anti-early antigen *(EA)*, and anti-nuclear antigen *(EBNA)*
   b. Appearance and duration of EBV specific antibodies differentiates acute from past infection
   c. IgG or IgM anti-VCA in absence of anti-EBNA indicates infectious mononucleosis

EBV Antibodies

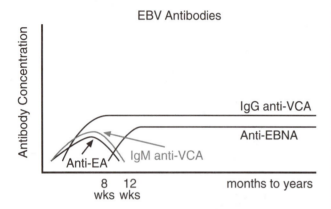

EBV Antibodies

EBV Specific Serology

METHOD: Immunofluorescence

RECENT OR CURRENT INFECTION
IgM Anti-VCA
Anti-EA
IgG Anti-VCA *without* Anti-EBNA

PAST INFECTION
Anti-EBNA
IgG Anti-VCA *without* IgM Anti-VCA

ANTISTREPTOLYSIN O (ASO)

1. Streptolysin O: hemolysin produced by Lancefield group A Streptococci

2. Procedure
   a. Dilute serum with buffer according to protocol
   b. Add antigen *(streptolysin O)*
   c. Incubate
   d. Add Group O red cells

   e. Incubate
   f. Read Todd units *(reciprocal of highest dilution showing no hemolysis)*
   f. Results
     ❖ *RBC control: RBC + buffer ➤ no hemolysis*
     ❖ *Streptolysin (SLO) control: SLO + buffer + RBC ➤ hemolysis*
     ❖ *If antibody is NOT present, streptolysin is not neutralized and will lyse red cells*
   g. Normal: < 166 Todd units
   h. High titers associated with streptococcal infections, active rheumatic fever, acute glomerulitis

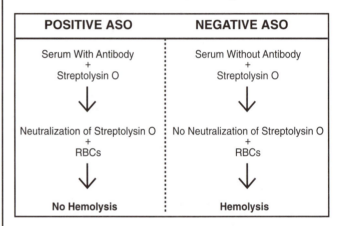

POSITIVE ASO	NEGATIVE ASO
Serum With Antibody + Streptolysin O	Serum Without Antibody + Streptolysin O
↓	↓
Neutralization of Streptolysin O + RBCs	No Neutralization of Streptolysin O + RBCs
↓	↓
No Hemolysis	**Hemolysis**

Evaluate ASO Controls to Determine Test Validity

ANTI DNASE-B TEST

1. Highly specific neutralization test for anti-DNase produced in group A *Streptococcus* infection

2. Better than ASO test for cases of glomerulonephritis *(anti-streptolysin O is often not produced in glomerulonephritis)*

3. Principle — DNase B reagent hydrolyzes DNA-methyl green conjugate reagent changing the color from green to colorless

4. Procedure
   a. Add patient serum to DNase B reagent and incubate
   b. DNA-methyl green conjugate added
   c. If anti-DNase B is present in the patient's serum, DNase B reagent is

neutralized and unable to decolorize the conjugate; green color persists and is graded from 2+ to 4+

STREPTOZYME

1. Slide agglutination test used to screen for antibodies to 5 streptococcal antigens *(streptolysin, streptokinase, DNase, NADase, and hyaluronidase)*

2. Procedure
   a. Reagent = Sheep red blood cells (SRBC) coated with the 5 streptococcal antigens
   b. Dilute patient serum and add to SRBC reagent
   c. If antibodies to any of these antigens are present, hemagglutination occurs

ANTINUCLEAR ANTIBODIES (ANA)

1. Present in autoimmune disorders and collagen diseases *(SLE, RA, scleroderma, Sjogren's syndrome)*, infectious diseases *(hepatitis)* and aging

2. Lab tests
   a. Indirect immunofluorescence (IIF)
      ❖ *Patient serum binds with tissue nuclei (human epithelial cells - HEp2 cells); wash, add fluorescent-labeled anti-human immunoglobulin; wash and read*
   b. Confirm by assaying for specific antibody *(anti-Sm, anti-ds DNA, anti- Scl-70, etc.)* using indirect immunofluorescence *(IIF)*, radial immunodiffusion *(RID)*, or double diffusion

Antinuclear Antibodies

ANA PATTERN	ANTIBODY	DISEASE
Homogeneous *(diffuse)*	Anti-histone	usually SLE
Peripheral (Rim)	Anti-ds DNA (double-stranded DNA)	SLE
Speckled	Anti-RNA Anti-ENA (extractable nuclear antigens)	SLE Scleroderma RA MCTD
Nucleolar	Anti-nucleolar RNA	Scleroderma Sjogren's

Testing for Antinuclear Antibodies

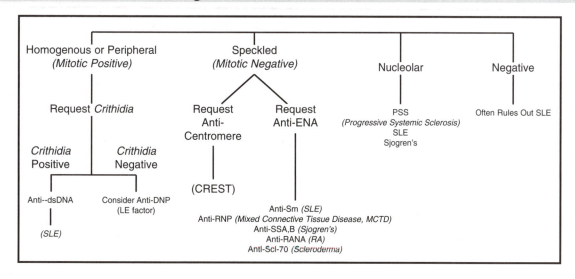

46

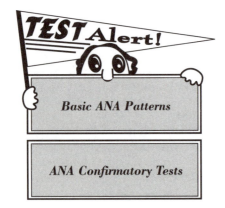

Basic ANA Patterns

ANA Confirmatory Tests

ACQUIRED IMMUNODEFICIENCY (AIDS)

1. HIV-1 retrovirus attacks CD4+ cells *(T helper)*

2. Clinical manifestations may include pneumococcus pneumonia, Kaposi sarcoma, recurrent infections

3. Lab tests
   a. Screen using ELISA procedure for HIV-1 antibody
   b. Confirm using Western Blot *(positive if bands for p24, gp41 and gp120 or gp160 are present)*
   c. T helper/T suppressor ratio is decreased

HUMAN T-LYMPHOTROPHIC VIRUS I (HTLV-1)

1. Retrovirus that infects T helper cells

2. Has little sequence homology with HIV

3. Usually asymptomatic

4. Rarely causes a form of T cell leukemia or tropical spastic paraparesis

5. Transmitted through contact with blood or blood products

6. Testing
   a. Routine ELISA
   b. Confirm with Western Blot

CYTOMEGALOVIRUS (CMV)

1. Asymptomatic infection

2. Very high incidence in humans

3. Causes Problems
   a. For immunocompromised patients
   b. In transfusions in infants

4. Presence of antibody does not prevent reinfection

5. Test by ELISA

VIRAL HEPATITIS

1. Inflammatory disease of the liver

2. Associated with increase in liver enzymes *(AST, ALT, GGT)*

3. Diagnosis depends on appearance of specific antigens and antibodies in serum

Serodiagnosis of Acute Hepatitis

HBsAg	HBeAg	Anti-HBe	Anti-HBc (IgM)	Anti-HBc	Anti-HBs	Anti-HAV (IgM)	Anti-HCV	Interpretation
−	−	−	−	−	−	+	−	Recent Acute Hepatitis A Infection
+	+	−	+ / −	+ / −	−	−	−	Acute Hepatitis B Infection *(highly infectious)*
+	+	+ / −	+ / −	+	−	−	−	Chronic Hepatitis B / Carrier State
−	−	+	−	+	+	−	−	Immunity to Hepatitis B Due to Past Infection
−	−	−	−	−	+	−	−	Immunity to Hepatitis B Due to Vaccination
−	−	−	−	−	−	−	+	Hepatitis C Infection

• *Adapted with Permission from Hepatitis Learning Guide, Abbott Diag., 1985*

REMEMBER!

Hepatitis *(Hepatitis B Antigens & Antibodies)*

Hep will help you remember the order of *Hepatitis B* antigens & antibodies!
Picture Hep with a shovel trying to dig to the center of the earth.

1) First, Hep starts at the surface (HBsAg)

2) Next, he goes through the earth (HBeAg)

3) Finally he reaches the core (Anti-HBc)

4) As Hep backs out he fills the hole with earth (Anti-HBe)

5) . . . and, finally reaches the surface (Anti-HBs)

Antibody Response in Hepatitis B

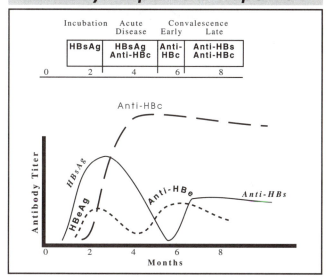

	Incubation	Acute Disease	Convalescence Early	Late
	HBsAg	HBsAg Anti-HBc	Anti-HBc	Anti-HBs Anti-HBc
0	2	4	6	8

Anti-HBc

HBsAg

HBeAg

Anti-HBe

Anti-HBs

Antibody Titer

Months

• *Adapted with Permission from Hepatitis Learning Guide, Abbott Diag., 1985*

Order of Hepatitis B Antigens and Antibodies

AUTOIMMUNE DISEASES

MULTIPLE SCLEROSIS (MS)

1. Autoantibodies to myelin sheath of nerves or myelin basic protein

2. Laboratory findings
   a. Oligoclonal IgG bands in CSF
   b. Helpful in diagnosis of MS - oligoclonal bands found in CSF but not in serum *(indicates CNS production)*

Disease Associated with Oligoclonal IgG Bands in Spinal Fluid

Antibodies Associated with Autoimmune Diseases

Specificity of Autoantibodies

DISEASE	AUTOANTIBODY DIRECTED AGAINST:
Graves Disease	Receptors for Thyroid Stimulating Hormone (TSH)
Goodpasture Disease	Basement Membrane (kidney, lungs)
Hashimoto Thyroiditis	Thyroglobulin
Multiple Sclerosis	Myelin Sheath of Nerves or Myelin Basic Protein
Myasthenia Gravis	Acetylcholine Receptors at Neuromuscular Junctions
Rheumatoid Arthritis	IgG (Fc) —19s anti-IgM autoantibody known as Rheumatoid Factor
Sjogren Syndrome	Salivary Duct / Tear Duct

Impaired Immune Function

DISEASE	DYSFUNCTION
Chronic Granulomatous Disease	Ineffective Phagocytosis
Chediak-Higashi Syndrome	Impaired Neutrophil Function
DiGeorge Syndrome	T Cell Deficiency *(Absence of Thymus)*
Human Immunodeficiency Virus *(HIV)*	↓ T-Helper Cell ↓Th/Ts Ratio ↓ T Cell Proliferation
Wiskott-Aldrich Syndrome	Partial Combined Immunodeficiency
Severe Combined Immunodeficiency Disease (SCID)	Complete or Marked Deficiency of T and B Lymphocytes

CANCER

TUMOR MARKERS

1. Substances synthesized and released by a tumor or produced by host in response to a tumor

2. Found in circulation, body cavity fluids, cell membranes or cytoplasm/nucleus of a cell

3. Absent or only trace amounts in normal population

4. Used in diagnosing, determining disease progression, monitoring response to therapy, and detecting recurrence

5. Testing commonly performed by EIA

Tumor Markers

TUMOR MARKER	ASSOCIATED DISEASE
Alpha-fetoprotein (AFP)	cancer of liver, ovary, testes (teratoblastoma)
Carcinoembryonic antigen (CEA)	cancer of colon, breast, lung
CA 15-3, BR 27.29	cancer of breast
CA 125	cancer of ovary
CA 19-9	cancer of pancreas
Estrogen/Progesterone receptors	cancer of breast
Immunoglobulins (M protein; paraprotein)	multiple myeloma Waldenstrom's macroglobulinemia
Prostate specific antigen (PSA)	cancer of prostate

IMMUNOLOGY PRACTICE QUESTIONS

1. A specimen is tested for antibodies to varicella resulting in a titer of 320. Two weeks later another specimen is drawn from the patient and the resulting titer is 640. A third test is done on a specimen drawn 4 weeks after the first specimen and the titer is 320. What is the disease status of the patient?

   A. Antibody levels are increased but titers indicate a past infection with chicken pox.
   B. Antibody levels are within normal reference limits.
   C. Elevated antibody levels indicate a current chicken pox infection.
   D. The second titer indicates a current infection with chicken pox.

2. A patient suspected of having cold agglutinin disease is tested and results indicate normal levels of cold agglutinins. The physician questions the result and the patient is retested the following day. The second test result is elevated for cold agglutinins. What is the most likely cause of the discrepancy in the two results?

   A. Patient was cold when the specimen 1 was drawn.
   B. Patient was overheated when specimen 1 was drawn.
   C. In specimen 1, serum was separated from the red cells and refrigerated before assay was performed.
   D. Specimen 1 was refrigerated before centrifugation and assay.

3. A patient is immunized for rubella. What type of immunity does this patient have?
   A. active
   B. passive
   C. adoptive
   D. natural

4. An immunofluorescence procedure is performed to test for specific antibodies to Epstein Barr Virus. The following antibodies were found:

   anti-VCA
   anti-EA
   anti-EBNA

How would these results be interpreted?
   A. Early infection
   B. Recent infection
   C. Current infection
   D. Past infection

5. ANA fluorescent techniques were performed and a speckled pattern occurred. The serum is then run on two-fold dilutions resulting in a titer of 320. What would you do next?
   A. Repeat the procedure.
   B. Test for extractable nuclear antibodies.
   C. Look for fluorescent mitotic cells.
   D. Test for DNA (*crithidia luciliae substrate*).

6. Multiple, homogeneous, narrow bands are seen in the gamma zone on electrophoresis of CSF on agarous gel. Immunofixation indicates that the bands are primarily IgG. This may indicate which of the following diseases:
   A. Addison's disease
   B. Myasthenia gravis
   C. Multiple sclerosis
   D. Multiple myeloma

7. Assess the disease state of the patient with the following results:

HBsAg	positive
HBeAg	positive
anti-HBc	positive
anti-HBe	negative
anti-HBsAg	negative

   A. Incubation period for Hepatitis B infection
   B. Very early infection with Hepatitis B
   C. Highly infectious stage of Hepatitis B infection
   D. Immunity to Hepatitis B

8. After exposure to measles, a patient is tested and has a 1:20 titer. This indicates:
   A. Current infection
   B. Immunity
   C. Immunization
   D. Test should be repeated in a few weeks

9. Given the following results for an ASO procedure, how would the patient result be reported?

Todd Units	12	50	100	125	166	250	333	500	625	833	1250	2500	RBC cont	SLO cont
Hemolysis	-	-	-	-	-	+	+	+	+	+	+	+	+	+

 A. Patient value is reported as 166 Todd units
 B. Patient value is reported as 250 Todd units
 C. Patient test should be repeated due to erroneous RBC control
 D. Patient test should be repeated due to erroneous SLO control

10. The best method for screening cerebrospinal fluid for syphilis is:
 a. VDRL
 b. RPR
 c. FTA-abs
 d. darkfield microscopy

11. A patient has a T helper:T suppressor ratio of 1:2. What disease state might you expect?
 a. infectious mononucleosis
 b. rheumatoid arthritis
 c. AIDS
 d. systemic lupus erythematosus

12. Multiple myeloma most commonly involves the following class of immunoglobulin:
 a. IgA
 b. IgD
 c. IgG
 d. IgM

13. To test for antibodies to specific allergens, the following procedure would be performed:
 a. RPR
 b. CRP
 c. RIST
 d. RAST
 e. VDRL

14. A patient suspected of having syphilis had various tests performed with the following results:
 Rapid plasma reagin (RPR) — reactive
 FTA-ABS — nonreactive
 VDRL (CSF) — nonreactive

These test results best reflect which of the following?
 a. neurosyphilis
 b. biologic false positive
 c. primary stage syphilis
 d. secondary stage syphilis
 e. tertiary stage syphilis

ANSWERS AND RATIONALE

1. A

To properly assess an infection as current, there must be a 4-fold rise in the antibody titer. If the first titer was 320, subsequent tests should give a titer of at least 1280 if infection is present.

2. D

Specimen handling is most often the cause of false negative results in testing for cold agglutinins. If the blood is refrigerated before separation of serum from erythrocytes, the cold agglutinins attach to the red blood cells. When the serum is tested, there are no antibodies left in the serum and the test will give low titers (false negative results). If the specimen is warmed before the serum is separated from the cells, the cold agglutinins will dissociate from the red cells and the results will not be affected.

3. A

Active immunity occurs after patient is presented with an antigen (*infectious organism or immunization*) and the patient produces antibodies.

Option B is incorrect since passive immunity occurs when antibody is produced by another person or animal and the antibodies are transferred to the patient giving the patient temporary immunity. (*The patient does not produce the antibodies.*) Option C occurs when adoptive immunity occurs when immunocompetent cells are transferred to the patient. Option D refers to the nonspecific mechanisms involved in fighting infection. It does not result in antibody formation.

4. D

The presence of antibody to Epstein Barr Virus nuclear antigen indicates a past infection. Anti-VCA is probably IgG rather than IgM.

5. B

Speckled patterns are confirmed using double immunodiffusion, radial immunodiffusion, indirect immunofluorescence or enzyme immunoassay to test for specific saline extractable nuclear antigens (*anti-Sm, anti-ds DNA, anti-Scl-70, etc.*) Option A is incorrect because the test has already been repeated with 2-fold dilutions. Option C is incorrect since mitotic cells are not seen in speckled patterns. Option D is incorrect because Crithidia substrate is used to confirm a homogeneous pattern.

6. C

In multiple sclerosis, IgG oligoclonal bands are often seen in CSF. Option A is incorrect because 40 - 70% of patients manifest antibodies against elements of the adrenal cortex and adrenal cell surfaces. Option B is incorrect since patients with myasthenia gravis demonstrate acetylcholine receptor blocking antibodies. *(IgG, C3 and C9 can be demonstrated at the neuro-muscular junction.)* Option D is incorrect because multiple myeloma *(plasma cell myeloma)* is characterized by neoplastic proliferation of a single clone *(monoclonal)* of plasma cells that produce a specific type of immunoglobulin *(usually IgG)*.

7. C

When HBeAg is present, the patient is considered highly infectious.

8. D

The patient's titer is not definitive. He/she could have antibodies from a past infection or from immunization. To determine if the infection is current, the test should be repeated in a few weeks with the results demonstrating a titer of at least 80 (4-fold increase).

9. C

The test is invalid because there is hemolysis in the RBC control. The purpose of the RBC control is to assure that the red cells are not hemolyzing in the presence of the buffer *(neither serum nor streptolysin has been added to this tube)*.

10. A

VDRL is the test of choice for testing CSF.

11. C

Due to reduced numbers of T cells in acquired immunodeficiency disease, there is a decrease in the T helper / T suppressor ratio.

12. C

Proliferation of a monoclonal antibody in multiple myeloma is usually of the IgG class.

13. D

Radioallergosorbent testing (RAST) is used to measure IgE antibodies to specific allergens.

14. B

FTA-ABS *(fluorescent treponemal antibody absorption)* is used to confirm positive screening tests (RPR, VDRL) for syphilis. Many diseases other than syphilis such as SLE, infectious mononucleosis, hepatitis, and malaria give false positive results for screening tests. Since the FTA-ABS is negative, this is probably a biologic false positive.

HEMATOLOGY

by Angela B. Foley

Hematopoiesis

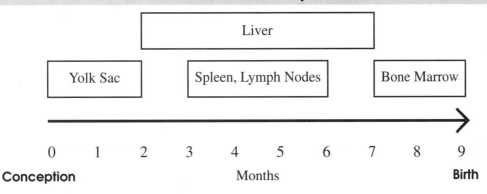

Prenatal Hematopoiesis

Liver

Yolk Sac

Spleen, Lymph Nodes

Bone Marrow

0 1 2 3 4 5 6 7 8 9

Conception

Months

Birth

Adult Hematopoiesis

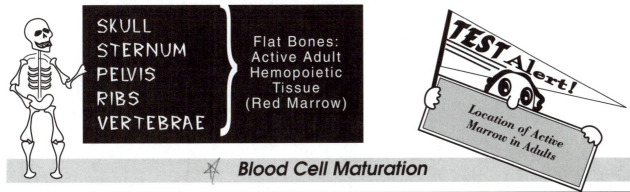

SKULL
STERNUM
PELVIS
RIBS
VERTEBRAE

Flat Bones:
Active Adult
Hemopoietic
Tissue
(Red Marrow)

TEST Alert!

Location of Active Marrow in Adults

Blood Cell Maturation

MULTIPOTENT STEM CELL					
	CFU - GEMM				LSC
COMMITTED PROGENITORS	CFU-E	CFU-GM [EO, BASO]		CFU-MEG	CFU-L
GROWTH FACTORS	GM-CSF, IL-3, EPO	GM-CSF, IL-3		GM-CSF, IL-3, TPO	IL-1,2,4,6,7
	Rubriblast ↓	Myeloblast ↓	Monoblast	Megakaryoblast ↓	Lymphoblast ↓
	Prorubricyte ↓	Promyelocyte ↓	Promonocyte	Promegakaryocyte	Prolymphocyte
	Rubricyte ↓	Myelocyte ↓			
	Metarubricyte ↓	Metamyelocyte ↓		Megakaryocyte	
	Reticulocyte ↓	Band Neutrophil ↓			
Peripheral Blood					
Peripheral Blood	Erythrocyte	Segmented Neutrophil	Monocyte	Platelet *(thrombocyte)*	Lymphocyte
		Basophil Eosinophil	Macrophage *(tissue)*		T Cell B Cell ↓ Plasma Cell

EPO = Erythropoietin
CSF = Colony Stimulating Factor
TPO = Thrombopoietin
GEMM = Granulocyte, Erythrocyte, Megakaryocyte, Monocyte
LSC = Lymphoid Stem Cell
IL = Interleukin

GM = Granulocyte, monocyte
CFU = Colony Forming Unit
Meg = Megakaryocyte
L = Lymphocyte

54

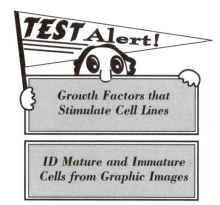
Hemoglobin

HEME SYNTHESIS

1. Must have iron and protoporphyrin

2. Iron storage and transport
   a. Excess iron will be stored in tissues and body organs → hemosiderosis, hemochromatosis (organ damage)
   b. Transferrin - Fe transport protein
   c. Ferritin - major Fe storage form
   d. Hemosiderin - H2O insoluble Fe storage form (long-term)

3. Protoporphyrin Synthesis
   a. Precursors *(see memory tool below)*
   b. Porphyrias - Enzyme deficiencies cause build-up of heme precursors – red or port wine colored urine
      ❖ *Early precursors (DELTA ala or PORphobilinogen) – neuropsychiatric symptoms, i.e. acute intermittent porphyria or AIP*
      ❖ *Later precursors (UR, COP, PROTO) – cutaneous sysmptoms such as photosensitivity, facial hair (werewolf legend)*

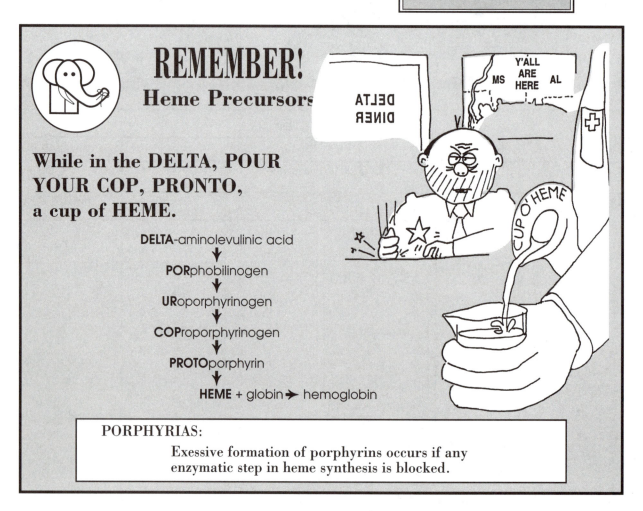

REMEMBER!
Heme Precursors

While in the DELTA, POUR YOUR COP, PRONTO, a cup of HEME.

DELTA-aminolevulinic acid
↓
PORphobilinogen
↓
URoporphyrinogen
↓
COProporphyrinogen
↓
PROTOporphyrin
↓
HEME + globin → hemoglobin

PORPHYRIAS:

Exessive formation of porphyrins occurs if any enzymatic step in heme synthesis is blocked.

TEST Alert!

Sequence of
Heme Precursors

GLOBIN SYNTHESIS

HEMOGLOBIN TYPES IN NEWBORN AND ADULT

CHROMOSOME		GLOBIN CHAINS	HGB	NEWBORN %	ADULT %
16	11	$\zeta_2 \varepsilon_2$	Gower I	0% (Embryonic)	0% (Embryonic)
	ε	$\alpha_2 \varepsilon_2$	Gower II		
ζ	γ	$\zeta_2 \gamma_2$	Portland		
		$\alpha_2 \gamma_2$	Hgb F	60-90%	1%
α	δ	$\alpha_2 \delta_2$	Hgb A_2	<2%	2%
	β	$\alpha_2 \beta_2$	Hgb A	10-40%	97%

HEMOGLOBIN-OXYGEN DISSOCIATION CURVE

1. Shift to left - O_2 NOT released to tissue adequately

2. Shift to right - O_2 released to tissue more easily

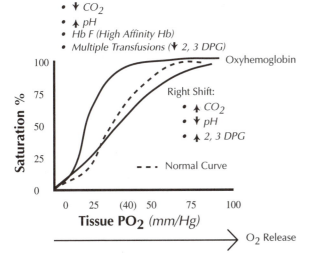

Left Shift:
- $\downarrow CO_2$
- $\uparrow pH$
- Hb F (High Affinity Hb)
- Multiple Transfusions ($\downarrow$ 2, 3 DPG)

Right Shift:
- $\uparrow CO_2$
- $\downarrow pH$
- $\uparrow$ 2, 3 DPG

- - - Normal Curve

Oxyhemoglobin

Saturation %

Tissue PO_2 (mm/Hg)

O_2 Release

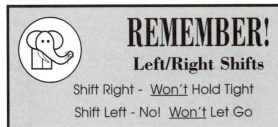

REMEMBER!

Left/Right Shifts

Shift Right - Won't Hold Tight

Shift Left - No! Won't Let Go

TEST Alert!

Conditions Causing
Left/Right Shifts

Normal Fetal and Adult
Hemoglobin Chains

Basic Laboratory Procedures

ANTICOAGULANTS

1. EDTA (ethylenediamine-tetra-acetate) - chelates Ca^{++} so it is unavailable to participate in the coagulation cascade

2. Heparin - anti-thrombin agent

HEMOGLOBIN

1. Principle - conversion of hemoglobin to cyanmethemoglobin by potassium cyanide and potassium ferricyanide

2. Sources of error
   a. Lipemia
   b. High white count
   c. Extremely icteric sample

3. Diluent - Drabkin solution

4. Reference range - male: 16 ± 2 g/dl
   female: 14 ± 2 g/dl

HEMOGLOBIN VARIANTS

HEMOGLOBIN	COMMENTS
Methemoglobin	Fe^{2+} Oxidized to Fe^{3+}, Brown, Cannot Bind O_2
Carboxyhemoglobin	$\uparrow$ in Carbon Monoxide Poisoning & Smokers, Cherry-Red

HEMATOCRIT

1. Measures packed cell volume in percent

2. Manual technique
   a. Can use fingerstick, EDTA or heparinized sample
   b. Sources of error
      ❖ Failure to seal tube adequately with clay
      ❖ Incorrect reading due to uneven clay plug
      ❖ Inappropriate centrifuge time

3. Automated techniques (usually indirect) - calculated from MCV and RBC

4. Reference range - male: 45 ± 5%
   female: 42 ± 5%

56

TEST Alert!

> **Mechanism of Action of Anticoagulants**

> **Sources of Error in Hemoglobin and Hematocrit Testing**

MANUAL CELL COUNTS - UNOPETTE

1. WBC/Platelet Count
   a. Diluent - 1.98 ml of 1% Ammonium Oxalate
   b. 0.02 ml or 20µl pipet
   c. 1:100 dilution *(0.02 ml in 2.00 ml)*

2. Hemacytometer *(Neubauer)*

1mm 1mm 1mm

1mm

1mm

1mm

Depth of Chamber - 0.1mm

3. Calculations

Formula:

$$\text{\# cells counted} \times \frac{1}{\text{tot vol*}} \times \text{dilution factor}$$

* NOTE:
Volume (of 1 square) = length x width x depth
Total volume = volume x # of squares counted

   a. WBC count
      ❖ *Count all 9 squares*
      ❖ *Total volume counted = 1mm x 1mm x 0.1mm x 9 = 0.9mm³*
      ❖ *Reference range - 5,000 - 10,000/ul*
   b. Platelet count
      ❖ *Count all 25 squares in center large square*
      ❖ *Total volume counted = 1mm x 1mm x 0.1mm³ = 0.1mm³*
      ❖ *Reference range - 150,000 - 400,000/ul*

❖ **WBC example**
   WBC's counted = 60
   $60 \times \frac{1}{.9} \times 100 = 6,667/mm^3$ or µL

NOTE: *You can eliminate the 1/.9 (volume factor) by multiplying 10% of cells counted and adding this value to the number of cells counted.*
Example:
60 cells counted x 10% = 60 + 6 = 66
Now: 66 x 100 = 6,600/mm³ or µL

❖ **Platelet example**
   Platelets counted = 150
   $150 \times \frac{1}{.1} \times 100 = 150,000/mm^3$ or µL

NOTE: *Multiply number of platelets counted by 1000.*

Red Cell Indices

INDICES	FORMULA	REF. RANGE	- - - - - - - - INDICATION - - - - - - -	
MCV	$\frac{HCT}{RBC} \times 10$	80-100fl (µ³)	<80 >100	Microcytic Anemia Macrocytic Anemia
MCH	$\frac{HB}{RBC} \times 10$	28-32pg (µµg)		Varies with Hemoglobin Content and Cell Size
MCHC	$\frac{HB}{HCT} \times 100$	32-36% (g/dl)	<32 >36	Hypochromic Cells Hyperchromic Cells *(Spherocytes)*, Lipemia, Hb SS, CC
RDW	$\frac{SD\ of\ MCV \times 100}{Mean\ MCV}$	11.5-14.5%	>14.5	Anisocytosis
• MCV is directly measured by automated methods; Hct is calculated from MCV and RBC count.				

Peripheral Blood Cells and Their Function

CELL	REFERENCE RANGE	FUNCTION
Red Cell	Females 3.8 - 5.2 x 10^6/µl Males 4.5 - 6.1 x 10^6/µl	O_2 Transport to Tissue and CO_2 Removal from Tissue; Cell Nutrition
Neutrophil	Relative 50-70% Absolute 2500-7000/µl	Phagocytic Response to Bacteria
Lymphocyte	Relative 20-40% Absolute 1000-4000/µl	Humoral and Cell Mediated Immunity
Monocyte	Relative 3-10% Absolute 150-1000/µl	Phagocytic Response to Bacteria
Basophil	Relative 0-2% Absolute 0-200/µl	Inflammatory Response Mediator
Eosinophil	Relative 0-3% Absolute 0-300/µl	Allergic Response Regulator
Platelet	Absolute 150,000-400,000/µl	Clotting

Dilution Factor, Diluent and Calculations for Manual Cell Counts

BLOOD SMEAR EXAMINATION

1. Wright stain
   a. Polychrome *(Romanowsky)* stain - phosphate buffer (pH 6.4), eosin, methylene blue and methanol
   b. Sources of error
      ❖ *Stain blue (pH of buffer or stain too basic, prolonged staining)*
      ❖ *Stain red (pH of buffer or stain too acid, prolonged washing)*

Constituents in Wright Stain

Sources of Error in Staining Smears

2. Leukocyte differential
   a. Reference ranges

CELL	PERCENT	INCREASED IN
Neutrophil	50-70%	Bacterial Infections
Lymphocyte	20-40%	Viral infections
Monocyte	3-10%	TB, syphilis, malignancies
Eosinophil	0-3%	Allergies, parasites, CML
Basophil	0-2%	Immediate hypersensitivity, CML

   b. Evaluate white cell morphology

MORPHOLOGY	ASSOCIATED WITH
Hypersegmented Neutrophil	Pernicious Anemia
Hyposegmented Neutrophil	Pelger Huet Anomaly Pseudo-Pelger Huet (AML, AIDS)
Toxic Granulation and Vacuoles	Bacterial Infections, Burns, Chemotherapy
Döhle Bodies (RNA)	Bacterial Infections, Burns, May-Hegglin
Atypical Lymphs (increased size and basophilia)	Infectious Mono (Epstein-Barr Virus), Other Viral Infections

58

3. Platelet estimate
   a. 8-20/oil immersion field
   b. If platelets seem low, check feather edge of slide for platelet clumping, check for satelitism
   c. Check platelet size
      ❖ *Large - Bernard-Soulier, May- Hegglin, myeloproliferative disorders, stress platelets*

4. Nucleated red cells
   a. Must correct white cell count
   b. Formula

$$\frac{\text{wbc count} \times 100}{100 + \text{\# nrbcs}} = \text{corrected WBC count}$$

5. Red cell morphology
   a. Size Normocytic - *(MCV of 80-100μ³ or fL)*
      ❖ *Microcyte (MCV < 80)*
      ❖ *Macrocyte (MCV > 100)*
      ❖ *Anisocytosis - variation in size*
   b. Color - Normochromic (MCHC of 32-36 g/dL)
      ❖ *Hypochromic - (MCHC < 32)*
      ❖ *Hyperchromic - (MCHC > 36)*

   ❖ *Polychromasia - blue color in rbc (if stained with reticulocyte stain, these would be reticulocytes)*
   c. Shape - Bi-concave disk
      ❖ *Poikilocytosis - variation in shape (see chart below)*
   d. Inclusions *(see chart page 49)*
   e. Crystals
      ❖ *Hemoglobin C - bar-shaped*
      ❖ *Hemoglobin SC - "hand in glove" or "Washington monument"*

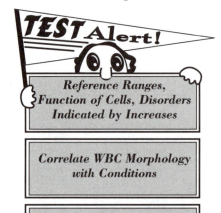

TEST Alert!

Reference Ranges, Function of Cells, Disorders Indicated by Increases

Correlate WBC Morphology with Conditions

Action Taken if Low Platelets Seen on Smear

Abnormal Red Cell Shapes

SHAPE	SEEN IN:	SHAPE	SEEN IN:
Acanthocyte	Abetalipoproteinemia, Severe Liver Disease	Sickle Cell *(Drepanocyte)*	Hb SS
Echinocyte "Burr" Cell	Uremia, Artifact *(Alkaline Glass Effect)*	Spherocyte	Hereditary Spherocytosis, (↑ *MCHC)*, ABO HDN, and Other Hemolytic Processes
Elliptocyte	Hereditary Elliptocytosis (>50%)	Stomatocyte *(Mouth Cell)*	Hereditary Stomatocytosis (>50%) Liver Disease
Macroovalocyte	Megaloblastic Anemia	Target Cell (Codocyte)	Liver Disease, Hb C and Other Hemoglobinopathies
Helmet (Keratocyte)	Hemolytic Processes	Teardrop Cell *(Dacryocyte)*	Extramedullary Hematopoiesis
Schistocyte *(RBC Fragment)*	DIC and Hemolytic Processes	*NOTE:*	HDN - Hemolytic Disease of the Newborn DIC - Disseminated Intravascular Coagulation)

Red Cell Inclusions

INCLUSION	COMPOSED OF:	STAIN	INDICATIONS
Howell-Jolly Body	DNA	Wright	Disturbed Erythropoiesis Hemolytic Anemias Megaloblastic Anemia Post-Splenectomy
Basophilic Stippling	RNA	Wright New Methylene Blue	Thalassemia Lead Poisoning
Pappenheimer Bodies Siderotic Granules *(siderocyte)*	Iron	Wright Prussian Blue	Sideroblastic Anemia Hemoglobinopathies
Heinz Body	Denatured Precipitated Hemoglobin	Supravital Stain such as Brilliant Cresyl Blue or New Methylene Blue **(NOT seen with Wright's stain)**	G6PD Deficiency Thalassemia Unstable Hemoglobins
Cabot Ring	Remnants of Mitotic Spindle	Wright	Megaloblastic Anemia
Parasites	Malaria Babesia Trypanosomes	Wright	Parasitic Infection

TEST Alert!

Correlate Abnormal RBC Shapes with Conditions

Correlate Abnormal RBC Inclusions with Conditions

RULE OF THREE

Correlation of Hb, Hct and RBC

Hb x 3 = Hct ± 3%

RBC *(in millions)* x 3 = Hb ± 0.5

If "Rule of Three" doesn't fit, consider:

1. Clotted sample
2. Cold agglutinin *(warm sample and rerun)*
3. Lipemic or icteric sample

NOTE:

☞ ⬆ *MCV,* ⬆ *MCHC and* ⬇ *red cell count are associated with cold agglutinin disease; warm sample and rerun*

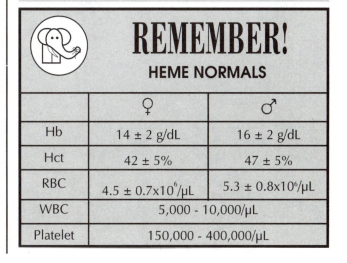

REMEMBER!

HEME NORMALS

	♀	♂
Hb	14 ± 2 g/dL	16 ± 2 g/dL
Hct	42 ± 5%	47 ± 5%
RBC	$4.5 ± 0.7 \times 10^6/\mu L$	$5.3 ± 0.8 \times 10^6/\mu L$
WBC	5,000 - 10,000/µL	
Platelet	150,000 - 400,000/µL	

60

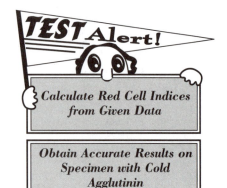

Calculate Red Cell Indices from Given Data

Obtain Accurate Results on Specimen with Cold Agglutinin

ERYTHROCYTE SEDIMENTATION RATE (WESTERGREN)

1. Principle - measures rate of fall of red cells through plasma

2. Reference ranges
   a. Female: 0-20 mm/hr
   b. Male: 0-15 mm/hr

3. Clinical correleation
   a. ↑ seen in presence of abnormal plasma proteins (*inflammatory conditions*)

4. Sources of error
   a. Increase - tilting tube, standing too long, ↑ temperature, excess EDTA
   b. Decrease - QNS specimen, ↓ temperature

RETICULOCYTE COUNT

1. Uses a supra vital stain which stains red cells in living state
   a. New methylene blue
   b. Brilliant cresyl blue

2. Monitors erythropoiesis

3. Calculations
   a. % reticulocytes =

   $$\frac{\text{\# retics in 1000 RBCs}}{10}$$

   b. Absolute retic = # RBCs x % retics
   c. Corrected retic count =

   $$\frac{\text{\% retics x patient hct}}{45}$$

4. Reference ranges - 0.5 - 1.5%

5. RPI (Reticulocyte Production Index =

   $$\frac{\text{Corrected retic count}}{\text{maturation time (usually use 2)}}$$

   a. >2 - adequate bone marrow (BM) response to anemia
   b. <2 - inadequate BM response to anemia

6. ↑ in hemolytic anemias, post-acute blood loss, following therapy (*i.e., iron, folate, B12*)

Reticulocyte Calculations
❖ **RBC = 3.0 x 10⁶/µL; HCT = 25%; 36 retics counted in 1000 RBCs**

❖ *Retic count example:*
$$\frac{36}{10} = 3.6\%$$

❖ *Absolute retic count example:*
$$3.0 \times 10^6/\mu L \times .036 = 108,000/\mu L$$

❖ *Corrected retic count example:*
$$\frac{3.6 \times 25}{45} = 2.0\%$$

❖ *RPI example:*
$$\frac{2.0}{2} = 1.0$$

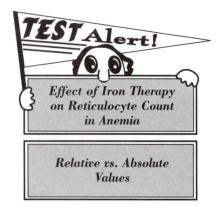

Effect of Iron Therapy on Reticulocyte Count in Anemia

Relative vs. Absolute Values

Calculations for Reticulocyte Counts

Special Hematology

BONE MARROW PREPS

1. Reference ranges
   a. Megakaryocytes - 5/lpf
   b. Myeloid: erythroid ratio - 3:1 - 4:1

2. Clinical correlations
   a. "Dry" tap - aplastic anemia, myelofibrosis
   b. ↓M:E ratio - erythroid hyperplasia, hemolytic anemia, erythroleukemia
   c. ↑M:E ratio - myeloid hyperplasia, myeloid leukemias

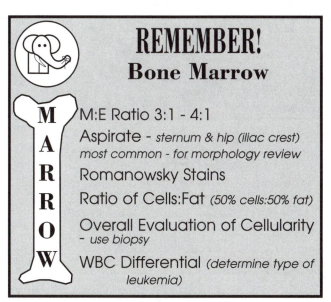

REMEMBER! Bone Marrow

M:E Ratio 3:1 - 4:1

Aspirate - *sternum & hip (iliac crest) most common - for morphology review*

Romanowsky Stains

Ratio of Cells:Fat *(50% cells:50% fat)*

Overall Evaluation of Cellularity - *use biopsy*

WBC Differential *(determine type of leukemia)*

HEMOGLOBIN ELECTROPHORESIS

1. Cellulose acetate, pH 8.6; from cathode to anode *(- to +)*

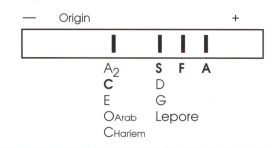

REMEMBER! Hemoglobin Migration

C *(crawl)*, **S** *(slow)*, **F** *(fast)*, and **A** *(accelerate)*

2. Citrate Agar, pH 6.2

(Most other hemoglobins migrate with A)

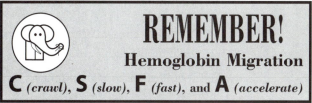

REMEMBER! What Migrates with A₂ & S (pH 8.6)

A₂, **CE O**f **C**lubs Harlem

Sad **D**og **G**ets **L**oved

Red Cell Disease States

HEMOGLOBINOPATHIES

1. Structural mutations (most common involve β-chain)

HEMOGLOBIN	COMMENTS
S	Valine for Glutamic Acid (6th Position, Beta Chain)
C	Lysine for Glutamic Acid (6th Position, Beta Chain)
D	East Indian Individuals, Migrates with HbS at 8.6
E	Southeast Asian Individuals, Migrates with Hb C and A2 at 8.6 (hypochromic, microcytic)

a. Hemoglobin S
   - *Heterozygous - asymptomatic (sickle cell trait)*
   - *Homozygous - severe chronic hemolytic anemia with many complications (sickle cell disease)*
   - *Primarily affects black population*
   - *See sickle cells on Wright (not in trait)*
   - *Sickle Dex - uses reducing agent (Nadithionite) to cause Hb S to precipitate producing turbid solution*
   - *Confirmed by electrophoresis*
     - Cellulose acetate - pH 8.6 *(migrates with D, G, Lepore)*
     - Citrate agar - pH 6.2 *(S separates from others)*

62

b. Hemoglobin C disease
- ❖ *Heterozygous - asymptomatic*
- ❖ *Homozygous - mild chronic anemia*
- ❖ *May see Hb C crystals (bar-shaped), and target cells*
- ❖ *In SC disease, crystals appear as "hand in glove" or "Washington monument"*
- ❖ *Confirm by electrophoresis*
  - ☞ *Cellulose acetate - migrates with A2, E, O, and C_{Harlem}*
  - ☞ *Citrate agar - (C separates from others)*

2. Decreased production of α or β chains
   a. β thalassemia - ↓ or absent production of β-chains
   - ❖ ↑ *Hb A$_2$ and F,* ↓ *or absent A*
   - ❖ *Microcytic, hypochromic anemia*
   b. α thalassemia - ↓ production of α-chains
   - ❖ *1 deleted α gene (- α/α α) - Silent carrier; normal CBC*
   - ❖ *2 deleted α genes (- α/-α) or (- -/α α) - Mild microcytic, hypochromic anemia*
   - ❖ *3 deleted α genes (- - /-α) - Hemoglobin H disease*

- ☞ Chronic hemolytic disease
- ☞ Hb H (β_4)
- ☞ Hb Bart's (γ_4) present at birth
- ☞ Hb H inclusions (*heinz bodies*)
- ❖ 4 deleted α genes (- -/- -)
  - ☞ *Hydrops fetalis*
  - ☞ Nonviable fetus

Classification of Anemias

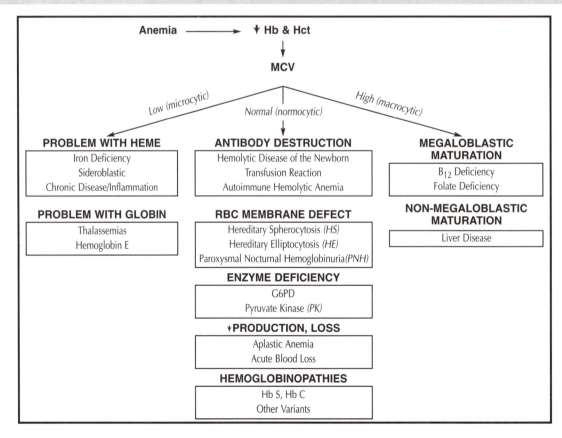

Anemia Types and Key Lab Findings

ANEMIA	LAB FINDINGS
MICROCYTIC/HYPOCHROMIC	
• Iron Deficiency	• ↓Fe, ↑TIBC, ↓% Saturation
• Chronic Disease / Inflammation	• ↓Fe, ↓TIBC
• Lead Poisoning	• Basophilic Stippling, ↑Blood Lead Level, ↑FEP
• Thalassemia Trait	• N Fe, N TIBC, ↑A2, ↑F
MACROCYTIC	
• B12 Deficiency	• ↓B12, ↓Retics, Pancytopenia, Oval Macrocytes, Hypersegmented Polys, Howell Jolly (HJ) Bodies
☞ Pernicious Anemia (PA)	☞ Anti-IF+ (Intrinsic Factor), ↑MMA (methylmalonic acid), ↑Homocysteine, Normal Schilling Test with IF
☞ Malabsorption	☞ Anti-IF−, Abnormal Schilling Test with and without IF
• Folate Deficiency	• ↓Serum/Erythrocyte Folate Levels, Oval Macrocytes, Anti-IF−, ↓Retics, Hypersegmented Polys, ↑Homocysteine, HJ Bodies
• Liver Disease / Alcoholism	• ↑Liver Enzymes, Target Cells, Round Macrocytes
NORMOCYTIC/NORMOCHROMIC	
• Antibody Mediated	• ↑Bilirubin, ↓Haptoglobin, DAT+
☞ PCH	☞ Donath Landsteiner Ab
☞ Cold Agglutinin Disease	☞ IgM Ab, Cold Agglutinin Titer+
☞ Warm Autoimmune Hemolytic Anemia	☞ IgG Ab
• Membrane Defect	
☞ Hereditary Spherocytosis	☞ ↑Osmotic Fragility, Spherocytes, ↑MCHC
☞ Hereditary Elliptocytosis	☞ Elliptocytes (>15% to 100%)
☞ PNH	☞ Ham's Test+, Sucrose Hemolysis+, CD55−, CD59−
• Enzyme Deficiency	
☞ G6PD	☞ ↓G6PD, Heinz Bodies
☞ Pyruvate Kinase (PK)	☞ ↓PK, No Heinz Bodies
• Decreased Production / Loss	
☞ Aplastic Anemia	☞ "Dry Tap" Bone Marrow (BM), Hypocellular BM, ↓Retics, Pancytopenia
☞ Acute Blood Loss	☞ Normal BM, ↑Retics
• Hemoglobin Defects	• Definitive Poikylocytes on Smear (HbC crystals, Sickle Cells, SC crystals, etc.), Hb Electrophoresis

REMEMBER!
Trust in yourself.
Your perceptions are often far more accurate
than you are willing to believe — *Claudia Black*

Correlate Lab Data to Determine Type of Anemia

Special Tests

TEST	MEASURES	INDICATIONS	COMMENTS
Osmotic Fragility	RBC Surface : Volume Ratio	↑ in Hereditary Spherocytosis ↓ in Thalassemia, Target Cells	Salt Tolerance
Ham's/Acid Hemolysis	Complement Mediated Lysis	PNH	Definitive
Sucrose Hemolysis (sugar water)	Effect of Complement (activated by sucrose) on RBC	PNH	Screen Only
Heinz Body Prep (supravital stain)	Effect of Oxidizing Agent on Hemoglobin	G6PD Deficiency Unstable Hemoglobins HbH	Formation Triggered by Oxidants such as Anti-Malarial Drugs, Fava Beans & Sulphur Drugs
Sickle Cell Screen	Reduced Solubility of Deoxygenated Hemoglobin S	HbS	Reducing Agent: Na Dithionate
Kleihauer-Betke Acid Elution	Resistance of Fetal Hemoglobin to Acid Elution	Fetal-Maternal Hemorrhage; Hereditary Persistence of Fetal Hemoglobin	Cells with ↑ HbF Stain Pink; Normal Adult Cells → Ghost Cells
Hemoglobin Electrophoresis	Migration of Various Hemoglobins	Suspected Hemoglobinopathies	May be Performed at Various pHs
Cold Agglutinin Screen	Presence of Cold Autoantibody	Cold Autoimmune Hemolytic Anemia	IgM Ab, Anti-I Specificity
Donath Landsteiner Test	Presence of Biphasic DL Antibody	Paroxysmal Cold Hemoglobinuria	IgG Ab, Anti-P specificity

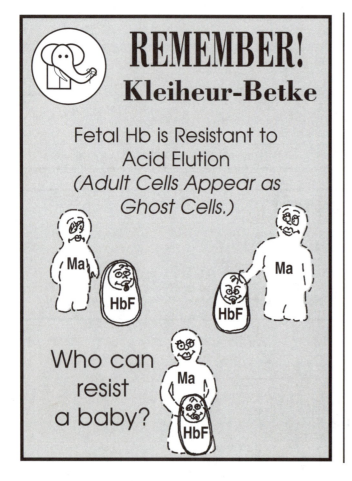

REMEMBER! Kleiheur-Betke

Fetal Hb is Resistant to Acid Elution (Adult Cells Appear as Ghost Cells.)

Who can resist a baby?

Principles and Indications of Special Tests

ERYTHROCYTOSES
1. ↑ number of red cells (↑Hb, ↑Hct)
2. Relative (↓plasma vol) - burns, dehydration, Gaisbock syndrome
3. Absolute (↑ red cell mass)
   a. Primary - ↓EPO, normal O₂ saturation (polycemia vera)
   b. Secondary - ↑EPO, ↓O₂ saturation (chronic obstructive lung disease, high affinity Hb)

White Cell Disease States

Hereditary Conditions

CONDITION	CHARACTERISTICS	COMMENTS
Chronic Granulomatous Disease (CGD)	Ineffective Killing of Bacteria	X-Linked
Alder-Reilly	Large Azurophilic Granules	↑Mucopolysaccharides (Hunter, Hurler)
Chediak-Higashi	Large Lysosomes (Fusion of Primary Granules)	Albinism, ↑Susceptibility to Infection
May-Hegglin	Large Platelet, ↓Number, Döhle Bodies in Segs, Monos, and Lymphs	Does Not Affect Leukocyte Function
Pelger-Huet	Hyposegmented Polys	Normal Function

MYELOPROLIFERATIVE DISEASES

1. Myelodysplastic Syndromes
   a. Refractory Anemia (RA) - <5% blasts
   b. Refractory Anemia with sideroblasts (RARS) - <5% blasts with ring sideroblasts
   c. Refractory Anemia with excess blasts (RAEB) - 5-20% blasts
   d. Refractory Anemia with excess blasts in transformation (RAEBIT) - 20-30% blasts
   e. Chronic Myelomonocytic Leukemia (CMMoL) - significant peripheral blood and bone marrow monocytosis

2. Myeloproliferative Disorders
   a. Myelofibrosis/Agnogenic Myeloid Metaplasia - "dry tap", tear-drop shaped rbc, bone marrow fibrosis
   b. Essential Thrombocythemia - ↑megakaryocytes, platelets (> 1 million/mm3)
   c. Chronic Myelocytic Leukemia (CML) - ↑myelocytic precursors (from blast to mature neutrophil), ↓LAP presence of Philadelphia chromosome
   d. Polycythemia Vera (PV) - ↑LAP, pancytosis

Leukemoid Reaction vs. CML

CHARACTERISTIC	LEUKEMOID	CML
LAP	↑	↓
Toxic Granulation	↑	↓
Döhle Bodies	Yes	No
Philadelphia Chromosome	No	Yes

3. Acute Myeloid Leukemias (FAB classification — >30% blasts in BM)

AML	PREDOMINANT CELL SEEN
M0	Myeloblast without differentiation
M1	Myeloblast with minimal maturation
M2	Myeloblast with maturation
M3	Promyelocyte (APL)
M4	Myeloblast and monoblast (AMMoL)
M5	Monoblast (AMoL)
M6	Erythrocytic series
M7	Megakaryocyte

TEST Alert!

Differentiate Leukemoid Reaction from CML

LYMPHOPROLIFERATIVE DISORDERS

1. Lymphocytic leukemias
   a. Acute lymphocytic leukemia (FAB Classification)
      ❖ L1 - small lymphoblasts
      ❖ L2 - large and small lymphoblasts
      ❖ L3 - large lymphoblasts with vacuoles (Burkitt lymphoma)

2. Chronic lymphocytic leukemia (CLL) - mature lymphocytes, "smudge" cells

3. Hairy cell leukemia (HCL) - mature lymphocytes with cytoplasmic projections, tartrate-resistant acid phosphatase positive

4. Lymphomas – Hodgkin vs. non-Hodgkin

Hodgkin vs. Non-Hodgkin

LYMPHOMA	REED STERNBERG CELL	INCIDENCE	SPREAD
Hodgkin	Present	Bi-modal	Stepwise (Predictable)
Non-Hodgkin	Absent	No Pattern	Unpredictable

5. Plasma Cell Dyscrasias
   a. Multiple myeloma
      ❖ Bone pain (multiple lytic lesions)
      ❖ Sheets of plasma cells in bone marrow
      ❖ Rouleaux - red cells appear as a "stack of coins" on blood smear
      ❖ ↑serum protein (IgG or IgA monoclonal spike), ↑Ca^{++}
      ❖ Urinary excretion of light chains (Bence Jones protein)

65

b. Plasma cell leukemia
  ❖ ↑ *plasma cells in bone marrow and peripheral circulation*
c. Waldenstrom macroglobulinemia
  ❖ *Normal bone scan*
  ❖ *IgM*
  ❖ ↑ *serum viscosity*

Multiple Myeloma vs. Waldenstrom

CHARACTERISTIC	MULTIPLE MYELOMA	WALDENSTROM
Bone Involvement	Yes	No
Serum Viscosity	±	↑↑
Immunoglobulin	IgG (Bence-Jones)	IgM (Heavy Chain)

WHO (WORLD HEALTH ORGANIZATION) CLASSIFICATION OF HEMATOLOGIC NEOPLASMS

1. Criteria for classification
   a. Cell lineage
   b. Combination of morphology, immunophenotyping, genetics, clinical presentation
   c. >20% blasts in BM defines acute leukemia

2. Acute lymphocytic leukemia (ALL) and lymphoma
   a. Classified as same disease with different clinical presentations
   b. Either B or T according to cell lineage
   c. Peripheral blood and BM involvement with >20% blasts defines ALL
   d. Solid tumor presentation defines lymphoma

Special Cytochemical Stains / Markers

STAIN/CELL MARKER	INDICATES:	SIGNIFICANCE:
Periodic Acid Schiff (PAS)	Glycogen	Erythroleukemia; ALL ("Chunky"+)
Prussian Blue	Iron	Sideroblastic Anemia
LAP	Alkaline Phosphatase	↑ Leukemoid Reaction, P. vera ↓ CML
Peroxidase/Sudan Black	Myeloperoxidase/Lipid	AML M1-M4+, AML M5– ALL–
Specific Esterase	Esterase in Granulocyte Precursors	AML M1-M4+, AML M5–
Non-Specific Esterase	Non-Specific Esterase in Monocyte Precursors	AML M4+, AML M5++ (with Fluoride Inhibition Step, M5–)
TRAP	Tartrate-Resistant Acid Phosphatase	Hairy Cell Leukemia
Abnormal NBT	Abnormal Granulocyte Function	Chronic Granulomatous Disease
Auer rods	Coalition of 1° granules	AML+ ALL–
CD13, CD33	Myeloblasts	AML+ ALL–
CD2, CD3, CD 5, CD7	T-lineage	T-ALL+, B-ALL– AML–
CD10 (CALLA), CD19, CD22	B-lineage	B-ALL+, T-ALL– AML–
t (15; 17)	Chromosome Translocation involving Retinoic Acid Receptor Gene	Acute Progranulocytic Leukemia (AML M3) Treat with ATRA (ALL Trans Retinoic Acid)
CD34	Stem Cells	Stem Cells for Transplantation
CD42, CD61	Megakaryocytes	AML M7
CD116, CD14	Monoblasts	AML M4 and AML M5

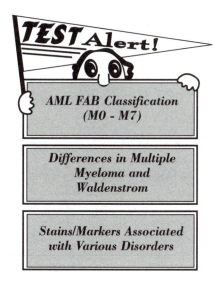

TEST Alert!

AML FAB Classification (M0 - M7)

Differences in Multiple Myeloma and Waldenstrom

Stains/Markers Associated with Various Disorders

WHO Classification of Acute Leukemia

REMEMBER!

WHO has acute leukemia? | >20% blasts in bone marrow

Lysosome and Lipid Storage Disorders

DISEASE	ACCUMULATED LIPID	LAB DIAGNOSIS	COMMENTS
Gaucher	Glucocerebroside	Macrophage	Macrophage Cytoplasm Looks Like an Unfolded Crumpled Piece of Paper
Niemann-Pick	Sphingomyelin	Macrophage	Macrophage Has Globular Cytoplasm, Sea-Blue Histiocytes
Tay-Sach	Sphingolipids (GM_2 Ganglioside)	Vacuolated Lymphocytes, Foam Cells (Bone Marrow)	Diagnosed by ↑ Startle Reflex, Cherry Red Spot in Macula of Eye & CNS Studies
Hurler, Hunter	Mucopolysaccharides	Large Granules in Lymphocytes (Alder Reilly Bodies); Also in Histiocytes and Lymphocytes (Bone Marrow)	Unmetabolized Products Detectable in Urine (Toluidine Blue Spot Test)

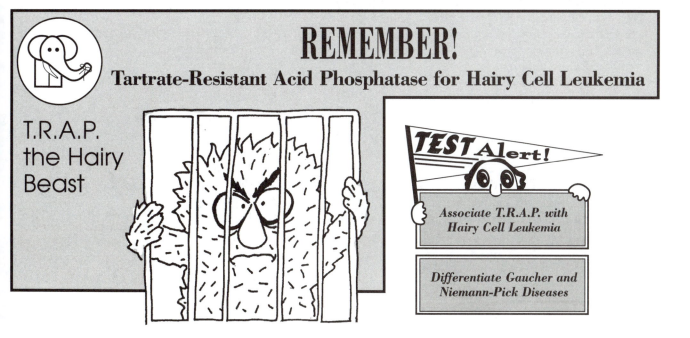

REMEMBER!
Tartrate-Resistant Acid Phosphatase for Hairy Cell Leukemia

T.R.A.P. the Hairy Beast

TEST Alert!

Associate T.R.A.P. with Hairy Cell Leukemia

Differentiate Gaucher and Niemann-Pick Diseases

HEMATOLOGY SAMPLE QUESTIONS

68

1. The major iron storage compound is
   A. Hemosiderin.
   B. Ferritin.
   C. Siderotic granules.
   D. Transferrin.

2. How would the following results on a 32 year old adult female be interpreted?

   Hemoglobin - 7.0 gm/dL
   MCV - 64 fl
   MCH - 20 pg
   MCHC - 31.5 g/dL
   RDW - 19.0 %
   Serum ferritin - 4 ng/ml (N=20-250 ng/mL)
   Serum iron - 29 µg/dl (N=70-200 µg/dL)
   TIBC - 590 µg/dl (N=250-435 µg/dL)
   % Saturation - 5

   A. Anemia of chronic disease
   B. Iron deficiency anemia
   C. Thalassemia minor
   D. Sideroblastic anemia

3. How would the following results on a 72 year old adult female be interpreted?

   Hemoglobin - 6 g/dL
   MCV - 114 fl
   MCH - 39 pg
   MCHC - 34 g/L
   RDW - 15.0 %
   Reticulocyte count - 1.2%
   Serum B_{12} - 55 pg/ml (N=200-1000 pg/mL)
   Serum folate - 7 ng/ml (N=2-10 ng/mL)
   Anti-IF (intrinsic factor) antibodies - positive
   Schilling test - Part I - 5% excretion (N > 7%)
       Part II (with IF) - 10% excretion
   Oval macrocytes on Wright stain

   A. Folate deficiency
   B. Liver disease
   C. Pernicious anemia
   D. Reticulocytosis

4. Which of the following results from decreased synthesis of globin chains?
   A. Beta-thalassemia
   B. Hemoglobin C disease
   C. Hemoglobin Lepore syndrome
   D. Sickle cell disease

5. The normal M:E ratio for an adult is
   A. 1:1.5
   B. 3:1
   C. 5:1
   D. 9:1

6. A patient with a negative dithionite solubility test has a band in the A region and a band in the S region on cellulose acetate hemoglobin electrophoresis at pH 8.6. On citrate agar there is only a band in the A region. Which of the following is compatible with these results?
   A. Hb AS
   B. Hb AE
   C. Hb AD
   D. Hb AC$_{Harlem}$

7. The failure of granulocytes to develop past the "band" or two-lobed stage is characteristic of
   A. Bernard-Soulier syndrome.
   B. Chediak-Higashi syndrome.
   C. May-Hegglin anomaly.
   D. Pelger-Huet anomaly.

8. A patient with a markedly elevated WBC count with a left shift, toxic granulation, vacuoles, dohle bodies and an increased LAP probably has which of the following?
   A. Chronic lymphocytic leukemia.
   B. Chronic myelogenous leukemia.
   C. Leukemoid reaction.
   D. Pelger-Huet anomaly.

9. A patient's lymphocytes demonstrate cytoplasmic projections and a positive tartrate-resistant acid phosphatase stain. What would the diagnosis most likely be?
   A. Chronic lymphocytic leukemia
   B. Acute lymphocytic leukemia
   C. Sezary syndrome
   D. Hairy cell leukemia

10. Plasma cells evolve from which cell line?
    A. Lymphocytic
    B. Monocytic
    C. Myelocytic
    D. Megakaryocytic

11. A manual white blood cell count using the Unopette dilution system and a Neubauer hemacytometer gave an average total count of 50 cells. What is the patient's white cell count?
    A. 5,000/µL
    B. 10,000/µL
    C. 5,500/µL
    D. 11,000/µL

12. A 7 ml EDTA tube was received in the laboratory containing approximately 2 ml of whole blood. If performed on this sample, which of the following manual laboratory test values might be in error?
    A. Hemoglobin of 10.5 gm/dl
    B. Retic count of 3%
    C. Sed rate of 22 mm/hr.
    D. WBC count of 10,500/mm^3

13. A peripheral blood smear stained with Prussian blue demonstrates siderocytes. On a Wright stained smear, what would be expected?
    A. Basophilic stippling
    B. Howell Jolly bodies
    C. Heinz bodies
    D. Pappenheimer bodies

14. A bone marrow differential performed on a patient showed 30% blasts. Flow cytometry studies demonstrated the blasts to be positive for CD10, CD19, CD22, and negative for CD13 and CD33. Which of the following diseases is most compatible with these findings?
    A. ALL
    B. AML
    C. CML
    D. CLL

15. Multiple myeloma may be suspected if which of the following is seen on a peripheral smear?
    A. Basophilic stippling
    B. Bizzare blast cells
    C. Hypersegmented neutrophils
    D. Rouleaux

ANSWERS AND RATIONALE

1. B

Option A is a long-term water-insoluble iron storage compound but not the major one. Hemosiderin can be found in found in macrophage lysosomal membranes and seen in bone marrow aspirates stained with Prussian blue. Option C are iron inclusions found in red cells stained with Prussian Blue. Option D is the transport protein specific for iron.

2. B

An RDW greater than 14.5%, decreased iron/increased TIBC and greatly decreased ferritin (indicating no iron stores) support this diagnosis. Option A is incorrect because ferritin would NOT be decreased and the TIBC would be decreased. Option C is incorrect because in - thalassemia minor, the Fe and TIBC would probably be normal and the anemia would be less severe. Also, the RDW would proabably be in the normal range. Option D is incorrect because the ferritin would be increased as would the serum iron.

3. C

Oval macrocytes, increased B$_{12}$, positive IF antibodies and a Schilling test less than 7% on the first day are all indicators of pernicious anemia. Option A is incorrect because the folate is normal. Option B is incorrect because the anti-IF antibodies would NOT be positive. Option D is incorrect because of the additional abnormal data.

4. A

All other options result from structural abnormalities.

5. B

The normal M:E ratio is between 3:1 and 4:1.

6. C.

Hb AS would give a positive solubility and would show a separate band in the S region on citrate agar. Hb E would give a negative solubility test but would migrate to the C position on cellulose acetate. Hb C$_{Harlem}$ would give a positive solubility test and would migrate to the C position on cellulose acetate.

7. D

Option A is a platelet adhesion problem characterized by giant platelets. Option B is characterized by giant lysosomes in leukocytes. Option C is characterized by giant platelets and Döhle bodies.

8. C

Option A is incorrect because there would be a predominance in the lymphocytic line and an LAP would not be performed. Option B is incorrect because the LAP score would be decreased. Option D would show a normal WBC count and LAP score with no Dohle bodies seen.

9. D

Option A would demonstrate lymphocytosis, but the TRAP stain would be negative. Option B would demonstrate an increase in lymphoblasts, but the TRAP stain would also be negative. Option C shows Sezary cells and the TRAP stain would be negative.

10. A

Plasma Cells evolve from B cells which are lymphocytes.

11. A

The formula using a Unopette with a Neubauer chamber is:

$$\text{\# cells counted} \times \frac{1}{\text{tot vol}} \times \text{dil factor}$$

The volume factor can be eliminated by taking 10% of the number of cells counted and adding this to the number of cells counted.

$$50 \times .1 = 5$$
$$50 + 5 = 55$$

So,

$$55 \times 100 = 5,500/mm^3$$

12. C

Excess anticoagulant causes red cells to shrink. This would cause the sed rate to be falsely increased and the spun hematocrit to be falsely decreased. The other values would probably not be affected.

13. D

Siderotic granules are composed of iron and on a Wright stained smear appear as Pappenheimer bodies within the red cell. They are frequently seen in sideroblastic anemia, alcoholism, thalassemia and some preleukemic states. Option A is composed of RNA remnants and does not stain with prussian blue. It is associated with lead poisoning, thalassemia, and hemolytic anemias. Option B is composed of DNA remnants and is associated with hyposplenism, pernicious anemia and thalassemia. Option C is denatured hemoglobin, is NOT seen on a Wright stained smear and is associated with G6PD deficiency, exposure to oxidizing drugs, alpha thalassemia, and unstable hemoglobins.

14. A

>30% blasts in the bone marrow is associated with acute leukemias. CD10, CD19 and CD22 are indicative of B- lineage ALL. Option B would be positive for CD13 and CD33. Options C and D would not have >30% blasts in bone marrow.

15. D

Rouleaux due to increased plasma proteins (monoclonal immunoglobulin) may be seen in Multiple Myeloma. The serum viscosity is increased and the albumin:globulin ratio is decreased. Option A is seen in conditions associated with disturbed erythropoeisis. Option B is seen in leukemia states. Option C is seen in Pernicious Anemia.

☞ Be able to identify mature and immature cells from graphic images. Correlate cells and inclusions with appropriate disease states.

COAGULATION

by Daniel Haun

Platelets

PRODUCTION

1. Produced from megakaryocytes

2. Distribution
   a. 30% spleen
   b. 70% peripheral blood
   c. Reference range - 150,000-400,000/mm3
   d. Life span - 9-12 days

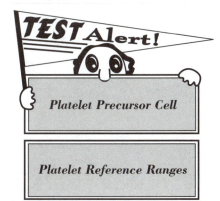

TEST Alert!

Platelet Precursor Cell

Platelet Reference Ranges

FUNCTIONS

1. Initial arrest of bleeding and formation of the platelet plug
   a. Adhesion
      ❖ *Glycoprotein Ib binds to exposed collagen*
      ❖ *Requires von Willebrand factor*
      ❖ *Results in release (secretion) of ADP and other granule components (including Factor V and fibrinogen)*
   b. Aggregation
      ❖ *Other platelets are stimulated by ADP to undergo shape change (disc to sphere to pseudopods) exposing the glycoprotein IIb / IIIa complex which binds fibrinogen*
      ❖ *Fibrinogen binding links the platelets; the first (and reversible) phase of aggregation*
      ❖ *With weak stimuli, the aggregates can disassociate but strong stimuli cause the aggregating platelets to release (secrete); with release, the aggregation is irreversible*

The bottom line..?

After adhesion and aggregation a platelet plug is built at the injury site. The bleeding time test asks the important question: Do the platelets properly adhere and aggregate at the injury site?

2. Localization of the platelet plug
   a. Secreting platelets release arachidonic acid which converts to prostaglandin, *(becomes Thromboxane A2)* in the platelet
   b. Arachidonic acid is processed by adjacent endothelial cells to form platelet-inhibiting prostacyclin

The bottom line..?

The platelet plug is limited to the injury site.

3. Assembly and localization of the fibrin clot
   a. Platelet release components include fibrinogen, Factor V and Factor VIII
   b. Fibrinogen is bound on the platelet surface during aggregation
   c. Factor VIII is bound to the platelet surface with von Willebrand factor
   d. Shape change exposes platelet membrane phospholipid (template for the assembly of the factor complexes)
      ❖ *Called Platelet Factor 3*
      ❖ *Binds the Factor VIII and IXa complex (requires Ca^{++}) - no wonder Hemophilia A and Hemophilia B (Factor VIII and IX deficiencies) are clinically identical*
      ❖ *Binds the factor V and Xa complex; also requires Ca^{++}*

The bottom line..?

The platelet plug is a wonderful place to produce a fibrin clot and without the platelet presence, the fibrin won't form. It is clot promotion and clot localization all in one.

Steps in Formation of
Platelet Plug

Plasma Coagulation Factors

FUNCTIONS

1. Substrate - factor I (*fibrinogen*)

2. Cofactors - accelerate enzymatic reactions
   a. Factors III, V and VIII
   b. Factor HMWK (*high molecular weight kininogen*)

3. Enzymes
   a. Serine proteases - cleave peptide bonds (*factors II, VII, IX, X, XI and XII*)
   b. Transamidase - XIII only

CHARACTERISTICS OF COAGULATION PROTEINS

Coagulation Groups

GROUP	CONTACT	PROTHROMBIN	FIBRINOGEN
Factors	XI, XII, PK, HMWK	II, VII, IX, X	I, V, VIII, XIII
Vitamin K Dependent	No	Yes	No
Consumed in Clotting	No	No (except for II)	Yes

1. Contact proteins
   a. Factors XII, XI, PK (*prekallikrein*) and HMWK (*high molecular weight kininogen*)
   b. Participate in the initial phase of the intrinsic system
   c. NOT consumed during clotting (*found in both serum and plasma*)
   d. NOT Vitamin K dependent

2. Prothrombin proteins
   a. Factors II, VII, IX, X
   b. Vitamin K dependent
   c. NOT consumed during clotting (*except II*)
   d. Present in fresh and stored plasma and serum

3. Fibrinogen proteins
   a. Factors I, V, VIII, XIII
   b. Consumed during clotting (*therefore not in serum*)
   c. ⬆ in acute phase (*pregnancy and inflammation*)

Characteristics of
Coagulation Proteins

FACTOR NAMES

1. Noted by Roman numerals

2. Exceptions:
   a. Prekallikrein
   b. High molecular weight kininogen

STABILIZED CROSSLINKED FIBRIN

1. Turn it on
   a. Activated intrinsically by the collagen (*via Factor XII*) contact system
   b. Activated extrinsically by disrupted endothelial cell membrane (*tissue factor or tissue thromboplastin*) complex with Factor VII to directly activate Factor X

2. Cofactors
   a. Factor VIII is bound with activated Factor IX by calcium to the platelet phopholipid membrane (*platelet factor 3*)
   b. Together these factors activate Factor X (*in the common pathway Factor V is the cofactor to Factor Xa in a similar arrangement with calcium and Platelet Factor 3*)
   c. This prothrombinase complex converts prothrombin to the active thrombin

3. Thrombin
   a. Cleaves peptides off of the fibrinogen molecule to form fibrin which polymerizes to form insoluble fibrin strands
   b. Thrombin also activates factor XIII which crosslinks the fibrin strands at the "D" region (*birth of the D-dimer*)

Coagulation Cascade

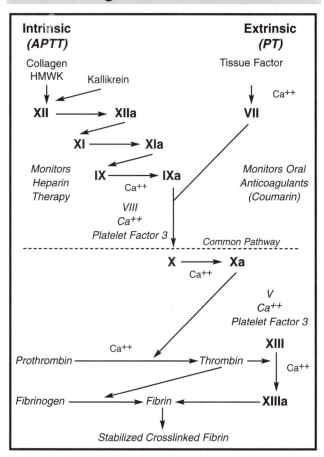

Intrinsic (APTT)

Collagen
HMWK

Kallikrein

XII → **XIIa**

XI → **XIa**

Monitors Heparin Therapy

IX → **IXa**
Ca⁺⁺

VIII
Ca⁺⁺
Platelet Factor 3

Extrinsic (PT)

Tissue Factor

Ca⁺⁺

VII

Monitors Oral Anticoagulants (Coumarin)

Common Pathway

X → **Xa**
Ca⁺⁺

V
Ca⁺⁺
Platelet Factor 3

Ca⁺⁺

Prothrombin ——→ Thrombin ——→

XIII
Ca⁺⁺

Fibrinogen ——→ Fibrin ←—— **XIIIa**

↓

Stabilized Crosslinked Fibrin

Other functions of thrombin

 Feeds back to "potentiate" factors V and VIII

 Recruits and aggregates platelets

 Turns on endothelial cell thrombomodulin *(receptor/activator for Protein C and Protein S system)* to inactivate Factors V and VIII

4. Turn it off
   a. Heparan sulfate on the endothelial cell binds antithrombin III which inactivates the activated serine proteases *(heparin works this way, too!)*
   b. Activated Protein C and its cofactor Protein S *(when bound to its receptor/activator thrombomodulin)* inactivates Factors VIII and V

Knowledge of Coagulation Cascade

FIBRINOLYTIC SYSTEM

1. Turn it on
   a. Activated intrinsically by collagen via the Factor XII / contact pathway that initiates intrinsic clotting or extrinsically by tissue plasminogen activator *(TPA)*
   b. Activators convert the precursor plasminogen to plasmin

2. What does it do?
   a. Plasmin cleaves fibrin strands to soluble fragments of fibrin *(fibrin degradation products are X, Y, D or E)*
   b. Can come from fibrin clot *(fibrinolysis)* or from unclotted fibrinogen *(fibrinogenolysis)*
   c. D-dimer comes from crosslinked clot *(clot specific)*

3. Turn it off
   a. TPA inactivated by tissue plasminogen activator inhibitor *(TPAI)* – stops activation
   b. Active plasmin inhibited by Alpha-2 Plasmin Inhibitor if it escapes the area of the clot. This prevents fibrinogenolysis

Excessive and inappropriate fibrinolysis

 Major feature of disseminated intravascular coagulation *(DIC)*; response to excessive clotting

 Also seen in liver disease *(activators are not cleared and the inhibitors are diminished)*

 Complications of cancer or surgery of the prostate or urinary tract where urokinase can leak into the circulation

74

"Clotbusters"

 Streptokinase (commercial)

 Urokinase (commercial)

 Tissue plasminogen activator (commercial and in vivo)

TEST Alert!

Role of Thrombin, Plasmin and Fibrin in Hemostasis

Specimen Collection/Handling

1. Sodium citrate, 3.8% or 3.2%(Ca^{++} *is necessary for both coagulation and platelet aggregation studies*); 3.2% is recommended

2. Whole blood - anticoagulant ratio = 9:1

3. Use plastic tubes or siliconized glassware (*glass activates factor XII and platelets will adhere to glass*).

4. Coagulation samples should NOT be drawn first when using evacuated tubes (*vacutainers*) because of contamination with tissue thromboplastin (*activates coagulation*) as needle pierces skin (*if only test ordered is coagulation study, draw a small amount in a tube that is discarded*)

5. Hemolyzed samples should NOT be used for platelet aggregation studies (*red cells contain ADP*).

6. Lipemic samples may cause problems with coagulation and aggregation studies (*may obscure changes in optical density*).

TEST Alert!

Anticoagulant Used for Coagulation Studies

Ratio of Anticoagulant : Blood

Routine Tests of Hemostatic Function

PROTHROMBIN TIME (*PT*)

1. Screen for extrinsic & common pathways

2. Measures factors I, II, V, VII and X

3. Monitors oral anticoagulants (*warfarin, coumarin, dicoumarol*)

4. Reagent - tissue thromboplastin & $CaCl_2$

5. Sensitive to Vitamin K factors

6. International normalized ratio: INR

$$INR = \left(\frac{patient\ result}{mean\ of\ reference\ range}\right)^{ISI}$$

(ISI = International Sensitivity Index from manufacturer)

7. Reference range = < 14 seconds
   a. Therapeutic goal: INR 2.0 - 3.5

ACTIVATED PARTIAL THROMBOPLASTIN TIME (*APTT*)

1. Screen for intrinsic & common pathways

2. Measures all factors except VII and XIII

3. Monitors heparin therapy

4. Reagents - activator (*kaolin, celite or ellagic acid*), platelet phospholipid (*PF3*) & $CaCl_2$

5. Reference range = 20 - 40 seconds
   a. Therapeutic goal: 1.5-2.5 times "normal" or use Heparin Response Curve

TEST Alert!

Therapy Monitored by PT and PTT

REMEMBER!
Monitoring by PT and APTT

APTT=2 T's Together Remind You of an "H"=Heparin
PT=<u>C</u>oumarin; Vitamin <u>K</u> Factors

FIBRINOGEN ASSAY

1. Quantitative measure of factor I

2. Reference range = 200-400 mg/dl

THROMBIN TIME (TT)

1. Does NOT measure defects in intrinsic/ extrinsic pathways

2. Affected by ↓ fibrinogen levels, and presence of heparin and other anti-thrombins

3. Reference range = < 20 seconds

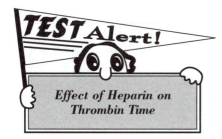

Effect of Heparin on Thrombin Time

BLEEDING TIME

1. Measures platelet function and numbers

2. Types
   a. Duke - earlobe; normal: 0 - 6 minutes
   b. Ivy - forearm; normal: 1 - 6 minutes
   c. Template - forearm; normal: 2 - 9.5 minutes

3. Prolonged with aspirin *(effects last 7 - 10 days)* and other drugs

CLOT RETRACTION

1. Evaluates platelet function, fibrinogen, red cell volume and fibrinolytic activity

2. Abnormal if platelet count <100,000/mm^3

3. Anemia and hypofibrinogenemia ↓ clot retraction

4. Rapid dissolution of clot = ↑ fibrinolytic activity *(example = DIC)*

5. Glanzmann Thrombasthenia - no clot retraction

Implication of a Rapidly Dissolved Clot

Correlate Conditions with Bleeding Time Results

Special Tests of Hemostatic Function

PLATELET AGGREGATION

1. Necessary for platelets to stick to each other

2. In vivo aggregating agents
   a. ADP
   b. Collagen
   c. Epinephrine
   d. Thrombin
   e. Serotonin
   f. Arachidonic acid
   g. Ristocetin
   h. Snake venom
   i. Antigen-antibody complexes
   j. Fibrin degradation products *(FDPs)*

3. In vitro aggregating agents
   a. ADP
   b. Collagen
   c. Ristocetin
   d. Epinephrine
   e. Thrombin
   f. Arachidonic acid

4. Measured with photo-optics
   a. As platelets aggregate, the turbidity of platelet rich plasma ↓
   b. Samples kept at RT, heated to 37C prior to testing
   c. Stirring necessary to bring platelets in contact for aggregation to occur

5. Aspirin inhibits secondary wave of aggregation *(destroys cyclooxygenase)*

Platelet Aggregration

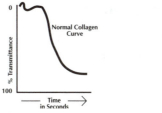

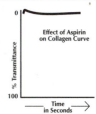

6. Abnormal ristocetin-induced aggregation
   a. Bernard-Soulier
   b. von Willebrand

Differentiating Platelet Disorders

DISORDER	NUMBER	MORPHOLOGY	ASSAYS
Glanzmann	N	N	Abn Agg (all agents ↓) vWF N
Bernard-Soulier	Moderate ↓	Giant Platelets	Abn Adhesion (ristocetin ↓) vWF N
von Willebrand	Usually N	N	Abn Adhesion (ristocetin ↓) vWF Abn

REMEMBER!
Platelet Adhesion Disorders

Wimpy Willie (*von Willebrand Disease*)
- normal platelets
- ↓Factor VIII
- ↓ vWF

Super Bernie (Bernard-Soulier) = **GIANT** Platelets

TEST Alert!
Diseases Associated with Abnormal Ristocetin Aggregation Curves

Effect of Aspirin on Platelet Aggregation Curve

FACTOR ASSAYS

1. PT and APTT tests performed with specific factor deficient plasma

2. % activity and amount of correction with normal plasma determined

3. Range of 40-150 % = normal

STYPVEN TIME

1. Russell's viper venom

2. Differentiates factor VII deficiency from common pathway deficiency
   a. Factor VII deficient plasma demonstrates "normal" results
   b. Deficiency of factors X, V, II demonstrate prolonged results

REPTILASE TIME

1. Snake venom enzyme

2. Test similar to thrombin time, but is not inhibited by heparin (*good to use for patients on heparin*)

3. Reference range = 18-22 seconds

FIBRINOLYSIS TESTING

1. Fibrin/fibrinogen degradation (*split*) products (*FDP/FSP*)
   a. Latex beads coated with anti-fibrinogen
   b. Positive screen in DIC

2. Latex D-Dimer - monoclonal antibody to crosslinked D fragment; positive in DIC, deep vein thrombosis and pulmonary embolism

TEST Alert!
Implications of a Positive D-Dimer Test

Hemostasis Disorders

1. Inherited Disorders
   a. Hemophilia A
      - ❖ *Deficiency of Factor VIII*
      - ❖ *Sex linked recessive - almost exclusive to men*
      - ❖ *Spontaneous bleeding into joints*
      - ❖ *Treat with commercial Factor VIII*
   b. Hemophilia B
      - ❖ *Deficiency of Factor IX*
      - ❖ *Sex linked recessive - almost exclusive to men*
      - ❖ *Clinically identical in inheritance and symptoms to Hemophilia A*
      - ❖ *Treat with Factor IX concentrates*
   c. Hemophilia C
      - ❖ *Deficiency of Factor XI*
      - ❖ *Incomplete autosomal recessive*
      - ❖ *Wide range in clinical severity*
      - ❖ *High incidence in Askenazi Jews*
      - ❖ *Only contact factor associated with bleeding*
   d. von Willebrand Disease
      - ❖ *Primary defect in the von Willebrand Factor (vWF)*
      - ❖ *Usually find secondary deficiency of Factor VIII*
      - ❖ *Autosomal dominant - males and females are affected equally*
      - ❖ *Platelet adhesion defect with prolonged bleeding time*
      - ❖ *Treat with cryoprecipitate or DDAVP (drug); Factor VIII concentrates do NOT contain vWF*
   e. Factor XIII deficiency
      - ❖ *Autosomal recessive*
      - ❖ *NOT detected by common coagulation tests*
      - ❖ *Results in a significant bleeding disorder*
      - ❖ *Detected with the 5M urea test*

2. Acquired Disorders
   a. Inhibitors - usually IgG antibody directed against a specific factor or phospholipids
      - ❖ *Lupus anticoagulant*
        - ☞ Directed against phospholipids
        - ☞ Seen in Lupus Erythematosis (about 5-10%) but also seen in malignancies, infections, drug therapy and other autoimmune disorders
        - ☞ Use platelet neutralization techniques to confirm presence *(platelet phospholipid neutralizes antibody and test will correct)*
      - ❖ *Factor VIII inhibitor - most common specific inhibitor, but others have been demonstrated; APTT mixing studies differentiate factor deficiency from inhibitor*
        - ☞ If corrected by normal plasma, a factor deficiency is indicated
        - ☞ If NOT corrected, an inhibitor should be investigated
   b. Vitamin K deficiency
      - ❖ *Functional deficiency of factors II, VII, IX and X*
      - ❖ *PIVKA molecules (proteins in vitamin K absence) - present but not functional*
      - ❖ *Vitamin K originates from diet and bacteria in gut*
      - ❖ *Deficiency seen in poor diet and with broad spectrum antibiotic use*
      - ❖ *Same result observed in coumarin and dicoumarol therapy*
   c. Liver Disease *(depending on severity or stage)*
      - ❖ *Deficiency of factors I, II, V, VII, IX and X*
      - ❖ *Factor VII deficiency most pronounced*
      - ❖ *↓ clearance of plasminogen activators*
      - ❖ *↑ FDP due to fibrin(ogen)olysis*
   d. Disseminated Intravascular Coagulation (DIC)
      - ❖ *Secondary to sepsis or obstetric complications*
      - ❖ *Thrombotic occlusion of micro-circulation*
      - ❖ *RBC fragments*
      - ❖ *Consumption of platelets and factors I, V, VIII*
      - ❖ *High levels of FDP and D-dimer*

Fibrinolysis

	PRIMARY	SECONDARY (DIC)
Platelet Count	N	↓
Red Cell Morphology	N	RBC Fragments
PT and APTT	Abnormal	Abnormal
Protamine Sulfate	—	+
FDP	+	+
Euglobulin Clot Lysis Test	+	—
D-Dimer	—	+

Thrombotic Diseases

1. Arterial Events - platelet driven *(arthlerosclerosis, prosthetic heart devices)*

2. Venous Events
   a. Blood flow problems *(superficial or deep vein thrombosis)*
   b. Clot inhibitor deficiency *(about 20%)*
      ❖ *Antithrombin III (ATIII)*
         ☞ Principle antagonist of active coagulation proteases
         ☞ Produced in the liver
         ☞ Activated by heparan sulfate on the endothelial cell and by heparin as therapeutic drug
      ❖ *Protein C*
         ☞ Vitamin K dependent serine protease
         ☞ Activated by thrombomodulin on the endothelial cell
         ☞ Requires Protein S cofactor
         ☞ Inactivates Factors V and VIII
      ❖ *Protein S*
         ☞ Vitamin K dependent
         ☞ Co-factor for Protein C
         ☞ Bound and free state
         ☞ Only free protein S is functional so measure total and free
   c. Factor V Leiden
      ☞ Mutant factor V
      ☞ Resists the action of Protein C/S
      ☞ Activated Protein C Resistance Test
   d. Antiphospholipid syndrome
      ❖ *Any of three classes of antibodies*
         ☞ Anticardiolipin antibodies
         ☞ Lupus anticoagulant
         ☞ Specific antibodies (e.g. beta-2-glycoprotein)
   e. Prothrombin mutation
      ❖ *Mutation at position 20210*
      ❖ *First described in 1996*
      ❖ *1-2% of general population are heterozygotes*
      ❖ *Results in ↑ thrombin formation*
      ❖ *↑ risk of thrombotic event*

TEST Alert!

Characteristics of Protein C and S

COAGULATION SAMPLE QUESTIONS

1. If one performs an aPTT on a patient on high-dose warfarin therapy, we would expect that the result would be:
   A. Normal because warfarin effects the PT only
   B. ↑ because of fibrinogen split products
   C. ↑ because of factor VII deficiency
   D. ↑ because of other factor deficiencies

2. Prolonged bleeding time and giant platelets best describe
   A. Bernard-Soulier syndrome
   B. Glanzmann thrombasthenia
   C. von Willebrand disease
   D. Wiskott-Aldrich syndrome

3. Which of the following would one suspect in afibrinogenemia?
   A. Bleeding time abnormal, reptilase time abnormal, thrombin time abnormal
   B. Bleeding time normal, reptilase time abnormal, thrombin time abnormal
   C. Bleeding time abnormal, reptilase time normal, thrombin time abnormal
   D. Bleeding time normal, reptilase time normal, thrombin time normal

4. A 22 year old female was seen in the emergency room with evidence of bleeding following a spider bite. Laboratory results show

   Blood smear: Schistocytes
   Platelet count: 50,000/mm3
   PT: 20 secs
   APTT: 60 secs
   D-Dimer: positive

The most likely diagnosis is
   A. Allergic reaction
   B. Primary fibrinolysis
   C. Secondary fibrinolysis
   D. Vitamin K deficiency

5. Which of the following is an immune mediated condition characterized by a low platelet count and is found primarily in children?
   A. Idiopathic thrombocytopenia purpura
   B. Thrombotic thrombocytopenia purpura
   C. May-Hegglin
   D. Wiscott-Aldrich

ANSWERS AND RATIONALE

1. D

The prothrombin time is used to monitor warfarin therapy, but warfarin results in deficiencies of factors II, VII, IX, and X. The correct answer is D because factors II, IX and X are also measured by the aPTT.

2. A

Options B and C are incorrect because platelet morphology is normal even though the bleeding time is prolonged. Option D is incorrect because this syndrome is characterized by tiny platelets and a prolonged bleeding time.

3. A

Bleeding time, reptilase time and thrombin time are all sensitive to deficiencies in fibrinogen.

4. C

Option A is incorrect as allergies do not result in coagulation abnormalities. Option B is incorrect because schistocytes, decreased platelets and a positive D-dimer test are not seen in primary fibrinolysis. Option D is NOT characterized by schistocytes and a positive D-dimer test.

5. A

ITP is an immune-mediated disorder characterized by a abrupt onset and spontaneous remission in several weeks. It is found predominately in children. Option B is a non-immune mediated condition usually characterized by microangiopathic anemia, thrombocytopenia, fever, renal disease and neurologic abnormalities. Option C is a non-immune mediated condition characterized by thrombocytopenia (decreased platelet production) with small hypogranular platelets. Option D is an immunologic condition characterized by immune deficiency (T and B cells). Thrombocytopenia with severely shortened platelet survival and platelets with absent dense bodies are also associated with this disease.

URINALYSIS/BODY FLUIDS

by Michele Zitzmann
and Libby Spence

Kidney

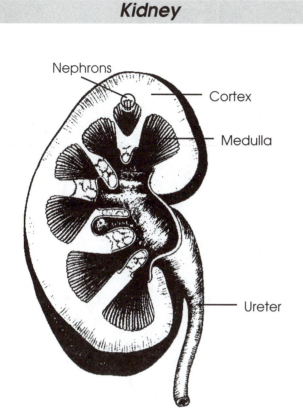

Nephron

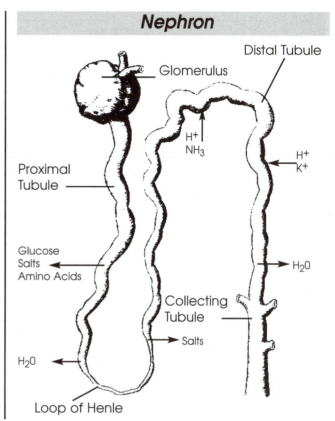

• Diagrams adopted with permission from Modern Urine Chemistry Manual; Bayer Corporation; 1996

Renal Physiology

NEPHRON

1. Major functional unit of the kidney

2. Approximately 1 million per kidney

3. Composed of glomerulus and renal tubules

GLOMERULUS

1. Coil of capillary vessels

2. Non-selective filter of plasma substances of less than 70,000 MW

3. Water, glucose, electrolytes, amino acids, urea, uric acid, creatinine, and ammonia comprise the glomerular filtrate

TUBULES	
Proximal Tubule	Reabsorbs water, Sodium Chloride, Bicarbonate, Potassium, Calcium, Amino Acids, Phosphates, Protein, and Glucose Glucose - Threshold Substance -Reabsorb at 160-180 mg/dl or less Secretes - Sulfates, glucuronides, Hydrogen ions and drugs
Loop of Henle Descending	Reabsorbs water No solutes reabsorbed
Loop of Henle Ascending	Reabsorbs Solutes (Sodium, Chloride, Calcium, and Magnesium No water reabsorbed
Distal & Collecting Tubules	Reabsorbs Sodium Secretes Potassium, Ammonia and Hydrogen ions Potassium ions exchanged for sodium ions

URINE VOLUME

	VOLUME	DISEASE AND CAUSES
Normal	Average of 1200-1500 ml/day	
Polyuria	>2500 ml/day	Diabetes insipidus, Diabetes mellitus, diuretics Caffeine, alcohol
Oliguria	<500 ml/day	Dehydration, Vomiting, Diarrhea, Burns, Perspiration
Anuria	Complete Cessation	Kidney Damage, Decrease blood flow to kidneys
Nocturia	Increase volume at night	

REMEMBER!
Urine Volume

Poor Polly
(polyuria)

- Diabetes mellitus

- Diabetes insipidus

Poor Ollie *(oliguria)*

- Dehydration Due To:
  - *Vomiting*
  - *Diarrhea*
  - *Burns*

Nocturnal Ned
(nocturia)

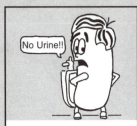

Absent Andy
(anuria)

- Damage to Kidney
- ↓Blood Flow to Kidney (↓*Cardiac Output*)

4. Filters 120 ml/min, or one-fifth of renal plasma

URINE COMPOSTITION

1. Urea *(non-protein nitrogen)*
   a. Metabolic waste product produced in liver from breakdown of protein
   b. 1/2 total urinary dissolved organic solids

2. Other organic solids *(non-protein nitrogens)*
   a. Uric acid
   b. Creatinine

3. Inorganics solids
   a. Chloride - primary constituent
   b. Na^+
   c. K^+

4. Water

HORMONES

HORMONES	SOURCE	ACTION
Aldosterone	Adrenal Cortex	Increases rate of sodium reabsorption
Antidiuretic Hormone (ADH)	Posterior Pituitary Gland	Reabsorption of water from the distal tubules Deficiency - Diabetes insipidus
Erythropoietin	Kidney	Stimulates production of erythrocytes

Role of Nephron in Urine Formation

Deficiency Causing Diabetes Insipidus

Specimen Collection and Handling

COLLECTION METHODS

1. Random
   a. Most common specimen type
   b. Easiest to collect
   c. Useful for routine screening tests

2. First morning
   a. First voided specimen upon waking
   b. Ideal screening specimen (*most concentrated*)

3. Midstream clean catch
   a. Clean external genital area
   b. First and last stream of urine voided; midstream collected
   c. Specimen of choice for bacterial culture in routine circumstances

4. Catheterization
   a. Insertion of catheter directly into bladder via urethra
   b. Avoids external contamination - may introduce infection

5. Pediatric
   a. Sterile, plastic collection bag placed over genital area with adhesive
   b. Bag checked every 15 minutes
   c. Many sources of contamination

6. Suprapubic aspiration
   a. Insert needle through suprapubic abdominal area directly into bladder
   b. Avoids external contamination - may introduce infection
   c. Optimum specimen for bacterial culture; invasive procedure

24 HOUR URINE

1. Collected over 24-hour period

2. First specimen discarded while all others collected

3. Used for quantitative urine studies

4. Completeness of collection monitored by creatinine levels (*should be > 1.0 mg/dl*)

ANALYSIS

1. Analyze within 1 hour of voiding (*NOT 1 hour after received in lab!*)

2. Effects of prolonged sitting of specimens at room temperature

⬆	⬇
Nitrite (*bacterial growth*)	Glucose (*glycolysis due to bacteria and yeast*)
pH (*urea converted to ammonia*)	Ketones (*volatization - exposure to air*)
Turbidity (*bacterial growth, red or white cells, or amorphous material*)	Bilirubin (*exposure to light*)
	Urobilinogen (*oxidized to urobilin*)
	Cells and Casts (*lysis*)

Changes in color occur due to oxidation or reduction of metabolites.

Urine Changes that Occur Upon Standing & Best Preservative to Use

REFRIGERATION

1. Preservation method of choice (*no more than 4 hrs*)

2. May result in precipitation of amorphous crystals

3. After removal from the refrigerator, let sample return to room temperature before testing (*approximately 15 min*)

Physical Examination

ODOR

1. Not evaluated, but may provide clue to constituents

84

2. Associations
   a. Fruity - ketones
   b. Ammonia - old urine
   c. "Mousy" - phenylketonuria (*PKU*)
   d. Maple syrup - Maple Syrup disease
   (*branched chain aminoaciduria*)

CLARITY

1. Normal urine is clear

2. Any of the urinary sediments (*cells, casts, crystals*), or bacteria may make urine cloudy

Color as a Clue

ABNORMAL COLOR	SUBSTANCE
Red	Hemoglobin Red Blood Cells Myoglobin Porphyrin Uroerythrin
Red-Brown	Hemoglobin Red Blood Cells Myoglobin
Yellow-Brown/Amber-Yellow-Green	Bilirubin Biliverdin
Yellow-Orange	Bilirubin Urobilin Pyridium (*drug*)
Bright Yellow	Vitamin C
Dark Yellow	Concentrated Specimen Bilirubin Urobilin
Brown-Black	Methemoglobin (*oxydized RBC's*) Homogentisic Acid (*Alkaptonuria*) Melanin
Blue	Indican (*Tryptophane Metabolic Disorder*)
Green/Blue-Green	Old Urine Psuedomonas
Port Wine	Porphyrin

Factors Contributing to Urine Clarity and Odor

COLOR

1. Normal urine is a pale yellow (straw) to yellow color

2. Urochrome gives urine its normal color

PH

1. Normal urine is slightly acid (*pH-6.0*), Random (*4.5-8.0*)
   a. Postprandial sample (*2 hours after eating*), urine may be alkaline (*alkaline tide*)
   b. When urine stands at room temperature (*or warmer*) for some time, it may become alkaline
   c. Acidic - Metabolic or respiratory acidosis, high protein diet, cranberry juice
   d. Alkaline-vegetarian

SPECIFIC GRAVITY (SG)

1. Offers the simplest way to check the concentration and dilution function of the kidney tubules

2. Normal urine: 1.002 - 1.035

3. 1.040 is the highest the kidney can concentrate
   a. Higher values are due to either large amounts of glucose or radio-opaque dyes from renal x-ray procedures
   b. ⬇ values - Diabetes insipidus (⬇ *ADH*)
   c. If the S.G. is higher than 1.035, dilute the urine 1:2 with distilled water and multiply the last two digits of the result by 2

4. S.G. is directly proportional to color; the higher the S.G., the deeper the color (*Exception: A pale colored urine with a high S.G. is probably due to glucose - urine is diluted due to loss of concentrating ability by diabetics*)

SPECIFIC GRAVITY MEASUREMENT		
METHOD	**MEASURED**	**NOTES**
Refractometer - TS	Refractive Index	No temperature corrections Correct for large amount of protein (1 g increases 0.003) and glucose (1 g increases 0.004)
Reagent Strip	Indirect - Colorimetric	pKa change of polyelectrolytes (relative to ionic concentration)

TEST Alert!

Define Specific Gravity and Refractive Index

Correlate Specific Gravity with Clinical Disease

Calculate Specific Gravity from Urine Dilution

Chemical Examination

PROTEIN

1. Dipstick
   a. Principle - "protein error of indicators"
      - *pH of the protein-testing portion is kept at 3.5*
      - *Albumin in urine binds to dye*
      - *Binding shifts the dye's spectrum so that it appears to change color from yellow to green*
   b. More sensitive to albumin than globulin

2. Some labs choose to confirm a positive dipstick with a quantitative protein method based on precipitation *(sulfosalicylic acid)*

3. Interfering substances
   a. Dipstick — highly alkaline urine *(false positive)*
   b. Sulfosalicylic acid — x-ray media, massive penicillin *(false positive)*

4. Proteinuria
   a. Best single indicator of renal abnormality *(glomerular involvement)*
   b. Associated with multiple myeloma, orthostatic proteinuria *(benign condition resulting in proteinuria after standing)* and strenuous exercise

5. Microalbuminuria
   a. Detected by sensitive albumin tests *(level too low to be detected by routine reagent strip)*
   b. Periodic monitoring benefits patients with diabetes, hypertension, and peripheral vascular disease
   c. Enables patients with low levels of albuminuria to begin treatment before kidney disease occurs
   d. Several commercial methods available for screening

GLUCOSE

1. Dipstick
   a. Analyzed for diabetes Renal Threshold 160-180 mg/dl
   b. Specific for glucose only
   c. Principle - glucose oxidase *(double sequential enzyme reaction)*
   d. Positive copper reduction test with negative dipstick = sugar *(or other reducing substance)* other than glucose
   e. Negative copper reduction test with positive dipstick possible because dipstick is more sensitive *(0.1% glucose)* than copper reduction method
   f. Interference by oxidizing agents *(bleach)* - false positive

2. Clinitest tablet
   a. For glucose and other reducing sugars
   b. Principle - Benedict's copper reduction test

   $CuSO_4 + NaOH + reducing\ substance = Cu_2O$
      - *Sugars (and other reducing substances) reduce the cupric ion to the cuprous state in the*

presence of alkali and heat
- ❖ Color of reaction ranges from blue-green to orange-red depending upon amount of sugar
  c. Sensitivity - 0.2% glucose (*dipstick can be positive with a negative tablet*)
  d. Screening test for galactosemia (*rare congenital carbohydrate metabolic condition in pediatric patients*)

DIPSTICK	COPPER REDUCTION	REASON
0	+	Non-Glucose Sugar or Other Reducing Substances
+	0	Dipstick More Sensitive to Glucose than Copper Reduction (.1% vs. .2%)

  e. Galactose, lactose, fructose, maltose and pentose give positive results
  f. Ascorbic acid (*vitamin C*) causes false positive results (*but only in extremely high doses!*)
  g. Use 2 drop method rather than 5 drop method to minimize "pass through" reactions (*reaction goes from negative* [blue] *to positive* [orange] *and back to negative*)

Evaluate Tests for Glucose and Other Reducing Substances

KETONES

1. Acetone, diacetic acid and beta-hydroxybutyric acid - (*end products of fat metabolism*)

2. Principle (*dipstick and tablets*) - Sodium nitroprusside + ketone = purple color

3. Dipstick specific for diacetic acid

4. Confirmation tests (*Acetest tablets*) specific for diacetic acid and acetone

5. Interference by highly pigmented urine and levadopa metabolites cause a false positive result

6. Uncontrolled diabetes mellitus, high protein diets and GI disturbances give positive results

BLOOD

1. 2-step enzymatic procedure
   a. Peroxide on strip + blood = O_2
      O_2 + color producer = color change

2. Bleach and other oxidizing agents can interfere - false positive results

3. Ascorbic acid (*vitamin C*) - false negative results (*newer reagent strips are more resistant to this effect*)

4. Hemoglobin and myoglobin have peroxidase activity

5. Positive results
   a. Hematuria associated with systemic bleeding disorders, renal diseases, cystitis, calculi and strenuous exercise
   b. Hemoglobinuria associated with hemolytic anemias, incompatible transfusions, malaria and strenuous exercise
   c. Myoglobinuria associated with muscle destruction

BILIRUBIN

1. Principle (*tablet or dipstick*) - Diazo Reaction: diazonium salt + bilirubin = bluish purple color

2. Ictotest (*tablet*) more sensitive than dipstick

3. False negatives
   a. Ascorbic acid
   b. Nitrite

4. Bilirubinuria associated with bile duct obstruction and liver damage (*hepatitis and cirrhosis*)

UROBILINOGEN

1. Principle (*dipstick*) - Ehrlich's reaction: Para-dimethylaminobenzaldehyde in acid buffer reacts with urobilinogen to produce a peach to pink color

2. False negatives
   a. Nitrite
   b. Formalin

3. False positives
   a. Highly pigmented urine
   b. Some medications

4. Normal: 1 mg/dl or less; 0.1 EU

5. ↑Urobilinogen
   a. Liver damage (*hepatitis, cirrhosis*)
   b. Hemolytic disease

6. Negative urobilinogen (*not detected on dipstick*) indicates bile duct obstruction

Normal Bilirubin Metabolism

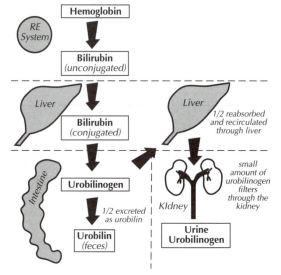

• Diagram Adapted with Permission from Urodynamics; Bayer, Inc.; 1979

	BILIRUBIN	UROBILINOGEN
Normal	0	0.1 EU
Hemolytic	0	↑
Liver Disease	0 or ↑	↑
Obstructive	↑	↓ (N on dipstick)

Correlate Bilirubin and Urobilinogen Results with Clinical Condition

NITRITE (DETECTS NITRATE-REDUCING BACTERIA)

1. Principle (*dipstick*) Griess's reaction
   a. Nitrite reacts with amine reagent at acidic pH forms diazonium compound
   b. This compound reacts with 3-hyroxy-1,2,3,4 tetrahydrobenz (*h*) - quinolin to produce a pink color

2. False negatives
   a. Lack of dietary nitrate

b. Urine not in bladder long enough (*4 hr min*) for bacteria to reduce nitrate to nitrite
c. Bacteria are present but not nitrate reducers
d. Ascorbic acid

3. Any shade of pink is considered to represent a clinically significant amount of bacteria

LEUKOCYTES

1. Principle (*dipstick*)
   a. Leukocyte esterase splits an ester to form a pyrrole compound which reacts with a diazo reagent to produce a purple color

2. Positive reactions indicate presence of leukocytes (*pyuria*)

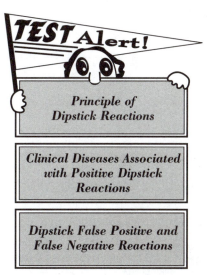

Principle of Dipstick Reactions

Clinical Diseases Associated with Positive Dipstick Reactions

Dipstick False Positive and False Negative Reactions

DIPSTICK CORRELATIONS	
POSITIVE TEST	CORRELATE OTHER TESTS
pH	Nitrite, Leukocyte esterase, Microscopic
Protein	Blood, Nitrite, Leukocyte esterase, Microscopic
Glucose	Ketone
Ketones	Glucose
Blood	Protein, Microscopic
Bilirubin	Urobilinogen
Urobilinogen	Bilirubin
Nitrite	Protein, Leukocyte esterase, Microscopic
Leukocyte esterase	Protein, Nitrite, Microscopic
Specific Gravity	None

Dipstick Reactions

Substance	Reaction Principle	False Positives	False Negatives	Clinical Significance
pH	2 Indicators Provide Wide Spectrum of Color Changes	None	None	Alkaline - May Indicate "Old" Urine; Seen after Eating (Response to HCl Secretion)
Protein	Protein Error of Indicators - pH of Strip = 3.5 Dye Changes Color of Strip	Highly Alkaline Urine	High Salt	Proteinuria - Best Single Indicator of early disease • Glomerular Involvement • Can be ↑ After Strenuous Exercise
Glucose	Glucose Oxidase Method (Double Sequential Enzyme)	Bleach	Ascorbic Acid (↑ Levels), Ketones, High SG with low pH	Diabetes Mellitus
Ketones	Sodium Nitroprusside + Ketones = Purple Color	Highly Pigmented Urine, Levadopa Metabolites	Ascorbic Acid (Newer Strips More Resistant), ↑SG	• Uncontrolled Diabetes Mellitus • High Protein Diet (Restricted Carbohydrates) • Dehydration (Excess Vomiting and Diarrhea)
Blood	Peroxide + Blood = O_2 O_2 + Color Indicator = Color Change	Bleach	Ascorbic Acid (↑ Levels), Ketones, High SG with low pH	• Hematuria - Systemic Bleeding Disorders, Renal Disease, Cystitis, Calculi, Strenous Exercise, Menstrual Contamination • Hemoglobinuria - Incompatible Blood Transfusion, Malaria, Strenuous Exercise, Hemolytic Anemias • Myoglobinuria - Muscle Destruction
Bilirubin	Diazonium Salt + Bilirubin = Bluish/Purple Color	Medication Color	Ascorbic Acid (Newer Strips More Resistant), ↑SG, Nitrite	• Bile Duct Obstruction • Liver Damage (Hepatitis and Cirrhosis)
Urobilinogen	Para-dimethylaminobin-zaldehyde + Urobilinogen = Peach to Pink Color (Ehrlich's Reaction)	Highly Pigmented Urine, Some Medications	Nitrite	• Liver Damage (Hepatitis and Cirrhosis) • Hemolytic Anemias
Nitrite	Nitrite + Amine Reagent = Diazo Compound Diazo Compound + 3-Hydroxy-1,2,3,4 Tetrahydrobenz-(h)-quinolin = Pink Color	Medication Color	Ascorbic Acid	• Bacteria (UTI)
Leukocytes	Leukocyte Esterase Splits Ester to Form Pyrrole Compound Pyrrole Compound + Diazo Reagent = Purple Color	Bleach	Glucose, Protein, High SG and Some Antibiotics	• WBC in Urine Which Most Likely Indicates the Presence of Bacteria • Reacts with granulocytes not lymphocytes
Specific Gravity	pK_a Change of Polyelectrolyte	Protein	Alkaline Urine	• ↓ Diabetes Insipidus (Consistently Low) • Radiopaque Dye

Microscopic Examination

STAINS

1. Sternheimer-Malbin - most frequently used supravital stain

2. Sudan III or Oil Red O - confirms the presence of fat or triglyceride

NORMAL URINE SEDIMENT CONSTITUENTS

1. 0-2 rbc/hpf

2. 0-5 wbc/hpf

3. 0-2 hyaline casts/lpf

4. Slight mucus

ABNORMAL URINE CONSTITUENTS

RED CELLS

1. May indicate glomerular damage or menstrual contamination

2. May be altered by pH and osmotic pressure to form "ghost", crenated or swollen cells

3. May be confused with yeast cells and oil droplets; add 2% acetic acid to lyse RBC

WHITE CELLS

1. May indicate inflammation or infection (*pyuria*)

CASTS

1. Cylindrical form having parallel sides

2. Formed in the lumen of the distal convoluted tubule and collecting duct

Location of Cast Formation

3. Major constituent of casts is uromodulin (*formerly known as Tamm Horsfall protein*), a glycoprotein secreted by renal tubular epithelial cells

4. Factors that influence cast formation
   a. ↓ pH
   b. ↓ output
   c. ↑ solute concentration (*increased S.G.*)
   d. ↑ protein

5. Types of casts
   a. Hyaline
      ❖ *Most frequently seen*
      ❖ *Primarily uromodulin protein*
   b. Red cell cast
      ❖ *Indicates bleeding from nephron; glomerular dysfunction*
      ❖ *Solid mass of tightly packed rbc with characteristic orange-red color (unstained sediment)*
      ❖ *Diagnostic of intrinsic renal disease (glomerulonephritis)*
   c. White cell cast
      ❖ *Signifies infection or inflammation within the nephron*

EPITHELIAL CELLS		
EPITHELIAL CELLS	**APPEARANCE**	**NOTES**
Squamous	Largest cell Abundant irregular cytoplasm Central nucleus (RBC size)	Least significant Most frequent seen
Transitional	Round or pear shape Central nucleus Absorb water - Swell to 3X normal size	Renal pelvis, bladder, upper urethra Renal carcinoma
Renal tubular	Most significant Round, eccentric nucleus Larger than WBC	Tubular necrosis
Oval fat bodies	Highly refractile fat droplets in Renal tubular epithelial cell	Nephrotic syndrome, "Maltese Cross" when polarized, stain with Sudan III or Oil Red O

❖ *Associated with pyelonephritis*
  d. Epithelial casts
     ❖ *Granular - disintegration of cellular casts*
  e. Waxy cast- older hyaline cast
     ❖ *Indicate prolonged urinary stasis*
     ❖ *Considered renal failure casts, if broad*
  f. Fatty casts - breakdown of epithelial cell casts tat contain oval fat bodies
  g. Broad casts
     ❖ *Form in collecting ducts that have become dilated (not a good sign!)*
     ❖ *All types of casts can occur as broad casts*

CRYSTALS

1. Formed by the precipitation of urine solutes subjected to changes in pH, temperature and concentration

2. Normal crystals
   a. Acid Urine
      ❖ *Amorphous urates - yellow-brown granules; pink sediment*
      ❖ *Uric acid - variety of shapes, usually a yellow rhomboid form*
      ❖ *Calcium oxalate*
        ☞ envelope-shaped
        ☞ may be seen in antifreeze poisoning *(young children)*

   b. Alkaline Urine
      ❖ *Amorphous phosphates - white precipitate in urine; microscopically identical to amorphous urates*
      ❖ *Triple phosphate - "coffin lid"*
      ❖ *Ammonium biurate - "thorn apple"*
      ❖ *Calcium carbonate - "dumbbell"*

ABNORMAL CRYSTALS

1. Indicate metabolic disorders or drug metabolites

2. Types
   a. Bilirubin - small clusters of fine needles
   b. Cystine - colorless hexagonal plates
   c. Cholesterol - rectangular plates with notched corners
   d. Leucine - yellow-brown spheres with concentric circles or radial striations
   e. Tyrosine - fine, delicate needles (*when seen with leucine crystals, liver disease is indicated*)
   f. Sulfonamide - needles or brown spheres
   f. Radiographic dye - plates
   g. Ampicillin - needles

REMEMBER!
Crystals Seen in "Normal" Urine

Acid Urine
Cal the Ox and Uri the Polar Bear are friends. They hang around Acid Urine.

Calcium Oxalate
• Envelope Appearance
Uric Acid
• Rhomboid shaped
• Polarizes

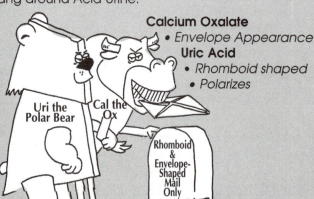

Alkaline Urine

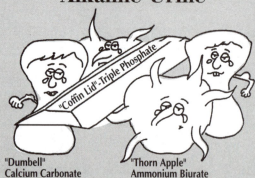

"Dumbell" Calcium Carbonate

"Thorn Apple" Ammonium Biurate

The Alkaline Funeral Party

Triple Phosphate
• Coffin Lid Shaped
Ammonium Biurate
• Thorn Apple Crystal
Calcium Carbonate
• Dumbell Shaped

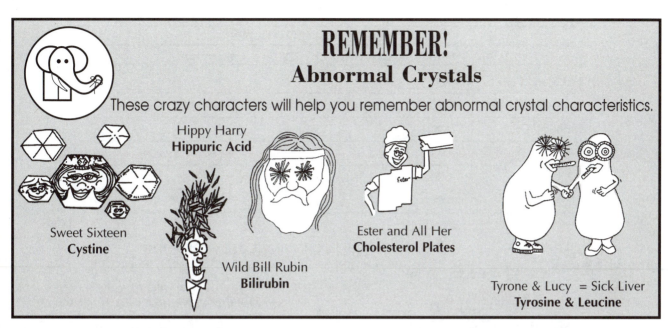

REMEMBER!
Abnormal Crystals
These crazy characters will help you remember abnormal crystal characteristics.

Sweet Sixteen
Cystine

Hippy Harry
Hippuric Acid

Wild Bill Rubin
Bilirubin

Ester and All Her
Cholesterol Plates

Tyrone & Lucy = Sick Liver
Tyrosine & Leucine

OTHER CONSTITUENTS PRESENT IN URINE

1. Bacteria - rod-shaped *(Bacilli)* most commonly present; correlate with presence/absence of leukocytes

2. Yeast - most often represents a vaginal infection; must correlate with clinical findings

3. Parasites *(Trichomonas vaginalis, Enterobius vermicularis)*

4. Sperm - may be seen in males and females

5. Mucus - no clinical significance

6. Clue cells - squamous epithelial cells with bacteria adhering to them; indicates bacterial vaginosis (BV)

Inclusion Bodies

1. In viral infections, such as Rubella and Herpes RTE cells may contain inclusion bodies.

2. CMV - produces large intranuclear inclusions in RTE

3. Lead poisoning produces cytoplasmic inclusions in RTE
   a. Cytocentrifuge and stain with Papanicolaou stain to visualize

4. Hemosiderin *(a form of iron)* contained in RTE or urine sediment indicates severe intravascular hemolysis, DTR, PCH, or as a result of Hemochromatosis
   a. Cytocentrifuge and stain with Prussian blue stain for iron

ARTIFACTS	
ARTIFACTS	CHARACTERISTICS
Powder *(Starch granules from gloves)*	May be confused with crystals
	Polarized light - Maltese Cross formation, but not round like cholesterol
Fat	Triglyceride stains positive with fat stain
	Cholesterol does not stain; produces Maltese Cross when polarized
Hair	May be confused with casts
Fiber	Fiber polarizes light - casts do not

MICROSCOPIC CORRELATIONS		
MICROSCOPIC ELEMENT	**PHYSICAL CHARACTERISTIC**	**CHEMICAL CHARACTERISTIC**
Red Blood Cell	Turbidity, red color	Blood
White Blood Cell	Turbidity	Protein, Nitrite, Leukocyte esterase
Epithelial Cells	Turbidity	Protein
Casts		Protein
Bacteria	Turbidity	pH, Nitrite, Leukocyte esterase
Crystals	Turbidity, color	pH

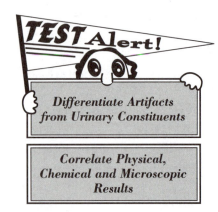

TEST Alert!

Differentiate Artifacts from Urinary Constituents

Correlate Physical, Chemical and Microscopic Results

Pregnancy Testing

1. Human chorionic gonadotropin (hCG), a glycoprotein composed of alpha and beta subunits, is secreted by the placenta. The appearance and rapid rise in concentration of hCG in the mother's serum and urine make it an excellent marker for confirming pregnancy.
   a. hCG can be detected as early as 8-10 days after ovulation (*1 day after implantation*)
   b. hCG peaks at 8-10 weeks of pregnancy
   c. First morning specimen preferred (*more concentrated*)

Renal Function Tests

1. Used to test for glomerular filtration and tubular function

2. Tests for glomerular filtration
   a. Clearance tests
   b. B2-Microglobulin
   c. Cystatin C

CREATININE CLEARANCE TEST

1. Most commonly used clearance test to assess GFR (*amount of blood filtered of a particular substance in a given time*)

2. Production and excretion of creatinine is fairly constant from day to day

3. Specimen collection
   a. 24 hour urine
   b. Creatinine > 1 mg/dl measures adequacy of collection

4. Mathematical formula:

$$\text{Creatinine Clearance} = \frac{U \times V}{P}$$

   U = Concentration of urine creatinine mg/dL
   V = Volume of urine in ml/time in minutes
   P = Concentration of plasma creatinine mg/dL

5. Normal Creatinine Clearance = 120 ml/min for adults; ↓ with age

6. Correction for Kidney Mass (*Kidney Mass Proportional to Body Size*)

$$\text{Clearance} = \frac{U \times V}{P} \times \frac{1.73}{A}$$

   A = Body Surface Area

7. Example:

   Plasma Creatinine = 1.5 mg/dL
   Urine Creatinine = 1.2 mg/dL
   Urine Volume = 1.2 L
   Surface Area = 1.30 mm^3
   Collection Time = 24 hours

$$\text{Volume} = \frac{1200 \text{ ml}}{1440 \text{ min}} = 0.833$$

$$\frac{1.2 \text{ mg/dL} \times (0.833 \text{ ml/min})}{.015 \text{ mg/dL}} = 66.67 \text{ ml/min}$$

$$\frac{66.67 \times 1.73}{1.30} = 88.71 \text{ ml/min}$$

B2-MICROGLOBULIN

1. Useful marker of renal tubular function.
2. ↑ plasma concentrations indicate a reduced GFR (not specific)

CYSTATIN C

1. May provide an equal or better detection of adverse changes in GFR
2. Disadvantages:
   a. Higher cost than creatinine clearance
   b. Possible variable results among individuals

Renal Diseases

Findings in Renal Disease

DISEASE	MICROSCOPIC FINDINGS
Acute Glomerulonephritis	Gross hematuria, Smoky Turbidity, RBC Casts, Waxy
Chronic Glomerulonephritis	Hematuria; All Types of Casts, but Only Occ to Few RBC Casts
Acute Pyelonephritis	Turbid, Pos Nitrite, Pos Leukocyte Esterase, WBC Casts, Bacteria
Chronic Pyelonephritis	Pos Nitrite, Pos Leukocyte Esterase; All Types of Casts, but Only Occ to Few WBC Casts
Nephrotic Syndrome	May See "Free" Fat Droplets; Fatty Casts; Oval Fat Bodies
Cystitis/Lower Urinary Tract Infection	Bacteria; WBC's

Body Fluids

CEREBROSPINAL FLUID (CSF)

1. Reasons for analysis:
   a. Meningitis
   b. Encephalitis
   c. Syphilis
   d. Brain abcess / Tumor
   e. Intracranial hemorrhage
   f. Leukemia / Lymphoma with CNS involvement
2. Normally clear, colorless
3. Xanthochromia - pink, orange, or yellow CSF supernatant (usually due to hemoglobin)
4. Important to differentiate between intracranial hemorrhage and traumatic collection
5. Normal Analyte Values
   a. Protein - 15-45 mg/dl

DISTRIBUTION OF CSF TUBES		
	LABORATORY SECTION(S)	POSSIBLE TESTS
Tube #1	Chemistry and/or Serology	Protein, Glucose, Lactate, VDRL, Latex agglutination tests
Tube #2	Microbiology	Gram stain, culture, India ink
Tube #3	Hematology	Cell count and differential

DIFFERENTIATION BETWEEN HEMORRHAGE VS. TRAUMATIC TAP		
	HEMORRHAGE	TRAUMATIC TAP
Appearance	All tubes equally red (bloody)	Subsequent clearing of blood in each tube
Supernatant	Xanthochromic	Clear
Presence of Clots	No	Yes, due to fibrinogen

Differentiating Causes of Meningitis - CSF Studies

	PROTEIN	GLUCOSE	WBC POPULATION	LACTATE
Bacterial	↑↑	↓	Neutrophils	↑
Viral	↑	N	Lymphocytes	N
Fungal	↑	N - ↓	Lymphocytes and Monocytes	↑

***TEST* Alert!**

Differentiate Traumatic Tap from Intracranial Hemmorrhage

b. Glucose - 60-70% plasma glucose
c. Cell Count - 0-5 WBCs/microliter(*ul*)
d. Differential - 70% lymphocytes; 30% monocytes

6. CSF Electropheresis - oligoclonal banding = multiple sclerosis (↓ *glucose* and ↑ *protein*)

MANUAL CELL CALCULATION FOR BODY FLUIDS

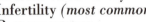

$$\frac{\text{\# Cells Counted X Dilution}}{\text{\# Squares Counted X Depth } (0.1)}$$

SEMINAL FLUID

Baby Shannon *(spermatid)*

1. Reasons for semen analysis
   a. Infertility *(most common)*
   b. Post vasectomy
   c. Forensic medicine — presence of acid phosphatase confirms presence of semen in alleged rape cases; flavin in semen fluoresces on clothing under UV light

Slim *(pinhead)*

Sylvester *(amorphous head)*

Sammy Sperm *(normal)*

Sigmund & Sergio *(2-headed)*

2. Reference ranges
   a. Volume - 2-5 ml
   b. Count - 20-250 million/ml
   c. Motility - > 50%
   d. Morphology - < 30% Abnormal Forms
   e. Viability > 75% live forms
      ❖ *Azoospermia - no sperm*
      ❖ *Oligospermia - < 20 million/ml*

Simone *(2-tailed)*

***TEST* Alert!**

Analyze Seminal Fluid to Determine Normality

SEROUS FLUIDS

1. Reasons for analysis:
   a. Sepsis
   b. Malignancy
   c. Systemic disease

SYNOVIAL FLUID

1. Reasons for analysis:
   a. Sepsis
   b. Hemorrhage
   c. Crystal induced inflammation

2. Normal appearance: clear, pale yellow

3. Monosodium urate crystals = gout

4. Calcium pyrophosphate crystals = pseudogout

5. Compensated polarization:
   a. Calcium pyrophosphate appears blue when parallel to compensator and yellow when perpendicular
   b. Monosodium urate appears yellow when parallel to compensator and blue when perpendicular

6. Cell count normal ranges:
   a. < 200 WBC/µL
   b. < 2000 RBC/µL

PLEURAL PERICARDIAL AND PERITONEAL FLUID

1. Effusion — build-up of fluid in a body cavity due to a pathologic process

2. Cell count and differential performed in same manner as CSF

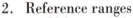

Transudates vs. Exudates

	TRANSUDATE	EXUDATE
Color	Colorless	Yellow-White, (inflammation); Red-Brown (hemorrhage); Yellow-Brown (bilirubin); Milky-Green (chylous fluid)
Turbidity	Clear, Watery	Cloudy, Viscous
Specific Gravity	< 1.015	> 1.015
Protein	< 3 g/dl	> 3 g/dl
LD (Lactic Dehydrogenase)	< 200 IU	> 200 IU
Cell Count	< 1000/µl	> 1000/µl
↑ Associated With	Congestive Heart Failure, Changes in Hydrostatic Pressure	Infections and Malignancies

AMNIOTIC FLUID

1. Reasons for analysis
   a. Fetal well-being
   b. Fetal lung maturity

2. Fetal lung maturity tests
   a. Lecithin/Sphingomyelin (L/S) ratio
      ❖ *Measures the phospholipids lecithin and sphingomyelin to assess fetal lung maturity*
      ❖ *If the L/S ratio is > 2.0, fetal lungs are usually mature (diabetic mothers — PG must be present for FLM)*
   b. Phosphatidylglycerol (PG)
      ❖ *Lipid component of pulmonary surfactants*
      ❖ *Not usually detected until 35 weeks of gestation*
      ❖ *Absence does not rule out mature fetal lungs*
   c. Lamellar body counts
      ❖ *Secreted into alveolar lumen at 20-24 weeks of gestation*
      ❖ *Amniotic fluid is analyzed on automated instrument by using the platelet count value*
      ❖ *Advantages*
         ☞ small sample volume
         ☞ short turnaround time
         ☞ low cost
         ☞ easily interpreted

3. Other amniotic fluid testing
   a. Alpha-1-fetoprotein (*AFP*)
      ❖ *↑ associated with neural tube disorders (such as Spina Bifida)*
   b. Bilirubin
      ❖ *Reliable estimate of fetal red cell destruction due to maternal antibody*
   c. Foam stability index
   d. Fluorescence Polarization Assay (TDx-FLM)

SWEAT

1. ↑ sweat electrolytes, sodium and chloride, confirms the diagnosis of cystic fibrosis

DETECTION OF MALIGNANCY

1. Benign tissue cells must be differentiated from malignant cells in body fluids.

DIFFERENTIATING BENIGN AND MALIGNANT CELLS

BENIGN CELLS	MALIGNANT CELLS
Distinguishable cell borders in clumps	Poorly defined
Flat clusters - not ball-like	Ball-like spherical clusters
Individual cells	Often cells within cells (cannibalism)
May be large, but not giant, tend to be uniform	Often bizarre, monstrous - non-uniform
N/C ratio low	Frequently high N/C ratio
Smooth, clear membrane	Irregular nuclear membrane
Even chromatin	Uneven chromatin
Can be multinucleated but nuclei uniform	Multinucleated forms with varied nuclear sizes
Nulei round or oval	Nuclear molding (mosaic)
Nucleus even, no clefts	Nuclear clefts
May be vacuolated	May be vacuolated with vacuoles over nucleus

Fluids with cells suspicious for malignancy always should be referred to cytology and for pathologist's review.

The cells should be reported as atypical and suspicious for malignancy on the differential cell report.

Summary of Body Fluids

FLUID	SOURCE	APPEARANCE	LAB TESTS	CLINICAL SIGNIFICANCE
Serous	*Ultrafiltrate of plasma; fills organ cavities*	*Normal; clear and pale yellow*		
PLEURAL	Thoracic Cavity *(around lungs)*	Turbid - white cells, bacteria Bloody - trauma, malignancy Milky - chylous fluid	Cell Counts:	↑ Red Cells - trauma, malignancy ↑ Neutrophils - bacteria ↑ Lymphocytes - tuberculosis, malignancy
			Glucose:	↓ Tuberculosis, rheumatoid inflammation, malignancy
			pH:	↓ Tuberculosis, malignancy, esophageal rupture
			Amylase:	↑ Pancreatitis
			CEA *(carcinoembryonic antigen)*:	↑ Malignancy
PERICARDIAL	Percardial Cavity *(around heart)*	Turbid - infection, malignancy Bloody - tuberculosis, tumor, cardiac puncture Milky - lymphatic drainage	Cell Counts:	↑ Red Cells - tuberculosis, tumor, cardiac puncture ↑ Neutrophils - bacterial endo cartitis
			Glucose:	↓ Bacterial infection
			CEA:	↑ Malignancy
PERITONEAL *(ascites)*	Peritoneal Cavity *(around abdomen)*	Turbid - peritonitis, cirrhosis Bloody - trauma Milky - chylous fluid Green - bile	Cell Counts:	↑ Red Cells - trauma ↑ Neutrophils - peritonitis
			Glucose:	↓ Tubercular peritonitis, malignancy
			Amylase:	↑ Pancreatitis, GI perforation
			Alkaline Phosphatase:	↑ Intestinal perforation
			Urea/Creatinine:	↑ Ruptured bladder
Other Fluids			*Other Fluids*	*Other Fluids*
SWEAT	Sweat Glands *(of skin)*	Clear and colorless	Sodium Chloride *(sweat test)*:	↑ in Cystic Fibrosis
SYNOVIAL	Synovial Membrane *(around joints)*	Clear, pale yellow, and viscous Bloody - hemorrhagic arthritis Milky - crystals, cells Green tinge - bacteria Deep yellow - inflammation	Cell Counts:	↑ Red Cells - hemorrhage ↑ Neutrophils (> 25%) - sepsis ↑ Lymphocytes - non-septic inflammation
			Crystals:	Uric Acid *(monosodium urate)* - gout
			Ropes Clot Test:	↓ clot - arthritis
GASTRIC	HCl and Pepsin *(secreted in stomach)*	Depends on diet	Titratable Acidity:	↓ in pernicious anemia *(no intrinsic factor)* ↑ in duodenal ulcer, Zollinger-Ellison Syndrome
AMNIOTIC	Amniotic Sac	Clear and colorless - normal Yellow-greeen - bilirubin, red cell destruction	Bilirubin:	↑ in HDN *(indicates red cell destruction)*
			L/S Ratio:	>2.0 = fetal lung maturity
			Phosphatidylglycerol:	↑ indicates fetal maturity *(similar to L/S ratio)*
			Creatinine:	Fetal age
			Alpha Fetoprotein:	↑ indicates neural tube disorders

URINALYSIS/BODY FLUIDS
SAMPLE QUESTIONS

1. Which of the following changes occur when a urine specimen is left at room temperature for longer than 1-2 hours?
   - A. Ketones ↓
   - B. Bilirubin ↑
   - C. Bacteria ↓
   - D. Glucose ↑

2. A urinalysis on a 3 year old revealed a positive copper reduction test and a negative glucose oxidase test. How would these results be interpreted?
   - A. A strong oxidizing agent is present
   - B. Copper reduction tests are more sensitive than glucose oxidase tests
   - C. Galactose is present
   - D. Glucose and lactose are both present

3. Chemical and microscopic analysis of a urine specimen yields the following results

   Protein: 4+
   RBC 0-10
   WBC 0-5
   Few hyaline casts
   Moderate fatty, waxy, and granular casts
   Many oval fat bodies

   These results are consistent with which diagnosis?
   - A. Hepatic insufficiency
   - B. Glomerulonephritis
   - C. Nephrotic syndrome
   - D. Pyelonephritis

4. An abnormally high specific gravity may be seen in which of the following conditions?
   - A. Chronic renal disease
   - B. Diabetes insipidus
   - C. Metabolic acidosis
   - D. Radiographic dye injection

5. The reagent strip reaction used to test for the presence of glucose is based on the principle of
   - A. A buffered reaction of mixed enzyme indicators
   - B. Acid precipitation of glucose salts
   - C. Double sequential enzyme reactions
   - D. Glucose producing a change in pH in a buffered system

6. An elevated urine urobilinogen and a negative test for urine bilirubin may indicate which of the following conditions?
   - A. Acute hepatic toxicity
   - B. Biliary obstruction
   - C. Hemolytic disease
   - D. Urinary tract infection

7. Calculate the creatinine clearance of a 24-hour urine specimen using the following data:

   Urine creatinine   500 mg/L
   Plasma creatinine 8 mg/L
   Urine volume   1.5 L

   - A. 6.5 ml/min
   - B. 0.75 ml/24 hours
   - C. 65 ml/min
   - D. 85 ml/min

8. An L/S ratio of 2.7 indicates
   - A. Fetal distress
   - B. Fetal lung maturity
   - C. Fetal red cell destruction
   - D. Inadequate fetal pulmonary surfactants

9. Cerebrospinal fluid results reveal an ↑ protein, normal glucose, normal lactate and ↑ lymphocytes. These results most likely indicate
   - A. Bacterial meningitis
   - B. Fungal meningitis
   - C. Multiple Sclerosis
   - D. Viral meningitis

98

ANSWERS AND RATIONALE

1. A

When a specimen is left unpreserved at room temperature, several changes take place. Option A is correct because ketones will ↓ due to bacterial metabolism of acetoacetate to acetone. Option B is incorrect because bilirubin ↓ as it is photooxidized to biliverdin. Option C is incorrect because bacteria multiply causing an ↑ result. Option D is incorrect because glucose ↓ as bacteria utilize the glucose for glycolysis.

2. C

The copper reduction method will detect any reducing sugar, whereas, the glucose oxidase method is specific for glucose. Option A is incorrect because oxidizing agents give false positive results with the glucose oxidase method and not the copper reduction method. Option B is incorrect because the glucose oxidase method detects minimum glucose levels of 100 mg/dl, while the copper reduction method only detects minimum levels of 200 mg/dl. Option D is incorrect because if these both sugars were present, both tests would be positive.

3. C

Hallmarks of the nephrotic syndrome include fatty casts, oval fat bodies, and markedly increased protein in the urine. Option A does not usually demonstrate cast formation. Option B would show a positive blood result and many red cell casts. Option D would have many WBC's and white cell casts.

4. D

Radiographic dyes are water soluble substances that are readily excreted in urine that cause a significantly increased specific gravity. In Option A, the kidneys are no longer able to concentrate or dilute urine causing a fixed specific gravity usually around 1.010. Option B is incorrect because persons with diabetes insipidus are unable to produce concentrated urine due to defective ADH production. In Option C, the body reacts to maintain acid-base balance by inducing the kidneys to eliminate H+ ions through the urine which does not affect the specific gravity.

5. C

The reagent strip reaction combines two separate reactions catalyzed by two different enzymes. Glucose is combined with oxygen in the presence of the enzyme glucose oxidase. Gluconic acid and hydrogen peroxide are formed from this reaction. Hydrogen peroxide formed in the first reaction oxidizes a chromogen in the presence of the enzyme peroxidase to produce a color change. Thus, this method is termed a double sequential enzyme reaction.

6. C

Increased hemoglobin degradation associated with hemolytic conditions such as transfusion reactions and sickle cell disease results in the production of large amounts of unconjugated bilirubin which is presented to the liver to be conjugated. This large amount of bilirubin then goes to the intestine and is broken down by bacteria into urobilinogen. Because larger amounts of bilirubin are excreted into the intestine and larger amounts of urobilinogen are made, increased amounts of urobilinogen are reabsorbed into the circulation. As a result, the urinary bilirubin remains negative but the urinary urobilinogen increases above its normal level. Option A would result in the production of increased levels of bilirubin and urobilinogen due to liver dysfunction. Option B is incorrect because bilirubin, due to the obstruction, could not be converted to urobilinogen. Less than normal amounts of urobilinogen would be excreted in the kidney. *(The dipstick will show normal urobilinogen because it cannot detect lower than normal amounts.)* Option D does not affect bilirubin metabolism.

7. C

To calculate the creatinine clearance:
$$\frac{U \times V}{P}$$

Where:
U= the concentration of urine creatinine in mg/ml
V= the volume of urine in ml/min
P= the concentration of plasma creatinine in mg/ml

The first step is to convert the results to the correct units. Because the volume of urine must be in ml/min, convert the volume of urine to ml then divide the ml by 1440 *(number of minutes in 24 hours)*. In this case, 1.5 L = 1500 ml = 1.04

ml/min. If the height and weight of the patient are known a correction for the kidney mass is calculated. Use this formula:

$$\frac{U \times V}{p} \times \frac{1.73}{A}$$

Where: A= the surface area of the body.

The surface area of the body can be determined by a nomogram which can be found in several reference books.

$$= \frac{500 \text{ mg/L} \times 1.04 \text{ mL/min}}{8 \text{ mg/L}}$$

$$= \frac{520 \text{ mL/min}}{8}$$

$$= \underline{65.1 \text{ mL/min}}$$

8. B

Lecithin and sphingomyelin are produced by the fetal pulmonary system in a relatively constant rate until the 35th week of gestation, at which time the concentration of sphingomyelin decreases and the concentration of lecithin increases in the amniotic fluid. Before this time, the L/S ratio is usually less than 2.0 which is associated with immaturity of the fetal lungs. When the L/S ratio reaches 2.0 or greater it is indicative of fetal lung maturity.

9. D

These results are indicative of viral meningitis. Option A would show an ↑ in neutrophils. Option B would show an ↑ lactate and possible monocytes. Option C would show a ↓ glucose and oligoclonal banding with electrophoresis.

☞ Be able to identify cells, casts, bacteria and yeast from graphic images. Correlate microscopic findings with chemical tests and disease states.

CHEMISTRY

by Mary Muslow and Larry Broussard

Sample Collection and Handling

1. Serum (*red top*) for most chemistry tests

2. Plasma — Heparin better than oxalate, EDTA, citrate

3. Heparin (*on ice*) - ammonia, blood gases

4. Sodium fluoride (*gray top*)
   a. Glucose (*prevents glycolysis*)
   b. NOT for BUN (*inhibits urease*)

5. Acid Phosphatase must be stabilized or ↓ pH

6. EDTA
   a. NOT for Na^+ or K^+ (*EDTA contains Na^+ and K^+*)
   b. Not for Ca^{++} since calcium is chelated in EDTA (*will cause a false ↓*)

↑ Hemoglobin =

• Protein Electrophoresis May Show Extra Band

• ↑ Fe^{++}

But, Bilirubin ↓
(*False ↓ with Diazo Method*)

REMEMBER!
Hemolysis . . .
as the cell bursts,
help (c)KLAMP the leak!

K K^+ ↑

L LD ↑

A Aldolase (*ALD* ↑)
Acid Phosphatase (*ACP* ↑)

M Mg^{++} ↑

P PO_4 ↑

PO_4   *ALD*   *ACP*   *K^+*   *HB*   *Mg*   *LD*

Carbohydrates : Glucose

1. Digestion, metabolism, regulation
   a. End product of carbohydrate digestion in the intestine
   b. Blood glucose is maintained at a fairly constant level by hormones (*Insulin ↓; all others ↑; see table on page 102*)
   c. Provides energy for life processes

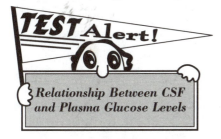

TEST Alert!

Relationship Between CSF and Plasma Glucose Levels

2. Specimen collection and handling
   a. Glucose levels decrease approximately 10 mg/dL per hour in whole blood (*7%*)
   b. Refrigerated serum is fairly stable
   c. Sodium fluoride (*anticoagulant*) prevents glycolysis (*gray top tube*)
   d. Fasting reference range for serum or plasma is 70-100 mg/dL
   e. Arterial and capillary values are 2-3 mg/dL higher
   f. "Normal" CSF values are two-thirds (*approximately 60-65%*) of plasma levels

*Original contribution by Melanie S. Chapman

HORMONAL ACTIVITY AFFECTING SERUM GLUCOSE LEVELS		
HORMONE	**SOURCE**	**ACTION**
Insulin	ß cells of Islets of Langerhans of pancreas	• ↓ serum glucose • Stimulates glucose uptake by cells
Glucagon	∂ cells of pancreas	• ↑ glucose • Stimulates glycogenolysis *(breakdown of glycogen → glucose)*
ACTH	anterior pituitary	• ↑ glucose • Insulin antagonist
Growth Hormone	anterior pituitary	• ↑ glucose • Insulin antagonist • Acromegaly = hyperglycemia
Cortisol	adrenal cortex	• ↑ glucose • Stimulates gluconeogenesis *(glucose from non-carbohydrate sources)*
Human Placental Lactogen	placenta	• ↑ glucose • Insulin antagonist
Epinephrine	adrenal medulla	• ↑ glucose • Stimulates glycogenolysis • Pheochromocytoma-tumor of adrenal medulla → hyperglycemia
T_3 & T_4	thyroid gland	• ↑ glucose • Stimulates glycogenolysis

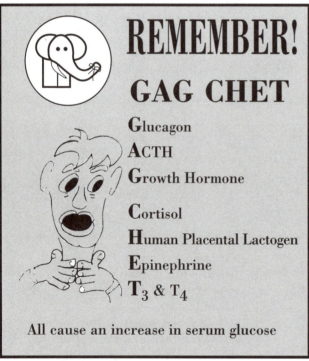

REMEMBER!
GAG CHET

Glucagon
ACTH
Growth Hormone

Cortisol
Human Placental Lactogen
Epinephrine
T$_3$ & **T**$_4$

All cause an increase in serum glucose

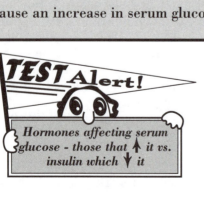

TEST Alert!

Hormones affecting serum glucose - those that ↑ it vs. insulin which ↓ it

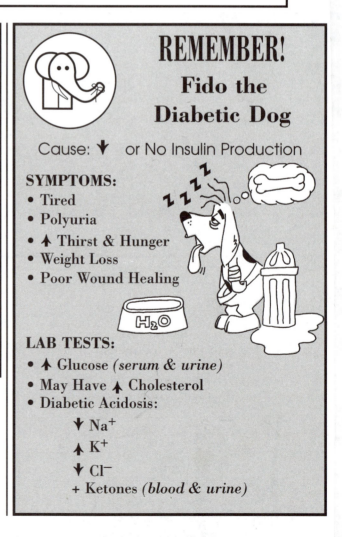

REMEMBER!
Fido the Diabetic Dog

Cause: ↓ or No Insulin Production

SYMPTOMS:
• Tired
• Polyuria
• ↑ Thirst & Hunger
• Weight Loss
• Poor Wound Healing

LAB TESTS:
• ↑ Glucose *(serum & urine)*
• May Have ↑ Cholesterol
• Diabetic Acidosis:
　　↓ Na^+
　　↑ K^+
　　↓ Cl^-
　　+ Ketones *(blood & urine)*

TEST INTERPRETATION TO DIAGNOSE DIABETES MELLITUS

STAGE	TEST		
	Fasting plasma glucose (FPG)	Casual plasma glucose	Oral glucose tolerance test (OGTT) *
Normal	FPG <100 mg/dL		2 hr PG <140 mg/dL
Diabetes Mellitus	FPG ≥126 mg/dL	≥200 mg/dL plus unexpected weight loss, polyuria, polydipsia	2 hr PG ≥200 mg/dL
Impaired Glucose Homeostasis	Impaired Fasting Glucose (IFG) FPG ≥100 <126 mg/dL		Impaired Glucose Tolerance (IGT) 2 hr PG ≥140 <200 mg/dL

* Oral Glucose Tolerance Test (OGTT) Dose:
Standard: 75 g • Children: 1.75 g/kg up to 75 g
Pregnancy (for Gestational Diabetes) - 50 g screen (O'Sullivan Test), if 1 hr glucose ≥140 mg/dL,
then give 100 g dose and compare fasting, 1, 2, 3 hr levels to acceptable limits

TESTS TO MONITOR DIABETES	NOTES
Glycosylated Hemoglobin; HbA$_{1c}$	• Assess Long-Term Goal • Glucose Attaches to Hemoglobin • Average Glucose Level Over 60 Days (1-2 Months)
Fructosamine	• Assess Intermediate-Term Control • Glucose Attaches to Proteins Including Albumin • Average Glucose level Over 2-3 Weeks
Urinary Microalbumin	• Detects Small Amounts of Albumin in Urine to Assess Early Renal Damage
C Peptide (reflects pancreatic secretion of insulin)	• Proinsulin Cleaved to Give C Peptide and Insulin • Reflects Endogenous Insulin Production if Patient is Taking Insulin

Glucose Tolerance Curve

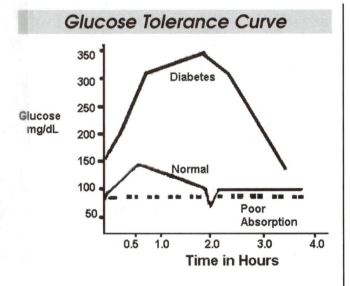

3. Glucose Methods : Enzymatic
   a. Glucose oxidase (Glu. Ox.)
      ❖ *Coupled Reactions*

Glu. Ox. converts glucose to gluconic acid + H_2O_2
Peroxidase converts H_2O_2 to O_2
O_2 + chromogenic acceptor gives color

      ❖ *Method used on urine dipsticks*
      ❖ *Modified method measures oxygen consumption with a pO_2 electrode*
      ❖ *Interfering substances - extremely high doses of ascorbic acid (vitamin C) - cause ▼results*
   b. Hexokinase
      ❖ *Reference method*
      ❖ *Coupled Reactions*

Hexokinase + ATP converts glucose to G6P + ADP
G6PD + NADP converts G6P to NADPH + H^+
NADPH measured directly at 340 nm or coupled to chromogen and measured in visible range

Carbohydrate Tests Other than Glucose

1. Lactose tolerance
   a. Evaluate deficiency of lactase in small bowel
   b. Ingest lactose and measure blood glucose to assess absorption and conversion to glucose
   c. May develop transient lactose intolerance when recovering from diarrhea or intestinal infection — avoid milk products until recovered
2. Xylose absorption
   a. Pentose absorbed and excreted into urine without need of pancreatic enzymes
   b. Helps distinguish intestinal malabsorption (*see low absorption of xylose*) and pancreatic-based malabsorption (*see normal absorption of xylose*)
3. Lactic Acid
   a. Indicator of oxygen deprivation (*exercise, drugs, diseases, etc.*)
   b. End product (*instead of pyruvate*) of glucose metabolism when oxygen deprivation occurs
   c. Build-up results in lactic acidosis
   d. Sample collection and handling critical
      ❖ *Glycolysis increases lactic acid levels*
      ❖ *No exercise before collection*
      ❖ *Separate plasma and refrigerate*

Lipids and Lipoproteins

CHEMISTRY AND PHYSIOLOGY

1. Organic substances insoluble in water, soluble in organic solvents
2. Human plasma lipids are cholesterol, triglycerides, phospholipids and non-esterified fatty acids
3. Transported in the form of lipoproteins (*lipids combine with proteins in the liver to form lipoproteins*)
   a. 60-70% by low density lipoproteins (*LDL*)
   b. 20-35% by high density lipoproteins (*HDL*)
   c. 5-12% by very low density lipoproteins (*VLDL*)
4. Apolipoproteins
   a. Protein portion of lipoproteins
   b. Apolipoprotein A is the major protein of HDL
   c. Apolipoprotein B is the major protein of LDL
   d. Apolipoprotein C is the major protein of VLDL and chylomicrons and a minor protein of HDL and LDL

LIPID	FUNCTION	TRANSPORTED BY:
Triglycerides	Primary form of lipid storage	Chylomicrons (*exogenous*) VLDL (*endogenous*)
Cholesterol	Important in cellular physiology Precursor to steroid hormones	LDL - to cells HDL - out of cells

LIPOPROTEINS CLASSES

1. 4 classes based on particle size, chemical composition, flotation characteristics and electrophoretic mobility; more protein higher density; more lipid, lower density

LIPOPROTEIN CLASSES	
CLASS	TRANSPORTED LIPIDS
Chylomicrons	exogenous (*dietary*) triglycerides
VLDL	endogenous triglycerides
LDL	cholesterol to cells (*heart*)
HDL	cholesterol out of cells (*heart*)

> ## REMEMBER!
> ## Lipoproteins
>
> - <u>H</u>DL is <u>h</u>elpful *(takes cholesterol from the cells)* Hooray Alpha!
> - <u>L</u>DL is <u>l</u>ethal *(brings cholesterol to the cells)* Boo! Hiss! Bad Beta
> - VLDL *(longest initials)* = pre-beta & endogenous triglycerides *(most letters)*

SPECIMEN COLLECTION AND HANDLING

1. 12 hour fast required
2. Non fasting may cause
   a. Turbid serum with layer of chylomicrons on top following refrigeration (an abnormal finding in fasting specimens)
   b. ⬆ triglycerides

LIPID METHODS

1. Cholesterol
   a. Enzymatic methods *(cholesterol oxidase)* have replaced colorimetric methods
2. Triglycerides
   a. Enzymatic methods best
      ❖ Involve liberation of glycerol by lipase
      ❖ Glycerol contamination from stoppers of evacuation tubes or ingestion of glycerol-coated medication can cause falsely ⬆ results
3. HDL-cholesterol (HDLc)
   a. Direct or homogenous assays — measure HDLc without pretreatment

b. Indirect — remove chylomicrons, VLDL, and LDL by precipitation; analyze supernatant for HDLc

4. LDL-cholesterol (LDLc)
   a. Direct or homogenous assays — measure LDLc without pretreatment
5. Electrophoresis
6. Ultracentrifugation
   a. Reference method
   b. Separates lipoproteins by their rates of flotation using ultracentrifugation
7. Friedewald method for the calculation of LDLc and VLDLc — cannot use when triglycerides (TG) >400 mg/dL

(Tot chol) = total cholesterol

a.
$$LDLc = (Tot\ chol) - (HDLc) - \frac{plasma\ TG\ in\ mg/dL}{5}$$

b.
$$VLDLc = \frac{plasma\ TG\ in\ mg/dL}{5}$$

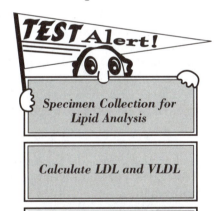

TEST Alert!

Specimen Collection for Lipid Analysis

Calculate LDL and VLDL

Lipid Cut-Off Action Levels

LDL-CHOLESTEROL (LDLc) DECISION LEVELS AND RECOMMENDED TREATMENT			
LDLc ACTION LEVEL	RISK CATEGORY	LDLc GOAL	TREATMENT
≥ 190 mg/dL	no CHD; < 2 risk factors	< 160 mg/dL	Drug
≥ 160 mg/dL	no CHD; ≥ 2 risk factors	< 130 mg/dL	Drug
≥ 160 mg/dL	no CHD; < 2 risk factors	< 160 mg/dL	Diet
≥ 130 mg/dL	no CHD; ≥ 2 risk factors	< 130 mg/dL	Diet
≥ 130 mg/dL	CHD	≤ 100 mg/dL	Drug
> 100 mg/dL	CHD	≤ 100 mg/dL	Diet

from National Cholesterol Education Program

TREATMENT GUIDELINES

1. Lipid Screening
   a. Can be nonfasting sample
   b. Goals
      - *Total Cholesterol < 200 mg/dL*
      - *HDLc ≥ 35 mg/dL*
      - *Triglycerides < 150 mg/dL*
   c. Follow-up testing if levels outside goals
      - *12 hour fasting sample*
      - *Lipoprotein analysis*
   d. Begin treatment based on LDLc results from lipoprotein analysis and other risk factors *(family history, age, smoking, diabetes, hypertension, etc.)*

Amino Acids

GENERAL

1. Aminoacidurias
   a. Overflow-plasma level above renal threshold as result of metabolic disorder
      - *PKU — enzyme deficiencies cause ↑ of phenylalanine in blood and ↑ phenyl compounds in urine*
      - *Branched chain ketoaciduria (maple syrup urine disease) — branched chain amino acids ↑ in blood and urine*
   b. Renal-normal plasma level but decreased renal threshold or reabsorption
      - *Cystinuria ↑ cystine, lysine, ornithine, arginine in urine*

METHODS

1. Screening Tests *(Initial Diagnosis)*
   a. Thin layer chromatography with ninhydrin
   b. Urine color tests
   c. Guthrie microbiological tests: PKU
2. Quantitative Tests
   a. Ion-exchange chromatography
   b. High performance liquid chromatography (HPLC)
   c. Gas chromatography mass spectrometry (GCMS)

AMINO ACID LEVELS IN BLOOD

1. Homocysteine
   a. ↑ levels associated with ↑ risk of cardiovascular disease, stroke, Alzheimer's and osteoporosis

Proteins

GENERAL

1. Most proteins are synthesized and catabolized in the liver

2. Carbon, hydrogen, oxygen and nitrogen: primary constituents of protein molecules

3. Basic unit - amino acids linked together by amide bonds to form protein

4. Protein breakdown in the body produces urea and ammonia; urea produced in liver and eliminated in urine by kidneys

METHODS : SERUM TOTAL PROTEIN

1. Kjeldahl
   a. Reference method
   b. Principle - measures nitrogen content
   c. Acid digestion converts nitrogen in protein to ammonium ion (NH_4^+) measured by titration or nesslerization

2. Biuret reaction
   a. Used most frequently
   b. Depends on presence of ≥2 peptide bonds which form a purple complex with copper salts in alkaline solution

METHODS : URINE AND CSF TOTAL PROTEIN

1. Dye — Coomassie brilliant blue

2. Turbidimetric methods
   a. Acid *(sulfosalicylic acid or trichloroacetic acid)* precipitates protein
   b. Measured spectrophotometrically or visually

METHODS : SPECIFIC SERUM PROTEINS

1. Dye-binding methods for albumin
   a. Bromcresol green *(BCG)*
   b. HABA *(2- [4' - Hydroxyazobenzene] - benzoic acid)*

2. Immunochemical methods for specific proteins other than albumin

Basic Tests for Protein

PROTEIN ELECTROPHORESIS

1. Direction of migration of proteins in an electrical field determined by surface charge of protein
   a. Protein at pH higher than its isoelectric point is negatively charged and migrates toward anode *(positive charge)*
   b. Albumin (smallest M.W.) has largest number of free negative charges and migrates most rapidly traveling greatest distance from application point
   c. Urine protein electrophoresis exactly same as serum except it must be concentrated before application

2. Electroendosmosis causes gamma globulins to migrate toward the cathode even though they are slightly negatively charged *(due to electrical charge on support medium)*

3. At pH 8.6, in order of migration, the 5 major bands are albumin, alpha-1, alpha-2, beta and gamma

4. Support media include cellulose acetate, agarose gel, and starch gel

5. Stains include Amido Black, Ponceau S and Coomassie Brilliant Blue

6. Relative concentration of each band determined by densitometry

7. Specimen collection and handling
   a. Plasma samples *(mistaken as serum)* result in fibrinogen peak migrating between gamma and beta fractions
   b. Recollect sample and repeat to verify that peaks not fibrinogen

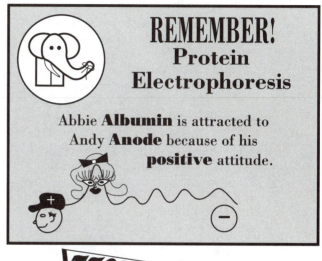

REMEMBER! Protein Electrophoresis

Abbie **Albumin** is attracted to Andy **Anode** because of his **positive** attitude.

TEST Alert!

Associate Electrophoretic Pattern with Disease

Some Common Protein Electrophoresis Patterns

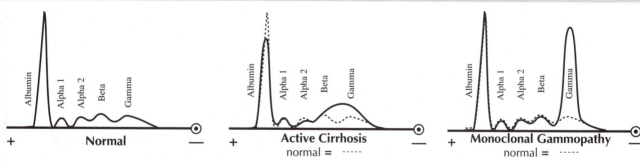

⊙ = Point of Application   • Beta Gamma Bridge

Normal

Active Cirrhosis — normal = - - - - -

Monoclonal Gammopathy — normal = - - - - -

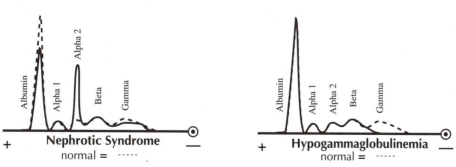

Nephrotic Syndrome — normal = - - - - -

Hypogammaglobulinemia — normal = - - - - -

• *Graphs Adapted with Permission from Helena Laboratories' Electrophoresis Reference Chart*

CLINICAL SIGNIFICANCE

1. Plasma proteins - albumin and globulins
   a. Liver produces albumin, alpha-1, alpha-2 and beta globulins
   b. RE system produces gamma globulin *(antibodies secreted by plasma cells)*

2. Albumin
   a. Largest plasma protein fraction *(52-62%)*
   b. Regulator of osmotic pressure
   c. Transport protein because of ease of binding with blood components
   d. Causes of ↓ values
      ❖ ↓ *synthesis (liver impairment)*
      ❖ *Malabsorption or malnutrition*
      ❖ *Nephrotic syndrome (renal loss)*
      ❖ *Severe burns*
   e. ↑ values generally have no clinical significance *(hemoconcentration, dehydration)*

3. Alpha-1-globulins
   a. Alpha-1-antitrypsin *(AAT)*
      ❖ ↑ *in acute phase and pregnancy*
      ❖ ↓ *associated with emphysema in neonates*
   b. Alpha-1-fetoprotein *(AFP)*
      ❖ ↑ *values*
      ❖ ↑ *in amniotic fluid and maternal serum in neural tube defects (spina bifida)*
      ❖ *liver cancer marker*
      ❖ ↓ *in maternal serum during pregnancy associated with Down's syndrome*

4. Alpha-2-globulins
   a. Haptoglobin
      ❖ *Binds free hemoglobin*
      ❖ ↑ *in acute phase and nephrotic syndrome*
      ❖ ↓ *in hemolysis and liver disease*
   b. Ceruloplasmin
      ❖ *Transports copper*
      ❖ ↑ *in acute phase and pregnancy*
      ❖ ↓ *Wilson's disease*

5. Beta globulin
   a. Carrier proteins for iron *(transferrin)* and lipids *(lipoproteins)*
   b. ↑ in:
      ❖ *Elevated beta lipoprotein (LDL)*
      ❖ *Iron deficiency anemia*

6. Gamma globulin
   a. ↑ in:
      ❖ *Chronic inflammation*

   ❖ *Cirrhosis or viral hepatitis*
   ❖ *Collagen diseases*
   ❖ *Paraproteins (monoclonal bands, gammopathies)*
   b. ↓ in congenital or acquired immuno-deficiency

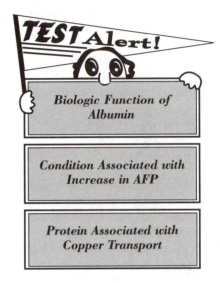

TEST Alert!

Biologic Function of Albumin

Condition Associated with Increase in AFP

Protein Associated with Copper Transport

Enzymes

GENERAL

1. Organic catalysts responsible for most reactions in the body

2. Enzyme reactions in laboratory measurements affected by:
   a. Concentrations of reactants
   b. pH *(optimum pH varies with each enzyme)*
   c. Temperature
      ❖ *Optimum 37°C*
      ❖ *Rate doubles every* ↑ *10 degrees*
   d. Ionic strength
   e. Presence of activators or inhibitors

3. Measurement
   a. Zero-order-kinetics — Large excess of substrate so that the amount of enzyme activity is only rate-limiting factor
   b. Catalytic activity *(not mass or concentration)* is directly measured
   c. One international unit *(IU)* = amount of enzyme that will cause utilization of substrate or production of product at the rate of 1 µM/ minute

Factors Affecting Enzyme Determination

Total CK (Creatine Kinase)

1. ↑ in muscle, cardiac or brain damage

2. Higher reference ranges in males due to greater muscle mass and physical activity

CK Isoenzymes

1. Different molecular forms of CK enzyme
    a. 2 subunits - M and B
    *   *CK1 = CK-BB - 2 B chains*
    *   *CK2 = CK-MB - 1 M & 1 B chain*
    *   *CK3 = CK-MM - 2 M chains*
    b. BB is most negatively charged; therefore migrates furthest toward anode
    c. Cardiac muscle = CK-MM and CK-MB
    d. Skeletal muscle = CK-MM
    e. Brain, GI, colon, prostate, uterus = CK-BB
    f. Trauma to skeletal muscle causes ↑ in total CK and MB isoenzyme, but % activity MB is < 3% (> 6% in MI)

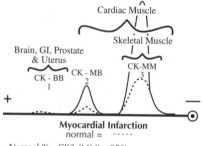

Normal %: CK3 *(MM)* = 95%
CK2 *(MB)* = 0-5%
CK1 *(BB)* = Usually Undetectable

⊙ = Point of Application

• *Graphs Adapted with Permission from Helena Laboratories' Electrophoresis Reference Chart*

Association of CK & Isoenzyme Results with Possible Disease

LD (Lactate Dehydrogenase)

1. ↑ in:
    a. Myocardial infarction (MI)
    b. Liver disease
    c. Muscle trauma
    d. Renal infarct
    e. Hemolytic diseases
    f. Pernicious anemia

2. Sources of error
    a. Hemolyzed specimens
    b. Prolonged contact of serum to cells

3. Spectrophotometric method
    a. LD converts pyruvate to lactate while oxidizing NADH to NAD
    b. Rate of decrease in absorbance of NADH at 340 nm is proportional to LD activity

4. LD isoenzymes
    a. 2 chains *(M and H)*
    b. 4 subunits
    c. 5 forms *(tissue-specific)*

AST (Aspartate transaminase)

1. Found in cardiac muscle, liver, RBCs and other tissues

2. ↑ in MI, liver disease, muscle trauma, renal infarct, hemolysis

Correlate AST with Various Diseases

ALT (Alanine transaminase)

1. ↑ in liver disease

2. More liver-specific than AST

GGT (Gamma-glutamyl transferase)

1. ↑ in liver disease *(highest in biliary obstruction and cirrhosis)*

2. Often ↑ after alcohol intake

3. Spectrophotometric method — measure nitroaniline released when GGT acts on substrate gamma-glutamyl-p-nitroanilide

10

ALP (Alkaline Phosphatase)

1. Optimum pH = 10; Mg^{++} activation

2. Found in bone, intestinal mucosa, renal tubule cells, biliary tree *(liver)*, leukocytes, placenta, some tumors

3. Isoenzyme separation acrylamide gel, electrophoresis, chemical, heat (56°C; 10 minutes):
   a. Regan *(cancer)* = rare, most heat stable
   b. Placental = most heat-stable of 4 most common
   c. Intestinal = inhibited by L-phenylalanine
   d. Liver = highest concentrations
   e. Bone = most heat-labile

4. ↑ in:
   a. Bone disorders with osteoblastic activity
      - *Paget's (highest ALP values)*
      - *Osteoblastic tumors*
      - *Rickets*
      - *Hyperparathyroidism*
   b. Disorders of hepatic biliary tree *(obstructive jaundice due to gallstones or malignancy)*
   c. Growing children - rapid skeletal growth *(bone)*
   d. Third trimester of pregnancy *(placenta)*

5. Methods
   a. Bessey-Lowry-Brock method
      - *P-nitrophenylphosphate* $\xrightarrow{ALP}$ *p-nitrophenylate + phosphate*
      - *P-nitrophenylate absorbs light at 404 nm*
   b. Immunoassay for bone isoenzyme

5'NT (5'-Nucleotidase)

1. ↑ in liver but NOT bone disease

2. ↑ ALP + Normal 5'NT = bone disease

3. ↑ ALP + ↑ 5'NT = liver disease

Amylase

1. Produced in salivary and pancreatic glands

2. Requires Ca^{++} and Cl^- *(dilute elevated samples with saline not water)*

3. Only common enzyme normally excreted in urine

4. Highest elevations seen in pancreatitis and obstruction to pancreatic ducts *(malignancy)*

5. Lower elevations seen in obstruction of salivary glands *(mumps)*

6. Methods
   a. Amyloclastic — measure disappearance of starch substrate
   b. Saccharogenic — measure reducing sugars *(glucose and maltose)* produced by enzymatic action
   c. Chromolytic *(dye)* — measure absorbance of soluble dye split from insoluble amylase-dye substrate

7. Isoenzymes - separated by electrophoresis *(cellulose acetate)*
   a. S1 = slowest salivary band
   b. P2
   c. P3 = Increased in pancreatitis

8. Urinary amylase remains elevated longer than serum in pancreatitis

9. Opiates *(Ex. morphine)* cause elevation

Lipase

1. ↑ in pancreatitis

2. Remains elevated longer than amylase

3. More specific for acute pancreatitis

4. Methods:
   a. Turbidimetric
   b. Cherry-Crandall: olive oil substrate; measure fatty acids product

Test Most Specific for Acute Pancreatitis

Clinical Significance of an Increased Amylase

ACP (Acid Phosphatase)

1. Sources: primarily prostate; other tissues erythrocytes, bone, liver, spleen, kidney, platelets

2. Clinical significance
   a. Highest elevations seen in metastasizing carcinoma of prostate; now use PSA instead
   b. ↑ in bone disease or cancers that metastasize to bone and in metastasizing breast cancer
   c. Tartrate-resistant portion elevated in hairy cell leukemia
   d. Presence in seminal fluid useful in forensic medicine for rape cases; now use PSA instead

3. Methods:
   a. Spectrophotometric for Total ACP
      ❖ *Phosphate substrate (Ex. p-nitrophenyl phosphate) cleaved by ACP to give colored product* (Ex. p-nitrophenol after OH⁻ added; yellow, read at 410nm)
   b. Spectrophotometric for Prostatic ACP:
      ❖ *Use substrates more specific for prostatic ACP* (Ex. thymolph-thalein monophosphate and alpha naphthyl phosphate)
      ❖ *Add tartrate buffer:*
         ☞ Prostatic ACP inhibited by tartrate
         ☞ RBC ACP <u>not</u> inhibited by tartrate
   c. Immunoassay for prostatic ACP

4. Specimen Collection and Handling
   a. Hemolysis results in falsely ↑ results
   b. Storage at room temperature results in loss of enzyme activity; must remove serum from cells immediately and stabilize (*add disodium citrate monohydrate or ↓ pH to 5.4 with acetic acid*)

Specimen Handling for Acid Phosphatase Determination

Cholinesterase

1. Erythrocyte acetylcholinesterase and plasma pseudocholinesterase

2. Destroys acetylcholine after nerve impulse transmission

3. Severe ↓ results in serious neuromuscular effects; one of few enzymes in which ↓ is clinically significant

4. ↓ in serum pseudocholinesterase useful in investigation of organophosphate poisoning

Test Helpful in Determining Pesticide Poisoning

Cardiac Markers to Evaluate Possible Acute Myocardial Infarction (AMI or MI)

1. Myoglobin
   a. Produced by muscles including heart
   b. ↑ in muscle damage including AMI
   c. Rises within 30 minutes of AMI; peaks within 4-10 hours and returns to normal within 24 hours
   d. Absence rules out AMI but ↑ does not diagnose AMI because may be due to other muscle trauma

2. CK2 (CK-MB)
   a. Immunoassays: mass CK2 assays measure concentration rather than activity
   b. Rises within 6-10 hours of AMI, peaks within 24 hours and returns to normal in 2-3 days

3. Troponin
   a. Troponin (Tn) is complex of 3 proteins in muscle fibers: troponin T (TnT), troponin I (TnI) and troponin C (TnC)
   b. Isoforms cTnT and cTnI are very specific to cardiac muscle and either may be used for detection of AMI
   c. cTnT and cTnI often called TnT and TnI or simply Tn
   d. Rises 4-8 hours after AMI, peaks at approximately 12-14 hours and remains elevated for up to 10 days

Evaluate Results to Determine Possible MI

Other Cardiac Function Markers

1. B-type Natriuretic Peptide (BNP) is active and N-Terminal pro-BNP (NT pro-BNP) is inactive
   a. B for brain because originally isolated from brain
   b. Natriuretic because BNP ↑ Na^+ and water excretion and causes vasodilation to ↓ blood pressure
   c. Released by ventricular walls in response to hypertension and volume overload
   d. pro-BNP cleaved to BNP and NT pro-BNP
   e. BNP and NT pro-BNP levels ↑ in congestive heart failure (CHF)
      ❖ *Levels correlate to classification of stages of CHF*
   f. BNP antagonist to renin-angiotensin-aldosterone system (RAAS) which ↑ blood pressure by vasoconstriction and retention of Na^+ and water
   g. NT pro-BNP cleared through kidneys so affected by renal function
   h. If BNP given as medication (Natrecor®) to ↓ blood pressure, must use NT pro-BNP to monitor ventricular BNP release

2. Ischemia-Modified Albumin (IMA)
   a. Early marker of AMI
   b. Serum albumin passing through ischemic vascular bed changes; affects ability to bind cobalt
   c. Rises (turns +) within 6-10 minutes of ischemic cardiac event and returns to baseline 6 hours after cessation of ischemic event
   d. Other causes of elevation
      ❖ *Cancer, acute infections, end-stage renal disease, liver cirrhosis, brain ischemia*
   e. Method: Spectrophotometric
      ❖ *Measures free cobalt binding to dithiothreitol*
      ❖ *Add cobalt to serum*
      ❖ *If IMA present, will not bind cobalt so more free cobalt available to react*

Liver Markers

1. AST - highest values in hepatitis
2. ALT - highest values in hepatitis, liver specific
3. LD - found in many tissues other than liver (*ex., heart, skeletal muscle*)
4. ALP - biliary obstruction; may be slightly elevated in hepatitis
5. 5' NT - biliary obstruction
6. GGT - liver-specific; highest ↑ from biliary obstruction or after alcohol ingestion

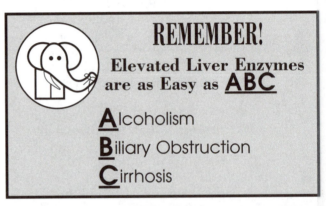

REMEMBER!
Elevated Liver Enzymes are as Easy as ABC

Alcoholism
Biliary Obstruction
Cirrhosis

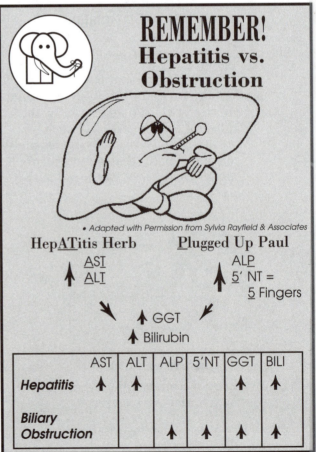

REMEMBER!
Hepatitis vs. Obstruction

• *Adapted with Permission from Sylvia Rayfield & Associates*

Hep**AT**itis Herb
↑ AST
   ALT

Plugged Up Paul
↑ ALP
   5' NT =
      5 Fingers

↑ GGT
↑ Bilirubin

	AST	ALT	ALP	5'NT	GGT	BILI
Hepatitis	↑	↑			↑	↑
Biliary Obstruction			↑	↑	↑	↑

Muscle Disorders

1. Duchenne's Muscular Dystrophy, trauma, surgery, IM injections, trichinosis

2. ↑ in:
   a. CK
   b. AST
   c. Aldolase

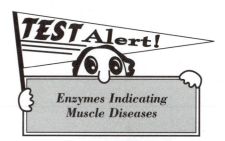

Enzymes Indicating Muscle Diseases

REMEMBER! Muscle Man

AST — CK — ALD

M
U — A T
S — S
C — C K
L — A L D
E — E

Acute Pancreatitis

1. ↑ amylase *(serum and urine)*; remains elevated longer in urine

2. ↑ lipase - more specific than amylase

REMEMBER! I Am Peter Pan with Lips

↑ in Pancreatitis
Amylase & Lipase

Electrolytes

SODIUM (Na⁺)

1. Major cation of extracellular fluid

2. 85% is reabsorbed in the kidney tubules

3. Reference range = 135-145 mM/L

4. Hyponatremia *(↓ serum Na⁺)*
   a. Diabetic acidosis (metabolic)
   b. Diarrhea
   c. Addison's disease
   d. Renal tubular disease

5. Hypernatremia *(↑ serum Na⁺)*
   a. Cushing syndrome
   b. Dehydration
   c. Hyperaldosteronism *(causes ↓ renal reabsorption)*
   d. Insulin treatment of uncontrolled diabetes

6. Method: Ion-selective electrode
   a. Glass electrod selective for Na⁺
   b. Direct reading
      ❖ *Sample not diluted*
   c. Indirect reading
      ❖ *Sample diluted*
      ❖ *Pseudohyponatremia if ↑ triglycerides or protein*

POTASSIUM (K⁺)

1. Major cation of intracellular fluid

2. Reference range = 3.5-5.0 mM/L

3. 23 times higher in cells than in plasma

4. Specimen collection and handling
   a. Separate serum from cells quickly to prevent K⁺ from shifting to serum *(shift ↑ at refrigerator temperature)*
   b. False ↑ in K⁺ *(pseudo-hyperkalemia)*
      ❖ *Hemolysis*
      ❖ *EDTA contamination (K⁺ is in EDTA)*
      ❖ *Prolonged tourniquet application*
      ❖ *Excessive heel or finger squeezing in capillary specimens*
      ❖ *Excessive fist clenching prior to veinpuncture*
      ❖ *500,000 WBC*
      ❖ *700,000 platelet count*
   c. Plasma K⁺, 0.1-0.7 lower than serum K⁺ *(K⁺ released from platelets during clotting)*

5. Hypokalemia ($\downarrow$ *serum K^+*) and hyperkalemia ($\uparrow$ *serum K^+*) may cause heart arrhythmias and/or neuromuscular symptoms including weakness and paralysis

6. Hypokalemia
   a. Insulin injections
   b. Alkalosis
   c. GI losses
      ❖ *Diarrhea*
      ❖ *Vomiting*
   d. Hyperaldosteronism ($\downarrow$ *renal reabsorption*)
   e. Cushing syndrome

7. Hyperkalemia
   a. Diabetic acidosis *(metabolic)*
   b. Intravascular hemolysis
   c. Severe burns
   d. Renal failure
   e. Addison's disease

8. Method: Ion-selective electrode
   a. Valinomycin membrane selectively binds K^+

Sources of Error in Potassium Analysis

CHLORIDE (Cl⁻)

1. Major anion of extracellular fluid

2. Maintains hydration, osmotic pressure and the normal anion-cation balance

3. Reference range = 98-106 mM/L

4. Chloride generally follows Na^+ so $\uparrow$ and $\downarrow$ in same conditions

5. Hypochloremia ($\downarrow$ *Cl⁻*)
   a. Diabetic acidosis *(excessive acid production)*
   b. Chronic pyelonephritis
   c. Prolonged vomiting *(loss of gastric HCl)*
   d. Aldosterone deficiency

6. Hyperchloremia ($\uparrow$ *Cl⁻*)
   a. Prolonged diarrhea (excess bicarbonate loss)

   b. Renal tubular acidosis
   c. Adrenocortical hyperfunction

7. Methods:
   a. Ion-selective electrodes - solid-state electrodes using membranes composed of AgCl *(silver chloride)*
   b. Schales and Schales *(mercurimetric titration)*
   c. Coulometric titration - generation of Ag^{++} ions which combine with Cl^- ions
   d. Colorimetry using $Hg(SCN)_2$ *(automated thiocyanate method)*; forms reddish color with peak at 480 nm

8. Sweat chloride
   a. $\uparrow$ in cystic fibrosis
   b. Sweat collected by iontophoresis using drug, pilocarpine, to induce sweating
   c. > 60 mM/L - cystic fibrosis

9. Chloride Shift
   a. Buffering system of the blood *(for acid-base balance)*
   b. HCO_3^- pulled out of erythrocytes and Cl^- moves into erythrocytes, resulting in $\downarrow$ serum Cl^-

Sources of Error in Chloride Analysis

Reagents Used in Sweat Chloride

Definition of Chloride Shift

CO₂ (TOTAL CARBON DIOXIDE)

1. $CO_2 + HCO_3^- + H_2CO_3$ = total CO_2

2. Reflects bicarbonate (HCO_3^-) concentration

3. Methods:
   a. Volumetric
   b. Manometric
   c. Colorimetric
   d. pCO_2 electrode measures change in internal pH due to CO_2

ANION GAP

1. Calculation that reflects differences between unmeasured cations and anions; used as analytical QC for measuring all electrolytes
   a. If abnormal gaps for multiple patients, suspect problem with electrolyte measurements

2. Major unmeasured cations
   a. K^+
   b. Ca^{++}
   c. Mg^{++}

3. Major unmeasured anions
   a. Albumin
   b. Sulfate
   c. Phosphate

4. Two calculations *(with or without K^+)*:
   a. $((Na^+) + (K^+)) - ((Cl^-) + (HCO_3^-))$
   b. $(Na^+) - ((Cl^-) + (HCO_3^-))$

5. Reference range
   a. 7-16 mM/L (using equation a above)
   b. 10-20 mM/L (using equation b above)

6. ⬆ Anion gap
   a. ⬆ in concentration of unmeasured anions
      ❖ *Ethanol*
      ❖ *Ketones*
      ❖ *Lactic acid*
   b. ⬇ in unmeasured cations
      ❖ *Low serum Mg^{++}*
      ❖ *Low serum Ca^{++}*

7. ⬇ Anion gap
   a. ⬇ in unmeasured anions- albumin loss
   b. ⬆ in unmeasured cations
      ❖ *High serum Mg^{++}*
      ❖ *High serum Ca^{++}*
      ❖ *Lithium therapy*
   c. Hemodilution

Evaluate Anion Gap and Take Corrective Action

OSMOLALITY

1. Measure of total concentration *(number)* of dissolved particles in a solution *(molecular weight, size, density or type of particle does not matter)*

2. Can be measured directly - most practical methods are freezing point depression *(most precise)* and vapor pressure depression — 2 colligative properties

3. One equation *(there are others)*
   $$\text{Calculated Osmolality} = 2Na + \frac{Glucose}{18} + \frac{BUN}{2.8}$$

4. Can compare calculated osmolality to measured osmolality; measured osmolality > 10 higher than calculated osmolality indicates presence of exogenous unmeasured anions *(methanol, ethanol, ketone bodies, etc.)*

   Both anion gap and calculated vs. measured osmolality assess unmeasured cations

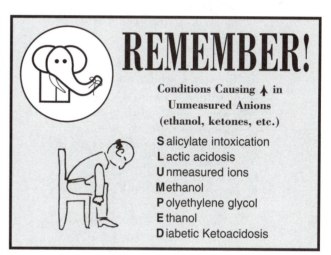

REMEMBER!

Conditions Causing ⬆ in Unmeasured Anions (ethanol, ketones, etc.)

Salicylate intoxication
Lactic acidosis
Unmeasured ions
Methanol
Polyethylene glycol
Ethanol
Diabetic Ketoacidosis

MAGNESIUM (Mg^{++})

1. Ca^{++} channel blocking agent *(affects heart)*

2. ⬆ in renal failure

2. ⬇ in:
   a. Cardiac disorders
   b. Diabetes mellitus
   c. Diuretics, alcohol and other drugs

4. Methods
   a. Atomic absorption
   b. Colorimetric method - calmagite, formazen or methyl thymol blue

CALCIUM (Ca^{++})

1. Combines with phosphate in bone

2. Controlled by 3 hormones:
   a. PTH *(parathyroid)* ⬆ Ca^{++}
   b. Calcitonin inhibits bone reabsorption (⬇ *Ca^{++}*)
   c. Vitamin D causes ⬆ absorption in intestines *(⬆ Ca^{++})*

3. Hypercalcemia *(⬆ Ca^{++})* - muscle weakness, disorientation
   a. Hyperparathyroidism
   b. Cancer with bone metastasis
   c. Multiple myeloma
   d. Renal failure

4. Hypocalcemia *(⬇ Ca^{++})* - tetany
   a. Hypoparathyroidism
   b. ⬇ serum albumin *(1 mg/dL Ca^{++} per 1 g/dL ⬇ albumin)*
   c. ⬇ vitamin D *(malabsorption, inadequate diet)* - impaired bone release, impaired renal reabsorption

5. Laboratory analysis
   a. Atomic absorption spectroscopy - reference method
   b. Colorimetric method - most common
      ❖ *Ca^{++} reacts with o-cresolphthalein to form reddish complex*
      ❖ *8-hydroxyquinoline is added to remove Mg^{++}*
   c. ISE - measures ionized Ca^{++}
      ❖ *pH dependent*
      ❖ *Collection — anaerobically to prevent CO$_2$ loss (⬆ pH)*
   d. Most methods measure total Ca^{++} including protein-bound Ca^{++} *(therefore ⬆ protein causes ⬆ Ca^{++}; ISE avoids problem)*
   e. Falsely ⬇ if using EDTA *(purple top)* or oxalate; EDTA and oxalate bind Ca^{++}

REMEMBER!

In Cases of Tetany, suspect Ca^{++} <u>first</u>, then Mg^{++} or K$^+$

PHOSPHOROUS

1. Majority of phosphate in body expressed as phosphorous; laboratory measures inorganic phosphorous *(PO$_4$)* only

2. Inverse relationship with Ca^{++} *(when Ca^{++} is ⬆, PO$_4$ is ⬇ and vice versa)*

3. ⬆ PO$_4$
   a. Hypoparathyroidism
   b. Chronic renal failure
   c. Excess vitamin D

4. ⬇ PO$_4$
   a. Hyperparathyroidism
   b. Impaired renal absorption

5. Methods
   a. Spectrophotometric methods use molybdate to combine with PO$_4$ ions
   b. Molybdenum blue is formed by the reduction of phosphomolybdate

IRON

1. Over 65% of total body iron is in hemoglobin - O$_2$ transport

2. Transported by transferrin, haptoglobin and hemopexin

3. Stored as ferritin and hemosiderin

4. Methods
   a. Serum iron - colorimetric - avoid hemolysis
   b. TIBC *(total iron-binding capacity)*
      ❖ *Reflects transferrin levels*
      ❖ *Excess ferric salts are added to serum to saturate binding sites on transferrin*
      ❖ *Unbound iron precipitated with magnesium carbonate*
      ❖ *After centrifugation, supernatant analyzed for iron*
   c. Direct methods for transferrin are immunochemical *(nephelometry)*
   d. Ferritin
      ❖ *Assess iron storage*
      ❖ *Immunoassay methods*
      ❖ *Sensitive for detection of iron deficiency*
      ❖ *⬆ in infection, inflammation, chronic diseases*

Laboratory Assessment of Iron

DISEASE	SERUM IRON (μg/L)	TRANSFERRIN SATURATION (%)	TIBC (μg/L)	SERUM FERRITIN (μg/L)
Normal	500-1600	20-55	2500-4000	15-200
Storage Iron Depletion (No Anemia)	N	N	N	↓
Iron Deficiency Anemia	↓	↓	↑	↓
Anemia of Chronic Disease (Inflammation)	↓	↓	↓	↑
Thalassemia	↑	↑	↓	↑
Hemochromatosis	↑↑	↑	↓	↑
Sideroblastic Anemia	↑	↑	N	↑

Acid-Base Balance

HENDERSON-HASSELBALCH EQUATION

1. Definition - logarithmic expression of ionization constant equation of a weak acid

2. Formula
   a. $pH = pKa + \log \dfrac{(HCO_3^-)}{(H_2CO_3)}$

   want this ratio to be $\dfrac{20}{1}$

   b. pH proportional to:
      - ❖ $\log \dfrac{HCO_3^-}{pCO_2}$
      - ❖ <u>kidney</u>
        lungs
      - ❖ <u>metabolic</u>
        respiratory

SAMPLE COLLECTION AND HANDLING

1. Anticoagulant - sodium heparinate (heparin)

2. Must use anaerobic collection for pH and blood gas studies

3. If blood is exposed to air:
   a. CO_2 and pCO_2 ↓
   b. pH ↑
   c. pO_2 ↑

4. If testing prolonged (> 20 minutes) blood should be kept in cracked ice to prevent glycolysis, which leads to:
   a. CO_2 and pCO_2 ↑
   b. pH ↑
   c. pO_2 ↓

Blood Gas Reference Ranges

PARAMETER	DEFINITION	'NORMAL'
pH	Negative Log of H+	7.35-7.45
pCO_2	Partial Pressure or Tension of CO_2 in Blood	35-45 mm Hg
HCO_3	Bicarbonate - Calculated	22-26 mM/L
pO_2	Oxygen Tension - Partial Pressure of Oxygen	85-105 mm Hg

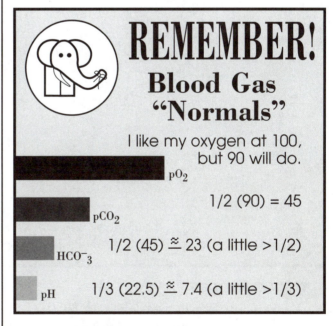

REMEMBER!
Blood Gas "Normals"

I like my oxygen at 100, but 90 will do.

pO_2

pCO_2 1/2 (90) = 45

HCO_3^- 1/2 (45) ≈ 23 (a little >1/2)

pH   1/3 (22.5) ≈ 7.4 (a little >1/3)

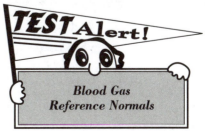

TEST Alert!

Blood Gas Reference Normals

Factors Affecting Blood Gas Analysis

	pH	pCO₂	pO₂
Bubbles in Syringe	↑	↓	↑
Sample Sitting More Than 30 Minutes *(Not on Ice)*	↓	↑	↓

REMEMBER!
Factors Affecting Blood Gases

Let me introduce the characters who will help you remember blood gases:

Phonetia *(pH)*,

Carbo *(Bicarbonate - HCO_3^-)*, and

Paco *(pCO_2)*

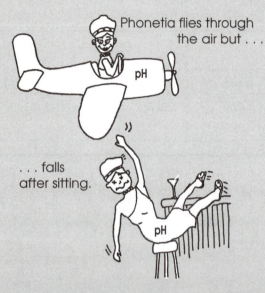

Phonetia flies through the air but . . .

. . . falls after sitting.

(Air bubbles in syringe ↑ pH, prolonged sitting at room temperature ↓ pH)

Paco, you forgot your parachute!

Paco falls from the air . . .

Help!!!

. . . but rises after sitting.

(Air bubbles in syringe ↓ pCO₂; prolonged sitting at room temperature ↑ pCO₂)

O_2 is simple: Exposure to air *(oxygen)* causes ↑ in pO_2; prolonged sitting causes loss of air, a ↓ in pO_2.

METABOLIC ACIDOSIS

1. Primary bicarbonate deficit *(↓ HCO_3^-)*
   a. Diabetic ketoacidosis *(↑ acid production)*
   b. Renal disease *(↓ H^+ excretion)*
   c. Prolonged diarrhea *(excessive HCO_3^- loss)*
   d. Late salicylate poisoning

2. Compensatory mechanisms
   a. Primarily respiratory
      ❖ *Hyperventilation*
      ❖ *↓ pCO2*
   b. Some renal *(if kidney function normal)*
      ❖ *↑ excretion of H^+*
      ❖ *Reabsorption of HCO_3^-*

3. Lab Findings
   a. ↓ pH, HCO_3^-, CO_2 and pCO_2
   b. Acid urine

METABOLIC ALKALOSIS

1. Primary HCO_3^- excess ($\uparrow HCO_3^-$)
2. Seen in:
   a. $NaHCO_3$ infusion
   b. Citrate *(anticoagulant in blood transfusions)*
   c. Antacids *(contain HCO_3^-)*
   d. Vomiting *(HCl loss; prolonged vomiting leads to alkalosis due to GI loss of HCO_3^-)*
   e. K^+ depletion
   f. Diuretic therapy
   g. Cushing Syndrome ($\uparrow$ *mineralocorticosteroids*)

3. Compensatory mechanisms
   a. Primarily respiratory
      ❖ *Hypoventilation*
      ❖ $\uparrow$ retention of CO_2
   b. Some renal -
      ❖ $\downarrow$ *excretion of H^+*
      ❖ $\uparrow$ *reabsorption of HCO_3^-*

4. Lab Findings - $\uparrow$ pH, HCO_3^-, CO_2 and pCO_2

RESPIRATORY ACIDOSIS

1. Primary CO_2 excess ($\uparrow pCO_2$)

2. Seen in:
   a. Emphysema
   b. Pneumonia
   c. Rebreathing air *(paper bag)*

3. Compensatory mechanisms
   a. Mainly renal -
      ❖ $\uparrow H^+$ *excretion*
      ❖ HCO_3^- reabsorption
   b. Some respiratory *(if defect is not in the respiratory center)*

4. Lab findings — $\downarrow$ pH and $\uparrow HCO_3^-$, CO_2 and pCO_2

RESPIRATORY ALKALOSIS

1. Primary CO_2 deficit ($\downarrow pCO_2$)

2. Seen in:
   a. Hyperventilation *(blowing off too much CO_2)*
   b. Early salicylate poisoning

3. Compensatory mechanisms
   a. Mainly renal
      ❖ $\downarrow H^+$ *excretion*

4. Lab findings - $\uparrow$ pH and HCO_3^-, $\downarrow pCO_2$ and CO_2

Compensatory Mechanisms

Resp. Acidosis	Renal	$\uparrow HCO_3$
Resp. Alkalosis	Renal	$\downarrow HCO_3$
Metabolic Acidosis	Lung	$\downarrow pCO_2$
Metabolic Alkalosis	Lung	$\uparrow pCO_2$

REMEMBER!
Compensatory Mechanisms

Compensation occurs in respiratory situations when Carbo gets mad at Phonetia for playing with Paco and hops on Paco's side of the seesaw! pH *(Phoentia)* goes up, pCO_2 and HCO_3^- *(Paco and Carbo)* go down. pH comes down, pCO_2 and HCO_3^- go up.

Compensation occurs in metabolic situations when Paco decides to crash the swinging twosome and hops on with Phonetia and Carbo. Now all go up or all go down.

Hey who needs Henderson or Hasselbalch!!!

REMEMBER!

Causes of Metabolic Acidosis vs Alkalosis

BASE EXCESS / DEFICIT

1. Defined as amount (dose) of acid or alkali needed to return pH to normal

2. Calculated using pH and pCO_2

3. Assess metabolic component of acid-base disorder
   a. Positive value (base excess) = metabolic alkalosis
   b. Negative value (base deficit) = metabolic acidosis

EVALUATING ACID-BASE DISORDERS

1. Look at pH; determine acidosis/alkalosis

2. Compare pCO_2 and HCO_3^- to "normals"
   a. pCO_2 seesawing with pH = respiratory
   b. HCO_3^- "swinging" with pH = metabolic

3. If pH normal, full compensation occurred

4. If main compensatory mechanism kicked in, but pH still out of normal range, partial compensation has occurred

5. Primary respiratory dysfunction results in change in pCO_2 (*seesaw*); main compensation is HCO_3^- (*metabolic*)

6. Primary metabolic dysfunction results in change in HCO_3^- (*swing*); main compensation is pCO_2 (*respiratory*)

REMEMBER!
Acid-Base Status

To determine acid base status (*respiratory or metabolic*) picture yourself in Rome. You are on a playground with Phonetia (*pH*), Carbo (*HCO_3^-*), and Paco (*pCO_2*).

R Respiratory

O Opposite

M Metabolic

E Equal

Phonetia and Paco hop on the seesaw and begin to play. Up and down, up and down. When the pH and pCO_2 are in opposite directions from "normal," the status is respiratory (*respiratory = opposite*).

Phoentia tires of playing with Paco and runs off to join Carbo who is on a swing. Both go up and both go down, always together. When pH and HCO_3^- are either both ↑ or both ↓, the status is metabolic (*metabolic = equal*).

pH > 7.45 = alkalosis
pH < 7.35 = acidosis

ACID-BASE PROBLEMS

Determine the acid-base status in each of the following examples:

1.

$$pH = 7.24$$
$$pCO_2 = 44$$
$$HCO_3^- = 18$$

Answer: Metabolic Acidosis *(uncompensated)*; Phonetia and Carbo are swinging down. pH < 7.35

2.

$$pH = 7.52$$
$$pCO_2 = 44$$
$$HCO_3^- = 39$$

Answer: Metabolic Alkalosis *(uncompensated)*; Phonetia and Carbo are swinging up. pH > 7.45

3.

$$pH = 7.26$$
$$pCO_2 = 56$$
$$HCO_3^- = 24$$

Answer: Respiratory Acidosis *(uncompensated)*; Phonetia and Paco are on the seesaw. pH < 7.35

4.

$$pH = 7.52$$
$$pCO_2 = 28$$
$$HCO_3^- = 21$$

Answer: Partially compensated respiratory alkalosis. Phonetia and Paco are seesawing. Carbo joins Paco to compensate.

5.

$$pH = 7.39$$
$$pCO_2 = 25$$
$$HCO_3^- = 15$$

Answer: Completely compensated metabolic acidosis or completely compensated respiratory alkalosis. For these situations, look at the pH. If it is on the low side of normal, choose acidosis. If it is on the high side of normal, choose alkalosis. In a like manner, completely compensated metabolic alkalosis cannot be distinguished from fully compensated respiratory acidosis. The Phonetia, Paco and Carbo story will work > 90% of the time in solving acid-base problems.

Hemoglobin Derivatives

1. Hemoglobin *(Hb)* breakdown products from aged or damaged RBCs include porphyrins, bilirubin and urobilinogen

LABORATORY ANALYSIS OF PORPHYRINS AND RELATED COMPOUNDS

1. Urines with large amounts of porphyrins show a red or "port wine" color

2. All porphyrins have a characteristic pink fluorescence *(can be quantitated using a UV spectrophotometer)*

3. Watson-Schwartz test
   a. Porphobilinogen *(PBG)* will react with Ehrlich's reagent, p-dimethyl-aminobenzaldehyde, to form red color
   b. Add chloroform to separate PBG from interfering compounds including urobilinogen *(UBG)*
      ❖ *Color in chloroform top layer = UBG and other interfering compounds*
      ❖ *Color in aqueous bottom layer = PBG*

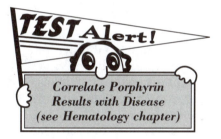

TEST Alert!

Correlate Porphyrin Results with Disease (see Hematology chapter)

LABORATORY ANALYSIS OF BILIRUBIN

1. Diazotization methods
   a. Evelyn & Malloy *(classic method)*
      ❖ *Bilirubin + diazotized sulfanilic acid ➤ azobilirubin (purple)*
      ❖ *Total bilirubin (conjugated + unconjugated) reacts slowly with diazo reagent*
      ❖ *Conjugated bilirubin (direct) reacts rapidly with diazo reagent in water*
   b. Jendrassik-Grof method *(same except accelerator is caffeine-benzoate)*
   c. Direct = conjugated = water soluble
   d. Indirect = unconjugated = relatively insoluble in water

2. Direct Spectrophotometric method
   a. Newborns only; they lack interfering compounds

122

3. Specimen collection and handling
   a. Bilirubin is light sensitive, therefore sample should be stored in dark *(amber-colored)* glass
   b. Lipemia - falsely ⬆ results
   c. Hemolysis - falsely ⬇ results

GENERAL INFORMATION

1. When unconjugated bilirubin is ⬆, there will be a ⬆ in urine urobilinogen *(due to ⬆ amount reabsorbed from intestine and filtered by kidney)*

2. When conjugated bilirubin *(water soluble)* is ⬆, it will appear in urine

CONDITIONS

1. Pre-hepatic jaundice *(i.e. hemolytic anemia)*
   a. ⬆ red cell destruction ➜ ⬆ unconjugated bilirubin
   b. Liver function is normal; conjugation occurs at normal rate ➜ normal conjugated bilirubin and no bilirubin in urine
   c. ⬆ unconjugated bilirubin ➜ ⬆ urine urobilinogen

2. Hepatic jaundice *(i.e. viral hepatitis, cirrhosis)*
   a. ⬆ unconjugated bilirubin, ⬆ conjugated bilirubin and ⬆ urobilinogen due to liver dysfunction
   b. ⬆ conjugated bilirubin ➜ ⬆ urine bilirubin
   c. ⬆ urine urobilinogen

3. Posthepatic *(obstructive)* jaundice
   a. Conjugated and unconjugated bilirubin cannot be metabolized properly; "back-up" into plasma
   b. ⬇ urobilinogen *(due to blockage)*

prevents conjugated bilirubin from entering intestine to be broken down into urobilinogen
   c. Stool may become clay colored

REMEMBER!

HDN . . .
Since bilirubin cannot be conjugated in neonates:

- serum indirect (unconjugated) bilirubin ⬆, conjugated bilirubin is normal for neonates

- **un**conjugated *(water insoluble)* cannot be excreted in the urine, so there is no urinary bilirubin

- **un**conjugated bilirubin cannot be broken down by intestinal bacteria so there is NO URINARY UROBILINOGEN *(appears as normal on "dipstick" - differs from other hemolytic processes where there is an ⬆ in urinary urobilinogen)*

Correlate Bilirubin Results with Disease

Bilirubin and Disease States

DISEASE	Plasma/Serum		Urine	
	UNCONJUGATED BILIRUBIN	CONJUGATED BILIRUBIN	BILIRUBIN	UROBILINOGEN
Prehepatic Jaundice *(hemolytic anemia)*	⬆	N	0	⬆
Hepatic *(cirrhosis, viral hepatitis)*	⬆	⬆	0 or ⬆	⬆
Posthepatic *(obstructive jaundice)*	N	⬆	⬆	⬇

Toxicology

METHODS

1. Immunoassay

2. Chromatographic Techniques
   a. Thin-Layer Chromatography *(TLC)*
      - *Separates drugs for identification*
      - *Urine best specimen for detecting drugs*
      - *Limited sensitivity*
      - *Results should be confirmed with another method*
   b. High-Performance Liquid Chromatography *(HPLC)*
      - *Separation and quantitation of drugs and their metabolites*
   c. Gas Chromatography-Mass Spectrophotometry *(GC-MS)*
      - *"Gold-standard" technique for confirmation of screening methods*
      - *Highly sensitive and reliable*

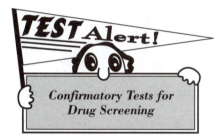

TEST Alert!

Confirmatory Tests for Drug Screening

Therapeutic Drug Monitoring (TDM)

1. Specimen collection
   a. Must wait until steady-state is reached to do therapeutic monitoring
   b. Takes 5 ½ half-lives to reach steady state and it takes 5 ½ half-lives to clear drug when medication stopped
   c. Trough specimen drawn immediately before next dose
   d. Most therapeutic ranges are for trough specimens
   e. Peaks for most drugs are drawn 1-2 hours after an oral dose, and vary for IV or IM procedures

2. Goal is to achieve therapeutic range, avoiding subtherapeutic or toxic concentrations

3. Each drug has own rate of absorption, peak time, extent of protein binding, metabolism and rate of excretion

4. Most common methods are immunoassays

5. HPLC and GC
   a. More sensitive and can measure parent drug and metabolites
   b. Disadvantages - expense, time and expertise required

6. Metabolism
   a. Most drugs metabolized in liver and excreted in urine
   b. Liver or kidney diseases affect drug levels
   c. If metabolites active, should monitor their levels also

AMINOGLYCOSIDES (ANTIBIOTICS)

1. Generic names
   a. Gentamicin
   b. Tobramycin
   c. Amikacin
   d. Vancomycin

2. Inhibit bacterial protein synthesis; treat severe infections by gram-neg bacteria

3. Monitor toxic range to prevent damage to hearing *(ototoxic)* and kidneys *(nephrotoxic)*

4. Measure peak and trough levels

ANTIARRHYTHMICS AND OTHER CARDIOACTIVE DRUGS

1. Digoxin
   a. If ↓ K^+ or ↓ Mg^{++}, may see toxic symptoms with therapeutic levels
   b. Treat overdose with Digibind *(antibody)*; cannot monitor digoxin levels unless assay measures free digoxin only *(most assays do not)*

2. Quinidine
   a. Adding quinidine if patient taking digoxin causes ↑ digoxin

3. Procainamide
   a. Monitor metabolite NAPA also

4. Disopyramide

5. Lidocaine
   a. Very short half-life

ANTICONVULSANTS

1. Phenytoin *(Dilantin brand name)*
   a. Highly protein bound

2. Phenobarbital
   a. Induces enzymes to ↑ metabolism of all drugs

3. Valproic acid
   a. Adding valproic if patient taking phenobarbital causes ↑ phenobarbital

4. Primidone
   a. Monitor metabolite, phenobarbital, as well as parent drug primidone

5. Carbamazepine

6. Ethosuximide

PSYCHOTROPICS (ANTIDEPRESSANTS)

1. Tricyclics
   a. Amtriptyline metabolized to nortriptyline *(can be given separately also)*
   b. Imipramine metabolized to desipramine *(can be given separately also)*
   c. Doxepin
   d. Methods
      ❖ *Immunoassays measure total* (parent plus metabolite)
      ❖ *Chromatography — HPLC, GLC* (measure parent and metabolite separately)

2. Lithium
   a. Used to treat bipolar disorders
   b. Methods
      ❖ *ISEs*
      ❖ *Atomic absorption*
      ❖ *Flame emission photometry*

BRONCHODILATORS

1. Theophylline
   a. Signs of toxicity include nausea, vomiting, headache, irritability, insomnia
   b. Severe toxicity can cause cardiac arrhythmias, seizures and death
   c. Caffeine is active metabolite in neonates *(monitor levels)*
   d. Methods
      ❖ *Immunoassays* (separate assays for theophylline and caffeine)
      ❖ *HPLC* (monitor both theophylline and caffeine simultaneously)

2. Caffeine
   a. Given to neonates

ACUTE POISONING

1. Substances
   a. Cyanide
   b. Carbon monoxide

c. Alcohols - Ethanol most common, enzymatic - alcoholic dehydrogenase
d. Heavy metals *(arsenic, mercury and lead)*
e. Lead *(blocks heme pathway; ↑ ALA but not PBG)*
f. Iron
g. Salicylates - metabolic acidosis - respiratory alkalosis
h. Organophosphates *(pesticides)*
   ❖ *CNS symptoms*
   ❖ *Lab findings* ↓ *cholinesterase* (RBC) *and pseudocholinesterase* (plasma)
i. Acetaminophen - liver damage from accumulation of toxic metabolite 48 hours after ingestion; antidote helpful if given in first 24 hours

TEST Alert!

Test to Confirm Pesticide Poisoning

Non-Protein Nitrogens (NPN)

GENERAL INFORMATION

1. All NPNs *(urea, creatinine, uric acid and ammonia)* are ↑ in the plasma in renal impairment; referred to as azotemia

2. In cases of suspected renal impairment, best laboratory evaluation = glomerular filtration rate *(GFR)*

3. Creatinine clearance evaluates GFR *(more sensitive than BUN or creatinine)*

4. Creatinine clearance

$$\text{Creatinine Clearance} = \frac{U\,creat}{P\,creat} \times \frac{\text{Volume 24 hr. Urine (mL)}}{1440\ (min/24\ hr)}$$

Creatinine clearance is expressed in mL/min

To correct for body surface area:
$$\text{Creat Clear} \times \frac{1.73}{\text{Area (nomogram)}}$$

5. Calculated GFR
   a. More sensitive than creatinine clearance
   b. Computer programs use serum

creatinine, BUN, demographic info (*age, gender, race*), and/or albumin
  c. 24-hour urine collection not needed

CREATININE

1. From creatinine in muscle

2. Can also be measured to evaluate renal function; NOT as sensitive as GFR

3. Classic method is the Jaffe reaction
   a. Creatinine reacts with picric acid in alkaline solution to form a red-orange complex that absorbs light at 490-540 nm
   b. Interferents (*non-creatinine chromagens*) include glucose, acetoacetate and ascorbic acid

BLOOD UREA NITROGEN (BUN)

1. ↑ in impaired renal function

2. Rises more rapidly than serum creatinine

3. Methods:
   a. Colorimetric method: urea reacts with diacetyl monoxime to form a colored complex
   b. Enzymatic method: Urease hydrolyzes urea into ammonia which can be measured spectrophotometically or with an ISE
      ❖ *Inhibited by the anticoagulant, sodium fluoride*
      ❖ *Must NOT use this anticoagulant for ANY enzyme analysis*

4. BUN/creatinine ratio is normally about 10:1-20:1

CYSTATIN C

1. Serum marker for GFR

2. Small protein produced by most nucleated cells in a consistent manner, unaffected by inflammation, gender, age, eating habits, or nutritional status

3. Method = immunoassay

URIC ACID

1. End product of purine metabolism

2. ↑ in gout, renal failure, leukemia, and chemotherapy treatment

3. Colorimetric method
   a. Uric acid reduces phosphotungstic acid to tungsten blue measured spectrophotometrically

   b. Interferents include lipids and several drugs

4. Enzymatic assays are based on the uricase reaction in which allantoin and H_2O_2 are produced and H_2O_2 is coupled to give a colored product

AMMONIA

1. Derived from action of bacteria on contents of colon

2. Metabolized by liver normally

3. ↑ plasma ammonia toxic to the CNS

4. Hyperammonemia (↑ *ammonia*)
   a. Advanced liver disease (*most common cause*)
      ❖ *Reye's syndrome*
      ❖ *Cirrhosis*
      ❖ *Viral hepatitis*
   b. Impaired renal function
      ❖ *Blood urea is ↑ (↑ excretion into intestine, site of conversion to ammonia)*

5. Causes of false ↑ due to specimen collection and handling
   a. Failure to place sample on ice, centrifuge and analyze immediately (*nitrogenous constituents will metabolize to ammonia*)
   b. Poor venipuncture technique (*probing*)
   c. Incompletely filling collection tube

Specimen Collection for Ammonia Analysis

Endocrinology

GENERAL

1. Hypothalmus / Pituitary / End Organ System — Hypothalmus produces releasing hormone which stimulates pituitary to produce stimulating hormone that causes end organ to produce hormones or initiate a process (*see table on page 126*)

2. Hyper and hypo conditions: end product hormone is ↑ (hyper) or ↓ (hypo)
   a. Primary caused by end organ problem
   b. Secondary caused by pituitary problem

c. Tertiary caused by hypothalmic problem

3. Regulation — end organ product or process feeds back to hypothalmus and pituitary to stop production of releasing and stimulating hormones

HYPOTHALMUS / PITUITARY / END ORGAN SYSTEM			
HYPOTHALMUS	**PITUITARY**	**END ORGAN**	**PRODUCT / ACTION**
TRH (thyrotropin releasing hormone)	**TSH** (thyroid stimulating hormone)	Thyroid	T_4 and T_3
CRH (corticotropin releasing hormone)	**ACTH** (adrenocorticotropic releasing hormone)	Adrenal Cortex	cortisol, aldosterone, estrogens, testosterone
GnRH (gonadotropin releasing hormone)	**LH** (leutinizing hormone) AND **FSH** (follicle stimulating hormone)	Ovaries OR Testes	ovulation OR spermatogenesis

THYROID HORMONES

1. Hypothalmus / Pituitary / Thyroid axis *(see table)*

2. Stimulate metabolic processes; necessary for normal growth and development

3. In the tissues T_4 is converted to T_3 *(physiologically active product)*: T_4 concentration much higher than T_3
   a. 99.97% of T_4 bound to thyroxine-binding globulin *(TBG)*, thyroxine-binding prealbumin *(TBPA)* and albumin; 0.03% is free
   b. T_3 is 99.5% bound and 0.5% free

4. Only free fractions metabolically active; bound is for storage and transport

5. Primary hyperthyroidism (↓ *TSH*; ↑ T_4 *and* T_3)
   a. Symptoms include weight loss, heat intolerance, hair loss, nervousness, tachycardia and tremor
   b. The most common cause is Graves disease
      ❖ *Autoimmune disorder*
      ❖ *Antibodies to thyroid-stimulating hormone (TSH) receptors*
      ❖ *Causes thyroid hyperactivity and suppression of TSH*
      ❖ *Lab findings*
         ☞ Normal or ↑ T_3 and ↑ T_4
         ☞ ↓ TSH

c. Pregnancy
   ❖ *TSH* ↓ *first trimester*
   ❖ *TBG* ↑ *due to estrogen*
   ❖ *FT_4 and FT_3* ↓ *second and third trimesters*
   ❖ *Total T_4 and T_3* ↑

6. Primary hypothyroidism (↓ T_4 *and* T_3; ↑ *TSH*)
   a. Symptoms include fatigue, weight gain, decreased mental and physical output, cold intolerance
   b. Cretinism - congenital
   c. Myxedema - severe thyroid deficiency in adults
   d. Hashimoto's Thyroiditis
      ❖ *Thyroid autoantibodies*
      ❖ *Lab findings*
         ☞ ↓ T_3 and T_4
         ☞ ↑ TSH

8. Tests for Thyroid Function
   a. TSH
      ❖ *Ultra-sensitive immunoassay*
      ❖ *Single best thyroid function test*
   b. Total thyroxine *(T_4)*
   c. Free T_4
   d. (Direct) T_3 measures triiodothyrinine *(T_3)*
   e. T_3 uptake
      ❖ *Indirect measurement of TBG*
      ❖ *No longer recommended*

ADRENAL CORTEX HORMONES

1. Hypothalmus produces CRH that stimulates pituitary to produce ACTH that stimulates adrenal cortex to produce steroid hormones made from cholesterol

2. 3 classes of steroids produced
   a. Mineralcorticoids
      ❖ *Aldosterone*
   b. Glucocorticoids
      ❖ *Cortisol*
   c. Sex hormones
      ❖ *Androgens: testosterone*
      ❖ *Estrogens: estradiol*

3. Regulation — cortisol feedback to hypothalmus and pituitary to stop production of CRH and ACTH

ALDOSTERONE

1. Maintains blood pressure, promotes sodium reabsorption and potassium secretion

2. Regulation of secretion through renin-angiotensin system
   a. Renin converts angiotensinogen to angiotensin I which is rapidly converted to angiotensin II which stimulates cortex to produce aldosterone

3. Hyperaldosteronism (↑ *aldostrone*) - Conn Disease
   a. ↑ Na^+
   b. ↓ K^+
   c. Hypertension

4. Hypoaldosteronism (↓ *aldosterone*) - Addison disease

a. ↓ Na^+ and Cl^-
b. ↓ cortisol
c. ↓ hemoglobin
d. ↓ urinary steroids
e. ↑ ACTH when primary hypoaldosteronism (*adrenal cortex problem*)
f. ↓ ACTH if secondary (*pituitary*) or tertiary (*hypothalamus*) problems

CORTISOL

1. Functions
   a. Causes ↑ glucose through gluconeogenesis and decreased carbohydrate use
   b. Inhibits protein synthesis
   c. Immunosuppressive and anti-inflammatory

2. ↑ cortisol (*without diurnal variation*) - Cushing syndrome
   a. Diabetes mellitus, ↓ plasma protein and hypertension
   b. Truncal obesity, facial hair, "buffalo hump", osteoporosis, scant menses

3. ↓ cortisol - Addison disease (*see Aldosterone*)

ANDROGENS

1. Male sex hormones, secondary sexual characteristics

2. Secreted by testes, adrenals and ovaries

3. ↑ testosterone - precocious puberty in boys, testicular tumors; masculinization in females

4. ↓ in hypogonadism

5. 17-ketosteroids (17-KS)
   a. Metabolites of androgens
   b. Zimmermann reaction
      ❖ *17-KS react with metadinitro-benzene in alcoholic alkali*
      ❖ *Produces red-purple color*

ESTROGENS

1. Female sex hormones

2. Secreted by ovaries
   a. Estradiol - secondary sexual characteristics
   b. Estrone - metabolite of estradiol

c. Estriol
   ❖ *↑ during fetal development in pregnancy*
   ❖ *Steady increase should occur in the third trimester*
   ❖ *24-hour urinary maternal estriol monitors integrity of feto-placental unit*
   ❖ *Decline or sudden change indicates a complication of the pregnancy*

3. ↑ estrogen - precocious puberty in girls, feminization in males, pregnancy, oral contraceptives, polycystic ovary disease

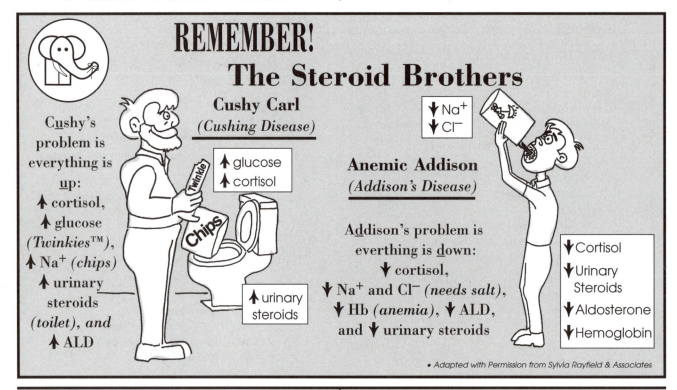

TESTS FOR ADRENAL CORTEX FUNCTION

1. Cortisol
   a. Diurnal variation *(highest in morning)*
   b. Can measure free *(unbound)* or total in serum, plasma or urine

2. Dexamethasone suppression
   a. Give dexamethasone to suppresses cortisol production
   b. Measure cortisol
   c. Interpretation
      ❖ *Cortisol ↓ (suppressed) = normal*
      ❖ *Cortisol ↑ (not suppressed) = Cushing*
      ❖ *Cortisol partially suppressed =*

depression, obesity, pregnancy, stress, infection

3. Aldosterone
   a. ↑ in upright position

4. Renin
   a. Produced in kidneys; may draw from either renal vein
   b. Tests
      ❖ *Renin activity* (angiotensin I generation)
      ❖ *Direct renin* (immunoassay for renin molecule)
   c. Very unstable *(sample must be frozen immediately)*
   d. ↑ in upright position
   e. ↓ in Conn

5. ACTH
    a. Distinguishes between primary and secondary hyperaldosteronism

6. Testosterone
    a. Hypothalmus / Pituitary / Testes and/or Adrenal Cortex
    b. Used for infertility testing
        ❖ *Males: ↓ causes infertility*
        ❖ *Females: ↑ causes infertility, hirsutism, masculinization*

7. Estrogens
    a. Measure estradiol and/or estriol in serum and urine

ADRENAL MEDULLA HORMONES : CATECHOLAMINES

1. Produced in chromaffin cells
    a. Epinephrine, norepinephrine and dopamine
    b. Homovanillic acid *(HVA)* = metabolite of dopamine
    c. Metanephrines and vanillylmandelic acid *(VMA)*= epinephrine metabolites

2. Pheochromocytoma
    a. Tumor of adrenal medulla
    b. Hypertension, headache

3. Neuroblastoma - fatal tumor in children

4. Tests for catecholamines
    a. Catecholamines *(plasma and/or urine)*
    a. Metanephrines in urine best screen for pheochromocytoma because catecholamine release is intermittent
    b. VMA - urine
    c. HVA - urine

GASTROINTESTINAL HORMONES

1. Gastrin - ↑ in Zollinger-Ellison syndrome *(peptic ulcers, excessive acid secretion)*

2. Serotonin
    a. Vasoconstrictor found in platelets, brain and other tissue
    b. Increased production in tumors of chromaffin cells of GI tract
    c. Measure breakdown product, 5-hydroxy-indole-acetic acid *(5-HIAA)*, in urine
    d. 5-HIAA falsely ↑ from some drugs or diet that includes bananas, pineapples and chocolate

CHEMISTRY SAMPLE QUESTIONS

1. A patient is administered an oral glucose tolerance test with the following results:

    Fasting - 75 mg/dL
    30 minutes - 82 mg/dL
    1 hour - 85 mg/dL
    90 minutes - 80 mg/dL
    2 hours - 78 mg/dL

    These results correlate with
    A. A normal curve
    B. Diabetes
    C. Hypoglycemia
    D. Poor gastric absorption

2. A physician calls to ask assistance in choosing a test to monitor a diabetic patient's long term control. You would suggest
    A. C-peptide of insulin
    B. Glycosylated hemoglobin(s)
    C. Fasting plasma glucose
    D. Postprandial plasma glucose

3. Which of the following set of test results indicates the greatest risk for coronary artery disease?

	Total Cholesterol mg/dL	HDL cholesterol mg/dL	LDL cholesterol mg/dL
A.	145	55	90
B.	165	60	105
C.	245	60	95
D.	345	30	205

4. Elevated conjugated bilirubin in both serum and urine, decreased urine urobilinogen, and decreased fecal urobilin is characteristic of
    A. Cirrhosis
    B. Hemolytic jaundice
    C. Hepatitis
    D. Obstructive jaundice

5. Calculate the LDL cholesterol from the following data:

    Total cholesterol = 250 mg/dL
    HDL cholesterol = 40 mg/dL
    Triglyceride = 210 mg/dL

    A. 140 mg/dL
    B. 168 mg/dL
    C. 210 mg/dL
    D. 237 mg/dL

6. A 65 year old male visits his physician complaining of fatigue, shortness of breath and difficulty breathing. He is 6 feet tall and weighed 200 pounds for many years, but has recently gained 30 pounds. His ankles and hands are swollen and he complains of feeling bloated. His blood pressure is markedly elevated.

What test should the physician order and why?
    A. Troponin
    B. Arterial blood gases
    C. BNP or NT pro-BNP
    D. Myoglobin

7. Which results will be falsely decreased in a hemolyzed sample?
    A. Acid phosphatase
    B. Bilirubin
    C. Iron
    D. Potassium

8. Which enzyme is decreased in insecticide poisoning due to organophosphates?
    A. Alkaline phosphatase
    B. Amylase
    C. Cholinesterase
    D. Creatine kinase

9. The biuret method for determining serum total protein is dependent upon
    A. Amino acid content
    B. Number of peptide bonds
    C. Nitrogen content
    D. Protein precipitation

10. An arterial blood sample is received in the laboratory 45 minutes after collection with a bubble in the syringe. The technologist should
    A. Perform the test immediately
    B. Reject the sample because the pO_2 will be falsely ↓
    C. Reject the sample because the pH will be falsely ↓
    D. Reject the sample because the pCO_2 will be falsely ↓

11. A patient in diabetic ketoacidosis would exhibit a/an
    A. ↑ pCO_2, ↑ HCO_3^-, ↑ pH
    B. ↓ pCO_2, ↓ HCO_3^-, ↑ pH
    C. Normal pCO_2, ↑ HCO_3^-, ↓ pH
    D. Normal pCO_2, ↓ HCO_3^-, ↓ pH

12. The best laboratory test for detecting cystic fibrosis is
    A. Lipase
    B. Sodium
    C. Sweat chloride
    D. Trypsin

13. A 25 year old female visits her physician with the following symptoms: feeling tired all of the time, recently gaining 15 pounds, swollen neck, dry skin, hoarseness, and delayed reflexes. The physician ordered thyroid tests with the following results:

    TSH = 3.0 mIU/L (ref. 0.2-4.0 mIU/L)
    Free T_4 = 0.4 ng/dL (ref. 0.8-1.8 ng/dL)

The physician performed a TRH stimulation test with the following results:
    30 minute TSH = 6.0 mIU/L
    60 minute TSH = 15.0 mIU/L

The results indicate that the patient is suffering from:
    A. Primary hyperthyroidism
    B. Primary hypothyroidism
    C. Secondary or "pituitary" hypothyroidism
    D. Tertiary or "hypothalamic" hypothyroidism

14. A blood ammonia level was ordered on a patient with Reye's syndrome. The results on the clotted sample were normal. The most likely explanation for these results is
    A. Inappropriate sample collection
    B. Incorrect diagnosis
    C. Patient is under treatment
    D. QC was out of acceptable limits

15. A patient with ↑ serum levels of creatine kinase (CK), aldolase (ALD) and aspartate aminotransferase (AST) but normal levels of alanine aminotransferase (ALT) most likely has
    A. Hepatitis
    B. Muscular dystrophy
    C. Myocardial infarction
    D. Pulmonary infarction

16. In drug testing using thin layer chromatography, why is a volatile organic compound mixed with urine specimens?
    - A. To preserve the drug
    - B. To remove interferences
    - C. To extract the drugs
    - D. To enhance the effect of the drug

17. Electrolyte values on 4 patients are as follows:
    - A. Na^+ 149 mmol/L; Cl^- 102 mmol/L; HCO_3^- 26 mmol/L
    - B. Na^+ 153 mmol/L; Cl^- 105 mmol/L; HCO_3^- 28 mmol/L
    - C. Na^+ 150 mmol/L; Cl^- 103 mmol/L; HCO_3^- 25 mmol/L
    - D. Na^+ 151 mmol/L; Cl^- 104 mmol/L; HCO_3^- 27 mmol/L

    Based on these results, what do you conclude about your electrolyte analyzer?

    - A. There is a problem with the chloride analysis.
    - B. There is a problem with the bicarbonate analysis.
    - C. All analyses seem to be accurate.
    - D. There is a problem with the sodium analysis.

18. Why should potassium levels be monitored prior to and during administration of IV insulin?
    - A. Insulin causes potassium to move into cells which may cause a drop in potassium levels.
    - B. Insulin concentrates potassium in the serum causing hyperkalemia.
    - C. IV fluids dilute electrolyte values causing hyponatremia and hypokalemia.
    - D. Exogenous insulin causes hemolysis which falsely elevate potassium levels.

ANSWERS AND RATIONALE

1. D

A flat curve, in which the normal peak at 1 hour does not occur, is seen in malabsorption or vomiting. In this case, an IV glucose load would reveal a normal *(or diabetic)* curve. In a normal curve *(option A)*, the glucose rises at 30 minutes and the highest level is seen at 1 hour. In diabetes *(option B)*, the peak level is greater than normal and glucose remains elevated. Hypoglycemia or hyperinsulinism *(option C)* exhibits glucose levels less than 65 mg/dL

2. B

Glycosylated hemoglobin is the specific hemoglobin fraction to which glucose molecules become irreversibly attached. Results of glycosylated hemoglobin are proportional to the average glucose level during the previous 1 to 2 month period. Option A is used to evaluate causes of fasting hypoglycemia. Options C and D give information about glucose levels for only a short period of time.

3. D

The treatment guidelines established by the Adult Treatment Panel of the National Cholesterol Education Program include recommendations that goals for cholesterol (assuming no other risk factors are present) should be less than 200 mg/dL for total cholesterol, <130 mg/dL for LDL cholesterol (the "bad" cholesterol), and >35 mg/dL for HDL cholesterol (the "good" cholesterol. All 3 values for Option D fall outside of the recommended levels and are considered independent risk factors. Options A and B have all values within the recommended levels. Although option C includes a total cholesterol of 245 mg/dL, an HDL cholesterol of 60 mg/dL and an LDL cholesterol of 95 mg/dL are not considered additional risk factors.

4. D

Obstruction in the bile duct results in conjugated bilirubin backing up into the circulation. Because it is water soluble, conjugated bilirubin is excreted into the urine. Since bile flow to the intestines is obstructed, urobilinogen and urobilin are found in the feces in less than normal amounts. Because of the liver damage, options A and C would result in increased levels of unconjugated and conjugated bilirubin in the serum. The increased conjugated fraction would be excreted in the urine. However fecal excretion of urobilinogen and urobilin would also be increased as the intestinal bacteria broke down the increased bilirubin. Option B would result in increased unconjugated bilirubin. Since the liver is undamaged, it could conjugate at the normal rate and there would be no excess to be excreted in the urine. There would be excess fecal urobilinogen due to the increased total bilirubin which would cause an increase in urine urobilinogen.

5. B

The Friedewald formula is:

$$\text{LDL chol} = \text{total chol} - \text{HDL chol} - \frac{\text{triglycerides}}{5}$$

$$= 250 - 40 - (210/5) = 168.$$

6. C

The patient is exhibiting symptoms of congestive heart failure (CHF). BNP (or NT pro-BNP) levels correlate linearly to the New York Heart Association's classification of the stages of CHF. The most commonly used cutoff for the diagnosis is 100 pg/mL, but some studies have used lower levels. Myocytes in the ventricles produce a 134 amino acid peptide, pre-pro-BNP, which is cleaved to pro-BNP (108 amino acids) and a signal peptide (26 amino acids). Hypertension and volume overload cause increased tension and stretching of the ventricular walls, and in response pro-BNP is cleaved to BNP and N-terminal pro-BNP (NT pro-BNP) which are secreted into the blood. BNP is biologically active whereas NT pro-BNP is inactive. BNP decreases blood pressure by vasodilation and renal excretion of sodium and water. Release of BNP is in direct proportion to ventricular wall tension, that is as the tension increases, the amount of BNP released also increases. Thus, BNP levels are an accurate reflection of the severity of heart failure.

7. B

Bilirubin is erroneously decreased in hemolyzed specimens. All other options are found in higher concentrations in the red cell than in plasma and are falsely increased in a hemolyzed sample. Hemolysis also falsely elevates magnesium and several enzymes such as LD, acid phosphatase, AST and ALT.

8. C

Analysis for cholinesterase is unique in that a decreased rather than an increased result is significant. Under normal conditions this enzyme is synthesized in the liver and circulated in high levels. Cholinesterase is most often measured to diagnose and monitor insecticide poisoning and to detect inhibition by succinylcholine, a muscle-relaxant used in anesthesia. It is also decreased in liver disease and other chronic diseases.

9. B

The biuret method, which provides an accurate determination of total protein based on the number of peptide bonds which join amino acids together in protein molecules. Option A is not used. Option C is measured by the Kjeldahl method (reference method), but it is more difficult and time-consuming to perform. Option D is the principle of the turbidimetric methods for urine or spinal fluid protein analysis.

10. D

When blood is exposed to air (air bubble in syringe), the pCO_2 decreases and the pO_2 and pH increase.

11. D

Ketoacidosis is a metabolic disorder. In metabolic acidosis both pH and HCO_3^- are decreased. In a compensated state pCO_2 would also be decreased.

12. C

Pilocarpine nitrate is electrically introduced into the sweat glands to induce sweating by a procedure called iontophoresis. Then sweat is assayed for chloride. In cystic fibrosis, both Na^+ and Cl^- are increased in sweat.

13. D

For the thyroid system, the hypothalmus produces TRH, which stimulates the pituitary to produce TSH, which stimulates the production of T_4 and T_3 by the thyroid gland. The decreased free T_4 level in this patient indicates hypothyroidism, but an elevated TSH is the expected result for primary hypothyroidism *(thyroid gland is dysfunctional)*. The TRH stimulation test involves injection of TRH and measuring baseline, 30 and 60 minute TSH levels. If the problem is a dysfunctional pituitary, the injected TRH will have no effect and the TSH levels will remain the same. If the problem is a dysfunctional hypothalmus *(tertiary hypothyroidism)*, the injected TRH stimulates the pituitary to produce TSH although this response is sometimes blunted or delayed. The results in this case are consistent with a diagnosis of tertiary or hypothalmic hypothyroidism.

14. A

Metabolism of nitrogenous constituents in blood is a source of plasma ammonia contamination. The anticoagulated blood sample *(usually collected in heparin)* must be put on ice immediately, centrifuged and analyzed without delay. Delays of greater than 15 minutes between sample collection and analysis have been shown to increase levels even when stored on ice. Option B is incorrect because in Reye's syndrome, ammonia blood levels are elevated since the liver is unable convert it to urea. Options C and D could be true, but given that the collection process was incorrect, option A is a better response.

15. B

Option A is incorrect because the ALD would not increase and the ALT would be increased. Options C and D are incorrect because the ALD would not be increased.

16. C

When using thin layer chromatography to test for drugs in urine the drugs are extracted into an organic solvent after adjusting the pH with a buffer. Most drugs are more soluble in the organic compound than in the urine. The drug extract is concentrated by evaporation of the volatile organic solvent. The concentrated extract is then separated by TLC and the drugs identified.

17. D

Calculation of the anion gap may be used as a quality control monitor of electrolyte analysis. In this case all 4 samples show an increased anion gap (21, 20, 22, 20) with an elevated sodium. It is unlikely that all 4 patients would have conditions causing an increased sodium and/or increased anion gap. More likely is the probability that there is a problem with the analysis of sodium. Presumably the control values for sodium would also indicate a problem but there are occasions when the controls are within range but an instrumental problem exists and may be detected by calculation of the anion gap for all patient samples.

18. A

Insulin promoted the entry of potassium into liver and skeletal muscle cells. During administration of IV insulin potassium levels should be monitored to detect and treat hypokalemia if it develops.

MICROBIOLOGY / Bacteriology

by Mary Lux

Bacterial Growth Requirements

1. Temperature
   a. Psychrophiles - cold loving; optimum temperature = 15°C
   b. Mesophiles - moderate temperature; optimum temperature = 37°C; (*most pathogenic organisms*)
   c. Thermophiles - heat loving; optimum temperature = 50-60°C

2. pH
   a. Bacteria 6.5-7.5
   b. Fungi 5.0-6.0
   c. Phosphate salts used to buffer media

3. Osmotic pressure
   a. Isotonic
   b. Halophiles - (*Vibrio*) - prefer higher salt concentration

4. Oxygen
   a. Aerobes - require O_2
   b. Facultative anaerobes - can grow with or without O_2
   c. Obligate anaerobes - harmed by O_2
   d. Formation of superoxide radicals, toxic; neutralized by catalase and superoxide dismutase (*possessed by aerobes and facultatives*)

5. Other atmospheric requirements
   a. Microaerophiles - prefer lower O_2 than in air
   b. Capnophiles - prefer higher CO_2 than in air

CULTURE MEDIA

1. Must meet growth requirements

2. Agar - polysaccharide derived from marine algae
   a. Melts at 100°C
   b. Solidifies at approximately 45°C

3. Complex media - most common; made of peptones and extracts

4. Anaerobic media - contain reducing agents which bind with dissolved O_2 (*thioglycollate, cysteine*)
   a. Broth tubes should be heated prior to use to drive out O_2
   b. Gas pak envelopes

   ❖ *Contain Na_2CO_3 and sodium borohydride*
   ❖ *Add water - produces H_2 and CO_2 (aids in growth)*
   ❖ *Palladium pellets catalyze the reaction*
   c. Some require hemin, Vitamin K, and yeast extract

5. Incubation
   a. 5-10% CO_2 (*incubator or candle jar*)
   b. 35-37°C
   c. 50-70% humidity

6. May be selective and/or differential

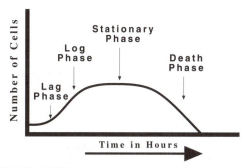

GROWTH CURVE

   a. Lag phase - enzyme synthesis and cell elongation
   b. Log phase - active reproduction
   c. Stationary phase - exhaustion of nutrients, ↑ waste, ↓pH, less viability
   d. Death phase - dead cells exceed new cells

STERILIZATION/INHIBITION TECHNIQUES

1. Heat - denatures protein
   a. Moist - autoclave (*steam under pressure*)
      ❖ *15 lbs pressure/sq. in., 121°C, 15 minutes*
      ❖ *QC - Bacillus stearothermophilus and B. subtilis*
   b. Dry heat
      ❖ *Flame, incinerator, hot air oven*
      ❖ *170°C, 2 hrs*
   c. Pasteurization, ultra high temperature
      ❖ *140°C, 3 seconds*
      ❖ *NOT sterilization*

136

2. Filtration
   a. Pore size 0.22 µ - 0.45 µ
   b. Used for sugar solutions, urea media, vaccines

3. Refrigeration - slows growth

4. Dessication - no multiplication, but organisms remain viable (*lyophilization*)

5. Osmotic pressure hypertonic solution
   a. Causes plasmolysis
   b. "Cured" meat, fruit preserves

6. Radiation
   a. Forms hydroxyl radicals
   b. Damages DNA

7. Disinfection
   a. Phenol - damages cytoplasmic membrane, denatures protein
   b. Halogens (*iodine and chlorine*) - oxidizers

c. Alcohols - denature protein and dissolve lipids

STERILIZATION	DISINFECTION
Kills All Microorganisms (*Including Spores and Viruses*)	Inactivation or Inhibition of Microorganisms (*May Not Affect Spores*)
Examples: • Autoclave (*121°C at 15psi for 15 min.*) • Incineration • Filtration (*Physically Removes Microorganisms*)	Example: • Bleach (*1:10 Hypochlorite*)

Autoclave Pressure, Temperature and Time

Antibiotics/Susceptibility Testing

Antibiotics and Their Actions

ANTIBIOTIC	EXAMPLES	ACTION	NOTES
ß-lactams	Penicillins Cephalosporins Carbapenams (*Imipenam*) Monobactams (*Azotreonam*) ß-lactamase Inhibiting Combinations (*Augmentin, etc.*)	Inhibits cell wall synthesis	Watch for methicilin resistant *Staphylococcus aureus* (MRSA)
Glycopeptides	Vancomycin	Inhibits cell wall synthesis	Drug of choice for *Clostridium difficile* and for methicillin-resistant staph (*MRSA*)
Aminoglycosides	Gentamicin Tobramycin Amikacin	Inhibits protein synthesis	Acts on 30S subunit; not active against anaerobes; used with a penicillin for *Enterococcus*
Tetracyclines	Tetracycline Doxycycline	Inhibits protein synthesis	Acts on 30S subunit; affects bone and teeth in children; may lead to superinfection of yeast
Chloramphenicol	Chloramphenicol	Inhibits protein synthesis	Acts on 50S subunit; can cause aplastic anemia
Macrolides	Erythromycin Clindamycin	Inhibits protein synthesis	Acts on 50S subunit; clindamycin for gram + and gram –anaerobes
Quinolones	Ciprofloxacin Norfloxacin	Inhibits nucleic acid synthesis	For *Pseudomonas aeruginosa* and other aerobes
Sulfa Drugs (*Sulfonomides*)	Sulfamethoxazole	Analogue of PABA (*intermediate in folic acid synthesis*)	For UTI, enteric infections; used with trimethoprim (*Bactrim, etc.*)

ANTIMICROBIAL THERAPY

1. Narrow spectrum - only certain groups covered

2. Broad spectrum - gram pos and gram neg coverage

3. Selective toxicity - action against only microbial structures (*70s ribosome, cell wall, etc*)

4. Bactericidal action - kills bacteria without host immune help

5. Bacteriostatic action - reversible inhibition (*ultimate destruction depends on host defenses*)

6. Drug combination
   a. Synergism - combined better than the sum: 1 + 2 = 4
   b. Antagonism - one decreases activity of other: 1 + 2 = 1

SUSCEPTIBILITY TESTING

1. Kirby-Bauer Method
   a. Mueller-Hinton agar
   b. Depth = 4mm
   c. pH = 7.2-7.4
   d. Physiologic concentration of Ca^{++} and Mg^{++}
   e. 35°C, ambient air
   f. 10^8 organisms (*McFarland 0.5*)
   g. QC weekly and with each new lot of agar or discs (*E. coli, S. aureus, P. aeruginosa*)

2. Broth methods
   a. MIC (*minimum inhibitory concentration*)
      ❖ Lowest concentration of drug that prevents in vitro growth
      ❖ First dilution tube with no visible growth
   b. MBC (*minimum bacteriostatic concentration*)
      ❖ Lowest concentration that results in >99.9% killing
      ❖ Subculture tubes near MIC to find first plate with no growth
   c. Schlichter test
      ❖ Serum bactericidal assay
      ❖ Tests patient serum (containing antibiotic) against the infecting organism

Sources of Error: Disk Diffusion

ABNORMAL RESULT	PROBABLE CAUSE
Tetracycline Zone Too Large and Clindamycin Too Small with *E. coli* or *S. aureus* Controls	pH of agar too low
Tetracycline Zone Too Small and Clindamycin Too Large with *E. coli* or *S. aureus* Controls	pH of agar too high
Aminoglycoside Zone Too Small with *P. aeruginosa* Control	Ca^{++} and/or Mg^{++} too high in agar
Aminoglycoside Zone Too Large with *P. aeruginosa* Control	Ca^{++} and/or Mg^{++} too low in agar
Zones Universally Too Large on Control Plates	Inoculum too light Nutritionally poor medium Slow-growing organism *(not seen with controls)* Agar depth too thin
Zones Universally Too Small on Control Plates	Inoculum too heavy Agar depth too thick
Methicillin Zone Decreasing over Days or Weeks with Control Organisms	Methicillin degrading during refrigerator storage
Methicillin Zone Indeterminate in Disk Test	Methicillin being degraded by strong ß-lactamase producing *Staphylococci*
Colonies within Zone of Inhibition	Mixed culture Resistant mutants within zone
"Zone within a Zone" Phenomenon	A swarming *Proteus* Feather edges of zones around penicillin or ampicillin disks usually occur with ß-lactmase neg. strains of *S. aureus* ß-lactamase pos. *H. influenzae* with penicillin or ampicillin

TEST Alert!

Preparation of Kirby-Bauer Plates and Inoculum

Interpretation of Kirby-Bauer Sensitivity Including QC and Troubleshooting

Organisms Used in Kirby-Bauer QC

Media

Routine Media

MEDIA	PURPOSE
Blood Agar (BA, BAP)	Most Bacteria; Determines Hemolytic Reactions
Chocolate Agar	*Haemophilus* and *Neisseria* sp.; Enriched with Hemoglobin or IsoVitalex
Phenylethyl Alcohol Agar (PEA)	Selects for Gram Negative Anaerobic Bacilli and Gram Positive Cocci; Inhibits Growth of Facultative Gram Negative Organisms
Columbia Colistin-Nalidixic Acid (CNA)	Selects for Gram Positive Cocci
Thayer-Martin Agar	*N. gonorrhoeae* and *N. meningitidis*
CAMPY-Blood Agar	*Campylobacter* sp.
Thioglycollate Broth	"Back-Up" for Anaerobes
Lowenstein-Jensen Agar	*Mycobacterium* sp.
Middlebrook 7H10 Agar	*Mycobacterium* sp.

Anaerobic Media

MEDIA	PURPOSE
Bacteroides Bile Esculin Agar (BBE)	Selects for *B. fragilis* Group (Black Colonies)
Kanamycin-Vancomycin Laked Blood (KVLB)	*Bacteroides* sp. (Enhances Pigment Production)
Cycloserine-Cefoxitin Fructose Agar (CCFA)	*C. difficile*
CDC Anaerobic Blood Agar	Anaerobes (Enriched with Hemin, Cystine, and Vitamin K)
Cooked or Chopped Meat Medium	Anaerobes

Special Media

MEDIA	PURPOSE
Bordet-Gengou Agar	*B. pertussis*
Buffered Charcoal Yeast Extract (BCYE)	*Legionella* sp.
Cystine-Glucose Agar	*F. tularensis*
Fletcher's Medium	*Leptospira*
Kelly's Medium	*Borrelia burgdorferi*
Skirrow Agar	*Helicobacter pylori*
Thiosulfate Citrate-Bile Salts (TCBS)	*Vibrio* sp.
Vaginalis Agar (V-Agar) (human blood)	*Gardnerella vaginalis*
Cystine-Tellurite Blood (Tinsdale)	*C. diphtheriae* (Black Colonies)
Loeffler's Medium	*C. diphtheriae* (Enhances Grouping and Metachromatic Granules)

Confusing Tests

TEST	DETECTS:
Schick	*Corynebacterium diphtheriae*
Dick	Susceptibility to Scarlet Fever (*Streptococcus pyogenes*)
Schlichter	Serum Bactericidal Level
Schultz-Charlton	Antiserum Injected into Rash; Blanches if Scarlet Fever
Elek	Confirms Toxin Production for *Corynebacterium diphtheriae* (in vitro)

COLD ENRICHMENT

- *Listeria monocytogenes*
- *Yersinia*

TEST Alert!

- Anaerobic Media and Associated Organisms
- Special Media and Associated Organisms Especially Legionella
- Purpose of Confusing Tests

Specimen Collection and Handling

GENERAL

1. Material from infection site

2. Optimal time (*ex.: Salmonella typhi- culture blood first week, culture stool second and third weeks*)

3. Sufficient quantity

4. Appropriate collection devices

5. NEVER refrigerate spinal fluids, anaerobic or GC specimens

6. Collect prior to antibiotic therapy

7. Set up within 2 hours of collection

CRITERIA FOR REJECTION

1. Preservatives used

2. Insufficient quantity

3. Dry swab

4. Leaky containers - contaminated specimen as well as biohazard

BLOOD CULTURE COLLECTION

1. Must prep skin properly with alcohol (*70%*) and iodine

2. Best time to draw is just prior to fever spike

3. Draw at least 2 cultures, but no more than 3 in a 24 hr period

4. May use antibiotic removal device (*ARD*) or resin bottles if patient on antibiotics

5. Isolator® best for fungi and acid fast organisms

6. Must have 1:10 dilution of blood to broth; on adults draw at least 10 ml if possible

Dilution of Blood for Blood Cultures

Collection and Handling of Blood Culture Specimens

Laboratory Diagnostic Methods

MICROSCOPY

1. Light microscopy
   a. Resolving power - 0.2 μm
   b. Ocular lens = 10X; oil immersion lens = 100X

2. Darkfield - for spirochetes; reflected light

3. Fluorescence - near UV range; auramine rhodamine, acridine orange and calco- fluor white stains

4. Electron microscopy - can resolve particles 0.001 μm apart; useful in viral I.D.

CULTURE CONDITIONS

1. Plates incubated at 35-37°C
   a. Campylobacter - 42°C
   b. Yersinia - 25-30°C
   c. 5-10% CO_2 (*Campy- microaerophilic*)
   d. 50-70% humidity

2. Anaerobic Conditions
   a. Broths with thioglycollate or cysteine
   b. Pre-reduced media
      ❖ *Gas pak jars or anaerobic chamber*
      ❖ *Environment: 10% H_2, 5% CO_2, 85% N_2, palladium crystals*

MEDIA

1. 1-2% agar

2. Non-selective
   a. Supports most organisms
   b. Blood agar, chocolate agar, trypticase agar

3. Selective agar
   a. Contains chemicals, dyes, antibiotics to inhibit certain organisms (*EMB, MAC, CNA, Campy-blood*)
   b. May also be differential (*HE, SS, XLD, EMB, MAC*)

INOCULATION

1. Streak for isolation with nichrome, platinum, or disposable loops

2. Calibrated 0.01 ml or 0.001 ml *(.001 ml for urine colony count plates)*

3. Number of colonies x 100 *(.01 loop)* or number of colonies x 1000 *(.001 loop)*

4. Read and report after 18-24 hrs

Stains Commonly Used in Microbiology/Mycobacteriology

	PRIMARY STAIN	DECOLORIZER	COUNTERSTAIN	RESULTS POS	NEG	PRINCIPLE
Gram Stain	Crystal Violet	Alcohol/Acetone	Safranin	Purple	Pink	• Iodine mordant • Methanol or heat fix • Violet dye & iodine form complex in cell; washes out of gram neg cells
Kinyoun & Ziehl-Nielson	Carbol Fuchsin	Acid Alcohol	Methylene Blue	Pink	Blue	• Acid fast • For *Mycobacteria*
Auramine-Rhodamine	Auramine and Rhodamine *(Fluorescent Stain)*	Acid Alcohol	Potassium Permanganate	Orange Fluoresc.	No Fluoresc.	• For *Mycobacteria*
Calcofluor White	Calcofluor White + 10% KOH			Bluish-white Fluoresc.	No Fluoresc.	• For yeast and fungi • KOH to break down debris and mucous

Gram Positive Cocci

STAPHYLOCOCCUS

1. "Grape-like" clusters

2. *S. aureus*
   a. Coagulase positive
   b. Most common pathogen of genus
   c. Common infections
      ❖ *Furuncles (boils) and carbuncles*
      ❖ *Bullous impetigo (blisters)*
      ❖ *Paronychia (nails)*
      ❖ *Post surgical wounds and bacteremia*
   d. Intoxications
      ❖ *Scalded skin syndrome (exfoliatin - neonates)*
      ❖ *Toxic shock syndrome (TSST-1) - women ages 12-52*
      ❖ *Food poisoning (enterotoxin) - symptoms in 1-5 hrs after ingestion (potato salad, cream dishes)*
   e. Exotoxins - hemolysins, leukocidins, coagulase and hyaluronidase *(spreading factor)*, nuclease, protease and lipase
   f. Resistance/sensitivity
      ❖ *Most resistant to penicillin due to plasmid mediated B-lactamase*
      ❖ *Some sensitive to penicillinase-resistant penicillins (PRP's) (methicillin, oxacillin, etc); if methicillin-resistant S. aureus (MRSA), vancomycin is drug of choice*
   g. Laboratory diagnosis
      ❖ *BAP - soft, opaque, regular colonies 2-3 mm in diam; some are beta hemolytic and some have pale golden color*
      ❖ *Growth in 7.5% NaCl and ferment mannitol*
      ❖ *Catalase positive*
      ❖ *Phage typing and susceptibility profile for epidemiologic studies*

TEST Alert!

Susceptibility Testing of Staphylococcus

3. Coagulase negative *Staphylococcus*
   a. Opportunist in immunocompromised hosts and patients with prosthetic valves and devices

Biochemical Tests

CATALASE TEST

1. Reagent: 3% H_2O_2

2. Add one drop to colony on slide

3. If catalase present, H_2O_2 is broken down to water and O_2 (*which bubbles off*)

4. Positive: *Staph*; negative - *Strep*

5. QC each day of use

COAGULASE TEST

1. Reagent - EDTA rabbit plasma

2. Bound coagulase - clumping on slide (*plasma and colony*)

3. Free coagulase - gels in tube test (*0.5 ml plasma and colony; 35-37°C 4-12 hrs*)

4. Agglutination tests - detect coagulase and protein A

5. Postitive: *S. aureus*; negative: other Staph (human pathogens)

Staphylococcus (Catalase Positive)

ORGANISM	COAGULASE	INFECTIONS	INTOXICATIONS	NOTES
S. aureus	+	Carbuncles, furuncles, paronychia, wounds, and bacteremia	Scalded Skin Syndrome, Toxic Shock Syndrome, and Gastritis (*enterotoxin, 1-5 hours after eating*)	Most beta lactamase +; many MRSA
S. epidermidis	—	Endocarditis, prosthetic device infections		Most methicillin resistant; sensitive to novobiocin
S. saprophyticus	—	UTI in young women		Resistant to novobiocin
Coag Negative Staph: Opportunistic Infections in Immunocompromised Patients and Those with Prosthetic Devices				

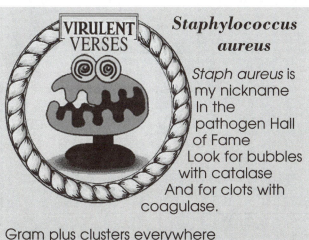

VIRULENT VERSES

Staphylococcus aureus

Staph aureus is my nickname
In the pathogen Hall of Fame
Look for bubbles with catalase
And for clots with coagulase.

Gram plus clusters everywhere
Skin and gut, nose and hair.

Protein A is my main trait
and Enterotoxin in what you ate.

Penicillin won't touch me
Methicillin, well . . . maybe?
Vancomycin killed in days of yore
But now that drug is not for sure.

Wash your hands, don't pick your nose.
Wear a lab coat over your clothes.

STREPTOCOCCUS

1. Spherical or oval; chains or pairs

2. Lancefield grouping based on C carbohydrate

3. *S. pyogenes* (*Group A*)
   a. Beta hemolytic
   b. Streptolysin S - stable in O_2; non-antigenic
   c. Streptolysin O - oxygen labile; antigenic
   d. Erythrogenic toxin - rash of scarlet fever
      - *Dick test - inject toxin to detect antibody*
      - *Schultz-Charlton test - antiserum injected into rash; blanches if scarlet fever*
   e. Highly sensitive to penicillin
   f. Infections
      - *Pharyngitis (Strep - most common cause)*
      - *Impetigo*
      - *Erysipelas*
      - *Wounds, burns*

- ❖ *Rheumatic fever (autoimmune sequelae to infection with Streptococcus group A)*
- ❖ *Lab diagnosis*
    - ☞ Sensitive to 0.04 units bacitracin disc
    - ☞ Typing

4. *S. agalactiae (Group B)*
   a. Narrow zone of beta hemolysis
   b. Neonatal sepsis and meningitis; UTI; vaginal infections
   c. Laboratory diagnosis
      - ❖ *Serotyping*
      - ❖ *CAMP reaction (with S. aureus)*
      - ❖ *Na hippurate positive*

5. *Streptococcus (Group D)*
   a. Enterococcus
      - ❖ *Growth in 40% bile and 6.5% salt*
      - ❖ *Alpha, beta or gamma hemolysis*
   b. Non-enterococcal - no growth in 6.5% salt
   c. Laboratory diagnosis - bile esculin positive

6. *S. pneumoniae*
   a. Alpha hemolytic crater-like colonies or mucoid, "water drop" colonies
   b. Lancet-shaped diplococci
   c. Check sensitivity to penicillin using OX *(oxacillin)* disc *(> 20 mm = sensitive)*
   d. Causes
      - ❖ *Primary lobar pneumonia (rusty sputum)*
      - ❖ *Meningitis*
      - ❖ *Bacteremia*
      - ❖ *Otitis media*
   e. Laboratory diagnosis
      - ❖ *Typical colony morphology*
      - ❖ *Quellung reaction*
      - ❖ *Sensitive to optochin*
      - ❖ *Bile soluble*

7. Other alpha *Streptococcus (viridans group)* - subacute bacterial endocarditis

(See Streptococci Chart on next page.)

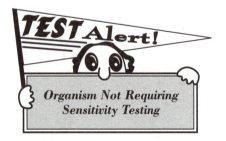

TEST Alert!

Organism Not Requiring Sensitivity Testing

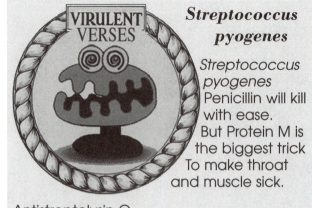

Streptococcus pyogenes

Streptococcus pyogenes
Penicillin will kill with ease.
But Protein M is the biggest trick
To make throat and muscle sick.

Antistreptolysin O
Will lay the heart and kidneys low.
Bacitracin is my sign
Zone of inhibition every time.

See what I do on B-A-P
Destroy the sheep R-B-C.

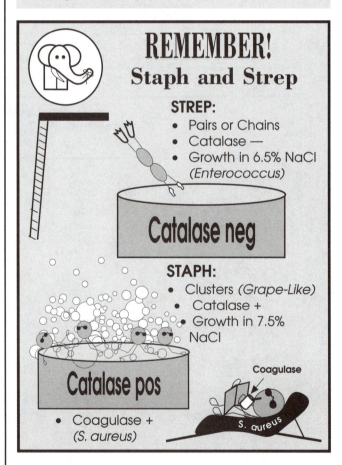

REMEMBER!
Staph and Strep

STREP:
- Pairs or Chains
- Catalase —
- Growth in 6.5% NaCl *(Enterococcus)*

Catalase neg

STAPH:
- Clusters *(Grape-Like)*
- Catalase +
- Growth in 7.5% NaCl

Coagulase

Catalase pos

- Coagulase + *(S. aureus)*

S. aureus

Streptococci (Catalase Negative)

	Hemolysis	Bacitracin	Na Hippurate	Optochin	Bile Solubility	Bile Esculin	6.5% NaCl	Infections
S. pyogenes (group A)	β	S	–	–	–	–	–	Pharyngitis, wounds, scarlet fever, impetigo, sequelae-rheumatic fever
S. agalactiae (group B)	β, δ	R	+	–	–	–	–	Neonatal septicemia and meningitis, UTI (*CAMP +*)
Enterococcus (group D)	α, β, δ	R	–	–	–	+	+	UTI, endocarditis (*treat with aminoglycoside+penicillin*)
Non-enterococcus (group D)	α, δ	R	–	–	–	+	–	Endocarditis (*rare*)
S. pneumoniae	α ("water drop"/ crater colonies)	R	–	+	+	–	–	Pneumonia, meningitis, bacteremia (*screen for penicillin sensitive with Ox; > 20 mm = sensitive*)
S. viridans	α, δ	R	–	–	–	–	–	Endocarditis (*rare*)

α hemolysis = greening around colony   β hemolysis = complete clearing around colony
δ hemolysis = no hemolysis   Shaded areas = Key Reactions

TEST Alert!

Growth Requirements of Streptococci

Key Characteristics of Pneumococcus

REMEMBER!
Victory Belongs to the Most Persevering.

Gram Negative Cocci

NEISSERIA AND MORAXELLA

1. Key characteristics
   a. Diplococci *(kidney bean shape)*
   b. Oxidase positive

2. *N. gonorrhoeae*
   a. Grows on chocolate and Thayer-Martin *(contains vancomycin, colistin, nystatin, hemoglobin and isovitalex)*
   b. Requires 5-10% CO_2; may take 48 hrs for growth
   c. Ferments glucose
   d. Gonorrhea
      ❖ *Sexually transmitted*
      ❖ *May be asymptomatic; may be mixed with Chlamydia*
      ❖ *Gram stain sensitive for males, but NOT for females*
      ❖ *May be confused with Moraxella or Acinetobacter*
      ❖ *Do NOT refrigerate prior to culture*
      ❖ *Penicillin or spectinomycin sensitivity; perform beta lactamase test to determine penicillin sensitivity*

Neisseria gonorrhoeae

Gonorrhea, the clap, GC I'm an old-fashioned STD.

I need CO_2 and chocolate agar And may not grow for 48 hours.

I ferment glucose, the only sugar for me, Do an oxidase and purple you'll see.

3. *N. meningitidis*
   a. Grows on blood agar, chocolate and Thayer-Martin
   b. 5-10% CO_2 enhances growth
   c. Ferments glucose and maltose
   d. Transmitted by respiratory droplets and requires close contact
   e. Meningitis
      ❖ *Seen mostly in children under 3*

      ❖ *Waterhouse - Friderichsen syndrome (scattered petechiae) = meningiococcemia*
      ❖ *Mainly caused by types A, B, C, Y and W*

4. *Moraxella (Branhamella) catarrhalis*
   a. Respiratory infections
   b. Grows well on chocolate and BAP but not on MacConkey's
   c. Colony hard and "moves over"; asaccharolytic
   d. Usually beta lactamase positive

5. Bacterial meningitis
   a. ↑ neutrophils
   b. ↓ glucose
   c. ↑ protein

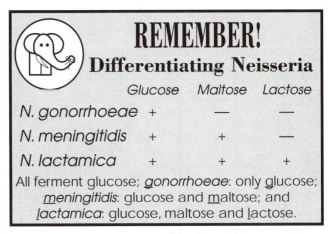

REMEMBER!
Differentiating Neisseria

	Glucose	Maltose	Lactose
N. gonorrhoeae	+	—	—
N. meningitidis	+	+	—
N. lactamica	+	+	+

All ferment glucose; *gonorrhoeae*: only glucose; *meningitidis*: glucose and maltose; and *lactamica*: glucose, maltose and lactose.

Gram Positive Rods

CORYNEBACTERIUM DIPHTHERIAE

1. Key Characteristics
   a. Small pleomorphic rods with clubbed ends
   b. Palisade or "chinese letter" arrangement
   c. Metachromatic granules *(stain red-purple with methylene blue)*
   d. Tinsdale agar - black colonies due to tellurite hydrolysis
   e. Elek test - determines toxin production by the isolate in vitro

2. Loeffler's - enhances development of metachromatic granules
   a. Palisade arrangement may be seen

3. Exotoxin production by only lysogenic organsims carrying a B phage

4. Produces pseudomembrane on tonsils, uvula or soft palate

5. Causes diphtheria

LISTERIA MONOCYTOGENES

1. Key Characteristics
   a. Small colonies with narrow zone of beta hemolysis
   b. Catalase positive
   c. Tumbling motility; "umbrella" motility in SIM at room temperature but NOT 37˚C
   d. Bile esculin positive

2. Causes neonatal meningitis and sepsis; sepsis in immunocompromised hosts

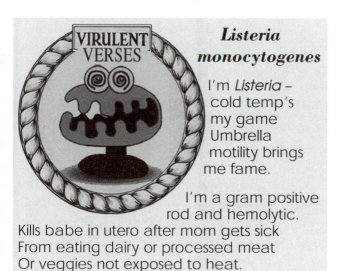

VIRULENT VERSES

Listeria monocytogenes

I'm *Listeria* – cold temp's my game
Umbrella motility brings me fame.

I'm a gram positive rod and hemolytic.
Kills babe in utero after mom gets sick
From eating dairy or processed meat
Or veggies not exposed to heat.

ERYSIPELOTHRIX

1. Key Characteristics
   a. Non-motile
   b. Catalase negative
   c. "Test tube brush" growth in gelatin; H₂S positive in TSI

2. Occupational infection for fishermen, butchers, veterinarians, rose growers

BACILLUS SP. (Sporeformers)

1. Key Characteristics
   a. Large, ground glass colonies
   b. Beta hemolysis (*EXCEPT B. anthracis*)
   c. Catalase positive
   d. Large gram positive to variable rods in chains with spores

2. *B. anthracis*
   a. Very long chains ("*bamboo shoots*")
   b. "Medusa head" colonies
   c. Non-motile, non-hemolytic
   d. Anthrax - cutaneous, pulmonary, or gastrointestinal

3. *B. cereus* - Food poisoning due to preformed toxin - "fried rice"

Gram Positive Rods

ORGANISM	CATALASE	ESCULIN	H₂S /TSI	ß HEMOLYSIS	NOTES
Corynebacterium	+	−	−	V	"Chinese Letter" Arrangement; Metachromatic Granules (*Loeffler's Slants*); Tellurite Hydrolysis (*Tinsdale Agar*); Elek Test Determines Toxin Production
Listeria	+	+	−	+	Tumbling Motility at 25C, but Not 37C; Cold Enrichment; Neonatal Meningitis and Sepsis; Sepsis in Immunocompromised Hosts
Erysipelothrix	−	−	+	−	"Test Tube Brush" Growth in Gelatin; Infection in Fishermen, Butchers, Veterinarians
Bacillus (*Spore Formers*)	+	V	−	V	"Ground Glass" Hemolytic Colonies; • *B. anthracis* (Non-Hemolytic, Non-Motile, "Medusa" Head Colonies); long, bamboo shoots • *B. cereus* (Food Poisoning, Enterotoxin) ß hemolytic

Gram Negative Rods

ENTEROBACTERIACEAE

1. General Characteristics
   a. Peritrichous flagella when motile
   b. Fement glucose
   c. Reduce NO_3 to NO_2
   d. Oxidase negative
   e. Antigens used in typing:
      - *Flagella = H Ag*
      - *Envelope = K Ag*
      - *Cell wall LPS (lipopolysaccharide) = O Ag*
      - *All possess LPS endotoxin; some produce exotoxins*

Escherichia coli

1. Key Characteristics
   a. Indole and lactose positive
   b. IMViC = ++ - -

2. Most common cause of UTI in females

3. Intestinal infections
   a. Enterotoxigenic E. coli (ETEC)
      - *LT toxin (heat labile)*
         - *ST toxin (heat stable) (EIEC)*
   b Enteroinvasive *E. coli*
      - *Penetrate epithelial cells in large intestine*
      - *May be lactose negative*
   c. Enterohemorrhagic *E. coli* (EHEC) - strain 0157:H7

- *Shigella-like toxin*
- *Food poisoning associated with undercooked meat (hamburger)*
- *Hemolytic uremic syndrome (HUS)*

4. K1 strains can cause neonatal meningitis

Shigella

1. Key Characteristics
   a. Lactose negative
   b. Non-motile
   c. Anaerogenic

2. Bacillary dysentery - penetrate epithelial cells in small intestine

3. *S. dysenteriae (Group A)* - most severe

4. *S. flexneri (Group B)*

5. *S. boydii (Group C)*

6. *S. sonnei (Group D)* - most common

7. < 200 organisms needed for disease

REMEMBER!
Shigella

S. dysenteriae = Group A *(1st alphabetically)*
S. flexneri = Group B *(not "B"oydii)*
S. boydii = Group C *("boyd ee ee" = "C")*
S. sonnei = Group D *(last alphabetically)*

Common Gram Negative Selective Media

AGAR	DIFFERENTIATING AGENT	SELECTIVE AGENT	H2S INDICATOR	LACTOSE POSITIVE	LACTOSE NEGATIVE
MAC MacConkey	Lactose	Crystal Violet, Bile Salts	None	Red	Transparent
EMB (Eosin, Methylene Blue)	Sucrose Lactose	Eosin Y Methylene Blue	None	Green Sheen, Purplish and Brownish Amber	Transparent
HE (Hektoen-Enteric)	Lactose Sucrose Salicin	Bile Salts	Sodium Thiosulfate	Salmon	Green to Blue (H2S+ = Black)
SS (Salmonella - Shigella)	Lactose	Brilliant Green Bile Salts	Sodium Thiosulfate	Red	Transparent (H2S+ = Black Center)
XLD (Xylose - Lysine Deoxycholate)	Lactose Sucrose Xylose	Bile Salts	Sodium Thiosulfate	Yellow	Transparent on Red Medium (H2S+ = Black)
Enrichment Broths = Selenite and G-N Broth					

Enterobacteriaceae: Primary Differentiating Tests

	TSI	Ornithine	VP	Urease	Lysine	Motility	H₂S	Deaminase	DNase
Citrobacter	K(A)/A, Gas	v	–	–	–	+	v	–	–
Enterobacter	A/A, Gas	+	+	–	v	+	–	–	–
Escherichia	A(K)/A, Gas	v	–	–	+	v	–	–	–
Klebsiella	A/A, Gas	–	+	v	+	–	–	–	–
Morganella	K/A, Gas	+	–	+	–	+	–	+	–
Proteus	K/A, Gas	v	–	+	–	+	+	+	v
Providencia	K/A, Gas	–	–	v	–	+	v	+	–
Salmonella	K/A, Gas	+	–	–	+	+	+	–	–
Serratia	K(A)/A	+	+	–	+	+	–	–	+
Shigella	K/A	v	–	–	–	–	–	–	–

v = variable

Shaded areas = Key reactions differentiating similar genera

TEST Alert!

I.D. Enterics from
Biochemical Tests

Klebsiellae

1. Opportunist; UTI, pneumonia; ampicillin-resistant

2. *Klebsiella*
   a. Non-motile
   b. Has capsule
   c. Urea positive
   d. Ornithine negative
   e. Can cause lobar pneumonia

3. *Enterobacter*
   a. Motile
   b. Ornithine positive

4. *Serratia*
   a. May produce red pigment
   b. DNase, gelatinase positive

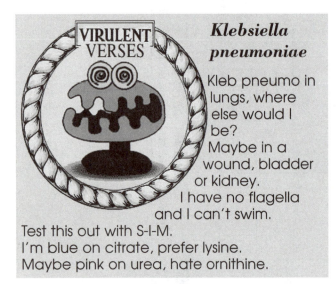

VIRULENT VERSES

Klebsiella pneumoniae

Kleb pneumo in lungs, where else would I be?
Maybe in a wound, bladder or kidney.
I have no flagella and I can't swim.
Test this out with S-I-M.
I'm blue on citrate, prefer lysine.
Maybe pink on urea, hate ornithine.

Salmonella

1. Large number needed for infection (> 100,000)

2. Biochemical reactions
   a. H$_2$S positive
   b. Lysine positive
   c. Indole negative
   d. Urea negative

3. *S. cholerasuis* - may cause septicemia

4. *S. typhi* - typhoid fever
   a. Blood positive early - 1st week
   b. Stool positive in 2nd to 3rd week

5. *S. arizona* - ONPG pos *(others neg)*

Citrobacter

1. Opportunist

2. Lysine negative

3. Similar to *Salmonella* biochemically

Proteus

1. Key Characteristics
   a. Urea positive
   b. Deaminase positive

2. *P. mirabilis*
   a. Most sensitive to penicillins
   b. Indole negative

3. *P. vulgaris*
   a. Indole positive
   b. H$_2$S positive

Yersinia

1. *Y. enterocolitica*
   a. Optimal growth = RT; cold enrichment
   b. Invasive and toxigenic

2. *Y. pseudotuberculosis* - Acute mesenteric lymphadenitis and "pseudotubercules"

3. *Y. pestis* - bubonic plague

BIOCHEMICAL TESTS

1. Oxidase test
   a. Reagent tetramethyl p-phenylenediamine dihydrochloride
   b. Positive = purple

2. Nitrate test
   a. Reagents - α-naphthylamine, sulfanilic acid
   b. Positive = pink *(use zinc powder to confirm)*

3. ONPG test
   a. Detects β-d-galactosidase
   b. Reagent - O-nitrophenyl-β-d-galactopyranoside
   c. Positive = yellow

4. TSI *(triple sugar iron agar)* slant
   a. 0.1% glucose, 1% sucrose, 1% lactose
   b. Yellow butt - glucose fermented
   c. Yellow slant - lactose or sucrose fermented
   d. Red slant - neither lactose nor sucrose fermented
   e. Black butt - H$_2$S produced

5. KIA - same as TSI but with only glucose, and lactose, no sucrose

6. Citrate test
   a. Media green
   b. Positive = blue

7. Decarboxylase tests
    a. Measures ability to decarboxylate amino acids
        ❖ *Lysine → Cadaverine*
        ❖ *Ornithine → Putrescine*
        ❖ *Arginine → Putrescine*
        ❖ *Indicator dye = bromcresol purple*
    b. Lysine iron agar (LIA)
        ❖ *Has H_2S indicator*
        ❖ *0.1% glucose and 1% lysine*
        ❖ *Positive = purple butt*
        ❖ *Slant of LIA turns red for lysine deaminase*
    c. Motility-indole-ornithine (*MIO*)
        ❖ *0.1% glucose and 1% ornithine*
        ❖ *Positive = purple butt*
        ❖ *Also tests for motility and indole (Kovac's)*

8. Indole test
    a. Indole split from tryptophan
    b. Reagent (*Kovac's*) - p-dimethyl-aminobenzaldehyde
    c. Positive = pink

9. Urease test
    a. Urea hydolyzed to ammonia and CO_2
    b. Phenol red indicator turns pink if positive

10. Voges-Proskauer (*VP*)
    a. Detects acetylmethylcarbinol (*acetoin*)
    b. Reagents = KOH and ∝-naphthol
    c. Positive = pink

11. Phenylalanine deaminase
    a. Reagent = ferric chloride
    b. Positive = green

Breakdown Products of Amino Acids

Indications of Positive Reactions in Biochemical Tests

REMEMBER! *Enterobacteriaceae* (TSI Reactions)

Picture yourself in a desert.
The <u>yellow</u> sun shining over the hot desert = A/A.
The moon shining over the desert = K/A.
The moon over the mountain = K/K.

A/A (Sun over Desert)	A/A, H_2S + (Sun over Desert)	K/A, H_2S + (Moon over Desert)	K/A (Moon over Desert)	K/K (Moon over Mountain)

S erratia	C itrobacter	C itrobacter	S higella	P seudomonas
E scherichia	A rizona	A rizona	Ci trobacter	Pseudo"moon"as
E nterobacter	P roteus	S almonella	P rovidencia	
K lebsiella		E dwardsiella	P roteus	
Seek shelter in the hot desert.	Wear a cap to protect yourself from the geyser (H_2S +).	A case of fire-crackers going off smells like sulphur. (H_2S +).	Y ersinia	
			Sk(*c*)ippy Coyote howls at the moon.	

TSI - Biochemical Reactions

A/A	A/A, H₂S+	K/A, H₂S+	K/A	K/K
Escherichia *(indole+)*	Proteus *(urea+, deam+)*	Salmonella *(mal-, ONPG-)*	Shigella *(citrate-, non-motile)*	Pseudomonas *(ox+, blue-green pigment, growth at 42° C, growth in cetrimide)*
Enterobacter *(ODC+, sugars)*	Arizona *(LDC+)*	Citrobacter *(LDC-)*	Providencia *(deam+)*	
Klebsiella *(ODC-)*	Citrobacter *(LDC-)*	Edwardsiella *(indole+, LDC+)*	Citrobacter *(citrate+)*	
Serratia *(sugars)*			Proteus *(urea+, deam+)*	
			Yersinia *(small colonies, urea+, deam-)*	

Enterobacteriaceae - A/A, Gas

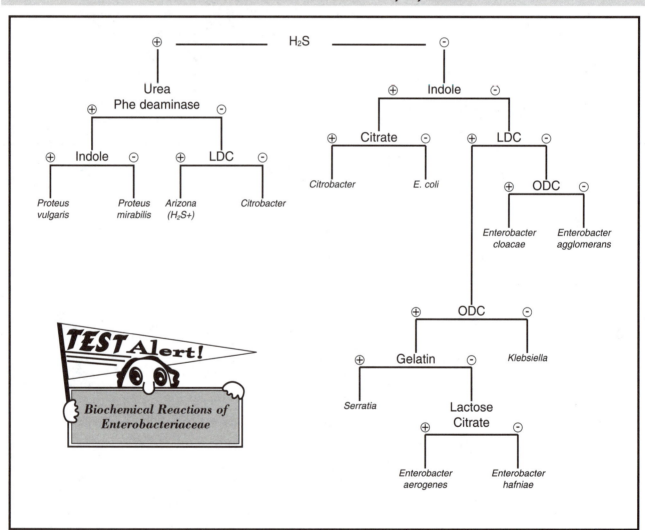

TEST Alert!

Biochemical Reactions of Enterobacteriaceae

Enterobacteriaceae - K/A, Gas, H₂S+

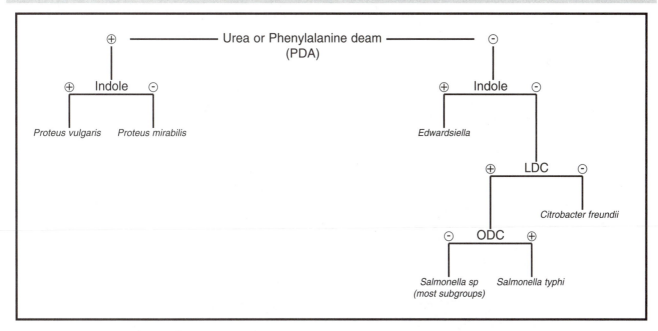

Tree diagram:

Urea or Phenylalanine deam (PDA)

⊕ (left branch):
- Indole
  - ⊕ *Proteus vulgaris*
  - ⊖ *Proteus mirabilis*

⊖ (right branch):
- Indole
  - ⊕ *Edwardsiella*
  - ⊖ LDC
    - ⊕ ODC
      - ⊖ *Salmonella sp (most subgroups)*
      - ⊕ *Salmonella typhi*
    - ⊖ *Citrobacter freundii*

GRAM NEGATIVE NON-FERMENTERS

1. Opportunists

2. Characteristics
   a. Glucose NOT fermented (*TSI=alk/alk*); lower acid production (*OF media = lower peptide content*)
   b. Oxidase positive (*some exceptions*)
   c. May not grow on MacConkey's agar

3. Pseudomonads
   a. Oxidase positive (*except Burkholderia cepacia and Stenotrophomonas*)
   b. Motile by polar flagella
   c. *Pseudomonas aeruginosa*
      ❖ *Most common*
      ❖ *Lactose negative on MAC*
      ❖ *May produce:*
         ☞ Pyocyanin (*blue-green*)
         ☞ Pyorubin (*rust*)
         ☞ Pyoverdin (*blue-white under UV*)
   ❖ *Mucoid strains found in cystic fibrosis patients*
   ❖ *Treated with aminoglycosides, 3rd generation cephalosporins and extended spectrum penicillins*
   ❖ *Infections - burns, pneumonia, swimmer's ear, eye infections, UTI*

Organism Associated with Cystic Fibrosis

Gram Negative Oxidase Positive Fermenters

VIBRIO

1. Characteristics
   a. Curved rods with polar flagella
   b. TCBS selective for *Vibrio*
   c. BAP - hemolytic colonies
   d. Lactose negative (*differs from enterics*)
   e. NO₃ positive (*NO₃ to NO₂*)

2. *V. cholera* (Serogroup 01)

   a. Gastroenteritis - rapid onset 3-10 hrs.; profuse diarrhea
   b. Need high concentration of organism unless hypochlorohydric
   c. Stools contain mucus flecks (*described as "rice water" stools*)
   d. Yellow on TCBS

3. *V. parahemolyticus*
   a. Green on TCBS
   b. Enteritis

4. *V. vulnificus*
   a. Green on TCBS
   b. Septicemia - can kill immunocompromised or diabetics

OTHER ORGANISMS

1. *Campylobacter jejuni*
   a. Small curved rods, "seagull appearance" (*light staining*)
   b. Microaerophilic, 2-4 days for growth
   c. Growth on CAMPY agar
   d. Found in raw poultry and contaminated water (*like Salmonella*)
   e. Erythromycin or tetracycline for treatment
   f. Biochemical reactions
      ❖ Catalase positive
      ❖ Oxidase positive
      ❖ Hippurate positive

2. *Helicobacter pylori*
   a. Associated with gastric and duodenal ulcers
   b. Produces large amounts of urease

3. *Aeromonas*
   a. Motile by polar flagella
   b. Most are indole positive
   c. Growth on MAC
   d. Cellulitis, wound infections and diarrhea

4. *Chromobacterium violaceum*
   a. Grows on MAC
   b. Motile by single polar and lateral flagellum
   c. Produces violet color (*seen best at room temperature*)

VIRULENT VERSES

Campylobacter jejuni

Just call me Jay June Eye.
I might be in water or chicken pot pie.
I like just a touch of O_2
More oxygen and I'll be through!

Campy-plates are best to grow
At 42 degrees or so
If I grow, gram stain me
And curved rods are what you'll see.

Zoonotic Diseases
(Acquired Directly or Indirectly from Animals)

ORGANISM	DESCRIPTION	DISEASE	NOTES
Brucella	Gram Neg Coccobacillus	Brucellosis	Blood Culture Pos in First Two Weeks (*Hold 21 days*)

	CO$_2$	H$_2$S	Thionine	Basic Fuschin
B. abortus (**cows**)	+	+	+/—	+
B. suis (**pigs**)	—	+/—	+	—
B. melentensis (**goats**)	—	—	+	+

REMEMBER! Brucella
Cows eat Basic Fuschin.
Pigs do NOT eat Basic Fuschin.
Goats eat Anything.

ORGANISM	DESCRIPTION	DISEASE	NOTES
Francisella tularensis **Francis the Rabbit Uses the Hood**	Gram Neg Coccobacillus Pinpoint Colonies *("mercury drop")* Cystine-Glucose Media H2S + with Lead Acetate	Tularemia "Rabbit Fever"	Infected by Tick Bite HIgh Risk to Lab Personnel *(Wear gloves and work under hood.)*
Yersinia pestis **Yersin the Safety Pin**	Gram Neg Bi-Polar Staining *(resembles safety pin)*	Plague	Transmitted by Fleas, Rats, Other Mammal Reservoirs
Pasturella multocida	Gram Neg Rod Bi-Polar Staining Oxidase and Indole Positive Ferments Glucose and Sucrose	Contracted from Cat and Dog Bites	"Mousy" Odor
Streptobacillus moniliformis	Long Filamentous Gram Neg Rods with Swellings (pleomorphic); "Puffball" or "String of Pearls" Colonies in Thioglycollate Broth	"Rat Bite Fever" Haverhill Fever	Acitic Fluid Sample Needed; SPS Inhibits

Fastidious Gram Negative Rods

GENERAL INFORMATION

1. Source - mouth flora

2. Pathogenic in immunocompromised hosts; causes:
   a. Peridontal and jaw abscesses (*Eikenella, Actinobacillus, Capnocytophaga*)
   b. Bacterial vaginosis (*Gardnerella*)
   c. Bacteremia (*Capnocytophaga, Cardiobacterium*)

4. Grow slowly and require 5 - 10% CO_2; NO growth on MAC

ORGANISM	OXIDASE	CATALASE	NITRATE	INDOLE	NOTES
Haemophilus aphrophilus	− / weak +	−	+	−	Colonies Similar to *Actinobacillus*; Endocarditis
Actinobacillus	+ / −	+	+	−	Peridontal & Jaw Abscesses; Center of colony has 4-6 Pointed Star
Cardiobacterium	+	−	−	+	Endocarditis
Eikenella	+	−	+	−	"Bleachy" Odor; Pits Agar; Peridontal & Jaw Abscesses
Kingella	+	−	+ / −	−	Endocarditis
Capnocytophaga	−	−	+ / −	−	Needs 5-10% CO_2 or Anaerobic Conditions; Gliding Motility; Fusiform Shape; Bacteremia

GARDNERELLA VAGINALIS

1. Bacterial vaginosis

2. "Clue cells" - high number of squamous epithelial cells colonized with gram variable rods

3. 10% KOH added to discharge causes "fishy" odor

4. Tiny colonies at 48 hrs on BAP and chocolate

5. Catalase and oxidase negative; hippurate and starch positive

BORDETELLA PERTUSSIS

1. Gram negative coccobacilli; causes "whooping cough"

2. Require special media
   a. Classic = Bordet-Gengou (*potato infusion with glycerol and 20% SRBc's*) and penicillin
   b. Regan and Lowe (*oxoid charcoal agar, 10% horse blood, cephalexin*); longer shelf life

3. Old method for collection - cough plate; better to collect NP swab and plate directly; fluorescent antibody technique more rapid

4. Colony
   a. Incubate 72-96 hrs, 35°C
   b. Pinpoint, "mercury droplet" colonies

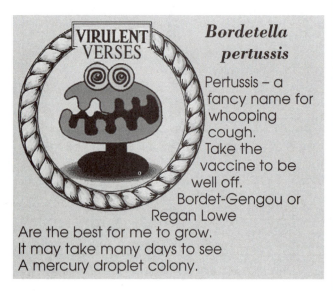

VIRULENT VERSES

Bordetella pertussis

Pertussis – a fancy name for whooping cough.
Take the vaccine to be well off.
Bordet-Gengou or Regan Lowe
Are the best for me to grow.
It may take many days to see
A mercury droplet colony.

HAEMOPHILUS

1. Small, non-motile gram negative rod

2. Requires growth factors

   a. X factor = hemin
   b. V factor = NAD
   c. Both factors found in blood, but need heat to break down red cells and release factors, so chocolate used
   d. Satellitism
      ❖ *S. aureus produces V factor and releases X factor by hemolyzing blood*
      ❖ *Haemophilus will grow in the hemolytic zone surrounding staph as satellite colonies on blood agar plate*
      ❖ *Need 5% horse or rabbit blood to see hemolysis*
   e. Infections
      ❖ *Meningitis - H. influenzae*
         ☞ 2-4 years
         ☞ Preceded by nasopharyngeal colonization and bacteremia
      ❖ *Epiglottitis*
         ☞ Ages up to 2 years; do NOT collect throat culture (*blood culture best*)
         ☞ May require intubation
      ❖ *Pneumonia <5 years, >60 years*
      ❖ *Conjunctivitis ("pink eye")*
         ☞ Very contagious
      ❖ *Chancroid - H. ducreyi*
         ☞ Painful genital ulcers or soft chancres
         ☞ Gram stain of drainage shows tiny gram negative coccobacilli with a "school of fish" arrangement

3. Characteristics
   a. Growth only on chocolate, NOT blood agar plate (*unless mixed with S. aureus*)
   b. Use X and V discs on Mueller-Hinton agar to detect growth requirements
   c. Susceptibility zone interpretations differ from conventional K- B zones (*use Haemophilus test media (HTM), supplemented Mueller-Hinton agar and incubate in 5-10% CO_2*)
   d. Perform beta lactamase to determine sensitivity to ampicillin; cefuroxime, ceftriaxone, cefotaxime (*meningitis*)

TEST Alert!

X and V Factors and Susceptibility Testing for Haemophilus

LEGIONELLA PNEUMOPHILA

1. Legionnaires disease - severe pneumonia; Pontiac fever = milder form

2. 75% illness due to L. pneumophila serogroups 1 and 6

3. Sources - potable water, faulty air conditioner vents, lakes and ponds

4. Identification
   a. Specimen - sputum, bronchial washing, pleural fluid, lung aspirate or biopsy
   b. Growth on BCYE (*buffered charcoal yeast extract*) with or without antibiotics but not on chocolate or blood
   c. Direct exam - Giemsa, Dieterle and Gram stain with basic fuschin counter stain

Isolation of Legionella

MYCOPLASMA AND UREAPLASMA

1. Smallest free-living microorganisms (*125-250 nm*)

2. Lack cell wall (*bound by single triple layered membrane*)

3. Does not stain with Gram's stain; can use Dienes stain

4. Center of colony grows into special media (*contains sterols*) giving appearance of inverted "fried egg"

5. *M. pneumoniae*
   a. Primary atypical pneumonia or "walking" pneumonia
   b. Causes positive cold agglutinin titer (*> 1:32*); false positive RPR
   c. Treat with erythromycin or tetracycline

6. *Ureaplasma urealyticum*
   a. Non-gonococcal, non-chlamydial urethritis, especially in males
   b. Produces urease
   c. Treat with tetracycline or spectinomycin

7. *M. hominis*
   a. May colonize GU tract; post partum fever
   b. Tetracycline; resistant to erythromycin (*all other Mycoplasma are sensitive*)

Other Fastidious Gram Negative Rods

ORGANISM	DESCRIPTION	DISEASE	NOTES
Gardnerella vaginalis	Tiny Colonies at 48 Hours on Blood and Chocolate; Catalase Neg; Oxidase Neg; Hippurate Pos; Starch Pos	Bacterial Vaginosis	"Clue" Cells; 10% KOH Added to Discharge = "Fishy" Odor
Bordetella pertussis	Gram Neg Coccobacillus; Pinpoint, "Mercury Droplet" Colonies	Pertussis (Whooping Cough)	Bordet-Gengou Media; NP Swab and Plate Directly
Haemophilus	Small, Non-Motile Gram Neg Rods • H. ducreyi - "School of Fish"	H. influenzae - Causes Influenza, Meningitis, and Epiglottitis H. ducreyi - Causes Genital Ulcers	Require X and V Factors
Legionella pneumophilia	Growth on BCYE	Legionnaires Disease	No Growth Routine Media
Mycoplasma/Ureaplasma	Colony Appears as Inverted Fried Egg	M. pneumoniae - Causes Primary Atypical Pneumonia (↑Cold Agglutinin Titer)	Dienes Stain NOT Gram Stain

156

Anaerobes

1. Clues to anaerobic infection
   a. Foul odor to specimen
   b. Location in close proximity to a mucosal surface
   c. Animal or human bite
   d. Gas in specimen
   e. Previous therapy with aminoglycosides
   f. Black discoloration of blood containing exudates
   g. Presence of "sulfur granules"
   h. Unique morphology on gram stain
   i. Failure to grow organisms seen on smear aerobically
   j. Growth in anaerobic zone or bubbles in fluid media

2. Specimen collection and transport
   a. Site containing a resident flora (*oral, GI, GU*) not appropriate for anaerobic culture
   b. Best to aspirate with syringe and needle and place in a transport vial or tube under reduced conditions (*swab samples not as good*)

3. Culture techniques
   a. "Classic" principle of anaerobic culture
      ❖ *Jar technique (Gas Pak jar)*
      ❖ *Catalyst - palladium pellets*
      ❖ *Envelope generates H_2 and CO_2 when water is added*
      ❖ *Methylene blue or resazurin - indicators (blue and pink, respectively when oxidized; clear when reduced)*
   b. Other methods
      ❖ *Anaerobic bags - clear bag with gas generating ampules; plates can be read without opening bag*
      ❖ *Roll tube technique*
        ☞ PRAS (*pre-reduced anaerobically sterilized media*) inoculated under constant flow of O_2 - free gas
      ❖ *Anaerobic chamber*
        ☞ Plates put in chamber through a pass box that is reduced
        ☞ Incubator in chamber; also contains palladium catalyst

Differentiating Gram Negative Anaerobes

	Vancomycin (5 µg)	Kanamycin (1 mg)	Colistin (10 µg)	Indole	Lipase	Esculin	Notes
Bacteroides fragilis	R	R	R	v	—	+	Catalase +, black colonies on BBE
Pigmented Gram Negative Rods	S	R	R	+	v	—	May fluoresce brick-red, may produce black pigment
Bacteroides ureolyticus	R	S	S	—	—	—	Pits agar; urease +
Fusobacterium nucleatum	R	S	S	+	—	—	Thin, fusiform rods, speckled colonies
Fusobacterium necrophorum	R	S	S	+	+	—	Rods variable in length and width
Fusobacterium mortiferum	R	S	S	v	—	+	Highly pleomorphic rods
R = resistant		S = sensitive			V = variable		

Differentiating Gram Positive Anaerobes

ORGANISM	CHARACTERISTICS
Clostridium difficile	Pseudomembranous Colitis; CCFA Agar *("Horse Stable" Odor)*; Spore Former
Clostridium perfringens	Double Zone of Hemolysis; Lecithinase +; Gas Gangrene; Spores Seldom Observed
Clostridium tetani	Terminal Spores *("Racquet-Shaped")*; Tetanus
Actinomyces israelii	"Molar Tooth" Colony; Branching Gram + Rods *("Lumpy Jaw")*; Sulphur Granules
P. anaerobius	Sensitive to SPS

TEST Alert!

Gram Negative Anaerobe Sensitive to Vancomycin

Organism Associated with Lumpy Jaw and "Sulfur" Granules

EXAMINATION OF PRIMARY PLATE

1. Pitting - *Bacteroides ureolyticus (could be Eikenella)*

2. Large colonies with double zone of hemolysis - *Clostridium perfringens*; set up egg yolk agar for Naegler test

3. Bread crumb or speckled colonies; gram negative slender fusiforms - *Fusobacterium nucleatum*

4. Molar tooth colonies of gram positive branching rods - *Actinomyces*

5. BBE - dark colonies, > 1 mm - *Bacteroides fragilis*

6. KVLB - look for pigment and examine under UV light
   a. Perform aerotolerance test on colonies by subculturing each colony type to an anaerobic blood plate and a chocolate plate

b. Incubate chocolate at 36°C under 5-10% CO_2 and the anaerobe BAP at 36°C in a gas jar or anaerobe chamber
c. If growth on both, the organism is facultative; if growth only on anaerobic blood, the organism is an anaerobe

SPIRILLACEAE

1. Rigid, helically curved rods with one or more turns; corkscrew motility by polar flagella; gram negative

2. *Spirillum minor* - "rat bite" fever
   a. Visualize by darkfield or stain with Giemsa
   b. 2-3 spirals and bipolar polytrichous tufts of flagella
   c. No growth on artificial media

Spirochetes

TREPONEMA PALLIDUM

1. Stain with silver impregnation
2. Darkfield - slow motility and flexion
3. No growth on artificial media
4. Sensitive to penicillin, tetracycline and erythromycin
5. Detected through serological tests (see Serology/Immunology for details)
6. Syphilis
   a. Primary lesion
      ❖ *2-10 weeks after infection, chancre appears*
      ❖ *Heals without treatment in 3-8 weeks; may perform darkfield or direct FA on fluid*
   b. Secondary lesion
      ❖ *Dissemination - skin rash erosions on genitalia*
   c. Latent stage
      ❖ *2-20 yrs later*
      ❖ *Affects skin, bone, joints, CNS*

LEPTOSPIRA

1. Spirals with hooked ends
2. Animal pathogen passed to humans via water contaminated with animal urine *(ex. sewer workers, farmers, vets)*
3. Positive darkfield or direct FA

158

4. Can grow in Fletcher's semi-solid media
   a. Incubate 6 wks at 30°C in the dark
   b. Perform darkfield from several centimeters into media

5. Weil's disease - severe form; CSF positive

Media for Culturing Leptospira

BORRELIA

1. *B. recurrentis*
   a. "Relapsing fever" from ticks or lice
   b. Looser coils; best seen with Giemsa or Wright's stain of blood smear
   c. Mutates during disease; relapse due to inability to recognize new antigen
   d. May exhibit cross reaction with Proteus OX K on febrile agglutinations with titer up to 1:80

2. *B. burgdorferi*
   a. Lyme disease
   b. Transmitted by *Ixodes* ticks *(deer or mouse tick)*
   c. Originally in northeastern US *(distribution spreading)*
   d. Chronic migratory erythematous rash, fever, muscle and joint pain; later meningioencephalitis, myocarditis and arthritis
   e. Culture in Kelly medium at 33°C - darkfield weekly for 1 month
   f. Serological diagnosis faster

Cause, Vector and Culture Media of Lyme Disease

Chlamydia

1. Obligate intracellular parasites

2. Gram negative cell wall, with no peptidoglycan; possess ribosomes for protein synthesis

3. Dependent on host for ATP

4. Laboratory diagnosis
   a. Giemsa stain *(purple inclusion bodies)* or iodine stain *(glycogen synthesized in large amounts by C. trachomatis and surrounds elementary body; stains brown with iodine; not produced with other species)*
   b. Direct FA, tissue culture or complement fixation

5. Growth in yolk sac of chick embryo or tissue culture *(McCoy cell)*

6. *C. psittaci*
   a. Psittacosis *(parrot fever)* - occupational hazard for pet bird handlers and poultry workers
   b. Acute lower respiratory infection

7. *C. trachomatis*
   a. Genital tract infections (sexually transmitted disease)
      ❖ *Non-gonococcal urethritis and epididymitis in males*
      ❖ *Cervicitis and salpingitis (PID) in females*
      ❖ *Can be passed to newborn as conjunctivitis or pneumonia*
   b. Eye infections
      ❖ *Trachoma - leading cause of blindness in underdevelped countries*
      ❖ *Inclusion conjunctivitis*
         ☞ Adults and newborns
         ☞ Can colonize nasopharynx (leading to pneumonia) and genital tract
         ☞ Appears 2-25 days after birth as a purulent eye discharge

Detection of Chlymadia

Rickettsiae

1. Small gram negative coccobacilli

2. Obligate intracellular parasites

3. Spread by arthropod vector

4. Seen better with Giemsa

5. Arthropod bite - causes fever, headache, rash (*Q fever - no rash and organism survives outside host*)

6. Weil-Felix test
   a. *Proteus* OX-19, OX-2 and OX-K used as antigens to detect Rickettsial antibody
   b. 4-fold rise in titer or 1:160 titer

Most Common Rickettsiae

ORGANISM	VECTOR	PROTEUS			NOTES
		OX 19	OX 2	OX K	
R. akari (Rickettsial Pox)	House Mites	—	—	—	
Coxiella burnetti (Q Fever)	Inhaled	—	—	—	Confirm with CF Test
R. prowazekii (Typhus Fever)	Louse	+	Variable	—	
R. rickettsiae (Rocky Mt. Spotted Fever)	Tick	+	+	—	Characteristic Rash on Palms of Hand and Soles of Feet
R. typhi (Murine Typhus)	Rat Flea	+	+	—	

Fungus-Like Bacteria

ORGANISM	ATMOSPHERE	CASEIN	TYROSINE	XANTHINE	ACID FAST
Actinomyces israelii	Anaerobic	N.A.	N.A.	N.A.	N.A.
Nocardia asteroides	Aerobic	—	—	—	Partially
Nocardia brasiliensis	Aerobic	+	+	—	Partially

Acid Fast Bacilli

Basic Test to Identify Nocardia

Mycobacteria

1. Morphology - slim gram variable rods; don't stain well due to high lipid content in wall

2. Acid fast stain
   a. Ziehl-Neilsen - "hot" stain
   b. Kinyoun - "cold" stain

3. Auramine-Rhodamine - fluorescent stain

4. All stains based on presence of mycolic acid (*lipid-waxy*) in cell wall

5. Any number seen on a smear is significant

6. Growth requirements
   a. Lowenstein-Jensen; 60% egg in nutrient base; malachite green; solidified into slants after inspissation (*heat to 85°C until protein coagulates*)
   b. Tween 80 (*oleic acid*) - aids in dispersing colonies in liquid media
   c. ↑CO_2 (*especially in first 24 hrs*)
   d. Most grow at 36°C; some require 30°C
   e. Takes 3-6 weeks for growth
   f. Automated culture systems give rapid indication of growth

7. Identification by nucleic acid probe

SPECIMEN COLLECTION

1. Sputum *(first morning; on 3 consecutive mornings)*, bronchial washing, gastrics, urines and tissue

2. Collect aseptically and place in sterile, tightly capped container

3. May be refrigerated overnight *(neutralize gastrics and urines if holding overnight)*

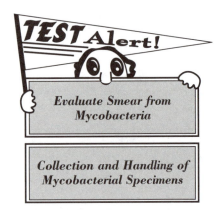

Evaluate Smear from Mycobacteria

Collection and Handling of Mycobacterial Specimens

SPECIMEN DECONTAMINATION

1. N-acetyl-L-cysteine *(NALC)* - mucolytic; NaOH decontaminates; time dependent

2. Stain and report slides within 24 hrs of processing

3. Centrifuge decontaminated specimen for 20 min at 3000 rpm prior to making smears and inoculating media *(use sediment)*

Processing Specimen for Mycobacteria

Associate Mycobacteria with Pigment Grouping

I.D. and Rapid Reporting of M. tuberculosis

(See Mycobacteria chart on following page.)

REMEMBER!
Mycobacterium tuberculosis

- May infect 1/3 of world's population
- Is spread by respiratory droplets
- Is resistant to drying
- Is resistant to many disinfectants
- Is best known for respiratory disease
- Has "cauliflower" colonies on LJ
- Requires long-term treatment
- Has MDR variants
- Can be grown in automated systems
- Can be identified by nucleic acid probes
- Use skin test for screening in U.S.

Mycobacterium avium complex

- Are environmental organisms
- May cause pulmonary disease
- May cause disseminated disease
- May infect immunocompromised patients
- Non-pigmented colonies on LJ
- Can be identified by nucleic acid probes

Mycobacterium leprae

- Causes leprosy (Hansen disease)
- Infects skin, mucous membranes, nerves
- Causes a progressive disease that is treatable
- Grows best in armadillo footpads

Differentiating Mycobacteria

	Growth < 7 days	Niacin	Nitrate Reduction	Tween 80 Hydrolysis	Tellurite (3 days)	Growth on MacConkey	Notes
M. tuberculosis	−	+	+	> 5 days	−	−	Rough & buff, serpentine cording on culture
M. bovis	−	−	−	> 5 days	−	−	Rough & buff colony, serpentine cording; susceptible to TCH
M. kansasii	−	−	+	< 5 days	−	−	Photochromogen
M. marinum	−	v	−	< 5 days	−	−	Photochromogen (30° C optimum temperature)
M. scrofulaceum	−	−	−		−	−	Scotochromogen
M. gordonae	−	−	−	5-10 days	−	−	Scotochromogen
M. avium	−	−	−		+	−	Non-photochromogen
M. ulcerans	−	−	−		−	−	Non-photochromogen (32° C optimum temperature)
M. fortuitum	+	−	+		v	+	Rapid grower
M. chelonei	+	v	−		v	+	Rapid grower

v = variable
Shaded areas = Key reactions differentiating similar genera

Photochromogen - produces pigment in light
Scotochromogen - produces pigment in dark
Non-photochromogen - produces no pigment
Rapid grower - growth in < 7 days

162

Specimen Source and Potential Pathogens

BODY SITES/SOURCE	"NORMAL" FLORA	EXPECTED PATHOGEN	NOTES
Throat, oropharynx	Alpha *Strep* *Staph* sp. *Neisseria* sp. Gram + Rods Anaerobes	*Strep* Group A	Pus pockets
		Corynebacterium diphtheriae	Pseudomembranes when toxin produced
		Bordetella pertussis	Whooping cough; confirm with DFA
		Haemophilus influenzae	Epiglottitis in children *(No culture.)*
Eye	Same as above except in lesser numbers	*H. influenzae*	"Pink eye"
		Neisseria gonorrhoea	Newborns
Ear	"	*H. influenzae*	
		Streptococcus pneumoniae	
Lower Respiratory Tract *(sputum)*	None	*H. influenzae*	Early morning sputum specimen best; <10 - 15 squamous epithelial cells per LPF
		S. aureus	"
		Streptococcus pneumoniae	"
		Klebsiella pneumoniae	"
		Mycoplasma pneumoniae	"
		Mycobacterium tuberculosis	"
		Legionella	"
		Fungi	
Transtrachial Aspirate	None	Anaerobes	
Bronchial Washing	Resident oral flora		No anaerobic set-up; AFB and mycology set-up
Gastric Specimens		*Helicobacter pylori*	Rapid urease test
Colon	Profuse flora	*Shigella*	Selective and differential media on stools (MAC, EMB, HE, XLD, selenite, or GN broth); subculture to selective media after 6 - 12 hours
		Salmonella	"
		Campylobacter jejuni	Microaerophilic bag at 42°C
		Yersinia enterocolitica	MAC after 48 hours at room temperature
		Vibrio cholerae	TCBS
		Toxigenic E. coli	Other tests better than culture
		Clostridium difficile	EIA best

BODY SITES/SOURCE	"NORMAL" FLORA	EXPECTED PATHOGEN	NOTES
Urinary Tract	Normally sterile *(May be contaminated with fecal flora)*	*E. coli*	Midstream catch with proper skin preparation; >100,000 organisms per ml for infection *(work up smaller number if pure culture and white cells present)*
		Other gram neg rods	"
		E. faecalis	"
		Staphylococcus sp.	"
Genital Tract		Neisseria gonorrhoea	Male - purulent discharge, do gram stain; Female - gram stain not sensitive or specific enough, do culture for GC *(Thayer-Martin: selective media for GC)*, nucleic acid probes
		Chlamydia trachomatis	Nucleic acid probe
		Group B *Strep*	Significant in pregnant women
		Herpes simplex	HSV-2
		Trichomonas vaginalis	Parasite, wet mount
		Treponema pallidum	Darkfield
		Gardnerella vaginalis	Implicated in vaginosis; look for "clue cells"
CSF	Normally sterile	*H. influenzae*	Children under 5
		Neisseria meningitidis	Children through young adults
		E. coli	Neonates
		Group B *Strep*	Neonates
		Cryptococcus	Immunocompromised patients
		Listeria	Immunocompromised patients
Deep Wounds/Abcesses		Anaerobes and Aerobes; depends on site	Bypass normal flora in collection; needle aspirate better than swab
Superficial Wounds *(pustules, dermatitis, rashes)*		*S. aureus*	
		Group A *Strep*	
		Pseudomonas aeruginosa Enterobacteriacea	
Blood	Normally sterile		In immunocompromised and prosthetic heart device patients, any organism isolated from more than 1 bottle is considered pathogenic

Gram Positve Cocci Found in Sputum

Organism Associated with Peptic Ulcers

Colony Count Indicating UTI

Specimen Collection and Handling of NP Swab

Virology

VIRAL STRUCTURE

1. RNA or DNA - not both

2. Does NOT contain structural elements required for protein synthesis

3. Replicates in host cells

SPECIMEN COLLECTION AND HANDLING

1. Pre- and post-convalescent sera - ship on dry ice

2. Specimen for viral culture - similar to transport media for bacteria but contains nutrients (*fetal calf serum or albumin*) and antibiotics

LABORATORY METHODS

1. EIA - presence of viral antibody or antigen (*ex. HbsAg and anti-HBsAb*)

2. Viral culture

3. Electron microscopy

4. Molecular techniques (*see below*)

SPECIAL PROCEDURES

1. DNA probes
   a. Molecular cloning of a specific DNA sequence

   b. If viral unknown "matches" clone, the viral identity is confirmed

2. Polymerase chain reaction (*PCR*)
   a. Method in which nucleic acid sequences can be amplified in vitro
   b. Carried out in cycles, each cycle doubling the amount of desired nucleic acid product

TEST Alert!

Collection and Handling of Viral Specimens

DNA Probe Technology

PCR Technology

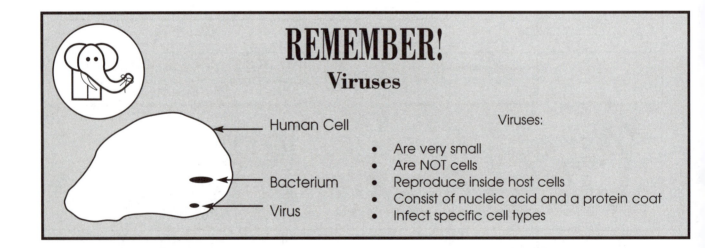

REMEMBER!
Viruses

Human Cell

Bacterium

Virus

Viruses:

- Are very small
- Are NOT cells
- Reproduce inside host cells
- Consist of nucleic acid and a protein coat
- Infect specific cell types

RNA Viruses

VIRUS	DISEASE	NOTES
Flavivirus	Yellow Fever; Dengue; St. Louis Encephalitis	Mosquito - Vector
Hantavirus	Pulmonary Syndrome; Hemorrhagic Fever	Rodent-Borne
Hepatitis A Virus (HAV)	Hepatitis A	Associated with Shellfish; One of Most Stable Viruses Infecting Humans
Hepatitis C Virus (HCV)	Hepatitis C	Formerly Non-A, Non-B Hepatitis
Influenzavirus	Influenza	
Morbillivirus	Measles	More Serious in Adults than Children
Mumps Virus	Mumps	
Parainfluenza Virus	Parainfluenza	
Poliovirus	Poliomyelitis; Aseptic Meningitis	Occurs Naturally Only in Humans
Respiratory Syncytial Virus (RSV)	Serious Respiratory Infection in Young Children	Giant Multinucleated Cells Due to Fusion of Infected Cells
Rhabdovirus	Rabies	Negri Bodies in Brain Tissue of Infected Animals; Rod or Bullet-Shaped; Wildlife - Reservoir
Rhinovirus	"Common" Cold	
Rotavirus	Acute Infectious Infantile Diarrhea	Can Cause Death in Infants
Rubivirus	Rubella	Vaccine Available; Contraindicated in Pregnancy; Spread by Respiratory Secretions; Serious Congenital Abnormalities
RETROVIRUS		
Human Immunodeficiency Virus (HIV I/II)	AIDS	EIA Techniques; Confirmed by Western Blot
Human T-Cell Leukemia Virus (HTLV I)	T-Cell Leukemia; Tropical Spastic Paraparesis (TSP)	EIA Techniques; Confirmed by Western Blot
Human T-Cell Leukemia Virus (HTLV II)	Hairy-Cell Leukemia	EIA Techniques; Confirmed by Western Blot

RNA Viruses and Associated Diseases

RSV-Associated Disease and I.D.

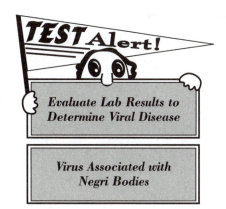

Evaluate Lab Results to Determine Viral Disease

Virus Associated with Negri Bodies

DNA Viruses

VIRUS	DISEASE	NOTES
Adenovirus	Respiratory Infections	
Cytomegalovirus *(CMV)*	Mental Retardation *(most common viral cause)*; Other Problems in Immunosuppressed Depending on Site of Infection	Most Common Congenital Infection
Epstein-Barr Virus *(EBV)*	Infection Mononucleosis; Chronic Fatigue Syndrome; Associated with Burkett's Lymphoma	Heterophile Antibody
Hepatitis B Virus *(HBV)*	Hepatitis B	ELISA Techniques; Vaccine Available
Herpesvirus *H. simplex* I *H. simplex* II	Oral Infections Genital Infections *(STD)*	
Human papillomavirus *(HPV)*	Genital Warts; Cutaneous Warts	Some Serotypes Associated with Cervical Cancer
Poxvirus	Smallpox	Supposedly Eradicated; Occasional Outbreaks in Labs Where Virus Cultures Are Stored
Varicella-Zoster	Chicken Pox *(children)*; Shingles *(adults)*	Diagnosed by Clinical Picture

DNA Viruses and Associated Diseases

Viral Cause of Cervical Carcinoma

REMEMBER!

The most important thing in science is not so much to obtain new facts as to discover new ways of thinking about them.

— Sir William Bragg

MICROBIOLOGY SAMPLE QUESTIONS

1. A "rice water stool" is characteristic of patients infected with
   - A. *Clostridium botulinum*
   - B. *Salmonella typhi*
   - C. *Shigella dysenteriae*
   - D. *Vibrio cholerae*

2. A sample of material from bluish purulent head lesions is submitted for analysis. A gram negative, motile, non-sporeforming oxidase positive rod was isolated. This organism is most likely
   - A. *Proteus mirabilis*
   - B. *Proteus vulgaris*
   - C. *Pseudomonas aeruginosa*
   - D. *Stenotrophomonas maltophilia*

3. A gram stained smear from a genital soft chancre demonstrated small gram negative rods arranged in tangled chains. You would suspect the cause of the chancroid to be
   - A. *Hemophilus ducreyi*
   - B. *Herpes simplex II*
   - C. *Neisseria gonorrhoeae*
   - D. *Treponema pallidum*

4. Organisms of this genus are gram negative, motile rods. A few are chromogenic and produce a red non-water soluble pigment. Some have been implicated in septicemia, pulmonary and urinary tract infections. One member of this genus is
   - A. *Pseudomonas aeruginosa*
   - B. *Sarcina lutea*
   - C. *Serratia marcescens*
   - D. *Staphylococcus aureus*

5. Which characteristic is most useful in differentiating *Citrobacter* and *Salmonella*?
   - A. H_2S production
   - B. Indole production
   - C. Lysine decarboxylase
   - D. Urease production

6. A gram stain from a sputum specimen demonstrates many gram positive cocci in chains and pairs. Numerous small alpha streptococci are observed on the primary blood agar plate. To determine if these organisms are *Streptococcus pneumoniae* which of the following tests should be performed?
   - A. Bacitracin susceptibility
   - B. Catalase
   - C. Esculin hydrolysis
   - D. Optochin susceptibility

7. Loeffler's medium is used as a primary isolation medium for
   - A. *Bordetella pertussis*
   - B. *Corynebacterium diphtheriae*
   - C. *Mycobacterium tuberculosis*
   - D. *Streptococcus pyogenes*

8. Autoclave sterilization of lab media requires which of the following pressure, temperature and time parameters?
   - A. 15 lbs pressure, 115°C for 10 min
   - B. 15 lbs pressure, 121°C for 15 min
   - C. 20 lbs pressure, 100°C for 15 min
   - D. 20 lbs pressure, 110°C for 10 min

9. Clinical diagnosis of rabies in infected animals is dependent upon brain tissue observation of
   - A. Metachromatic granules
   - B. Multinucleated cells
   - C. Negri bodies
   - D. Viral capsids

10. Which of the following results is typical of *Campylobacter jejuni*?
    - A. Catalase negative
    - B. Non-motile
    - C. Optimal growth at 42°C
    - D. Oxidase negative

11. The use of penicillin/aminoglycoside to treat endocarditis due to *Streptococci* Group D represents a
    - A. Broad spectrum susceptibility
    - B. Multi-drug resistance
    - C. "Shotgun" approach
    - D. Synergistic relationship

12. Characteristics indicating an appropriate sputum collection would be microscopic findings of
    - A. > 25 epithelial cells, > 25 white cells
    - B. > 25 epithelial cells, < 25 white cells
    - C. 10-25 epithelial cells, 10-25 white cells
    - D. < 10 epithelial cells, 10-25 white cells

13. A clean catch urine specimen from a female with a suspected UTI showed gram positive cocci that were catalase positive, coagulase negative and Staph latex negative. On the Microscan panel, growth in the novobiocin well was noted. The most likely organism is
    - A. *Staphylococcus aureus*
    - B. *Staphylococcus epidermidis*
    - C. *Staphylococcus saprophyticus*
    - D. *Enterococcus fecalis*

14. The treatment of choice for methicillin resistant *Staphylococcus* is
  A. Cephalothin
  B. Nafcillin
  C. Oxacillin
  D. Vancomycin

15. The most likely cause of subacute bacterial endocarditis is
  A. *Staphylococcus aureus*
  B. *Staphylococcus epidermidis*
  C. *Streptococcus Group A*
  D. *Streptococcus viridans*

16. The organism known for its "stormy fermentation" and double zone of beta hemolysis under anaerobic conditions causes
  A. Botulism
  B. Gas gangrene
  C. Pseudomembraneous colitis
  D. Tetanus

17. The bacteremic Waterhouse-Friderichsen syndrome is associated with
  A. *Corynebacterium jeikeium*
  B. *Listeria monocytogenes*
  C. *Mycoplasma pneumoniae*
  D. *Neisseria meningitidis*

18. The specimen of choice in a case of suspected epiglottitis is collected from the
  A. Blood
  B. Spinal fluid
  C. Sputum
  D. Throat

19. A specimen from a female complaining of vaginitis emitted a "fishy" odor when mixed with 10% KOH. A wet prep showed some white cells and epithelial cells covered with small gram variable rods. The most likely organism is
  A. *Chlamydia trachomatis*
  B. *Gardnerella vaginalis*
  C. *Neisseria gonorrhoea*
  D. *Treponema pallidum*

20. A photochromogenic mycobacterium isolated at 30°C is most likely
  A. *M. gordonae*
  B. *M. marinum*
  C. *M. ulcerans*
  D. *M. xenopi*

21. A scotochromogenic mycobacterium showing hydrolysis of Tween 80 in 7 days is probably
  A. *M. avium*
  B. *M. fortuitum*
  C. *M. gordonae*
  D. *M. marinum*

22. A gram negative rod, isolated from the urine of a female with recurrent UTI, was oxidase negative, urease positive showing A/A with H2S on TSI and red/black on LIA is most likely
  A. *Escherichia coli*
  B. *Klebsiella pneumoniae*
  C. *Proteus mirabilis*
  D. *Pseudomonas aeruginosa*

23. An organism recovered from a diarrheal stool was K/A with no gas or H2S on TSI, lysine negative, oxidase negative, urease negative and citrate negative. The most likely organism is
  A. *Aeromonas hydrophila*
  B. *Escherichia coli*
  C. *Proteus vulgaris*
  D. *Shigella sonnei*

24. A cause of acute infectious infantile diarrhea is
  A. Hantavirus
  B. HIV
  C. Rhabdovirus
  D. Rotovirus

25. Specimens for viral culture should be transported in
  A. Anaerobic containers
  B. Bovine albumin (22%)
  C. Nutrient medium with antibiotics
  D. Sheep blood (5-10%)

ANSWERS AND RATIONALE

1. D

    Though options B and C may cause diarrhea, only *V. cholera* causes the characteristic "rice water stool". Option A may cause infant botulism which is characterized by 2-3 days of constipation followed by flaccid paralysis.

2. C

    Pseudomonas aeruginosa is the only oxidase positive organism listed.

3. A

    Option B is a virus not visible on a gram stain. Option C are gram negative diplococci. Option D is a spirochete that causes a hard chancre.

4. C

    The only organism listed which produces a red pigment is *Serratia*. Options B and D are cocci.

5. C

    The classic biochemical reaction which separates these two genera is lysine. The other biochemical reactions can be variable.

6. D

    Optochin susceptibility separates *Streptococcus pneumoniae* from the other *Streptococci*. Option A is a characteristic of *Streptococcus pyogenes*. Option B separates *Staphylococcus (catalase positive)* from *Streptococcus (catalase negative)*. Group D *Streptococcus* are positive with option C *(esculin hydrolysis)*.

7. B

    Microscopic morphology is best demonstrated on Loeffler's medium though cystine-tellurite agar is also used *(C. diphtheriae colonies demonstrate a grey-to-black color on this media)*. Option A is seen on Bordet-Gengou media. Option C is associated with Lowenstein Jensen media. Option D grows well on blood agar.

8. B

    Autoclave sterilization requires 15 psi, at 121˚C for 15 min.

9. C

    Demonstration of Negri bodies *(cytoplasmic inclusion bodies)* in brain tissue is the hallmark of rabies diagnosis. Option A is not seen in viruses. Option B is associated with measles virus. Option D is seen in electron micrographs of many viruses and bacteria.

10. C

    Campylobacter jejuni is oxidase positive, motile, catalase positive and grows optimally at 42 C.

11. D

    These drugs in combination enhance bactericidal activity.

12. D

    Greater than 10 epithelial cells indicates the specimen is heavily contaminated with oral flora.

13. C

    S. saprophyticus is resistant to novobiocin and can cause urinary tract infections.

14. D

    Vancomycin is the drug of choice for methicillin resistant *Staphylococci*.

15. D

    Streptococcus viridans is most commonly associated with subacute bacterial endocarditis.

16. B

    Clostridium perfringens is the cause of gas gangrene and is noted for its stormy fermentation and double zone of beta hemolysis. Option A is caused by *C. botulinum* and is diagnosed by demonstration of botulism toxin. Option C is caused by *C. difficile* which grows on CCFA agar. Option D is caused by *C. tetani* and is identified by its "racquet' or "drumstick" shaped terminal endospores.

17. D

    Overwhelming DIC *(due to large amounts of endotoxin)* with shock and destruction of adrenal glands is caused by *N. meningitidis*.

18. A

Options B and C are not related to the diagnosis. Collecting a throat culture *(option D)* could cause the airway to close.

19. B

Gardnerella is associated with the haracteristic "fishy" odor when vaginal discharge is mixed with KOH. Option A is diagnosed by EIA, DNA probes or FA. Option C are gram negative cocci. Option D is a spirochete seen with darkfield microscopy.

20. B

Option A is a scotochromagen. Option C grows at 30°C but is a non-photochromagen. Option D is a scotochromagen and grows best at 37°C.

21. C

Option A is a non-photochromogen and does not show hydrolysis of Tween 30. Option B is a rapid grower and does not show hydrolysis of Tween 80. Option D is a photochromogen which hydrolyzes Tween 80 in less than 5 days.

22. C

Options A and B are H_2S negative and deaminase negative. Option D is K/K on TSI and oxidase positive

23. D

Option A is oxidase positive. Option B is A/A on TSI and indole positive. Option C is H_2S positive and urease positive

24. D

Option A causes hemmorrhagic fever. Option B causes AIDS. Option C causes rabies.

25. C

Media for transporting specimens for viral culture are similar to bacterial transport media but must contain additional nutrients such as albumin or fetal calf serum and antibiotics *(to prevent bacterial growth)*.

MYCOLOGY

by Mary Lux*

Characteristics of Fungi

1. Reproduction
   a. Sexual - fusion of 2 haploid nuclei; spores - teleomorph
   b. Asexual - mitotic division of haploid nucleus and budding production of conidia - anamorph

2. Growth and morphology
   a. Diverse; from bacteria-like yeast to mushrooms
   b. Hyphae
      ❖ *Tube-like structures with thick parallel walls*
         ☞ Septate - has cross walls
         ☞ Aseptate *(coenocytic)* - has rare cross walls
      ❖ *Several types: racquet, favic chandeliers, pectinate, nodular, spiral*
      ❖ *Mycelium is a matt of hyphae*
         ☞ Vegetative growth into medium
         ☞ Aerial growth above the medium
   c. Pseudohyphae are elongated budding yeast cells *(blastoconidia)* with constrictions between cells *(buds)*
   d. Fruiting bodies
      ❖ *Sexual (perfect, teleomorphic)*
         ☞ True sporulation
         ☞ Fusion of haploid nuclei
         ☞ Homosexual - zygospore
         ☞ Heterosexual - oospore
         ☞ Spore sacs *(asci)*
            ★ *Cleistothecium (round, closed)*
            ★ *Perithecium (flask-shaped, open)*
            ★ *Apothecium (saucer-shaped, open)*
      ❖ *Asexual (imperfect, anamorphic)*
         ☞ From specialized supportive hyphae
            ★ *Chlamydoconidia - round, thick-walled structures located terminal, intercalary, sessile*
            ★ *Arthroconidia - hyphal fragmentation at cross walls*
         ☞ Aerial structures
            ★ *Conidiophore, vesicle, phialiade, conidium*
            ★ *Sporangiophore, columella, sporangium, spore*
   e. Mycelial structures for *Zygomycetes* - stolon, rhizoid

CLASSIFICATION

1. *Zygomycota* - ribbon-like aseptate hyphae; sexual and asexual
2. *Ascomycota* - septate; sexual and asexual; produce asci
3. *Basidiomycota* - septate; sexual; mushrooms; club fungi
4. *Deuteromycota* (Fungi Imperfecti) - no sexual stage; many common pathogens

Laboratory Methods

1. 10% KOH wet prep - clears debris and breaks down keratin from nails and hair
2. Lactophenol cotton blue
   a. Stains and kills organism
   b. Use with culture material
3. India ink - capsule of *Cryptococcus neoformans*
4. Calcofluor white - fluorescent
5. Primary growth agars
   a. Sabouraud's Dextrose agar *(SAB)* - glucose, peptone, pH 5.6
   b. Mycosel - similar to SAB but contains cycloheximide, BHI with 5% SRBC's, gentamicin and chloramphenicol
      ❖ *Inhibits some Candida and Cryptococcus; also Aspergillus fumigatus and Pseudallescheria boydii*
6. Specialty growth media
   a. Bird-seed agar - *Cryptococcus neoformans* (brown colonies)
   b. Corn meal agar - *Candida albicans* (chlamydoconidia)

Specimen Collection and Handling

1. Optimum temperature - 25-30°C
2. Hold 6 weeks
3. Use screw-cap tubes or tape plates to avoid accidental opening and drying
4. Work under a biologic safety hood

*Original contribution by Susan M. Marler (deceased)

TEST Alert!

Processing Samples for
Fungal I.D.

SUPERFICIAL MYCOSES
(HAIR, SKIN, NAILS)

Dermatophytes

Microsporum	Microconidia - Small Club-Shaped Macroconidia- Many, Rough, Spindle-Shaped (except M. audouinii)	Tinea (Mostly in Children); Hair and Skin; Hair Fluoresces	
M. audouinii		Rare Distorted Macroconidia; Terminal Chlamydoconidia	
M. canis		Thick-Walled Macro-conidia; Knobby End	
M. gypseum		Thin-Walled Macroconidia	
Trichophyton	Microconidia - Many Macroconidia - Few; Thin, Smooth Walls	Mostly in Adults; Hair Skin and Nails; NO Fluorescing Hairs	
T. mentagrophytes		Urease Pos; Rose-Brown Reverse	
T. rubrum		Urease Neg; Red Reverse	
T. tonsurans		Black Dot Ringwom; Balloon Forms; Yellow-Red Reverse	
Epidermophyton	Microconidia - None Macroconidia - 2-4 Cells in Clusters or Singles, Smooth Walls, Club-shaped	Skin and Nails; Especially Feet, Hands and Groin	
E. floccosum			

DERMATOPHYTES

1. Use keratin as nitrogen source

2. Tinea - ringworm

3. Septate hyphae; micro- and macroconidia

4. Cause tinea capitis
   a. Endothrix *(inside shaft)* - temporary hair loss
   b. Ectothrix *(outside shaft)* - permanent hair loss

5. KOH prep of scales from advancing margin of lesion, hair or nails

6. Wood's lamp - some dermatophytes fluoresce with UV light *(Microsporum in hair)*

7. Treatment - miconazole, clotrimazole, griseofulvin

MICROSPORUM

1. Affects hair and skin

2. Mostly in children

3. Macronidia - large, spindle shaped, rough with 4-15 septa

4. Microconidia - small, club shaped

M. audouinii

1. Epidemic tinea capitis

2. Hyphae usually sterile

3. Terminal chlamydoconidia

4. 10-21 days for growth

5. Reddish - brown color on reverse side of colony

6. Hairs fluoresce yellow-green

7. Salmon colored mycelia

M. canis

1. Causes dog and cat ringworm which is passed to humans

2. Macroconidia - abundant with 4-8 septa, knoblike, echinulate (rough) ends

3. Thick walls

4. Growth 4-5 days

5. Yellow color on reverse side of colony

6. Ectothrix

M. gypseum

1. Many macroconidia with 3-5 septa and echinulate surface *(rounded ends, not knobby)*

2. Thin walls

3. Orange-brown color on reverse side of colony

4. Ectothrix

TRICHOPHYTON

1. Affects skin, hair and nails

2. Primarily in adults

3. NO fluorescing hair

4. Few or no macroconidia - thin, smooth walls

5. Many microconidia

T. mentagrophytes

1. Microconidia - numerous, spiral and nodular bodies; white, cottony mycelium

2. Rose-brown color on reverse side of colony

3. Endothrix

4. Urease positive in 2-3 days

T. rubrum

1. Microconidia - tear shaped and dispersed along hyphae

2. Cherry red color on reverse side of colony

3. Urease negative

4. Ectothrix

T. tonsurans

1. Causes black dot ringworm *(hair breaks off)*

2. Endothrix

3. Yellow-red color on reverse side of colony

4. Microconidia - numerous, clavate varying in size *(balloon forms and "matchstick" forms)*

5. Chlamydoconidia in older cultures

174

6. Spores not commonly seen, only hyphae

T. schoenleinii

1. Causes favus (*severe tinea capitis*)

2. Endothrix

3. Slow growth, waxy colonies, favic chandeliers (*look like "deer antlers"*) and chlamydoconidia

T. violaceum

1. Affects scalp and body

2. Wrinkled, yeast-like purple colony

3. Hyphae and chlamydoconidia in chains

EPIDERMOPHYTON

E. floccosum

1. Skin and nails (*especially feet, hands and groin*)

2. Macroconidia
   a. Large, smooth, club-shaped
   b. Found in singles or clusters at end of hyphae
   c. 2-4 septa

3. No microconidia

4. Olive green or khaki color

Tinea versicolor vs. nigra

	Tinea versicolor	Tinea nigra
Cause	*Malassezia furfur*	*Phaeoannellomyces werneckii* (Dematiaceous)
Clinical Description	Brown, Scaly Areas on Trunk, Arms, Face	Brown Patches on Hands
Description	Hyphae & Yeast-Like Spore on Direct Prep ("Spaghetti & Meatballs")	Black Yeast-Like Colonies; Mold-Like with Age; 1-2 Clavate Cells
Miscellaneous	Overlay SAB with Olive Oil Prior to Inoculation	

Black vs. White Piedra

	Black Piedra	White Piedra
Cause	*Piedraia hortae* (Dematiaceous)	*Trichosporon beigelii*
Description	Black Nodules of Hyphae at Hair Shaft	White Nodules of Hyphae at Hair Shaft; White Mycelia; Arthroconidia and Blastoconidia

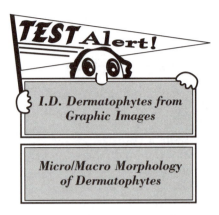

SYSTEMIC FUNGI

YEAST

Cryptococcus neoformans

1. Yeast; no pseudohyphae; brown colonies on bird seed agar

2. Mucoid colonies - capsule (*detected with India ink*)

3. Urease positive

4. Inhibited by cycloheximide

5. Found in pigeon and bird droppings

6. Meningitis (*found in spinal fluid*) and septicemia in immunocompromised hosts

7. Amphotericin B or flucytosine for treatment

Candida albicans

1. Yeast, pseudohyphae

2. Germ tube positive

3. Chlamydoconidia on cornmeal agar (CMAT)

4. Human flora

DIMORPHIC FUNGI

1. Yeast or tissue phase at 36°C; mold phase at 30°C

2. Treatment - Amphotericin B

Histoplasma capsulatum

1. Small yeast forms in tissue

2. Mycelial form exhibits tuberculate macroconidia - diagnostic

3. Found in bird and bat droppings

4. Infects RES - bone marrow specimen of choice

5. Primary focus pulmonary

6. May be confused with *Sepedonium (show dimorphism by converting to yeast phase at 36°C on BHI with blood and without antibiotics)*

Blastomyces dermatitidis

1. Large yeast cells with broad based buds and double contoured wall; mold phase produces "lollipop" forms

2. Primary focus pulmonary; skin lesions common

3. Confused with Scedosporium apiospermum *(do conversion studies)*

Coccidioides immitis

1. Tissue form - large, round walled spherule containing endospores *(spherules vary in size)*

2. Mold phase - thick walled, alternate staining arthroconidia *(very infectious to lab personnel)*

3. Difficult to convert from mold to yeast phase in routine lab

4. Endemic in desert southwest and semiarid regions

5. Primary focus pulmonary

Paracoccidioides brasiliensis (South America blastomycosis)

1. Yeast form diagnostic - multiple blastoconidia budding from sides of large blastospore ("*Mariner's Wheel*")

2. Primary focus pulmonary; can simulate TB

3. May have cutaneous or mucocutaneous lesions

Subcutaneous Fungi

Sporothrix schenckii (Dimorphic)

1. Found in soil, plants, decaying matter

2. Traumatic inoculation through skin *(gardeners via rose thorns)*; usually on hand

3. Pyogenic and granulomatous inflammatory reaction

4. Yeast phase - ovoid, "cigar" bodies

5. Mycelial phase - delicate branching hyphae with ovoid conidia clustered at tip in "rosette" head or along side like a "sleeve"

Dimorphic Fungi

Histoplasma capsulatum	Yeast -Very Small Mycelial - Tuberculate Macroconidia	Bat and Bird Droppings; Ohio and Mississippi River Valley; Infects RES (Bone Marrow Specimen of Choice)	 Confused with Sepedonium
Blastomyces dermatitidis	Yeast - Broad-Based Bud; Double-Contoured Wall Mycelial - "Lollipop" Forms	Along Ohio, Mississippi Valley and Appalachia; May Cause Skin Lesions	 Confused with Scedosporium apiospermum
Coccidioides immitis	Yeast - Spherules Containing Endospores Mycelial - Alternately Staining Arthroconidia	Desert Southwest and Semiarid Regions	
Paracoccidioides brasiliensis	Yeast - Multiple Buds ("Mariner's Wheel") Mold - Similar to "Lollipop" Forms	"South American Blastomycosis"; Simulates TB; Cutaneous Lesions	
Sporothrix schenckii	Yeast - "Cigar" Bodies Mold - Delicate Hyphae with Ovoid Conidia Along Side ("Sleeve") or in Rosette Heads	Found in Dirt and On Plants ("Rose Gardener's" "Mycosis")	

176

Chromoblastomycosis

1. *Phialophora* and *Cladosporium* - foot or leg

2. Scaly, wart-like lesions

3. Brown pigmented hyphae

4. Characteristics
   a. *Cladosporium (C. carionii)* - conidia in branched chains
   b. Phialophora (*P. verrucosa*) - conidia produced in a flask-like conidiophore or phialide
   c. Acrotheca (Rhinocladiella-like) (*Fonsecaea pedrosoi*) - conidia formed along side of irregular, club

shaped conidiophores; this genus exhibits all three types of sporulation

Mycetoma

1. Found in the tropics

2. Foot trauma; draining sinuses

3. Purplish discoloration and tumor-like deformities that drain pus with granules

4. Actinomycotic - *Nocardia, Actinomadura*

5. Fungal
   a. *Pseudallescheria boydii (perfect stage)*
   b. *Scedosporium apiospermum (imperfect stage)*

6. White cottony mycelium; turns brown with age; oval conidia borne on conidiophores ("*lollipop*")

7. May also be found in eye, sinuses, brain abscess

8. Opportunist in compromised patients

YEASTS AND OTHER OPPORTUNISTS

Organism	Characteristics	Notes	Illustrations
Candida albicans	Numerous Blastoconidia Along Pseudohyphae; Germ Tubes Formed; Terminal Chlamydoconidia	Germ Tube Test - Pos in 2 Hrs. at 37C in Rabbit or Human Plasma; Urease Neg; May be Isolated in Blood of Immunosuppressed	
Candida tropicalis	No Chlamydoconidia Sparser Blastoconidia	Germ Tube Test - Neg (But, Forms Structure Between Tube & Spore)	
Geotrichum	Arthroconidia	"Hockey Stick" Bud on One Corner of Arthroconidia	
Trichosporon	Arthroconidia and Blastoconidia	Budding from Both Corners of Arthroconidia Urease Pos	
Candida (torulopsis) glabrata	No Pseudohyphae	Assimilates Only Glucose & Trehalose	
Cryptococcus neoformans	No Pseudohyphae; Encapsulated; India Ink Pos	Urease Pos; Brown Colonies on Birdseed Agar; May be Isolated in Blood of Immunosuppressed	

Microscopic Observations

Description	Possible Organism
Small Extracellular Yeast	*Candida sp.* *Sporothrix schenckii*
Small Intracellular Yeast	*Histoplasma capsulatum*
Yeast with Capsule	*Cryptococcus neoformans*
Yeast with Pseudohyphae	*Candida sp.*
Large Yeast with Broad-Based Buds	*Blastomyces dermatiditis*
Large Yeast with Multiple Buds	*Paracoccidioides brasiliensis*
Endospherules and Endospores	*Coccidioides immitis*

I.D. Yeast from Graphic Images

Yeasts Found in Blood Cultures

Opportunists

Organism	Characteristics	Illustrations/Notes
Penicillium	Green or Blue-Green Colonies; Branching or "Penicillus" Head; Sterigmata Blunt	
Acremonium	Delicate Hyphae; Elliptical Conidia with Appearance of Brain Surface	
Fusarium	Colonies Lavender to Purple; "Banana" - Shaped Macroconidia	
Aspergillus	Conidiophore Ends in Swelling ("Vesicle") Which Carries Sterigmata and Chains of Conidia	Respiratory Infections "Farmer's Lung"
fumigatus	Green Conidia	
flavus	Yellow Conidia	
niger	Black Conidia	

I.D. Most Common Opportunists from Graphic Images

Differentiate Penicillium and Aspergillus from Graphic Images

Dematiaceous Molds

Organism	Characteristics	Notes	Illustrations
Curvularia	Macroconidia - 4-6 Cells; Center Cell Larger; Gives a Curved Appearance	Saprobe	
Alternaria	Macroconidia Have Transverse and Longitudinal Septa in Chains	Saprobe	
Bipolaris	Similar to Drechslera; Slightly Protruding ("Squared-Off" Hilum)	Germ Tube Forms along Conidial Axis	
Aureobasidium	Produces White Yeast-Like Colonies and Black Yeast-Like Colonies	Large, Segmented Hyphae; Appear as Oreo® Cookies	
Cladosporium	Branching Conidiophores with Chains of "Tree-Like" Conidia	Cladosporium-Type Sporulation; Shield Cells; Scars Where Conidia Attach	
Phialophora verrucosa	Flask-Shaped Phialides With a Distinct Collarette at the Apex; Conidia in Clusters at Apex	Phialophora-type Sporulation; Looks Like "Vase of Flowers"	
Fonsecaea pedrosoi	Short Chains of Conidia from Sides of Conidiophores (Initial Appearance - "Rabbit Ears")	Acrotheca or Rhinocladiella-Type Sporulation; May See Cladosporium or Phialo-phora-Type Sporulation	
Exophiala jeanselmei	Initially Form Black Yeast Cells; Eventually Form Hyphae	Forms Conidiophores Which Terminate in Tapered Annelids; Does NOT Grow at 40C	
Wangiella dermatitidis	Initially Form Black Yeast Cells; Eventually Form Hyphae	Opposite of Above	
Pseudallescheria boydii (Perfect or Sexual Form)	"Lollipop" Forms; Cleistothecia (Only in Sexual Form)	Scedosporium apiospermum (Asexual or Imperfect Form); Can be Confused with Blastomyces (Mycelial Phase)	

TEST Alert!

I.D. Black Mold from Graphic Image or Description

Phycomycetes

Organism	Characteristics	Illustrations
Rhizopus	Nodal Rhizoids; Sporangiophore Ends in Swelling ("columella")	
Mucor	No Rhizoids	
Absidia	Internodal Rhizoids	

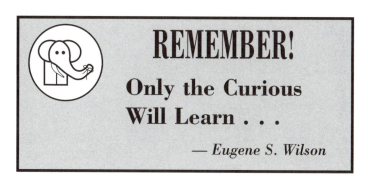

REMEMBER!

Only the Curious Will Learn . . .

— *Eugene S. Wilson*

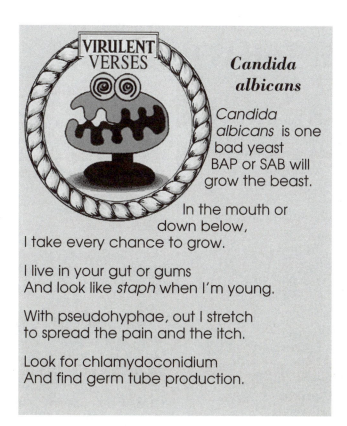

VIRULENT VERSES

Candida albicans

Candida albicans is one bad yeast BAP or SAB will grow the beast.

In the mouth or down below, I take every chance to grow.

I live in your gut or gums And look like *staph* when I'm young.

With pseudohyphae, out I stretch to spread the pain and the itch.

Look for chlamydoconidium And find germ tube production.

MYCOLOGY SAMPLE QUESTIONS

1. A fungal specimen isolated from the bone marrow of a patient with a pulmonary infection showed tuberculate macroconidia at 30C and yeastlike cells at 36C. Identify the most likely dimorphic fungi with these characteristics.
   - A. Aspergillus fumigatus
   - B. Blastomyces dermatitidis
   - C. Histoplasma capsulatum
   - D. Trichophyton mentagrophytes

2. A yeast-like organism was isolated from a sputum specimen. On cornmeal agar, this yeast produced mycelia with thick-walled terminal chlamydoconidia. This organism is most likely
   - A. Blastomyces dermatitidis
   - B. Candida albicans
   - C. Candida tropicalis
   - D. Geotrichum candidum

3. Thick-walled yeast cells bearing single buds attached by a broad base are observed in an aspirated clinical specimen. The organism is most likely
   - A. Blastomyces dermatitidis
   - B. Candida albicans
   - C. Cryptococcus neoformans
   - D. Geotrichum candidum

4. Crust from a cauliflower-like lesion on the hand microscopically exhibited brown spherical bodies. After 3 weeks incubation at room temperature, a black mold grew on Sabou-raud's agar. Microscopic examination revealed cladosporium, phialophora and acrotheca sporulation. The most probable identification is
   - A. Cladosporium carrionii
   - B. Fonsecaea pedrosoi
   - C. Phialophora verrucosa
   - D. Pseudallescheria boydii

5. In order to prove a yeast is dimorphic, which of the following tests is performed?
   - A. Carbohydrate assimilation
   - B. Growth on cornmeal agar
   - C. Incubate yeast subculture at 37C
   - D. Urease

ANSWERS AND RATIONALE

1. C

   Option A causes "Farmer's Lung" but is NOT a dimorphic fungus and is usually identified from a sputum sample (branching hyphal filaments in a characteristic Y shape). Option B is a dimorphic fungus but, as a mold, it bears spherical conidia from the sides of the hyphae frequently appearing in "lollipop" forms. It is usually identified from a sputum sample or may spread via thebloodstream and infect the skin (identified from a skin scraping). Option D is a dermatophyte and NOT a dimorphic fungus and is identified from skin, hair or nail scrapings.

2. B

   Option A is a dimorphic fungus and as a yeast produces broad-based buds with a double contoured wall. Option C does not produce chlamydoconidia. Option D produces characteristic rectangular arthroconidia.

3. A

   Option B produces small oval yeasts which may be single cells or often appear with buds, hyphae or pseudohyphae (elongated yeast cells that remain attached to each other). Option C is a yeast which forms a large capsule (seen on India ink preps) and may be isolated from spinal fluid. Option D produces a "hockey stick" bud on rectangular arthroconidia.

4. B

   F. pedrosoi is the only mold which produces all three types of sporulation.

5. C

   Dimorphic fungi demonstrate yeast forms at 36C and mycelial (mold) forms at 28-30C. Option A identifies yeast isolates. Option B (with Tween 80) allows for enhanced formation of hyphae, blastospores and chlamydospores. Option D is positive with many yeasts (C. albicans is NEGATIVE for urease while C. neoformans is positive).

PARASITOLOGY

by Michele Zitzmann and Mary R. Hebert

Specimen Collection and Handling

GENERAL

1. Recommended to examine 3 specimens within 10 day span; every other day if possible

2. Examine liquid specimens within 30 minutes of passage or place in preservative

3. Examine soft specimens within 30 minutes of passage or place in preservative

4. Examine formed stools within 3-4 hours; place an aliquot in preservative and refrigerate the remainder

TYPES OF SPECIMENS

1. Feces - 95% parasite specimens
   a. Collect in clean, dry container with a secure lid
   b. Do not accept specimens contaminated with urine *(may destroy motile organisms)*, water *(may contain free living organisms)* or oil or barium enemas *(intestinal protozoa may be undetectable 5-10 days after barium is given)*

   c. Antibiotics *(such as tetracycline)* modify intestinal flora and may prevent parasite recovery for 2 weeks after drug cessation

2. Sputum - early morning specimen is best *(most concentrated)*

3. Urine - early morning or 1st void

4. Genitalia - saline wet swabs

5. Tissue and skin - sterile container

6. Blood
   a. Fresh blood from fingerstick *(Best NOT to use EDTA)*
   b. Prepare thick smear for concentration and thin smear for identification

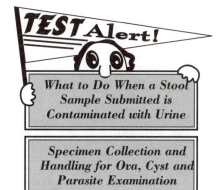

TEST Alert!

What to Do When a Stool Sample Submitted is Contaminated with Urine

Specimen Collection and Handling for Ova, Cyst and Parasite Examination

OVA, CYST & PARASITE EXAMINATION

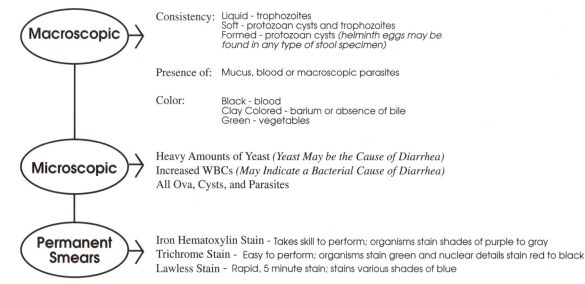

Macroscopic →

Consistency: Liquid - trophozoites
Soft - protozoan cysts and trophozoites
Formed - protozoan cysts *(helminth eggs may be found in any type of stool specimen)*

Presence of: Mucus, blood or macroscopic parasites

Color: Black - blood
Clay Colored - barium or absence of bile
Green - vegetables

Microscopic →

Heavy Amounts of Yeast *(Yeast May be the Cause of Diarrhea)*
Increased WBCs *(May Indicate a Bacterial Cause of Diarrhea)*
All Ova, Cysts, and Parasites

Permanent Smears →

Iron Hematoxylin Stain - Takes skill to perform; organisms stain shades of purple to gray
Trichrome Stain - Easy to perform; organisms stain green and nuclear details stain red to black
Lawless Stain - Rapid, 5 minute stain; stains various shades of blue

TYPES OF PRESERVATION

1. Refrigeration - good for eggs, larvae and amoebic cysts; **Do not refrigerate if you suspect amoebic trophozoites**

2. 10% formalin - good for eggs, larvae and amoebic cysts

3. MIF *(Merthiolate-Iodine-Formalin)* concentration procedure as well as preservative; good for eggs larvae and amoebic cysts

4. PVA *(Polyvinyl Alcohol)* best for amoebic trophozoites; can prepare permanent stain slides from specimens preserved this way

5. SAF *(Sodium Acetate-Acetic Acid-Formalin)* good for amoebic trophozoites; environmentally safer than PVA

CONCENTRATION TECHNIQUES: (USED TO DETECT SMALL NUMBERS OF PARASITES)

1. Formalin-Ethyl Acetate Sedimentation:
   a. Forms four layers:
      - *Ethyl acetate*
      - *Debris*
      - *Formalin*
      - *Sediment (parasites)*;
   b. Ethyl acetate removes fats and oils and formalin preserves organisms
   c. Advantages: Can stay in formalin stage indefinitely; easy to perform
   d. Disadvantages: preparation contains more debris

2. Zinc Sulfate Flotation Technique
   a. Specific gravity of zinc sulfate is greater than ova, cysts and larvae, therefore they float on top of the zinc sulfate solution
   b. Specific gravity of zinc sulfate solution should be 1.18
   c. Advantages - does not use flammable chemicals; produces a cleaner preparation
   d. Disadvantages - large eggs *(schistosomes)* and operculated eggs *(D. latum)* may sink quickly

MODES OF TRANSMISSION

1. Ingestion - eggs, cysts or larvae; examples:
   a. Ascaris
   b. Paragonimus
   c. Trichinella
   d. Giardia

2. Penetration - larvae penetrates directly through the skin; examples:
   a. Strongyloides
   b. Hookworm

3. Vector - vectors inject parasites into blood/tissue; examples:
   a. Mosquito
      - *Plasmodium, Brugia, Wuchereria,*
   b. Tse Tse fly
      - *Trypanasoma gambiense*
      - *T. rhodesiense*
   c. Tick
      - *Babesia*

Helminths

TERMS

1. Intermediate host - host which contains the larval form of the parasite

2. Definitive host - host which contains the adult sexual form of the parasite

3. Hermaphroditic - contain both sexes in one helminth; cestodes and trematodes *(except Schistosomes)*

4. Gravid proglottid - segments filled with eggs

Intestinal Nematodes (Roundworms)

GENERAL CHARACTERISTICS

1. Males smaller than females and have a curved tail

2. Unsegmented

3. Length varies from a few millimeters to meters in length

4. Complete digestive tract *(mouth to anus)*

5. Worldwide distribution

Ascaris lumbricoides (Large Intestinal Roundworm)

1. Largest nematode

2. If no male present in small intestine, female will lay unfertilized eggs

3. Diagnosis
   a. Demonstrate characteristic egg in feces *(round egg containing albuminous coating)*

b. Recovery of worms from anus, nasal passage or sputum

5. Clinical disease
  a. "worm ball" - blockage in intestines
  b. "ascaris pneumonitis" - due to larvae migration in lungs

6. Second most common nematode infection in U.S.; 5-9 year old group most prevalent in U.S.

7. Visceral Larval Migrans - dog and cat ascarid *(toxocara canis and cati)* migration through viscera resulting in eosinophilia

Cause and Symptoms of Visceral Larval Migrans

Enterobius vermicularis (Pinworm)

1. Eggs become embryonated within hours resulting in a high rate of autoinfection; treat entire family of an infected individual

Autoinfection Associated with Pinworms

2. Diagnosis
  a. Scotch tape *(cellulose tape)* preparation - eggs and larvae stick to tape; since migration of female occurs at night the prep is performed after patient has been sleeping or early in the morning
  b. Adults may become "stuck" to the outside of the stool as it passes the perianal folds where the female migrates to lay eggs

3. Most common helminth parasite of humans; frequently in children due to poor sanitation habits

Trichuris trichiura (Whipworm)

1. Diagnosis - demonstrate characteristic egg in feces *(football shaped with mucoid polar plugs)*

2. Clinical disease — prolapsed rectum may occur in heavy infections

Strongyloides stercoralis (Threadworm)

1. Smallest nematode

2. Rhabditiform larva *(noninfective)*
  a. Short buccal cavity *(approximately 1/3-1/2 width of body)*
  b. Prominant primordial genitalia

3. Filariform larva *(infective)*
  a. Short buccal cavity
  b. Notch at end of tail

4. Eggs hatch in mucosa of intestine; rarely seen in feces

5. Has both a free living cycle and a parasitic cycle

6. Autoinfection - some of the rhabditiform larvae develop into filariform larvae in the bowel and reinfect the host

7. Clinical disease
  a. 3 stages based on life cycle
    ❖ *Cutaneous - initial skin penetration*
    ❖ *Pulmonary - larval migration through lungs*
    ❖ *Intestinal - symptoms depend on worm load; immunocompromised patients may exhibit leukocytosis and eosinophilia*
  b. Hyperinfection syndrome- may lead to death from tissue damage
    ❖ *Occurs in the immuno-compromised (AIDS, drugs)*
    ❖ *Can be transferred through organ transplantation*

8. Diagnosis - demonstrate rhabditiform larvae and/or filariform larvae in feces

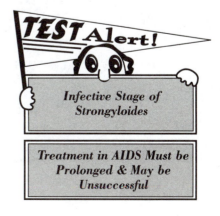

Infective Stage of Strongyloides

Treatment in AIDS Must be Prolonged & May be Unsuccessful

184

Necator americanus (New World Hookworm) and Ancylostoma duodenale (Old World Hookworm)

1. Adults
   a. May live 2-14 years
   b. Rarely seen in stools since firmly attached to mucosa

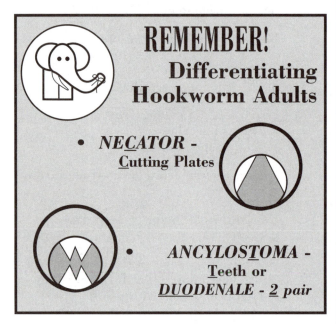

REMEMBER!
Differentiating Hookworm Adults

- *NECATOR -* **Cutting Plates**

- *ANCYLOSTOMA -* Teeth or *DUODENALE - 2 pair*

2. Rhabditiform larvae
   a. Long buccal cavity *(approximately as long as width of body)*

3. Infective stage - filariform larvae
   a. Long buccal cavity
   b. Pointed tail

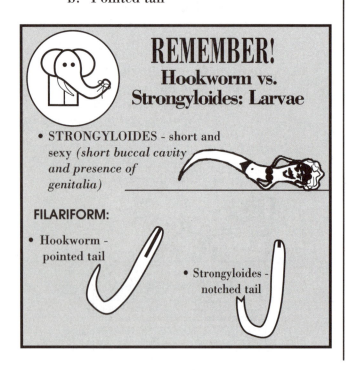

REMEMBER!
Hookworm vs. Strongyloides: Larvae

- STRONGYLOIDES - short and sexy *(short buccal cavity and presence of genitalia)*

FILARIFORM:

- Hookworm - pointed tail

- Strongyloides - notched tail

4. Clinical disease
   a. Pneumonitis
   b. Allergic reactions - "ground itch"
   c. Anemia - each adult worm consumes 0.2 ml of blood/day
   d. Cutaneous larvae migrans - migration of dog hookworms (*ancylostoma, braziliensis, and caninum*) through subcutaneous tissue causing intense itching

5. Diagnosis
   a. Demonstrate characteristic egg in feces
   b. Do not see larvae in feces (*unless specimen left at room temperature*)

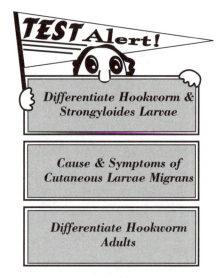

TEST Alert!

Differentiate Hookworm & Strongyloides Larvae

Cause & Symptoms of Cutaneous Larvae Migrans

Differentiate Hookworm Adults

BLOOD AND TISSUE NEMATODES

Trichinella spiralis (Trichina Worm)

1. Adults
   a. Females bear larvae **NOT** eggs

2. Infective stage - ingestion of encysted larvae in undercooked pork

3. Diagnostic stage - muscle biopsy showing encysted larvae in striated muscle

4. Clinical disease
   a. Destruction of muscle cell
   b. High eosinophilia *(may reach 90%)*
   c. Myocardial involvement possible

MICROFILARIAE

GENERAL CHARACTERISTICS

1. Require an arthropod as an intermediate host; when infected arthropod takes a blood meal, the microfilariae are released into human host

2. Diagnosis made by examining Giemsa stained thick and thin smears *(except Onchocerca volvulus - skin scraping from nodules)*

Wuchereria bancrofti

1. Microfilaria
   a. Sheathed
   b. NO nuclei in tip of tail
   c. Nocturnal periodicity — 10pm-4am greatest concentration in blood

2. Elephantiasis - permanent blockage of lymphatic system; usually occurs in the lower extremities and genitalia

3. Diagnosis - demonstrate in blood smear

Brugia malayi

1. Microfilaria
   a. Sheathed
   b. 2 terminal nuclei at tip of tail; separate from rest of body nuclei
   c. Nocturnal periodicity

2. Elephantiasis restricted to the lower extremities

3. Diagnosis - demonstrate in blood smear

Loa Loa (Eye Worm)

1. Microfilaria
   a. Sheathed
   b. Nuclei to the tip of tail
   c. Diurnal periodicity — 10am-4pm greatest concentration in blood

2. Causes calabar swellings (allergic reaction to worm migration in tissue)

3. Diagnosis
   a. Demonstrate in blood smear
   b. Worm may migrate across conjunctiva

Onchocerca volvulus (Blinding Worm)

1. Microfilaria
   a. Only pathogenic microfilaria which is NOT sheathed
   b. NO nuclei in tip of tail
   c. Found in nodules under skin, NOT in peripheral blood

2. Clinical disease
   a. Severe dermatitis *(50-70% eosinophilia)*

b. Microfilariae in ocular structures may result in blindness; leading cause of blindness in Africa

3. Diagnosis - demonstrate from skin "snips"/tissue scrapings

REMEMBER!
Capt. Mic Ro Filariae

- **ONCHOCERCUS VOLVULUS -** Only pathogenic microfilariae with no sheath, no nuclei in tip of tail (*"on"* is *"no"* *backwards*)

- **WUCHERERIA BANCROFTI -** No nuclei in tip of tail

- **BRUGIA MALAYI -** B is second letter of alphabet (*2 nuclei in tip of tail*)

- **LOA LOA -** Name repeats and so do nuclei, continuously to tip of tail

TEST Alert!

Differentiate microfilariae based on morphology

Characteristics of Microfilariae

Microfilaria	Disease	Arthropod Vector	Diagnostic Stage Found In:	Diagnostic Characteristics
Wuchereria bancrofti	Elephantiasis	Mosquito (*Culex & Anopheles*)	Blood	Sheath, no nuclei in tail
Brugia malayi	Elephantiasis	Mosquito (*Mansonia*)	Blood	Sheath, 2 nuclei in tip of tail
Loa loa	Calabar Swellings Blindness	Fly (*Chrysops*)	Blood	Sheath, continuous nuclei in tail
Onchocerca volvulus	Blindness	Fly (*Simulian*)	Tissue from Nodule	No sheath, no nuclei in tail

TEST Alert!

Infective and Diagnostic Stages of Nematodes

CESTODES (TAPEWORMS)

GENERAL

1. Flat, ribbon-like, segmented worms

2. Shape of proglottids, presence or absence of armed rostellum and size aid in identification of adults

3. Hermaphroditic - mature proglottids contain both male and female reproductive organs

4. 4 cup shaped suckers on scolex (*except Diphyllobothrium latum which has 2 suctorial grooves*)

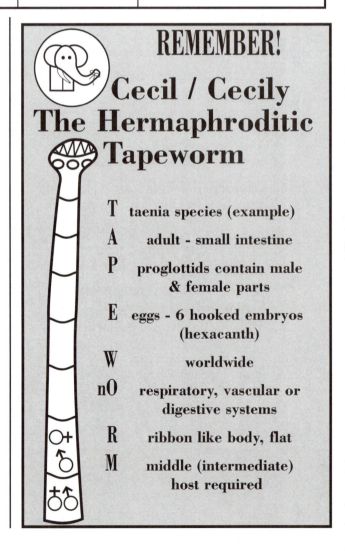

REMEMBER!
Cecil / Cecily
The Hermaphroditic Tapeworm

T taenia species (example)

A adult - small intestine

P proglottids contain male & female parts

E eggs - 6 hooked embryos (hexacanth)

W worldwide

nO respiratory, vascular or digestive systems

R ribbon like body, flat

M middle (intermediate) host required

Taenia saginata (Beef Tapeworm)

1. Adults
   a. Scolex has an unarmed rostellum
   b. Consists of as many as 2000 proglottids *(10-15 ft long)*
   c. Adults may live 25 years

2. Infective stage - ingestion of undercooked beef containing larval stage

3. Diagnostic stage
   a. Find characteristic egg in feces
   b. Proglottids can be stained; note number of major uterine branches *(15-30 in T. saginata)*

Taenia solium (Pork Tapeworm)

1. Adults
   a. Scolex has armed rostellum
   b. Consists of as many as 1000 proglottids; 6-10 ft long

2. Cysticercosis - human is intermediate host
   a. Man ingests the egg of T. solium
   b. Egg passes through the stomach and hatches in the intestine
   c. The embryo penetrates the mucosa and becomes a cysticercus; most commonly found in the subcutaneous connective tissue, eye, brain, muscles, heart and lungs

3. Diagnostic stage
   a. Find characteristic egg in feces
   b. Proglottids can be stained; note number of major uterine branches *(7-13 in T. solium)*

Differentiating Taenia Species

T. solium	T. saginata
Pork 7-13 Uterine Branches Armed Cysticercosis	Beef 15-30 Uterine Branches Unarmed Rare Cysticercosis

REMEMBER! Taenia Species

T. solium
- "soul" food = pork
- "soul" sister = cysti(*sister*)cercosis
- parasite causing this serious condition must be armed

T. saginata
- has more letters in its name and more uterine branches

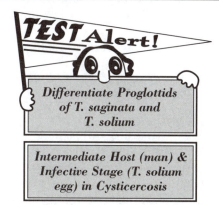

TEST Alert!

Differentiate Proglottids of T. saginata and T. solium

Intermediate Host (man) & Infective Stage (T. solium egg) in Cysticercosis

Hymenolepis nana (Dwarf Tapeworm)

1. Most common human tapeworm in the U.S.

2. Adults
   a. Small tapeworm; 40 mm long
   b. Contains approximately 200 segments
   c. Armed rostellum *(short with hooks)*

3. Does not require an intermediate host; may have intermediate host such as flea or beetle

4. Infective stage - ingestion of eggs

5. Diagnostic stage - demonstrate characteristic egg in feces; eggs contain polar filaments

6. Heavy infections can occur through autoinfection

188

Hymenolepis diminuta (Rat Tapeworm)

1. Adult - unarmed rostellum

2. Man is accidental host via ingestion of infected intermediate arthropod host (*Ex. grain beetles in pre-cooked cereals*)

3. Rat is definitive host

4. Infective stage - ingestion of flea

5. Diagnostic stage - demonstrate characteristic egg in feces; eggs look similar to *H. nana*, except lack polar filaments

Diphyllobothrium latum (Broad Fish Tapeworm)

1. Adults
   a. Scolex consists of two longitudinal suctorial grooves known as bothria, giving it a spoon shape
   b. Uterus in gravid proglottid appears as a rosette
   c. May have as many as 3000 proglottids

2. Infective stage - ingestion of larvae in infected undercooked freshwater fish

3. Clinical disease
   a. Can cause megaloblastic anemia, since vitamin B_{12} is absorbed by worm
   b. Sparganosis - disease caused by drinking water containing infected copepod; larva develops in human who is the intermediate host instead of the fish
   c. High incidence in Finland, Alaska, and Canada

4. Diagnostic stage - demonstrate characteristic egg or proglottids (*often in chains of a few inches to several feet*) in feces (*may NOT be seen in flotation techniques; operculated ova may sink*)

5. Only cestode to produce operculated eggs

6. Egg possesses a small aboperculear knob

Echinococcus granulosus - (Hydatid Tapeworm)

1. Adult
   a. Very small; 3-6 cm long
   b. Consists of only three proglottids - immature, mature and gravid
   c. Scolex has an armed rostellum

2. Normal life cycle
   a. Sheep (*intermediate host*) ingest eggs
   b. Dog (*definitive host*) infected from eating infected viscera of butchered animals

3. Infective stage - man (*intermediate host*) ingests egg

4. Diagnostic stage
   a. Hydatid cysts seen in routine x-rays or exploratory surgery (*form in various parts of the body - most commonly the liver, lungs, brain, heart*)
   b. Serological tests (*ELISA, IHA*)

Hydatid Disease - Man Ingests Egg & Becomes Intermediate Host

Dipylidium caninum - (Dog Tapeworm)

1. Adults
   a. Scolex has an armed rostellum
   b. Proglottids resemble pumpkin/cucumber seeds when moist and rice grains when dry

2. Normal life cycle - dog and cat ingest infected fleas containing larvae

3. Infective stage - human (*accidental intermediate host*) ingests infected flea

4. Diagnostic stage - demonstrate characteristic egg packet (*5-30 eggs are in a hyaline non- cellular egg sac*) in feces

5. Found predominantly in children

TREMATODES (FLUKES)

GENERAL

1. Flat leaf-shaped organisms

2. Hermaphroditic - contain both male and female reproductive parts (*except Schistosomes*)

3. Require an intermediate host

Man is the Definitive Host in Trematode Infections

4. Snail is always 1st intermediate host

5. Eggs are operculated (*except Schistosomes*)

Fasciolopsis buski - (Giant Intestinal Fluke)

1. Infective stage - ingestion of raw aquatic vegetation (Ex. water chestnuts) with encysted metacercaria

2. Diagnostic stage - demonstration of characteristic eggs in feces (*eggs resemble F. hepatica*)

3. Clinical Disease
   a. Diarrhea, epigastric pain
   b. Symptoms relate to number of worms present

4. Found in Asia

Fasciola hepatica - (Liver Fluke)

1. Infective stage - ingestion of raw aquatic vegetation (Ex. water chestnuts) with encysted metacercaria

2. Diagnostic stage - detect characteristic eggs in feces (*eggs resemble F. buski*)

3. Clinical disease
   a. Larvae elicit inflammatory response in liver
   b. Stone formation may occur
   c. Eosinophilia may occur during larvae migration

4. Sheep and cattle are reservior hosts; therefore, high incidence in sheep raising countries

Clonorchis sinensis - (Chinese Liver Fluke)

1. Infective stage - ingestion of raw fish infected with metacercariae

2. Diagnostic stage - demonstration of characteristic eggs in feces (*operculated with shoulders and small knob at abopercular end*)

3. Found in Japan, Korea, China, Taiwan and Vietnam (*cats and dogs serve as reservoir hosts*)

Paragonimus westermani - (Oriental Lung Fluke)

1. Infective stage - human ingestion of crustacea (crabs, crawfish, etc.) infected with metacercariae

2. Diagnostic stage - demonstrate characteristic egg in feces or sputum (*may appear macroscopically in sputum as reddish-brown flecks resembling iron filings*); (*operculated with shoulders and thick abopercular shell*)

3. Clinical disease
   a. Light infections asymptomatic
   b. High eosinophilia
   c. Chronic cough and abundant mucus in heavy infections

4. Found in Japan, Korea, China, Philippines, and Southeast Asia

Blood Flukes (Schistosomes)

1. Most important trematode in man because of severity of infection

2. Separate male and female adult worms

3. Adult flukes live in venules (*S. japonicum and S. mansoni in mesenteric venules and S. haematobium in bladder venules*) and may live 4-35 yrs

4. Snail is intermediate host

5. Infective stage - cercariae in water directly penetrate skin of man (*definitive host*)

TEST Alert!

Cause of "Swimmer's Itch" is Human Infection with Bird Shistosomes

6. Diagnostic stage - demonstration of characteristic egg in feces or urine (*S. haematobium*); may NOT be seen in flotation techniques (*large eggs may sink*)

7. Eggs possess a characteristic spine (*used to speciate*)
   a. *S. mansoni* = conspicuous lateral spine
   b. *S. japonicum* = inconspicuous lateral knob
   c. *S. haematobium* = terminal spine

8. Clinical disease
   a. Progressive chronic inflammatory disease involving liver, small intestine, large intestine and bladder
   b. Tissue damage
   c. Cirrhosis of liver (*S. mansoni*) and associated with bladder cancer (*S. haematobium*)

190

d. High eosinophilia
e. Skin urticaria
f. Bloody diarrhea

9. Found in Western hemisphere
   (transmission does not occur in U.S.
   because lack of appropriate snail)

SCIENTIFIC NAME	COMMON NAME
Ancylostoma caninum	Dog hookworm
Ancylostoma duodenale	Old World hookworm
Ascaris lumbricoides	Large intestinal roundworm
Clonorchis sinensis	Oriental/Chinese liverfluke
Diphyllobothrium latum	Broad fish tapeworm
Echinococcus granulosus	Hydatid tapeworm
Enterobius vermicularis	Pinworm
Fasciolopsis buski	Large intestinal fluke
Fasciola hepatica	Sheep liver fluke
Hymenolepis diminuta	Rat tapeworm
Hymenolepis nana	Dwarf tapeworm
Loa loa	Eyeworm
Necator americanus	New World hookworm
Onchocerca volvulus	Blinding worm
Paragonimus westermani	Oriental lung fluke
Schistosoma haematobium	Bladder fluke
Schistosoma japonicum	Oriental blood fluke
Schistosoma mansoni	Manson's blood fluke
Strongyloides stercoralis	Threadworm
Taenia saginata	Beef tapeworm
Taenia solium	Pork tapeworm
Toxocara canis/cati	Dog/Cat Ascarid
Trichuris trichiura	Whipworm

REMEMBER!
Helminth Names

Common name of worms give you clues
to the distribution and/or location of
adult worms.
(Ex. Clonorchis-Chinese Liver Fluke,
adults found in the liver)

REMEMBER!

Beyond Stools: Look for me in:

BLOOD
Microfilariae (larvae)
- except Onchocerca (skin)

URINE
Enterobius vermicularis (eggs)
Schistosoma haematobium (eggs)

SPUTUM
Paragonimus westermani (eggs)
Ascaris lumbricoides (adults),
Strongyloides stercoralis (adults, larva, or eggs)

MUSCLES
Trichinella spiralis (larvae)

LIVER / BILE FLUID
Echinococcus granulosus (larvae)

Key Characteristics of Helminth Eggs

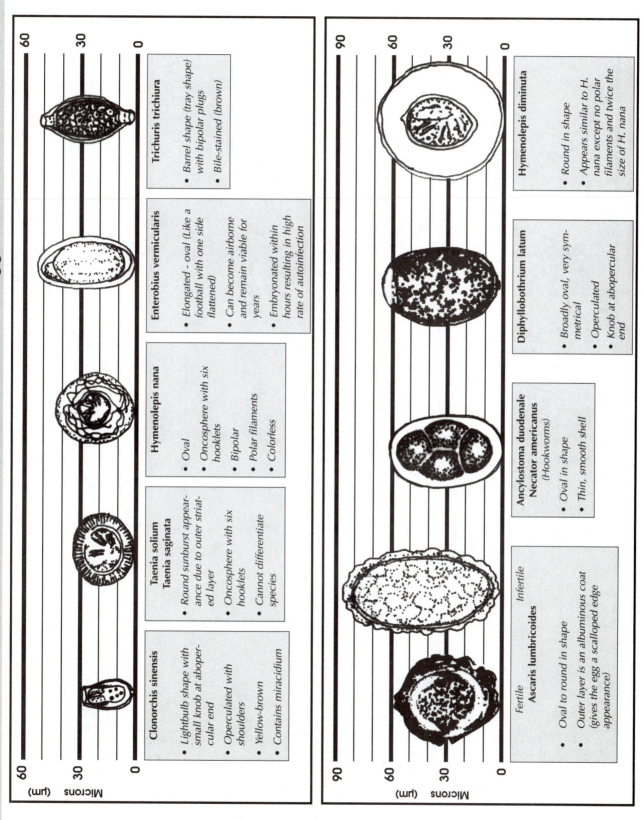

Microns (μm)

Trichuris trichiura
- Barrel shape (tray shape) with bipolar plugs
- Bile-stained (brown)

Enterobius vermicularis
- Elongated - oval (Like a football with one side flattened)
- Can become airborne and remain viable for years
- Embryonated within hours resulting in high rate of autoinfection

Hymenolepis nana
- Oval
- Oncosphere with six hooklets
- Bipolar
- Polar filaments
- Colorless

Taenia solium
Taenia saginata
- Round sunburst appearance due to outer striated layer
- Oncosphere with six hooklets
- Cannot differentiate species

Clonorchis sinensis
- Lightbulb shape with small knob at abopercular end
- Operculated with shoulders
- Yellow-brown
- Contains miracidium

Microns (μm)

Hymenolepis diminuta
- Round in shape
- Appears similar to H. nana except no polar filaments and twice the size of H. nana

Diphyllobothrium latum
- Broadly oval, very symmetrical
- Operculated
- Knob at abopercular end

Ancylostoma duodenale
Necator americanus
(Hookworms)
- Oval in shape
- Thin, smooth shell

Infertile

Fertile
Ascaris lumbricoides
- Oval to round in shape
- Outer layer is an albuminous coat (gives the egg a scalloped edge appearance)

192

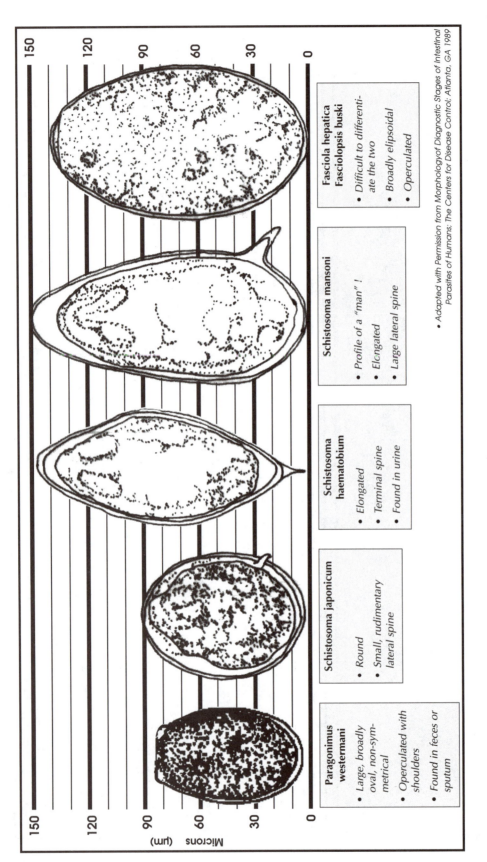

Microns (µm)

150 120 90 60 30 0

Paragoninus westermani
- Large, broadly oval, non-symmetrical
- Operculated with shoulders
- Found in feces or sputum

Schistosoma japonicum
- Round
- Small, rudimentary lateral spine

Schistosoma haematobium
- Elongated
- Terminal spine
- Found in urine

Schistosoma mansoni
- Profile of a "man"!
- Elongated
- Large lateral spine

Fasciola hepatica Fasciolopsis buski
- Difficult to differentiate the two
- Broadly elipsoidal
- Operculated

- Adapted with Permission from Morphology of Diagnostic Stages of Intestinal Parasites of Humans; The Centers for Disease Control: Atlanta, GA 1989

REMEMBER!
Congratulate Yourself !

You are almost through!!!

TEST Alert!

Identify Helminth Eggs from Graphic Images

Protozoa

Classification of Intestinal Protozoa

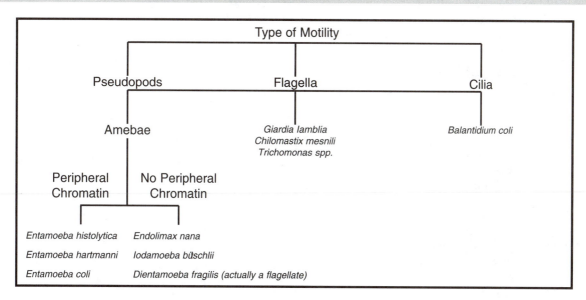

INTESTINAL AMEBAE

GENERAL CHARACTERISTICS

1. Motility by pseudopods

2. Infective stage - cyst *(usually ingested in contaminated food/water)*

3. Diagnostic stage is cyst or trophozoite *(troph)* in feces

Entamoeba histolytica

1. Pathogenic - causes ulcers of the intestinal tract; and liver or lung abscesses

2. Cyst
   a. Up to 4 nuclei, uniform peripheral chromatin; central karyosome
   b. May contain chromitoidal bars which are cigar-shaped
   c. Size 10-20 μm

3. Troph
   a. 1 nucleus, peripheral chromatin, central karyosome
   b. May have ingested rbc's
   c. Size 12-60 μm
   d. Progressive motility

Entamoeba dispar

1. Nonpathogenic

2. Morphologically identical to *E. histolytica*

3. Trophs cannot ingest red blood cells

4. Serological testing used to differentiate species

Entamoeba coli

1. Nonpathogenic

2. Confused with E. histolytica

3. Cyst
   a. Up to 8 nuclei; irregular peripheral chromatin; eccentric karyosome
   b. May contain chromatoidal bars which have splintered ends
   c. Size 10-35 μm

4. Troph
   a. 1 nucleus; peripheral chromatin; eccentric karyosome
   b. Ingested bacteria, yeast
   c. Sluggish motility
   d. Size 15-50 μm

E. histolytica vs. E. coli

E. histolytica	E. coli
Central Karyosome Uniform Peripheral Chromatin	Eccentric Karyosome Irregular Peripheral Chromatin
Troph	
Active, Progressive Motility May Have Ingested RBCs	Sluggish Motility May Have Ingested Bacteria
Cyst	
1,2, or 4 Nuclei Chromatoidal Bars (Cigar-Shaped)	Up to 8 Nuclei Chromatoidal Bars (Pointed-Shaped)

Entamoeba hartmanni

1. Identical appearance to E. histolytica *except* smaller
   a. Cyst: less than 10 µm
   b. Troph: less than 12 µm

2. Nonpathogenic

Iodamoeba butschlii

1. Nonpathogenic

2. Cyst
   a. 1 nucleus, no peripheral chromatin, blot-like karyosome
   b. Glycogen vacuole present
   c. Size - 12 µm

3. Troph
   a. 1 nucleus; no peripheral chromatin; blot-like karyosome
   b. Glycogen vacuole may or may not be present
   c. Size 15 µm

Endolimax nana

1. Nonpathogenic

2. Cyst
   a. 4 nuclei, no peripheral chromatin, blot-like karyosomes
   b. Clear halo around karyosomes
   c. Size 8 µm - smallest ameba

3. Troph
   a. 1 nucleus, no peripheral chromatin, blot-like karyosomes
   b. Size 10 µm

FREE LIVING AMEBAE

Naegleria fowleri

1. Pathogenic; causes primary amebic meningoencephalitis *(P.A.M.)* and is usually fatal

2. Man becomes infected via cysts entering nasal passage while swimming and diving in ponds; cysts invade the CNS

3. Diagnostic stage - demonstrate cysts or trophs in CSF

Differentiating Amebae

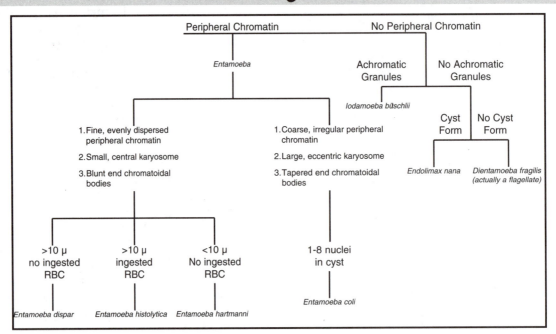

Acanthamoeba spp.

1. Usually affects immunocompromised patients

2. Causes keratitis and chronic form of meningoencephalitis

Disease Associated with Naegleria fowleri

Identification of Amebae from Graphic Images

Amoeba Trophs and Cysts

	Entamoeba histolytica/dispar	Entamoeba hartmanni	Entamoeba coli	Endolimax nana	Iodamoeba büschlii
Trophozoite					
Cyst					

Brooke MM, Melvin DM. *Morphology of Diagnostic Stages of Intestinal Parasites*, 2nd ed., CDC, 1984

FLAGELLATES

GENERAL CHARACTERISTICS

1. Motility by flagella

2. Infective stage - cyst *(usually ingested in contaminated food/water)* except when no cyst stage, then troph

3. Diagnostic stage - demonstrate cysts or trophs in feces

Dientamoeba fragilis

1. Studies indicate this is actually a flagellate and not an ameba as the name might suggest

2. No cyst stage is known

3. Troph
   a. Usually has 2 nuclei
   b. Nucleus - has a blot-like karyosome composed of 4-8 granules
   c. Lacks flagella

D. fragilis Has No Known Cyst Stage

Giardia lamblia

1. Pathogenic; causes duodenitis and malabsorption of fats

2. Cyst
   a. 4 nuclei
   b. Retracted flagella, axostyle and parabasal body
   c. Ovoid shaped
   d. Size 12 μm

3. Troph
   a. "Falling leaf" motility
   b. 2 nuclei
   c. Axostyle and parabasal body
   d. 4 pairs of flagella
   e. Sucker on underside of organism attaches to mucosa
   f. Tear-drop shaped
   g. Size 12 μm

4. Common in day-care centers and AIDS patients

Chilomastix mesnili

1. Nonpathogenic

2. Cyst
   a. 1 nucleus
   b. Lemon shaped
   c. Size 10 μm

3. Troph
   a. 1 nucleus
   b. Spiral groove - which gives it a "cork screw-type" motility

   c. Cytostome
   d. 6 flagella
   e. Tear-drop shaped
   f. Size 15 μm

Trichomonas sp.

1. T. vaginalis - pathogenic; others - nonpathogenic

2. No cyst stage

3. Species can be identified by source
   a. T. vaginalis - vagina or urethral discharge
   b. T. hominis - feces

Identification of Trichomonas Species by Specimen Source

4. Troph
   a. Tear drop shaped
   b. Undulating membrane attached to flagella; length of membrane used in differentiation
      ❖ *T. vaginalis - 1/2 length of organism*
      ❖ *T. hominis - full length of organism*

Intestinal Flagellates: Trophs and Cysts

	Trichomonas hominis	Chilomastix mesnili	Giardia lamblia
Trophozoite			
Cyst	No cyst Scale: 0 5 10 μm		

Characteristics of *Dientamoeba fragilis*

	Dientamoeba fragilis*
Trophozoite	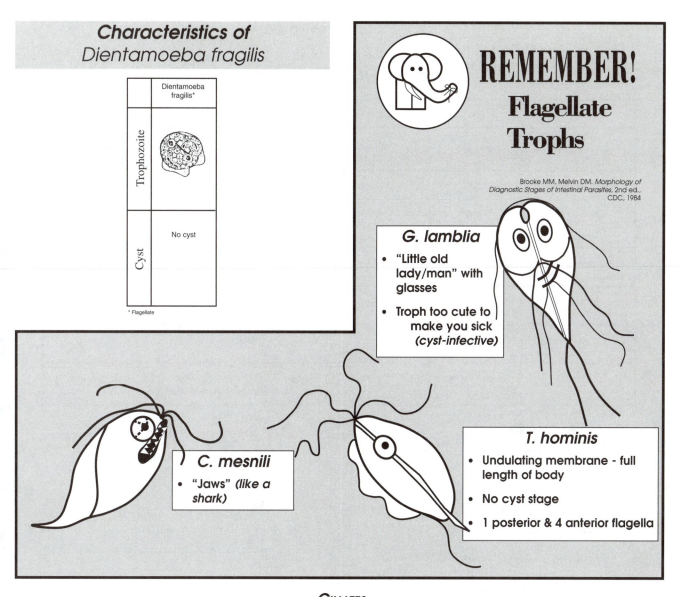
Cyst	No cyst

* Flagellate

REMEMBER!
Flagellate Trophs

Brooke MM, Melvin DM. *Morphology of Diagnostic Stages of Intestinal Parasites*, 2nd ed., CDC, 1984

G. lamblia

- "Little old lady/man" with glasses
- Troph too cute to make you sick (cyst-infective)

C. mesnili

- "Jaws" (like a shark)

T. hominis

- Undulating membrane - full length of body
- No cyst stage
- 1 posterior & 4 anterior flagella

CILIATES

GENERAL CHARACTERISTICS

1. Motility by cilia

2. Infective stage - cyst *(ingestion of contaminated food/water)*

3. Diagnostic stage - cysts or trophs in feces

Balantidium coli

1. Largest protozoan to infect man

2. Pathogenic

3. Cyst
   a. 2 nuclei
   b. Shape - round
   c. Double cell wall
   d. Size 50 µm

4. Troph
   a. Completely covered with cilia
   b. 2 nuclei *(one large kidney bean shaped macronucleus and one small round micronucleus)*
   c. Shape - oval
   d. Size 100 µm

Sole Ciliate:
Balantidium coli Troph and Cyst

	Trophozoite	Cyst
Balantidium coli		40 µm / 20 / 0

Brooke MM, Melvin DM. *Morphology of Diagnostic Stages of Intestinal Parasites*, 2nd ed., CDC, 1984

BLOOD AND TISSUE PROTOZOA

Plasmodium sp.

Characteristics of Plasmodia

	P. vivax	P. ovale	P. falciparum	P. malariae
Appearance of Red Cell	Enlarged	Enlarged	Normal	Normal
RBC Inclusions	Yes	Yes	Maurer's Dots	Zieman's Stippling
Trophozoite	Ameboid	Red Cell Containing Troph May Have Fimbriated Edges	Accole' or Applique' Forms (Troph at Margin of Red Cell); May Have Multiple Rings	Band
Average Number of Merozoites in Schizont	16	8	24	8
Stages Seen in Peripheral Blood	All	All	Young Ring and Few Gametocytes (Crescent or Banana-Shaped)	Few Rings, Mostly Trophs and Schizonts
Age of Infected Red Cells	Young	Young	All Ages	Old
Disease	Benign Tertian	Ovale Fever	Tertian Malaria, Blackwater Fever (Release of Hemoglobin into Urine)	Quartan Malaria

GENERAL CHARACTERISTICS

1. Causes malaria with bouts of fever and chills

2. Infective stage - sporozoites liberated into the bloodstream via bite of an infected female anopheline mosquito

3. Diagnostic stage - demonstration of characteristic parasite in Geimsa-stained blood smears (thick and thin); collect blood prior to fever spike

4. Resistance to infection
    a. Duffy negative red cells (Fy4Fy4) are resistant to P. vivax invasion
    b. HgbS resistance to invasion by P. falciparum
    c. G-6-PD deficient cells are more resistant to invasion by P. falciparum

Characteristics of Malarial Parasites

Identify Plasmodia Based on Graphic Images

Babesia

1. B. microti causes most infections in U.S. (Texas Cattle Fever)

2. Blood parasite of domestic animals

3. Infective stage - trophozoites liberated via the bite of deer tick

4. Confused with ring forms of P. falciparum

5. Tiny ring forms are in packets of four called "Maltese cross"

6. Can be transmitted via blood transfusion

7. Diagnostic stage - demonstration of characteristic ring forms in Giemsa stained blood smears (thick and thin)

Trypanosoma and Leishmania: Stages Seen Most Often

STAGE	DESCRIPTION	COMMON NAME:	FOUND IN:
Amastigote	No Flagella	Leishmanial Form	*L. donovani* *L. tropica* *L. braziliensis* *T. cruzi*
Trypomastigote	Flagella Originates at Posterior End of Organism	Trypanosomal Form	*T. rhodesiense* *T. gambiense* *T. cruzi*

GENERAL INFORMATION: TRYPANOSOMES

1. Hemoflagellates living in human blood and tissues

2. Clinical disease
   a. Chagas Disease - *T. cruzi*
   b. West African sleeping sickness - *T. gambiense*
   c. East African sleeping sickness - *T. rhodesiense*

Trypanosoma rhodesiense and gambiense

1. Infective stage - trypomastigote injected when Tse Tse fly takes a blood meal

2. Diagnostic stage - demonstration of trypomastigote from Giemsa stained thick and thin smears as well as aspirate from chancre at the site of the insect bite, enlarged lymph node and spinal fluid in human blood

Trypanosoma cruzi

1. Infective stage - trypomastigote injected when feces of reduvid bug are rubbed into bite wound when host scratches the bite

2. Diagnostic stage
   a. Demonstration of trypomastigote from Giemsa stained thick and thin smears as well as aspirate from chancre at the site of the insect bite, enlarged lymph node, and spinal fluid
   b. Demonstration of amastigote in macrophage

Characteristics of Trypanosomes

	T. cruzi	T. gambiense	T. rhodesiense
Diagnostic Stage	Amastigote (*Striated Muscle-Heart and GI Tract*) Trypomastigote (*Blood*)	Trypomastigote (*Blood*)	Trypomastigote (*Blood*)
Characteristics:	Trypomastigote - "C" or "U" shape	Long and Slender with Undulating Membrane	Long and Slender with Undulating Membrane
Type of Smear	Blood Smear: Giemsa-Stained Thick/Thin Aspirate: Chancre, Lymph Node or CSF	Blood Smear: Giemsa-Stained Thick/Thin Aspirate: Chancre, Lymph Node or CSF	Blood Smear: Giemsa-Stained Thick/Thin Aspirate: Chancre, Lymph Node or CSF
Human Infected By:	Feces from Reduvid Bug (*Kissing Bug*) Rubbed into Bite Wound; Blood Transfusions and Placental Transfer	Bite of *Tse Tse* Fly	Bite of *Tse Tse* Fly
Disease	Chagas' Disease South American Sleeping Sickness	West African Sleeping Sickness	East African Sleeping Sickness

200

GENERAL INFORMATION: LEISHMANIA

1. Clinical disease
   a. L. donovani - causes Visceral Leishmaniasis or Kala Azar
   b. L. tropica - causes Cutaneous Leishmaniasis or Oriental sore
   c. L. braziliensis - causes Mucocutaneous Leishmaniasis or Espundia

2. Infective stage - promastigotes released via bite of a sandfly

3. Diagnostic stage - demonstration of amastigote in macrophage in Giemsa stained smears from aspirates or biopsies of skin lesions

INTESTINAL COCCIDIA

GENERAL CHARACTERISTICS

1. Prevalent in AIDS patients / immunocompromised persons

2. Diagnostic stage: oöcysts passed in feces

3. Infective stage: oöcysts

Cryptosporidium parvum

1. Method of infection
   a. Infective oöcysts transmitted via fecal-oral route

2. Clinical disease
   a. Illness is self-limiting in

immunosufficient persons
   b. Immunodeficient persons experience severe diarrhea, fever, nausea, abdominal pain and weight loss

3. Diagnosis
   a. Modified acid-fast stain
      ❖ Oöcysts stain red against blue background (acid fast positive)
      ❖ Average size is *4-6 µm*

Cyclospora cayetanensis

1. Method of infection
   a. Infective oöcysts ingested in contaminated food or water
   b. Outbreaks have been associated with contaminated berries

2. Clinical disease - indistinguishable from cryptosporidiosis

3. Diagnosis
   a. Modified acid-fast stain
      ❖ *Oöcysts stain from light pink to deep red (acid-fast variable)*
      ❖ *Average size is 8-10 µm (larger than C. parvum)*

Isospora belli

1. Method of infection
   a. Direct transmission to humans via fecally contaminated food or water

2. Clinical disease
   a. Often asymptomatic and self-limiting
   b. Symptoms range from mild gastro-intestinal distress to severe dysentery

3. Diagnosis
   a. Modified acid-fast stain
      ❖ *Sporoblasts and/or sporocysts stain deep red (acid-fast positive)*

Microsporidia

1. Newest group of obligate intracellular protozoa

2. *Enterocytozoon bieneusi* - most common microsporidia causing enteritis in AIDS patients

3. Organism is very small *(1.5 - 4 µm)*

4. Characteristic feature - spores containing a polar tubule, used to inject infective spore contents into host cells

5. Method of infection
   a. Most likely by ingestion of spores
   b. Inhalation of spores, ocular exposure and sexual intercourse may also be routes of transmission

6. Clinical disease
   a. Similar to cryptosporidiosis
   b. Spores are very resistant

7. Diagnosis
   a. Modified Trichrome stain
      ❖ *Concentration 10 x higher than traditional trichrome stain*
      ❖ *Spore wall stains bright pink; background stains green or blue (depending on counterstain)*
   b. Serological testing
   c. PCR - research labs only
   d. Electron microscopy - necessary to speciate; not available in most clinical laboratories

TISSUE COCCIDIA

GENERAL CHARACTERISTICS

1. Prevalent in AIDS patients / immunocompromised persons

2. Worldwide distribution

Toxoplasma gondii

1. Method of infection
   a. Definitive host: house cat
   b. Accidental ingestion / inhalation of oöcysts from cat feces *(when cleaning litter box)*
   c. Ingestion of undercooked meat *(cattle, sheep, pigs)* - intermediate hosts
   d. Transmitted across the placenta to fetus from mother who acquires first infection during pregnancy

2. Clinical disease
   a. Infection in immunosufficient persons usually asymptomatic
   b. Symptoms resemble infectious mononucleosis
   c. Can cause death of fetus, mental retardation or blindness when transmitted across placenta

3. Diagnosis
   a. Serological testing *(EIA, IFA)*; important in detecting neonatal toxoplasmosis *(IgM antibodies)*

Pneumocystis carinii

1. Recently classified as a fungus, based on DNA studies

2. Causative agent of atypical interstitial plasma-cell pneumonia (PCP)

3. Identified with Gomori's methenamine silver stain *(silver impregnation stain)*

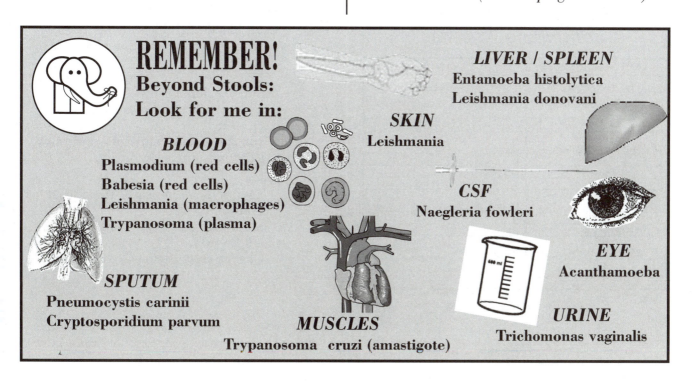

REMEMBER!
Beyond Stools:
Look for me in:

BLOOD
Plasmodium (red cells)
Babesia (red cells)
Leishmania (macrophages)
Trypanosoma (plasma)

SPUTUM
Pneumocystis carinii
Cryptosporidium parvum

SKIN
Leishmania

CSF
Naegleria fowleri

MUSCLES
Trypanosoma cruzi (amastigote)

LIVER / SPLEEN
Entamoeba histolytica
Leishmania donovani

EYE
Acanthamoeba

URINE
Trichomonas vaginalis

202

Some Diseases Caused by Human Parasites

DISEASE	PARASITE
Amebiasis	*Entamoeba histolytica*
Anemia	Hookworms
Blindness	*Onchocerca volvulus*
Chagas' Disease	*Trypanosoma cruzi*
Cysticercosis	*Taenia solium*
Cutaneous Larval Migrans	Dog and cat hookworms (*Ancylostoma braziliensis*)
Visceral Larval Migrans	Dog and cat ascarids (*Toxocara canis and cati*)
Dum Dum Fever (kala-azar)	*Leishmania donovani*
Elephantiasis	*Wuchereria bancrofti, Brugia malayi*
Espundia	*Leishmania braziliensis*
Hydatid Disease	*Echinococcus granulosus*
Malaria	*Plasmodium* spp.
Meningioencephalitis	*Naegleria fowleri*
Oriental Sore	*Leishmania tropica*
Sleeping Sickness, East African	*Trypanosoma rhodesiense*
Sleeping Sickness, West African	*Trypanosoma gambiense*
Sparganosis	*Diphyllobothrium latum*
Trichinosis	*Trichinella spiralis*
Toxoplasmosis	*Toxoplasma gondii*

Vectors & Insects Transmitting Parasites

VECTORS & INSECTS	PARASITES
MOSQUITOES	
Anopheles	Malaria, Wuchereria bancrofti
Culex	Wuchereria bancrofti
Mansonia	Wuchereria bancrofti, B. malayi
FLIES	
Simulium (*black fly*)	Onchocerca volvulus
Chrysops fly	Loa Loa
Sandfly	Leishmania
Tse Tse fly	T. gambiense, T. rhodesiense
FLEAS	
Dog flea	Dipylidium caninum
Rat flea	Hymenolepis diminuta
Copepods (*water flea*)	D. latum
TICKS	
Deer tick	Babesia
BUGS	
Reduvid bug	T. cruzi

MISCELLANEOUS TESTS

1. Occult blood - "Hidden Blood"
   a. Used for early detection of colorectal cancer
   b. Principle - pseudoperoxidase activity of hemoglobin releases oxygen from hydrogen peroxide to oxidize guaiac reagent
   c. Interpretation - blue color indicates gastrointestinal bleeding
2. Fecal fat
   a. Steatorrhea - indicated when fecal fat excretion > 6g/day
   b. Stain with Sudan III, Sudan IV, or Oil Red O
   c. Characteristic orange-red staining

PARASITOLOGY SAMPLE QUESTIONS

1. Which of the following organisms causes Visceral Larval Migrans?
   A. *Ancyclostoma brazilensis*
   B. *Ascaris lumbricoides*
   C. *Strongyloides stercoralis*
   D. *Toxocara canis*

2. Enterobius vermicularis infection is usually diagnosed by finding eggs from
   A. Cellulose tape preps
   B. Concentrated stool samples
   C. Iodine wet mounts from fresh stool
   D. Sedimented stool samples

3. The infective stage for *Strongyloides stercoralis* is the
   A. Ova
   B. Filariform larvae
   C. Rhabditiform larvae
   D. Free living adult

4. If humans ingest the egg of *Taenia solium*, they may develop
   A. Hydatid Disease
   B. Sparganosis
   C. Trichinosis
   D. Cystercercosis

5. A silver methenamine stained slide of a bronchial washing from an AIDs patient is examined. Which of the following parasites is most likely to be identified?
   A. *Cryptosporidium parvum*
   B. *Toxoplasma gondii*
   C. *Strongyloides stercoralis*
   D. *Pneumocystis carinii*

6. A blood smear showed crescent shaped gametocytes in several red cells. What is the most probable identity of the organisms?
   A. *Babesia microti*
   B. *Plasmodium falciparum*
   C. *Plasmodium malariae*
   D. *Leishmania donovani*

7. Which organism is transmitted to humans by ticks and blood transfusions?
   A. *Babesia*
   B. *Wuchereria bancrofti*
   C. *Leishmania donovani*
   D. *Trypanosoma cruzi*

8. The ameba which can cause liver or lung abscesses is
   A. *Balantidium coli*
   B. *Dientamoeba fragilis*
   C. *Endolimax nana*
   D. *Entamoeba histolytica*

9. Which of the following can cause a fatal meningoencephalitis?
   A. *Balantidium coli*
   B. *Entamoeba histolytica*
   C. *Naegleria fowleri*
   D. *Toxoplasmosis gondii*

10. The trophozoite of which organism is characterized by "falling leaf motility", two nuclei, an axostyle, 4 pair of flagella and a sucker on the underside of the organism?
    A. *Chilomastix mesinili*
    B. *Giardia lamblia*
    C. *Trichomonas hominis*
    D. *Trichomonas vaginalis*

11. Which of the following eggs may not be detected in zinc flotation procedures?
    A. *Ascaris lumbricoides* (fertile)
    B. *Trichiura trichuris*
    C. *Schistosoma mansoni*
    D. *Taenia solium*

12. Which trophozoite is suspected if ingested red cells are seen on a saline wet prep?
    A. *Entamoeba coli*
    B. *Entamoeba histolytica*
    C. *Endolimax nana*
    D. *Iodamoeba butschlii*

13. Pregnant women are to avoid cleaning litter boxes of their house cats until after delivery to prevent congenital infection of
    A. *Ancylostoma caninum*
    B. *Dipylidium caninum*
    C. *Toxocara cati*
    D. *Toxoplasma gondii*

14. A patient visiting from overseas is hospitalized due to suspected tuberculosis. The sputum sample submitted to the laboratory is bloody with orange-brown flecks. Preliminary TB tests are negative. Which of the following parasites may be suspected?
    A. *Ascaris lumbricoides*
    B. *Fasciolopsis buski*
    C. *Schistosoma japonicum*
    D. *Paragonimus westermani*

15. Which of the following cysts has a nucleus with a prominent karyosome, a clear halo, no achromatic granules, no peripheral chromatin?
    A. *Entamoeba histolytica*
    B. *Entamoeba hartmanni*
    C. *Endolimax nana*
    D. *Iodamoeba bütschlii*

16. Differential diagnosis of *Cryptosporidium parvum* and *Cyclospora cayetanensis* is based on:

A. Clinical symptoms
B. Oöcyst size - Cyclospora is larger
C. Oöcyst morphology
D. Acid fast stained smears - Cyclospora is NOT acid fast

ANSWERS AND RATIONALE

1. D

Dog & Cat Ascarids *(Toxocara canis and cati)* cause Visceral Larval Migrans. Option A *(Dog and Cat Hookworms)* causes Cutaneous Larval Migrans. Option B may cause pneumonia from migration through liver and lungs or bowel obstruction. Option C may cause abdominal pain, vomiting and diarrhea.

2. A

The female migrates to the anal opening (usually at night) and lays eggs in the perianal opening. The cellulose tape *(scotch tape)* prep will pick up the eggs and when stuck to a slide will allow microscopic viewing.

3. B

The filariform larvae produces a proteolytic enzyme which allows it to penetrate man's skin.

4. D

Taenia solium causes cystercercosis. Option A results from an infection with *Echinococcus granulosus.* Option B occurs when man is the intermediate host of *Diphyllobothrium latum.* Option C occurs when the larval forms of *Trichinella spiralis* encysts in the muscle.

5. D

Pneumocystis carinii causes interstitial plasma cell pneumonia and is life threatening to immunocompromised patients. Option A can cause profuse diarrhea in AIDS patients and is identified using an acid fast stain. Option B leads to involve the CNS with various neurological symptoms and is diagnosed using serologic techniques. Option C may cause death and has a high rate of autoinfection in immunocompromised hosts but is diagnosed by characteristic ova or larvae in stool samples.

6. B

The crescent shaped gametocytes is characteristic of *P. falciparum.*

7. A

There is documentation of *Babesia* transmission via blood transfusion as well as deer ticks. The other three options are not transmitted by a tick bite (*Wucheria* - mosquito, *Leishmania* - sandfly, *T. cruzi* - reduvid bug).

8. D

A hallmark of *E. histolytica* is its ability to form extraintestinal abscesses. Options A and B are not amebas and do not cause extraintestinal abcesses. Option C is an ameba but is nonpathogenic.

9. C

Naegleria fowleri can cause primary amebic meningoencephalitis; infections may go undetected unless a direct wet prep of the CSF is performed.

10. B

Other choices have one nuclei and no sucker.

11. C

The eggs of *S. mansoni* are too large and heavy to float. Other eggs which may not be demonstrated in the zinc flotation procedure are those with operculi such as *Diphyllobothrium latum*

12. B

The diagnostic feature of *E. histolytica* is the finding of ingested red cells in trophs. Options A, C and D may exhibit ingested bacteria.

13. D

The definitive host of *T. gondii* is the cat. Immunocompromised patients as well as pregnant women are advised to avoid cleaning litter boxes to prevent exposure. Most people exhibit few or no symptoms due to infections, but immunocompromised patients may experience cyst rupture leading to internal lesions while pregnant women may pass the infection transplacentally leading to congenital problems.

14. D

P. *westermani*, a lung trematode found in the far East and Aftica, encapsulates in the lungs. The brownish-yellow eggs may be found in sputum or fecal samples. Eggs of options A, B and C are found in the stool.

15. C

Options A and B exhibit peripheral chromatin. Option D has achromatic granules.

16. B

Cyclospora is about twice the size of Cryptosporidium. Both organisms are acid fast *(Cyclospora is variable)* and have similar morphology and clinical symptoms.

☞ Be able to recognize the more common parasite eggs, cysts or trophozoites from graphic images.

MOLECULAR DIAGNOSTICS AND GENETICS

by Marcia Firmani

Key Terminology

Agarose – a gelatinous carbohydrate made up of seaweed

Allele – alternative forms of a gene or genetic marker

Cell nucleus – carry genetic information but only express about 20% of genes at any particular time

Codon – 3 bases in mRNA that code for amino acid production

Diploid - cells that carry two genome copies

Exon - coding sequence

Gene Expression - protein synthesis - is tightly controlled and regulated

Genetic Code – combination of nucleotides that build the different codons

Genome - an organisms total DNA contents

Genotype – the observed alleles for an individual at a genetic locus

Haploid- -cells that contain a single copy of the genome such as germ cells or gametes

Haplotype – series of alleles on a single chromosome

Heterozygous – two different alleles at a locus

Homozygous – two identical alleles at a locus

Intron- non-coding sequence between 2 exons

Ligation – joining reaction between DNA molecules involving 3'-hydroxy and a 5'phosphate termini as well as the covalent joining of two segments into one uninterrupted strand in a DNA duplex

Linkage disequilibrium – allelic association when closely linked alleles are inherited together during many generations

Locus – location in the genome of a gene or genetic marker

Molecular Diagnostics - the use of DNA, RNA or mRNA to identify and/or characterize diseases caused by infectious agents or gene abnormalities

Mutations - changes in the DNA sequence

Penetrance - the probability of expressing a phenotype, given a particular genotype

Phenotype – observable characteristics

Polymorphism – a difference in a nucleotide

Proteins – made up of amino acids

Protein expression - Different proteins are expressed in different cells according to the function of the cell

Sequence - the order of nucleotide bases along a DNA strand

STR - short tandem repeats (di-, tri-, tetranucleotide repeats)

Susceptibility gene – a gene which influences the risk of developing a characteristic or disease, but is not causative

Transcription – process where genetic information in DNA is copied into messenger RNA (mRNA) utilizing the RNA polymerase enzyme

Transgene - a gene that is introduced randomly somewhere in the genome

Translation – mRNA used as a template to synthesize protein within the endoplasmic reticulum of the cell cytoplasm

VNTR - variable number of tandem repeats (14–30 bp repeats)

Molecular Diagnostics

PURPOSE

1. Monitor diseases more accurately
   a. Allows for early treatment and better patient care

2. Determine most appropriate treatment
   a. Reduces or eliminates unnecessary treatment
   b. Reduces or eliminates inadequate treatment
   c. Yields greater cost effectiveness

3. Reduce patient morbidity and mortality

Genetics in Molecular Biology

DNA—THE CHEMICAL BASIS OF HEREDITY

1. Biological "blueprint"
   a. Carries information for cells to live, grow, differentiate, and replicate
   b. Provides consistency and variability

GENETIC UNITS OF HUMAN DNA

1. Nuclear DNA
   a. Diploid genome *(two sets of chromosomes)*
   b. Packaged in 23 pairs of chromosomes
   c. 22 homologous pairs *(autosomes)*
   d. 2 sex chromosomes (XX or XY)
   e. 6 billion bases
   f. Approximately 30,000 genes

2. Mitochondrial DNA
   a. 16,569 base pairs
   b. 37 genes
   c. Higher mutation rate
   d. 128 naturally occurring polymorphisms
   e. Maternal inheritance

3. DNA is comprised of 4 building blocks or nucleotide bases:

   A = adenine;   T = thymine

   C = cytosine;   G = guanine

4. DNA double helix
   a. Nucleotide bases pair together to form "base pairs"

   A always binds to T   A – T
   C always binds to G   C – G

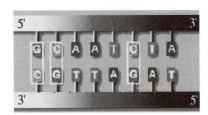

   b. The two strands of the DNA double helix are oriented in opposite directions.
   c. The beginning of a DNA strand is called the 5' end
   d. The end of a DNA strand is called the 3' end

REMEMBER!
4 Nucleotide Bases

G–CAT

CELLULAR DIVISION:

1. DNA strands separate

2. Complementary DNA strands are generated

3. Two duplicate DNA sequences produced

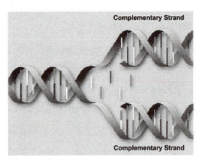

THE HUMAN CHROMOSOME

1. Single linear duplex DNA

2. Numerous protein interactions

3. DNA from a single cell measures approximately 2 meters in length

4. Histones – Nucleosomes – Solenoids

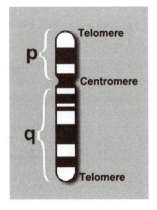

HUMAN GENE STRUCTURE

1. Genes
   a. Discrete sections of chromosome called exons which are separated by introns
   b. Sequence of base pairs encodes information for proteins.
   c. Different sequence = different protein

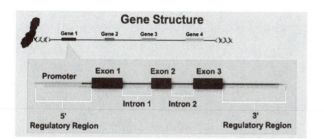

TRANSCRIPTION

1. The mRNA sequence - complimentary to the DNA template
   a. Except that uracil (U) bases replace thymine (T) bases.

2. During transcription, mRNA is processed by:
   a. Splicing – removal of introns
   b. Capping – modify the 5' end
   c. Polyadenylations – add adenines to the 3' end (also called the poly-A tail)

REMEMBER!

INtrons remain IN the nucleus; EXons EXit the nucleus

Polly splices the neutrons

Puts on her cap *(capping the 5' end)*

Adds her name to the 3' end *(the "Polly" or poly-A tail)*

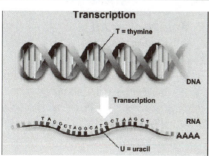
Transcription

The Central Dogma of Molecular Biology

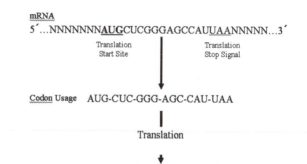

DNA → (transcription) → RNA → (translation) → PROTEIN

TRANSLATION / GENETIC CODE

mRNA
5´...NNNNNNN**AUG**CUCGGGAGCCAU**UAA**NNNNN...3´

Translation Start Site / Translation Stop Signal

Codon Usage   AUG-CUC-GGG-AGC-CAU-UAA

Translation

Peptide Sequence   Met-Leu-Gly-Ser-His

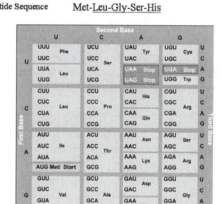

Genes

REMEMBER!

Order of Nucleotides = Amino Acid

Order of Amino Acids = Protein

GENETIC MUTATIONS

1. General types of Mutations
   a. Large scale mutations
   b. Gain and loss of chromosomal region
   c. Translocation of parts of a chromosome
   d. Small scale mutations

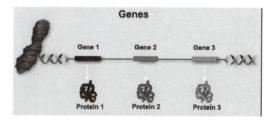

210

e. Nucleotide base substitutions, deletions or insertions

2. Specific types of Mutations
   a. Germ-line mutations
      ❖ *Can be inherited and transmitted*
      ❖ *Considered a polymorphism if germ line mutation present in a population at a relative frequency of 1%*
   b. Missense mutation
      ❖ *Nucleotide in a sequence altered such that amino acid changes*
   c. Silent mutation
      ❖ *Nucleotide in sequence altered such that amino acid does not change*
   d. Nonsense mutation
      ❖ *Nucleotide changes such that a stop codon is introduced*
   e. Frameshift mutation
      ❖ *Nucleotide either deleted or added to a sequence such that protein produced is altered*

	MUTATION TYPE	WHAT HAPPENS
	Germ-Line	Can be inherited and transmitted
	Missense	Nucleotide in a sequence is altered such that the amino acid changes
	Silent	Nucleotide in a sequence is altered such that the amino acid does not change
	Nonsense	Nucleotide changes such that a stop codon is introduced
	Frameshift	Nucleotide is either deleted or added to a sequence ➜ the protein produced is altered

SOMATIC MUTATIONS

1. Alterations in somatic cells, mutations can accumulate in daughter cells, causing the cells to divide uncontrollably, enhanced cellular division can result in tumor development

2. Mutations occur:
   a. During DNA replication
      ❖ *Incorporation of the wrong bases*
   b. When exposed to mutagens (*DNA damaging agents*)
      ❖ *Radiation, UV, x-rays, radioactivity*
      ❖ *Chemicals that bind to or react with DNA*
      ❖ *Chemicals that metabolize to generate reactive oxygen compounds that damage DNA*

DNA REPAIR

1. Mechanisms that prevent accumulation and propagation of most mutations

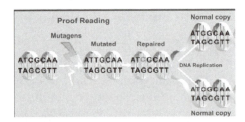

2. Genetic diseases can be divided into three main categories:
   a. Chromosomal defects
      ❖ *Chromosomal defects include gain or loss of a chromosome (aneuploidy)*
      ❖ *Part or parts of a chromosome (deletion)*
      ❖ *Transfer of a segment of one chromosome to another (translocation)*
      ❖ *Reversal of a segment of a chromosome (inversion)*
   b. Single-gene disorders
      ❖ *Usually classified as either dominant or recessive, sex-linked, or autosomal*
   c. Multigenic traits
      ❖ *Disorders which are difficult to analyze genetically because they do not show clear inheritance patterns and environmental factors can contribute to disease development*

TYPE OF DEFECT	DESCRIPTION	DESCRIPTION
Aneuploidy	Gain or loss of a chromosome	
Deletion	Loss of part of a chromosome	
Translocation	Transfer of a segment of one chromosome to another	
Inversion	Reversal of a segment of a chromosome	

MENDELIAN GENETICS

1. Genes are inherited in pairs: one copy from mom and the other from dad

2. Autosomal traits are inherited on an autosome (*not the X or Y chromosome*)
   a. Autosomal dominant
      - *A single gene is sufficient to generate a specific phenotype*
      - *Affected individuals have an affected parent*
      - *Each child of an affected parent has a 50% risk of inheriting the abnormal allele*
      - *Unaffected individuals do not have affected children*
      - *Males and females are affected equally*

Example 1:
Two carrier parents of an autosomal dominant disease (D):

	D	d
D	DD	Dd
d	Dd	dd

Genotype
1/4 (25%) = Normal – dd
1/2 (50%) = Heterozygous affected– Dd
1/4 (25%) = Homozygous affected – DD
Phenotype
1/4 (25%) = Normal – dd
3/4 (75%) = Affected – DD, Dd

Example 2:
One affected parent and one carrier parent of an autosomal dominant disorder (D):

	d	d
D	Dd	Dd
d	dd	dd

Genotype and Phenotype
1/2 (50%) = Normal - dd
1/2 (50%) = Affected - Dd

   b. Autosomal recessive
      - *Requires two genes, one from each parent, for the recessive phenotype*
      - *Located on an autosome*
      - *Carriers – one dominant gene and one recessive gene – masks recessive phenotype*
      - *Carrier parents have a 25% chance of having an affected child*
      - *Affected individuals may have unaffected parents (disease skips generations carried by but not displayed by carriers)*

Example 1:
Two carrier parents of an autosomal recessive disease (r):

	R	r
R	RR	Rr
r	Rr	rr

Genotype
1/4 (25%) = Normal – RR
1/4 (25%) = Affected – rr
1/2 (50%) = Carriers – Rr
Phenotype
3/4 (75%) = Normal – RR, Rr
1/4 (25%) = Affected – rr

Example 2: One normal and one carrier parent of an autosomal disorder:

	R	r
R	RR	Rr
R	RR	Rr

Genotype
1/2 (50%) = Normal – RR
0 = Affected
1/2 (50%) = Carriers – Rr
Phenotype
All (100%) = Normal – RR, Rr

3. X-linked traits occur from mutations in the X-chromosome
   a. X-linked recessive
      ❖ *Affected individuals are primarily male*
      ❖ *All female offspring of an affected male will be carriers of the disease gene (obligate carriers)*
      ❖ *Male offspring of affected men are always unaffected*
      ❖ *Require two copies of the defective gene in females, but in males only one copy is needed as they only have one X chromosome*
   b. X-linked dominant
      ❖ *All female offspring of affected males will be affected*
      ❖ *No male offspring of affected males will be affected*
      ❖ *An affected female has a 50% chance of having an affected child*
      ❖ *All affected individuals have an affected parent*

REMEMBER!
Mendelian Genetics

Dominant: 1 of me is ENOUGH.

Recessive: It takes 2 of us.

RECOMBINATION

1. Exchange of genetic material between homologous chromosome pairs

2. Segments of DNA exchanged with the other chromosome of the pair

3. Shuffling of genetic material

4. The basis of genetic diversity in sexually reproducing organisms

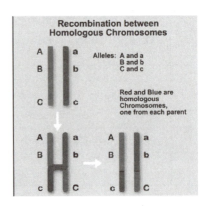

Recombination between Homologous Chromosomes

Alleles: A and a
B and b
C and c

Red and Blue are homologous Chromosomes, one from each parent

MITOSIS

1. Cell division of somatic cells

2. A diploid cell generates an identical diploid cell

3. Normally no recombination takes place

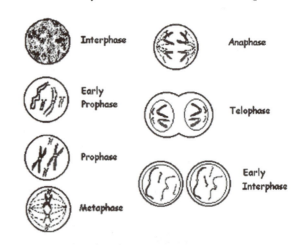

Interphase

Early Prophase

Prophase

Metaphase

Anaphase

Telophase

Early Interphase

REMEMBER!
Mitosis

The **Pro** **Met** **Ana** at the **Tele**phone to **Introduce** himself.

Prophase
Metaphase
Anaphase
Telophase
Interphase

MEIOSIS

1. Occurs during gamete formation

2. A diploid progenitor cell generates four haploid gametes

3. Meiotic recombination is frequent

Interphase

Early Prophase I

Prophase I

Metaphase I

Anaphase I

Telophase I

Prophase II

Metaphase II

Anaphase II

Telophase II

Molecular Techniques

BASIC STEPS IN ISOLATING DNA FROM CLINICAL SPECIMENS

Separate WBCs from RBCs, if necessary

↓

Lyse WBCs or other nucleated cells

↓

Denature / Digest proteins

↓

Separate **contaminants** (e.g., proteins, heme) from DNA

↓

Precipitate DNA, if necessary

↓

Resuspend DNA in final buffer

REMEMBER!
Isolation of DNA from Clinical Specimens

Some = Separate
Lazy = Lyse
Dogs = Denature
Can = Contaminants
Play = Precipitate
Right = Resuspend

RESTRICTION ENDONUCLEASE

1. Bacterial enzymes that cut or nick specific sites of a DNA sequence

2. Restriction site defined by short sequence, usually 4, 6, or 8 bases in length

3. Short sequences recognized by restriction enzymes, usually palindromes

Staggered Ends	Staggered Ends	Blunt Ends
BamH1	**KpnI**	**HaeIII**
↓	↓	↓
G GATCC	GGTAC C	GG CC
CCTAG G	C CATGG	CC GG
↑	↑	↑

REMEMBER!
Palindromes

Palindromes are the same sequence on both DNA strands when read in either direction:
5' – GGTACC – 3'
3' – CCATGG – 5'

DENATURATION

1. Denaturation of DNA describes separation of duplex strands through one of several conditions:
   a. Alkaline pH
   b. Ionic strength of high salt solution
   c. Elevated temperature

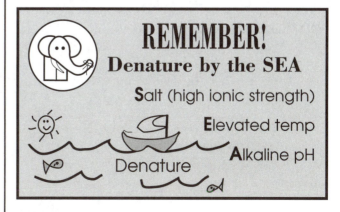

REMEMBER!
Denature by the SEA

Salt (high ionic strength)

Elevated temp

Alkaline pH

Denature

DNA SEQUENCING

1. Ability to determine nucleotide sequences of DNA molecules
   a. Gold standard for mutation detection
   b. Gold standard for histocompatibility typing
   c. Manual vs. automated methods
   d. Uses high-resolution denaturing polyacrylamide gels

2. Resolution of large fragments of ssDNA that differ by a single base

DNA MICROARRAYS

1. Useful technique to study gene expression of thousands of genes at the same time

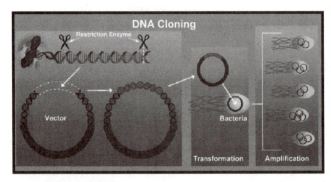

GENE CLONING

1. Cloning is the process of isolating and amplifying a specific gene or DNA fragment using a vector, such as a plasmid and a cell (i.e. *Escherichia coli* bacteria).

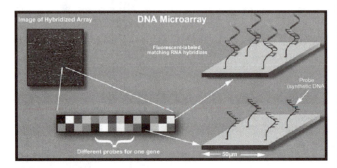

POLYMORPHIC MARKERS

1. Areas in the chromosomal DNA that contain polymorphisms or alterations in a way that can be used to identify a specific trait

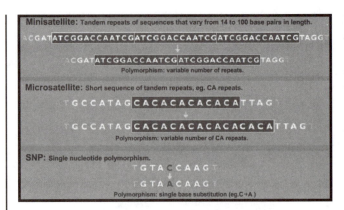

SINGLE NUCLEOTIDE POLYMORPHISMS (SNP)

1. Changes in a nucleotide sequence at specific points throughout genomic DNA; these alterations do not usually produce changes in an individual's physical appearance, but are shared in groups of people. SNP's can provide valuable information for a variety of clinical applications.

IN-SITU HYBRIDIZATION

1. Hybridization of a probe to DNA in morphologically preserved tissue or cells

Amplification Techniques

COPY NUMBER AMPLIFICATION

1. Polymerase chain reaction (PCR)

2. Ligase chain reaction (LCR)

3. Nucleic acid sequence-based amplification (NASBA)

4. Transcription-mediated amplification (TMA)

5. Strand-displacement amplification (SDA)

SIGNAL AMPLIFICATION TECHNIQUEES

1. Branched DNA (bDNA)

2. Hybrid capture assay (HCA)

THE POLYMERASE CHAIN REACTION (PCR)

1. PCR proceeds by incubation at three different temperatures:
   a. Denaturation (95°C) – unwinds the target dsDNA
   b. Annealing (60°C) – hybridize the primers to the single-stranded template
   c. Extension (72°C) – polymerize the primer into the full-length gene of interest
   d. Each cycle doubles amount of DNA

ORNL-DWG 91M-17476

DNA Amplification Using Polymerase Chain Reaction

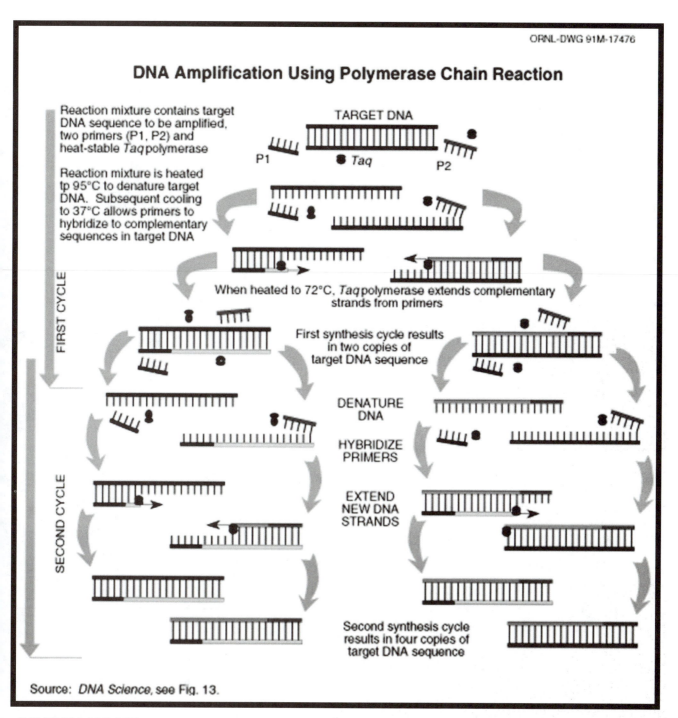

Source: *DNA Science*, see Fig. 13.

CONTROLS FOR PCR

1. Blank reaction
   a. Controls for contamination
   b. Contains all reagents except DNA template

2. Negative control reaction
   a. Controls for specificity of the amplification reaction
   b. Contains all reagents and a DNA template lacking the target sequence

3. Positive control reaction
   a. Controls for sensitivity
   b. Contains all reagents and a known target-containing DNA template

REVERSE TRANSCRIPTION POLYMERASE CHAIN REACTION (RT-PCR)

1. Creates a complementary piece of DNA (cDNA) from an RNA target sequence followed by basic PCR to amplify the cDNA target sequence

REAL-TIME PCR

1. A qualitative and/or quantitative technique – allows visibility of amplification process in real time

STRAND DISPLACEMENT AMPLIFICATION (SDA)

1. Target amplification that uses heat denaturation, annealing and extension to create an altered target with a restriction endonuclease recognition site.

NUCLEIC ACID SEQUENCE BASED AMPLIFICATION (NASBA)

1. A nucleic acid sequence based amplification technique that amplifies RNA and rRNA

HYBRID CAPTURE

1. Nucleic acid amplification technique used for RNA or DNA applications

BRANCH CHAIN DNA (BDNA)

1. Uses a series of hybrid probes to elicit a signal amplification to detect specific RNA sequences

Electrophoresis Technology

ELECTROPHORESIS OF NUCLEIC ACIDS

1. Nucleic acids separated based on size and charge

2. DNA molecules migrate in electrical field at a rate inversely proportional to molecular size *(number of base pairs)*

3. Employs a sieve-like matrix *(agarose or polyacrylamide)* and an electrical field

4. DNA possesses net negative charge and migrates towards positively charged anode

POLYACRYLAMIDE GEL VARIATIONS

1. Vertical electrophoresis

2. Can detect
   a. Very small pieces of DNA
   b. A single nucleotide mutation

FACTORS AFFECTING MIGRATION RATE

1. Matrix type and porosity (%) of the gel (gel casting)

2. Net charge of nucleic acid molecule

3. DNA conformation

4. Electric field strength

5. Temperature of gel

6. Nucleic acid base composition

7. Presence of intercalating dyes

8. Type and strength of buffer

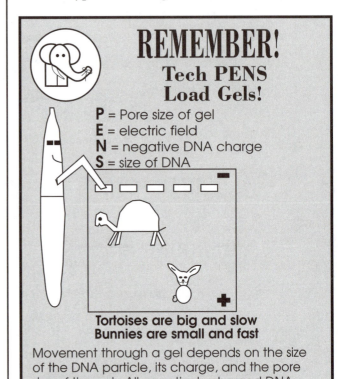

REMEMBER!
Tech PENS Load Gels!

P = Pore size of gel
E = electric field
N = negative DNA charge
S = size of DNA

Tortoises are big and slow
Bunnies are small and fast

Movement through a gel depends on the size of the DNA particle, its charge, and the pore size of the gel. All negatively charged DNA particles move toward the anode, but the larger pieces have a harder time squeezing through the small pores in the gel and cannot move as fast, i.e., as far, as the smaller pieces.

PULSED FIELD GEL ELECTROPHORESIS OF DNA (PFGE)

1. PFGE employed in the analysis of DNA fragments up to 100 kb in size

2. Separation accomplished using a pulsed electrical field

3. PFGE commonly used for genotyping prokaryotes

Blotting Techniques

SOUTHERN BLOT

1. Detects specific DNA sequences

2. DNA denatured in the gel by an increase in pH

3. DNA transferred to a membrane by capillary action with a high salt solution

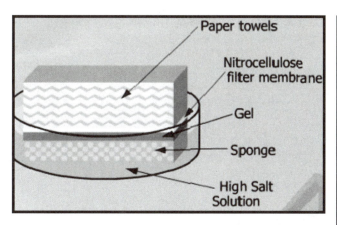

Paper towels

Nitrocellulose filter membrane

Gel

Sponge

High Salt Solution

4. Labeled complimentary probe used for detection

5. Procedure:
   a. Genomic DNA cut with restriction enzymes
   b. DNA electrophoresed
   c. Gel submerged in an alkaline solution to denature the DNA
   d. DNA transferred onto a nitrocellulose membrane by capillary action
   e. Membrane mixed with a solution containing labeled probe
      ❖ *Probe will hybridize to complimentary piece of DNA on gel*
   f. Membrane washed to remove excess, unbound probe
   g. Membrane developed and visualized using either radioactive isotopes, chemiluminescent dyes, or colorimetric techniques

REMEMBER!

Southern Blot – DNA

Southern Belle named "Dee" for DNA

NORTHERN BLOT

1. Detect specific sequences of RNA

2. RNA transferred to membrane by capillary action using a high salt solution

3. Labeled complimentary probe used for detection

REMEMBER!

Northern Blot – RNA

Northern Eskimo with an RNA Virus because it's Cold

Ah-Choo!

WESTERN BLOT

1. Protein run on SDS- polyacrylamide gel electrophoresis (PAGE)

2. Protein electrically transferred to membrane (electro-transfer)

3. Membrane incubated with a primary antibody and blocking solution

4. Membrane washed and incubated with secondary antibody and blocking solution

5. Membrane washed and rinsed with substrate buffer

6. Substrate added and developed

REMEMBER!

Western Blot – Protein

Western Cowboy Eats his Protein

Molecular Diagnostics Sample Questions

1. Molecular diagnostics utilizes principles of molecular biology to do all of the following except:
   a. Identify individuals at risk for acquiring disease
   b. Diagnose infectious diseases
   c. Determine appropriate treatments
   d. Increase morbidity

2. Human genome consists of:
   a. Haploid copy number
   b. 22 chromosomes
   c. Circular structure
   d. Approximately 6 billion bases

3. The migration rate of a macromolecule through a gel matrix during electrophoresis depends on:
   a. Net charge on the molecule
   b. Size of the molecule
   c. Gel casting
   d. All of the above

4. The order of a polymerase chain reaction (PCR) cycle usually is:
   a. Denaturation, digestion, detection
   b. Denaturation, annealing, extension
   c. Annealing, denaturation, extension
   d. Digestion, annealing, extension

5. RT-PCR involves all of the following except:
   a. DNA isolation
   b. Reverse transcription
   c. PCR amplification
   d. Product analysis

6. If someone has one normal and one mutant gene, they are referred to as:
   a. Heterozygous
   b. Compound homozygous
   c. Homozygous
   d. Wild type

7. The coding sequences of a gene are known as:
   a. Introns
   b. Exons
   c. Splice sites
   d. Frameshifts

8. Restriction endonucleases recognize specific:
   a. Methylation patterns
   b. Trinucleotide repeats
   c. Palindromic DNA sequences
   d. DNA-damaged sites

9. Western Blotting is a method used to detect which of the following:
   a. DNA
   b. Protein
   c. RNA
   d. Mutations

10. What are the chances that individual number 27 *(in the diagram below)* will be affected with an autosomal dominant trait?
    a. 0%
    b. 25%
    c. 50%
    d. 100%

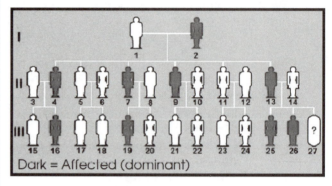

Dark = Affected (dominant)

11. What are the chances that individual number 13 *(in the diagram below)* will be affected with an autosomal recessive trait?
    a. 0%
    b. 25%
    c. 50%
    d. 100%

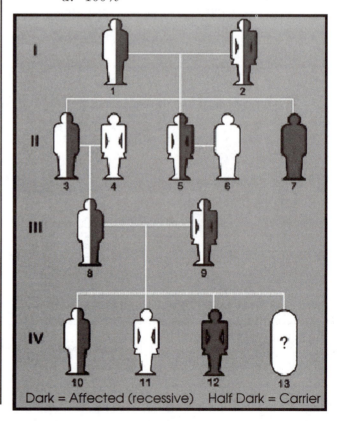

Dark = Affected (recessive)   Half Dark = Carrier

12. X-linked recessive traits are more common in:
   a. Males
   b. Females
   c. Children
   d. None of the above

13. What type of inheritance pattern is represented in this pedigree? *(shown below)*
   a. Autosomal dominant
   b. Autosomal recessive
   c. X-linked recessive
   d. X-linked dominant

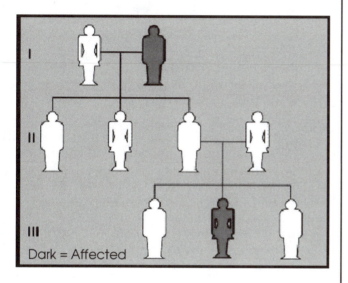

Dark = Affected

14. Using the picture below, which is the SNP?
   a. t/a
   b. c/c
   c. c/a
   d. t/g

| ATTCGCATGCCTAGTCAAATGC | Abnormal Allele |
| ATTCGAATGCCTAGTCAAATGC | Normal Allele |

15. What are microarrays used for?
   a. Gene expression in response to external stimuli
   b. Pharmacogenetics
   c. Toxicogenetics
   d. All of the above

16. According to the following western blot, which vegetables contain chlorophyll?
   a. Green bean, carrot and asparagus
   b. Green bean, squash, and asparagus
   c. Green bean, asparagus, and spinach
   d. Green been, carrot and squash

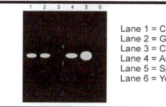

Lane 1 = Control protein - chlorophyll
Lane 2 = Green bean extract
Lane 3 = Carrot extract
Lane 4 = Asparagus extract
Lane 5 = Spinach extract
Lane 6 = Yellow squash extract

Answers and Rationale

1. D

Molecular diagnostics utilizes principles of molecular biology to identify individuals at risk for disease, to diagnose infectious disease, and to determine treatment efficacy. However, molecular diagnostics is not used to increase morbidity (cause illness) since that would defeat the purpose of using molecular diagnostics in the laboratory.

2. D

The human genome is dipoid, not haploid. It has a total of 23 chromosome pairs, not 22. It is linear, not circular. But it does have about 6 million bases.

3. D

The migration rate of a macromolecule through a gel matrix during electrophoresis depends on the net charge, the molecules size as well as the way the gel is cast *(the percentage and thickness of the agarose can affect the rate at which DNA can migrate)*.

4. B

One cycle of a polymerase chain reaction (PCR) includes a denaturation step to break the strand apart, an annealing step so that the primers can sit down on the appropriate area of the DNA, and an extension so that the Taq polymerase can make a copy of the strand of DNA.

5. A

RT-PCR involves PCR amplification of the product, reverse transcriptase is the enzyme that is used in RT-PCR, and the product must be analyzed. However, RT-PCR requires isolation of RNA, not DNA.

6. A

If someone has one normal and one mutant gene, they are referred to as heterozygous. Homozygous individuals have identical patterns. Wildtype refers to the "normal" or prototype cell.

220

7. B

The coding sequences of a gene are known as exons. The introns are spliced out before the gene is translated. A frameshift mutation is when a nucleotide is either deleted or added to a sequence such that an altered protein is produced.

8. C

Restriction endonucleases recognize specific 4 – 5 nucleotide palindromic *(reads the same in either direction)* DNA sequences.

9. B

Western Blotting is used to identify proteins through the use of SDS-PAGE. Southern Blotting identifies DNA and Northern Blotting identifies RNA. Mutations are usually identified in the genomic DNA, therefore, a western would not be used.

10. C

If the parent is heterozygous for the dominant trait *(i.e., #13 from the chart)*, the chance of being affected is always 50%. If you quickly sketch a punnett square Aa x aa for this pedigree – you will see that half will have the trait (Aa).

11. B

In the case of an autosomal recessive trait, the chances of being affected when both parents are heterozygous (Aa) will be 25%.

12. A

X-linked traits are always more common in males because males have one X chromosome (XY) as opposed to females who have two (XX). In females the other X chromosome carries the dominant genes so as carriers, they do not display the trait. Males with only one X chromosome display whatever traits are on that chromosome, dominant or recessive.

13. B

This pedigree is an example of an autosomal recessive trait. In an autosomal recessive disorder, an individual must have two copies of the abnormal gene in order to be affected. Also, autosomal recessive traits commonly skip generations. It is not an X-linked recessive trait because there is male to male transmission – father in generation I would have to have passed it to his son in generation II for him to pass to his daughter in generation III. Fathers can only pass the X linked recessive genes to their daughters *(they get the X chromosome)* not to their sons *(they get the Y chromosome)*.

14. C

A polymorphism is a change in the DNA sequence. In this example, the SNP or single nucleotide polymorphism is an A that changes to a C. If you match the top and bottom sequences, they are identical except for the sixth nucleotide in from the left.

15. D

Microarrays are a powerful tool that can be utilized for various diagnostic purposes, including measuring the levels of gene expression or to determine the affects of a drug or a toxin. Hence all of the answers are correct.

16. C

A western blot is used to analyze the presence of protein in a sample. Therefore, if the specific protein is present, you will see a product on the western blot. Lanes 1, 2, 4, and 5 have a product. Lane 1 is the positive control and should have a product. Lane 2, 4, and 5 are extracts from green beans, asparagus and spinach. Hence, these are the vegetables that contain chlorophyll.

REFERENCES

Tsongalis, Gregory T. and William B. Coleman. *Molecular Diagnostics – A training and study guide.* Copyright 2002. American Association for Clinical Chemistry Press. Washington, DC.

Pictures and Instructional Materials were obtained from the following:

Roche Diagnostics. *Molecular Technology Education Program.* Copyright 2003 CD-rom version 1.0 (Roche.MDxS.Certification.Net)

Hoffman F. – LaRoche Ltf. *Molecular Diagnostics Services.* Roche Genetics Education Program. CD-rom version 4.0

LABORATORY OPERATIONS AND INSTRUMENTATION

by Patsy Jarreau, Mary Muslow, Angela Foley, Larry Broussard, Michele Zitzmann, Mary Lux

Quality Assurance

1. QA takes into consideration all factors that may affect the treatment of a patient
   a. Pre-analytical variables
      - *Specimen collection*
      - *Transport*
      - *Preservatives used*
   b. Analytical variables
      - *Test processing*
      - *QC data*
   c. Post-analytical variables
      - *How results are reported and acted upon*

Quality Control

DEFINITIONS

1. Accuracy - agreement of results with true value for substance in given specimen
   a. Statistical measures of accuracy
      - *Mean ($\bar{x}$) = average*
      - *Mode = most common value*
      - *Median = middle value*

2. Precision - ability to produce series of results on the same sample that agree closely with each other (*reproducibility*)

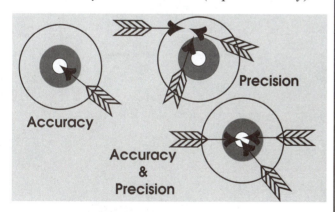

Accuracy

Precision

Accuracy & Precision

Determine Accuracy and Precision from Data

a. Statistical measures of precision
   - *Standard deviation (s or SD)*

$$SD = \sqrt{\frac{\sum (X - x)^2}{n - 1}}$$

$\sum$ = sum
n = number of values
X = individual value
$\bar{x}$ = mean

Information Needed to Calculate SD (mean, number of samples, etc.)

Minimum of 20 analyses are needed to determine standard deviation.
Normal distribution (*Gaussian*)
- *68% of values will fall within ± 1s*
- *95% of values will fall within ± 2s*
- *99% of values will fall within ± 3s*

Correlate Percentage and Standard Deviation

- *Coefficient of variation (CV) (Relative Standard Deviation) Expressed as percent*

$$CV\ (\%) = \frac{s\ (100)}{\bar{x}}$$

3. Sensitivity - ability to detect small concentrations of a substance

4. Specificity - ability to measure only the substance of interest (*no interfering substances*)

5. Reference range - range in which a certain percentage of the population is expected to fall; random samples from a

given "normal" population will fall within the mean ± 2s range of values for that population

6. Standards - substances whose exact concentrations, purity or quality are known
   a. Primary standard - chemically pure, can be weighed or measured directly
   b. Secondary standard - assayed value established by a reference method or comparison to a solution of known concentration *(less expensive)*

7. Controls - substances having a known or determined range of values
   a. Assayed - values stated by manufacturer
   b. Unassayed - values not given, determined by user

8. Confidence interval *(control range)* - range of values within which control result must fall
   a. Usually established by analyzing the control at least 20 times and

calculating mean, standard deviation, and ±2s range

9. Delta check - compare most recent patient result with previous result(s)
   a. Large disparity usually indicates error in one of the results

10. Comparison to external quality control
    a. Standard Deviation Index (SDI) or Z-score

$$SDI = \frac{\text{Your Lab's Result - Group } \bar{x}}{\text{Group Standard Deviation}}$$

SDI should be less than 2
    b. Youden plot
       ❖ *Plot Level I control vs Level II control*

EXAMPLE OF YOUDEN PLOT

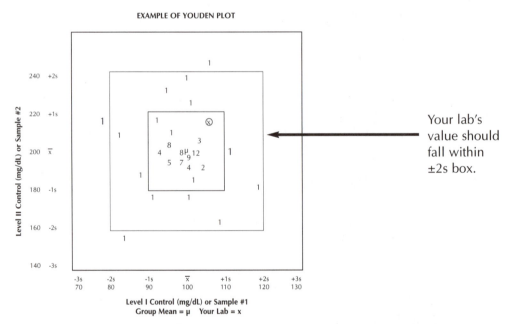

Your lab's value should fall within ±2s box.

---

11. Sources of Variation or Error
    a. Random error - may be due to: instrument errors *(voltage fluctuations, incorrect sample volume)* sample error *(anticoagulant or drug interference, lipemia, hemolysis)*, or human error *(mixing of control samples)*

    b. Systematic error - may be due to: instrument errors *(dirty photometer, faulty ISE)*, decomposition of standards or reagents *(evaporation or contamination)*
    Systematic errors may be constant bias *(y-intercept is not zero)* or proportional bias *(slope is not 1.000)*

223

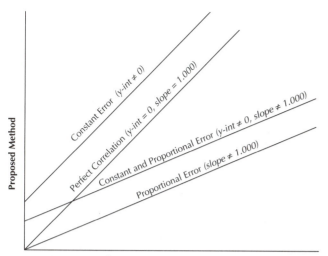

Current or Reference Method

12. t-test - comparison of the means of two populations or two test method means; used to compare the *accuracy* of two methods.

13. F-test - comparison of standard deviations of two populations or two test methods; used to compare *precision* of two methods

Purpose of t-Test

INTERPRETATION OF QC

1. Trend - values for the control that continue to either increase or decrease over a period of 6 consecutive days (*a trend may be due to reagent deterioration or instrument wear*) - Determine by visual inspection of Levey-Jennings quality control chart

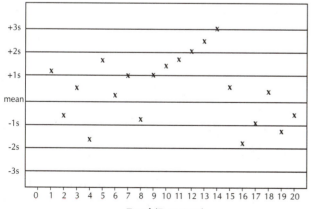

Trend (Days 9-14)

2. Shift - 6 or more consecutive daily values that distribute themselves on one side of the mean value line, but maintain a constant level (*a shift may be due to deterioration of a standard or a change in reagent lot*) - Determine by visual inspection of Levey-Jennings quality control chart

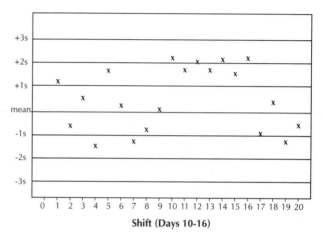

Shift (Days 10-16)

3. Westgard Multi-Rules - used to accept or reject a "run" of samples
   a. Warning Rule -
      1:2s - Evaluate previous controls when one observation exceeds the mean ±2s limit. If no other rules are broken, accept results

   b. Reject Rules (Out-of-Control)
      1:3s - Reject when one observation exceeds the mean ±3s limit

      2:2s - Reject when two consecutive observations exceed the same mean +2s limit or the same -2s limit

      R:4s - Reject when one control observation in the run exceeds its mean +2s limit and the next exceeds its mean -2s limit (*The two points are more than 4s apart*)

      4:1s - Reject when four consecutive control observations exceed the same mean +1s limit or the same mean -1s limit

      10x - Reject when ten consecutive control observations fall on one side of the mean

   Only apply "reject rules" if the WARNING RULE has been broken

Evaluate Data to Determine Shifts and Trends

REFERENCE RANGES (NORMAL VALUES)

1. Definition - range of usual values for constituent of clinical interest in a healthy population
   a. From a group of persons who are in a state free from obvious abnormalities
   b. 95% of the population of normal persons or mean $\pm 2s$

2. Considerations - physiological differences due to race, age, sex, weight, nutritional and absorptive states, degree of physical activity, position of body during blood sampling, menstrual cycle, emotional state, geographic location, and time of day *(diurnal variation)*; also differences in analytical methods

3. Establishing reference ranges
   a. Large population preferable
   b. (100 individuals minimum) from community in which lab is located
   c. Values for analyte must follow Gaussian distribution
   d. Determine 95% confidence limits $(\bar{x} \pm 2\,s)$ *(1 "normal" person in 20 will fall outside of this range)*

Laboratory Mathematics

MEASURING CONCENTRATION

1. Can be measured in one of three ways:
   a. Weight per unit weight (w/w)
   b. Weight per unit volume (w/v)
   c. Volume per unit volume (v/v).

2. A common way to express concentration is in per cent (%), which simply means parts per 100

WEIGHT PER UNIT WEIGHT (W/W)

1. Most accurate type of % concentration; not often used in the clinical laboratory

2. Example:

   Make a 30% w/w NaCl aqueous solution

   Answer:

   Mix 30 gm of NaCl with 70 gm H_2O

3. Example:

   Make 100 gm of a 30% NaCl aqueous solution

   Answer:

   30% of the total must be NaCl
   100 gm X .30 = 30 gm
   To make 100 gm of this solution, mix 30 gm NaCl with 70 gm H_2O

WEIGHT PER UNIT VOLUME (W/V)

1. Most commonly used method in the clinical laboratory; a solid solute is mixed with a liquid solvent
   (1 mL H_2O = 1 gm H_2O) (1% = 1gm/100mL)

2. Example:

   Prepare 0.5% NaCl solution

   Answer:

   Measure 0.5 gm NaCl and add H_2O up to 100 mL

VOLUME PER UNIT VOLUME (V/V)

1. When a solution has a liquid solute in a liquid solvent

2. Example:

   Prepare a 25% H_2SO_4 solution

   Answer:

   A 25% H_2SO_4 solution = 25 mL of concentrated H_2SO_4 in 100 mL of solution. Add 25 mL of concentrated acid to 75 mL H_2O

REMEMBER! Acid to Water NEVER add water to acid. Do what you "oughta", ADD THE ACID TO THE "WATA".

CHANGING CONCENTRATION AND ACID-BASE NEUTRALIZATION

1. The volume of one solution times the concentration of that solution equals the volume of a second solution times the concentration of the second solution

$$V_1 \times C_1 = V_2 \times C_2$$
(Units on both sides of the equation must be equal.)

2. Example:

How much 95% alcohol is required to make 200 mL of 5% alcohol?

Answer:
$$V_1 \times C_1 = V_2 \times C_2$$
$$200 \times 5 = V_2 \times 95$$
$$1000 = 95 (V_2)$$
$$V_2 = 10.5$$
(10.5 mL of 95% alcohol diluted up to 200 mL)

NOT CHANGING CONCENTRATION

1. Involves variation in the amount of total solution.

2. Easiest method is the ratio-proportion procedure.

$$\frac{\text{unit weight 1}}{\text{unit volume 1}} = \frac{\text{unit weight 2}}{\text{unit volume 2}}$$

Cross-multiply to solve.

3. Example:

Prepare 500 mL of 0.5% NaOH.
Answer:
$$\frac{0.5 \text{ gm NaOH}}{100} = \frac{X}{500}$$

$$100X = 500 (.5)$$
$$100X = 250$$
$$X = 2.5 \text{ gm NaOH diluted up to 500 mL}$$

Example:
A solution contains 45 gm of solute in 240 mL of solution. What is the % concentration?
Answer:
$$\frac{45 \text{ gm}}{240} = \frac{X \text{ gm}}{100}$$

$$240X = 4500$$
$$X = 18.75 \text{ gm per 100 mL} = 18.75\% \text{ solution}$$

MOLARITY

1. A mole of a substance = number of grams equal to the atomic or molecular weight of the substance

2. Gram molecular weight (*GMW*) is often used as a definition of mole; a 1 molar solution contains 1 mole of solute per liter of solution

3. Example:

What is the GMW of H_2SO_4?

Answer:
$$2 H = 1 \times 2 = 2$$
$$1 S = 32 \times 1 = 32$$
$$4 O = 16 \times 4 = 64$$

$$GMW = 98$$

4. Molarity (*M*) expresses the number of moles of substance in 1 liter (*1000 mL*) of solution.
   a. Molarity (M) = # of moles
   b.
   $$M = \frac{\text{grams/liter}}{GMW}$$
   $$M = 1000 \text{ millimoles (mmole)}$$
   $$\text{mmole} = 1/1000 \text{ mole} = \frac{\text{mg/L}}{GMW}$$

   c. # grams/liter = GMW $\times$ M

   d. $M = \dfrac{\% \times 10}{GMW}$
   e. $\% \times 10 = GMW \times M$

5. Example:

Make 500 mL of 2M NaCl.

Answer:
Atomic wt of Na   = 23
Atomic wt of Cl   = 35.5
GMW   = 58.5

GMW $\times$ M = # gms/L

$58.5 \times 2 = 117$ gm/L

Dilute 117 gms NaCl up to 1000 mL. Use ratio-proportion to adjust total volume to 500 mL.
$$\frac{117 \text{ gm}}{1000 \text{ mL}} = \frac{X \text{ gm}}{500 \text{ mL}}$$
$$1000X = 58500$$
$$X = 58.5 \text{ gms NaCl diluted to 500 mL}$$

6. **Example:**

What is the molarity of a solution in which there are 25 gms of Na_2SO_4 in 500 mL solution?

Answer:

2 Na = 2 X 23 = 46
1 S = 1 X 32 = 32
4 O = 4 X 16 = 64
GMW = 142

$$M = \frac{gm/L}{GMW}$$

First, use a ratio-proportion to change 500 mL to 1 L.

$$\frac{25\ gms}{500\ mL} = \frac{X\ gms}{1000\ mL}$$

X = 50 gms/L

$$M = \frac{50}{142} = .35\ M$$

NORMALITY

1. Based on the same principle of molarity except **M** is based on GMW and **N** is based on gram equivalent weight *(GEW)*

2. As a general rule, the GEW of a substance is equal to the GMW divided by the valence; GEW is always equal or less than GMW

3. Gram equivalent weight (GEW) = gram molecular weight/valence

4. Normality (N) = $\frac{\text{\# grams/liter}}{GEW}$

5. # grams/liter = GEW X N

6. $N = \frac{\% \times 10}{GEW}$

7. % X 10 = GEW X N

8. **Example:**

Make 200 mL of a 0.5 N H_2SO_4 solution.

Answer:

2 H = 2 X 1 = 2
1 S = 1 X 32 = 32
4 O = 4 X 16 = 64
GMW = 98

$$GEW = \frac{GMW}{valence} = \frac{98}{2} = 49$$

gms/L = GEW X N

gms/L = 49 X 0.5 = 24.5 gms/L

$$\frac{24.5\ gms}{1000\ mL} = \frac{X\ gms}{200\ mL}$$

X = 4.9 gms of H_2SO_4 diluted up to 200 mL

CONVERSION OF MOLARITY TO NORMALITY

1. N = M X valence

2. $M = \frac{N}{valence}$

3. **Example:**

Express 0.4 N H_3PO_4 as molarity.
$$M = \frac{0.4}{3} = .13$$

CONVERSIONS BETWEEN MEQ/DL AND MG/DL

1. Mg/dL means mg/100 mL; multiply the number of mg/100 mL by 10 to get the number of mg/1000 mL

2. $mEq/L = \frac{mg/L}{GEW} = \frac{mg/100mL \times 10}{GEW} =$

$$\frac{mg/dL \times 10}{GEW}$$

3. $mg/dL = \frac{mEq/L \times GEW}{10}$

4. **Example:**
Express 200 mg/dL Cl as mEq/L

Answer:
$mEq/L = \frac{200 \times 10}{35.5} = \frac{2000}{35.5} = 56.34\ mEq/L$

NOTES

1. mg% = mg/dL

2. % = parts/100 = gm/100 mL

3. 1 gram mol. wt. (GMW) = 1 mole

4. 1 mg. mol. wt. = 1 mmole

5. 1 mole = 1000 mmole

6. M = mmole/mL

7. mM/L = mEq/L

8. Molarity is based on grams per 1000 mL of solution; for any volume other than 1000 mL, use a ratio/proportion formula to solve the problem

Preparing Standard Solutions

Conversion to Decimals

PREFIX	SYMBOL	DECIMAL
Primary Unit	No Prefix	1.0
Milli	m	0.001
Micro	μ	0.000001
Nano	n	0.000000001
Pico	p	0.000000000001
Femto	f	0.000000000000001

Conversion Between Units

MULTIPLE	MASS	VOLUME
One (standard)		Liter (L)
$1/10$		Deciliter (dl)
$1/1000$	Milligram (mg)	Milliliter (ml)
$1/1,000,000$	Microgram (μg)	Microliter (μl)
$1/1,000,000,000$	Nanogram (ng)	
$1/1,000,000,000,000$	Picogram (pg)	

Example:

Convert μl to mL
Step 1: μl = .000001 = 10^{-6}
　　　　mL = .001 = 10^{-3}
Step 2: $10^{-6} - 10^{-3} = 10^{-3}$ = .001
Step 3: 1 μl x .001 = .001 mL

Conversion of mL to μl

Chemistry / Immunology Instrumentation

SPECTROPHOTOMETRY

1. Principle - measurement of light in a narrow wavelength range; wavelength selected by prisms, gratings or filters
   a. Chemical reaction produces a substance that absorbs light
   b. Measurements may be made in the visible range (*most common*), ultraviolet range or in the infrared region
   c. Under suitable conditions, the amount of light absorbed by a solution when illuminated with light of a proper wavelength, is directly proportional to the concentration of its color component (*Beer's Law*)
   d. Basically, the same principle for all analytical methods that measure radiation (*Ex., gamma counters*)

2. Mathematical formula for Beer's law:

$$A = abc = \log \frac{100}{\%T} = 2 - \log \%T$$

A = absorbance
a = absorptivity
b = light pattern of the solution in cm
c = concentration of the substance
%T = transmittance

   a. If measurement is made in absorbance, plot on linear graph paper; concentration of substance is directly proportional to amount of light absorbed

228

Concentration

b. Beer's law is usually used to measure absorbance and calculate the concentration by rearranging the formula above:

$$c = \frac{A}{ab}$$

where a and b are constants

c. Ratio of standard to unknown - the simplest type of concentration measurement involves determination of the absorbance values for a known concentration of the substance measured *(standard)* and the measurement of that substance in a patient or control sample *(unknown)*

If Abs. of std. = abc(std.)
and
Abs. of Unk. = abc(unk.)
then

$$\frac{Abs.\ of\ std.}{Abs.\ of\ unk.} = \frac{abc(std.)}{abc(unk.)}$$

or

$$\frac{Abs.\ of\ std.}{Abs.\ of\ unk.} = \frac{c(std.)}{c(unk.)}$$

or

$$c(unk.) = \frac{Abs.\ of\ unk.}{Abs.\ of\ std.} \times c(std.)$$

Example:

Unknown absorbance = 0.252
Standard absorbance = 0.640
Conc. of standard = 200 mg/dL

$$c(unk.) = \frac{0.252}{0.640} \times 200 = 79\ mg/dL$$

Calculations Based on Beer's Law

d. Deviations from Beer's Law
  ❖ *Simultaneous absorption at multiple wavelengths*
  ❖ *Absorption of light by interfering substances*
  ❖ *Light transmission by stray light*

  ❖ *Measurement of very high concentrations (dilute sample multiply results by dilution factor)*

3. Components of a Spectrophotometer
  a. Light source
    ❖ *Visible range - tungsten lamp*
    ❖ *Ultraviolet range - hydrogen discharge or deuterium lamp*
  b. Monochromator
    ❖ *Filter*
    ❖ *Diffraction grating - range from near-UV to near-infrared*
    ❖ *Prism - quartz for visible and UV range; glass for visible light only*
  c. Cuvette - glass, quartz or plastic
  d. Photomultiplier tube detector
  e. Measuring device/meter

4. Standardization of Spectrophotometers
  a. Wavelength calibration
    ❖ *H^+ or deuterium radiant energy lamps have built-in sources for checking wavelength accuracy*
    ❖ *Holmium oxide or didymium filters may be used to check wavelength calibration*
    ❖ *Solutions of stable chromagens can be used to determine if wavelength accuracy of instrument has changed after wavelength accuracy has been determined by one of preceding primary methods*
  b. Stray Light
    ❖ *Detected by using filters or solutions with sharp cutoff wavelength for transmission (Ex., $NiSO_4$)*
    ❖ *Corrected by changing light source, verifying wavelength calibration, sealing light leaks, realigning instrument components or cleaning optical surfaces*

Spectrophotometer Maintenance & Adjustment

5. Bichromatic Analysis
  a. Automation procedure in which absorbance is measured at two different wavelengths

b. Minimizes background interference *(such as hemolysis or icteria)* by providing a blank for each specimen

Principle of Bichromatic Analysis, Including the Purpose of the Blank

Sources of Error in Spectrophotometry

FLUOROMETRY

1. Principle
   a. Energy emission that occurs when certain compounds absorb electromagnetic radiation, become excited and return to energy levels slightly lower than their original energy levels
   b. Emitted energy is less than absorbed energy, so the wavelength of emitted light is longer than absorbed light
   c. Extremely sensitive, up to 1000 times as sensitive as colorimetric methods
   d. Disadvantage is quenching interference *(occurs when the excited molecule interacts with a substance in the solution and loses some of its energy)*

Characteristics of Light Emitted in Fluorometry *(longer wavelength lower energy)*

TURBIDIMETRY

1. Principle - measures the amount of light blocked by particulate matter as light passes through the cuvette by a colorimeter or spectrophotometer

2. Sources of Error
   a. Particle size of standard is not the same as the particle size in samples
   b. Particles may settle out as measurements are being made

NEPHELOMETRY

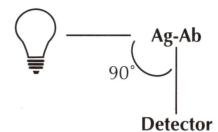

Ag-Ab

90°

Detector

1. Principle
   a. Measures light that is scattered by small particles at right angles to the beam incident to the cuvette
   b. Amount of scatter is related to the number and size of the particles
   c. More precise than turbidimetry

Principle of Nephelometry

2. Used to measure antigen-antibody complexes *(IgG, IgA, IgM, CRP, RF, C3, C4, haptoglobin, etc.)*; provides high specificity

OSMOMETRY

1. Osmolality – measure of total number of dissolved particles in a solution *(molecular weight, size, density or type of particle does not matter)*

2. Any substance dissolved in a solvent will do the following *(called colligative properties)*
   a. Depress the freezing point
   b. Elevate the boiling point
   c. Decrease the vapor pressure
   d. Increase the osmotic pressure

3. Most practical methods for measuring the concentration of dissolved particles are freezing point depression *(most common method)* and vapor pressure depression

4. Significant differences between methods is a means of determining if a volatile solute such as alcohol is present
   a. Osmolality is increased in the presence of ethanol, methanol and glycol by the freezing point depression method only

230

b. Vapor pressure techniques do not measure volatiles *(therefore, lower values would be seen with this method)*

5. Sources of error
   a. Cooling bath temperature too cool or too warm
   b. Particulate matter in sample does NOT allow sufficient supercooling to occur before freezing takes place

Sources of Error in Osmolality

CHROMATOGRAPHY

1. Principle - Separates mixture into individual components on basis of specific differences in physical characteristics

2. Types
   a. Liquid-liquid chromatography - separation is based on differences in solubility between two liquid phases - one aqueous, one organic
   b. Ion exchange chromatography - separation depends on the molecular weight, size and charge of the ions or molecules *(ions with the greater charge densities are held most strongly on ion exchange material)*
   c. Gas-liquid chromatography *(GLC)* and gas chromatography *(GC)* - separation depends on sample volatility and rate of diffusion into liquid layer *(partition coefficient)* or inert gas *(mobile phase)*
      ❖ *Retention time is used to identify volatiles (methanol, isopropyl alcohol), drugs, organic acids in urine and catecholamines*
      ❖ *Best method for blood alcohol*
      ❖ *Confirmatory testing - GC with mass spectrometry (MS) required for regulated drugs of abuse*
   d. Thin-layer chromatography *(TLC)* - separation depends on rate of diffusion and solubility of the substance in the solvents as the components migrate through media
      ❖ *Used to identify drugs, lipids,*

carbohydrates and amino acids
   ❖ *$Rf = \dfrac{distance\ moved\ (constituent)}{distance\ moved\ (solvent)}$*
   e. High-performance liquid chromatography *(HPLC)*
      ❖ *Aqueous or organic solutions are pumped through columns under high pressure, which allows high resolution with fast and accurate quantitation*
      ❖ *Trouble shooting:*
         ☞ Recorder- noisy baseline may be due to bubbles or particulate matter entering the flow cell or a leaking filter; drifting baseline can result from an overloaded column or from contamination in solvent reservoir
         ☞ Loss in column resolution may be due to overloading column with sample or degradation of column packing

ELECTROPHORESIS

1. Principle
   a. Method for the physical separation of proteins based on their ionic charge and molecular size
   b. When placed in an electrical field, electrically charged molecules migrate in a direction that depends on the isoelectric point of the molecule and the pH of the buffer
   c. Factors that affect the rate of migration are molecular weight and size, ionic strength of the buffer and the type of support medium

2. Types of electrophoresis
   a. Paper
   b. Agarose gel
   c. Cellulose acetate
   d. Polyacrylamide gel
   e. Starch gel
   f. Isoelectric focusing

3. Components commonly separated
   a. Amino acids
   b. Serum proteins
   c. Lipoproteins
   d. Glycoproteins
   e. Nucleic acids
   f. Hemoglobins
   g. Isoenzymes
      ❖ *Lactate dehydrogenase*
      ❖ *Creatine kinase*
      ❖ *Alkaline phosphatase*

h. Immunoglobulins
i. Specific antigens by immunological electrophoretic techniques such as rocket IEP or immunofixation

Sources of Error

PROBLEM	LIKELY CAUSE:
No Migration	Instrument Not Connected Wrong pH Electrodes Connected Backwards
Bands Too Large/Small	Over/Underloading
Very Slow Migration	High Molecular Weight Low Charge Ionic Strength Too High Voltage Too Low
Sample Precipitates in Support	pH Too High or Low Voltage Too High
Split or Broken Bands	Excessive Pressure Applied to Wire Applicators
Crescent-Shaped Bands	Bent Applicators Overloading

TEST Alert!

Sources of Error in Electrophoresis

ELECTROCHEMISTRY (POTENTIOMETRY, AMPEROMETRY, COULOMETRY)

1. Potentiometry - pH meters, ion-selective electrodes *(ISEs)*
   a. Based on the measurement of potential *(voltage)*
   b. Difference between reference and indicator electrodes when no current is passing through the cell; changes in voltage occur in proportion to ionic activity of the solution in which the electrodes are immersed
   c. Reference electrode is usually either saturated calomel *(HgCl$_2$ and KCl)* or silver/silver chloride *(Ag/AgCl)*
   d. Indicator electrode should interact with the analyte of interest and not with other compounds
   e. pH electrodes- glass sensitive to H$^+$
   f. Na$^+$ electrodes - glass sensitive to Na$^+$
   g. K$^+$ electrodes - liquid ionophore, valinomycin

h. Gas-sensing electrodes - the membrane is permeable to the gas measured; the CO$_2$ electrode for the measurement of blood pCO$_2$ is a pH glass electrode that has a silicone rubber membrane which is permeable to CO$_2$

$$CO_2 + H_2O <====> H_2CO_3 <====> H^+ + HCO_3^-$$
H$^+$ is the measured ion

i. Enzyme electrodes - electrodes are covered by a layer of immobilized enzymes that catalyze a chemical reaction measured by the electrode

2. Amperometry
   a. Measurement of the current flowing through an electrochemical cell when a constant electric potential is applied to the electrodes
   b. pO$_2$ electrode for blood gases; cathode is made of platinum, anode is Ag/AgCl
   c. Current directly proportional to the pO$_2$ in solution is observed

3. Coulometry
   a. Titration in which the titrant is electrochemically generated
      ❖ *Silver ions are produced by electrolysis from a silver wire used as an anode*
      ❖ *Chloride ions from the sample complex with silver (Ag$^+$)ions*
      ❖ *Indicator electrode senses the excess silver ions*
      ❖ *When an excess of Ag$^+$ is detected, the titration stops*
   b. Length of time that it takes for the titrator to generate excess Ag+ is directly proportional to the Cl$^-$ concentration because the current has been kept constant

TEST Alert!

Principles of Each Type of Instrumentation

Summary of Instrumentation Principles

INSTRUMENTATION	MEASURES:
Spectrophotometry	Light in a **Narrow** Wavelength Range
Bichromatic Analysis	Light Absorbence at **2** Different **Wavelengths**
Fluorometry	Light Emitted from Compounds that **Absorb Electromagnetic Radiation**, Become Excited and Return to Energy States Slightly Lower than Their Original Energy States
Turbidimetry	Light **Blocked** by Particulate Matter as Light Passes Through the Cuvette by a Colorimeter or Spectrophotometer
Nephelometry	Light **Scattered** by Small Particles at **Right Angles** to the Beam Incident to the Cuvette
Osmometry	Total **Number of Dissolved Particles** in a Solution Based on Colligative Properties *(freezing point depression and vapor point depression most commonly measured by instruments)*
Chromatography	**Separation** of Mixtures into Individual Components **Based on** Specific Differences in **Physical Characteristics**
Electrophoresis	**Separation** of Proteins **Based on Ionic Charge & Molecular Size**
Potentiometry - pH meters, ion-selective electrodes *(ISE)*	Potential *(voltage)* **Difference Between Reference and Indicator Electrodes** when **No** Current is Passing through the Cell
Coulometry	**Titration** in which the Titrant is **Electrochemically** Generated
Amperometry	**Current** Flowing through an Electrochemical Cell when a **Constant Electric Potential** is Applied to the Electrodes

Hematology Instrumentation

METHODOLOGIES

1. Electronic impedance *(Coulter Principle)*
   a. Cell passing through electric current creates pulse proportional to cell size
   b. Used in cell counting/sizing and creating 3 part differential *(lymphs, monos, granulocytes)*
   c. RBCs and platelets counted in RBC bath
      ❖ *Differentiation based on size by using thresholds*
      ❖ *MCV measured directly (size of pulse proportional to cell size)*
   e. WBCs and nRBCs *(if present)* are counted in WBC bath *(RBCs are lysed)*

2. Laser light (Flow cytometry)
   a. High intensity light of a single wavelength
   b. Used in cell analysis and differentiation
   c. WBC population identification based on differential light scatter (forward vs. side)

   d. Generates a 5 part differential

3. Cytochemical staining
   a. Myeloperoxidase stain
   b. Aids in identification of WBC's based on degree of peroxidase activity

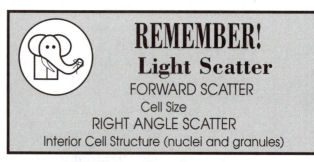

REMEMBER!
Light Scatter
FORWARD SCATTER
Cell Size
RIGHT ANGLE SCATTER
Interior Cell Structure (nuclei and granules)

Associate Laser Light Scatter with Cell I.D.

Histograms / Scattergrams

RED CELL NORMAL HISTOGRAM

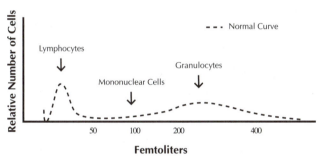

BIMODAL CURVE - 2 POPULATIONS OF RED CELLS

1. Example:
   Left shift + Normal population = Fe deficiency anemia receiving transfusion

WHITE CELL NORMAL HISTOGRAM

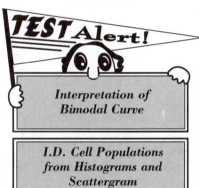

TEST Alert!

> *Interpretation of Bimodal Curve*

> *I.D. Cell Populations from Histograms and Scattergram*

WBC SCATTERGRAM

- *Beckman Coulter*
- *Impedence*
- <u>*V*</u>*olume,* <u>*C*</u>*onductivity, light* <u>*S*</u>*catter* (VCS technology)

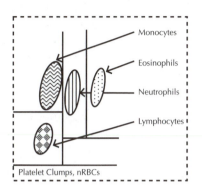

WBC/PEROXIDASE SCATTERGRAM

- *Bayer*
- *Light Scatter*
- *Peroxidase staining*

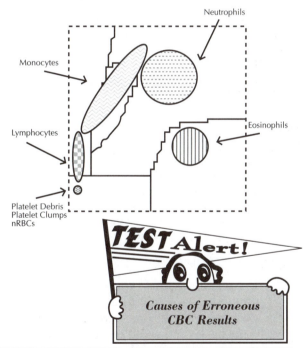

TEST Alert!

> *Causes of Erroneous CBC Results*

ERRONEOUS CBC RESULTS

PARAMETER	FALSE ⬆	FALSE ⬇
RBC	⬆⬆⬆ WBC count, giant platelets, RBC agglutination	Scistocytes, microcytes, cold agglutinins
WBC	nRBCs, lyse resistant RBCs (HbS, HbC), giant platelets, platelet clumps, abnormal precipitant	Aggregates counted as single cells
Platelet	Schistocytes, microcytes	Platelet clumps, giant platelets
Hemoglobin	Lipemia, ⬆⬆⬆ WBC count, resisting Hb (S,C), abnormal globulins, Icterus	Sulfhemoglobin
MCV	⬆⬆⬆ WBC count, cold agglutinins	Hypochromic RBCs

Coagulation Instrumentation

CLOT DETECTION METHOD - FUNCTIONAL ASSAY

1. Electromechanical
   a. Formation of fibrin strand across two electrodes completes electrical circuit causing timing device to stop
   b. Clot times not affected by lipemic, hemolyzed or icteric samples
   c. Probes must be cleaned between samples to prevent specimen carry-over

2. Optical density
   a. Formation of fibrin clot causes change in optical density which is monitored by photodetector and triggers end point
   b. Lipemia, hyperbilirubinemia, extreme hemolysis may interfere with clot detection

CHROMOGENIC METHOD - FUNCTIONAL AND QUANTITATIVE ASSAY

1. Activated coagulation factor (enzyme) cleaves substrate releasing color tag

2. Color change is directly related to factor concentration and is measured photometrically

TEST Alert!

Sources of Error in Electromechanical vs. Optical Density Clot Detection

Microbiology Instrumentation

SPECTROPHOTOMETRY

1. Principle *(see Chemistry/Immunology Instrumentation section)*

2. Infrared region - used in some blood culture methods to measure increases in CO_2 generated

FLUOROMETRY

1. Principle *(see Chemistry/Immunology Instrumentation section)*

2. Used in stains for microscopic exam

3. Used as labels in manual and automated systems for identification of organisms

CHROMATOGRAPHY

1. Used to determine type and relative amounts of organic acids produced by anaerobic organisms. Computerized data-base compares "tracing" from unknown to stored "tracings" of known organisms for identification

2. Used on cell wall extracts to identify organisms such as *Legionella* to species level

PULSE-FIELD GEL ELECTROPHORESIS (PFGE)

1. Evaluate nucleic acids for identification of sub-species typing

2. Important in epidemiology

CHEMILUMINESCENCE / NUCLEIC ACID PROBE

1. Principle
   a. Luminescent marker is attached to nucleic acid probe
   b. When probe hybridizes with target nucleic acid sequence, the bond with the luminescent marker is protected
   c. Bond between luminescent marker and unbound (not hybridized) probe is not protected and is easily hydrolyzed at 60° resulting in loss of chemiluminescent potential
   d. Luminescence is stimulated by a reagent that degrades the luminescent marker, resulting in a flash of light
   e. Light is measured using luminometer in relative light units (RLU) and is proportional to amount of bound (hybridized) probe

AUTOMATED BLOOD CULTURE

1. Determination of an increase in CO_2 in the culture bottle
   a. Increase in CO_2 results from increase in metabolism that occurs when organisms are growing

2. Increase in CO_2 is monitored at intervals
   a. Relative level of CO_2 is "growth index"
   b. Significant change is growth index results in culture flagged as positive

3. Increase in CO_2 can be measured by several methods
   a. Invasive
      ❖ *Radiolabeled CO_2*
      ❖ *Infrared spectrophotometry*
   b. Non-invasive
      ❖ *pH indicators imbedded in bottles (as level of CO_2 increases, pH decreases)*
      ❖ *Fluorescent sensors*
      ❖ *Increase in pressure*

AUTOMATED BACTERIOLOGICAL IDENTIFICATION AND SUSCEPTIBILITY TESTING

1. Test panels consist of set of wells containing desiccated reagents for either biochemical or susceptibility testing

2. Panels of different types *(for organisms with different gram reactions or growth requirements)* are bar-coded for identification by instrument

3. Wells are inoculated with bacterial suspension which also rehydrates the wells

4. Control wells are used to detect contamination and potential for growth

5. Reactions are determined by several methods
   a. Turbidity
   b. Colorimetry
   c. Fluorescence

6. Identification is accomplished by comparison with computerized data base
   a. Most probable identification is reported at a predetermined confidence level
   b. Recommendations for additional tests may be made for organisms which cannot be identified at the confidence level

7. Some systems allow for rapid identification *(<6 hours)*

8. Most systems include incubator, automated reader, data terminal, and printer and can be linked to hospital information system

Automated Urinalysis Instrumentation

1. Include individual strip readers, semi-automated, fully automated, and complete urinalysis workstations

2. Use reflectance photometry to determine each analyte concentration

3. Most commonly used analyzers:
   a. Clinitek *(Bayer Diagnostics)*
   b. Chemstrip *(Roche-Boehringer Mannheim Diagnostics)*
   c. Rapimat *(Behring Diagnostics, Inc.)*
   d. Yellow Iris *(International Remote Imaging Systems)*

LABORATORY OPERATIONS AND INSTRUMENTATION SAMPLE QUESTIONS

1. Bichromatic analysis is used in automation to
   A. Blank for background interference.
   B. Decrease testing time.
   C. Measure samples twice at timed intervals.
   D. Verify wavelength calibration.

2. The most common light source for spectrophotometry in the visible range is the
   A. Didymium lamp.
   B. Deuterium lamp.
   C. Hydrogen discharge lamp.
   D. Tungsten lamp.

3. What type of instrumentation is based on the principle of measuring energy emission that occurs when compounds absorb electromagnetic radiation, become excited and return to energy levels lower than their original energy levels?
   A. Atomic absorption spectrophotometry
   B. Flame emission photometry
   C. Fluorometry
   D. Nephelometry

4. The protein fraction that migrates most rapidly toward the anode is
   A. Albumin.
   B. Alpha-1.
   C. Beta.
   D. Gamma.

5. While performing an electrophoresis, it is noted that crescent-shaped bands develop. The next course of action is to repeat the electrophoresis and
   A. Use a new lot number of support media.
   B. Reduce the application pressure.
   C. NOT overload the sample.
   D. Use serum instead of plasma.

6. Kinetic assay of a serum enzyme gives the following data:

Time (min.)	Absorbance
0	0.005
1	0.035
2	0.075
3	0.135
4	0.195
5	0.215

   This assay demonstrates
   A. Lag phase.
   B. Linearity.
   C. Substrate exhaustion.
   D. Zero order kinetics.

7. How should a clinical laboratorian interpret the QC data shown below?

   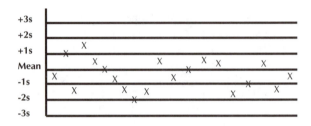

   A. Acceptable
   B. Loss of precision
   C. Shift
   D. Trend

8. When staining a serum protein electrophoresis plate, the normal and abnormal controls as well as the patient samples showed no bands. What might cause this problem?
   A. Staining time too long
   B. Voltage too high
   C. Electrodes were reversed
   D. Excess pressure was used in serum application

   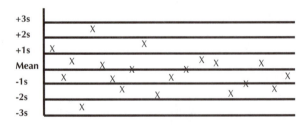

9. Using Westgard rules, evaluate the QC results above?
   A. 10x rule broken, out-of-control
   B. 4(1s) rule broken, out-of-control
   C. R4s rule broken, out-of-control
   D. 2(2s) rule broken, out-of-control

10. An EIA procedure for HCG was performed. Low and high controls were run. Two standards (0 mIU/mL and 200 mIU/mL) were run in duplicate and results were calculated using average absorbances according to Beer's Law. Results on both controls were slightly higher than their respective control ranges. If one of the standard absorbances was eliminated, both controls would read near their respective control range means. Which standard absorbance was eliminated to accomplish this?
  A. 0 mIU/mL standard
      Absorbance 0.056
  B. 0 mIU/mL standard
      Absorbance 0.059
  C. 200 mIU/mL standard
      Absorbance 0.752
  D. 200 mIU/mL standard
      Absorbance 0.696

11. Which of the following disorders would be associated with a right shift in the red cell histogram?
  A. Thalassemia
  B. Fe deficiency anemia
  C. Pernicious anemia
  D. Aplastic anemia

12. Which of the following may be a source of error in electromechanical clot detection methods?
  A. Lipemia
  B. Bilirubinemia
  C. Hypercoagulable sample
  D. Sample carryover

13. Which of the following is associated with a false increase in hemoglobin as well as the MCV and RBC count?
  A. Schistocytes
  B. Marked leukocytosis
  C. Microcytosis
  D. Lipemia

ANSWERS AND RATIONALE

1. A

In bichromatic analysis, absorbance is measured at two wavelengths. The baseline measurement is taken near the base of the peak, and the other is taken at the peak. The difference in absorption is proportional to concentration. This corrects for background interference (e.g. lipemia, hemolysis, etc.) in each sample.

2. D

The tungsten lamp produces a wavelength spectrum from the near infrared through the visible to the near ultra-violet region. Option A is ??? Deuterium and Hydrogen discharge lamps (options B and C) are used to provide continuous spectra in the ultraviolet region.

3. C

The principle of flame emission photometry (option B) is that excitation of an atom's electrons by heat energy from the flame causes unstable electrons to change from a higher energy state to a lower energy state. The principle of atomic absorption (option A) is the inverse of this, in which light is absorbed by ground state atoms. The principle of nephelometry (option D) is that the measured light is that scattered by particles in solution.

4. A

Albumin migrates the fastest because of its small size and negative charge. Separation of the major five bands, in order of migration, is albumin, alpha-1, alpha-2, beta, and gamma. The gamma fraction migrates slightly toward the cathode because of electroendosmosis.

5. C

Crescent-shaped bands are usually caused by sample overloading or bent applicators. Option A may result in cracked or excessively dry material which may show distorted zones. Option B causes split bands. Option D will produce a fibrinogen peak which migrates between the gamma and beta fractions.

6. D

Plotting the absorbance vs time of the data presented shows a rapid increase between minutes 0 - 3 and a constant rate of reaction for minutes 3 - 5. Zero order kinetics occurs when a reaction follows the following process: 1) At the moment the enzyme and stustrate are mixed, the rate of reaction is zero but, 2) over time, the rate increases sustantially and 3) remains constant for a period of time. Option A occurs when there is an initial period of time after the enzyme and substrate are mixed when the rate of reaction is zero. Option B occurs when the absorbance vs time increases proportionately throughout the assay. Option C is the point in time when the reaction rate begins to decrease due to lack of substrate for the enzyme.

7. D

Days 4 - 9 show consistently decreasing values. A trend occurs when a single control value increases or decreases for 6 consecutive days. (Or, two control values increase or decrease for 3 consecutive days.) Option B occurs when there is an increased distribution of control values beyond the + or - 2 S.D. limit. Option C is incorrect because a shift occurs when there is an abrupt change to a new mean.

8. B

If voltage is too high, proteins may be denatured (option B). If the plate remained in stain too long (option A), bands will stain but may be darker. If electrodes were reversed (option C), bands would appear but may not be well separated. If excess pressure were applied (option D), the medium may be cut and protein fractions may not migrate, but a band would be visible at the application point.

9. C

R4s (option C) is correct because the values on days 4 and 5 are 4s apart, one below the mean and one above the mean. 10x (option A) would require 10 values on the same side of the mean. 4(1s) (option B) requires 4 values to be outside 1s (all either above the mean or all below the mean. 2(2s) (option D) requires both values to be outside 2s on the same side of the mean.

10. C

Using the 200 mIU/mL standard with the higher absorbance would increase the slope of the curve, give lower control results, and lower results for the patient samples. Absorbances for the two 0 mIU/ML standards (options A and B) are too close to affect the slope of the curve. The 200 mIU/mL standard with the lower absorbance (option D) would decrease the slope and increase the concentrations of the controls and unknowns.

11. C

Options A and B are microcytic anemias and the red cell histogram would show a left shift.

In option D, the red cells are usually normocytic, normochromic.

12. D

Options A and B may interfere with photo-optical clot detection methods but will not affect electromechanical methods. Option C may result in an erroneously long clotting time using photo-optical methods if the clotting time is shorter than the guard interval.

13. B

Since WBCs are counted in the same bath as RBCs, markedly increased numbers of WBCs (>100,000/μL) will cause a false elevation of the RBC count as well as the MCV since they will be sized along with the RBCs. Also, a high WBC count will increase turbidity thereby increasing the hemoglobin value. Schistocytes are often too small to be counted even as red cells and their presence will not have any effect on the hemoglobin determination since they will be lysed along with the normal red cells. Microcytic red cells can be counted accurately, will cause a decreased MCV and do not falsely effect the hemoglobin measurement. Option D may cause a false elevation in the hemoglobin but will have no effect on the MCV or RBC count.

LABORATORY SAFETY & REGULATIONS

by Louann Lawrence and Mary Hebert

BLOOD BORNE PATHOGENS

1. Universal (standard) precautions - All blood and body fluids are considered potentially infected with blood-borne pathogens

Concept of Universal Precautions

2. Examples of blood-borne pathogens:
   a. HIV - Human Immunodeficiency Virus
   b. HBV - Hepatitis B Virus
   c. HCV - Hepatitis C Virus

3. OSHA "Blood-Borne Pathogens" standard requires written "Exposure Control Plan"

4. Categories of exposure:
   a. Category 1 - exposed to blood and body fluids on a daily basis
   b. Category 2 - regularly exposed to blood and body fluids
   c. Category 3 - never exposed to blood and body fluids

5. Employers must offer hepatitis B vaccine at no cost to all personnel in Category 1 and Category 2

6. Identify tasks causing exposure to blood or body fluids
   a. Use engineering controls (*work shields, needle safety devices, pipeting devices, etc.*) to minimize risk of exposure
   b. Employers must provide PPE (*personal protective equipment*) at no cost when needed (*ex. gloves, lab coats and safety glasses*)

7. Good work practices
   a. Wash hands before leaving the lab, before using the biologic safety cabinct (*BSC*) and after removing gloves; first line of defense in infection control
   b. Do NOT mouth pipet
   c. Do NOT eat, drink, smoke, apply cosmetics, lip balm or contact lenses in clinical areas
   d. Do NOT bend, break, shear or recap used needles and syringes
   e. Clean up blood/body fluid spills immediately with 1:10 dilution of household bleach (*hypochlorite*) solution
   f. Clean counter tops, phones, keyboards on a regular basis with 1:10 dilution of household bleach (*hypochlorite*) solution
   g. Report all blood and body fluid exposures, document via incident report and have exposed person's blood tested as well as source patient's blood
   h. Employees have right to know lab results of source patient but must observe confidentiality
   i. Employees are entitled to medical consultation
   j. Use universal precautions with all reagents prepared from human blood or body fluids

Appropriate Disinfectant for Viruses

8. Biological safety cabinet
   a. Facilitates safe manipulation of infectious material
   b. Reduces risk of exposure to personnel and laboratory area
   c. Directs airflow through high efficiency filter

REMEMBER!
Biological Safety Cabinets

MUST monitor airflow

Use BSC with samples potentially containing pathogens transmitted by aerosolization. Ex., *M. tuberculosis, C. imitus, F. tularensis* and *B. anthracis*

HAZARDOUS CHEMICALS

1. OSHA "Right-to-Know" *(Hazard Communication)* standard states employees have a right to know what hazardous chemicals they work with and how to protect themselves when using them

2. Prepare a chemical inventory of all chemicals used

3. Material Safety Data Sheets *(MSDS)*
   a. Information provided by the chemical manufacturer stating risks of exposure, what to do if exposed and other important medical information
   b. Must have MSDS on all chemicals used

Purpose of MSDS

4. Separate chemicals according to National Fire Protection Association *(NFPA)* coding:
   a. Flammable Solvents - store in flame cabinet; 1 gal or smaller containers may be kept under fume hood
   b. Corrosives - separate from other non-compatible chemicals *(alkali)* for storage
   c. Acids - separate from other non-compatible chemicals for storage

 STOP NEVER store chemicals above head height.

Appropriate Storage of Chemicals

5. Chemical Hygiene Plan
   a. Written plan stipulates what to do in case of a chemical spill, fire or exposure to chemicals in lab
   b. Plan also requires training and the appointment of a chemical hygiene officer
   c. Fume hood *(used to protect workers from noxious or hazardous chemical reagents)* must be monitored periodically
   d. General information
      ❖ *If a chemical is splashed in eye, go to the nearest eye wash and wash eye for 15 minutes; seek medical attention*
      ❖ *If a chemical is splashed on person or clothing, go to nearest body shower and rinse for 15 minutes; seek medical attention*
      ❖ *Any chemicals considered carcinogenic should only be used while wearing gloves; consult MSDS*
      ❖ *Any chemical considered a respiratory health threat should be handled under a fume hood*

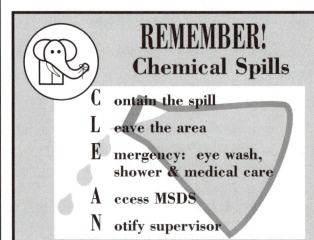

REMEMBER!
Chemical Spills

C ontain the spill
L eave the area
E mergency: eye wash, shower & medical care
A ccess MSDS
N otify supervisor

WASTE DISPOSAL

1. Types
   a. Hazardous waste - solid waste or mixture of sold wastes which may pose a threat to human health or the environment when improperly handled
   b. Infectious waste - equipment, utensils or substances that may harbor or transmit pathogenic organisms from individuals who may have a communicable disease
   c. Medical waste - any solid, semisolid or liquid waste generated in diagnosis, treatment or immunization of humans or animals in research or production or testing of biologics

2. Identified by orange or red seamless plastic bags labeled with the biohazard symbol

Biohazard   Radiation

3. Sharps containers must be rigid, puncture-proof and leakproof

4. Treat infectious or medical wastes by incineration or autoclaving *(public trash collection NOT suitable for disposal of raw infectious waste)*

5. Secured storage area for infectious material to prevent accidents in handling

RADIATION SAFETY

1. Dispose of all radioactive material in appropriate labeled container

2. Report any exposure to radioactive material and seek medical attention

3. Radiation monitoring
   a. Film badge or survey meter
   b. Exposure limits *(maximum permissible dose equivalents - 5000 mrem/yr; whole body)*
   c. Wipe test *(leak test)* - laboratory work surfaces wiped with moistened absorbent material *(wipe)*; radiation contained in each wipe counted

FIRE SAFETY

1. What to do
   a. Alert staff
   b. Rescue any injured
   c. Pull nearest fire alarm
   d. Contain fire - close doors
   e. Call institution emergency number
   f. Find nearest fire extinguisher; only attempt to put out fire if it is small

REMEMBER!
Fire Safety

Rescue injured
Alarm
Contain fire
Close doors
Emergency number;
Extinguish only if small

2. How to use a fire extinguisher
   a. Use appropriate class of extinguisher
      ❖ *Class A - wood and paper fires*
      ❖ *Class B - flammable liquid fires*
      ❖ *Class C - electrical fires*
      ❖ *Class D - reactive metals*
   b. Most fire extinguishers can be used on A, B, and C fires
   c. Halon Gas
      ❖ *Heavier than O_2; displaces O_2 near fire which extinguishes fire*
      ❖ *Will not harm lab equipment*
   d. Remove pin from fire extinguisher; slowly squeeze the handle
   e. Aim at base of fire; walk slowly up to fire while moving extinguisher in sweeping motion

NEVER use water on flammable liquids or electrical fires.

ELECTRICAL SAFETY

1. Lock out/tag out malfunctioning electrical or mechanical equipment until serviced

2. Report any small shocks; unplug and tag equipment until serviced

3. Replace all frayed wires and plugs

4. If a severely shocked person cannot let go of instrument, unplug it *(without touching it)* or knock person loose with nonconductive material, such as wood

5. If the shock victim stops breathing, perform CPR

REGULATORY AGENCIES

1. Occupational Safety and Health Administration *(OSHA)*- federal agency that regulates employee safety in the workplace

2. U.S. Food and Drug Administration *(FDA)* – regulates use of numerous products including medical devices and blood products; approves new laboratory tests, technology and instruments

3. Centers for Medicare and Medicaid Services *(CMS)* – federal agency responsible for administration of Clinical Laboratory Improvement Act of 1988 *(CLIA 88)*, Medicare / Medicaid services, and contains the Office of the Inspector General *(OIG)*

4. Department of Transportation *(DOT)* - administers the Hazardous Materials Standard which requires specific procedures for shipping of biohazardous materials and employee training

5. U.S. Postal Service *(USPS)* - administers "Mailability of Etiologic Agents" - -instructions on correctly packaging specimens, biological products and clinical specimens

6. Centers For Disease Control and Prevention *(CDC)* – national advisory agency that develops disease prevention standards and guidelines and promotes environmental health; does not have regulatory or enforcement authority

7. U.S. Department of Health and Human Services *(DHHS)* – oversees FDA, CMS, and CDC

8. Equal Employment Opportunity Commission *(EEOC)* – enforces laws prohibiting job discrimination

9. Office of the Inspector General *(OIG)* – governmental agency that investigates Medicare / Medicaid billing fraud and abuse
   a. Compliance program – voluntary plan to assure laboratory's adherence to regulations established by CMS to prevent fraud and abuse

10. Health Insurance Portability and Accountability Act *(HIPAA)* – federal law that protects the security and confidentiality of healthcare information
    a. Protected Health Information *(PHI)* – individually identifiable information *(electronic, paper or oral)* relating to a patient's health condition or payment for healthcare

TEST Alert!

What do these regulate?
CDC, CLIA, EEOC, HHS, OSHA

CLINICAL LABORATORY IMPROVEMENT ACT OF 1988 (CLIA 88)

1. Federal law that established minimum standards for laboratory practice and quality; applies to all laboratories in U.S. performing tests on humans for the purpose of medical treatment

2. Purpose – to ensure accuracy, reliability and timeliness of patient test results regardless of where test was performed

3. Extent of regulation based upon complexity level of testing *(waived, moderately complex, and highly complex)* and risk of harm to patient when incorrect results are reported

4. Provisions include
   a. Quality control and quality assurance
   b. Use of proficiency tests
   c. Personnel qualifications
   d. Performance improvement
   e. Patient test management

5. All labs must be certified every 2 years

VOLUNTARY ACCREDITING AGENCIES

1. Joint Commission on the Accreditation of Health Care Organizations *(JCAHO)* – inspects and accredits hospitals and other health care facilities

2. College of American Pathologists *(CAP)* – voluntary accrediting agency for clinical laboratories

3. American Association of Blood Banks *(AABB)* – voluntary accrediting agency for blood banks

4. Deemed status – alternative to direct federal oversight granted to the above agencies to enforce CLIA regulations

Name 3 Voluntary Accrediting Agencies

SAFETY SAMPLE QUESTIONS

1. The concept that laboratory personnel should treat all blood and body fluids as capable of transmitting infectious diseases is known as
   A. Infection control
   B. Quality control
   C. Safe practice standards
   D. Universal precautions

2. Of the following, which would be considered personal protective equipment?
   A. Biologic safety cabinet
   B. Latex gloves
   C. Sharps container
   D. Work shields

3. What type of fire extinguisher would be best to use on computer equipment?
   A. CO_2
   B. Foam
   C. Halon
   D. Water

4. A clinical laboratorian's first respone to a formalin spill in the laboratory is to
   A. Call 911
   B. Consult the MSDS
   C. Evacuate all personnel from the area
   D. Notify the supervisor

5. Which of the following is a voluntary accrediting agency?
   A. CDC
   B. DHHS
   C. JCAHO
   D. OSHA

6. If an employee suspects that the employer is violating safety standards, which agency should be notified?
   A. OSHA
   B. OIG
   C. CDC
   D. CLIA

ANSWERS AND RATIONALE

1. D

The Centers for Disease Control and the Clinical and Laboratory Standards Institute *(CLSI)* have developed a laboratory personnel protection system that is comprised of engineering controls, personal protective equipment and work practice controls. These are designed to guard workers from the potential of exposure to blood-borne pathogens. Option A is a hospital promoted concept primarily focusing on washing hands as a way to prevent hospital spread infections. Option B is those procedures that ensure the accuracy of test results and includes but is not limited to testing control materials with known value ranges, equipment maintenance and proficiency testing of personnel. Option C sounds good but doesn't mean much in terms of a specific concept.

2. B

Options A, C and D are examples of engineering controls.

3. C

Halon is heavier than air and will displace the O_2 putting out the fire. It will NOT damage equipment, which is a major advantage.

4. C

Evacuate personnel first. Then notify the supervisor and consult the MSDS for appropriate information.

5. C

The Joint Commission for Accreditation of Health Care Organizations (JCAHO) is the only agency listed that is voluntary and that accredits health care organizations

6. A

The Occupational Safety and Health Administration (OSHA) oversees standards that regulate safety in the workplace, including the Bloodborne Pathogen and Chemical Hazard Standards. An employee may request an OSHA inspection if violations are suspected.

Congratulations on completing your review!!!

We hope this book has been helpful in preparing you for your courses and exams.
Please send suggestions or ideas for future editions to:

Patsy Jarreau
LSU Health Sciences Center
Department of Clinical Laboratory Science
1900 Gravier Street
New Orleans, LA 70112

INDEX

248

Order Form

Order your copy of *Clinical Laboratory Science Review* Now!

To order: call (504)568-4276 **or mail** the form below and your check or money order to:

> LSUHSC Foundation
> Department of Clinical Laboratory Sciences
> 10th floor
> 1900 Gravier Street
> New Orleans, LA 70112

Yes, I wish to order _____ copies of **Clinical Laboratory Science Review** priced at $39.95/each. Please include $4.00 shipping and handling per book. *(Louisiana residents pay additional taxes– Orleans Parish add $3.96 city and state sales tax, outside Orleans Parish add $1.76.)*

Payment:

___ Check/Money order enclosed Payable to: LSUHSC Foundation

Charge to: ____ Visa _____ MasterCard _____ Discover _____AMEX

Account # _____ Exp. date _____

Authorized Signature _____

Name _____

Address _____

City/State _____

Zip Code _____ Phone # (_____)_____

Alternate Phone # (_____)_____

e-mail _____

or fax this order form with your credit card information to:

(504) 568-6761

Thank you for your business. We look forward to your success.